MOROCCAN SUCCESS; THE KADA WAY

Greg Rowlerson

chipmunkapublishing
the mental health publisher

Greg Rowlerson

All rights reserved, no part of this publication may be reproduced by any means, electronic, mechanical photocopying, documentary, film or in any other format without prior written permission of the publisher.

>	Published by
>	Chipmunkapublishing
>	PO Box 6872
>	Brentwood
>	Essex CM13 1ZT
>	United Kingdom

http://www.chipmunkapublishing.com

Copyright © Greg Rowlerson 2009

Chipmunkapublishing gratefully acknowledge the support of Arts Council England.

MOROCCAN SUCCESS; THE KADA WAY

Dedication

To Mum, Dad and Stephen ~ my life constants

Greg Rowlerson

MOROCCAN SUCCESS; THE KADA WAY

Contents

Acknowledgements

Introduction

Enter Salah & Hicham

Kada's David's First Serious Battles With Their Goliaths

When In Rome ~ Great, When In Nice ~ Nice, When In Atlanta…

Brilliance In Brussels By The New Desert Prince

Reaching The Top ~ The Kada Way

Athens ~ Confirmation Of What We Already Knew

Injuries, Development And Domination

The Toughest Barrier Is The Kenyans

An Initiation, A Masterpiece And A Final Exam

The Dream: To Emulate Said, Brahim And Khalid

Testing Times For So Many Reasons

Edmonton And Abrupt Endings

The Three Letters That Taint Distance Running

Should It Always Be Guilty Until Proven Innocent?

Hicham Attempts To Outdo The Great Said

From The Greatest Never To The Greatest Ever?

Afterword

References

MOROCCAN SUCCESS; THE KADA WAY

Acknowledgements

My initial interest in the sport of track and field comes from my father. Neil was a decent runner himself, having completed seven marathons with a personal best time of 2:36 and change. Despite him vacating the house often to train, it wasn't the activity itself that first sparked my love of the sport. It was Neil - the fan. He didn't only concern himself with his own pursuits for improvement, but paid much attention to the world's best, particularly during the era of Australian Robert De Castella.

This led onto the Steve Moneghetti era, and my first viewing experience (that I recall) is the 1988 Olympic marathon (my Dad had me chained up). More vivid are my memories of the 1990 Commonwealth Games marathon, by which time I was a massive 'Mona' devotee. Unfortunately Douglas Wakihuri got the better of him, something we were used to. I also vaguely remember the 5,000 metres from the same Games, when Andrew Lloyd staged an almighty upset by defeating the favoured Kenyans, John Ngugi and Yobes Ondieki. While most would just recall the sprint finish, I always remember that the two favourites fell (quite remarkable) during the event. To me, it wasn't just that Lloyd *had* won, but *why* he had done so.

I started running myself in 1991, just prior to my tenth birthday. Helped by some encouragement from my Boronia Primary School teacher Robert Bates (also a family friend and runner), I competed in cross country school events and found that with my slender frame, running came easier to me than most. I soon became hooked. In the not too distant future I was tagging along on some of my father's shorter runs. This further encouraged my love of the sport as a fan. In later times the Knox Athletics Club would also contribute to my love of running, led by the likes of marathon (and pole vault!) man George Dyer."

The 1992 Barcelona Olympics bought about the sadness of Moneghetti's result in the marathon, but also the excitement and controversy of the 10,000 metres, where Morocco's Khalid Skah out kicked Kenya's Richard Chelimo. By the 1993 World Championships in Stuttgart I was a fanatic, and for the next decade I would get up on many occasions during the middle of the night to see most of the distance races from the World Championships and Olympic Games. Despite my brother stating that, "it's just putting one foot in front of the other," I always believed that there was a little more to distance running than that!

I am a lot less clear as to how my initial interest in writing came about. My mother has always had a liking for the written word, so perhaps I inherited it from her. Throughout my schooling I enjoyed writing short stories when the opportunity presented itself, and I even remember doing a basic project on Robert De Castella at primary school. In secondary school I took literature as one of my subjects with my teacher Anna Hall, offering good support.

From there I became erratic with my writing until I decided to put my energies into "Moroccan Success; The Kada Way." Before that I was still writing, though not putting my talents to any particularly good use.

I must firstly thank Salah Hissou for providing the inspiration to kick start this book project. I also thank him for allowing me into his home in Beni Mellal. Salah was polite, helpful and impressed (rather than freaked out) by the knowledge I possessed of his career.

I could not have met Salah without knowing Driss Dacha, and it was he who introduced us, as well as acting as translator during our discussion. This is much appreciated. Driss also took care of me during my near five month stay in Morocco, allowing me to live on his premises and also helping me adapt to the differences in culture and language.

My one fan from the beginning of this project has been my mother, Marion. Right from the get go she showed interest in the Hissou story, even if not an avid fan of Salah herself. This helped me to think of myself as a writer, and the confidence gained has contributed to the end product of around 200,000 words, hopefully much of which is worthwhile content. Mum has also acted as a proof reader/editor for this book, allowing this to be a generally smooth read, even before it reached my publisher. She has put in countless hours for this cause, for which I am most grateful.

Giving me further motivation to strive for greater things with this book was Jason Pegler of Chipmunka Publishing. Jason liked the positive message of life success that the book spoke of and decided that he wanted to publish it. Having never written a book before, I was very grateful for the interest that he showed. I thank him for not just encouraging the completion of my first book, but hopefully the others that follow.

The most relevant race information that I garnered came from Andreas Janssen from Germany. Andreas is also an avid fan of distance running. His knowledge of the sport is unsurpassed, as far as anyone I've ever known is concerned. He forwarded me, what must be virtually the entire racing catalogue of Hicham El Guerrouj and Salah Hissou's careers. At least 10% of these results I could not have found out myself. While I already had most of Salah's career mapped out (from the first phases of writing I had done on the book), Hicham's I didn't. Having Andreas send me his career results with the dates included was most helpful, for at the time I was just beginning to write about El Guerrouj. Hence it became much easier for me to insert his story. Andreas is also a fan of the likes of Ron Clarke and Haile Gebrselassie, but his favourite athlete is Said Aouita. Being aware of his enormous knowledge and passion for Aouita's career, it is my hope that Andreas puts this to good use and writes the story of Said.

As this is my first book, I would also like to add some general acknowledgments. I extend further thanks to Driss Dacha for providing me with the opportunity to travel to Morocco. He and the Zakhir family showed me very good hospitality time and time again, helping to make my stay an enjoyable and safe one. Being very much an introverted individual, I can be selfish and an anti-social freak sometimes, but these guys put up with me! Thank you very much for giving me a rewarding life experience and opening my mind to other possibilities. Another 'family' I've appreciated have been my Victorian employers, Bowens. The timber company employed me for most of my adult life, and apart from giving me vast wealth (when I convert to Moroccan Dirhams!), have provided me with experience, knowledge and many good memories over the years. Most of all, thank you to the one who called me Fox for inspiring much of my great writing, even if you never do that for my benefit!

Finally, to my immediate family - Dad, Mum and younger brother, Stephen – I appreciate the love and support that you have always given me. They're always there for their son and brother.

MOROCCAN SUCCESS; THE KADA WAY

Introduction

The story of the story..............

When I first started this project it was titled, "Salah Hissou: Battling The Giants, his complete yet incomplete career story." My initial idea was to simply write about the career of Hissou.

As well as asking, 'why such a long book title?' you might also ask, 'why write about Salah Hissou?' Admittedly he was never the best track distance runner in the world, though he was arguably one of the best five going around during his best seasons and somewhat of a force for almost a decade (when he was fit to compete).

I liked the idea of writing the story of an athlete who was great, but not *the* greatest, as most sports biographies tend to focus on the number one in a discipline, while ignoring those next in line. I also enjoy exploring the career of a sportsperson who doesn't necessarily succeed 'all' the time. For me, it is the down periods of their career, which make their journey every bit as fascinating as the high periods. Of course, having the high periods are still essential, since without them, the athlete (in this case, Salah Hissou) wouldn't be a champion and hence, probably not worth writing about! By the way, the complicated book title was in direct relation to Hissou's successful career, which nevertheless contained some difficult times.

I started work on the Salah Hissou story in November 2006. For about eight months I completed enormous research on his background and had the main body of a book written on his running career. I hadn't attempted to contact a publisher but perhaps felt that I would do so nearing the end of 2007 when I anticipated that the book would be completed. These plans changed in mid 2007 when I was researching Hissou on a running website message board. On "letsrun" I found in the archives a post from a Moroccan named Driss Dacha, who in reply to a thread had mentioned what Khalid Skah and Salah

Hissou were up to in retirement (this was from late in 2005). Driss stated that he was a neighbour of Salah's. Fortunately for me, Driss left his email address so I contacted him and let him know about my book project. Driss expressed some interest in what I was doing and from that point, regular emails transpired. This culminated in my decision to travel to Morocco in early 2008 to undertake further extensive research on Hissou.

Before reading of Driss, I was unaware that he himself was a top international (marathon) runner. Also during this period I was conversing with German Andreas Janssen, who I'd also met via "letsrun". Andreas is a massive fan of long distance running from various eras and he supplied me with a full list of Salah Hissou's career results. Some of these races I did not previously know about. I'd been attempting to get in touch with various publishers and a suggestion was made by one to widen my topic to gain more reader attention. However, I felt that a book focusing on all of the great runners of North Africa would be too much. Nevertheless, I knew that Hissou was coached by Abdelkader Kada (himself a former runner of some note) and that Kada had also coached the great miler Hicham El Guerrouj. I was aware that Driss knew Kada, so from there I considered the idea of writing about Kada's best athletes (Driss also thought this a good idea). Once I discovered that Morocco's best steeplechaser, Ali Ezzine, was also coached by Kada, I had the basis for my book. Salah, Hicham and Ali had all been highly successful Moroccan runners from a similar era, but with different strengths and event focuses. It now became a case of adding to my Hissou story, the careers of El Guerrouj and Ezzine. I wanted to be careful that the book didn't become too El Guerrouj dominated, which it could have been, considering his incredible level of success. Hopefully I have achieved a nice balance, giving a similar volume of content to both Hicham and Salah, particularly in the early chapters when their career achievements were on a similar scale. Less content is provided on Ali, which is understandable, given his shorter career.

Over the course of his coaching career, Abdelkader Kada has

MOROCCAN SUCCESS; THE KADA WAY

overseen many Moroccan distance runners. Hicham El Guerrouj, Salah Hissou and Ali Ezzine were his most successful students, hence the decision to focus on them. To discuss his entire squad in great detail would have meant too many athletes to focus on, and may have restricted the book space given to the star runners.

Introducing rival athletes at different phases of the book was a tactic I employed in an attempt to keep things fresh, realising that sometimes there is perhaps too much of an overload on statistical data and race results. I broke this up with regular runner biographies, so that you are never just reading about the same athletes over again. There is almost as much information on the careers of Daniel Komen, Haile Gebrselassie and Noureddine Morceli as the major book subjects themselves! For this I make no apologies, as I wanted to write about the major runners of the era, rather than focus on one or two.

My extensive in depth race details also differ from other books, where often, significant information will be sadly missing. I also cover all bases with my decision to include as many race results as possible. As such, I do not focus solely on the main races, which by the way, I do not view as only occurring every four years!

Whilst being mightily proud of "Moroccan Success; The Kada Way," I am the first to acknowledge its shortcomings.

I did not care to write greatly about running technique, diets/nutrition, etc, though I would have enjoyed providing more specific details of the training sessions of El Guerrouj, Hissou and Ezzine. Unfortunately I did not have these at my disposal, though did include what I was able to research. In my interview with Salah I asked more about his race tactics and his actual opponents than specific training. I did not interview Abdelkader Kada, which is regrettable, as far as the credibility of the book is concerned. Yet even if I had gained access to the entire training logs of my three athletes I would not have put the majority of it into the story, since this book is not based on how to become a great distance runner, or even of how to improve your running regardless of your level. It is more about the international class athlete, and how they go about defeating their other highly talented foes. In this respect I would love to have included key speed sessions that took place before world and national record attempts, plus of course the major championships. The benefits to the writer and reader would be a greater knowledge and understanding of the training (and not just racing) form and therefore the exact level of expectation from the coach and athlete for the big race. I see the stark absence of the majority of these details as the books major failing. Regardless, I view the finished product as a tremendous personal success. Far from perfect, but still pretty, pretty, pretty, pretty good.

I am also aware of my penchant for too much writing, which is to say that I can sometimes lean more on the side of quantity, rather than quality when it comes to the written word. I have certainly included virtually every race detail that I could get my hands on! Nevertheless, I should relate somewhat to the sports fan geek, who is in the mould of say, a star trekker (I'm not a trekker myself, not that there's anything wrong with that!). I am confident that my literature will, "Make your mouth water *if* you love distance running!"

By writing in this fashion I have stayed true to myself.

Many books do not dare to mention the use of performance enhancing drugs in their sport, but as this is a topic discussed by most fans, I thought it relevant enough to discuss in some detail. Some may think that by encouraging thought on the topic, that I am bringing undeserved suspicion to Kada's athletes. However, I believe that by not brushing over this topic, I've actually enhanced their reputation. Moroccans have tested positive to performance enhancing drugs, so to not mention this at all would indicate that there's something to hide. Therefore, the points that I've raised, which distance El Guerrouj, Hissou and Ezzine from the likes of Boulami and Mourhit, give them their own positive result.

As many of the races include direct quotes made during the events, I thought it sensible to describe some of them in the

MOROCCAN SUCCESS; THE KADA WAY

present tense. I endeavour to have the reader feeling like they are there, as the races take place. It is an attempt to put the reader trackside at Brussels, Zurich, Athens, etc.

In "Moroccan Success ~ The Kada Way," I discuss why the bulk of the world's top runners come from just a couple of areas of the globe.

My greater love for the sport has always been in the 5,000 and 10,000 metres events, rather than say the 1,500 metres. Another reason for starting a book on Salah Hissou (as well as being one of his fans), is that Paul Tergat and Haile Gebrselassie already had books published about them. These stories are decent reads in their own way, but differ to this text in the subjects tackled. The Tergat book has a lot in the way of good training information and Gebrselassie's book goes into great detail of Haile's personal life, telling us of the man behind the running legend.

To my knowledge, not many running books have been written in a way that celebrates *both* the athlete's career and those who surrounded it. To fill this void I give much more space to other athletes, specifically the most significant runners that El Guerrouj, Hissou and Ezzine competed against. My book is therefore about an era of a sport as much as it is about the outstanding careers of three runners and their coach who made it all possible. From a personal perspective, I would also prefer to read about the great contests in races than simply read of an occasional result, before the next few pages revert back to 'mileage'.

So this book is certainly not a scientific read, nor one that is filled with training logs for the average fun runner. It is not a book that attempts to teach you how to run like the best Moroccans. My target audience is sports fans, specifically the fans of distance running, and why shouldn't it be, since I am a fan myself and not an athlete, coach or doctor? My target is not the runners themselves, though I realise that in many cases a runner and a fan of the sport are one and the same. This publication was never going to be about page after page of training information. There are more than enough books, which have been written for the fun runner or serious athlete for self improvement.

I am writing to celebrate the runners' success, the excitement of the sport, the thrill of competition, the rivalries of the individuals and the countries that make it a terrific spectacle. If you are a devotee of distance running, and want to learn more about the Moroccan success in men's distance running, then read on. I hope you enjoy it.

Abbreviations used ......

kms – kilometres
kgs – kilograms
ng – nanogram
ml – milligram
PB – personal best

MOROCCAN SUCCESS; THE KADA WAY

A brief background on the sport........

When Salah Hissou was born on the 16th of January 1972, his nation of Morocco had little in the way of a distance running pedigree. However, when Hissou stepped onto the world stage in the mid 1990's, this had changed significantly. In 1972, Africa as a whole had in fact only just begun to make an impact in middle and long distance running. Yet by the mid '90's Africa had practically conquered the world. With America's African descended negros dominating the sprints, it was rare to find world or Olympic track champions who did not have African origins.

International athletics has a long history of course, going back to the 1896 Olympic Games in Athens. On the track, the longest event conducted was the 1,500 metres, though there was a much longer race than this held on the road. The 42.195 kms marathon was an original Olympic event and it remains an integral part of the Games to this day.

In the early years, only men competed in competition and the competitors were generally from wealthy nations. In the early 20th century, most athletics events involved those from the likes of Europe, America and Australia. Yet considering the very little 'professionalism' that was displayed from athletes, some of the feats of these early stars were quite phenomenal.

The first big 'star' in distance running was Paavo Nurmi. In fact the Fin's achievements transcend athletics. His nine gold medals make him one of the greatest Olympians of all time. Even with the enormous improvements in race times, the greats of the day still need to be given respect. How would one go about winning nine Olympic gold medals?!

Being an amateur sport, things were completely different than to today. There were no specialized training techniques and most athletes didn't even have a coach! Some of the eating and drinking habits of the early 20th century runners were less than favourable to good performances and most of them had full time employment, giving them little time for effective training. Being far less professional than today, athletes were also allowed to focus on more than one event at an Olympics. In the modern era most distance runners consider doing a double (racing in two events) as too daunting a task. These doubts would not have entered the mind of Nurmi as he won many medals in the distance running events that were on offer in 1920, 1924 and 1928. This is not to say that today's stars are not as strong minded as Nurmi. It simply illustrates that the intensity and demands of current day sport are so much greater than in yesteryear.

If Paavo Nurmi was the first legendary distance runner, then Emil Zatopek was probably the second. The Czech was an out and out superstar. In the 1952 Games he won the 5,000 metres, the 10,000 metres and then the marathon. This must be considered one of sports' all time greatest achievements. I can guarantee that it will never be repeated. At this time, African athletes had not arrived on the scene and the distance running events were very much the domain of the 'white man'. But this wouldn't last too much longer.

The big breakthrough for African distance running came during the 1960 Rome Olympics. A little known Ethiopian streeted the field in the marathon, while in the process, smashing the world record. Abebe Bikila was his name and he would forever have the distinction of winning this race without the assistance of shoes. Bikila ran the roads in bare feet for 42.195 kms! Truly astonishing.

Four years later he won the marathon again, though it was taking a while for the rest of Africa to jump on the bandwagon. 1968 at Mexico City would be more significant for its results with Ethiopia's neighbours Kenya, coming onto the distance running scene with some note. While Ethiopia won the marathon again with Mamo Wolde, Kenya dominated the track in men's competition. Kip Keino won the 1,500 metres, Naftali Temu the 10,000 metres and Amos Biwott the 3,000 metres steeplechase at an Olympics where distance running events were more about survival than performance. Mexico City was one of many circumstances where the well being of the athletes was given very little thought and consideration by Games' organizers. Many future Olympics would be staged in

MOROCCAN SUCCESS; THE KADA WAY

oppressive conditions, not conducive to top distance running.

There were further African athletes coming through in the 1970's but there was no continued dominance by the continent. Europe was still the reliable force at the Olympics. In 1972 and 1976, Finland's Lasse Viren did the 5,000/10,000 metres double, carrying on his nation's great tradition in the sport. Four gold medals in two Games was obviously a terrific achievement.

Following Viren, the next major star to burst onto the distance running stage was Henry Rono. The enigmatic Kenyan was a versatile genius. At one point he held the world records for the 3,000, 5,000 and 10,000 metres events as well as the 3,000 metres steeplechase. He was a colossus of the sport.

Unfortunately politics has got in the way of many an athlete's career. Rono was denied the opportunity to compete at the 1980 Moscow Olympics when at the peak of his powers, due to a Kenyan boycott. It is disappointing that we would never know how Henry would have performed against the Ethiopian Murits Yifter who completed the traditional track distance double of Viren. The ageless African had a devastating kick, which gave him his victories. Rono may have been capable of destroying him before the last lap but alas, we will never know the outcome had Henry competed in Russia. Four years later the Kenyan was washed up, after spending too much time enjoying the high life in America. Despite not going to an Olympics, Henry Rono is remembered as one of the greatest Kenyan athletes of all time.

Sometimes the importance of the Olympic Games can be overrated when analysing an athlete's career. A problem with the sport of athletics was that the Olympics were so much bigger than any other form of competition. The Commonwealth had its Games as did Europe, but these events were on a small scale compared to the Olympic Games, which of course were only held once every four years. It can be frustrating when sports enthusiasts will only consider Olympic success in analysis, for this can be so misleading. Why should an athlete have just a single opportunity every four years to prove their greatness while elite tennis players and golfers receive four opportunities *each* year (grand slams and majors). And don't get me started on tennis in the Olympics!

Track and Field took a big step forward in 1983 with the introduction of the World Athletics Championships, a competition that would rival the Olympics in importance, whilst giving the best athletes more opportunity to achieve glory, and ultimately prove themselves to sports fans and themselves. Initially the World Championships were held every four years but this has since changed to every two years. This has been a good adjustment as it separates them from the Olympics (the Games hold slightly more weight because an athlete gets less opportunities at Olympic gold). It also gives an athlete three chances in every four years to be the champion of the world. The current set up is perfect as the non major championships year allows the smaller championships to enjoy some status. Not having a World Championships or Olympic Games on which to concentrate can also encourage the best athletes to focus their energies on world record attempts, as Haile Gebrselassie would do during 1998.

By 1983 Eastern Africa had made its mark with Ethiopia, Kenya and to a lesser extent, Tanzania excelling in distance running. At the first World Championships a new talent from North Africa arrived on the scene. His name was Said Aouita and he was about to improve distance running standards still further. Said was from Morocco and it was from this point that his country's track history began. In the 1,500 metres, Aouita ran third, but this was only the beginning of one of athletics' great careers. A year later, Said Aouita was Africa's best long distance runner. The nation of Morocco had a hero and as a whole, the continent of Africa was again on the rise in the men's distance running scene. The supply of great runners from this continent would prove plentiful.

MOROCCAN SUCCESS; THE KADA WAY

Enter Salah & Hicham

On the 26th of March 1994, a young Moroccan athlete named Salah Hissou was ready to make his mark on the international stage. For a distance runner he was tall, (about 5 feet 10 in) and weighed around 62 kilograms. At twenty two years of age and with sufficient training in the Atlas Mountains (only 750 metres from his home in Kasbat Tadla) under his belt, it was his time to shine. Under the guidance of his coach Abdelkader Kada, he had made the necessary improvements required to be competitive against the best. He knew that success at the highest level was possible. Aouita, Boutayeb and Skah had shown him the way.

Salah Hissou grew up in a very poor neighbourhood. While Morocco was not quite considered a third world country, much of it remained impoverished. Like many of his countrymen, Hissou was raised on a simple but essential diet, consisting of rice, vegetables and meat. Salah had, and still has a particular liking for chicken, which is appropriate, for his training style is very much to run with others. Often he'd refuse to jog on a trail alone, being scared for his safety!

At the age of seventeen, Hissou clocked times of 14:15.0 for 5,000 metres and 8:17.63 for 3,000 metres. These weren't astonishing times but enough for the Moroccan Athletics Federation to take notice. He was then given the opportunity to focus solely on running at the National Institute Of Sport in Rabat where Abdelkader Kada took him under his wing. Under his guidance, his career started to blossom.

Salah's talents first became apparent to non Moroccans when he finished twelfth in the World Junior Cross Country on March 25, 1990. However this did not necessarily mark him down as a runner to watch on the world stage. An eighteen year old who can run eight kms over cross country terrain in 23:27 might impress some, but there was an abundance of Kenyans who could do that and much better. Quite frankly, there were junior Kenyans who were putting in more than respectable performances against senior athletes! Hissou had a lot of improving to do if he was to impress most astute distance running judges.

Two Kenyans that were over one minute faster than the young Moroccan in the championships were Kipyego Kororia and Richard Chelimo, the first finishers from the junior race. In third position was Ethiopian Fita Bayissa. Fourth was another Kenyan and despite missing a medal, it was this runner who stood out. Ismael Kirui looked set to become a superstar. He had only turned fifteen in 1990! To be so competitive at such a young age was quite extraordinary. Later that year, Salah Hissou improved his 5,000 metres personal best to 14:05.9 and registered a 3:42.5 for the 1,500 metres. He also entered the World Junior Championships, competing in the 5,000 metres. Unfortunately on August 10 he failed to finish his heat, which was won by Bayissa.

Salah's improvement would be slow going. A year later he would only finish fourteenth in the World Junior Cross Country, a sign that he had taken a step backwards in his development. This was going to take time. A little way ahead of him in eighth place was another Ethiopian, Haile Gebrselassie.

On the 3rd of July 1991, there were some of distance running's best athletes competing over 5,000 metres in Stockholm, Sweden. Italy's enigmatic Salvatore Antibo won in 13:13.66, a performance in defiance with the trends of African distance running dominance. Antibo edged out Kenyans, Ibrahim Kinuthia and Richard Chelimo by less than a second. Behind them came seasoned Moroccans, Brahim Boutayeb and Hammou Boutayeb. This was where the action was, but if we had panned back 150 metres, we would have seen a younger Moroccan showing signs of future potential.

Salah Hissou finished only tenth but importantly ran a 13:37.40, a time that made him the fourth fastest junior *in the world* at the distance for 1991. This good performance wasn't a once off either. During the year, Hissou also won the 5,000 metres at the Moroccan National Championships in a time of 13:59.82. The time might appear slow, but the winner of Morocco's National 5,000 metres Championship rarely ran

MOROCCAN SUCCESS; THE KADA WAY

under fourteen minutes, since conditions were often so hot. Hissou was only nineteen when he won this senior race. It was a sign that one day he could be good enough to compete strongly against some of the best in Europe.

However, Hissou's emerging career seemed to stall during the next two years. Soon after his twentieth birthday he won a significant race, defeating fellow Moroccan Hammou Boutayeb in a 12 kms cross country race held at his local city of Rabat. Salah now seemed ready to step up to the senior event of the World Cross Country, but this competition was a major setback with only a lowly fifty seventh place finish in the 1992 championships in Boston on March 21. It was a disappointing race for Morocco all around with reigning champion Khalid Skah, relegated to fourth as Kenyan, John Ngugi won a record fifth title. The athletes had difficulty coping with the freezing conditions, illustrated by the paths on the course having to be cleared of snow in order for the event to take place. This affected the Moroccan more than most, as his long stride was more conducive to a firmer surface.

He soon found himself in the much warmer confines of Flagstaff, Arizona. Here he stayed with his Moroccan friend Driss Dacha, himself a runner of real pedigree. Driss had recorded a 2:13.03 marathon to place third in St. Paul, Minnesota, during October last year and was living in the United States. He would go on to clock a 2:11.43 in Berlin the following year. Dacha did not have the natural track speed of Hissou but he had strength in abundance, so Salah was able to work on this side of his development while residing with him. As was common in Moroccan training, Hissou would run twice on most days, with the afternoon session often being the tougher. General aerobic endurance sessions usually occupied the morning, with Salah sometimes focusing on the track in the afternoon, completing interval workouts at distances ranging from 400 metres to 2,500 metres repetitions. He and Driss also trained with Elarbi Khattabi during this period. Elarbi had potential as a steeplechase runner and like Salah, would soon be endeavouring to break into the major Moroccan teams. Hissou raced on the road during this period, winning a 5 kms event in 14:18 and also a half marathon in Ontario, California where he led Dacha to the line.

There wasn't a lot to talk about regarding Hissou's other performances during 1992. On May 16 he recorded a respectable time of 13:41.55 for a 5,000 metres event in Princeton, although that wouldn't cut it in the big time of Europe's Grand Prix meetings. Kada then had his athlete compete in a series of 10,000 metres races. The first of these was in Dedham when on the 24th of May, Hissou recorded a victory in a solid time of 28:31.62. He was again victorious on June 25, defeating teammate Khalid Boulami in Bukarest with a winning time of 28:33.58.

To continue his development, Salah wanted to experience the tactical racing of a championship event on the track so he prepared for the Pan Arab Games, being held later in the year in Latakia, Syria. He decided to compete in both the long distance events, the first of which was the 10,000 metres on September 5.

The race was slow, but notably Hissou won in 29:23.0. Perhaps the win sapped some of his energies for the 5,000 metres that was to be conducted only four days later where Salah came second, recording a reasonable time of 13:56.32. The winner Mohamed Suleiman from Qatar, was far too strong in the latter stages, registering a 13:53.13. Yet Hissou was in good company. Mohamed had just recently won the bronze medal in the Barcelona Olympic 1,500 metres. It had been a productive championship for the Moroccan but better times were needed if he wished to compete in the big European races.

Salah next prepared for a race in Casablanca. Competing against his countrymen, Hissou displayed his abilities in running a decent time of 13:43.42 and winning the 5,000 metres event.

1992 had been an average year in performance. He had certainly enjoyed an increase in confidence from a number of victories and had proved his capabilities at 10,000 metres, but

MOROCCAN SUCCESS; THE KADA WAY

he couldn't remotely consider running against the world's best until he was clocking sub twenty-eight minutes. In the 5,000 metres he had yet to run under 13:30. There was still a lot of work to do. Despite his relative lack of improvement in '92, becoming a decent international distance runner still remained a possibility. He was young enough for time to be his friend and not his enemy.

Unfortunately, 1993 was a barren year for the twenty one year old Moroccan. In the World Cross Country on March 28, he finished a horrific 80th! Hissou ran the 11.8 km course in 35:00, whereas the winner William Sigei ran 32:51. Salah was a long way off the pace.

On the 6th of June, he ran a 5,000 metres time of 13:49.5 in Rabat. It was nothing to write home about and in this race, was beaten by fellow youngster Mohammed Mourhit. Two weeks later he was thrashed in the Mediterranean Games. The following were the top four finishers from the 5,000 metres:

Thierry Pantel	13:39.04
Aissa Belaout	13:41.65
Mohammed Mourhit	13:50.12
Salah Hissou	13:55.31

Hissou was still racing slower times than he had run in Stockholm two years earlier. That performance alone proved that he had the necessary ability. Would all his training ever enable him to reach the top?

Following this setback, Abdelkader Kada set out an updated training program that included more miles and tougher speed sessions. His twenty one year old runner had better be ready for it. It was make or break time.

It was now that Salah saw his hard work start to pay off. He wasn't proving himself in races, but during the second half of 1993, he produced training of a quality that he hadn't managed previously. He was also able to back up better from the hard sessions and turn out more of them. He could feel his stride become more powerful as the next session of 400 or 1,000 metres repetitions was completed. Abdelkader could see it all coming together.

Later in the year, we would see confirmation of Hissou's improvement when he won a 20 kms road race in Madrid with a good time of 59:33. It was the first race in a long time where he showed more than just talent. This was a genuinely good result. It was the equivalent of a sixty-three minute half marathon. Hissou had become a much stronger runner following his great block of training.

On December 26, 1993, Salah went to France and competed in a high class road race in Houilles. He was more than just competitive against some big names. Over the 9.6 km course, Hissou finished third behind Skah and Abebe, men who were 10,000 metres medallists from Barcelona. Salah even beat home Ismael Kirui who had recently become the 5,000 metres world champion. He was now stamping himself as a truly elite distance runner.

It seemed apparent following the 1993 World Championships in Stuttgart that Morocco was in desperate need of new talent. Khalid Skah failed to perform to his very high standards of the past and there was nobody else worthy of speaking about in its men's athletics team. Morocco had medalled in either the 5,000 metres or 10,000 metres in every major championship since 1984, but in 1993 its best result was Skah's fifth in the 5,000 metres. The world standard wasn't greatly improving. Morocco was simply falling away.

But things were about to change. It was the day of the 1994 World Cross Country Championships. Salah Hissou hoped that he was someone who could give Moroccan distance running a shot in the arm. As he stood on the grass in Budapest, waiting for the starter's gun, thoughts may have turned to his coach Abdelkader Kada, and all the training he'd completed. The ability to make his mark on world distance running may also have been foremost in his mind.

MOROCCAN SUCCESS; THE KADA WAY

As Salah readied himself for the challenge of Budapest, he had good reason to now do more than just hope for a good performance. The off season had proved beneficial and Hissou had taken his improved self to race in Italy in a 10.5 km cross country event. It was his warm up race for today.

Thirteen days earlier, on the 13th of March, the Moroccan defeated some significant names in the world of distance running. In fact he beat everyone who competed, running a time of 30:23.7. Behind Salah were Brahim Boutayeb (Olympic 10,000 metres champion from Seoul), Ismael Kirui (world 5,000 metres champion from Stuttgart), Vincenzo Modica and Moses Kiptanui (world steeplechase champion from Tokyo and Stuttgart). This was more like it, more like the talent he had displayed in 1991. It was a good test, but was still only a lead up race to Budapest. Could Salah Hissou prove himself against the best distance runners in the world?

The race in Hungary on March 26 saw the world witnessing the first signs of a new Moroccan star on the rise. In the 1994 World Cross Country Championships, Salah Hissou accounted well for himself in the freezing conditions, finishing eleventh, an enormous improvement from the 57th placing that he occupied in 1992. This was much better than 80th. It was also conclusive proof that he had arrived as a top class distance runner. Clearly, a lot had changed in nine months. This was the confidence builder that Hissou had desperately needed to kick start his international career. All of a sudden he believed in himself. The best were not so far ahead of him now with repeating champion, William Sigei some fifty four seconds up the road. Critically we are talking gaps of seconds now, and not minutes.

But the best were very good and many of them were only going to get better. Sigei had beaten home compatriot Simon Chemoiywo. But look back behind these two athletes and the names become more interesting, more significant to Salah Hissou's future ambitions. World 10,000 metres champion Haile Gebrselassie made up the podium, denying Paul Tergat from making it a Kenyan trifecta. Finishing fifth was Khalid Skah. He was still the top Moroccan, however the world appeared to be slowly but surely going past him. From now on Hissou would be gunning for him as well. The 1992 Olympic 10,000 metres champion was in Salah's sights.

It was a marvellous race for Morocco. The team recorded its highest ever finish, defying all expectations by finishing second behind Kenya. Skah was the only runner in the top ten but the nation's depth was impressive. Behind Hissou came Khalid Boulami fifteenth, Mohamed Issangar sixteenth, Brahim Lahlafi twenty second, Brahim Boutayeb twenty sixth and Hammou Boutayeb thirty first.

Morocco was suddenly blessed with tremendous depth and now appeared a good event on the running calendar in which it would be able to show it off. On the 17th of April, Morocco competed in the World Road Relay Championships in Litochoro, Greece and the results were surprisingly fantastic. It wasn't long since Morocco had been humiliated in the Stuttgart World Championships, yet here they won the gold medal! These Ediken Relay Championships involved six runners from each team, with each athlete running a different leg from the others. Each Moroccan performed as well as, or better than expected. The standout display came from Hissou. Salah had only run a 28:31.62 PB for 10 kms on the track. Despite this, he ran a 27:57 for 10 kms on the road! This was a world class performance. He put enormous time into the Ethiopian Bayissa, 28:52, and the Kenyan Yego, 29:56. The belief found in Budapest seemed to be having a tremendous flow on effect. Khalid Skah ran the 7.2 km leg in a time of 20:04. Running much faster than him was Haile Gebrselassie. The Ethiopian ran the same section in a blistering 19:27. Overall it was Ethiopia and Kenya winning the silver and bronze medals respectively.

The standard of Morocco's efforts was reflected in a new record time for the relay event. Its overall time was 1:57:56, although as a record, this was fairly irrelevant as the event was only in its second edition, having first been held in 1992 when Kenya was victorious. What wasn't irrelevant was that Morocco had showed that it was going to remain a major force in men's distance running. The results in Litochoro

MOROCCAN SUCCESS; THE KADA WAY

proved that the Stuttgart World Championships were simply a bad week in Moroccan Athletics. A lull if you like. Nothing more. Morocco could realistically hope to continue to challenge Kenya and Ethiopia in the major races.

Morocco's main rivals took the championships fairly seriously. As well as Gebrselassie, Ethiopia had fielded Fita Bayissa and Worku Bikila in its team. Morocco was simply too good. It boded well for the rest of the year and the European track season.

The Moroccans had Said Aouita with them as team coach, a man whom many considered an idol. You could argue that they were even inspired by his presence.

Aouita had been the real pioneer for Moroccan distance running, at least on the track. The nation's only previous international star was Rhadi Benabdesselem who had won the silver medal behind the famously bare footed Ethiopian Abebe Bikila. While Bikila received many deserved plaudits, Benabdesselem's performance barely earned any public recognition, despite his 2:15.42 run being just twenty five seconds adrift of Africa's first distance running legend.

Rhadi's great achievement did not inspire the next generation of Moroccans to follow in his footsteps. By the 1980's, Africa had developed a rich history in the sport, but in distance running this had mostly been due to the efforts of East African nations Kenya and Ethiopia. It didn't take long for Said Aouita to change that.

Born on November 2, 1959, Aouita started to take running very seriously in the late '70's, where he had much success in his home country. For a long time however, it seemed that he wouldn't be able to make the grade internationally. Said's times were not quite fast enough, although he did show great potential over a variety of distances.

In 1978, Aouita won Morocco's Junior Cross Country event but when he tested himself against the world's best juniors, he could only manage a thirty fourth placing in Glasgow.

However there was plenty of time to improve.

In 1979, Said produced excellent times at 5,000 metres and 1,500 metres of 13:48.5 and 3:42.3 respectively. However when he raced in the African Championships in Dakar, he only finished ninth in the 1,500 metres in a disappointing 3:49.0. This was well behind the great Kenyan Mike Boit's 3:39.9.

Despite this setback, Aouita continued to test his speed and in 1980 became a regular competitor over 800 metres. Now we were seeing the early signs of the man who would one day become regarded as having the best range in track running. He posted a national record of 1:47.8 in Grasse, France and immediately in his next race ran a huge personal best of 3:37.08 over 1,500 metres in Paris. These times were not going to allow Aouita to contend for Olympic medals but they were big, positive steps forward.

A most difficult period was then endured, as no noticeable improvements were made throughout 1981 and 1982. Said would either race in European 'B' races and be highly competitive, or be blown away by the elite in the 'A' races. He was soon able to settle in Italy, where much of his training would be conducted with the benefits of an Italian base as opposed to a Moroccan one, soon becoming apparent.

Aouita had been hovering around the 1:50 and 3:40 standard during most of his races but after a tremendous training period in the winter of 1982/83 he returned to racing, a different athlete. Firstly there was a 2:16.9 over 1,000 metres, which sliced more than two seconds from his national record. Two races later came a sensational 3:32.54 at 1,500 metres. This four second plus improvement brought him up to an international standard. Then, twenty two days later he recorded an amazing 1:44.38 for 800 metres. This time the improvement was more than two seconds. Suddenly the Moroccan was truly world class.

From there the rest is history. Later that year, Said won the bronze medal at the inaugural World Championships in

MOROCCAN SUCCESS; THE KADA WAY

Helsinki over 1,500 metres. The following year Aouita became arguably the world's greatest runner as he went through the season undefeated. Returning some focus to the 5,000 metres, Said quickly registered a stunning 13:04.78 in Firenze and would go on to win the Olympic race easily in 13:05.59. In Los Angeles, Aouita showcased to the world the running talent of North Africa.

1984 was littered with awesome performances but perhaps the best of these was at Brussels. The Belgium city was somewhat of a Mecca for distance running and here Aouita competed in the 3,000 metres. Despite never having broken eight minutes he clocked 7:33.3, winning by a massive 14.1 seconds. The Moroccan had fallen just short of Kenyan legend Henry Rono's world record of 7:32.1.

The rest of the decade was more significant for the races that Aouita *didn't* win! There were so few. Steve Cram required a world record to edge him out in a Nice 1,500 metres during 1985. At the end of 1987 he tried his hand at the steeplechase, only losing to the talented Italian Alessandro Lambruschini. In 1989 he put in his sole poor performance during this entire lengthy period, when he was defeated comprehensively by Yobes Ondieki in the Seville 5,000 metres. Clearly this was a case of simply underestimating the experienced Kenyan who had made big improvements in a short space of time. Later in the season the two met again twice at 3,000 metres. The Moroccan won both contests, which included his world record of 7:29.45 in Koln, when he gave the entire world class field an absolute hiding.

The only other race that Aouita did not win during his years of dominance was the Olympic Games 800 metres in Seoul when he took the bronze medal. This was certainly not a blight in the slightest on his career. In fact it were his achievements at the shorter distance during 1988 which best highlight Said's greatness.

Aouita had only competed over 800 metres sparingly since 1983. When he did race, it was in a smaller meeting. He would sensibly just race the world's best at the longer events which best suited him. But for 1988 Said had a grand plan. He wanted to win the 1,500 metres gold medal, since he already had the 5,000 metres gold from Los Angeles. For this he would start the hot favourite, but in the Moroccan's mind he felt himself capable of also contending in the 800 metres, so he decided to go for that as well!

It was unheard of for a successful 5,000 metres runner to start racing at 800 metres. The events were totally different. Another factor was his age. Aouita was twenty eight years old. It was most common for an athlete to move up in distance in the latter stages of his career, not move down. Anyone who even considered what Aouita was planning would be thought of as most egotistical. But Said was no ordinary athlete and he proved that his drastic career move was indeed a correct one.

He raced at Verona, Budapest, Brussels and Koln at his new distance, winning on every occasion. He defeated all the pre Olympic favourites. This was truly incredible. Aouita's best result was a 1:43.86 in Koln. He went to Seoul as the slight favourite for gold in this event.

Said performed well in the Olympic final but was defeated by better runners on the day. His time of 1:44.06 was good, but Paul Ereng and Joaquim Cruz were faster. There was no shame in that. The shame was that he was unable to contend for the 1,500 metres, which he was expected to win. Too much racing led to an injury, which forced Aouita to sit out his semi final.

The athletics world still recognised the enormity of what the Moroccan had accomplished and at year's end he was deservedly ranked number one in the world at 800 metres.

Aouita's legacy wasn't only left in Seoul with his own achievement (no man had previously won Olympic medals in the 800 and 5,000 metres). For Morocco still ended up with an Olympic gold medal courtesy of Brahim Boutayeb who was a surprise winner of the 10,000 metres. This was the beginning of the flow on effect of Aouita, the Moroccan hero.

MOROCCAN SUCCESS; THE KADA WAY

Said wasn't going to be a once off.

Brahim produced an outstanding performance to win comfortably in an Olympic record of 27:21.46. This was a very fast time in the warm conditions, not far short of Fernando Mamede's 27:13.81 world record. For a while the Portuguese's mark was under threat, after a 5,000 metres split of 13:36.47. At 2,000 metres Moses Tanui had taken off at a tremendous speed, dragging along his team mate Kipkemboi Kimeli and Italy's Salvatore Antibo. Boutayeb was a little slow to react, but gradually worked his way up to the front, smartly expending his energies a little more wisely than his opponents. Keeping a consistent pace, Brahim soon found himself running with only Kimeli, well before the halfway point. With still 4,600 metres remaining he took the lead himself after Tanui had re-established contact. Running the fifteenth lap in 64.64 seconds, the Moroccan was able to distance himself from Kimeli and completely end the resistance of Tanui. From thereafter Brahim held a significant gap and was never threatened. It was a commanding front running display. As well as winning the Olympic title Boutayeb became the Moroccan record holder, as he had bettered Aouita's once off effort at the event of 27:26.11 in Oslo 1986. That year Brahim Boutayeb additionally won the 5,000 and 10,000 metres at the African Championships.

Although he finished third and fourth in the Tokyo World Championships and Barcelona Olympic Games in the 5,000 metres, Brahim's career was a minor disappointment considering his performances in 1988. However Morocco had another Boutayeb who also reached the elite level. Hammou Boutayeb clocked a 27:25.48 over 10,000 metres in Oslo, 1990 and the next year placed eighth in the World Championships. Mohamed Issangar also arrived on the scene, winning a big 5,000 metres race in London with a 13:08.51. He defeated the world record holder at 10,000 metres, Arturo Barrios, by one hundredth of a second! At the 1992 Barcelona Olympics, Rachid El Basir shocked many when he won the silver medal in the 1,500 metres. By 1993 Brahim Jabbour was also making an impact, finishing sixth in the World Championship 5,000 metres. Each of these runners was sending clear signals that Morocco was becoming a major force in men's distance running.

But the real runner that took over the mantle from Said Aouita was Khalid Skah.

Born on the 29th of January 1967, Khalid spent his major developing period in the shadow of Aouita. At the end of the 1980's Said was still the best athlete around. But all of a sudden age and injuries caught up with him. Fortunately for Morocco, Skah was ready to make an impact in a way that few imagined possible.

The 1990 World Cross Country was expected to be a Kenyan dominated race. It had won the last four events, all thanks to John Ngugi, but had also shown tremendous overall depth, as Kenya had triumphed in the team's competition throughout those years as well. Ngugi was troubled with injuries this time around and would only place twentieth, but most felt that it would make little difference as to the winning nation. Enter a pesky little Moroccan to start a new rivalry. Khalid had placed only sixty eighth in the junior race in 1986 and fifty sixth in the senior race last year, but in Aix-les-Bains Skah kept with team Kenya's strong pace throughout, then used his superior kick to defeat Moses Tanui and win the gold medal. This was a massive achievement.

Khalid proved that he was no flash in the pan by later dominating the European Grand Prix circuit. He won 5,000 metres races at Stockholm and Zurich, and then won the 10,000 metres at Brussels. All these venues were traditional places of excellence for distance running.

Skah defended his title by winning the World Cross Country again in 1991 at Antwerp, with Tanui once more frustrated to place second. He continued his good form on the track with a personal best 27:23.29 victory in the 10,000 metres at Oslo in the lead up to the World Championships in Tokyo. The Kenyans had a serious problem on their hands. How could they stop this man from dominating in Japan?

MOROCCAN SUCCESS; THE KADA WAY

Khalid had an outstanding finishing kick, which the Kenyans didn't seem to be able to match. Somehow they needed to break away, or at least make the pace tough enough in order to reduce the kick of the Moroccan, should the race boil down to a sprint. Already Kenya had a tradition for aggressive front running. Such tactics had led to comfortable victories for Paul Kipkoech in Rome '87 and John Ngugi in Seoul '88. But there hadn't been a runner of Skah's abilities to contend with in those races.

The Tokyo Championships were the height of the Khalid Skah vs. Kenya rivalry. Skah was attempting to win both the 10,000 and 5,000 metres. First up was the longer event and his cross country rival Moses Tanui and new talent Richard Chelimo were waiting for him.

The race was a minor classic. This wasn't directly due to Skah but was very much indirectly due to him. If he hadn't been in the race then it is likely that the Kenyans would have taken the first half much easier. As it was, Chelimo took off like a mad man, opening up a huge lead as he passed through 5,000 metres in 13:30, which was under world record pace. There was no way that Khalid could have gone with this and not blown up, so he sensibly stayed with the main pack.

The key to the race was when Tanui made his move and Skah chose not to, or was unable to follow him. Once the Kenyan caught his teammate, they were able to work together, even though Chelimo was doing it tough after his earlier tempo. Their pace slowed substantially as conditions were warm, thus not great for distance running. Skah displayed good form in the dying stages but he left his run too late. Tanui out sprinted Chelimo for the gold in a winning time of 27:38.74. Skah finished exactly three seconds back and had to settle for the bronze medal.

A successful double was always unlikely and Khalid needed a slow early pace to give him a chance in the 5,000 metres. But with Yobes Ondieki in the field this didn't happen. Not long after the gun the Kenyan charged off at an incredible speed. To gain his huge lead over the field he ran approximately a four minute mile! Skah was toast. Ondieki slowed a great deal after his initial surge, but his winning time of 13:14.45 was only challenged by Ethiopia's Fita Bayissa who chased hard to run 13:16.64. Brahim Boutayeb placed third but was well beaten in 13:22.70. Skah would have been better off not running. Finishing sixth was a false indication of his standing in the world of distance running, as was his time of 13:32.90.

The Kenyans now had the confidence against Skah and this only increased when Ngugi returned to form to win his fifth World Cross Country in 1992 (he had failed to finish in '91). Skah was run out of the medals in fourth place. Despite these defeats, by the time the Barcelona Olympics were held, he was arguably still the favourite to win the 10,000 metres.

There was no doubling up on events this time as conditions were even more oppressive than Tokyo. Khalid would have to contend with Tanui and Chelimo once more. However Moses had a shocker and was not a factor in the latter stages. Richard was on form but finding that on this occasion he was unable to rid himself of Skah.

The two had cleared well out from the rest of the field and as the contest entered its final few laps it seemed as if the pair were preparing themselves for a sprint finish. Skah had been sitting in behind the Kenyan but he briefly took over the lead as they lapped his teammate Hammou Boutayeb approaching three laps to go.

The laps were slow and Hammou kept pace with the leaders. But on the back straight, to everybody's surprise, he accelerated past the *competing* athletes. Suddenly Chelimo was sandwiched between the two Moroccans! The Spanish crowd did not like this at all and a great feeling of unease overtook the stadium.

Both Chelimo and Skah regained the lead but still Boutayeb kept pace. On the back straight for the second last time, Hammou went past them once more as a chorus of boos rang out from the crowd. The two competitors went back to the front but as they approached the bell, the lapped athlete was

MOROCCAN SUCCESS; THE KADA WAY

still attempting to stay in contact. In scenes never witnessed before, an official tried to physically stop him from involving himself any further in proceedings.

Fortunately, there were no interruptions on the last lap and it was Skah who had the finishing speed to win in 27:46.70, with Chelimo clocking 27:47.72. However Khalid was immediately disqualified and Richard was awarded the gold medal. What Boutayeb had done was against the rules. Skah put forward a protest, claiming that he had nothing to do with Boutayeb's strange actions. He even stated that the two were rivals, insinuating that Hammou might have been wanting to disrupt Skah as much as Chelimo. The case hinged on the interpretation of whether the lapped runner had impeded Chelimo. Whether or not Skah had been involved in creating some quite brilliant team tactics we will probably never know. Regardless, most people felt that he would have won the race with or without Boutayeb's help. Common sense prevailed and Skah was reinstated as the Olympic champion. It was the culmination of a three year period where on the basis of excellent consistency, he had been the world's best long distance runner.

In 1993, Skah continued his winning form on the track with big wins in the Zurich 5,000 metres and the Brussels 10,000 metres. However his cross country form was lagging as his sixth and fifth placings in the 1993 and 1994 World Cross Country events showed. For now, he remained clearly Morocco's best long distance track runner and arguably the world's best.

But one Moroccan youngster was hungry and after his crown.

1994 turned into a tremendously satisfying year for Salah Hissou. Following his productive cross country and road running he returned home for a brief stint of training. He warmed up for his European adventure by running a 3:43.40 for 1,500 metres in Meknes on May 28. This was far from a world class time but Salah wasn't a middle distance runner and now he freshened up for a massive race at 5,000 metres in Saint-Denis, France, on June 10.

He had already shown some good form in cross country and on the road. Now he intended to show it on the track. Hissou had never competed in a World Athletics Championships or Olympic Games, but on this day he was to first experience a level that was close to that on the track. This race contained the reigning world and Olympic 10,000 metres champions. Both had been comfortably ahead of Salah in Budapest. Could Hissou close the gap in Saint-Denis?

This was a fascinating confrontation. In one corner was Haile Gebrselassie, the young majestically talented Ethiopian. In the other was Khalid Skah, the Moroccan who had been arguably the world's best distance runner over the past few years. He had experienced great successes in many various disciplines, such as cross country, track races in Europe's Grand Prix meetings, plus the major track championships themselves. However Haile had defeated Khalid twice at major championships, those being the Stuttgart 5,000 metres and most recently, the World Cross Country. Skah needed to turn the tables now or face the prospect of never defeating the improving Gebrselassie again.

It didn't take long for Salah Hissou to realise that he was running at a track level far above what he was used to. His fastest ever 5,000 metres race had been conducted at approximately sixty five, sixty six second lap pace. Many of his races had averaged close to sixty eight second lap tempo. Now in France, he was striding out the sixty four second laps with some of distance running's elite, spending most of the race keeping up with Khalid Skah. This was the moment that Abdelkader Kada may have realised that his runner belonged in such esteemed company.

In the latter stages, Salah slipped away from the best but he wasn't the only one. By the last lap, only Skah and Gebrselassie had survived to battle for the race win. It was a close encounter, with somewhat surprisingly Khalid gaining victory in a time of 13:10.51. Haile was only just behind with a 13:10.79. Everyone else had been dropped.

MOROCCAN SUCCESS; THE KADA WAY

Hissou was relatively competitive with the rest of the field, finishing seventh and clocking a personal best of 13:19.42. He had taken *eighteen* seconds off his pre race best!

There were many other Moroccans displaying their distance running talents. Brahim Lahlafi and Brahim Jabbour both defeated Hissou, finishing third and fifth respectively. Just behind Salah in eighth place was Ismail Sghyr, who like Hissou, was twenty two years old. It was the third race in 1994 that Hissou and Moroccan men's running as a whole had shown that they were a force to be reckoned with.

Abdelkader and Salah decided to remain in France for a championship event that would provide good practice for future major championships. Hissou would add further to his burgeoning reputation at the Francophone Games, a championship for French speaking nations. These Games were held in Paris during July. The championship had only been held once before, with the inaugural Games taking place in 1989. In that edition, the 5,000 metres event was of great interest with the best runner in the world, Said Aouita beating Khalid Skah. Khalid went on to bigger and better things and Salah hoped that Francophone would have a similar impact on his career. The 10,000 metres and 5,000 metres races were held on the 11th and 13th of July. It didn't allow much time for recovery, but feeling in great form Hissou chose to compete in both events. The medallists from the races were:

10,000 metres

Salah Hissou	28:34.25
Hammou Boutayeb	28:35.88
Khalid Boulami	28:48.43

5,000 metres

Salah Hissou	13:22.08
Brahim Lahlafi	13:25.91
Brahim Jabbour	14:01.64

Salah Hissou had won both the 5,000 metres and 10,000

metres against quality opposition. This double was a major accomplishment. Winning the longer race was good enough in itself but it was the shorter race that he had to truly excel in to win. And how well he won it! Salah went close to his recent 5,000 metres PB, while comfortably beating fellow Moroccans Brahim Lahlafi and world championship representative Brahim Jabbour. Defeating two runners who he'd lost to in his previous race again highlighted that Salah was constantly improving during this period. Hissou finished the 5,000 metres emphatically, gapping Lahlafi by more than three seconds while he destroyed Jabbour by nearly forty! This showed that he didn't require a pure fast kick to win. Future races would reveal that it was much easier for Hissou when he didn't have to rely on his sprint finish. Often, it wasn't very reliable!

The 10,000 metres time wasn't impressive but this was a championship so good times were not imperative. A fast time could come later in the year. It was at these Games where Salah made others believe that he was to be the next top Moroccan distance man. The nation was looking for its next world beater. Many eyes would now be focussed on Salah Hissou.

Hissou did not have to contend with Skah in Paris. Khalid had surprisingly run the 3,000 metres steeplechase and won it, in a respectable time of 8:19.30. The great Moroccan had plenty of strings to his bow. It is fair to say that it's unlikely Salah would have beaten him if he'd chosen to run in the 5,000 metres or 10,000 metres. Skah was world standard. Hissou was *nearly* there, but not quite. Yet.

At the same time, Abdelkader Kada was also coaching another young runner who performed well at the championships.

Nineteen year old Moroccan Hicham El Guerrouj placed third in the 1,500 metres. It was a slow race with the winner Azzedine Sediki clocking 3:42.57. Frenchman Abdelkader Chekhemani ran 3:43.08 with Hicham not far behind in 3:43.54. While his result did not match that of Salah's, Kada's middle distance runner was at least as talented, as his junior

MOROCCAN SUCCESS; THE KADA WAY

results reflected. With age on his side there was plenty of time to improve on 3:43.54.

Hicham El Guerrouj was born on the 14th of September 1974, in Berkane, a city at sea level, which was situated in North Eastern Morocco. Hicham first displayed his immense ability to Morocco's running elite when he won the National Cross Country junior event in 1990. This was a great surprise to many as he'd only started training regularly the previous year (he ran his first ever 1,500 metres race in 4:01), having earlier put most of his sporting energies into football, although as a goalkeeper, his endurance can't have been enhanced too much during that phase. Even though Hicham only took up distance running from a serious perspective quite late, he had always taken an interest in the world's best. Years later he spoke of his middle distance heroes, "I have always liked the British athletes - Steve Ovett, Seb Coe and particularly Steve Cram. I remember the contests between them very well and I know all about their rivalry. But, of course, I have also always followed Said Aouita, who has a great following in Morocco." He had also displayed real ability in amongst his football career, having finished second in a cross country race at the age of twelve. Even decades later Hicham recalled this experience fondly, "My best memory is the day I started running." He said that finishing second was "a great, great thing for me, something I never thought that I could do."

By 1991, he was training at the National Institute of Athletics in Rabat where he started his association with coach Kada. Initially he was forced to conduct his work under one of Abdelkader's assistants, which Hicham wasn't too pleased about. He had seen that Salah Hissou trained under Kada and he wanted to be involved with the elite of Morocco's youthful talent. Kada later remembered, "He saw that I was coaching Salah Hissou and he said he wanted to work with me also or he would go home."

Years later, Salah fully understood the young runner's determination and fierce commitment as he commented, "He is a very serious professional runner. He doesn't want to be a normal athlete. He wants to be a great athlete. He could do twenty competitions a year, but he only does seven to ten, so they will always be high level."

That season El Guerrouj managed to run a time of 3:51 for the 1,500 metres. This was a good performance for a sixteen or seventeen year old.

1992 was the significant year in El Guerrouj's junior development. Rabat played host to the Moroccan Cross Country Championships on February 8 and Hicham placed second in the 8 kms junior race. He finished the course in twenty five minutes dead. Pretty good at seventeen. It was on this day that Salah Hissou ran the senior race, winning the 12 kms event in 35:37.

The next month El Guerrouj travelled to America, aiming at a high place in the World Junior Cross Country Championships. Hicham ran at a similar standard to his Rabat effort (24:26 for 7.8 kms) but that wasn't going to be good enough in this class of field. The winner, Ismael Kirui of Kenya, ran the course in 23:27. Taking the silver and bronze medals were Haile Gebrselassie and Josephat Machuka, outstanding junior runners. The Moroccan was nearly a minute behind and finished fourteenth.

Later in the year the World Junior Championships were held in Seoul. Having just turned eighteen, Hicham was still unsure about where his future lay, event wise. Here, he entered the 5,000 metres where he again encountered Kirui and Gebrselassie.

The heats were raced on September 17, 1992, and the standards were very high. Hicham qualified comfortably enough, finishing fifth in a decent time of 14:03.93. First to cross the line was Gebrselassie in 14:00.10.

The final was on the 19th of September and El Guerrouj experienced a career highlight. He was unable to keep in touch with the two big guns but defeated the rest of the best young athletes to win the bronze medal. His time was an excellent 13:46.79. Gebrselassie out kicked Kirui to take the

MOROCCAN SUCCESS; THE KADA WAY

gold in 13:36.03. Haile did the distance double at the championships, establishing himself as a superstar of the future.

Hicham knew that becoming a top international distance runner was now possible. So did Kada. He acknowledged, "You will be a great champion some day. Just be patient."

El Guerrouj did not over race during this period of his youth. On the contrary, his training was more important than his racing, though he did race on November 29, but it was another junior cross country event. The 6.98 kms distance was covered in Torres Vedras and Hicham's time of 23:04 was slow, but he won. It was a good confidence builder.

A track race was scheduled next at the distance of 3,000 metres in Dar el Beida, Morocco. On the 14th of February, El Guerrouj defeated many of his fellow countrymen in a good time of 7:56.3. The win was impressive but much more improvement was required before he could contemplate taking on the senior athletes.

Hicham entered the World Junior Cross Country Championships again when they were held in Amorebieta, Spain, on March 28, but it seemed that he didn't quite have the makings of a really top class runner on the uneven terrain. The race was Kenyan dominated. The distance running super nation filled the podium, led by sixteen year old Philip Mosima. The eighteen year old Moroccan was smashed by him and many others. Finishing fifteenth must have been slightly disappointing for Kada and El Guerrouj. Together they decided that in order to reach the next level, more time needed to be dedicated solely to training.

Any plans to contest the European Grand Prix season were scrapped as many months of hard training were completed. Once 1994 arrived, El Guerrouj was a much better runner. He first displayed this in a 3,000 metres race on March 19 in Meknes, Morocco. Running a time of 7:49.84 and getting the race win was a tremendous start to the year. It was the start of his regular competition in the senior ranks.

Hicham El Guerrouj skipped the Cross Country in Hungary and next appeared as a part of Morocco's successful team in the World Road Relay Championships on April 17. He ran a 5 kms leg in a time of 13:43 that the fastest for that section. It was a faster time than he had run for the same distance on the track in the World Junior Championships nineteen months earlier. To run quicker on the road, where times are generally slower, showed his improvement. He also enjoyed the company of the national coach at the time, Said Aouita. In 1999 Hicham was full of praise as he reflected, "Said Aouita was my hero. A hero and a myth for the whole of Morocco. He brought Moroccan athletics to the front of the international stage and I want to bring all of his records back to Morocco."

Having equal regard for Hicham, Said predicted that this young man would go on to become the best 1,500 metres runner in history.

It was during these Road Relay Championships that Abdelkader Kada's boys really shone. Hicham was the third of the Moroccan runners and by the time he took the baton, he was already giving up ground to the Kenyan and Ethiopian teams. Kenya was approximately twenty seconds clear with Ethiopia thirteen seconds ahead. However El Guerrouj quickly reeled them in, and by the time he handed the baton to Salah, Morocco led Kenya by thirteen seconds. Hissou then increased the margin substantially during his fourth leg. Morocco's gold medal team consisted of El Guerrouj, Hissou, Skah, Brahim Jabbour, Elarbi Khattabi and Brahim Boutayeb.

It was now time for El Guerrouj to focus on the track. It was a mystery to most as to what event Hicham would focus his attentions on. There was no mystery to he and Abdelkader. Information gathered from years of training told them that the Moroccan's future lay as a middle distance athlete. Kada entered him in the 1,500 metres at the Francophone Games where he performed well for third place.

El Guerrouj felt ready to take his ambitions on to the big stage of the European circuit. There was an important meeting coming up on July 18 and Hicham was keen to test himself

MOROCCAN SUCCESS; THE KADA WAY

against another great young talent, Burundi's Venuste Niyongabo.

Hicham could not have hoped for much better from the event. The race contained many of the world's best middle distance runners and surprisingly, the young Moroccan more than held his own. The top four in the Nice 1,500 metres were:

Venuste Niyongabo	3:30.95
Azzedine Sediki	3:32.71
Hicham El Guerrouj	3:33.61
Eric Dubus	3:34.75

El Guerrouj even defeated the reigning Olympic champions at 800 and 1,500 metres, with William Tanui and Fermin Cacho lagging behind in eighth and ninth places!

The time of 3:33 was outstanding. It was easily his best performance to date, his first result that was of a top international standard at senior level. Only the man from Burundi was in a class above Hicham. Morocco was well represented in Nice with Sediki's excellent second place ahead of El Guerrouj.

The next European athletics meeting was an even bigger one. On July 22, Oslo hosted its annual Bislett Games, always regarded as a highlight on the track and field calendar.

The meeting was famous for its golden mile, the event having been made famous by many runners, including Sebastian Coe. Hicham wanted to improve on his already spectacular form. A similar standard of performance to Nice would see him come close to the 3:50 barrier. It was a barrier that not many had broken, considering that it was first done by John Walker on the 12th of August, 1975 in Gothenburg. The world record then was 3:49.4. Others to have conquered 3:50 since are:

Sebastian Coe
Steve Ovett
Jose Luis Gonzalez

Steve Scott
Mike Boit
Steve Cram
Sydney Maree
David Moorcroft
Ray Flynn
Thomas Wessinghage
Said Aouita
Jim Spivey
Peter Elliott
Jens-Peter Herold
Abdi Bile
Joe Falcon
Wilfred Oanda Kirochi
Simon Doyle
Noureddine Morceli
William Kemei

A total of twenty one men. Close enough to one per year since Walker's mark. The mile's golden age had been the early '80's with the British runners setting new standards. Since then, there hadn't been much improvement until an Algerian came along. As of July 22, 1994, the world record stood at Noureddine Morceli's 3:44.39. In nearly twenty years the record had vastly improved but running sub 3:50 remained only possible for the truly elite.

Another runner was added to the above list when Venuste Niyongabo won the Oslo race in an excellent time of 3:48.94. His result made him the tenth fastest of all time. The 1987 1,500 metres world champion, Abdi Bile was a distant second in 3:50.67, almost two seconds adrift.

Hicham El Guerrouj managed a good time of 3:53.71, yet this only left him in eighth place, such was the quality of the field. This was no reason to become dispirited as not many teenagers are able to break the four minute mile so easily.

Niyongabo was proving to be an athlete of real calibre. He was clocking the sort of times that would force Noureddine Morceli to take notice. Everything seemed to be falling into

MOROCCAN SUCCESS; THE KADA WAY

place for a tremendous battle between the two at next year's Gothenburg World Championships.

Four days later in Saint Petersburg, Morceli would better him with a mile winning time of 3:48.67. The twenty seven hundredths of a second difference would only give Niyongabo more encouragement.

Kada's other runner was also in attendance at the Bislett Games. Confident after his excellent double at the Francophone Games, Salah Hissou felt he was ready to go to another new level in the 5,000 metres. Could his lungs and legs now handle a sixty three second lap pace and could he now defeat Khalid Skah?

Skah's good form had continued on from Saint-Denis. On July the 8th he again displayed the apparent difference between himself and Morocco's next best runners when he had a good crack at the 5,000 metres world record in Lille. Khalid wasn't far off Gebrselassie's recent world record as he came very close to removing Said Aouita's Moroccan mark, but to no avail. The time of 13:00.54 was nevertheless a magnificent personal best and suggested that the top Moroccan was still improving at the age of twenty seven. He was far from a spent force and 1995 and in particular the World Championships, could have a lot to offer him.

Khalid was his nation's top runner but Morocco's next best were fast catching up. The Oslo 5,000 metres provided a classic encounter with a race that was run at close to a world record time. Salah Hissou put in another ground breaking run, running a 13:04.93. This was averaging sub sixty three's and was a personal best time by 14.49 seconds! Yet in Norway this was only enough for fourth place. Hissou wasn't even the first or second Moroccan. Another improving Moroccan named Brahim Lahlafi reversed the result from the Francophone Games, running 13:03.36. Ahead of him was a surprise packet from America in Bob Kennedy, who clocked 13:02.93, a time that made him the fastest white man in the world and one of the fastest overall. Defeating them all was Khalid Skah. With a 13:01.89, he was running as well as ever.

The big change for Skah was that there was now strong competition coming from his native Morocco. This only added to the regular challenges he got from the usual suspects of Kenya and Ethiopia. For now Khalid was coping very well with all the opposition.

Time wise, this was as close as Salah had come to the world's best at any distance. Only Said Aouita and Haile Gebrselassie had ever broken thirteen minutes. Salah was already close to reaching his optimum abilities. His late race speed was something that needed to be improved if he was to start winning distance races on the highly competitive European Grand Prix circuit but that could come later. Despite finishing fourth, there were mostly positives to take from the race. Plenty of daylight existed between him and the rest. Paul Bitok ran a 13:12.10 for fifth place and he was the silver medallist from Barcelona. Ismael Kirui was even further behind, finishing eighth. Hissou was competing against high quality opposition and discovering that he belonged.

Born on April 15, 1968, Brahim Lahlafi was slow to show the world signs of his potential. His junior career produced nothing of significance but in 1990 he placed thirtieth in the World Cross Country and posted a personal best for 5,000 metres of 13:21.11. His career then hit a brick wall and didn't prosper until 1993 when he recorded an excellent eleventh place finish in the World Cross Country. Later that year, he improved his 5,000 metres personal record to 13:15.85 in Oslo. Given his age of twenty five years, he was unlikely to produce another big improvement which he'd require if he wanted to compete with the world's best.

His latest result in Norway was a big surprise and changed everything. Suddenly he was hot on the heels of Khalid Skah.

Yet in Oslo, the mile and 5,000 metres were just minor events in the bigger scheme of things. World cross country champion William Sigei surprised many by running a new 10,000 metres world record. The time was a sensational 26:52.23, six seconds faster than teammate Yobes Ondieki's old time. He had completed the second half of his record run in 13:19.52!

MOROCCAN SUCCESS; THE KADA WAY

Now being the world cross country double champion and 10,000 metres world record holder, much would be expected of Sigei. Surely 1995 would hold great things for him. Could he win the '95 10,000 metres world title in Gothenburg?

Perhaps if he didn't dwell in Kenya he would have been able to have a say in proceedings. Being a Kenyan athlete brings great prestige, but it also brings incredible competition, not just from the world, but also from within your own nation. In 1994, William Sigei was one of the best long distance runners in the world, but he only had to slip a little to fall off the face of the Kenyan distance running earth. Sigei got injured prior to the '95 World Cross Country and was unable to compete, leaving Paul Tergat to take his title without William getting a chance to defend it. As things eventuated, Sigei would not make the Kenyan team for Gothenburg and he never did anything else of great significance. It was just one of many examples of the quick rise and fall of a Kenyan runner.

At this time there was little argument as to who was the best middle/long distance runner in the world. On August 17 the world's best at 1,500 metres took on the best over 5,000 metres and won in a canter. The kick down in Zurich from Noureddine Morceli was unforgettable. Simply explosive. After 4,000 metres were reached in 10:37.44, the Algerian recorded better than a 2:26.41 final km to win in 13:03.85. His last lap was timed at 52.20, which was the fastest ever recorded for this distance! His margin of victory over Fita Bayissa was almost four seconds, with the other names further back being a who's who of long distance running. Skah, Bikila, Lahlafi, Kennedy, Sigei and Kirui.

Previously on the 2nd of August, Morceli had set another world record. This time he took a large chunk off the 3,000 metres standard when he ran 7:25.11 in Monaco. The Algerian was in a class of his own. In his wake he'd left another newly crowned world record holder. Haile Gebrselassie came in second, but he was light years away in 7:37.49. For the young Ethiopian, this was nothing to be embarrassed about. Morceli had done this to many quality athletes in the last few years. But beware, the longer an athlete remains at the top, the closer he is to being knocked off his perch.

On the 4th of June, Haile Gebrselassie had conquered the long standing 5,000 metres world record of Moroccan Said Aouita. His 12:58.39 wasn't the greatest of records, but it had become an almost mythical time, because it had survived for nearly seven years. This in itself was a surprise. Dave Moorcroft from Great Britain had set a world record of 13:00.41, way back on the 7th of July 1982, in Oslo. In nearly twelve years the 5,000 metres had improved by only 2.02 seconds! Somebody was going to break it soon. That it was Haile didn't necessarily mean that the Ethiopian was destined for real greatness. Like Roger Bannister breaking the four minute mile, it didn't mean that much more was to follow. Of course Gebrselassie would become a much more significant athlete than Bannister but at the time, few knew. Haile and his agent Jos Hermens believed that greater things were possible.

Haile's time in Hengelo was 12:56.96. This wasn't ground breaking but Gebrselassie had already won gold and silver medals at last year's World Championships. The title of world record holder made his an imposing resumé.

But in 1994 the Ethiopian was proving to be beatable. He had suffered two losses at 5,000 metres since Hengelo, as well as Morceli's crushing victory at 3,000 metres. In between times he had recorded a personal best for 10,000 metres, when he ran 27:15.0 for victory in Lausanne. He was arguably the world's best at this distance.

Salah Hissou had won races over 10,000 metres, but he had yet to record a world class time. The venue of Brussels would provide an opportunity for the in form Moroccan to rectify this on August 19. Rectify it he did, running a superb personal best of 27:21.75. But his performance was about so much more than the time. This was an extremely high quality field and it was Hissou's best career run so far. Lining up alongside him was the world champion Haile Gebrselassie. Next to Haile, Salah's pedigree was clearly outmatched. On the track

MOROCCAN SUCCESS; THE KADA WAY

though, there was little difference. Consider that in his first breakthrough race, the '94 World Cross Country, Gebrselassie had beaten Hissou easily. Over 10,000 metres in Brussels it came down to a sprint finish, so alas, if you watched the Stuttgart races then you know the final outcome.

Haile Gebrselassie	27:20.39
Salah Hissou	27:21.75
Aloys Nizigama	27:22.06
Paul Tergat	27:23.89
Ondoro Osoro	27:28.36
Mathias Ntawulikura	27:36.15
Vincent Rousseau	27:47.79

The Ethiopian was too good, but to finish less than two seconds in arrears must have made Salah feel like a real winner, not to mention the quality of competitors left trailing him. There were some other big names not mentioned above who cracked in a big way. Brahim Boutayeb and Moses Tanui finished eighth and thirteenth in Brussels. However these were the champions of the past. We were in the midst of a new era.

This upgrade in performance made Salah Hissou the sixth fastest 10,000 metres runner in 1994. Significantly he was ahead of Khalid Skah in the charts and had definitely made it to the big time. The Memorial Van Damme meeting was to be a highly influential venue in Salah Hissou's career.

In hindsight, we can look back and see that this was possibly Hissou's best ever chance to defeat Gebrselassie on the track. At least out of those times when he made it to the start line. Little did we know, that Brussels '94 would be the start of something special for Haile Gebrselassie. An amazing period of dominance would take place. Gebrselassie would race many times on the track, against the best distance runners in the world. Yet from 3,000 metres up to 10,000 metres, indoors and out, he would lose only once in a time span of over six years! Haile *never* performed badly. It is probably his greatest quality. His consistency of high performance.

But that was all in the future. The 1994 season was far from over for Salah Hissou and Hicham El Guerrouj.

Kada's middle distance man was also competing in Brussels but was not expecting a great result. Hicham's earlier season form had disappeared. Two days prior to Brussels he raced at Zurich and performed dismally in the 1,500 metres.

The race was a slow one, which made it even more surprising as to just how much Hicham had tailed off at the end. It was one mighty struggle for the athletes, but in particular the Moroccan as he slumped to an eventual time of 3:48.63, nearly the length of the straight behind Niyongabo who recorded another big win with his 3:36.16. The time wasn't as bad as it looked, for the conditions were monsoon like. The torrential rain made it a real slog, not a race for the pure track runner. Nevertheless, Venuste seemed to be coping well with everything that was being thrown at him in 1994 as he continued to go from strength to strength.

The Belgium meeting offered an opportunity for the Moroccan to improve on his previous poor showing. Tenth place was his actual result from Zurich. To improve a few positions would be encouraging. Kada knew not to have early high expectations as he realised that inconsistency is not unusual in a young athlete on the rise.

Consequently Abdelkader might not have been overly distraught with what eventuated in the Brussels 1,500 metres. The result was arguably worse than Zurich. El Guerrouj was pushed even further down the pecking order into thirteenth position. The one small consolation was an improvement in time. Still, a 3:41.60 wasn't fast enough to deny that this Moroccan was done for the season. Still shy of his twentieth birthday, Hicham needed another off season with many miles of exhaustive training which would then hopefully give him the strength to see out a European season.

The constant of Niyongabo winning (he ran 3:34.35) continued without Morceli in the field. El Guerrouj's teammate Azzedine Sediki ran well, recording another second place

MOROCCAN SUCCESS; THE KADA WAY

finish behind the barnstorming Burundi blazer. Placing third was Cacho, a respectable result for him after what had been a horrible year.

Despite obvious fatigue, El Guerrouj kept racing without a break. On August 21 he went to Germany with Hissou and Kada to race in Koln. The coach probably felt that this racing period would consist of Hicham's toughest challenges. If he could just remain positive and committed after many a battering, it would make him tougher for the future. Right now his student was in heavy study mode. The exams were going to come, but not till much later. The top performers from the Koln 1,500 metres were:

Venuste Niyongabo	3:31.98
Mohamed Suleiman	3:32.73
Azzedine Sediki	3:34.03
Atoi Boru	3:34.43
Benson Koech	3:34.72

Sediki once again scored high marks with a good placing. Azzedine wasn't a star but he was enjoying a very productive 1994, defeating many quality middle distance runners. It was only that elite level, the next level up, that he couldn't quite reach at the moment. Still, his competitiveness was impressive.

Hicham El Guerrouj wasn't yet an A grade student but this, another thirteenth placing did have a silver lining as the Moroccan was back under 3:40. His time was 3:37.60 to be exact, so he was much closer to Niyongabo when compared to the more recent races. That there remained many opponents still ahead of him shouldn't overly disgruntle Hicham.

Kada's number one athlete had speed on his mind, stepping down to the 3,000 metres only two days after a fast 10,000 metres. A high class field had assembled for the event and Salah Hissou produced a decent performance, finishing fifth in a time of 7:38.14. In great form was the '92 5,000 metres Olympic champion Dieter Baumann. The German won in

7:34.69 and proved that he still possessed one of the most devastating kicks in distance running. He was one man that you had to be well ahead of before the bell. The men that he beat were not amateurs. The steeplechase world record record holder Moses Kiptanui, the Olympic 10,000 metres champion Khalid Skah and America's fast 5,000 metres man, Bob Kennedy. Hissou himself had beaten some reasonable names. Fita Bayissa, Aloys Nizigama, Abdi Bile and Paul Bitok all came in behind Salah. But these were not the names that were likely to challenge Hissou in the future. On the timesheets, Salah may have been the fastest Moroccan over 10,000 metres in 1994, but head to head Skah was still beating him.

For many years the 3,000 metres had been basically a part time event in athletics. It was an occasionally raced distance that would offer the middle distance runners and the long distance runners some variety to their usual schedules. Some great names had held the world record such as Henry Rono and Said Aouita but the distance held little in the way of prestige and meaning to most. During the season, distance runners and fans alike would tend to look forward to a fast 10,000 metres in Oslo and perhaps a quality 1500 metres/mile to go with it. Or to Zurich, where the 5,000 metres was usually of high quality. Or perhaps Brussels where the 10,000 metres had become almost a championship in itself, much like Fukuoka was for the marathon in the late 1970's, early 1980's.

Despite not being a championship event, the men's 3,000 metres would become a glamour event in track and field. So much so that it took some of the focus away from the 5,000 metres and 10,000 metres. Runners like Morceli and Kiptanui first gave the event some momentum with their high quality performances in the mid '90's. Then it became time for Gebrselassie and Komen to take over and give the distance even more emphasis. With each passing season, the 3,000 metres seemed to be held with more and more regularity and on most occasions there were many of distance running's best in attendance, putting their form and reputation on the line in their version of the 100 metres sprint. It even drew the

MOROCCAN SUCCESS; THE KADA WAY

best cross country and 10,000 metres runners. Athletes like Tergat, Koech and of course Hissou. Although this wasn't their best distance, they still competed hard and often quite well, against some of the faster men. Later, Salah would at times race over 3,000 metres as much as he would the 5,000 metres. The same could be said for Gebrselassie.

The night of August the 22nd, 1997 would be best remembered for the world record breaking feats that took place, with two world records being taken from a certain Ethiopian, yet he was not defeated in the process of losing either record. This wasn't because Gebrselassie wasn't competing. As well as those longer distance events, Brussels also held a 3,000 metres. At the venue where the 10,000 metres is king, the world's best distance runner *chose* to run the 3,000 metres. That in itself shows how far the event had come in just a few years. It wasn't as if Haile was alone in his choice to race this distance in Brussels. Finishing behind him, a long way behind him, were athletes who had been 5,000 metres medallists at the highest level. By then, seven and a half laps of the track held a stature that nobody would have thought possible at the start of the decade.

But that was the future and in '94 it were the longer distances that were most commonly raced. In the best shape of his life, Salah Hissou raced in Rieti over 5,000 metres on August the 28th. As he had done so in Brussels, he came close to achieving his first ever European Grand Prix victory. By the latter stages he had burned everyone off, with the exception of the most intimidating opponent of the day. Middle distance maestro Noureddine Morceli was in his usual great form and Hissou didn't stand a chance. When the Algerian put on the after burners in the final stages of the race, it was no contest. Morceli won in 13:07.88, with Hissou clocking 13:10.95. Salah could look at Noureddine bolting away at the finish and know that he could never reach that level of kick.

Explosive speed at that level is something you are born with. You certainly need to harness it to reach the Algerian's level, but basically you either have it or you don't. What Hissou *did* have was a tremendous capacity to run at a high threshold for long periods, a type of running which would soon become synonymous with a Kenyan named Daniel Komen. What Salah needed to do was increase his threshold running capacity a little further, then he could look to implement plans to rid himself of the Morcelis of world distance running before the final kick. The bell needn't always sound like a death knell for the Moroccan.

The performance in Rieti was another positive step forward in Hissou's development. On the 30th of August Salah went back to Germany for another 5,000 metres event in Berlin. The meeting was a part of the Golden Four (along with Oslo, Brussels and Zurich) so it attracted most of the best runners. The Golden Four was what would become effectively known as The Golden League in the late '90's.

After many excellent performances it was perhaps time for a bad one. This was arguably it for Hissou as he managed only ninth in 13:16.28 although this wasn't as bad as it sounds, considering it was a big bunch sprint finish. Dieter Baumann again produced the goods with a withering sprint to triumph in 13:12.47. He just defeated Moroccans Khalid Skah, Khalid Boulami and Ismail Sghyr who ran 13:12.74, 13:12.95 and 13:13.47 respectively. 1994 was a tough year to beat Skah, and Baumann had just knocked him off in back to back races. He was the one European flying the flag against the might of Africa.

Hicham El Guerrouj also competed in Berlin. Unfortunately it was the third consecutive 1,500 metres race in which he finished thirteenth. A superstitious man would be getting a little freaked out by these strange coincidences! The time of 3:38.39 showed no improvement from the Koln race so that was it for Hicham's first serious season competing in the upper echelons of middle distance running. Abdelkader sent him back home. There was plenty to work on but also plenty to look forward to. A relatively small improvement could see a big gain in 1995.

Incredible speed was shown from Venuste Niyongabo who destroyed the field by a massive margin. Great Britain's

MOROCCAN SUCCESS; THE KADA WAY

Matthew Yates was more than twenty metres behind the winner's 3:31.18. He was streets ahead of everyone, bar Morceli.

Noureddine and Venuste were the best at Hicham's chosen event, the 1,500 metres. They were a level or two up on El Guerrouj but the rest weren't consistently defeating him by huge margins. There was an opening there for a regular high placed finish. Take a few seconds off his last two races and Hicham would have found himself entrenched in the first three, rather than seemingly struggling in an ugly thirteenth. Abdelkader Kada would drum this into him during the months of hard training that were sure to follow.

For some there were still events to be hotly contested. Next up for Salah Hissou was the Grand Prix Final.

At the Grand Prix Final in Paris he showed a marked improvement in his finishing speed, though it wasn't enough to enable a win. On the 3rd of September Hissou finished a creditable fourth place in the 5,000 metres. It was another strong indication that his first big track victory wouldn't be far away. His time wasn't super fast, just a 13:15.16, but the first three athletes were less than a second ahead. This again showed that Salah's lack of basic speed was proving decisive in his overall result. Khalid Skah was still the top dog, winning in 13:14.63, but only just. He defeated another Moroccan Khalid Boulami, by one hundredth of a second. Finishing third was Moses Kiptanui. Some big names really struggled with Ismael Kirui tenth and Willam Sigei twelfth. Boulami was yet another Moroccan making his mark in 1994 though at a later age. He had just turned twenty five on August 7.

Salah Hissou's season concluded on the road. He ran in the World Half Marathon Championships in Oslo on September 24 and produced a reasonable time of 62:20. The eighteenth place finish wasn't great but Salah's focus was mainly on the track and cross country. Khalid Skah had no trouble adapting. He took the gold medal in the tremendous time of 60:27. 1994 was proving to be arguably his best year.

Salah wanted to continue testing himself so he competed again in a low key event in Rennes, France on October 3. The 10 kms on the road suited Hissou and he won with a time of 30:20, however this was just a warm up for a bigger race a week later.

Salah spent almost half of his 1994 season racing in France and so he found himself back in Paris on October 10. The outcome of this road race confirmed that Salah's immense talents weren't only confined to the grass and rubber. The field wasn't the greatest ever assembled so when the gun went off there was little fan fare, but fifty eight minutes and twenty seconds later, distance running's best kept secret was out. Morocco would have an adequate successor to Khalid Skah.

Hissou had performed superbly over the 20 kms road course and won the race in the process, beating the likes of Thomas Osano from Kenya and his fellow Moroccan Brahim Boutayeb. There was an even bigger surprise in the aftermath of his run. Despite a victory margin of only four seconds, Salah had broken the world record! Sure, 20 kms on the road was not a regularly run distance event, but to go from a little known athlete to a world record holder was a big deal. Hissou had run the equivalent of a low sixty one minute half marathon, indicating his performance was a very good one. This was back in the days when the top road runners were struggling to break one hour, so Hissou wasn't far away from those top guys such as Skah. This was a bonus run really, as Salah really saw himself as a track runner, not a road runner (beep, beep!). It was a good display of his strength, a quality that he would need in abundance if he was to continue to do well on the track and in cross country.

Surprisingly, his 20 kms world record was not beaten until fellow Moroccan Khalid Khannouchi smashed it on September the 7th, 1998, when he ran 57:37 in New Haven.

1994 had been a fantastic year for variety in Salah Hissou's racing. It was the year when he discovered how good he could be. He had competed well over 3,000 metres, the half

MOROCCAN SUCCESS; THE KADA WAY

marathon and everything else in between. He had excelled in most of his races, showing his competitors that he would be a runner to be reckoned with in future years. There were suddenly high expectations for Hissou in next year's World Cross Country and later the World Athletics Championships. Would he live up to them?

Greg Rowlerson

Kada's David's First Serious Battles With Their Goliaths

Kada planned a very hectic racing schedule for Salah Hissou and Hicham El Guerrouj in the early part of 1995. Salah was to race in numerous cross country events, designed to prepare him for the World Cross Country Championships on March 25. Hicham was to race many events indoors, with his eventual goal being the World Indoor Championships. The 1,500 metres final was scheduled for March 11.

Despite finishing his '94 season late, Hissou raced again on December 27. It was the season to be jolly but it wasn't the merriest of times for Salah who finished third over the 9.2 km course in Durham. Perhaps he wasn't race ready, but this was the venue for the upcoming World Championships and Kada wanted Hissou to experience the surroundings three months out from the big day. The Moroccan ran a time of 30:14, some eleven seconds off the pace of Kenyan winner Ismael Kirui. Ismael had struggled at times during the '94 European track season but he always liked competing over the cross country terrain.

Kirui was still only nineteen and considering all that he had achieved, this was a little hard to believe. In later years his birth date of February 20, 1975, would in fact come under question, after the revelations of his late brother's real age.

This brother of Ismael just so happened to be Richard Chelimo, the multiple medallist and former world record holder at the 10,000 metres. One of Kirui's cousins was also Moses Kiptanui, the world champion and world record holder at the steeplechase. No wonder this boy could run!

He first stunned the running world when he finished second in the 10,000 metres at the World Junior Championships in 1990, placing behind his brother Chelimo. This was unheard of for a fifteen year old. His first major title came at the 1992 World Junior Cross Country, when he comfortably beat Haile Gebrselassie to the line. Later that year it was clear the two enjoyed a rivalry after the Ethiopian defeated the Kenyan by

MOROCCAN SUCCESS; THE KADA WAY

just five hundredths of a second in the World Junior Championships 5,000 metres final in Seoul.

Kirui continued to make massive strides forward in his career. Early in 1993, he shocked many by claiming the bronze medal in the World Cross Country senior race. Later he set a world record on the road for 12 kms in San Francisco and moved into top track form with an excellent 13:06.71, giving him victory over 5,000 metres in Lausanne. On the 4th of August Kirui improved on this further by clocking 13:06.50 at Zurich. However, having finished fifth and a significant distance behind the winner Khalid Skah, he wasn't seriously expected to challenge for the world title, which was decided twelve days later in Stuttgart.

That race on August 16, 1993, will always be remembered as one of the greatest races at a major championship. The Moroccan Skah was the favourite and if he faltered, then Kenya's Paul Bitok was expected to come through and win. As it turned out, the pace was too fierce for either to have an impact.

The least fancied of the Kenyans, Michael Chesire completed the first 800 metres in 2:00.24, a suicidal speed. The pack stayed reasonably close to him, and by the time he reached 1,600 metres in 4:08.39, they were on his heels. But there was no respite for Skah and the Ethiopians. Soon Ismael was in the lead and former New Zealand Olympic champion John Walker made the accurate call with his comment, "Kirui knows only one way to run and that's fast from the front." After passing 2,000 metres in 5:11.27 Kirui took off, running the next lap in 60.21. With the others not really trying to chase him, his lead quickly grew to twenty five metres. Ismael stayed in front for the remainder of the race and at the bell still held a gap of around thirty metres. Bayissa and Gebrselassie made good attempts at chasing him down but their efforts were to no avail as Kirui held on to record a championship and junior record time of 13:02.75.

The atmosphere during this race was spine tingling, no doubt helped by the German fans, some of the sport's most knowledgeable. Australian broadcaster, Bruce McAvaney called the conclusion superbly, "Kirui's twenty metres in front. Bayissa and Gebrselassie work together. The two Ethiopians are going to try and run Kirui down. Can they do it? Kirui's lead is fifteen metres. The stadium is alight. Everybody's on their feet. This has been a magnificent race. And Kirui leads, Gebrselassie's after him, Kirui's hanging on, the eighteen year old. It's one of the greatest victories of all time. That's as good as you'll ever see. It will bring the house down."

John Walker chimed in with, "What gutsy front running and only a Kenyan could do it."

Though Kirui did win the 1994 5,000 metres race in Stockholm, he was less active during the season. But this victory in Durham showed that he was likely to be a major force again in 1995.

Kirui also had other family members in Willy Kirui, Catherine Kirui and William Mutwol who were all international calibre runners or would be in the future. There was something about a person's genes that made it more likely for some to become a champion distance runner. Famous family names roll off the tongue such as Konchellah, Keino, Soh, Shahanga, Castro and Boulami. Later would come Bekele and Songok. On a larger scale, it is the Kalenjin Kenyans in the Rift Valley who have, and would continue to provide an extraordinary number of world class distance runners, despite the tribe of people making up just a small percentage of the Kenyan population itself.

Most of the good running genes in the Hissou family tree had been handed down to Salah and he was making the most of his God given gift. He next travelled to Spain to race in Fuensalida on the 4th of January. A good line up had been assembled yet Hissou was able to defeat them all. Victory was achieved with a 29:44 over the 10.2 kms, but only after a titanic battle with Kenya's Paul Tergat. In the close finish, both were given the same time. Tergat was a good scalp now and would be an even better one in the future. Behind them were Domingos Castro and Worku Bikila, then the best from Spain.

MOROCCAN SUCCESS; THE KADA WAY

Hissou turned twenty three on January 16 but there was no luxury afforded for much celebrating. He raced again two days later in Seville. He completed the 10 kms cross country in a good time of 28:53 but lost out to the Portuguese athletes, Paulo Guerra and Domingos Castro by a few seconds. This loss wasn't disheartening because Salah hadn't reduced his training as it was too early to taper with his target race over two months away.

Fellow Moroccan Brahim Lahlafi finished fourth in this event with young Kenyan Daniel Komen fifth.

A week later Hissou took on Guerra once more and again the Portuguese won in Saint-Sebastian. The 10 kms course was a much tougher one with the winning time being 32:13. On this occasion Salah was only a second adrift as he moved up one position from Seville. It was time for a brief break from racing and a few weeks totally dedicated to training. Then he could begin to ease off to freshen up for Durham.

It was on this same day of January 25 that Hicham El Guerrouj commenced his season. The race in Grenoble had Kada throwing him to the lions. Abdelkader knew that his runner was far superior to 1994 following a productive off season. He could have entered him in a race where he was likely to win and grow in confidence, but on the start line, Hicham El Guerrouj looked across and saw Noureddine Morceli for the first time.

Born on February 28, 1970, Morceli had developed into one of the greatest runners of all time. Whilst having a range in his abilities, it was always as a miler where he was destined to have the most success. In 1988, Noureddine finished a respectable tenth in the World Junior Cross Country but a much higher second position in the World Junior 1,500 metres, later that year on the track.

The Algerian began to base himself in the United States and in his early years made nice, steady progress. During 1989 he finished fourth in the African Championships and ran a 3:37.87 personal best to win in Verona, Italy. Both of these races were at his preferred 1,500 metres.

At the time, Said Aouita was clearly the world's best middle distance runner and was clearly the man to beat throughout 1990. However after starting the year with some victories indoors, he suffered injury setbacks that required compartment syndrome surgery. When he returned he wasn't the same. He ended his season with a disastrous fifteenth placing in a big mile race in New York. The number one position suddenly became vacant.

It was Morceli who stepped into that vacancy and assumed the number one world ranking. Noureddine wasn't unbeatable. In fact he lost at Brussels, Koln and Rieti late in the year. Yet most of the time when he competed at 1,500 metres or a mile, he won. Morceli had a kick down over the final lap that could be devastating to his opposition. He was most consistent in his performances and had a season's best time of 3:32.60 in Bologna. Not too bad for a twenty year old.

The performances of Aouita from the previous season were slightly superior to Morceli's, so all middle distance running fans were excited about the confrontation for the 1991 season. If the Moroccan got himself fit, could he regain his spot as the world's best?

The early signs were that Said was finished but to his credit, despite losing repeatedly at various distances, he didn't give up on the year nor his career. In his first significant race over 1,500 metres, Aouita was beaten comprehensively into sixth place at Hengelo. However three weeks later, Said enjoyed confidence building wins in Nice and Paris. Now he was to face Morceli in Monaco just before the World Championships.

The results of the season indicated that Morceli would humble Aouita by at least five seconds. For starters his personal bests were down to 3:31.00 and 3:49.12. Nobody could get close to defeating him in his specialist events as his smallest victory margin was 0.96 seconds. Noureddine was proving to possess other Said type qualities also. After a dominant indoor season, Morceli surprised many by opening his season

MOROCCAN SUCCESS; THE KADA WAY

outdoors at 800 metres in Germany. The surprises continued as not only did he win, but recorded an excellent time of 1:44.85. Later he decided to step up to 3,000 metres for a race in Nice, which comprised many of the world's best 5,000 metres runners. Noureddine was not overawed and met the challenge with supreme confidence. Showing that his endurance levels were almost a match for his speed, Morceli kept pace with Brahim Boutayeb, Khalid Skah and Dieter Baumann, before leaving them more than a second in his wake at the finish. The time was a very impressive 7:37.34. The concluding km and lap were run in 2:24.64 and 53.8 respectively. Scary.

Aouita was no threat to Morceli in Monaco, though the world record holder's pride did extract out of him a tremendous effort, as he placed second in a massive season's best of 3:33.28. Morceli, running 3:32.04, was simply too young, too fast and now too good. Despite the Algerian's final lap of 53.7, Said didn't necessarily think so. His post race comments showed that he still retained a champion's arrogance, "Now all my world championships adversaries have to understand that I'm a potential medallist. I had trouble getting to the front, so I had to eat up all my energy in the straightaway. But the great Aouita has returned, and you won't be disappointed. As for Morceli, I will have my revenge."

They sounded more like the words of a world heavyweight champion than a distance running track one!

The Tokyo World Championships were more a celebration of the Algerian's special abilities than a confirmation of them. In the final he won the gold with consummate ease, running an extraordinary last lap of 51.55 to complete the event in 3:32.84, a full two seconds ahead of the rest. The thirty one year old Aouita no longer possessed the ability to step up the pace and finished in eleventh place.

Morceli said, "I was very confident, because I knew that sprinting was my strength."

Nobody had ever run such a fast final lap off that sort of

tempo. Not Coe, not Cram, not even Aouita.

A new era had well and truly emerged. Morceli concluded his year with another easy win in the Grand Prix Final in Barcelona. This is where he would surely become the Olympic champion next year. Coming back well in this race to finish second was Aouita. Noureddine put an exclamation mark on his 3:34.48 with a scorching 52.10 last lap.

Another outstanding indoor season followed in 1992, highlighted by his 2:15.26 world record over 1,000 metres. He appeared a certainty for Barcelona gold. Unfortunately Morceli became injured and at the commencement of the European season, he was suddenly back with the pack.

Noureddine suffered defeats in Rome and Oslo before he won his final lead up race in Lausanne. However his season's best was a fairly slow 3:34.16 and he'd won by a mere two hundredths of a second. In this form it was highly unlikely that he could win in Spain, but the 1,500 metres final was thirty one days away. Was there enough time to prepare in order for the real Morceli to be on display for the big race?

Morceli won both his preliminary rounds and reestablished himself as the athlete to beat in the final, but he ran a poor tactical race and allowed himself to be boxed in at the crucial stage on the last lap. He eventually finished a devastating seventh, well behind the home country hero, Fermin Cacho. The Spaniard's kick had been very good, but considering the very slow winning time of 3:40.12, a final lap of 50.40 wasn't as incredible as it might have sounded. The athletes had jogged through 800 metres in over 2:06, a split that was slower than the women's 1,500 metres final! Despite not at his best, Morceli should have then had the good sense to go to the front and build up a long, sustained drive for home. He still may not have won, but anything would have been better than the non contest that he gave on this most important of days.

Despite this performance, his form was good enough to challenge for gold, as just three days later he won in Monaco with a top time of 3:32.75, his best performance since the

MOROCCAN SUCCESS; THE KADA WAY

indoor season. This was the real Morceli. Eight days later he went to Zurich and destroyed the best from Barcelona on his way to a national record of 3:30.75. Later he would conclude his year in Rieti, where he not only won the 1,500 metres convincingly, but broke Said Aouita's long standing world record with a magnificent time of 3:28.86. Barcelona was just an anomaly in this man's domination of the 1,500 metres.

Over the next two years, Morceli was undefeated at distances ranging from 1,000 to 5,000 metres. Amongst his many highlights was the retention of his world title in Stuttgart, where he recorded an incredible 50.62 final lap (3:34.24 overall time), world records for the mile and 3,000 metres, plus that awesome 5,000 metres win in Zurich. He was also named the winner of the overall Grand Prix title (incorporating athletes from all track and field events) in 1994.

Consequently at the dawn of the 1995 season, it was most unlikely that Hicham El Guerrouj could defeat Noureddine Morceli. What was important would be the deficit.

The Moroccan did not win but showed improvement despite clearly being out of the Algerian's league. Last season Hicham might have been five to ten seconds in arrears. Here in France, the gap was significant but not so substantial. Morceli clocked 3:34.29 to El Guerrouj's 3:37.10. Noureddine's kick remained every bit as fearsome as previously but Hicham was much stronger now. No question. He even picked up the Moroccan national record for good measure.

El Guerrouj came up against another world champion when he competed in Stuttgart only seven days later. To see this athlete was a surprise, for it was Kenyan Moses Kiptanui, renowned for his steeplechase dominance, not his middle distance ability. In this 1,500 metres race indoors he was treading on Hicham's ground. So who would win? The specialist or the proven world beater?

It was not a close result. Kada's young star opened up the month of February in style, destroying his new record by running 3:35.70. Kiptanui wasn't disgraced. A 3:38.21 indoors for 1,500 metres isn't to be scoffed at, particularly when you understand that the event is his fourth favourite! It now looked apparent that El Guerrouj was only going to be beaten by specialist milers and only the really elite ones. To beat someone so great was fitting, as this was the Moroccan's first victory outside of home as a senior athlete. It was a momentous occasion.

Later that month he had his final lead up race before the World Indoor Championships. Hicham performed outstandingly well in Birmingham, but competing against only the locals gave him no competition. He defeated Anthony Whiteman by over five seconds, winning in commanding fashion in 3:36.22. Three races in a month, all under the old national record!

With Morceli and Niyongabo likely to skip the World Indoors, El Guerrouj was fast becoming a potential gold medallist in Barcelona.

Salah Hissou was back in action on March 4, competing in the famous Cinque Mulini cross country event in Italy. The race did not go as planned with Fita Bayissa defeating him comfortably. The times respectively were 34:25.9 and 34:35.4. The Ethiopian had seemed a little past it in 1994, so this loss was a step backwards for Hissou. A positive sign was that Paul Tergat had also lost out to Fita, though he also beat Salah, condemning him to third place. The Durham battle was still three weeks away. That was what mattered.

What mattered to El Guerrouj came sooner. The heats of the 1,500 metres at the World Indoor Championships were held on the 10th of March. The heat was no sweat for Hicham, as he breezed into the final, winning the first qualifier in 3:42.72. This was a fairly standard sort of time for a non final.

The final took place the very next day, giving El Guerrouj little rest. Could Hicham become a world champion, admittedly in an inferior event to the Outdoor Championships?

MOROCCAN SUCCESS; THE KADA WAY

Only one athlete in the final had a clearly better pedigree than El Guerrouj. Lining up on the start line in his home country, was Fermin Cacho. The Spaniard held his greatest memory in this city of Barcelona. It gave him his Olympic gold medal in 1992. That 1,500 metres victory remains one of track and field's greatest ever upsets.

Hicham had yet to run at that sort of level, but 1994 had been a poor year for Fermin. Plus this final was so early in the season. Who knows what shape he was going to be in? As it turned out, Cacho's form was sub standard. Despite thousands of people cheering him on, Cacho placed a disappointing sixth in the final.

This was in spite of the fact that the race was conducted in a very '92 Olympic final type manner. The pace was slow, even for indoor standards. The athletes jogged around, covering the early 200 metres circuits in over thirty seconds. This wasn't a test of El Guerrouj's strength. It was a true test of his finishing speed. The Moroccan had strength-endurance. The bronze medal at the World Junior Championships over 5,000 metres proved that. But did he have that real explosion, the last lap burst that generally separates the great milers from the rest?

Yes, yes, yes! It wasn't explosive enough to challenge the best yet, but this twenty year old proved his middle distance calibre by out kicking some seasoned professionals. The final results from Barcelona on March 11, 1995 were:

Hicham El Guerrouj	3:44.54
Mateo Canellas	3:44.85
Erik Nedeau	3:44.91
Niall Bruton	3:45.05
Vyacheslav Shabunin	3:45.40
Fermin Cacho	3:45.46
Rudiger Stenzel	3:45.64
Dominique Loser	3:46.09

Hicham was showing that he could win under varying circumstances. Becoming a world champion was an enormous boost to his self belief. He could take his magnificent indoor season and use it for the most important races that were later in the year in Europe outdoors. It was back to Morocco for over two months of training, much of it at high altitude. Before this year the aim for the Gothenburg World Championships was to make the 1,500 metres final and then see what happens. Now a medal seemed possible.

Was a medal of the same calibre a possibility even sooner for another Moroccan? In 1994, Salah Hissou had improved in leaps and bounds, but this improvement went largely unnoticed by the distance running world. Without a major track championships taking place, Salah had been able to slide onto the world stage, rather than explode onto it under a spotlight. It had been the twelve months that could set up his career. Statistically he was the sixth fastest in the world for both the 5,000 metres and 10,000 metres. But could he carry it on? The 1995 World Cross Country Championships would provide a good guide. Hissou had improved to an eleventh place finish in Budapest on March 26, 1994. The '95 Championships were taking place in Durham on March 25. It would be interesting to see just how much Salah Hissou had really improved in the last twelve months.

After the running of the 12 km's classic, the answer was clear, for the Moroccan had discovered that he was one of the best going around. Third! On the podium! It was a very pleasant surprise. Salah was also the first 'non' Kenyan, proving indeed complimentary as Kenya was clearly the dominant nation over the cross country terrain.

Paul Tergat was in a class of his own, winning in 34:05, well clear of his diminutive twenty year old teammate Ismael Kirui who clocked 34:13, and Hissou who finished in 34:14. Salah still had little in the way of a finishing kick but he had proved to the world that he possessed good strength and could maintain a fast sustained running tempo. In fact to have 'good strength and thus be able to sustain a fast tempo' were the attributes of any quality cross country runner. Hissou's third place carried plenty of merit, this being back in the days when there was only the longer event held and not the 4 kms that

MOROCCAN SUCCESS; THE KADA WAY

would occur in later years. This gave these runnings of the 12 kms more substance as it drew almost anyone who was anyone in distance running to compete in it.

Somebody who wasn't just anyone was Haile Gebrselassie. The young Ethiopian had already accomplished so much, yet there was so much more to come. Despite his best efforts, he couldn't quite compete with Tergat in the World Cross Country. Surprisingly, he was also dropped by Kirui and Hissou. Haile came in fourth in 34:26, with Salah's Moroccan teammate Brahim Lahlafi next with a 34:34. Hissou was amongst the cream of the crop at a time when distance running was going through a great transition phase. It was suddenly clear that he could compete with the best. The 10,000 metres seemed the obvious event to focus on for the upcoming World Championships in Gothenburg, Sweden. In hindsight though, the 5,000 metres would have been a more sensible choice.

Salah's cross country bronze medal carried greater value than Hicham's indoor gold. The best milers weren't in Barcelona, while in Durham the field was of the highest quality. What's more, Hissou had to contend with no less than nine Kenyans!

Kenya was nigh on impossible to beat over the cross country terrain. But this dominance wasn't only as a result of its individual star runners. The high emphasis that it placed on the team factor of the World Cross Country was extraordinary to see, considering that athletics is very much a sport that encourages selfish ambition. No matter how good a Kenyan runner is, if he is not the best, then he runs for the best. No questions asked. The Durham race highlighted this brilliantly. Despite being the 5,000 metres world champion and an enormous talent in cross country, Ismael Kirui ran as one of Paul Tergat's pacemakers. Not a bad pacemaker. Despite not racing for himself, he *still* finished second! There is no question that Paul Tergat was the best cross country runner of the '90's, so his winning streak would be no surprise, when you factor in that he also had the best teammates. Tergat realized the importance of this support as much as anyone and he always acknowledged his countrymen after his victories.

All of a sudden it had become common knowledge that Abdelkader Kada had some serious quality under his reign. Now the pressure was on to produce even more improvement and high finishers at the World Championships. Could Kada harness his talent and utilize it to its maximum potential? The next three months of hard training and early season European races were going to be most critical.

Saint-Denis often held the first significant track distance race of the year and Salah took to the venue in France with ambitions of a good placing in the 5,000 metres on the 1st of June. However, the race turned into a fairly dismal one. His competitors weren't close to the levels of those he'd met in Durham and Hissou lacked the necessary speed to play a major part in proceedings.

It wasn't a fast race and when Salah had to kick, he couldn't. The winner was fellow Moroccan Ismail Sghyr who clocked the decidedly slow time of 13:16.80. What mattered however was the victory. It was yet another Moroccan winning a European track distance event. Was this a Moroccan revolution?

Perhaps Hissou simply required more racing. His finishing time in France was 13:20.01. It was the lowly tenth placing that was more concerning. There were many athletes ahead of him who did not possess the same credentials as this world cross country medallist.

There was still substantial time until the next lot of medals were handed out in Sweden, allowing many weeks to build to a peak performance. Salah could also find comfort in the eleventh placed runner just behind him. It was Olympic 5,000 metres champion, Dieter Baumann.

In need of a confidence boost, Salah raced in Rehlingen, Germany on June 5, again over 5,000 metres. The meeting was a low grade one. None of the nine athletes who had his measure in Saint-Denis were on the start line. Hissou was

MOROCCAN SUCCESS; THE KADA WAY

clearly the most talented distance runner in the field, and by rights, he should win comfortably. This he did. The victory in a slow 13:23.54 wasn't ever likely to be one of Salah's most decorated moments but it carried some importance for he won with a decisive kick, leaving Stephane Franke (who clocked 13:24.81) in his dust. Winning was vital because his next race was going to be a major step up in class.

The Moroccan would not have won if he'd competed in Holland on the same day. The athletics meeting in Hengelo also symbolically signified the start of the European outdoor track season. As the years went by it became synonymous with the regular high quality performances from Haile Gebrselassie. It was here a year ago that he broke the 5,000 metres world record. On June the 5th, 1995, he didn't just break a world record. He obliterated it. Haile Gebrselassie turned the athletics world on its head when he destroyed Willem Sigei's 10,000 metres world record. The old mark was 26:52.23. Haile's time was an extraordinary 26:43.53! This sort of performance was unheard of. He was clearly going to be the man to beat in Sweden.

Haile Gebrselassie was born on April 18, 1973 and like many Ethiopians, had been initially inspired to run through the exploits of Murits Yifter. It was appropriate that Yifter's nickname of 'the shifter' could have easily been applied to Gebrselassie also.

Haile demonstrated enormous potential when he won both the 5,000 and 10,000 metres at the 1992 World Junior Championships. Only a special talent could win both events considering the toughness of the competition. The Ethiopian enjoyed great battles against Kenyan's Ismael Kirui and Josephat Machuka in the respective races.

As soon as he stepped into senior ranks Gebrselassie was world class. In 1993 he placed an excellent seventh in the World Cross Country and by the arrival of the European track season he was even better. The performances that Haile produced were enough to gain him selection for the Stuttgart World Championships in both the 5,000 and 10,000 metres, but he wasn't expected to do as well as he did. In the 5,000 metres he won the silver medal, though clearly displayed on the final lap that he was the most gifted runner in the field. It could be argued that inexperience cost him the gold medal. In the 10,000 metres he did not let a Kenyan escape from him and was able to use his superior kick to become the world champion. The Kenyan whom Haile frustrated was Moses Tanui, the reigning title holder. The race was quite uneventful until the bell. Tanui had been setting the pace and it was to his annoyance that Gebrselassie refused to offer him support once the two had broken clear of their opposition. With 400 metres remaining, the Ethiopian stepped on the heel of the Kenyan's right foot, slightly dislodging his shoe. In a moment of anger Tanui kicked off his shoe and took off, gapping Gebrselassie greatly in the process. With half a lap remaining, it appeared that he would retain his championship, but his initial burst was too great, and he ran out of steam. Running more evenly, Haile came past on the home straight to record what Tanui certainly felt was an undeserved win. Attempts by Gebrselassie to congratulate or console Tanui were rebuked, as the Kenyan angrily pointed a shoe at the victor. Coming on the back of the concluding stages of the corresponding race in Barcelona last year, one would be hard pressed to say that the 10,000 metres event was boring at present!

The longer track distance was Gebrselassie's favourite and in 1994, he enjoyed good wins in the event at Lausanne and Brussels. However he continued to prove himself versatile, with that 5,000 metres world record in Hengelo, as well as earlier also winning the bronze medal at the World Cross Country. In 1994 he was one of the best long distance runners in the world. His latest world record in Hengelo had shown that he had gone up a notch and was perhaps ready to assume the mantle as the best.

Kada's other Moroccan was there to witness the Haile Hengelo proceedings. The 1,500 metres event was to be Hicham El Guerrouj's first major test outdoors in 1995.

Three days beforehand he'd opened his season in an unconventional style by racing over 800 metres in Torino,

MOROCCAN SUCCESS; THE KADA WAY

Italy. To place third was a satisfactory outcome. His time of 1:47.18 was about what you'd expect of a top miler. It showed that whilst getting closer to his idol's old levels, Hicham probably wouldn't ever possess the top gear of Said Aouita. Winning with the time of 1:46.56 was the specialist Moroccan two lapper, Mahjoub Haida.

This race barely deserved to be rated as an entrée when compared to the importance of Hicham's Hengelo engagement. It was his first significant win outdoors and could be rated a touch above the Barcelona gold medal. The victory was just so emphatic.

This was El Guerrouj signifying that he had truly arrived as a miler to be feared by anyone who was, or desired to be the best in the world.

He went close to his personal best, as he careered away to his 3:34.28, thrashing Olympic medallists Rachid El Basir and Mohammed Suleiman by over three seconds! Watching Hicham El Guerrouj power away down the back straight was a joy to watch and was something athletics fans were to get most used to in the years ahead.

Hicham's track program had his next race scheduled for thirteen days time.

Salah had his own track program to focus on. On the 8th of June, Hissou went to Rome to test his form and newfound reputation as a cross country star. This was a good opportunity to show some star quality on the track. Competing again over 5,000 metres, Salah added to his pedigree with a 13:02.25, a new personal best. Unfortunately for Hissou, he found that he still wasn't quite as competitive as he had been in the World Cross Country. This was hardly devastating considering the standard of the race. Kenyan steeplechase legend Moses Kiptanui ran a time of 12:55.30. He had broken Haile Gebrselassie's world record. The Ethiopian had held the two track distance records for a grand total of three days! Also going inside the old record was a young Kenyan named Daniel Komen. The little known athlete clocked 12:56.15. This was a stunning breakthrough for a nineteen year old. There would be many more stunning performances during Komen's next two seasons. Gebrselassie's fellow countryman Worku Bikila nearly became Ethiopia's fastest ever, as he ran 12:57.23. For Salah, it was a great sign to be running close to thirteen minutes early in the season. Behind such quality, fourth place wasn't too bad either.

Salah forced himself to a new level in this race. He ran at his absolute maximum tempo for as long as was humanly possible. In doing so, he crept a little into the red zone and had nothing left in the final laps. This was a good thing in a way because by running at a world record pace, Salah discovered more about himself and his capabilities.

What Hissou did in Rome was establish the current limits of his aerobic capacity. To run aerobically is a term used for long distance running, whereas the shorter the distance, the more the athletes are said to reach into their anaerobic supplies. Therefore an 800 metres athlete runs more anaerobically while a 5,000 metres athlete runs more aerobically.

Daniel Komen had taken them through 3,000 metres in 7:47.0. Hissou was third at the time, sandwiched between Kiptanui and Bikila. The rest of the twenty-two man field was already a huge distance in arrears. Salah's split of 7:47.3 was quite close to his personal best for 3,000 metres, which was 7:38.14. Moses on the other hand was running more comfortably, with the benefits of having a 7:28.96 personal best for 3,000 metres soon becoming apparent. The Kenyans still had a little stored away for a big finish while Salah would need to improve on his shorter distance speed to give him a realistic chance at breaking thirteen minutes.

The 'red zone' is a term often used in endurance sports, particularly in cycling on a mountain stage of a grand tour. If a rider goes too hard too early they can blow up and lose enormous chunks of time. Sometimes it is not advisable to go with the best but to instead ride at your own pace. The same philosophies apply in long distance running.

MOROCCAN SUCCESS; THE KADA WAY

The term 'hitting the wall' means the same thing and has been a common way of describing marathon runners who have fallen apart late in the gruelling race. Runners of varying abilities, talk about feeling comfortable until they reach the twenty mile mark, when suddenly a metaphoric wall appears and they feel sapped of all their energies. The elite runner might blow out to 3:30 km pace. The three hour runner might blow out to 5:00 km pace (not that a three hour marathon runner is slow!). In these circumstances, no matter how mentally strong, the body refuses to do what the brain tells it and the runner loses all his/her form.

This same wall can appear in shorter races, perhaps even at 3,000 metres. The difference is that the body (and in some cases the mind) will take a lot longer to recover from the marathon than a track race. At various stages of his career, Salah Hissou would come across this wall in all the major long distance events.

The concept of getting the best out of yourself without going into the red zone is a great balancing act. You never want to push yourself past your limits, but if you never totally exert yourself, how will you know what those limits are? By racing with tremendous commitment in Rome, Hissou knew where he stood amongst the best in the world. He was a 13:02.25 runner over 5,000 metres. There were no ifs or buts about that.

Just like Salah had done in Rehlingen, Hicham did in Duisburg. Abdelkader Kada had his miler also race in a lower grade German meeting and the result was the same, only El Guerrouj won even more easily. It was a great credit to the in form Moroccan that he nearly ran a personal best with little help, coming seventeen hundredths shy of his Nice '94 time. His 3:33.78 was well ahead of Britain's Gary Lough who clocked 3:36.39. The only concern was that it was June the 18th. The heats of the 1,500 metres in Gothenburg weren't until August the 10th. It was always possible to peak too early.

Peaking for many top international sports people is much the same. You have an event or a match that is your target goal and you do everything possible to be in the best shape for that important sporting moment. For a track and field athlete the major targets are usually the World Outdoor Championships and the Olympic Games. Hicham El Guerrouj and Salah Hissou had their racing/training program designed around getting the best possible performances out of themselves in Gothenburg.

The responsibility of getting these Moroccans to peak at the right time was more up to the coach Abdelkader Kada than Hicham and Salah. The runners would compete as hard as they could for every race, so it was up to Kada not to burn them out by racing them too much. This was potentially more of a pitfall for Hissou because his distances were longer. Abdelkader made the decisions on training quantity and quality, so it was in his control as to how much he pushed them. The general consensus was that it could be a good thing to combine a hard training period with racing. The athlete was unlikely to perform at his best but would feel all the more better for the most important race or races once he'd tapered off. The downside to training hard all the time while racing was the likely poorer results that lead to a loss in confidence. It is hard for a coach to convince his runner to believe that he can medal in a major championship if his performances have been well off that standard all season.

It was another of distance running's balancing acts.

There were other issues too. Other big athletics meetings were held from June through to September. The coach and the athlete both wanted to get great results from Europe's most distinguished track and field venues. Rome and Monaco were always big. Oslo, Zurich, Brussels and Berlin were arguably even bigger. The money that came with it also carried its fair share of incentive.

For how long after tapering off, can a distance runner hold his top form?

To taper off, is to reduce the mileage and often the intensity of

MOROCCAN SUCCESS; THE KADA WAY

your training. El Guerrouj usually trained about 120 kms per week, running twice on most days. When freshening up he may even halve the total quantity and his usual training run will be at less intensity. Instead of running at five minute mile pace he may jog (in comparison) at six minute mile pace. Some of the high intensity effort in training will remain in the speed sessions that are critical for keeping El Guerrouj in race shape. In the final week before a target race these intervals may be made easier even as the quality remains high. For example instead of running something similar to 20 x 400's in 51 seconds with one minute recovery, Hicham might only complete eight of them. In that way he keeps his body conditioned to the last lap speed of a mile but doesn't exhaust himself in the process.

To be in supreme form from June through to September was difficult. The best athletes could often win all their races, not because they always performed at their best, but because they were so much better than the opposition. The best almost always carried more self belief into a race than the hopeful challenger so sometimes despite lesser form a victory could still be still achieved. Even distance runners who have dominated an entire season usually have a race somewhere where there's a lull in performance. Staying healthy and injury free was a big factor in limiting the difference between an athlete's absolute peak period and their racing during harder training.

It was almost impossible for a runner to stay in his peak racing shape for more than three months straight. Most struggled to be in peak form for more than a month at a time. This is due to the base training that is required to build up an athlete's strength. The base training consists of longer distances and higher overall mileage that aren't necessarily conducive to getting the athlete into tremendous racing form. But from this 'base' the runner can build on the quality of his training with faster tempo runs and harder track sessions. Once in racing shape and having tapered off, the runner should be super fit and ready to perform. However after a period, that fitness will lag and eventually another base will need to be built in order to again return to peak form. That's the circle of life of a distance runner!

This concept holds true for all running standards if you're training really hard and have great commitment.

Hicham and Salah warmed up for the 1994 and 1995 European seasons with heavy training from January to May. The only brief respites came with the target races indoors and in cross country. By the start of June, they were in fantastic shape and ready to tackle meetings in Rome and Hengelo. The decision that Abdelkader had to make was whether to continue their hard training, and therefore sacrifice a possible breakthrough performance, or to let them show their improvement and gain the belief that comes with a good result.

It was possible to peak at a few different times during the year. Being an ex athlete of real calibre himself, Kada knew that he needed to give his runners a down period during the lengthy European season. He reasoned that it was best to let Hissou and El Guerrouj loose in June. As such, both had achieved great results recently in Rome and Duisburg. Their confidence was at an all time high.

To attempt to remain in racing shape all the way to mid August and beyond was unlikely and risky. Yet an athlete still needs to race to be ready for a major championship. To solve this dilemma, Abdelkader would sometimes give his runners short periods of approximately two week lengths to train hard during the racing season. The athlete may still race during this time. He may not. Hissou or El Guerrouj might include two or three of these short hard training periods in order to keep some sort of base and in a way cheat the system. With this idea in place it was possible to create the illusion that you were in great shape for the whole season. Whereas it's highly unlikely for any top distance runner to race weekly for three straight months. What are they doing during those 'off' periods? Usually very hard training at a high altitude.

There was another issue that the coach always had to delicately balance. The fitter his distance runners were, the

MOROCCAN SUCCESS; THE KADA WAY

closer they were to falling ill. It might sound strange, but the world's fittest athletes are the most susceptible to picking up bugs which can lead to the flu or something else which can destroy an entire training period and racing season. Top distance runners don't only go to bed early so that they have loads of energy for the following days' training. They don't only eat the best foods for this very same reason. To avoid sickness is as good a reason as any. One late night for example would have a limited impact if an athlete stayed fit. The next couple of days might result in a drop in standards of training. But getting sick can bring months of good hard work undone. If a runner becomes badly ill with say a chest infection, he will probably have to take time off and resume again from scratch, building another base. All elite endurance athletes fear of getting sick. Just a sniffle or a cough is a great concern.

As far as their results went, Hicham El Guerrouj appeared in much better shape than Salah Hissou for the upcoming World Championships. But did Hicham genuinely know where he stood with the elite? He was about to get some sort of an answer. On July 5 he competed in Lausanne and there was a familiar face on the start line.

Venuste Niyongabo had destroyed Hicham on many occasions last season, but coming into their latest battle the Moroccan had reeled off five consecutive victories at 1,500 metres. The Burundi star would need to be more wary of him in Switzerland and in other future competitions. Was Kada's boy ready to challenge his event's second best?

Born in Burundi on December 9, 1973, Venuste Niyongabo was the rare African distance runner of serious talent who did not hail from Kenya, Ethiopia or Morocco. His junior credentials were as good as most of his rivals in the senior ranks, for Niyongabo took on the challenge of running the 800 and 1,500 metres at the World Junior Championships in Seoul 1992. After finishing fourth in the shorter event, he backed up the next day with a silver medal in the 1,500 metres. Along with Haile Gebrselassie and Ismael Kirui, he was one of the stars of the competition.

1993 was at times a difficult learning curve for the teenager, as he failed to qualify for finals at the World Indoor and Outdoor Championships. But post Stuttgart, there were better results. The Brussels mile in particular was significant. Sure, he finished over seven seconds behind a rampaging Noureddine Morceli, but his time of 3:54.71 was a national record and his third position was easily his best result thus far at such a big meeting. Niyongabo again finished seven seconds adrift of Morceli at Rieti but still placed second, then concluded his season with wins over 800 and 3,000 metres at smaller meetings. Morceli was way ahead of Niyongabo, but he usually enjoyed such dominance over everyone that the number two spot was clearly there for the taking.

Venuste established himself as arguably the world's number two early in 1994, not because of any particularly outstanding performances but Niyongabo had caught onto the winning habit. He lost only once during an extensive indoor season and that was over 1,000 metres. Once outdoors, Venuste reeled off five consecutive victories at 1,500 metres, the final two coming in Rome and Paris against good fields. His quickest time during this stretch was a national record 3:35.10, which wasn't special at all, but he possessed an excellent kick that resulted in substantial winning margins.

The international competition was very poor at this point. With Cacho having an off year and Morceli racing elsewhere, Niyongabo was left to enjoy the victory spoils.

In fact Morceli had only raced once thus far and that was at 3,000 metres where he'd produced a magnificent run to smash his opposition by over four seconds in clocking 7:34.74 at the Mediterranean Games. Noureddine was to open his season proper in a 1,500 metres race at Lille, France. Venuste decided to join him.

It was less than a month since his latest win in Paris, but the times that he had registered thus far would not have concerned the Algerian in the slightest. But in this race Niyongabo really pulled one out of the bag, smashing his own national record and nearly defeating the seemingly invincible

MOROCCAN SUCCESS; THE KADA WAY

Morceli in the process. He clocked a 3:30.66 to 3:30.61. It was oh so close. Finally, Noureddine Morceli had a worthy rival!

Venuste's effort in slicing the massive chunk of 4.44 seconds from his personal best was one of the most extraordinary improvements seen in track and field. Usually such a performance would bring with it dubious doubt, as to its legitimacy, but I think that in Niyongabo's case it was most probably genuine.

Generally the most suspicious runs from athletes come when a big improvement is made at a late age. This is particularly so if the runner has had a career that has stagnated for a lengthy period, rather than a consistency in improvement. Most common is for the jump in standard to occur over an off season. The athlete has a substantial period of time to train with the added assistance of illegal performance enhancers, then comes out and produces a performance that is unexpected. This latest Burundi record came under different circumstances. Niyongabo was only twenty years old and big natural improvements are common for the younger athlete. Also, it's more realistic that the four second improvement did not entirely come in the twenty seven day period between the Paris and Lille races. Venuste was probably in 3:33 form from the start of the outdoor season (after some normal improvement over winter and then the indoor season) but the races he'd been running in had been run at a slower pace than he was capable of keeping to. Hence the ease with which he had been able to run away from the field at the end of those races. In Lille he found someone to push him to his limits and to his and many others pleasant surprise, discovered that they were now sub 3:31. Effectively Venuste had improved by almost six seconds over about a twelve month period at the age of nineteen and twenty. This is not uncommon and equates to about a twenty second or forty second improvement for a 5,000 or 10,000 metres runner. Sometimes an athlete just needs to be given the right race and Lille was certainly that for Niyongabo.

Venuste enjoyed relatively easy wins in every one of the big

1,500 metres races that followed including at Monaco, Zurich, Brussels and Berlin without Morceli involved. Many made the claim that Noureddine was avoiding him, though the truth was more that this was a non major championship year and thus Morceli was racing less often, as well as competing at other distances. His form was hardly lacking. When he avoided him in Monaco the result was a world record for 3,000 metres. The same could be said at Zurich when Morceli, clearly concerned about his abilities, ran scared from Niyongabo by racing in the 5,000 metres. He also happened to run away scared from his opposition, which was virtually a who's who of long distance running, with that supersonic fifty two second last lap!

When the two big guns finally raced each other again, it was in the Grand Prix Final in Paris. As often happens in the Grand Prix final, the event was an anti climax. Morceli won comfortably enough but the time was only 3:40.89 to Niyongabo's 3:41.72. It was pretty clear though that the Algerian remained the best, but the Burundi athlete had closed the gap substantially from where things had stood at the end of 1993.

Entering the Lausanne 1,500 metres in 1995, nothing had changed. This was the first outdoor race of the season at the distance for Venuste, who had enjoyed a most successful indoor campaign, including a sensational 3,000 metres in Birmingham when he registered a 7:37.81 and smashed the great Moses Kiptanui by 4.25 seconds. Niyongabo ran that final 1,000 metres in 2:27.27 and was unbeaten in five races this year.

At least in Switzerland we found out exactly where Hicham El Guerrouj stood. He was no match for Venuste but no disgrace either. Again he came close to a personal record with a time of 3:33.88. Ahead of him were Niyongabo in 3:32.37 and Kenya's William Kemei in 3:33.42. Hicham's improvements over the last twelve months had made him a worthy opponent. There were some decent names behind him in the fifteen man field, including El Basir, O'Sullivan and Bile.

MOROCCAN SUCCESS; THE KADA WAY

Also racing in Lausanne was Salah Hissou, who was about to take on some of the best that Kenya had to offer in the 5,000 metres.

After a brief respite from racing, Hissou had gone to England to race at Gateshead on the 2nd of July. Again he'd competed over 5,000 metres and with the field of a lesser quality, the race was slower. It was a good opportunity for Salah to test his finishing speed and to see if there been any improvement in this critical area from '94.

The answer was unfortunately no. Matched in a last lap sprint against an unknown South African, Hissou was found out, again! Shadrack Hoff was the man who got the better of him. The winning time was only 13:14.16. Hissou ran 13:14.72. Behind him were a host of honest but nevertheless B grade 5,000 metres runners. They were B grade in comparison to what he was to face in Lausanne anyway.

The competition was hot, the race bringing back together the three placegetters from the World Cross Country. It was a setting that Europe would see often during the remainder of the '90's. Hissou doing battle with a bunch of Kenyans. Salah put in a very good performance, but it was Ismael Kirui who had the fast twitch fibres when it mattered. The world champion won in 13:07.80, with Hissou well behind in 13:09.60, but happy to have collected the scalp of Tergat, with the World Championships just over a month away. The world cross country champion ran 13:10.12. On the track Tergat didn't seem to have the necessary leg speed, at least that was the general consensus at this time. Losing to Hissou in sprint finishers wasn't going to help change that!

This really was the World Cross Country on the track with grass specialists Simon Chemoiywo and William Sigei placing fourth and fifth. Sigei was attempting to get back to the form that took him to the 1993 and 1994 titles.

There were many other scalps for Salah. Others finishing well back included Bob Kennedy, Shaun Creighton, Todd Williams, Aloys Nizigama, Paul Bitok, Moses Tanui and

Yobes Ondieki. The former world champion was just a shadow of his former self, placing fifteenth. Retirement beckoned.

Hissou's busy schedule continued when he raced in Nice on July 12. The world titles were less than a month away as Salah stepped down to the 3,000 metres, perhaps hoping to improve a little on his leg speed. A high placing would be a bonus at this non favourite distance.

The race was a relatively fast one and the Moroccan went through 2,000 metres in about 5:05, running behind the pacemaker and Bob Kennedy. Once the rabbit dispersed, the American made the tempo and had the entire field beaten, bar Hissou by the last lap. Could Salah win in a sprint finish on this occasion? The top placings in France were:

Salah Hissou	7:35.66
Bob Kennedy	7:37.69
Paul Bitok	7:38.55
Vyacheslav Shabunin	7:39.24
Atiq Naaji	7:39.57
Yahia Azaidj	7:41.84
Shaun Creighton	7:42.02
Manuel Pancorbo	7:42.81
Mathias Ntawulikura	7:43.09
Todd Williams	7:43.86
Khalid Boulami	7:49.85
Mohamed Issanger	7:49.87

Yes, and it was highly convincing, considering that Salah only turned up the screws in the final 200 metres. When he kicked, Bob stood no chance. A personal best was an added bonus. A 7:35.66 in 1995 was a pretty impressive time, as the only guys running sub 7:30 were Morceli and Kiptanui. Hissou hadn't beaten any of those men in Nice. Who he had defeated were two of his usual rivals. In a strung out field Paul Bitok had placed third. The Kenyan was one of those runners that you dare not have with you going into a last lap so it was nice in Nice that Kennedy disposed of him earlier.

MOROCCAN SUCCESS; THE KADA WAY

Like any sportsperson competing at an international level, Hissou would keep mental notes on his main opposition. What their strengths were, what their weaknesses were, if they had any. There would be a list of names swimming around Salah Hissou's head under the topic, 'runners I must be away from before I hear the bell'. These names would include Paul Bitok, Khalid Skah, Khalid Boulami, Ismael Kirui, Dieter Baumann and HAILE GEBRSELASSIE. In July '95, that would have been the gist of it.

Abdelkader was keeping both his athletes with him as Gothenburg became closer. As a result Hicham El Guerrouj also competed in Nice, though somewhat out of his comfort zone in the 1,000 metres. This was a rarely run distance that would be an excellent test of the Moroccan's basic speed.

Competing against athletes whose preference was the two lap event, the outcome perfectly displayed El Guerrouj's limitations, yet it didn't produce a result which would necessarily concern his coach. The first six after the two and a half laps were:

Mahjoub Haida	2:14.69
Joseph Tengelei	2:14.73
Arthemon Hantungimana	2:15.48
Vincent Malakwen	2:16.20
William Tanui	2:16.26
Hicham El Guerrouj	2:16.85

A sub 2:15 is serious running, yet neither Haida nor Tengelei had ever accomplished much at 1,500 metres. Over 800 metres they were very strong and both would run 1:43.57 in Zurich the following month. These five athletes ahead of Hicham were unlikely to worry him in a mile, except for William Tanui who was the Olympic champion at 800 metres and later moved up in distance with some success.

It was during the final 500 metres of his pet events where El Guerrouj damaged the opposition. When he broke away from his competitors it appeared to be done with pure speed when in actual fact, it was more with pure strength. Don't get me wrong, Hicham's kick was impressive enough, but in a slowly run 1,500 metres race, even at his career best, he would struggle mightily to defeat the likes of Coe, Aouita and Morceli.

To some extent the personal best times of these runners over 1,000 metres show this. But it's not totally accurate because the distance is raced over far less than even the mile and perhaps only as often as the two mile. As of the 12th of July, 1995, only these runners had broken 2:14.

Sebastian Coe	2:12.18
Steve Cram	2:12.88
Noureddine Morceli	2:13.73
Rick Wohlhuter	2:13.90

It was a very exclusive list and many of the world's greatest middle distance runners could fairly claim that they'd never once targeted a great time in this event. Aouita himself had *only* clocked a 2:15.16 and surely his potential best would be within two seconds of Cram and probably within two seconds of Coe. With El Guerrouj currently a 3:33 athlete, it was a credit to him that he'd come within two seconds of Aouita's personal record. Again, this is a blight on the master Moroccan's achievements at this event.

Even if this new challenge improved his speed, finishing sixth wasn't something that Abdelkader wanted Hicham to make a habit of. On July 21, he and Salah travelled to Oslo where El Guerrouj reverted to his favourite event, while Hissou took on the task of attempting to win another 3,000 metres race.

Once again El Guerrouj clashed with Niyongabo in what was to be his final race before the World Championships. Morceli was not at the meeting, so the Moroccan would go into Gothenburg having raced just once in two years against the world record holder.

Perhaps the decision to compete in a shorter event in Nice was not based solely with the purpose of trying to improve Hicham El Guerrouj's speed. There was a 1,500 metres race

MOROCCAN SUCCESS; THE KADA WAY

that evening, one that contained an Algerian ace in imposing shape. Morceli had come into the meeting in career best form, having just broken the 2,000 metres world record in Paris with a 4:47.88. This result completely obliterated Aouita's 4:50.81 standard. Even for a relatively weak record, this was an enormous chunk of time to take off. The victory was achieved in great style, with a final lap time of 55.06. The first km was *only* timed at 2:26.15. How much faster could Morceli have run off a more even pace?

In Nice, Noureddine set about improving his own world record of 3:28.86. He now held four outdoor records, from the 1,500 metres to the 3,000 metres. There was no better athlete in the world, yet with little to prove he again raised the standards.

Needing to average under fifty six second laps to challenge the record, Morceli went out hard, completing the first lap, with the help of rabbits, in about 55.50. His brother Ali was the pacesetter and had gone through in 54.89. A little strange though, was the fact that Noureddine sat in fifth position, running on the shoulder of the fourth placed athlete William Kemei, who incidentally was a competitor and not a rabbit. Not wanting to clip his opponent's heels, Morceli would spend the majority of his first four bends situated on the outside of lane one. It doesn't sound like much, but *any* extra distance covered only adds greater difficulty to the already almighty task of breaking a world record. It makes sense to hug the curve, yet for approximately 400 metres the Algerian ran wider than he had to. The Kenyan had every right to be positioned where he was, but at the end of the day he did finish some four seconds in arrears.

Ali was able to take the field through to 700 metres but during the fourth bend Morceli was clearly "drifting slightly" as Kemei lost ground on the new leaders. Noureddine reached 800 metres in approximately 1:51.8. Still very fast, but in reality he had given up ground that he shouldn't have. On the back straight he finally made his way past Kemei and began to use "that incredible stride length he generates for such a small man" to full effect.

Morceli was able to keep to the inside as the two leaders cleared a path, moving out while the speedster took the lead for the final 580 metres or so. Nevertheless, when the 1,000 metres split registered approximately 2:21.2, a new record looked unlikely, given that Noureddine was slightly adrift of the 2:20 mark that was 3:30 pace. The last 500 metres had to be covered in less than 1:07.7, give or take a few hundredths. This amounted to about a fifty four second lap speed for the final half a km. Most world records were set with only a minor kick down, since the athlete was running at his limit. They weren't storing much away for a big sprint. But Noureddine had produced a definitive kick in Paris. Could he do the same again in Nice?

There was never any doubt, as arguably the greatest miler of all time ran arguably his greatest race. When the bell was rung, he could be forgiven if he'd not heard it, such was his speed at this point. He was running at a final lap type tempo for a slow, 3:40 sort of race. But this was sub 3:30 tempo and in fact turned out to be well under.

The French knew that they were witnessing something special as the Algerian flew around the circuit. Morceli's pace slowed slightly during the last 200 metres but his form never wavered. He crossed the line in 3:27.37, over four seconds clear of his entire irrelevant opposition. Surely this record could not be broken in the next decade. Could anyone currently competing remotely hope to run as fast as Morceli had just done?

The final half a km burst was averaged out at sub fifty three second lap pace. He had run a 200 metres split from 1,000 metres to 1,200 metres in approximately 25.8 seconds (the official 1,200 metres split was 2:47.02)! This was sub fifty two second lap speed. With better economical running during the first two laps Morceli could have run an even faster time. Hypothetically, he had a full second up his sleeve and perhaps could have run even faster still.

Nevertheless 3:27.37 was going to be more than fast enough to satisfy Noureddine and his fans. Despite the significant

MOROCCAN SUCCESS; THE KADA WAY

improvements of Niyongabo he remained clearly the best miler going around. Morceli's confidence (some might say arrogance) was sky high as he declared: "If everything is right for me then I can break every record between 800 and 10,000 metres before I finish my career. Really, I feel extraordinary and I have no doubt that I can do this."

If El Guerrouj could be accused of avoiding Morceli, then Niyongabo was in the same boat. Venuste had yet to put all his cards on the table in 1995 but like Hicham he too was competing in Nice. This meeting was a middle distance extravaganza as the Burundi runner made an attempt on Morceli's nine day old 2,000 metres record.

The attempt was a very good one as Niyongabo came quite close to Morceli's Paris time. He proved his status of worthy challenger by clocking 4:48.69, also well inside Said Aouita's old record. On most other nights it would be the major story, but nobody was going to steal Noureddine Morceli's thunder on this night in Nice. He ran with the speed of lightning thus bringing after it thunderous applause.

Niyongabo was in great shape for the Bislett Games and expected to win the 1,500 metres rather comfortably. How would he adapt with moving down in distance? How would El Guerrouj adapt with moving up?

Both runners answered in the affirmative and the final positions were not a surprise. But for the first time in his career Hicham took it up to Venuste and made it a contest. He raised his game greatly and with it produced a big personal best time.

Niyongabo ran 3:30.78, while El Guerrouj ran 3:31.53. In doing so the twenty year old became the second fastest Moroccan of all time. The heats in Gothenburg were only twenty days away and Hicham was in the best form of his life. Abdelkader appeared to have got the timing right.

Niyongabo now had something else to think about. Rather than purely focussing on trying to defeat Morceli, he might have to glance over his shoulder at a rapidly improving star. The World Championships 1,500 metres had been given another dimension.

The field for Salah's race was of a similar quality to his Nice win, only it did include Dieter Baumann, the German who possessed one of distance running's most fearsome finishes. Dieter still required to be in good form in order to hang on until the last lap and have the opportunity to utilize his kick.

Salah begun the race with new confidence but was unable to reproduce his standards of nine days earlier. Finishing fifth in 7:38.12 was not a disaster. Just a minor setback. The first three finishers were good 5,000 metres athletes. Dieter Baumann did win, with a very good time of 7:33.56, with Paul Bitok improving from Nice with a 7:34.50 and Morocco's Ismail Sghyr clocking an impressive 7:35.51. Hissou was well behind, so it wasn't just a matter of being beaten for basic speed. It was an average run, plain and simple.

The 10,000 metres heats were fifteen days away so it wasn't such a bad result. The full taper would only take place in the final week. Right now Hissou and others were probably in heavy training mode. Ismael Kirui only managed seventh place and a 7:41.21.

Four days later Salah raced in his third consecutive 3,000 metres. It seemed a somewhat unconventional way to prepare for a World Championship 10,000 metres. Kada's view was that racing the twenty five lap heat would give Hissou more than enough racing miles before the final. The Monaco meeting was his final serious hit out before Gothenburg. One of his main opposition was in the field also. Hissou had edged out Tergat in Lausanne. Could he do the same on July 25?

The grind of all the training showed even more so and it was worrying to see Salah Hissou so lethargic. Paul Tergat only finished fifth in a time of 7:36.68, but this was outstanding in comparison to Hissou's dismal thirteenth place and 7:41.54. In just thirteen days since Nice, things seemed to have gone

MOROCCAN SUCCESS; THE KADA WAY

pear shaped for the Moroccan. But things aren't always as they seem to the outsider.

As far as assembling a group of elite runners is concerned, this was the biggest Grand Prix distance race of the season. But who had eased off in their training and who was still putting in the hard miles, the hard speed sessions, two weeks out from the World Championships? Of course nobody knew, but I would suspect that many big names under performed in Monaco because they were looking at the bigger picture. If you had taken this one race as a strict guide to Gothenburg, you would have been surprised on many fronts. It was no surprise who won this particular 3,000 metres. Kenya's best, Moses Kiptanui, went close to the world record with a 7:27.18. He was comfortably ahead of Ismail Sghyr, who again showed that he was in good form clocking 7:30.09. Next there were noticeable gaps back to Khalid Boulami third, and Bob Kennedy fourth. But look at some of the names behind Tergat. Shem Kororia ninth, Brahim Lahlafi tenth and Ismael Kirui twelfth!

So maybe things weren't quite so bad for Salah Hissou after all.

The major highlight in Monaco was another majestic display by Noureddine Morceli. In his final race before the championships, it would be reasonable to think that the Algerian would be content to race only to win, having just smashed his own world record. This was far from the case. Maybe he studied his splits from Nice and also thought that he could run faster. He certainly endeavoured to do so. The result was almost another world record. The incredible time of 3:27.52 was agonizingly close to his last performance. His brother ran at a slightly better suited pace this time, reaching 800 metres in 1:51.6, having clocked a 1:50.5 for the same sectional in Nice. Barring any major mishaps, there was no way that Noureddine Morceli was going to be defeated in Gothenburg. Morceli on Monaco, "And then in life, you always have to try, and today, I may not have succeeded, but I am happy to have tried to beat my record."

Greg Rowlerson

The countdown was well and truly on. Hissou would participate in the big battle for the 10,000 metres crown instead of entering the potentially easier 5,000 metres. It is doubtful that anyone could have beaten the 'emperor' in Gothenburg, not even Kenenisa Bekele in his pomp. Going into the race Gebrselassie had recently made the big statement with his nine second pounding of Sigei's world record. There was nothing scarier than to have the athlete with arguably the most devastating kick in history to also claim the world's fastest time. What it basically amounted to was unbeatable.

But it wouldn't stop his rivals from trying. Hissou went into the championships with poor recent track form, but at least he knew that he had the ability to be competitive, following his good runs in Rome and Nice. He also knew that he had beaten Gebrselassie. Granted, it was over the cross country terrain but against someone who has run 26:43 one would use any result as motivation. Or just live in denial! Hissou had *only* run 27:21. At least he knew that he had come reasonably close to the Ethiopian on that occasion. There had been that 5,000 metres to consider too. Not many guys could run faster than 13:02, so the temptation to run that event had to be there. Maybe those 3,000 metres thrashings had concerned him. With that in mind it was probably the speed factor that scared him away from the 5,000 metres. As it turned out the finishing kick at the close of the 10,000 metres was more emphatic than in the 5,000 metres. Far more.

For the world titles Morocco had a high quality team. In the 1,500 metres it had Rachid El Basir and Azzeddine Seddiki as well as Hicham El Guerrouj. In this event it was clearly the strongest group of any nation. In the steeplechase it was not as strong but was nevertheless improving. Elarbi Khattabi, Abdelaziz Sahere and Brahim Boulami made up its team here that wasn't remotely close to the quality of the Kenyan line up. There was no shame in that. In the 5,000 metres Morocco had Khalid Boulami, Brahim Lahlafi and Ismael Sghyr to contend for the medals. These runners were expected to be able to match it with the Kenyan and Ethiopian contingent. In the 10,000 metres it had Khalid Skah, the Olympic champion

MOROCCAN SUCCESS; THE KADA WAY

who wanted to prove that he was still a major factor in the major championships after he was battered into submission at the '93 World Championships in Stuttgart. Skah would probably need some help which was perhaps one reason why Salah Hissou entered the longer track race with his country having little depth at the distance. Secondly, Morocco had three other strong runners to compete in the 5,000 metres. Salah may not have made the Moroccan team. In any case it would have been intriguing to see how he would have performed. Despite not being truly battle hardened having never run at a major track championships, I can safely say that the 5,000 metres was slightly winnable in Gothenburg. If he had competed in that he might have missed a medal, but he might also have won. In entering the 10,000 metres he was virtually cancelling out his chances of gold but he would also play a part in one of the best races in the modern era.

The field was of the highest quality and it continued on the recent great rivalry of Kenya vs. Ethiopia vs. Morocco. Joining Gebrselassie, Skah and Hissou was Paul Tergat, the world cross country champion, whose ability on the track was still relatively unknown. His teammates were top road runner Joseph Kimani and youngster Josephat Machuka. Machuka had gained prominence after he had literally come to blows with Gebrselassie in the World Junior Championships in '92. The 10,000 metres came down to a final sprint between the pair and as Haile went past, Josephat was so angry that he punched him in the back of the neck and was subsequently disqualified. The Gothenburg race was the first clash between the pair since their controversial meeting so it was one that athletics enthusiasts were looking forward to. Josephat had recently displayed tremendous form when he ran the fastest ever time at altitude. In Nairobi on July 1 he clocked 27:53.0. But it would be his older Kenyan teammate who was the real one to watch.

On the 5th of August, 1995, Paul Tergat was twenty six years old. It was a late age for one to be competing in his first major track championships but Tergat had only entered the athletics arena late after spending time in the Kenyan army. He quickly developed into one of the greatest running machines ever seen, excelling from 3,000 metres to the marathon. His career boasted everything except for a gold medal from an Olympic Games or a World Athletics Championships. Nobody would again question his track ability after the 10,000 metres final.

Paul Tergat only took up running in the early '90's, but by 1992 he was arguably the best cross country runner in the world. In lead up races to the '92 world titles, Tergat won the Kenyan National Cross Country Championships at Ngong racecourse and a week later won at the same venue in the IAAF Cross Country event. He seemed to be the favourite for the World Cross Country Championship in Boston, USA. But with snow everywhere in Massachusetts, the Kenyans went for a training run on the hard tarmac, which Tergat had never experienced before. He suddenly felt pain in his calf muscle and by day's end he could not even walk. He was left shattered and out of the big race. It would be two long years before Tergat would get back to near his level pre Boston.

By September later that year and now under the guidance of Italian coach Dr. Gabriele Rosa, Tergat, over the calf injury, finished fifth in the World Half Marathon Championships in Newcastle. This was the first time that a World Championship had been held for the half marathon. Tergat's teammate Benson Masya was the inaugural winner. Not only did he take gold, but he ran 60:24, which sliced three seconds off Australian Steve Moneghetti's world record.

In the 1993 World Cross Country in Amorebieta, Spain, Tergat placed *only* tenth. Perhaps he would never regain the form that had made him Kenya's best cross country runner only a year ago. In the meantime William Sigei had stolen his thunder. Taking over from Ngugi, Sigei was another Kenyan who seemed to have come from nowhere to become a world beater. Though placing a solid eighth in '92, he didn't appear to have the talent to win the title, having a 10,000 metres personal best of just 28:35.00. Yet later in 1993 Sigei would right this wrong, improving his personal record to 27:16.81.

As the '93 season wore on, Tergat also made some nice improvements. He showed that he had some speed on the

MOROCCAN SUCCESS; THE KADA WAY

track. His 5,000 metres best of 13:20.16 wouldn't scare many, but the longer the distance, the more effective Tergat became. His 10,000 metres personal best of 27:18.43 was the sixth fastest time in the world in 1993. Despite his efforts it was hard to be a prominent stand out when four of those ahead of him were also Kenyans.

It was throughout 1994 when Tergat displayed his immense potential on the road. He won the Stramilano Half-Marathon in Milan and also recorded a 15 kms road world record of 42:13 in Paris. Yet later in the year he only managed an eleventh place finish in the World Half Marathon Championships in Oslo. His progression on the track had also stalled. Paul's fastest 5,000 metres and 10,000 metres times of 1994 were 13:15.07 and 27:23.89 respectively. He was one of many who were thrashed by Sigei when the 10,000 metres world record was broken in Oslo. There, Tergat placed fifth in 27:29.45.

Nevertheless by 1995 Paul Tergat was a feared athlete. He was the new world cross country champion and had defended his Stramilano half marathon title with a time of 59:56, only nine seconds shy of the world record held by Moses Tanui. But there remained doubts about his capabilities on the synthetic surface.

Whilst proving to be a regular victor on the road, transferring that winning habit to the track was difficult to establish. In early June Tergat won 5,000 metres races in Seville and Moscow but with a fastest time of just 13:22.12. He was only able to place third on June 29 in the 10,000 metres at the Kenyan Championships, though his time of 28:04.30 was good for the altitude of Nairobi. After his decent performance in Lausanne he'd backed up with another personal best over 5,000 metres in Stockholm on July 10, but 13:09.34 wasn't as competitive a mark as what it used to be and Paul finished only sixth. There he finished well behind the elite with Shem Kororia winning in 13:02.80. Was Tergat's strength good enough to test Gebrselassie's speed on the track in Gothenburg?

We wouldn't find out the answer to that just yet. The two were matched up in the first of the 10,000 metres heats and both qualified easily. The first eight runners from each of the two heats automatically made it through to the final, so for the top athletes, a lot of shadow boxing went on. The heats weren't there to show your opposition how good you were. A 10,000 metres event can be quite gruelling so the general rule is to qualify with the minimum of fuss, and do this in as slow a time as possible. Of course this is not always easy. Athletes who are not confident in their finishing speed will often try to make a heat relatively fast, so that they have a greater chance of finishing in the first eight, or if this fails, they can hope to qualify as one of the four fastest losers. The four fastest times outside of the first eight from each heat also made it through to the final. With Gebrselassie's super ability and sprint, he wouldn't care if his heat was run in thirty-five minutes!

As it turned out, Gebrselassie won heat 1 in Gothenburg. His time was a pretty much standard 28:10.66. Tergat was just behind in 28:10.78 with Skah sixth in 28:11.99. It wasn't too fast, but certainly wasn't slow either. It was a good warm up for the final, this first heat that contained all the big stars of the event.

The second heat carried little if any big names. Any sub 27:30 runner should have no difficulty in qualifying. Things were made even easier for the others when the sole Ethiopian Fita Bayissa didn't make an appearance.

The heat in which Salah Hissou made his debut in a major track championship was conducted in a much different fashion to heat 1. It was much faster and saw two Kenyans sprint away from the field, racing like it was the final. When the smoke cleared, Josephat Machuka had clocked 27:29.07! This was crazy. It was even faster than each of the last three major championship 10,000 metres finals! The second Kenyan, Joseph Kimani, was equally unrestrained, as he ran 27:35.20. The main pack kept up a good pace while the Kenyans were having their fun. Salah Hissou placed third in a still very fast time of 27:47.20. Abdelkader Kada was delighted, for the Moroccan qualified easily, but without showing his hand. Sure, Machuka and Kimani had showed

MOROCCAN SUCCESS; THE KADA WAY

tremendous form, but had they taken too much out of themselves for the final in only three days time?

Salah Hissou's first real moment of truth as an international distance runner came at 6:35 pm on Tuesday the 8th of August, 1995. In the final Haile Gebrselassie would probably receive very little help, although he was unlikely to require any. Ethiopia didn't currently have a top 10,000 metres runner to support him.

This is a classical race from start to finish. Salah starts from the outside group. On his right is Machuka. To his left is Ntawulikura of Rwanda. To the left of him is Gebrselassie. The pace is initially slow with a first lap of 70.44 as Salah mingles with the group, though more towards the front end. In the second lap American Todd Williams, who has a personal best of 27:31 takes off, but the second lap time of 67.31 tells us that he hasn't really kicked it down. The main pack is still taking things very easily because his lead is already thirty metres. 2:49.01 is the first km pace as the lead extends to close to fifty metres. Williams completes the third lap in a very fast 62.55.

The American's brave (some might say unwise) attempt to charge away from this field, is never going to last but it does make the race a fast one and will give the Kenyans an early opportunity to attack.

Kimani leads Machuka followed by Hissou at the head of the pack. Todd's fourth lap is a 64.58 and his lead has blown out to sixty metres. Gebrselassie now moves up behind Kimani, taking closer notice of proceedings, suggesting that he is becoming more tactically astute in his racing. The next lap is much slower, only a 66.44 which gives a 2:42.31 km and a split at 2,000 metres of 5:31.32, just over 27:30 pace.

Williams begins to sit on around twenty eight minute pace which indicates that it's only a matter of time before he is reeled in. The next three laps are sixty sevens and there is plenty of activity going on behind him. By the end of lap seven, Joseph Kimani starts to stride out and opens a ten metres gap on Hissou that encourages others to go around the young Moroccan. Kimani is within forty metres of the leader and on lap eight (third km in 2:48.06) he really opens up and runs about a sixty three second lap, bringing him to within just ten metres of the fading American. The Kenyan has a margin of twenty five metres on the bunch that is now lead by Skah. Early into lap nine and Kimani swoops past Williams, hoping to establish a tremendous lead of his own. However there is one man in particular that isn't going to let a Kenyan escape too easily.

Haile assumes responsibility to set things right, going to the front of the pack and setting a searing tempo. Kimani runs the ninth lap quickly but Gebrselassie doesn't just limit the damage, for he has brought the group that has gone past Williams to within fifteen metres of the front runner. The chasers run this lap in approximately sixty two to sixty three seconds. No wonder they closed!

Meanwhile this acceleration has destroyed the field and Williams is spat out by the bunch. Even some of the more highly regarded runners are struggling to hang on. Before the end of lap ten they have caught Kimani. There are incredibly only seven survivors at the 4,000 metres split of 11:02.85 after a 2:43.35 km with most of the athletes having run considerably quicker than that. Kimani's tenth lap is clocked at 64.13, meaning that the pack has produced another sub sixty three!

Haile Gebrselassie is the man who had restored unity to the race. It was probably the memory of a famous 5,000 metres battle in Stuttgart that had now forced Gebrselassie's hand. That was the 1993 World Championships final in which the Ethiopian left his final run too late. In that race Ismael Kirui had charged away from the field after only five laps and amazingly stayed away to record one of athletics greatest victories. At that moment his 13:02.75 was only four seconds off the world record. In distance running it is rare for a major championship to be run at anywhere near world record pace. Warm temperatures and race tactics usually make world records impossible. Joseph Kimani wasn't considered as big a

MOROCCAN SUCCESS; THE KADA WAY

threat but he did wear a Kenyan uniform and Gebrselassie wasn't going to make the same mistake again.

The fireworks have finally ended now as the pack settles into a sixty five, sixty six second lap rhythm. Not a bad rhythm at around 27:15 tempo! By 5,000 metres its lead is about fifty metres over the ensuing athletes. The halfway split is 13:46.20. Kimani continues to lead though he looks to be waiting for someone else to take it up as they round a 65.05 thirteenth lap. Tergat is running his own race at the back in seventh position.

The next lap is a 65.46 and then Kimani kicks again for a 64.39, which is awfully fast for this period of the race but the Africans appear to be jogging! The km is run in 2:42.38, fast enough to dispose of the German Stephane Franke. Now there are six. Salah looks in good shape in fifth position still ahead of Tergat.

The contenders for the medals are down to Gebrselassie, Kimani, Machuka, Tergat, Skah and Hissou. Two years ago Salah was struggling to make the grade in his local Morocco. Now he is competing at the highest level possible. Abdelkader likely watched in great anticipation and thought of what might be.

Kimani's pace setting can no longer hurt the others. Machuka is running at times on the outside of Haile, half boxing him in. Now Josephat edges to the front as a time of 65.20 is clocked with eight laps remaining. There is no kick down from Machuka as he and Kimani exchange the lead as the steady pace continues. The seventh km is run in 2:43.12, then the eighth km in 2:44.76 after a slower 65.96 sixth last lap. The tension starts to increase. Will these runners settle for a bunch sprint?

Salah looks composed in fifth position but must be near his upper limits. At the back, perhaps straining to remain in contact is Paul Tergat. With 1,900 metres to go, Australian broadcaster Bruce McAvaney makes a comment about the race's delicately poised situation, "You feel that if anyone is going to make the decisive move, it must be Machuka. Kimani has done the work for him and Tergat, I just don't think on the track has the pedigree of Machuka."

However, there is a little more speed in Paul Tergat than what others realize. But still he sits waiting for his moment. The pack is now really bunching up after a 66.48 lap. With 1,500 metres to go, Tergat goes!

His fierce attack instantly drops Kimani and seriously hurts Machuka, though this isn't his plan to only destroy his teammates! Gebrselassie and Skah seem to respond easily while Hissou hangs on tenaciously. Salah is in some trouble, falling back about eight metres, but is smart enough not to go with the surge initially, preferring to gradually build his speed to match the Kenyan. He rounds Machuka and is able to tack back on with 1,300 metres remaining. As the first three athletes look like getting away, McAvaney makes a more appropriate remark, "Have a look at this. World cross country champion leads world champ leads Olympic champ. It's enough to make your mouth water if you love distance running." Spot on!

Salah *is* good enough to hang with these guys. This must have impressed and excited Abdelkader. Now could Hissou also kick with them?

The surge results in a 64.01 lap time as Machuka works hard to recover, making it a battle of five. The twenty third lap is a slower 65.32, during which Josephat is constantly teetering on the edge of dropping off and hanging on. Usually in these cases it is the former that wins out.

Hissou moves up around Gebrselassie and into second spot. Now with 650 metres left, Salah takes up the lead as Machuka is dropped for good. The Moroccan still leads at the bell as crunch time approaches after a 64.56 second penultimate lap.

Is he really good enough to challenge in a sprint finish? Salah leads into the back straight with Haile sitting on his shoulder.

MOROCCAN SUCCESS; THE KADA WAY

Still nobody makes a decisive move. It is getting awfully tense. Now at the top of the curve the Ethiopian lets fly. Even with wings it would have been hard to keep up!

These final 200 metres must have been one hell of a shock for Salah and Abdelkader. For running fans it is a case of simply watch and enjoy, in total awe and amazement. It is as if Gebrselassie is attached to a rocket launcher. At the top of the bend he storms past Hissou whose move to the front of the pack is actually his sprint. Skah and Tergat take off in pursuit but this is similar to Fredericks and Bolden trying to compete with Johnson in Atlanta. They stand no chance. Gebrselassie clocks 25.1 seconds for the last 200 metres, the sort of speed that is stunning at the end of a 1,500 metres, never mind a 10,000 metres race. Skah and Tergat are over a second behind with Hissou a further five seconds back. He displays a dejected look on his face as he crosses the line having been run off his feet. This has been his induction into real running. It isn't going to be easy to win a major title if this is any guide. Gebrselassie's time of 27:12.95 is the fastest ever 10,000 metres at a major championship. The final km is timed at 2:33.70. The competition is so very tough. Too tough right now for Hissou. Salah would need to get better.

These were only the beginnings of the career of Salah Hissou but already he was one of the world's fastest 5,000 metres and 10,000 metres runners, as well as one of the top performers over the cross country terrain. His 27:19.30 in the World Championship final was a personal best. Skah's 27:14.53 and Tergat's 27:14.70 were also career bests. In Skah's case his time was a Moroccan record that emphasized the high quality of the race. The depth in the field was so good that sixteen runners broke twenty eight minutes in the final! One of them was fourteenth placed Assefa Mezgebu from Ethiopia. Why mention him you ask? Assefa was only seventeen years old. Haile Gebrselassie had some help coming his way.

The Kenyans and Moroccans had been able to isolate Haile Gebrselassie early on, so they may have given themselves a big chance of victory, although in hindsight, there really was no chance at all.

Nevertheless, Morocco had raised its reputation further following the top runs of Skah and Hissou, but in the steeplechase there were none of those similar lofty placings. The final that was held on August 11 was a memorable one for athletics fans, though not ones hoping for another Morocco vs. Kenya battle in men's distance running. Not a single one of the three Moroccan representatives made the final. It was a setback in this discipline for the nation.

Not that anyone in the history of the event (yes even Henry Rono) could have come close to stopping world record holder Moses Kiptanui from winning his third straight world title. The winning time was magnificent, 8:04.16, a championship record, but it was the margin of victory that was more astounding. The Kenyan defeated second placed teammate Christopher Koskei by 5.14 seconds. That's the equivalent to a 2.57 second margin in a 1,500 metres. Every World Athletics Championships has its few really ultimate performances and its few really ultimate champions. In Gothenburg, Moses slotted nicely into both categories.

The 1,500 metres commenced a day earlier. The most notable of the four heats was the first, which was run at a very slow pace, all but guaranteeing that only five of the eleven participants would qualify for the semi finals. This didn't worry Venuste Niyongabo who finished closely behind the winner Ali Hakimi of Tunisia. However 1987 world champion Abdi Bile was knocked out, as was Kenyan Jonah Birir. Hakimi's winning time was 3:48.40. Niyongabo's 3:48.58 left him with little to spare over the unlucky sixth runner Branko Zorko who clocked 3:48.83.

Morceli won heat 2 in 3:42.58 and Seddiki impressed by winning the faster third heat with a 3:38.24. In heat 4 El Guerrouj nearly matched him with his 3:38.93. He also won his heat so all was well in the Kada camp. However the semis were going to be more serious.

Back to August 11 and the men's 1,500 metres semi finals.

MOROCCAN SUCCESS; THE KADA WAY

Again only the first five across the line were automatic qualifiers and this time there were only two fastest losers. The results of the first heat were not surprising with Morceli winning very easily in 3:38.37. Olympic champion Fermin Cacho finished fifth. His 3:39.35 was only five hundredths ahead of Hakimi. This wasn't a fast time, so the Spaniard could consider himself fortunate to be safely through to the final.

Heat 2 pitted Venuste against Hicham and for the first time the Moroccan won out, although being a preliminary it wasn't a true victory. Kada's youngster looked at ease with the high pressure stakes as he grounded out a 3:37.47 to Niyongabo's 3:37.62. It was just as well that both had edged under Noureddine Morceli's time. For it was all that they could take into the final with them in order to believe that there was any semblance of chance of a gold medal. No matter how else you looked at it, the Algerian was a whopping red hot favourite for the August 13 final.

This Sunday was a big day for Abdelkader Kada, almost as much as it was for Hicham El Guerrouj. They had come a long way in a relatively short period and after years of great planning and dedication there lay this opportunity to become a medallist at the highest level. Salah Hissou had achieved this, via his bronze collect in Durham. The 1,500 metres final started at the fairly early time of 4:20 pm.

El Guerrouj was joined by El Basir in the twelve man line up. Morocco and Spain were the only countries with two athletes in the field. Noureddine Morceli looked unbeatable. As Australian Bruce McAvaney said, "If they sit and sprint, it looks impossible to beat him. If it's just even it looks impossible to beat him." But you never know what could happen. If he had a bad day, if he ran a bad tactical race, if he fell.......

The gun sounded but the race did not start with a bang. The runners were dawdling, crawling along at a jog for their relative abilities. For Morceli, he may have thought briefly of Barcelona, but any of those thoughts are quickly extinguished as the big beefy American Paul McMullen takes the lead and appears willing to make it more of a true miler's race.

With the pace on from the 300 metres mark, the top athletes can relax and get into their stride. From the middle stages Morceli sits permanently on the American's shoulder in a menacing fashion. It is clear to all that McMullen does not pose a threat but is merely a sitting duck. The first 400 metres split is 57.43. Niyongabo is next with Morceli sitting right on him. El Guerrouj follows in the path of the favourites.

The next lap is much slower with Niyongabo racing alongside McMullen at 800 metres in 1:59.69 after a 62.26 lap. This is his chance to go. As a 3:30 runner it is possible to make a long run for home off this pace but of course you need supreme confidence against this calibre of opposition.

But he doesn't make his move yet as Robert De Castella makes the comment with 650 metres to go, "I think they've almost accepted that the gold is gone. They're racing now probably for silver and bronze. I don't see how Morceli can be beaten off this slower pace."

Venuste continues to sit on the American's shoulder and doesn't move ahead until 500 metres remained. As he takes the lead, he clips the American, causing himself to stumble slightly and lose his impetus. Running a perfect tactical race, Noureddine makes his move at the same time and surges past the man from Burundi. As he hits the bell he goes into overdrive. This is something to watch.

The split at 1,100 metres is 2:42.45. El Guerrouj also accelerates but is kept out by Niyongabo going into the bend and has to settle into third position. Can Venuste drag Hicham along with the accelerating Algerian?

The 1,200 metres split is 2:55.37 after a 55.68 lap with only half of that of real running. Niyongabo makes a valiant attempt to go with Morceli but is clearly found wanting. As Morceli motors along the back straight the elastic stretches and then snaps. The pace is very special. Bruce McAvaney,

MOROCCAN SUCCESS; THE KADA WAY

"He's stretching them now. Look at him go already Morceli. Five metres Niyongabo, three metres El Guerrouj. He won by a record margin in Tokyo, he nearly matched it in Stuttgart. He'll better it here. Look at this man go!"

Niyongabo isn't a completely broken man and bravely fights on. He enters the home straight running well enough to expect the silver medal.

Behind him though is a young Moroccan, running powerfully himself. With his strength showing out El Guerrouj passes Niyongabo in the dying stages to become a world championship silver medallist! The top eight finishers were:

Noureddine Morceli	3:33.73
Hicham El Guerrouj	3:35.28
Venuste Niyongabo	3:35.56
Rachid El Basir	3:35.96
Kevin Sullivan	3:36.73
Abdelkader Chekhemani	3:36.90
Mohamed Suleiman	3:36.96
Fermin Cacho	3:37.02

Hicham and understandably the entire Moroccan athletics team were thrilled with his breakthrough achievement. Still shy of twenty one, El Guerrouj had improved from the many thirteenth place finishes at the end of '94 to this. It was a massive rise in the ranks and now the question was being asked for the first time. Could Hicham improve even more and close on Noureddine next season?

The snapping of the elastic is another popular term bandied about in distance running circles when a runner breaks the resistance of another. It's a way of describing how a runner is being dropped by another or losing contact with the main pack. When the elastic is being stretched it is a very dangerous sign for the runner losing contact, however it doesn't always end in disaster. Sometimes the pace will slow at a critical moment, allowing the struggling opponent to get back on and in touch. It's vital that when a strength runner has a speed runner in trouble, that he maintains the pressure and finishes him off. Otherwise he may be punished in a sprint finish. Of course it's not only strength runners that break the elastic. Noureddine Morceli certainly wasn't lacking in speed. His final lap was timed at 51.28. The Algerian gave his thoughts on the race, "I never know what to expect in a race. The race was a little bit fast, not like what I had expected. I expected it to be a little bit slow."

It was a great pleasure to view the performance of the victor for all but Morceli's destroyed opponents. He was like a greyhound, sleek and slender with an incredible top end speed. He had the race won in Gothenburg half a lap out, such was his supremacy. Noureddine eased over the final twenty metres, his final victory margin flattering his rivals.

The 5,000 metres final took place on the same day. It turned out to be a reasonable race and for Morocco it was fantastic, but it was not earth shattering in standard. Ismael Kirui defended his title from Stuttgart, this time winning in a sprint finish, after doing a lot of the heavy front running work. This showed his versatility and displayed his cross country strength. Plus it made a mockery of his twelfth place result in Monaco. The winning time was only 13:16.77 with a last lap of 56.55. Finishing within a second of him were Moroccan Khalid Boulami and Kenyan Shem Kororia. Boulami's teammates were also in the battle for the podium with Sghyr and Lahlafi finishing fourth and fifth. Ismail's 13:17.86 was an agonizing twenty seven hundredths short of a bronze medal after he faded badly over the final fifty metres. The race was conducted in a similar manner to the 10,000 metres in that by the latter stages there were only six runners in contention. Three Moroccans in the top five firmly demonstrated what a major factor the team was now and was set to be in the future. A Moroccan did not win the 5,000 metres but who knows, perhaps it was winnable for Salah Hissou who had run that 13:02 earlier in the season in Rome.

But as Brussels showed, perhaps not. On August 25, many of the best from Gothenburg fought it out over 10,000 metres and surprisingly it was the 5,000 metres men who triumphed. Worku Bikila proved that Gebrselassie wasn't the only

MOROCCAN SUCCESS; THE KADA WAY

Ethiopian capable of winning a big 10,000 metres race. He clocked 27:06.44, a great time, as he edged out the double world champion Ismael Kirui who ran 27:06.59. Coming in third was Hissou, delighted to have run 27:09.30, another personal best and more significantly a Moroccan record. This was Hissou symbolically taking over from Skah. Salah was the future of Moroccan distance running, even if he had yet to defeat Khalid on the track. He may have *only* finished third, but his future looked very bright when you consider the Kenyans he defeated. Josephat Machuka ran 27:10.34, Paul Tergat 27:14.08, Shem Kororia, 27:18.02 and William Sigei 27:31.54. Brahim Lahlafi was also well back in the field with a 27:43.05, as was former world champion Moses Tanui who ran 27:45.86. Paul Koech rounded out the top ten in 27:50.06. This was a truly high quality race and again Hissou was in the thick of the action. It was only that lack of a finishing kick that was proving a problem. It would be Salah's future endeavour to forever try to get rid of those sit and kickers. Run to his strength, which was the ability to go hard from a long way out, or to put in various punishing laps in the early stages of races and be able to recover from them. Speed meant a lot but it didn't have to mean everything. Not only did he become the fastest Moroccan ever but Salah also moved up a number of places on the all time list. This list was a rapidly changing one. Here's how the top ten looked after Brussels '95:

Haile Gebrselassie	26:43.53
William Sigei	26:52.23
Yobes Ondieki	26:58.38
Worku Bikila	27:06.44
Ismael Kirui	27:06.59
Richard Chelimo	27:07.91
Arturo Barrios	27:08.23
Salah Hissou	27:09.30
Josephat Machuka	27:10.34
John Ngugi	27:11.62

Hicham El Guerrouj was also at the Van Damme Memorial meeting. He was set to race Venuste Niyongabo in the 1,500 metres. During the last two months the pair had developed arguably the most interesting rivalry in track and field.

The Moroccan hadn't spent any time bathing in his glorious silver from Gothenburg. The massive athletics night in Zurich was held only three days after the World Championships, on August the 16th, yet Hicham wanted to justify his suddenly elite status. The men's mile was always of great interest, particularly for this edition because Noureddine Morceli was competing and in the mood to attack his own 3:44.39 world record.

But there were also other races of great significance being played out at the Weltklasse stadium. Moses Kiptanui became the first man to break eight minutes in the 3,000 metres steeplechase. His time of 7:59.18 was a big breakthrough. Similar to the four minute mile, sub eight minutes in the steeplechase had been something of a barrier. Consider that Henry Rono ran 8:05.40 in 1978, yet it took more than seventeen years to improve the time just that little bit more. Kiptanui's world record was arguably better (not just faster) than Rono's but it would not last nearly as long. There were more talented Kenyans following him through.

As a just reward for breaking through the eight minute wall, Kiptanui was selected as the overall Grand Prix winner for 1995. He could not have won this prize from one performance, but without this, he surely wouldn't have won it ahead of the likes of Gebrselassie and Morceli. Moses achieved his record feat without the assistance of pacemakers. His km splits were 2:41.25, 2:40.95 and 2:36.98. His final lap was covered in just 60.09! It was his seventh world record run, having previously also lowered marks in flat distances of 3,000 metres, 2 miles, 5,000 metres, plus 3,000 metres indoors.

Yet despite having just created such monumental athletics history, Moses Kiptanui was *not* the biggest story of the night.

It was anyone's guess as to who was the number one 5,000 metres runner in the world. After Ismael Kirui defended his world championship in Gothenburg, Bruce McAvaney speculated, "The distance talent at the moment is

MOROCCAN SUCCESS; THE KADA WAY

phenomenal. If Morceli goes to 5,000, Kiptanui goes to 5,000, Gebrselassie, Kirui."

Robert De Castella elaborated, "It's incredible competition and threats in terms of who exactly is the number one 5,000 metres runner in the world. There's so many who can lay claim to that title."

The Zurich 5,000 metres gave us a clear answer.

Apparently one earth shattering world record in a year is not enough for Haile Gebrselassie. The Ethiopian smashed Kiptanui's own 5,000 metres world record to smithereens with a 12:44.39, taking 10.91 seconds off the Kenyan's best. It was possibly the greatest performance in the history of distance running. At least some felt so at the time. Right now he was unstoppable.

The latter stages of this performance were incredible as Gebrselassie demolished this highest quality of line ups. Finishing well over 100 metres adrift would be Olympic champion Baumann, world champion Kirui, then came Kennedy, Franke and Sghyr. His 10,000 metres opponents Machuka and Tergat were to place seventh and eighth. Still further back were former world cross country champion Sigei, Gothenburg silver medallist Boulami and sub thirteen minute man Komen. It was a who's who of long distance track running in the mid '90's. All that were missing were Skah, Hissou, plus part time supremos Kiptanui and Morceli.

The concluding stages of the race are worth reminiscing over. The rabbit Worku Bikila, took Haile through to four laps remaining. At this point his lead was approximately twenty five metres over the next man Ismael Kirui. Now given the task of setting the pace himself, Gebrselassie rose to the task and increased this margin substantially from then on.

It is not long thereafter that we realise that we might be witnessing something very special. It is the moment that Haile passes through 4,000 metres in 10:14.15, with a lead of over fifty metres. The km split has registered as 2:31.23. This is extraordinary! A new record is assured. The only question is how much will he take off?

The rhythm is so smooth, yet he is moving so quickly. Haile's cadence is absolutely unbelievable as he ticks off the final laps like a machine. 60.3, 60.4, 59.69. Though he never appears to be sprinting, Steve Ovett describes him as "cruising." The crowd is going berserk, standing and applauding this great athlete. Who says that non competitive races are boring? This is the most exciting performance in men's distance running for many years. Or perhaps just since Hengelo!

There was also a mile to be conducted on this amazing night of men's distance running. This was even better than the World Championships for the Algerian as he ripped away from what little challenge El Guerrouj had to offer. It was still a top run from Hicham, but that just goes to show how awesome Noureddine was. On this occasion there was no record although most milers would happily settle for a 3:45.19. Abdelkader Kada wasn't disillusioned with the somewhat thrashing that El Guerrouj had copped. The clock said 3:48.69, which was a big positive. He was likewise delighted with his youngster backing up with a second high quality performance only three days after the Gothenburg final. With Hicham showing an increasing ability to race regularly and well, Kada entered him in another monster race, in Koln on August 18.

The Burundi bronze medallist was back, looking to turn the tables on this upstart Moroccan. Would he be able to reclaim his spot as the next best miler behind Morceli?

The race wasn't able to provide us with an accurate answer. But what a race it was! It was fast and provided El Guerrouj with yet another personal best time. The two rivals were neck and neck down the final straight. Either would have been a worthy winner but it was the Moroccan who was judged the victor by the narrowest of margins. Hicham was given a 3:31.16 and Venuste a 3:31.17! Azzedine Sediki was also magnificent. The unheralded Moroccan also ran a personal

MOROCCAN SUCCESS; THE KADA WAY

best with his third placed time of 3:31.48.

Now in Brussels, it was unclear who was better. El Guerrouj or Niyongabo? Hicham had come out on top in their last two clashes but Venuste still had a faster 1,500 metres time plus a superior overall record during the last two seasons. Most experts were split on this one and looked forward to the race that didn't include Morceli.

Hicham El Guerrouj's last three races had arguably produced his three greatest ever results. Could he make it a fourth straight outstanding performance in Brussels?

On this night Niyongabo had it and El Guerrouj didn't. Venuste proved that he really was the second best 1,500 metres runner in the world, despite the Gothenburg glitch. It was a majestic display from him and a rout over Hicham, much like Morceli's victory in Zurich. He really opened up on the final lap and hit the line in 3:31.68, miles ahead of everyone bar American Steve Holman who clocked 3:33.34. El Guerrouj still managed to take third, but the time of 3:35.72 said it all. It was his slowest outdoor time this season.

Both of Abdelkader Kada's stars had finished third at the huge meeting. The results were misleading, for one had broken the national record, the other had simply been broken.

On this same night in Brussels, Moses Kiptanui almost ran another world record in the 3,000 metres steeplechase. The performance of 7:59.52 was incredible as he thrashed another top quality field. Noureddine Morceli also capped off another magnificent year by winning the 3,000 metres in 7:27.50, the third fastest of all time. Only himself and Kiptanui had gone faster. More than eleven seconds adrift were Khalid Boulami, Ismail Sghyr, Dieter Baumann, Paul Bitok and Bob Kennedy. These runners were amongst the best 3,000 metres/5,000 metres competitors in the world. Yet Morceli, a natural miler, had completed destroyed them. He was an amazing machine.

The Algerian competed three more times during the European

season and his standards remained remarkably high. There was a 3:48.26 mile in Berlin, a 7:29.36 3,000 metres in Rieti where he had over fifteen seconds to spare on Paul Bitok and a whopping 4.34 second victory margin in the 1,500 metres at the Grand Prix final in Monaco. It's worth mentioning the winning time of 3:28.37. It was only one second off his world record best and nobody had *ever* come within a full second of this run in Monaco. His form had scared off his toughest competitors as neither Hicham El Guerrouj nor Venuste Niyongabo bothered to take him on post Zurich. Noureddine completed the final lap in 54.20.

In Rieti, Morceli proved that his 7:25.11 world record was far from invincible. At halfway he was four seconds under world record pace thanks to brother Ali's efforts. From there on he fell away but the Algerian felt that the less than perfect conditions were the main contributing factor in him failing at his record attempt, "The rain makes me heavy. You can't always run a record." Noureddine had also been quoted as saying, "I think my 3:27 for 1,500 metres is worth 7:21 for 3,000 metres..."

Having just won his third world 1,500 metres championship in his usual commanding fashion, the general consensus was that we were watching the greatest miler of all time. But sporting standards are usually on the improve and world records often don't last as long as expected. Little did we know what surprises 1996 and beyond held in store.

The season wasn't over yet for Salah Hissou but it would have been better if he'd gone home.

Haile Gebrselassie continued on his merry way, running a 12:53.19 in the Berlin 5,000 metres on the 1st of September. This much *slower* time than his Zurich exploits was nevertheless the second fastest in history! But it was just another victory for the great man.

Moses Kiptanui took his astounding form into the race but even he couldn't get near the Ethiopian. He placed second and his time was very good. Suddenly 13:00.90 wasn't as

MOROCCAN SUCCESS; THE KADA WAY

good as what it used to be.

Salah Hissou blew up in Germany, his good form having definitely deserted him. The end result was ninth position and a 13:16.74. The other Moroccans were able to restore the nation's pride with Khalid Boulami and Ismail Sghyr finishing third and fifth behind the Gebrselassie show.

Hissou continued racing, finishing off his European season with a marginally better run, finishing eighth in the Grand Prix Final on September 9 in Monaco. The lowly placing wasn't so bad with Salah racing in the shorter 3,000 metres. After incredibly punishing 10,000 metres races in Gothenburg and Brussels, plus the poor showing in Berlin, it was no surprise that Hissou would find the step down too great a challenge. Running a 7:38.51 while being slightly jaded wasn't too bad a way to close off a good season. In reality, even at his best, Hissou was unlikely to win major races over 3,000 metres, particularly those that had Haile Gebrselassie in the field. The Ethiopian added another victory to his rapidly growing resumé but perhaps even the long season had finally taken its toll on him. His time was 7:35.90 and in an extraordinary finish he held out Burundi's 1,500 metres man, Venuste Niyongabo by just one hundredth of a second! The first six were separated by only 1.11 seconds. Behind Niyongabo came Boulami, Sghyr, Kororia and Bitok. Just ahead of Hissou, in a time of 7:38.09 was Daniel Komen. The two would enjoy many battles over the ensuing years. Komen had struggled since his great 5,000 metres run in Rome but he was only nineteen years old. Another off season of hard altitude training and the Kenyan would be ripe for improvement in 1996. Just how much though, nobody could have predicted.

Hicham El Guerrouj had skipped the concluding stages of the 1995 European track season. In place of that he'd travelled to Asia to compete in some lower grade meets. On the 15th of September he raced in Tokyo and edged out Mohamed Suleiman by nine hundredths in a slowly run 1,500 metres. The clock was finally stopped at 3:40.96. But so late in the season, slow times could be forgiven. After the Brussels experience it was good to get back in the winner's circle.

His final race in 1995 was two days later, also in Japan in Kobe. He finished his outdoor season where it had started, surprisingly at 800 metres. It was super slow but the victory over a non favourite distance was certainly savoured by athlete and coach. Hicham's 1:50.16 was too good for Suleiman who was again his nearest challenger.

At the end of 1995 distance running was at a fascinating stage. There were a number of athletes who had claims to the 'best in the world' tag. Gebrselassie was a popular candidate, having both 5,000 metres and 10,000 metres world records plus being the double world champion at the longer distance. Then there was Ismael Kirui, the amazing Kenyan who had just become the double world champion over 5,000 metres, at twenty years old! Kirui also had taken second place at the '95 World Cross Country Championships. On top of this he had run that fast 10,000 metres in Brussels. Moses Kiptanui was a freak in his own right. He had dominated the 3,000 metres steeplechase having won the last three World Championships and being the only man to break the magical eight minute barrier. He'd missed out on the '92 Barcelona Olympics through injury, this being the only blight so far during an amazing career. He had formerly held both the 3,000 metres and 5,000 metres flat world records as well. He was unarguably the greatest steeplechaser of all time. Khalid Skah had one of distance running's greatest pedigrees. He was a double world cross country champion from 1990 and '91, an Olympic 10,000 metres champion from Barcelona, a bronze medallist for the same event in Tokyo '91 and he had just taken that second place behind Gebrselassie in Gothenburg.

These distance runners were all greats of the sport but there was one who right now probably surpassed them all. Few would dispute the Algerian ace Nourredine Morceli's already legendary status. Like Kiptanui, Morceli was now a triple world champion who had suffered the great disappointment of not performing at his best in the 1992 Olympic Games. However he hadn't let that get him down. His numerous fast times since then spoke for themselves. At the end of 1995 he held the world records at 1500 metres, the mile, 2,000 metres and 3,000 metres. His last lap kick was breathtaking and he

MOROCCAN SUCCESS; THE KADA WAY

had the stamina to back it up.

It is clearly evident there were a lot of superstars in men's track distance running during the mid 1990's. Two Kenyans not mentioned above were about to add themselves to the list. Salah wasn't far in the background either and Hicham was right there with him.

Finishing second in the World Championships showed El Guerrouj that becoming the world's best was possible. Only Morceli appeared unbeatable, while Niyongabo was still a rival and potential factor in the amount of success that would come during Hicham's future.

But Hissou appeared to have even greater obstacles to cross on his path towards winning a major gold medal. He still needed to defeat Skah on the track. Tergat was undeniably a major rival and potential problem in all, upcoming championships. Plus there was another issue. How do you solve a problem named Haile Gebrselassie?

Greg Rowlerson

When In Rome - Great, When In Nice - Nice, When In Atlanta...

Gebrselassie was proving to be nigh on unbeatable on the track, but over the cross country terrain he was just another top African runner. He didn't stand out from the rest on the grass as he did on the rubber. Even Salah Hissou had defeated Haile in cross country.

Hissou started 1996 on the road with a 10 kms event in Bolzano, Italy on January 2. He displayed decent early season form by clocking a 28:20 and in the process, just went down to Shem Kororia by one second. Also making an early start to his year was Daniel Komen who finished fourth.

Salah next competed on the 29th of January in a 10 kms IAAF (International Association of Athletics Federation) cross country race in Saint-Sebastian. His early season form was solid but not spectacular. In this warm up event, he placed third in a time of 29:41. His conquerors were Kenyan James Kariuki and Ethiopian Worku Bikila who defeated him by one and two seconds respectively.

Hissou continued with his preparations for Stellenbosch's World Championships with a stellar victory in Torrejoncillo, Spain on February 13. Salah covered the 10.8 kms course in 32:24, defeating Portugal's Paolo Guerra.

Hissou would have a lot on his plate in this Olympic year. For 1996, his initial focus would be on the World Cross Country Championships where he hoped to at least replicate his third place of a year before. The race was being held in Cape Town, South Africa on March 23.

While Salah focused on cross, Hicham focused on the indoors. El Guerrouj's improvement in 1995 had been substantial and immediately he went about showing that 1996 would continue with the same upward trend. Racing in Stockholm on the 25th of February, Hicham destroyed a weak field with a fast time of 3:34.97. Once again he had broken

MOROCCAN SUCCESS; THE KADA WAY

the Moroccan record. His winning margin was an enormous 4.58 seconds over Christophe Impens from Belgium and he was closing in on Morceli's world record of 3:34.16. However, this record was not of great importance as indoor races were held less often and were not the major focus like the races outdoors. What did matter were the warning signs that El Guerrouj was sending out to the rest of the world. 'Venuste and Noureddine, I'm coming to get you.' Come the summer, these guys were going to have an almighty challenge on their hands.

Most athletes used the indoor season to test their racing form during a period of often hard training. The relatively short season runs through February and March. It offers runners a second racing period, adding to the outdoor season which generally takes up the time between June and September.

The world records for indoor distances are much slower than their outdoor counterparts. This in part, is due to the configurations of the circuit. The bends are tight and with a lap covering only 200 metres, each straight only gives the runners approximately 50 metres each time in a direct line. Running down the straight in 100 metres segments has proven to be a faster practice.

This equates for some of the record differentials, but not all. The indoor records could be a little stronger if all the top athletes raced and had their major focus on the races in February and March. This is hardly ever the case. A 1,500 metres event indoors, even at the World Championships will be lucky to have forty percent of the world's best on the start line. Those that are competing will still consider the World Outdoor Championships (or Olympic Games) to be their main goal for the year. The major outdoor championships will have everyone who is good enough on the start line, save for injured athletes or those that are jeopardized by unfair selection committees.

There was only this one indoor race for El Guerrouj, so Kada sent his star back home for months of intensive training, with everything being geared towards a shot at Olympic gold in

Atlanta. The games were taking place in late July, early August. Hicham wanted to be in top shape once June arrived and with it, some highly significant Grand Prix races.

Kada's other star was putting his eggs in more than one basket. It was impossible for Salah Hissou to focus only on the Olympics. The World Cross Country Championships meant too much to him. Finishing third last year had been momentous enough. Now Salah and Abdelkader dreamed of more. Standing in the way of such dreams was the class of '96, arguably the strongest cross country field ever assembled.

The defending champion Paul Tergat was there, as was his little teammate Ismael Kirui. The Kenyans had a host of other quality runners in their team. One reason why the World Cross Country is considered such a tough race to win is that there are lesser restrictions on distance running's best nations. At an Olympic Games, countries can only select three athletes whereas in the World Cross Country, this number jumps to nine. Instead of battling against the best nine runners from Kenya, Ethiopia and Morocco, other athletes must compete against the best twenty seven from distance running's super powers. Even with twenty seven in the event, this still isn't really a true indication of all the world's best runners, since Kenya usually has about twenty of the best thirty distance runners going around. However, it is a better all in war than the major track championships.

Hissou was perhaps the only worry for the always dominant Kenyan team, although Haile Gebrselassie was giving the event another crack. You could never totally count out the 'emperor' from Ethiopia.

But this was one discipline that Gebrselassie would never conquer. The uneven terrain didn't suit his bouncy track style and Tergat was far too strong for him. So was Salah Hissou.

Hissou put in a top run, but Tergat was far and away the best for the second straight year. Salah's second place was one small place up from last year, but was another giant leap in

MOROCCAN SUCCESS; THE KADA WAY

his running career. May have to pay royalties for that line!

Despite the Moroccan's efforts, the Kenyan had won by a large amount. Twelve seconds to be exact. Ismael Kirui made it the same podium finishers from '95 with a third place finish, only two seconds behind Hissou. The little man remained a star and he was barely twenty one years old. A fortune teller would surely tell of great success, years of competing for the world cross country title as well as glories at future World Championships and Olympic Games. Alas, it was all down hill from here for Ismael. In arguably an unfair decision, Kirui missed selection for the Atlanta Games and never recovered. As it turned out, Kenya's two best 5,000 metres runners in the '90's never went to an Olympic Games. Sometimes there is little justice in sport.

There had been large gaps between many of the top runners in the race, which wasn't always the case. It demonstrated Tergat's domination of the field. His nemesis on the track, Haile Gebrselassie, finished fifth, though he did have a rare excuse, having tripped over a log during the event. It's doubtful that he could have finished much closer to the winner regardless. Tergat clocked 33:44, Hissou, 33:56, Gebrselassie, 34:28. Finishing fourth between Ismael and Haile was the impressive late bloomer, Paul Koech. The key section came during the eleventh km, which Tergat ran in a supersonic split of 2:30! Not sure if anyone in the history of the sport could have gone with that.

During his performance in the World Cross Country, Hissou had proven to the world that he was a real force, not a flash in the pan. He was the man to take over from Skah, to carry the Moroccan flag with pride in the major long distance races. Incidentally, Salah had thrashed Khalid in South Africa. The former champion could *only* manage a seventh place result. He had just celebrated his twenty ninth birthday and right now the general rule was that long distance running (on the track and grass) was proving to be a young man's game. It was nearly time for twenty four year old Salah Hissou to make his mark on the track. The 1996 Atlanta Olympics were fast approaching. For now, it was back into hard training with his mate Hicham. They had to continue to apply themselves one hundred percent if their dreams of becoming Olympic champions were to be realized.

Rating the careers of Hicham and Salah against each other made for an intriguing comparison. As far as victories and top three finishes in European Grand Prix meetings were concerned, El Guerrouj had the far more successful results. His best time at his favourite distance, the 1,500 metres, made him the third fastest in the world for 1995 and he even moved up to second ranked in the lesser raced mile. Hissou in contrast, could *only* manage a fourth placed ranking for 1995 in the 10,000 metres. But Salah was now the Moroccan record holder at this distance, while Hicham had to be content to sit behind Said Aouita's former world record time. Hissou had also proven to be more versatile, winning at 3,000 metres (where his time ranked eighth in '95) and performing wonderfully well in the World Cross Country. His recent bronze and silver medals suggested that he had the ability to improve on his ranking in the 10,000 metres. That cross country strength combined with decent speed at 3,000 metres showed that he could also improve in the 5,000 metres where he ranked sixth last season.

Depending on how highly you rate the World Cross Country, Salah Hissou had achieved arguably more to date than Hicham El Guerrouj. Their ages were a significant factor in the similar level status that both were held in at this time.

With so much already accomplished, it was easy to forget that Hicham El Guerrouj was only twenty one years old. Once an athlete has reached the elite level it is usually very hard to extract further improvements from them. That is often because it takes them until their mid twenties to reach such a level. On the other hand, it was not uncommon for runners in their early twenties to still make big leaps in standards from the top level of the sport. Just look at Haile Gebrselassie who last year had taken massive chunks off his already excellent 5,000 metres and 10,000 metres personal bests.

As the big European track races drew nearer, it was expected

MOROCCAN SUCCESS; THE KADA WAY

that Noureddine Morceli would continue his domination, but there was one major advantage that Hicham El Guerrouj and Venuste Niyongabo had on their side. Youth.

Venuste was twenty two. Noureddine was twenty six. Twenty six could be a good age for peak performance. It's just that it was less likely for Morceli to improve on the level he'd attained. Still, even with some improvement from his rivals, he was going to be too good, as long as he maintained his high standard.

For the 1996 Atlanta Olympic Games, Morceli was logically going to be the toughest runner to defeat for El Guerrouj. But looking further ahead, even as far as the Seville 1999 World Championships and the Sydney 2000 Olympics, his focus was likely to shift to Niyongabo. Getting the better of this Burundi runner was critical in whether Hicham became a regular winner or a regular bridesmaid. The age gap was minimal enough to basically be irrelevant and so far Niyongabo had the edge on El Guerrouj. In whose favour would the advantage in this rivalry go to during 1996?

The athletics season is not a particularly long one. Tennis players and golfers try to stay at a high level of performance for eleven months each year but it is different for track and field athletes. A top track performer will try to peak for the European season which runs approximately from June-September. For a distance runner it is hard to maintain top form for such a time, so someone like Salah Hissou will focus on a few races, usually some that lead up to a major championship and then the major championship itself. Then he will attempt to maintain his form for the final track meetings of the season. A two month peak period is more realistic for most runners. Hence the Grand Prix final often throws up odd results. Results that don't paint a true reflection on the season passed. The 'final' comes too late in the year with the athletes having already expended their physical and emotional energies in Rome, Oslo, Zurich, Brussels, etc.

As the '96 European season arrived, Hissou decided to put his form on the line early. Rome was the venue and 5,000 metres was the distance as Salah joined a field that included the legendary Moses Kiptanui. It was here just twelve months ago where Moses had broken the world record with Salah finishing well off the pace. That field comprised of many great runners. For the 1996 Rome race this was even more the case, but Salah Hissou was not overawed. His running would soon prove that it had very few flaws.

There were close to 50,000 spectators in the stadium on June 5, 1996. The fans would be privileged to see the highest quality 5,000 metres 'contest' ever. Zurich '95 could not be described as any sort of a contest!

In Rome the race was contested by twenty two athletes, quite a large contingent, but one that did not have cause for concern due to the manner in which it was run. The distance races in the big European meetings are usually run at a fast pace. There isn't the bunching up that you often see in a championship event. As a result, the runners were likely to spread out into single file very quickly.

Most of the runners wear white, so it isn't hard to spot Salah Hissou, dressed in an all yellow uniform, standing in the middle of the inside lanes. Symbolically, standing to the right of him are Moses Kiptanui and Daniel Komen.

The gun sounds, sending the runners into an early sixty three second lap tempo. Salah is content to settle into a mid pack position. The fourth and fifth laps are fast as the Moroccan moves up to seventh at 2,000 metres, the leader going through in 5:07.57. On pace for around 12:50! The third km slows fractionally, but the average speed of approximately sixty-two second laps remains far too fast for most of the twenty-two competitors.

At the split it is Kiptanui leading the way in 7:44.26. He is followed by Daniel Komen, Salah Hissou, Thomas Nyariki, Shem Kororia and Philip Mosima. This race is being dominated by the Kenyans. In seventh place we find David Chelule, who is in the process of being dropped as he goes through in 7:46.60.

MOROCCAN SUCCESS; THE KADA WAY

Hissou had never gone under thirteen minutes over 5,000 metres. On two previous occasions he had threatened to break the barrier at this venue. Last year, the situation had been almost identical with Salah sitting on the heels of Komen and Kiptanui. In '95 he faded in the closing stages. How would he fare in the closing stages of '96, with the race being run at an even faster pace?

The precocious young talent of Daniel Komen now takes up the front running, keeping the pace at a high threshold of pain tempo. He passes through 3,400 metres in 8:45.89, with his five rivals still keeping on his tail. Hissou looks composed, even whilst in the middle of a Kenyan sandwich. It is one Moroccan vs. five Kenyans. This is Michael Jordan type stuff!

Suddenly Komen switches off as Kiptanui retakes the lead and Hissou goes with him. Moses doesn't surge and the pack eases through in 9:50.40 after a lap of 64.51. Three laps to go. It is a time when the runners are hurting. It's a perfect time for a strength runner to make his opposition really hurt as Salah Hissou takes over the lead for the first time.

He starts to apply the pressure. It is only now that he's able to truly display his improvements made over the off season. Previously it was a question of could he stay with the Kenyans? Now Hissou is the runner asking the questions.

With two laps to go (which is split in 10:52.45), Salah has broken the resistance of Nyariki, Komen and Kororia. Only Kiptanui and the nineteen year old Mosima can stay in contact. The Moroccan's form appears fantastic. He seems set to break Said Aouita's national record.

For the penultimate lap, Hissou stays on sixty two second lap pace which is enough to prise open a gap on the former world record holder, Kiptanui. With 400 metres to go (11:54.38 at 4,600 metres) he is really kicking it down. It's apparent that he is on his way to his first major victory. The last lap isn't just a celebration as Salah shows that he *does* have a finishing sprint to be feared. He runs a 56.42 last lap on his way to a winning time of 12:50.80!

He was scorching hot, so much so that he immediately went to remove his shoes to allow his feet to breathe after crossing the line. The last km was timed at 2:29.86. In such a fast race this was too much to cope with for anyone but Haile Gebrselassie.

After disposing of his shoes, Salah stood up, but shortly after, the enormity of what he had just done must have started to sink in, as he knelt to the track, said a prayer and then kissed the same rubber surface upon which he has just made his track reputation.

The Moroccan had just reached a new level of running. To dominate against most of the best from Kenya was a rare thing to see. The time of 12:50.80 was stunning. If it had been run twelve months earlier, Salah would have held the world record! Of course a certain Ethiopian had beaten him to the punch. Gebrselassie's amazing 12:44.39 at Zurich in August '95 was the only performance ahead of Hissou's on the all time list.

The Moroccan's victory was most impressive. Racing in Europe during '94 and '95 had let him know that he wasn't going to have a chance of winning big track races in bunch sprints. But not all the big races were run at the slower paces that encouraged bunch sprints. Also, the faster the entire race is, the harder it is for the fastest kickers to produce their sprint, that's if they are even still in contact. Hissou had proved that he could sprint just as well off a sub thirteen minute pace as opposed to say a thirteen thirty pace. As such, his last lap sprint could become competitive if the race was fast enough. In Rome the 5,000 metres event was raced hard all the way, in effect making it into a strength race like a 10,000 metres or a cross country race would be. This was always going to be Hissou's greatest strength, that is, running at a high threshold for long periods. When he had the form to put it into practice, few could match it.

Running at a high threshold is to run at very close to your optimum level. For example in this race, Salah went through 3,000 metres in 7:44.8. His personal best at 3,000 metres

MOROCCAN SUCCESS; THE KADA WAY

was *only* 7:35.66, so he was running awfully close to his maximum 3,000 metres speed. However, his cross country strength allowed him to maintain the fast tempo for the remaining 2,000 metres and eventually pull away from the rest of the field.

With this performance, Salah had officially joined the list of names laying their claim to that 'greatest distance runner in the world' tag. He had arrived, you could say and he had to be considered a serious threat at the Olympics. Now the decision. Should he enter the 5,000 metres or 10,000 metres in Atlanta?

Hissou had won easily in Rome, but he wasn't running against mugs. To get a good indication of the high standard of this 5,000 metres race is easy. As the first three athletes crossed the line, they became the second, third and fourth fastest in history! Mosima had overtaken Kiptanui on the final lap and run 12:53.72. This was a stunning time for anyone, let alone a teenager, but again he would be another Kenyan who would fade from the spotlight. Kiptanui clocked a career best 12:54.85. Incredibly this race simply proved that the distance running world was going past him. At the grand old age of twenty five!

There was a fourth runner who also ran under the thirteen minute barrier. Another new Kenyan on the scene, named Thomas Nyariki. He ran 12:59.19, usually a performance that would attract plenty of notice, but in these circumstances, he was able to fly under the radar. By Atlanta, he would be in the spotlight.

Salah attempted to downplay his victory in Rome by saying, "I was not on a special time out. About it I want to only think about Olympics."

Noureddine Morceli also raced at the Rome meeting and he didn't disappoint. The 1,500 metres event was won in his usual cakewalk. The time was 3:30.93 and the gap over the rest was nearly four seconds. The Algerian remained self assured of his dominance. On May 21 he'd said, "I think I can run about 3:25 in the 1,500 and 3:42 or 3:43 in the mile," regarding planned record assaults later in the season at Monaco and Zurich.

Hicham El Guerrouj commenced his season in Seville, Spain the following day (June 6). It was a good race to open his season. There were a number of quality Spaniards in the 1,500 metres, including the Barcelona champion Fermin Cacho. How would the Moroccan cope in hostile territory?

Easy as you like. Hicham was an absolute superstar. He left the others in his dust in the way that only Morceli and Niyongabo did. He ran 3:32.94, but it was the kick down which was most impressive. Cacho ran second, in a distant 3:35.40. Behind him were his teammates Canellas and Estevez. Kada and El Guerrouj should have been very happy with the way the season was progressing but there remained a lot to do. There was much time and many races to play out before Atlanta.

Another Moroccan decided to try his own Hicham El Guerrouj impersonation and it wasn't a bad one. On the 7th of June in Nuremberg, Salah's focus shifted to pure speed where his magnificent form was once again highlighted.

Racing over 1500 metres, Hissou bided his time early, sitting in sixth place after lap 1, clocked in 56.70. The pace stayed solid with an 800 metres split of 1:54.30, by which time Salah was up to third position. Soon he found himself at the head of the pack, making a long drive for home in an attempt to defeat the middle distance specialists. He reached 1,200 metres in 2:52.13 and continued to kick down to sub fifty six second lap pace to win emphatically.

Hissou clocked a personal best time of 3:33.95, good for a middle distance runner, outstanding for a long distance one. In the process he had destroyed a reasonable field. Second and third were Ali Hakimi of Tunisia, 3:36.08, and Anthony Whiteman of Great Britain, runners with decent mile pedigrees. These weren't the stars of the discipline, yet this victory remained quite an achievement for someone who was

MOROCCAN SUCCESS; THE KADA WAY

generally thought of as a 10,000 metres athlete. At the end of their careers, how many runners could say that they had run a podium place in the 12 kms World Cross Country and won a 1,500 metres in 3:33.95? This was versatility of which Said Aouita would be proud.

Abdelkader's runners were everywhere with Morocco's real middle distance runner back racing and winning on June 12 in Duisburg. This time Hicham clocked 3:33.89. This time the victory margin was a whopping 5.36 seconds to Zaki of Sweden. It was almost too easy and Kada knew that he needed to take on some real competition before Atlanta.

With each new outstanding win, the huge pressure to succeed at the Olympic Games was applied more to Abdelkader Kada. It was becoming apparent that in El Guerrouj and Hissou, he coached two of the best handful of distance runners in the world. Both were in magnificent, career best form. It was good timing, for the Olympics only came along every four years. Kada and his crew might never have another good chance at Olympic glory. The final weeks of planning had to be meticulous. His students had to perform but it was Abdelkader who would make some crucial decisions. Does he race here? Has he raced enough? Has he raced too much? When do Salah and Hicham begin to fully taper off? Should Hicham race over 800 metres or 3,000 metres for variety before the games? After his remarkable win in Rome, should Salah enter the 5,000 metres in Atlanta?

These were just some of the many tough questions that Kada needed to answer. Being correct was imperative. His nation expected medals. Of a gold colour if possible.

Abdelkader took his stars away from the Grand Prix circuit for a couple of weeks. On June 28 he returned with his 5,000 metres man. The venue was Paris but it seemed more like a Moroccan National Championship. Hissou had beaten the Kenyans but was he really the best from Morocco? This was a good opportunity to prove so.

Proving so was straightforward for Salah as he blew the top

field away with a classic front running display in its purest form. Once again he went under Said Aouita's old record. He reached the 3,000 metres split in 7:48.20, by which time he was running well clear of all his rivals. The race had been decided after 4,000 metres with the Moroccan opening up a massive lead. Salah says about his tactics in 5,000 metres races, "I like to run the fourth km hard because my finishing kick is not great." Like a snake, Hissou's surge was often venomous and this was certainly the case in France. His eventual winning time of 12:55.93 was again highly impressive and made his choice of events in Atlanta all the more easier.

Unfortunately this made the situation all the more difficult.

After fighting a lone Moroccan battle against Kenya in Rome, he had to fight against his own in Paris. The race demonstrated just how well his country was performing in men's distance running. Their stocks had recently soared. Seven of the first thirteen athletes in this Paris 5,000 metres were from Morocco. It was Hissou who stood head and shoulders above the rest. Salah left his teammates in his wake as he won by forty metres. Khalid Boulami was the best of the rest, clocking 13:02.30, just ahead of Ismail Sghyr's 13:02.94. Baumann of Germany finished fourth but had been no match for the North Africans with his time of 13:09.47 paling in comparison. Hissou had left the field in tatters. He was proving to be far too accomplished for these 5,000 metres men.

Well back in the field, in seventh position, with a time of 13:15.32, was Khalid Skah. The takeover was complete.

After two years of shadowing the stars, Salah Hissou had suddenly become one himself. Becoming the second fastest 5,000 metres runner of all time was a good way to acquire the fans' attention. Winning just as well in Paris cemented his name as one to watch in Atlanta. Knowledgeable distance running fans appreciated his latest victory, for it was a wonderfully rare thing to see an athlete go out hard from a long way out and be able to sustain it. For it to have been

MOROCCAN SUCCESS; THE KADA WAY

done by a non Kenyan athlete was even rarer. Usually these top class 5,000 metres races came down to a last lap sprint but Hissou knew that to beat the best, he had to kick it down well before the bell. There was no other way that he could succeed. Try as he might, he just couldn't match the big guns in a pure sprint finish.

So there you have it. Three races in June. Three career best victories. If the IAAF gave out Athlete of the Month awards, Hissou may well have got it in June '96. But the medals were to be handed out in July.

Another significant race took place during the same Paris meeting. A certain Algerian won the 1,500 metres in a scorching time of 3:29.50. The split from his brother Ali at 800 metres was 1:52.90 so the finishing speed was very much there, even off a strong early tempo. Right now Noureddine Morceli remained the clear favourite to win the Olympic gold medal that he richly deserved. Importantly he had proved that he had sub 3:30 form.

Salah Hissou was also in tremendous form for the upcoming Olympic Games. He now needed to maintain this form through to the end of July. The Moroccan had two more races before Atlanta, the first of which took place when he carried his winning streak to Oslo on July 5 to resume his battle with Kenya. On this occasion, the distance was 3,000 metres and Hissou was matched up against Paul Bitok and Shem Kororia. Both had been 5,000 metres medallists at the highest level.

Also in the race was the former world record holder, Moses Kiptanui. The triple steeplechase world champion obviously had some concerns leading into Atlanta. He was unable to keep pace with the leaders and ended up finishing fourth in a disastrous time of 7:43.39. This was from a runner who managed a 7:27.18 less than twelve months ago. He had little time to get himself right and win Olympic gold. Moses was a non factor in Oslo. Kororia also wasn't a problem for Hissou. Shem had been one of the many Kenyans beaten by the Moroccan in Rome where he had finished sixth. In this 3,000 metres race the same thing happened. With some sustained power running from Salah, Shem was out the back door, on his way to a 7:37.46.

Bitok was a different kettle of fish. The Barcelona silver medallist was in top shape and nothing that Hissou did could shake him. This race was very fast, with Hissou helping to drag Bitok through to a sub 7:30 (7:29.55). Despite being out kicked, Salah could be extremely happy with his 7:30.46, another massive personal best. It was a time that wasn't far short of Aouita's Moroccan record of 7:29.45.

All of Said's national records, if not being broken were constantly under threat. El Guerrouj returned with a 1,500 metres triumph in Hechtel, Belgium on July 7. It was yet another big win, with the time being a fast 3:31.61. It was close to a personal best, though this still remained some way from Aouita's 3:29.46. Similar to his early season indoor win in Stockholm, the runner up was local boy, Christophe Impens.

Hicham returned to Stockholm the next day for his biggest race this season. For the first time in 1996 he would race the world's best, with the exception of Morceli who was absent from the meeting. Noureddine had yet to display the devastating form that was so evident throughout 1995, but his Paris performance still confirmed that he was the one to beat. But who was avoiding whom in the Atlanta lead up?

Even without the Algerian competing there was a sense of expectation in the stadium on the 8th of July, 1996. On the start line was Burundi's best, Venuste Niyongabo. Even Salah Hissou was here, ready to test his strength against these speedsters. But what did Abdelkader Kada hope to gain from throwing Hissou into this lion's den? There was a 5,000 metres event on tonight as well. Wouldn't that be a much more sensible final lead up race to enter before the Olympics? Time would tell.

Perhaps Kada secretly hoped that he could achieve a one-two in this race. If so he was kidding himself. Salah wasn't

MOROCCAN SUCCESS; THE KADA WAY

competitive but the race itself was superb as the two middle distance kings in waiting put on a great display.

The race was fast all the way which is how Hicham liked it. Even as he began to dominate this event he was still mostly known for his great strength. He was becoming feared for his ability to take a race 600 metres out and push it hard to the tape. Most middle distance runners could only kick for about 300 metres. Morceli could run an amazing last 400 metres, but El Guerrouj seemed to be able to kick for even longer. Not with quite the same explosion, but it was powerful all the same.

Niyongabo led El Guerrouj in the early stages, as the 400 metres and 800 metres splits were approximately 55.30 and 1:53.60 respectively. From 450 metres out, the Moroccan pushed ahead of the Burundi runner and to the front as the final rabbit exited. The 1,200 metres split was a very fast 2:49.51, meaning the third lap was covered in a scorching 55.91. A fast third lap was becoming a staple of El Guerrouj's tactics.

In Sweden he was firing on all cylinders, so much so that he headed into uncharted waters. Yet entering the final bend he was still facing enormous pressure from Venuste who retook the lead, while hindering Hicham's rhythm a little, as he cut in on him just before the turn. But El Guerrouj refused to panic and fifty metres from the line he powered past again to win convincingly. On his way to this tremendous victory, Hicham broke the 3:31 barrier. But just achieving this would not have been enough to win, so with some credit going to Niyongabo for pushing him, El Guerrouj had broken the 3:30 barrier also, running a time of 3:29.59. It was agonizingly close to Aouita's fastest time but that record could come to him at a later date. The time of 3:30 is the unofficial barrier that separates the great 1,500 metres runners from the rest. Hicham became only the sixth man to join the sub 3:30 club. The exclusive club as of July 8, 1996:

Noureddine Morceli   3:27.37
Said Aouita   3:29.46

Hicham El Guerrouj	3:29.59
Steve Cram	3:29.67
Sydney Maree	3:29.77
Sebastian Coe	3:29.77

Venuste Niyongabo ran a personal best himself and almost joined the club with a 3:30.09. In third place was Kenyan Laban Rotich with a 3:32.00. Finishing eighth was Salah Hissou. The time of 3:35.38 was good, but finishing in such a lowly position couldn't possibly be the best way to go into a major championship.

El Guerrouj could have run even faster in Stockholm. A clocking of 40.08 for the final 300 metres was exceptional, especially in light of Niyongabo impeding his stride. This slight handicap probably cost Hicham the Moroccan record. That aside, with this fast time Hicham had certainly thrown a spanner in the works.

So Abdelkader. It seems that there are no questions required in regards to El Guerrouj. If he continues to get the better of Niyangabo, only Morceli poses a problem. But what of Hissou? Should he do battle with the Kenyan cross country great and the Ethiopian legend in the 10,000 metres? Or what about competing in a more open 5,000 metres? A distance he raced twice for two wins last month. This event decision could seriously affect the type of medal that hangs around Salah's neck in Atlanta.

Hissou had made up his mind. His wins in Rome and Paris had been enough to convince him that he could win the 5,000 metres at the Olympic Games. Being clearly his nation's best athlete at this event this season, Salah would be an automatic starter at this distance. Right? Wrong.

The Moroccan Athletics Federation had a problem with Salah Hissou competing in the 5,000 metres because it had other athletes who could also run strongly at this distance, whereas in the 10,000 metres it had nobody of note but Khalid Skah, whose form had dropped off this season. Khalid Boulami, Ismail Sghyr and Brahim Lahlafi had all placed in the first five

MOROCCAN SUCCESS; THE KADA WAY

at last year's World Championships. Nobody was saying that any of these runners were a match for Hissou, but each of them could be competitive in Atlanta. If Salah raced the 5,000 metres, one of them would have to make way.

The technical director, Aziz Daouda had the final say and the verdict was in. Salah Hissou would compete in the Atlanta 10,000 metres. He felt that his athlete could still win this event, despite never having seriously threatened Haile Gebrselassie in a track race. However he had defeated the Ethiopian in cross country and had overcome Kenyan star Paul Tergat a number of times on the track. Besides, it wasn't as if Hissou would start the 5,000 metres as the red hot favourite.

Atlanta was always likely to provide the athletes with hot conditions and Salah didn't particularly enjoy the heat, so it made further sense for him to compete in the shorter track event. This would mean less racing time for the conditions to adversely affect him. Regardless, the decision had been made.

Hicham El Guerrouj had one more race before the most important one of his young career was upon him. Kada had selected the meeting in Nice on July 10 as the venue. The Grand Prix was held just two days after Stockholm and the 1,500 metres had the distinct smell of a rematch. Niyongabo wanted revenge before Atlanta. Could he turn the tables on the Moroccan in France? It was essential that he did so if he was to stand a realistic chance of winning the 1,500 metres gold medal.

Hicham was the runner who risked the most by racing here. The win in Stockholm had given him more than enough confidence against Venuste for the Games. Racing him again and losing would only detract from the gains made two days ago. Racing in Nice seemed like a no win scenario but we weren't to know what was in Venuste Niyongabo's thoughts. Perhaps Hicham could encourage Venuste to consider his other Atlanta options.

The 3:29.59 clearly had not exhausted El Guerrouj. He was just as impressive in Nice. This time he was far superior to Niyongabo. The results from the 1,500 metres were as follows:

Hicham El Guerrouj	3:30.61
Venuste Niyongabo	3:31.65
Laban Rotich	3:32.62
Anthony Whiteman	3:34.92

The Moroccan was stamping his authority with a worrying regularity. Worrying, if you had to try to take him down in Atlanta. No doubt that Noureddine Morceli was paying close attention to the man who was a very serious threat to his Olympic ambitions. The Algerian had not encountered anyone of this quality during his domination of the 1990's.

Like in Stockholm, Niyongabo led El Guerrouj early with the splits being around 56.50 and 1:54.00. At the bell Hicham went to the front and passed 1,200 metres in 2:50.31. A gap was beginning to open up, and with another impressive final split of 40.30, it was no surprise to see his rival trail helplessly in his wake.

Abdelkader Kada could not have been happier with his man. He had enormous belief that El Guerrouj could now defeat Morceli. The major issues to counter were that the Algerian would be desperate, having conquered the event for a long time yet missing out in Barcelona. There was also the fact that Morceli had not lost a race to El Guerrouj. The two hadn't met since Zurich '95, when Noureddine ran a stunning 3:45.19 mile.

The lead up races had all been completed. It was time to hand out some medals.

The 10,000 metres took place before the 5,000 metres heats so it is conceivable that some athletes planned on running both events. But conditions were warm and the track surface was hard. The Atlanta organizers had set up a track specifically suited to their star sprinters. In a way this was a

MOROCCAN SUCCESS; THE KADA WAY

good thing, as it helped to produce the greatest sprinting performance of all time. But they shouldn't have had to put Haile Gebrselassie's Olympic status in jeopardy in order to further confirm Michael Johnson's greatness. The hard track played such havoc with Gebrselassie's feet that he was almost forced to abandon his quest for Olympic gold. Now that would have been a shame.

Not for Hissou. He would have been happy to have seen the back of the Ethiopian, or to better put it, not to see the back of him at all. Haile's problems had come not from his heat, but simply from a session he had done on the surface a week earlier. Subsequently he had not trained at all in the week before the 10,000 metres. Only the best could have this problem, yet still be good enough to disguise it from their opposition.

Not a single athlete was prominent in both the 10,000 metres and 5,000 metres. Any plans that an athlete such as Hissou may have had on competing in the 5,000 metres were dismissed after the punishing 10,000 metre heats and final. Salah had thrown all his eggs in the Atlanta 'too hard' basket.

The heats were held on the 26th of July and Hissou was in heat 1 with Tergat. Worku Bikila of Ethiopia won with a decent time of 27:50.57. Tergat was next in 27:50.66, with Hissou a comfortable fifth. His 27:53.32 was more than two seconds ahead of the rest. Gebrselassie won the second heat in a slower 28:14.20, leaving his opponents none the wiser as to his recent struggles.

The heats of the 1,500 metres were on the same day as the 10,000 metres final and Abdelkader Kada and Hicham El Guerrouj were happy to see that Venuste Niyongabo had abandoned the distance in favour of a crack at the 5,000 metres, an event which he hoped would be a weaker race. Venuste was earlier quoted as saying about Morceli that, "As long as Morceli is in the race, it is always second place."

As it turned out, avoiding Morceli and El Guerrouj was a blessing in disguise for Niyongabo. It also made things a little easier for Hicham who now only had one runner to really concern himself with.

El Guerrouj had to wait until the fourth heat to show his stuff. Before him, the fastest qualifier had been Laban Rotich running a 3:35.88. Morceli had clocked a very slow 3:41.95 but qualified safely. In his heat Hicham looked good, calmly crossing the line in 3:37.66, just ahead of William Tanui, the 800 metres Barcelona champion. It was a matter of getting through the rounds with the minimum of fuss. So far, so good.

Haile Gebrselassie went into the Atlanta 10,000 metres final on July 29 as the overwhelming favourite, despite the impressive credentials of Tergat and Hissou, his world cross country conquerors. It was difficult to think of a distance runner who had such an amazing resumé for his first appearance at a Games. Haile was a double world champion and world record holder, the latter at both the 10,000 metres and 5,000 metres. These facts aside, no one had ever known of a distance runner with a better kick than the Ethiopian, save for possibly a Moroccan from the '80's. In recent times there had been good distance runners with outstanding kicks, but those runners rarely held the world record. They were beatable because they were breakable. On the track it was unknown if Gebrselassie could be beaten. Sure, he did *only* take silver in the 5,000 metres at the '93 World Championships, but that was his first major final. Haile didn't then know his own extraordinary capabilities. Watching replays of that classic race (over and over again), you can see that Gebrselassie didn't know when to take the initiative, when to take it up to Kirui. He only showed his pure brilliance in the final 100 metres when it was too late. In any case, that finishing burst was scintillating. If Haile had possessed the confidence of '95 in that '93 final he would have won. He could have left his teammates with about 600 metres to go and made it a solo trip in pursuit of the eighteen year old Kenyan. This is not to take anything away from Ismael Kirui's run. It was one of athletics' great performances. But from '93-'99 it could be argued that Gebrselassie should not have lost to anyone over 5 kms, except for Daniel Komen who reached those truly elite levels for about eighteen months.

MOROCCAN SUCCESS; THE KADA WAY

He was even harder to defeat over 10,000 metres. This point was never better illustrated than in Atlanta when America saw Paul Tergat at his best, but the great Kenyan still couldn't shake off his nemesis. Even though Tergat didn't beat Gebrselassie, he earned respect in bucket loads from distance running fans and no doubt Haile himself, who knew that he would have to watch for Tergat in future track races. Unknowingly the effort Gebrselassie had to expend went some way towards helping Tergat's teammate Komen defeat Gebrselassie later in Zurich. But how do we know who truly defeated Haile Gebrselassie in Zurich. Was it Daniel Komen or the Atlanta track?

Back to the 10,000 metres Olympic final itself and the field was a similar one that headlined the Gothenburg final. Josephat Machuka rejoined Tergat in the Kenyan lineup, with Paul Koech replacing Joseph Kimani as the so called work horse for the other two. Khalid Skah backed up from his silver a year ago to accompany Hissou, so Morocco was expected to strongly challenge. The race would go in a similar fashion to last year's championship. Once the pace had gone on mid race there were only Africans remaining, with Gebrselassie being left as the sole Ethiopian.

Salah is considered to be the event's second favourite, although still a long way behind *the* favourite in the pecking order. Rob De Castella explains the difficulties in defeating Haile, "How do you beat the man? He's got the world record and he's also got a devastating kick. Almost invincible."

It's 27 degrees and 72 percent humidity, so far from perfect conditions. Bruce McAvaney makes the following comments throughout lap five, "There's Hissou, one of the big dangers. He's run twice this year for 5,000 metres inside thirteen minutes and run a 3:33 1,500, so he is one man who might match the Gebrselassie kick if it comes down to it." Sorry Bruce, it doesn't necessarily work that way!

McAvaney, "Interesting Rob, just behind these five, Hissou leads the next group and Gebrselassie sits right on him. They're sixth and seventh place as they come to screen now.

So Gebrselassie believes that Hissou's the man and Machuka sits behind them, so three of the favourites, and Tergat's only one back. These favourites all around one another." Nizigama is the athlete doing most of the early front running.

Hissou is rated a better chance than Tergat in Atlanta because of his outstanding track form. Post Gothenburg, the Kenyan had shown little on the track, having been blown away by Gebrselassie in Zurich, then defeated by many including Hissou in Brussels. In 1996 Paul had avoided the European circuit, preferring to compete in cross country and on the road.

In the 1995 World Championship Final the field had reached halfway in 13:46. In Atlanta it is 13:55.22 but these are tougher conditions. Shortly after the 5,000 metres split the pace begins to pick up with Paul Koech doing most of the work. Once the race had truly developed there are only six contenders remaining, the same number that were also left to survive a year ago. The men who hope to deny Gebrselassie were Koech, Machuka, Tergat, Hissou and Nizigama. Machuka and Tergat are working off Koech's Kenyan pace making. Hissou is flying solo as Khalid Skah can no longer compete at this level and is left to battle it out for seventh place. But Salah looks comfortable enough. Is he going comfortably enough to be a realistic winning chance?

What is Abdelkader's and Salah's plan of attack from here? Is it simply to stay in touch and rely on Hissou's new found finishing kick?

Aloys Nizigama is the odd man out, the surprise packet. Burundi isn't exactly known as a long distance running stronghold and it is strange to see an athlete still in contention at this stage of the 10,000 metres who doesn't wear a Kenyan, Ethiopian or Moroccan singlet. Track fans had not seen a runner from another nation remain in touch with the leaders past fifteen laps of a 10,000 metres championship final in the '90's. Nizigama wasn't a complete unknown having placed sixth in Tokyo and then fifth in Stuttgart. In 1994 he was high in the time charts with good performances of

MOROCCAN SUCCESS; THE KADA WAY

27:20.51, and 27:22.06. He'd also won a 10,000 metres race in London during 1995 in 27:20.38. Still, this event has gone up a level in the past couple of years and he is clearly everybody's first pick to get dropped from the remaining six. Salah isn't concerned by Aloys, having disposed of him with ease in the Paris Grand Prix race.

Koech runs the fourteenth lap in 62.87 and this starts to sort the men out from the boys. The pace is pretty consistent from then on. With Machuka helping Koech set the tempo, the seventeenth, eighteenth and nineteenth laps are run in 64.72, 64.93 and 64.79. It will be extremely difficult to kick down off around twenty seven minute pace.

Most of the runners are already doing it hard, as you would when you have the pace being pushed by the fourth placed finisher of the World Cross Country and the man who has run the fastest ever time at altitude. Water is offered to the competitors each time they traverse the back straight. Watching proceedings with eight laps to go, you can actually see Gebrselassie hurting. In retrospect we can understand the difficulty he had trying to perform with injured feet. You could continually see a pained grimace throughout the latter stages with perspiration pouring off him.

Nevertheless on the twentieth lap Rob De Castella observes, "Doesn't Gebrselassie look sensational? A nickname has been generated back home for him. They call him the rocket launcher because of his devastating acceleration and kick."

With 2,200 metres to go Machuka takes a sponge and hands it to Tergat. They are fourth and fifth with Nizigama now behind them. Hissou is third behind Koech and Haile.

Tergat sits towards the tail of the lead pack, just waiting for the right moment. His rivals are about to get the shock of their lives with five laps to go. Down the home straight, Tergat takes off at an incredible speed, storming past his rivals. McAvaney announces, "Now Tergat makes the move, and here he goes with five laps to go and Gebrselassie chases him."

Gebrselassie has to give it everything to get onto his back. He had never had to produce such an effort in Gothenburg, but here he was against a legend. A legend with a cunning plan and he was following it through to the letter.

McAvaney, "I think the key here is whether Hissou can respond too. The key to the race will be if Hissou can get onto the back of Gebrselassie. Tergat knows that it's a long way from home and he's going to have to try to take everything out of Gebrselassie legs and Hissou knows Deek that if he can't get onto the back and he's chasing hard. This is the big move of the race."

The term 'a decisive move' is often spoken about in distance running and under this definition could read 'Paul Tergat's move to the front twenty laps into the 1996 10,000 metres Olympic Final.' A runner's job is to either make the decisive move or respond to it once it is made. Salah Hissou realizes that this is the decisive move but perhaps his reactions aren't fast enough. That first 200 metres surge is timed at approximately twenty nine seconds and Tergat runs the full twenty first lap in 60.55, with the Ethiopian hanging on and the Moroccan ten metres off the back, trying desperately to latch on. The other three contenders are well beaten with Koech having done so much of the work, while Machuka and Nizigama aren't quite in the same calibre.

The kick down was also helped by the twentieth lap being run in a slightly slower 66.13. The difference in intensity between a thirty three second half lap and twenty nine second half lap, 8,000 metres into a 10,000 metres race is huge. Once Tergat went, Gebrselassie was able to respond immediately but for Hissou this challenge was too great. Salah passed Koech fifty metres into the lap by which time he'd lost close to fifteen metres to the leaders! But he worked hard on the back straight and kept them in sight. At 1,700 metres to go he was almost back on, tantalizingly close, perhaps eight metres down on the Ethiopian who was clipping the Kenyan's heels. Already the others are close to thirty metres behind the Moroccan.

MOROCCAN SUCCESS; THE KADA WAY

With four laps to go Salah still looks relatively relaxed. His style is perfectly fluent yet he's extracting everything out of himself. But a 13:12 second half in oppressive conditions on a hard track. How do you keep up with that?

McAvaney, commenting with 1,500 metres to go, "Still Hissou can't quite reel them in, but maybe he knows that if he can just hang on, that Tergat will slow down after that thumping lap."

Abdelkader's man gives it his all to get back into the contest but Tergat is not going to slow down much, even after a 60.55 second lap. If he wants to beat Gebrselassie then he has to keep pushing himself and the Ethiopian to their limits. With 1,400 metres to go Salah remains about ten metres behind. However he soon heads into the red zone and starts to fall away, until with 1,200 metres remaining he is a broken and beaten man, twenty metres back and running for bronze after a 62.09 lap from Tergat. One golden dream of Kada's is over. McAvaney, "I think Hissou's gone Deek. It looks like it's just Tergat and Gebrselassie for the major spoils. They've put eighty metres on the rest of them."

Tergat's pressure is relentless, but even on the way to such a quick second 5 kms split he is unable to break Haile. The ninth km is timed at 2:33.90! No wonder Salah is now thirty metres adrift. The third last lap is again fast at 62.37, but Gebrselassie is never more than a metre behind. The Ethiopian grimaces even more so, clearly hurting. It's just that Tergat never quite has the great enough kick. With 450 metres left Gebrselassie surges, making it a 62.87 penultimate lap. This is not with the venom of his move in Gothenburg, but is still with enough speed to prise open a small gap. Deek, "A sly look at Tergat saying is that all you've got? Well let me show you something really good."

With 300 metres remaining Tergat is within ten metres of him but on the back straight Haile really digs in and establishes a winning break of about twenty metres. Tergat chases him home hard over the final 200 metres but he is never going to get him. With a final lap of 57.49 the little master has done it again. The eighteen finishers were:

Haile Gebrselassie	27:07.34
Paul Tergat	27:08.17
Salah Hissou	27:24.67
Aloys Nizigama	27:33.79
Josephat Machuka	27:35.08
Paul Koech	27:35.19
Khalid Skah	27:46.98
Mathias Ntawulikura	27:50.73
Stephane Franke	27:59.08
Jon Brown	27:59.72
Armando Quintanilla	28:09.46
Marko Hhawu	28:20.58
Abel Anton	28:29.37
Carlos de la Torre	28:32.11
Alejandro Gomez	28:39.11
Zoltan Kaldy	28:45.48
Worku Bikila	28:59.15
Stefano Baldini	29:07.77

The winning time was staggering, with the second half being run in under world record pace! Tergat had run the perfect race yet it wasn't enough for gold. The world cross country champion ran the final 2,000 metres in around 5:05. What a kick down! Unfortunately for Tergat it was possible that he was trying to break the unbreakable. Still unbreakable, despite the problems he'd encountered with the track surface.

Hissou held on for third and looked pleased when crossing the line with the bronze medal. It was a good run. A 13:29 back half in those conditions was excellent. Nizigama did tremendously well to beat the Kenyans of Machuka and Koech. Skah kicked away from Mathias Ntawulikura from Rwanda for seventh place. The first eight finishers were all from Africa.

As things turned out it is possible to say that Hissou's great form peaked too early before the Olympics. His run in Atlanta wasn't quite up to that 12:50 Rome standard, even if that level of running would still have left him unlikely to challenge the

MOROCCAN SUCCESS; THE KADA WAY

top two stars here. The final five laps of this race were of the highest quality.

In hindsight, the decision to have Salah compete in this event seemed like a bad choice. But this is the hindsight that followed from Atlanta. If you were to give an opinion in a month's time comparing it to Brussels, then maybe Hissou simply under performed slightly in Atlanta.

From his viewpoint, Salah wasn't too happy with the track either. It wasn't only Haile who had problems coping with the hard surface. It was unfortunate that such important races were conducted under these conditions. Despite the surface it is still hard to imagine Hissou keeping pace with his two rivals over those final 2,000 metres.

Perhaps Salah Hissou may have been a little dejected with the race but I'm sure that receiving an Olympic bronze medal would have somewhat tempered his disappointment. It was hardly a disgrace to be dropped by Tergat and Gebrselassie. The key for him was that he never gave up, even after being dropped. He held on for the bronze when others may have hit the wall completely. In the great scheme of things, it was another small step up from fourth at last year's World Championships.

Maybe Salah wouldn't see it in the same light, considering he had been right in the mix only 200 metres from home in Gothenburg. This time he had no time to even think about a sprint finish. It was clear that Tergat had made big improvements from last year and he was going to be possibly as hard to beat on the track as Gebrselassie in the future. Perhaps Hissou and the Moroccan Federation should focus entirely on Salah running the 5,000 metres in future major championships.

However after Atlanta, the 5,000 metres was no longer an open event either.

To have won the 10,000 metres would have meant all time legendary distance running status. To win the 5,000 metres would mean that you are simply an Olympic champion. But an Olympic gold medal is still an Olympic gold medal, no matter the circumstances. Its meaning remains immense. It can be strongly argued that Salah Hissou was the third best long distance runner at the Atlanta Games. It's just that he was forced to race against the best two.

Kada still had his best chance to do battle for gold. On August the 1st, El Guerrouj raced in the semi finals of the 1,500 metres. The first semi had been lightning fast, with Morceli crossing first in 3:32.88. Cacho, Bile, Tanui and Rotich all were in the 3:33's. The second semi was more sedate and Hicham had no problems, winning in 3:35.29. As usual he raced impressively and all awaited his match up with Morceli in two days time. Noureddine was the favourite but Hicham had a chance. A very real chance.

It was interesting to note that both had won their semis by the same margin of twenty four hundredths of a second. It was very hard to split this pair.

Abdelkader Kada awoke on the morning of August 3, 1996, knowing that by the end of the day he could be the coach of an Olympic champion. Things could change forever, for him and his student. The last few months had gone beautifully. How could this one day possibly go so wrong?

Hicham seemed relatively calm, even excited at the final ahead. It wasn't going to be easy, as he would have to beat the best. There were none better than the world record holder and world champion.

The Algerian's career form line had peaked and was perhaps even dipping. The Moroccan's was still going skyward. Two careers going in opposite directions. The question was when would the lines cross over?

As they toed the line Rob De Castella spoke of the young runners' chances as a crowd of approximately 83,000 eagerly awaited this confrontation, "He's been running so well Bruce and if anyone is going to upset Morceli, then I think it's going

MOROCCAN SUCCESS; THE KADA WAY

to be that young Moroccan." As they readied themselves Bruce McAvaney set the scene, "Will he win, Morceli? Will it be fast? Let's hope it is."

The race was a fairly slow one. Not quite the crawl that was Barcelona, but Atlanta wasn't exactly like Los Angeles either. Still, it looked set up to give the two combatants each and every chance to prove themselves. To prove who was now the best.

Morceli immediately pushes to a good position, unlike Barcelona when he let himself get boxed in. Initially El Guerrouj is mid pack on the outside. Two Kenyans lead after 300 metres. It is Rotich just ahead of Kipkorir with Morceli third and the final Kenyan Tanui on his outside.

The first split is 1:01.03 with Noureddine back behind the Kenyans in fourth place on the outside of Moroccan Driss Maazouzi. Hicham follows on the outside of Fermin Cacho. Deek on Morceli, "They'll be doing everything that they can to upset his rhythm and his style because they know that he really is the man to beat. He's in great form coming in. Had a whole series of tremendous races. Has already raced here in this stadium and set the fastest time in America over a mile so he knows what it's like. He's prepared himself for the big humidity. He actually went down to Florida. Normally trains at altitude at Alburcuque, but he came down to Florida to spend time training in the heat and humidity and he's really focused on this event."

Nothing eventuates until Abdi Bile makes a strong move with 800 metres to go. Here, Morceli almost gets into trouble, having to put a hand on the Somalian as he crosses over. The next split is 2:01.63, just solid pace, not fast. The Algerian remains in the box seat.

El Guerrouj has been biding his time and is now poised to contend. With 600 metres to go the tempo is picking up and Morceli moves to the front, passing Kipkorir. Cacho tries to go with him. In the process of doing so he holds up Hicham slightly, who is also attempting to make his bid for glory.

Cacho moves to the outside of Morceli. The twelve man field remains quite bunched with 500 metres left. We await the explosion of power about to be unleashed.

As the runners enter the final straight approaching the bell, Morceli does what he has always done. He strides to the lead, readying himself for his famous venomous kick. At this precise moment El Guerrouj is taking off, ducking out from Cacho and into lane two. With 450 metres to go Noureddine can feel the shadow looming up on him. It is Hicham the challenger, ready to do just that. We are set for a classic final lap but we don't get it. The race is decided before the bell. The Algerian has the inside lane but the Moroccan moves in on him, half behind and half alongside. Morceli fights back to ensure he retains the lead at the bell.

The two milers however, are too close for comfort.

Hicham's left knee makes slight contact with Noureddine's right heel, impeding and affecting the leader's rhythm. On the following stride Morceli's right leg hits his left calf and then rebounds out from his normal stride pattern into the path of Hicham, who has nowhere to go. It all happens so suddenly without any time to react. Down he goes and with him, his Olympic dream. The last lap is almost an anti climax. The finishing results were:

Noureddine Morceli	3:35.78
Fermin Cacho	3:36.40
Stephen Kipkorir	3:36.72
Laban Rotich	3:37.39
William Tanui	3:37.42
Abdi Bile	3:38.03
Marko Koers	3:38.18
Ali Hakimi	3:38.19
Mohammed Suleiman	3:38.26
Driss Maazouzi	3:39.65
John Mayock	3:40.18
Hicham El Guerrouj	3:40.75

Cacho puts his left arm around Morceli's shoulders in a show

MOROCCAN SUCCESS; THE KADA WAY

of congratulations. At first Morceli doesn't look particularly thrilled because of the manner in which he has won. Maazouzi also embraces him. Now Noureddine acknowledges his victory. Hicham El Guerrouj is in tears as he walks across the track and puts his head on the barriers of the stands in front of crowd. The new Olympic champion later reflected, "This makes me forget what happened in Barcelona. This is the greatest athletic achievement of my career." He was also prepared for anything that might eventuate in the final. "I had ten different tactical plans in my head before the race. When I saw the pace was slow, I knew I could kick in the last lap."

Subsequent to the fall, the Algerian already had a winning gap as he heard the bell. He found himself five metres clear of Cacho with Bile third. The incident certainly didn't only affect Hicham. Bile who was on the inside had briefly jumped onto the grass to avoid falling over the grounded Moroccan. Cacho's evasive action was to leap over him. The split at 1,100 metres was 2:42.28. This became 2:55.12 at 1,200 metres, so don't worry, Morceli was seriously moving as he increased his lead further, with that 100 metres being run in 12.84 seconds, or sub fifty two second lap pace. This came at the end of a 53.49 split between 800 and 1,200 metres which is outstanding. The first half of the last lap was timed at 25.90 seconds, still sub fifty two pace. Yet with 200 metres left, Cacho was still within range but could never get close enough to seriously threaten. Morceli eased up over the last twenty metres and recorded a last lap of 53.51. Cacho's split was 53.70. Even after slowing down, the final 800 metres were clocked in a fast 1:48.80. However nobody will ever know for certain if Morceli would have won the gold had El Guerrouj not fallen.

As a result unfortunately, the win was a slightly dubious one. Despite this black mark, nobody denied that he deserved to become the Olympic champion. Since the start of the decade he had been clearly the best miler in the world since taking over from Said Aouita. It was only in recent weeks that his dominance was questioned. Morceli said, "I wanted to run a tactical race, to save energy and finish with a very strong last lap. If I was challenged that final 200 would have been 25 instead of 27. I was ready to run 1:46 off that pace."

What wasn't in doubt was his reduced superiority. The way he won in Atlanta bared no similarities to his victory in Gothenburg. The winning gap that separated him from Cacho was basically the advantage he'd gained from El Guerrouj's fall.

The devastated Moroccan was unable to speak to the press after his disaster. Morceli felt for the young man, saying, "I feel sorry for him, Hicham is a great athlete with a great future." Perhaps the Algerian fully understood as to just how great a future he was likely to have as he said, "I am 26 years old and it is time I must start thinking about moving to the 5,000."

McAvaney added, "Look, it's only the naked eye telling me this. He just didn't look to me to be as devastating as he did last year Morceli." Deek continued, "Certainly didn't have that explosive acceleration and that devastating speed that we've come to expect from this man, but he's been running so well and keeping in mind that Cacho is so fast to, so that may well have been a little deceptive. Maybe to actually hold and pull away by a metre or two on Cacho over that last 200 is an indication of just how fast he was running." McAvaney, "The thing that I liked about El Guerrouj was that he was prepared to go past Cacho and attack Morceli at the bell. He was running to win."

When it came to the Olympic Games, all the victories of June and July had counted for little. Kada had expected more than just a bronze medal. Olympic redemption was definitely going to be hard to come by, but the beauty of international sport is that there is always a further competition to focus on. There were other races to come. The truth was that the European athletics Grand Prix season was really only just warming up.

MOROCCAN SUCCESS; THE KADA WAY

Brilliance In Brussels By The New Desert Prince

Athletics didn't stop for a break after the Olympic Games and the action became frantic during the season's final weeks, with the distance events in particular being at an extremely high standard. Kenya's top Olympians went to Monaco after the games to race over 3,000 metres on the 10th of August. They would all perform magnificently with Tom Nyariki, Paul Bitok and Paul Tergat all running career best times and clocking sub 7:30. Their respective results were 7:27.75, 7:28.41 and 7:28.70. Up ahead of them though, was another Kenyan. Seething over missing Atlanta, this man burnt up the track with a 7:25.16. This was Daniel Komen, a runner too good for all these Atlanta participants. The night was almost perfect for him. He beat two of the men who kept him out of the Olympic Games but missed Morceli's world record by a mere five hundredths of a second. By the 2,000 metres mark Komen was already in full flight, passing the split leading in 4:56.1, almost ten metres up on Tergat, 4:57.4. It was such a high standard race that Bitok was only seventh, 4:58.8, and Nyariki eighth, 4:58.9, at this juncture.

This was only the beginning of what was to become Komen's near complete domination of the distance running world.

Daniel Komen was born on May 17, 1976. He quickly established himself as a runner to watch with his performances at the 1994 World Junior Championships in Lisbon where he replicated Haile Gebrselassie's effort in winning both the 5,000 and 10,000 metres. His victories were even more impressive as they were achieved by big margins. That year Komen produced another victory that even bettered those feats. At the African Junior Championships in Algiers he won the 5,000 metres with a good time of 13:31.10. The gap back to future top senior runners, Habte Jifar and Mohamed Amine was over twenty seconds. Komen did have a go in a senior championship that year, racing in the 5,000 metres at the Commonwealth Games, but showing his inexperience (and youthful exuberance), he went out like a madman and clocked 57.42 for the first lap. He would fade to an eventual ninth place finish.

Komen's first full senior season of 1995 was a patchy one, but it did include the second fastest 5,000 metres ever in Rome on June 8, when he was just defeated by his local hero, Moses Kiptanui. In his first big European track race, Komen went from a 13:20.51 personal best to a 12:56.15. This improvement wasn't that great a surprise when you considered his junior credentials. Komen had also recently run a world leading 13:29.33 for a high altitude race at Nairobi. However after Rome his form fell away. This guy clearly had extraordinary abilities, even for a Kenyan. Now could he put it all together with consistent performances?

Unfortunately Komen could only place fourth in the 5,000 metres at the Kenyan Olympic trials, meaning that he was unlikely to be selected for Atlanta. Nevertheless from that time on, he went from strength to strength. Firstly he finished second to Bitok in a 5,000 metres in Eugene. He improved greatly on that time with a 13:01.38 for fifth place in the hotly contested Rome race. In the remaining time before the Games, Komen won four consecutive races, starting with a relatively slow (for him) 7:39.43 for 3,000 metres in Moscow. On July 3 he proved that he was the real deal when he ran superbly in Lausanne to take the 3,000 metres in 7:31.33. Five days later Daniel ran the third fastest 5,000 metres ever with his easy 12:51.60 victory in Stockholm. Placing second behind the Kenyan was American Bob Kennedy. His time of 12:58.75 made him the first white man ever to run sub thirteen minutes. It was difficult enough to create this significant piece of history, but defeating Komen right now was even more difficult, a nigh on impossibility. On the 14th of July he competed in Lappeenranta over the rarely contested two miles. It was now that Daniel really started to make the sports headlines as he broke the world record with a time of 8:03.54. It seemed that he would be the man to beat for the Olympic 5,000 metres gold medal.

However, Komen never made it past the Kenyan selection process.

MOROCCAN SUCCESS; THE KADA WAY

The Olympic 5,000 metres had the potential to be a far more potent race. Kenya had the double world champion Ismael Kirui, an in form Paul Bitok, plus new sub thirteen minute man Philip Mosima in its stable. This was all on top of the sport's latest superstar, Daniel Komen.

The difficulties lay with the fact that none of these four best credentialled athletes had placed in the first three positions in the Kenyan trials. Those runners were Shem Kororia, David Chelule and Thomas Nyariki. It would take a cruel man to not pick Kororia, for he was the bronze medallist from the Gothenburg World Championships and had won the trial's race. But his recent form wasn't great, having been defeated comprehensively by Bitok and Hissou in the fast 3,000 metres in Oslo.

Nyariki had decent form in Europe to go on. He'd finished ahead of Komen in Rome but been thrashed by him in Stockholm, despite still running a very respectable 13:01.79. Komen then followed up with the record at two miles. Nobody with common sense would have argued that Thomas was in better shape for Atlanta than Daniel. But crucially he had placed third to Komen's fourth at the trials. The Kenyan selectors knew that Kororia and Nyariki were in reasonable form and so felt that they could not drop them for the Olympic Games.

David Chelule on the other hand, had not produced anything of note in Europe. Going against usual Kenyan traditions, he was not selected. This was unfortunate but at the same time, a sensible decision.

However a problem still existed. Four or more deserving runners do not go into one spot! The selectors had got the first step partly right. For a change, it appeared that common sense may rule. With the runner up from the trial's race cancelled out, Daniel Komen seemed to be the next man in line having placed fourth. Added to this was the minor fact that he was the most in form Kenyan distance runner!

Despite being the double world champion, Ismael Kirui would

have to sit out the Games. Sounds ridiculous doesn't it? It wasn't as if he'd suddenly put on twenty kgs or was carrying an injury. This season Kirui had run a respectable time of 13:06.86 in Paris. But respectable doesn't cut it when you are a Kenyan runner.

Mosima had his fourth fastest 5,000 metres performance of all time in Rome to go from, but since then Komen had bettered that time, and Philip hadn't produced anything else of real substance. He'd been injured in a car accident and in Stockholm only finished sixth in 13:10.27, so he was out of the reckoning also. The two candidates that remained were Bitok and Komen.

Paul had the pedigree. He was the Olympic silver medallist from Barcelona. He also had good form, defeating Komen earlier in Eugene and recently having defeated the red hot Hissou in Oslo. He very much deserved a spot. But should you select a runner whose personal record is 13:07.30, at the expense of a runner who has just recorded a 12:51.60?

Whatever your opinion, it was Bitok who was given the final 5,000 metres birth. As the results in Atlanta showed, selecting him was not a mistake. But the selection process as a whole is the problem. Why select from the results of a one off trial's race in Kenya? It would be fairer to look at the best performances being run in Europe, which is track and field's homeland. Komen probably would have defeated Bitok at the Olympic Games. He almost certainly would have placed higher than Thomas Nyariki and Shem Kororia.

It could be argued that selection would be fairer if it were based on overall performances during the six months prior to the major championships. If that is too complicated then picking the three best times would be more sufficient. But since that doesn't give the sit and kickers much chance, how about the two fastest over the particular distance plus the winner of the Kenyan trial? If need be, qualifying times could only be recorded from that year's European season, so then Kenya is guaranteed to get in form runners selected, from races that have taken place in the two months prior to the

MOROCCAN SUCCESS; THE KADA WAY

championships.

The Kenyan trials are always held in Kenya so are usually conducted in oppressive conditions, conditions which the team is not going to face in European Grand Prix meets and unlikely to face in the major championships. These finals are often held in warm climates but not at high altitude. The major championships are often held in Europe so it would make sense to generally select the athletes that are doing the business in athletics' homeland. The trials are sometimes run during a time when big Grand Prix meetings are taking place so many of the top Kenyans don't even go back for the trials. Cases of superstar Kenyans missing out on Olympic Games are numerous. It has sometimes made the world champion more creditable than the Olympic champion. I do not see why Kenya cannot hold a trial race in Europe from which to select the best performer.

The decision makers of Kenyan athletics teams have/are taking the easy way out in holding a single race that usually selects the first three finishers for its team. David Chelule's omission was an exception. It's the easiest way because it's simplistic but this doesn't mean that it is the fairest way. A common sense approach based on opinion would be controversial, but I guarantee that it would have resulted in a stronger Kenyan team for the 5,000 metres in Atlanta.

Granted, Kenya still fielded one of the strongest teams for the event, but it wasn't by far *the* strongest, which it should have been. I would have selected Paul Bitok, Daniel Komen and Ismael Kirui for the Kenyan team. You have an athlete with winning form and experience from the past Olympics. You have an athlete with winning form who is running the best times and finally, you have an athlete who, as the double world champion, has proved himself in the past to be a good performer under the greatest of pressure.

Each of the athletes selected had an obvious weakness, or at least no obvious strength, which makes the non selection of Daniel Komen all the more frustrating. Paul Bitok could be deadly if the race was run to his liking, but if the pace was on he could be dropped. This was demonstrated at the '93 World Championships where he was destroyed big time in Stuttgart when Kirui tore the field apart and he finished only eighth. There was no opportunity in that race for him to use his fast finishing kick. Shem Kororia was neither a speed nor strength runner, but was pretty adept in both areas. He had therefore built up a resumé of solid, consistent results without many big wins. He was highly unlikely to win a major championship. Thomas Nyariki was in the process of making his mark on the world stage, but he hadn't achieved what Komen had time wise, nor did he possess a finishing kick when compared to his world class rivals. It was debatable whether Komen had a terrific kick himself, but it didn't really matter, since he had won his last four races so easily!

Thomas was a quality strength runner, but as the '97 World Championships proved, he was far from a Daniel Komen. Let's face it, not many are close to a Daniel Komen. In Atlanta, Nyariki had the ability and the opportunity to make an impact but lacked the confidence to do so. He briefly kicked it down in the middle stages. Surprisingly the field allowed him to get about a twenty metres lead. But Thomas chose not to continue his surge and settled back into the pack. He was never a factor thereafter and was not competitive in the last lap sprint that left him in fifth place. What would have happened if Komen had been in Nyariki's position? If you take the races just prior to Atlanta and anything that went on afterwards as a guide, then you would have certainly got plenty of fireworks. It's a great shame because Komen could have done something really special at the Games.

It is my belief that the Kenyan selectors got this very wrong. Perhaps so too, did the Moroccan selectors.

There were other athletes besides Komen who didn't race the Atlanta 5,000 metres who could have won, such as Salah Hissou. He had outstanding form at the distance and wouldn't have been intimidated by anyone on that start line. At the end of 1996 Komen and Hissou claimed the top two ranking positions for the event despite not competing in the biggest race.

MOROCCAN SUCCESS; THE KADA WAY

The standard of the Olympic 5,000 metres final was quite good, but the medallists were simply good long distance runners, not really great ones. The winner was Venuste Niyongabo who had cashed in on some weaker opposition. It was a super smart career decision to step up in distance, despite his much superior pedigree at 1,500 metres. He never accomplished anything else at 5,000 metres after Atlanta, but he made the most of a glorious opportunity. Always keep in mind that these Games only come around every four years.

Second was Paul Bitok, the Kenyan making it two Olympic silver medals at the distance. This was a great achievement as a) Kenyans often don't last at the top for four years, b) it is hard to make one Kenyan Olympic team let alone two and c) he came up with the goods twice in the pressure cooker of Olympic competition. Still, in my opinion, that doesn't put him within a bull's roar of Daniel Komen. Third was Khalid Boulami. The Moroccan was a very consistent performer who would medal in three straight major championships but he was never a superstar. Salah Hissou was a better 5,000 metres runner than all of these three. He had thrashed Boulami in Paris and Niyongabo and Bitok were not pure 5,000 metres runners. They had not clocked under thirteen minutes. That's not to say that Hissou would have won the 5,000 metres final in Atlanta. It's just to say that he very well *could* have. The winning time was a decent 13:07.97, with a last 800 metres of 1:55.01. This came on top of a harsh schedule that forced the runners to progress past two preliminary rounds. Salah certainly could not have matched Niyongabo and his kick in the final 500 metres. The question is could he have done what Nyariki had threatened to do, and that was make the race faster in the middle stages, thus breaking the middle distance specialist? I believe this to be a missed opportunity even if some Moroccans in higher places felt that avoiding the 10,000 metres would have been taking an easier way out. I guess they wanted David to take on Goliath to see if he could measure up. For the record, Salah felt that nobody in the Atlanta 5,000 metres field could have gone with him over the last 2,000 metres.

Consequently, the Monaco 3,000 metres victory by Daniel

Komen was a nice suggestion to the Kenyan decision makers that they may have got it wrong in ignoring him. Nonetheless, he still wanted to make a few more subtle suggestions.

On August 14, Haile Gebrselassie went to Zurich expecting to continue his long unbeaten run at the long distance track events. Coming off Olympic gold, Haile was stepping down to the 5,000 metres distance where he was virtually as dominant.

In fact maybe he was more so. Tergat had nearly knocked him off in Atlanta but over the shorter distance Gebrselassie held the world record with a stunning 12:44.39, more than six seconds faster than the next best, Salah Hissou. Of course the Ethiopian had proven on more than one occasion that he clearly had the Moroccan's measure.

So Zurich would surely see another sub thirteen minute, cruise to victory for the undisputed number one distance runner in the world. Or would it?

Gebrselassie's shadow Paul Tergat was again on the scene, though he seemed to be less likely to defeat Haile over the shorter distance. But that non Olympian Daniel Komen was also in Zurich, ready to put some dispute on that 'undisputed number 1 distance runner in the world' tag.

The distance world was stunned when the Kenyan ran the Ethiopian ragged, surging throughout and taking the sting out of Gebrselassie's famous finishing kick. In the last lap it was Komen who was flying away to a famous victory. It was the second time in four days that he had missed a world record by less than a second. His 12:45.09 made everyone take notice, including the 'emperor' who limped home in 12:52.70. To put this in some perspective, realize that for Haile, this was one of his worst runs. Yet at the time only two runners had ever gone faster in history. That is the greatness of Haile Gebrselassie.

Tergat continued his excellent form with a 12:54.72, not too far behind his nemesis. Morocco had been in the mix too, with

MOROCCAN SUCCESS; THE KADA WAY

Khalid Boulami backing up well from his Olympic bronze with a 12:55.76. The three men in front of him were not even in his Atlanta final! Zurich was the more realistic guide as to the world's best 5,000 metres runners. In the meantime, another of the world's best 5,000 metres runners who had not been in that Atlanta final was cooling his heels and readying himself for his next battle. The 10,000 metres race in Brussels was next on Salah Hissou's agenda.

Skipping a meeting as highly regarded as Zurich was a career risk for Salah. An elite athlete was unlikely to stay elite for very long. Opportunities to run fast 5,000 metres races weren't always going to be available. He had mostly made his own fast times in Rome and Paris. Here he had Komen and Gebrselassie to push things along. It was a chance to run under 12:50 and defeat a tired Ethiopian, though not necessarily defeat a superstar Kenyan. Both Tergat and Boulami were dragged through to career best times.

Then again, perhaps Hissou was going to make the most of the opportunities that presented themselves in Brussels.

Salah's Moroccan mate wasn't interested in taking any breaks. He was restless, which was totally understandable after the disaster that was the Atlanta final. He arrived in Zurich angry and fiercely competitive. The only problem was that Morceli wasn't in attendance.

Everybody else was racing in Zurich. The Atlanta medallists Cacho and Kipkorir, plus the 5,000 metres champion Niyongabo. Venuste was happy to immediately step back down to his familiar event. He had renewed confidence that this would be third time lucky in his battles with Hicham in 1996.

But El Guerrouj was having none of that. Despite the best efforts of the man from Burundi, the Moroccan remained undefeated this season. That's in races where he stayed upright for the full three and three quarter laps.

The victory was comfortable enough as the results show:

Hicham El Guerrouj	3:30.22
Venuste Niyongabo	3:30.90
William Tanui	3:31.20
Laban Rotich	3:33.01
Elijah Kipruto Maru	3:33.53
Fermin Cacho	3:34.43
Ali Hakimi	3:34.95

The feeling that overcame the victor as he crossed the line was that it was going to take a lot more to extinguish the Atlanta demons. Hicham El Guerrouj was going to remain unsatisfied for a very long time but winning at Zurich was a great start to make towards his path of redemption.

He wanted to keep racing and keep winning. So two days later he did it all again in Koln, Germany. The race showed that the long season might be starting to take its toll. Hicham kept the winning streak going, but he didn't have his usual dash and in the end, was nearly defeated by William Tanui. The time gap was small. 3:33.45 to 3:33.62.

There was a much more interesting Kenyan in this field. Finishing third in a decent time of 3:34.17 was Daniel Komen, the man who only two days earlier had run the second fastest 5,000 metres ever. This athlete was on fire, with every performance produced being of the highest quality. Like Hicham he was seeking redemption for Atlanta emptiness. Brussels was the next big meeting on every athlete's calendar. It was only a week away. Any wait would prove to be well worth it.

The men's distance races promised to be extraordinary, even with Haile Gebrselassie finished for the season. There was Daniel Komen versus the clock in the 3,000 metres. Hicham El Guerrouj versus William Tanui in the 1,500 metres. The final event on the schedule was the 10,000 metres, always the Brussels highlight. This was being billed as Paul Tergat versus Salah Hissou. It was the biggest single night in Abdelkader Kada's coaching career so far.

MOROCCAN SUCCESS; THE KADA WAY

The Belgium crowd always produced an exciting atmosphere for the runners to feed off. Being the last big Grand Prix meeting of the season meant that it was a last chance to set records, so fast times were usually a result. Neither El Guerrouj nor Hissou had won here before. This time they had more self belief. This time they were focusing on more than just a victory.

Daniel Komen wasn't the only top runner competing in the 3,000 metres but he sure made it look like he was. Again he came so close to achieving a world record but Morceli's mark survived again. The clock stopped at 7:25.87. For the third straight race he had missed a world mark by less than one second. It was yet another breathtaking display of rhythmic running. He was proving to be unstoppable over seven and a half or twelve and a half laps. That he came so close to the record was made all the more incredible by the slow (for Komen standards) early speed. The first km was passed in 2:32.25, with Komen pouring on the power by the 2,000 metres split which he led in 5:00.53. Daniel had run the final 1,000 metres in 2:25.66! With better pacing Noureddine's record would have surely been his. Behind him were some good performances by Khalid Boulami, Bob Kennedy and El Hassan Lahssini. The three ran 7:31.65, 7:31.69 and 7:32.44 respectively although I don't think anyone noticed. One athlete who most certainly was noticed was the sixth place finisher who recorded a 7:36.81. It was a great surprise to see Noureddine Morceli struggle so valiantly, following his Atlanta gold. Previously he had been unbeatable at this distance so this run did not augur well for his future in trying to hold onto his crown as the world's best over 1,500 metres. Komen summed up the race perfectly with his post race comment, "Tonight the first kilometre was far too slow to beat the record. And Morceli wasn't really giving any help."

The 1,500 metres event in Brussels turned into a total non contest, though it was momentous nevertheless. El Guerrouj smashed the field by a margin rarely seen in such a short event. On the final lap it was clear that he was on for something special. It was special indeed. When Hicham stopped the clock at 3:29.05 it took a while to sink in. But it was true. El Guerrouj had run faster than Said Aouita. The twenty one year old was the Moroccan record holder!

In the process he had become the second fastest in history, replicating Hissou's achievement from Rome. Abdelkader Kada was so proud of his miler. He had known for a while that this boy was going to be a superstar. Now it was reality. El Guerrouj finished a massive 3.95 seconds ahead of Isaac Viciosa of Spain, with Tanui third. It was a good quality field but like Daniel Komen he made them look decidedly second rate.

The learned crowd applauded ecstatically at Hicham's performance. They didn't need Noureddine Morceli anyway. This young man was the future of the event. The general consensus now was that he was also the best currently. It was up to the Algerian to come out of hiding and put the Moroccan back in his place.

El Guerrouj and Komen were the hottest runners on the Grand Prix circuit proving that Olympic medals are not required to build a reputation. These two runners were going to be the big stories of the night. Nothing could top these performances. Or could it?

The 10,000 metres took place on a fantastic night in Belgium on August the 23rd, 1996. Once again Paul Tergat was on the start line having recently run that gem in Atlanta, as well as those personal bests over 3,000 metres and 5,000 metres. Right now he wasn't far from that coveted 'best long distance runner in the world' tag, with only Gebrselassie ahead of him. Well it was *only* Gebrselassie ahead of him. Daniel Komen's repeated excellence was impossible to ignore and right now he was the best long distance runner in the world. He was the talk of the distance running world but the 10,000 metres race would also demand the attention of athletics fans, and surprisingly a new name would be added to the above list.

Joining Tergat in Brussels was his fellow Kenyan Paul Koech, the man who finished sixth in that Atlanta final. A good cross country competitor with great strength, Koech was coming

MOROCCAN SUCCESS; THE KADA WAY

into his own and would surely be of great help to Tergat in his latest confrontation with Hissou.

But recent history said that he shouldn't need any.

Their two careers had travelled along almost identical paths with the Kenyan usually standing in the Moroccan's way. While Tergat was frustrated at not being able to beat Gebrselassie on the track, Hissou was frustrated at not being able to beat Tergat in the major championships on both the track and cross country. At the '95 World Cross Country, Hissou was third but Tergat was first. At the '95 World Championship 10,000 metres, Hissou was fourth but Tergat was third. At the '96 World Cross Country, Hissou was second but Tergat was first. At the '96 Olympic 10,000 metres, Hissou was third but Tergat was second. I gather you can see a trend here.

So why would this race be any different? Tergat was seemingly in career best form and Hissou's best seemed not quite good enough.

Others were thinking in the same way. Brussels meeting director Wilfried Meert had promised an attack on Haile Gebrselassie's world record from Tergat and Koech. The bronze medallist from Atlanta was seen to be an extra, a support act.

But Salah was quietly confident about the race and his chances of recording a fast time. He had defeated Tergat twice before at Brussels. In fact, Hissou's best 10,000 metres performances had come at the Van Damn Memorial Stadium. He even had designs on Gebrselassie's world record, his belief founded from his fast 5,000 metres in Rome. He was also well prepared and race rested. It was twenty five days since his Olympic final. Plenty of that time had been spent at his favourite high altitude city in Morocco.

Salah needed a top result to remind the athletics world of his class. After his great performance at the World Cross Country and world leading time in the 5,000 metres, Salah seemed close to the cream of the distance running crop. But with the result in Atlanta and arrival of Daniel Komen, Hissou looked to have slipped a notch.

Belgium would witness the breakthrough of all breakthroughs for the mighty Moroccan who took on a nemesis head to head. Standing toe to toe, Salah and Paul battled it out on neutral ground and surprisingly on this night it was Hissou who stood head and shoulders above Tergat. This was a career defining moment for Salah as he blew Tergat and Koech away, while heading into new territory. Sub twenty seven minutes.

Conditions were perfect for the race. It was twenty degrees, with very little wind. Two hours earlier it had rained, so the air was filled with rich oxygen as the 10,000 metres runners took their marks. Despite all that had preceded, Kada may have sensed that his night was far from complete.

Hissou has a Moroccan pacemaker Larbi Zeroual, who he wants to take him through 5,000 metres in 13:20 but they go through in 13:25.45 along with Tergat and Koech. It doesn't seem like the world record is on. This is still however, a super fast pace and providing Hissou doesn't blow up, he will still set a new national record. Salah is kept up to speed on the splits throughout the race by his coach. Even if a world record isn't possible there is still the race to be won. With Koech and Tergat with him this is going to be difficult enough. But with Zeroual out of the way the pace quickens slightly and after seven kms, Hissou is only three seconds off the Gebrselassie world record pace. This split is 18:46.99 with the last 1,000 metres being covered in 2:42.30.

It's now that Salah really reaches a new standard in Moroccan distance running. The eighth km is clocked at 2:39.48, then the ninth km at 2:35.50! Instead of struggling to run with the Kenyans, he is actually running away from them. Haile Gebrselassie's world record in Hengelo is 26:43.53, a "record for the eternity" some had said. Performed by a "miracle runner". But as Hissou storms clear, it becomes apparent that the record is in danger. Salah Hissou the world

MOROCCAN SUCCESS; THE KADA WAY

record holder over 10,000 metres? Surely he does not have the class? I'm sure that Tergat and Koech are convinced that he does, as they watch him romping away, while running under twenty seven minutes themselves. The athletics world will have to believe it too, as Hissou crosses the line in 26:38.08, over sixteen seconds ahead of Tergat and five seconds inside the Gebrselassie standard!

This was truly amazing for Salah who had never before attained this quality of performance. He had beaten a giant of the sport in Tergat and while he hadn't beaten Gebrselassie, bettering his best time was the next best thing.

Hissou celebrated in grand style, taking four laps of honour! An hour later he sat in the press conference soaking in his career best achievement.

"On the last kilometres, I flew," he commented. His final km was timed at 2:36.11.

The Belgium crowd had realized it too. As a world record became a possibility, the 40,000 spectators started chanting, "Hissou, Hissou, Hissou!" Combined with the traditional African drum roll, the atmosphere was electric. Salah had done the most damage between the 7 km and 9 km splits. He was three seconds off world record pace, but reversed this in spectacular fashion. Following some scintillating laps, he was suddenly seven seconds under world record pace at 9 kms. In the process of breaking the record, he had run the second 5,000 metres in 13:12.63. That was the official split. Since Salah had gone through 5,000 metres in about 13:26.20 his second half was approximately 13:11.90. Incredible.

This was all a bit of a surprise. Few had thought that Hissou was quite this good and Haile's world record was considered very special. Salah had witnessed the Hengelo run himself, describing it as "moving" and "simple of fabulous." How could Salah Hissou take five seconds off Haile Gebrselassie's "fabulous" run?

However his Moroccan manager Aziz Daouda was *not*

surprised.

"It was Salah's first record run, which we wanted but he was not necessarily under pressure to set," he said. He stated that Hissou's season was designed around Brussels and he was convinced that he could break the record after he ran the second fastest 5,000 metres of all time in Rome.

Salah's breaking of the "miracle runner's" record made people take stock, for nobody was talking of miracles anymore, since the Kenyans Tergat and Koech had also gone inside the twenty seven minute mark. It was little over three years ago that the barrier was first broken. Now it was being smashed.

Tergat ran 26:54.41, Koech 26:56.78. The others were a long way behind with fellow Kenyan William Kiptum Muigei 27:18.84, Aloys Nizigama 27:25.13 and Mathias Ntawulikura 27:25.48. This Brussels race had five of the first eight finishers from the Atlanta 10,000 metres final but with a very different outcome.

"How long will the world record remain?" Hissou was asked. "At least until 1997," came Salah's reply. "In this year there are no more 10,000 metres races."

Even if the record didn't last, Aziz Daouda was convinced of his pupil's credentials.

"Salah Hissou is better than Said Aouita, already now. Salah Hissou is our new desert prince."

The margin that the Atlanta silver medallist enjoyed over the bronze medallist was virtually reversed in Brussels. This was a monumental turn of events. Every runner has good and bad days but the major factor was in planning and preparation. While Tergat had gone straight to Europe after the Games, Hissou had gone straight to Ifrane. Training at altitude, his sole focus was the Brussels encounter. During that period Tergat was stretching the limits of his peak racing season by clocking personal bests at 3,000 and 5,000 metres in Monaco and Zurich. Nobody can go on producing his best

MOROCCAN SUCCESS; THE KADA WAY

performances race after race without doing some base training to start the cycle again. Not that Tergat's run in Belgium was poor. It was another huge personal best but most people in distance running would regard his Zurich, Monaco and most definitely his Atlanta runs as superior in quality. For Salah it was vital to make the most of his yearly minor championship since it was not easy to skip a meeting as big as Zurich. He had certainly done that!

Morocco had previously had Olympic champions at 10,000 metres but Salah Hissou became the first Moroccan to hold the world record at the historic distance. World records from Moroccans weren't going to shock running enthusiasts anymore. Said Aouita had regularly rewritten the record books in the 1980's.

Belief from Brussels. That is what Salah Hissou collected from his 26:38.08. It was even more important than the world record. It was the inspiration he needed to give himself a chance of winning a major championship, next year and beyond. Having the world record would give Salah stature, something to intimidate his rivals. It would also give him added pressure. Could he handle it?

Abdelkader Kada could hardly believe it all. The manner in which he destroyed the best from Kenya made him smile. He had done the same thing to their best 5,000 metres runners in Rome. Salah Hissou had defeated all the best long distance track runners in 1996 apart from Haile Gebrselassie.

Hicham El Guerrouj had defeated all the best middle distance runners in 1996 apart from Noureddine Morceli. Milan was to host the Grand Prix final and it was here that he would get this chance. Before that there was a performance of monumental proportions.

September 1, 1996, was to be a date to remember in men's distance running. There were no major meetings on this day, just some competition in Rieti, Italy. Whilst not being one of Europe's renowned track and field venues, it had produced world records in the modern era. In 1992 Morceli set a new benchmark in the 1,500 metres and he did likewise in the mile the following year.

Daniel Komen had recorded the second and third fastest times in history over 3,000 metres during August. Yet he still believed that he was capable of better. His great performances at 5,000 metres suggested that he may well be, but after nearly two months at the top of his game, how much longer could he sustain this level for?

Only two days earlier Komen had again pushed his body to its limits in a 5,000 metres race in Berlin. Going for the world record that he had just missed in Zurich, Komen reached 3,000 metres in 7:42.1, though having blown most of the field to pieces he had nobody for support. He fell away from a super fast time and had to settle for a 13:02.62. Paul Koech had tried to stay with him, running a 7:42.8 split, but he fell apart even more so. Despite the drop off, Daniel still defeated second placed Bob Kennedy by over three seconds.

Having looked so tired in Germany, a world record did not appear to be a realistic goal in Italy. But as this 3,000 metres time trial (it was never much of a race!) commenced, we quickly became aware that he was taking this attempt seriously. He had two fellow Kenyans to pace him for as long as possible and he settled in behind them, while the small but packed stadium settled in to watch history in the making.

Conditions are virtually ideal with very little wind. It is the pace that is mind blowing as the rabbit passes 1,000 metres in 2:25.89! From 1,200 metres Komen has just one assistant, though he is doing an outstanding job. The split at 1,400 metres is 3:23.55 after a stunning lap of 57.66! Daniel Komen and exclamation marks went hand in hand during 1996.

He is just a metre or two off the rabbit and doesn't look to be over striding. His split at 2,000 metres for his fast Monaco run was 4:56 but now it is 4:53.18 after Komen passes the pacemaker just prior to the split. The amazing tempo that he is setting is best described by the fact that this time comes within one second of Moses Kiptanui's Kenyan record for a

MOROCCAN SUCCESS; THE KADA WAY

flat out 2,000 metres!

Mere mortals might have naturally slowed now, if they were in Komen's position of having to go it alone. Yet this Kenyan gets back into a faster rhythm and at 2,200 metres the split is 5:21.83, the last 400 metres being covered in 58.37!!! Surely on this occasion, Morceli's world record is not going to survive.

Daniel does not fall apart, but he isn't able to produce a kick at all in the final laps. Who knows what sort of time he would have registered then? The penultimate lap is timed at 59.75 with the final lap at 59.09 as Komen retains his form. He has smashed the world record with a time of 7:20.67!

These figures would soon become almost mythical in track and field, like 8.90 or 19.32. But were Komen and his management team too greedy during this period? It seemed that every week the Kenyan superstar was attempting a world record. Surely the Berlin race had taken something out of his legs. With a little more sensible planning I think that the Rieti run could have been even faster and we might be talking about a sub 7:20.

Nevertheless, it was intimidating for anybody to have to race against this well oiled machine. Who would be the next star to pit his credentials against Komen?

Milan was a meeting of match ups. Finally we were getting to see Morceli versus El Guerrouj at 1,500 metres. Also, only six days after Morceli's 3,000 metres record fell and just fifteen days after Gebrselassie's 10,000 metres record fell, came a confrontation of the two new world record holders at 5,000 metres. It was Komen versus Hissou. The two battles took place on September the 7th during the Grand Prix final.

Could Hicham prove that he was now the best? He was undefeated and had the fastest time for the year. The pieces were all in place for the handing over of a crown. How easily would Noureddine give it up, if at all?

Morceli had experienced an extraordinary period of dominance. Since his rise to prominence in 1990 he had been vulnerable to defeat on only a few occasions. This was during 1992 when he hurt his hip in the lead up to the Barcelona Olympics. The world champion hadn't recovered in time for his moment of truth and the final was a great disappointment. He finished seventh in a slow race won by Fermin Cacho.

Only four weeks later he smashed Said Aouita's world record when he ran 3:28.86 in Rieti on September 6. The following year he also broke the mile record as well as retained his world title. But Noureddine was to get even better. During the next two years he improved his 1,500 metres record further, to a staggering 3:27.37. He added the 3,000 metres record to his resumé when he ran 7:25.11 while also proving his capabilities at 5,000 metres with some great victories. Capping it all off was a third 1,500 metres world championship in 1995.

Now in 1996 he was being challenged. His Olympic win was the least impressive of all his major championship victories. Many now felt that this young Moroccan Hicham El Guerrouj was ready to defeat him. For various reasons their only contest this year had been the Atlanta final which of course was a non contest. But thankfully the Grand Prix Final was bringing them together for another showdown.

The Algerian wasn't taking this lightly. He had sharpened up well following his lacklustre run in Brussels with good wins in Berlin and Rieti. In Germany Noureddine defeated Venuste Niyongabo on August 30 in the mile. The winning margin was very emphatic. 3:49.09 to 3:51.01. He commented on his win here while also providing an explanation for his Brussels performance: "I am very satisfied with my race. You know I was ill for about three weeks and a little bit uneasy about whether I could return to my early form. Today's race showed me that I'm back."

In Italy on September 1 he'd defeated the Olympic 5,000 metres champion convincingly again, clocking a 1,500 metres time of 3:29.99 while the Burundi runner trailed home in

MOROCCAN SUCCESS; THE KADA WAY

3:31.01. The pace was on close to world record schedule throughout and Morceli managed a last lap of 55.68. This excellent performance was fairly comparable to El Guerrouj's outstanding win in Brussels.

The Milan field included everyone of relevance except for Cacho. The race was slow, but it still came down to the two best runners over the final lap.

In non championship outdoor races, Hicham El Guerrouj had run under 3:34 in every 1,500 metres he'd competed in during '96. It showed fantastic consistency of high performance. It was somewhat equivalent to going out and racing a 5,000 metres every week or two and clocking a sub 13:05. Of course a longer distance runner is unlikely to race as often as El Guerrouj, with the extra race miles taking more out of the athlete. Hicham's racing schedule was quite crowded. As a comparison, he raced fifteen times on the track in 1996 with thirteen finals. Salah Hissou raced ten times on the track with nine finals.

As Hicham toed the start line in Milan, you could picture Abdelkader watching with admiration and anticipation. His student appeared calm, yet he knew that this race meant more to him than to the other athletes. This was the closest he could get to a rerun of the Atlanta final. He felt no animosity towards Morceli. Noureddine simply had what he craved. That metaphoric crown as the 'king' of the mile. The Algerian had an imposing winning streak of fifty five dating back to 1992 when competing over 1,500 metres or the mile.

The race started with everyone seemingly uneasy. The speed was awfully slow. This was appropriate. Who was meant to dictate the terms? The runners didn't know who to keep an eye on. The one with the titles or the one with the youthful confidence.

Logically the slow pace should have allowed others to contend for what was a prestigious race win in itself. But the last lap was like a rite of passage for Hicham El Guerrouj. Nobody dared stand in his path, not even Noureddine Morceli.

The build up in tempo was gradual and predictable. The Algerian was a disappointment. This race was the definitive proof that he didn't contain the same kick as in seasons past. Morceli at his best would have won this race. That he didn't was a career disaster. It gave his rival so much confidence that by their next meeting there was a clear gap between them. A gap that would only widen.

Not that Noureddine was too concerned on the outside, "It's okay. I've dominated the 1,500 for many years. Sometimes you're exhausted and don't have a good result and that's normal." He also said that the flu was still bothering him. Later this month the Algerian declared that he was looking at clocking even faster times during 1997. "I have the capacity to run the 1,500 metres in three minutes 24 seconds or three minutes 25, and the 3,000 in seven minutes 18 or 19 seconds. I am still young and I am able to take other titles and achieve other records."

Though Morceli did have the time after the Milan race to provide a statement on his conqueror, describing El Guerrouj as, "the new generation. I think he'll dominate that event for years to come."

That El Guerrouj didn't require his best race to win was the let down. A let down to track fans. Not a let down to Hicham and Abdelkader though. As the Moroccan strode clear on the final straight and crossed the line in first place, they knew that he was now the world's best miler. Hicham didn't require a medal for that confirmation.

The final times were uninspiring. El Guerrouj, 3:38.80. Morceli, 3:39.69. The gap however was enough to be convincing and the final 800 metres was clocked at 1:47.10. It was a strange race, with Niyongabo only managing fifth place behind the Kenyans Rotich and Tanui. It's true that the Grand Prix final rarely brings the best out of track's distance runners.

The 5,000 metres would offer an exception to the rule.

The event showed that men's distance running had come a

MOROCCAN SUCCESS; THE KADA WAY

long way in the last couple of years, yet it also showed that a lot of things had stayed the same. Whether it was Aouita versus Ngugi, Skah versus Chelimo, or Hissou versus Tergat. Morocco versus Kenya had been an exciting staple in men's distance running for a decade. It was set to continue in Italy.

If Salah could beat Daniel than he could offer an argument for being the best performed distance runner of 1996. This might seem an outrageous claim as he only finished a distant third to Gebrselassie and Tergat in Atlanta. But as well as that bronze medal, he had that silver medal from the World Cross Country and he had run faster over 5,000 metres and 10,000 metres than both Gebrselassie and Tergat. Yes, that statistic even surprises me! Only Komen had bettered him over 5,000 metres, but Milan would offer an opportunity for Salah to end Daniel's winning streak and replicate his earlier defeat of him in June. Easier said than done of course.

Beating Komen in Rome was different to beating him at present, now that he was a 12:45 runner and had defeated the 'emperor' from Ethiopia. The Moroccan gave a good account of himself in Milan, running 12:54.83. Only four runners besides himself had gone faster this year. But that was never going to be enough to defeat Daniel Komen, who was riding one of the hottest streaks of form ever seen in the modern era of distance running. The Kenyan clocked 12:52.38, for him just average, nothing particularly special. He may not have gone to Atlanta, but in my eyes, Komen was clearly the men's distance runner of the year in 1996 (I cannot say men's runner of the year full stop, as there was a certain Michael Johnson going around, really really fast). He beat anybody who was anybody. For Hissou, losing out to Komen by two and a half seconds was actually a great run, for Komen's form for the past month was something for not just the athletics world, but the entire sporting world to behold.

Komen went through 3,000 metres in 7:40.90, with Koech and Hissou desperately hanging on in 7:41.30. To put this in perspective, this was faster than Salah's first 3,000 metres in Rome. It was too quick for Koech, who was soon dropped but still hung on for a more than respectable time of 13:00.67. He finished ahead of some quality athletes. Khalid Boulami was fourth in 13:03.85, and then behind him were Bob Kennedy, Ismail Sghyr, El Hassan Lahssini, Shem Kororia and Thomas Nyariki. For Hissou, it was a very good performance backing up from Brussels.

For Daniel Komen, this victory clinched his position as the overall winner of the Grand Prix season for 1996. The IAAF fully recognised and appreciated his remarkable performances. I am sure though, that Komen would have given back all of the $250,000 that he was awarded, for a shot at the Olympic 5,000 metres gold medal.

Both of Kada's athletes were in such good shape that they didn't want their seasons to end. Salah and Hicham went to Sarajevo on the 9th of September with El Guerrouj racing his usual event and Hissou racing over the rarely run distance of 2,000 metres.

In the 1,500 metres Hicham out kicked a pack of Kenyans led by the remarkable Komen who came within a second of the dominant Moroccan. Daniel liked the look of himself as a miler. He would dabble in the shorter distances on many occasions over the coming years.

The winning time was better, 3:34.38. This race was a higher standard than the Milan one, even with a much less hyped build up. Conspicuous by his absence was Morceli. The King had relinquished his crown, at least for the moment.

The field in Salah's race was an average one and Hissou nearly pulled off another victory at a middle distance. Britain's John Mayock, a specialist miler, just pepped him, running 5:00.91 to the Moroccan's 5:00.95. Another Moroccan distance man, Ismail Sghyr finished third with a 5:02.69. This race wasn't at the level of those that preceded it, but it was a fine way to cap off a truly wonderful year for Salah Hissou. This was going to be hard to top in the future. For the twenty four year old Salah might have reached his limits, limits which might stop just short of those of a certain Kenyan and Ethiopian. The truth appeared to be that when Komen and

MOROCCAN SUCCESS; THE KADA WAY

Gebrselassie were really on, Hissou couldn't hope to defeat them. They were at another level, on another stratosphere. For how long remained to be seen. Salah needed to remain at his own exceptionally high level, and hope that those above him dropped their performances just a little.

For if they slipped just a little, there would be a quality athlete ready to pounce and strike. 1997 was going to be a vital year in the career of Salah Hissou. He had proved to be a great competitor in the big Grand Prix meets, but could he win a major championship? The upcoming World Cross Country Championships in Turin would provide another opportunity and later in the season would come the World Athletics Championships in Athens. Salah's confidence was at an all time high but with Gebrselassie, Komen and Tergat on the scene, it was a nightmarish era to be trying to win major men's long distance running events. The 'emperor' from Ethiopia was now the 10,000 metres Olympic champion and Olympic record holder. Despite this, 1996 was one of his worst ever years, such are the man's achievements. He did not break the world record in his two pet events. He nearly lost one to Komen and did lose the other one to Hissou. This only made Gebrselassie more determined to regain his 10,000 metres world record.

El Guerrouj wanted to keep winning. It was a great habit to get into and it was proving hard to break free of. He returned to Italy and the Torino international meeting on September 14 and clocked 3:33.51, defeating a lesser class field. It was a fine way to celebrate his twenty second birthday. That made it thirteen finals, all raced over 1,500 metres for the year. Hicham had won twelve times, unlucky thirteen being his fall in Atlanta.

The Moroccan had taken on all comers and beaten them with aplomb. He was still young with further sizeable improvement possible. He was committed, determined and supremely gifted and was being guided by a knowledgeable coach. It was a dangerous combination for the rest of the world's milers to combat.

Hicham's issue was a similar yet different one to his training partner. Both wanted to win a major championship. Salah didn't fully know that he was capable of attaining one. Hicham knew for certain that he had the capabilities. It was a case of keeping things simple. Continue training with the same discipline. Don't get sick. Don't get injured. All logic pointed to a gold medal in Athens next year.

MOROCCAN SUCCESS; THE KADA WAY

Reaching The Top ~ The Kada Way

"Salah Hissou is better than Said Aouita, already now."

Aziz Daouda, are you sure? Better than an athlete who went undefeated at 5,000 metres for nearly ten years and who was an Olympic and world champion and a world record holder at multiple distances?

Some people have short memories. Or perhaps they simply get carried away with current performances.

Salah Hissou wasn't yet better than Said Aouita, the Moroccan who was the best track distance runner of the 1980's, but at the end of 1996, he was amongst the cream of the crop in distance running circles. Excluding the road runners, Hissou was being spoken about as one of the best distance runners in the world. He was being mentioned in the same breath as Gebrselassie, Komen and Tergat. It was pretty heady stuff. It was also highly deserved.

Hicham El Guerrouj was being spoken about in much the same light. In fact before Atlanta many were calling him Morocco's 'new desert prince'. The 10,000 metres Brussels record had partly overshadowed his own remarkable year. To some followers he was a far more successful athlete than Salah. He had achieved many more wins but just not the medals in cross country, nor a bronze from Atlanta, nor a world record from a classic track distance. Abdelkader Kada didn't mind who others regarded as his best runner. He was simply happy that they were both his. He could make a convincing argument that at the end of 1996 he had two of the seven wonders of the distance running world.

If you were to rate the best male runners over any discipline from the 1,500 metres to the 12 kms cross country then only Daniel Komen, Haile Gebrselassie, Paul Tergat, Noureddine Morceli, Venuste Niyongabo and Moses Kiptanui would be in the same league right now as Hicham El Guerrouj and Salah Hissou. Hicham didn't have the world titles of a Morceli,

Kiptanui or Gebrselassie but he did have an unbeaten season in '96 when he managed to stay on his own two feet. Salah's best arguably didn't reach the heights of some of those names mentioned above, but his versatility was unmatched by all, except for perhaps Gebrselassie and Kiptanui.

All these eight athletes had advantages over others in certain areas. The following is a somewhat hypothetical group of lists, stating the various strong points of each runner.

The Classic Distances

1,500 metres / mile	Morceli, El Guerrouj, Niyongabo, Gebrselasie, Komen, Kiptanui, Hissou, Tergat
5,000 metres	Gebrselassie, Komen, Hissou, Kiptanui, Morceli, Niyongabo, Tergat, El Guerrouj
10,000 metres	Gebrselassie, Tergat, Hissou, Komen, Kiptanui, Morceli, Niyongabo, El Guerrouj

Other Significant Disciplines

3,000 metres	Komen, Gebrselassie, Morceli, Niyongabo, Kiptanui, Hissou, Tergat, El Guerrouj
12 kms cross country	Tergat, Hissou, Gebrselassie, Komen, Kiptanui, Morceli, Niyongabo, El Guerrouj

Many of these lists are based purely on speculation, as these runners have not competed recently or in some cases ever, over some of these distances. Who knows who would win a 12 kms cross country between Morceli, El Guerrouj and Niyongabo? Nobody. What these lists do is highlight the differences in abilities that these runners have in varying

MOROCCAN SUCCESS; THE KADA WAY

disciplines when compared to one another. Hicham El Guerrouj rates as one of the world's best because he seems on the verge of becoming the best miler. Salah Hissou rates as one of the world's best because he has reached a high standard in all of the above disciplines. My ratings have taken into account personal bests, performances in major championships and any significant victories. More than anything, they reflect on recent results. Based solely on 1996, Hicham could rate first in the mile but because the decision was 'lineball', I went with Noureddine due to his previous years of dominance.

Moses Kiptanui is the only runner with known expertise over the 3,000 metres steeplechase and rating the rest would be a total guess because the event is totally different to all the others mentioned above. For the 10,000 metres and cross country, I can go a little from the runners' abilities over 5,000 metres for a clearer estimation. If I were to step down to 800 metres, then Noureddine Morceli would be a clear cut winner.

The 5,000 metres was the hardest to analyse, since in this case, it is the middle distance and is where the abilities of the milers and the cross country runners come to a head. Gebrselassie and Komen are clear cut and so is 'last' placed El Guerrouj. All the others apart from Tergat, have attributes that they can bring to the table to mount a case for 'third' place in the rating. The rating comes down to best times, performances at major championships, victories and *recent* results. Hissou ticks three of those boxes (no performance in a major championship) and that is why he rated ahead of the rest. Above former world record holder Kiptanui, former Zurich winner Morceli, Olympic champion Niyongabo and sub thirteen minute man Tergat. Salah has run faster than all of them and has done so, in winning performances against top class fields, performances that came during 1996. Hicham El Guerrouj has been treated harshly because his history so far is almost exclusively as a miler. He could rate above some of these runners in the 3,000 metres but I have nothing to go from, to justify moving him up that list.

Some questions were unanswerable. What Kada did know

was that he had two runners who could potentially win major championships. Take note that I don't count the World Indoors as a major championship. 1997 was mostly about getting Hicham and Salah ready for gold medal pursuits at the World Athletics Championships in Athens during August. Salah also had the Turin World Cross Country Championships where he dreamed of winning gold against the might of team Kenya.

Just two years ago, Hicham and Salah were very much at an international level. But that level was quite a distance from where they now sat. So how had Salah Hissou and Hicham El Guerrouj reached such a high status? How had they run such great times? How had they placed highly in such big races so often?

It has been well documented that runners from Kenya and Ethiopia have a distinct advantage from others because they were born and raised at high altitude. Morocco is not as high above sea level, yet this nation has produced many outstanding long distance runners. Nepal is not noted for its distance running excellence so it isn't just altitude that goes into the makings of a record breaking athlete. Nevertheless as distance running followers well know, it certainly helps.

Altitude training has become increasingly popular for the world class distance runner in recent times. Spending time at a higher elevation naturally increases the percentage of red blood cells in the body. Since these cells carry oxygen, a greater red blood cell count enables a human to have better endurance. Specifically in distance running, this simply means the capacity to run harder for longer. Running at a high altitude not only naturally improves an athlete physically, but also mentally. The positive impact of racing at sea level, where there is more oxygen in the air, soon after training at altitude can be significant.

Morocco is one of the hottest countries in the world. This gives a certain edge to its runners, as many of the major championships are conducted in warm conditions. A Moroccan like Khalid Skah is used to running hard in conditions like he experienced in Barcelona. Many of his

MOROCCAN SUCCESS; THE KADA WAY

opposition are not so well acclimatized. Morocco is not one of the poorest African countries, but most of its citizens are not rich. Approximately half of its 30 million people live off less than $600 a year. Most people survive on a basic natural diet. It is not the fast food lifestyle of their European and American counterparts. Like Kenya and Ethiopia, Morocco gains an advantage in distance running, from this way of life.

If most Africans lead a basic lifestyle then why aren't other African nations in the mix for medals in distance races?

Firstly, you can cancel out Western Africa, whose people are a different breed to their Eastern African neighbours. These nations produce many of the world's top sprinters. Of course, this part of the continent is where African-Americans descended. The genetics of the Eastern and Northern Africans go a long way to explaining their superiority to the majority of the world in distance running.

But what of a nation like Sudan? It's based in Eastern Africa and is one of the poorest countries in the world. Yet it doesn't produce any world beaters in distance running. Once again, there is more to this than meets the eye.

Who do most young boys look up to? Who do they admire and aspire to be? Many would give their answer as sports stars from their own country. Ethiopia had Bikila then Yifter. Kenya had Keino, then Rono. Morocco had Aouita. These trailblazers showed their countrymen that international sporting success in athletics was possible. To win an Olympic gold medal or to break a world record could be more than just a dream. I wonder how many thousands of Ethiopians, Kenyans and Moroccans were inspired to run and race, by their exploits.

As these countries have developed more depth in the quality of their distance runners it has all snowballed. The initial phases of organised Kenyan group training dated back to camps created to prepare for the World Cross Country Championships during the John Ngugi era. By the early 1990's, most of the best Kenyan runners were training with each other throughout the year. Having the best athletes training with each other is of course going to have a highly motivating effect on everyone involved.

The thought process of a talented youngster who has been given the opportunity to run with one of their heroes would be along the lines of, 'I am training with a world champion. This is what he does in training to race at this level. This is what I must do. This is what I will do.'

This bringing together of top distance runners to push each other is perhaps the biggest advantage that the 'big three' nations in distance running has over the rest. By the mid '90's, Moroccans were training in a similar vein to their Kenyan opponents. In big training camps, specifically focused on bringing their runners up to top form for the major championships. Salah Hissou could see what Brahim Boutayeb and Khalid Skah did to become 10,000 metres Olympic champions.

There are still other factors that contribute to a country's success or lack thereof, in distance running. Tanzania, being a neighbour of Kenya, has a history of distance running success. In the 1970's and early '80's it was the third best performed distance running nation from Africa. Yet it slipped away and stopped producing quality athletes. Tanzania has been a war torn country for some time and this obviously has had an effect on its depleted running stocks.

Morocco's neighbour Algeria has also enjoyed success in distance running, mostly through Morceli and Boulmerka. Generally speaking, when a commentator talks about the East Africans, they are referring to the Kenyans and Ethiopians. When they mention the North Africans, the reference is to Morocco and Algeria.

Hopefully a country like Sudan finds a hero, a trailblazer, someone to burst onto the European athletics scene and make an impact. It may start the snowball effect.

The many poor people of Kenya, Ethiopia and to a lesser

MOROCCAN SUCCESS; THE KADA WAY

extent Morocco, now also see that running can be a way out of poverty. To earn a reasonable living for themselves and their families is arguably the biggest motivator towards the success of Africa's athletes. Those who are naturally very talented know that if they work hard and make full use of their ability, that there is a good possibility of being rewarded with success and food on the table for their families. This silent encouragment speaks volumes to many of Africa's youth.

Another factor is that most African countries do not have a lot of sporting interests outside of soccer, otherwise known as football. Morocco for example boasts track and field as its second most popular sport behind soccer. An Australian might dream of becoming a test cricketer, a Wimbledon tennis champion or an Olympic swimmer. An American might dream of playing in the world series, or the NBA finals, or the super bowl. An Italian might dream of playing in the san siro, racing at Monza or riding in the giro or tour. For most nations, becoming an Olympic 10,000 metres champion is well down the list of sporting priorities. Since the 1980's, for Salah Hissou and many of his Moroccan countrymen, this has become a popular dream. One that they've seen is attainable.

Salah Hissou and Hicham El Guerrouj lived in hot, humid weather, with Salah also growing up in relatively mountainous terrain, at a reasonably high altitude. Kasbat Tadla, where Salah grew up, is at around 1,000 metres in altitude. They had heroes to aspire to be, who gave them dreams. Dreams which they knew contained the small ounce of a possibility in becoming reality. Both came from quite poor families. Morocco has been a stable nation during its development, enabling Abdelkader's boys to focus on their dream. They have been encouraged and supported in their endeavours because of their natural ability. Rather than be recruited to the armed forces, Hicham and Salah were recruited to train in Morocco's highly focused national training centre, as just some of the many young Moroccans identified as having sufficient natural talent to potentially prosper as an adult in the international sporting arena.

Moroccan scouts are always keeping an eye on school cross

country races, hoping to spot the next champion, but their dedication and the Moroccan system goes much deeper. From the ages of twelve to sixteen, students are systematically subjected to three types of tests. These tests rate a kid's ability in sprinting, middle distance and long jump. Obviously if a teenager is a good middle distance runner, there is a good chance that he/she can also develop into a quality long distance one. The most talented youngsters are recruited to Morocco's national training centre in Rabat. This recruiting process is the legacy of Said Aouita who in 1988 asked the King of the day to fund a talent identification development system for track and field. Now overseeing the Moroccan Athletics Federation was Aziz Daouda, the Moroccan technical director. He comments on the recruiting program, "We never put pressure on athletes to leave school. That has to be the decision of their parents. But if they have the kind of potential that could allow them to make a living in track & field and they make that decision, we provide support for that at the Institute."

Another man who was instrumental in the improvements of Moroccan running was Lahcen Samsam Akka, a former top shot putter. He had preceded Aziz Daouda as the Moroccan technical director and a lot of the credit for all the success now going to Daouda should also be given to Akka. Even with Aziz in charge, Lachen was still doing some work for him behind the scenes. A coaching course that was completed by Abdelkader Kada was taught to him by Akka.

By 1996 Morocco's training camps had become very intense and very scientific. The training programs were now being specifically designed around the major championships. The basic system involved a large block of training at sea level followed by a smaller batch of training at high altitude. This cycle would repeat itself a number of times, only being interrupted when an athlete's program approached a major championship and/or a period of racing. At such a time an athlete's program or workload would often be reduced, thus allowing the runner to be fresh for racing.

Aziz Daouda describes the training techniques of the

MOROCCAN SUCCESS; THE KADA WAY

Moroccans and the requirements for training as an individual and in a group, "These days the major competitions have reached such level of intensity that we can not think that we can prepare the athletes like they used to train in the '60's. People sometimes confuse personalizing training with following an individual training program. We do not have two athletes training the same way, but we have a method we adapt to each athlete. We are not creating anything new, but we are making improvements to something that already exists by utilizing scientific data."

Aziz also comments on Hissou's improvement and training, "In Brussels in '95, when Hissou broke Skah's Moroccan 10,000 metres record with 27:09.30, we thought he should have run much faster in the last two kms, but he got tired, so we analysed him thoroughly and now he runs with more economical style. The movement of his arms is different from a biomechanical perspective, and his stride is more efficient. It comes from the need to prepare a training plan for the group (about 30 athletes), respecting each athlete's individualism. It is a compulsory behavior line for the group. An example: they run by time, 20, 30, 40 minutes, but Salah Hissou never runs more than one hour of continuous running, yet Khalid Skah runs very often over 75-80 minutes. Same event, same level of performance, different loads."

Much of what Daouda sprouted was not rocket science or revolutionary and he admits as such. It was a matter of applying general common sense and then making additions to proven theories. Most of the Moroccan training system used the training philosophies of the great British milers of the 1980's. What Aziz has done is acknowledge the importance of the modern day major championships. In earlier eras, the focus was mostly on the Olympic Games. The Olympics still remained significant but now has to contend with the World Athletics Championships and the World Cross Country Championships, not to mention the huge annual track and field extravaganzas that were held in Zurich and Brussels.

It is interesting to note that the Moroccans run by time in training and not by distance. For example most of the western world will say that they're going for a ten mile run rather than a sixty minute run. The comparisons of Skah and Hissou's training volumes show perfectly that what works for one runner may not necessarily work best for another. It is up to the individual (and his coach) to discover which training ingredients are required to get the best out of the athlete.

As well as having the support of Daouda and the Moroccan Athletics Federation, Hissou and El Guerrouj also had their own personal coach to take care of their development and current day form. That man of course was Abdelkader Kada, one of two head coaches (supported by six assistants) in the Federation and himself an ex runner of some note. Kada had been Morocco's national champion over 5,000 and 10,000 metres as well as in cross country. Salah and Hicham were not being advised by fools. Yet he refused to big note himself, "Myself, I was an athlete. I was not a big athlete. I was a national athlete, four times Moroccan champion. I didn't do big things in my life as an athlete but with my athletes together, maybe we do good things."

Abdelkader not only talks, but also listens. In 2000 he was asked by Sebastian Coe, "What makes you different as a coach?" His answer, "Because I learn from the athletes. I learn from everyone, from the coaches, from the journalists, from the old athletes."

Kada was doing a lot more than advising just the 1,500 metres world silver medallist and the 10,000 metres world record holder. Throughout the 1990's he had command of around 20-30 Moroccan athletes. On this aspect he said that they are "specialising in different distances, although they are complementary to each other and they inspire each other."

Morocco's athletics squad first started official preparations for August '97's World Championships on October 15, 1996. Distance runners do not have an off season. The period of 15/10/96 to the 20/02/97 was very much a non racing period. During this time the runners were to focus on aerobic endurance, strength and power. For Salah, this was a heavy period of training aimed at getting himself in the best possible

MOROCCAN SUCCESS; THE KADA WAY

condition for Turin's World Cross Country Championships in March.
Kada speaks a little on the training phases, "You have maybe at the beginning of the year we have two weeks of adaptation first and we have accumulation first. We do road mileage and weights in the weight rooms and we begin hill training and then we have another phase. It is a conditioning phase, more rhythm and speed and competition phase."

Hicham was gearing up for the World Indoor Championships. Even in the early phases of his 1997 season, El Guerrouj was doing many miles of very fast running. His aerobic endurance sessions were done as either:

standard runs of 30-45 minutes or 50-60 minutes
or
interval sessions of 6 x 1,000 metres in approximately 2:30 and 4 x 2,000 metres in approximately 5:10.

The standard runs were completed at about three minute km pace. This would vary slightly depending on how Hicham was feeling. The intervals both allowed for two minutes recovery time between each rep.

The initial base training involved six weeks training at sea level in Rabat, followed by three weeks at altitude in Ifrane, which is only two hundred kms from the nation's capital. The city of Ifrane is located 1,600 metres above sea level. The plateau, on the Hebrie Mountain, reaches approximately 2,100 metres in height. Later, altitude training programs were also conducted at Davos, Saint Moritz and Mexico City. Team Morocco was leaving no stone unturned in order to get the best out of its athletes for Athens.

The runners were split up into various groups of approximately ten athletes with Hicham El Guerrouj leading the middle distance runners, Khalid Boulami leading the 5,000 metres runners and Salah Hissou leading the 10,000 metres/cross country runners. These men were now the heroes that Morocco's next generation of stars would aspire to be.

This group training was similar to the mentality adopted by Kenya and Ethiopia, which differed to many other elite athletes from the western world who preferred to go it alone. Later El Guerrouj spoke of how he remained motivated through all "the pain and suffering." "My motivation comes from my training partners, my rivals, my family and my fans. My training group is particularly important. They respect me but they really push me too."

The lead runners of each group had their own rabbits that assisted them on interval speed sessions. Starting in 1997, Houcine Benzriguinet began work as Hicham El Guerrouj's main pacemaker. In the years ahead Houcine would become a friend and advisor to the Moroccan, whilst never racing himself. In future years Hicham was also assisted in his training by his brother Fethi and Mohammed Amyn, among others.

With athletes having varying targets and focusing on different distances, it's obvious that some runners will differ slightly to the standard preparation set out by Aziz Daouda.

Aziz had specified the period from 21/02/97 to 10/05/97 was to be the second major training phase for the upcoming European track season. This did not apply to Morocco's world cross country team who had that significant interruption of Turin. For the likes of El Guerrouj, this training period involved a stronger focus onto specific endurance and race pace. Then from May 11 it would be time to ease off a little with the sessions in order to get race ready for the first competition period, which Daouda had bracketed as the 30th of May to the 10th of June. Another short training phase would take the athletes to the start of July and from there, it was all going to be big race after big race. The World Championships were at the start of August and other big Grand Prix meetings then closed out the season. For most Moroccans, the basic plan was to be peaking around August. The World Championships were obviously a major target. Specifics about the Moroccan training program and training sessions of Hissou and El Guerrouj will be discussed in a later chapter.

MOROCCAN SUCCESS; THE KADA WAY

Salah Hissou would not stick specifically to this preparation phase but would use it as a guideline. Even when the track season started, he would do his own thing. Salah did not always race in the biggest Grand Prix meets. After Turin, whatever he did would have the aim of improving his form and his chances for the big 10,000 metres races that he was to take part in at Athens and Brussels.

The racing program that Abdelkader Kada had devised for Hicham El Guerrouj and Salah Hissou showed little variance to their 1996 schedules. Both had the World Athletics Championships as their major goal, replacing the Atlanta Olympics. Salah also had the World Cross Country that he considered almost to be of equal importance. Hicham had 1,500 metres competition lined up in Stockholm, Zurich and Brussels. Salah continued to have Brussels as a target meet, as well as Rome. The only real addition was that the World Indoor Championships were on this year in Paris and Hicham wanted to defend his title from 1995.

The two runners continued to stick to the general racing/training schedule that had served them so well. In fact this sort of basic program was adhered to, by most of the world's best distance runners. It went a little something like this:

October - January	General base training where athletes get a lot of miles under their belt.
February - March	This is a combination of racing and heavy training with the indoor and cross country seasons taking place. Hicham and Salah won't want to reduce their training intensity too much, even for a vital race because of the need to be in peak form for the European summer season.
April - May	This is the most important training period of the year with a major focus on high quality, gut busting speed sessions. The completion of these interval tasks over and over again is designed to improve speed endurance as well as increase pain tolerance! These tasks specifically get El Guerrouj into such shape that he can sit on sub fifty seven second lap pace for up to a mile. Likewise, they enable Hissou to sit on sixty one second lap pace for up to two miles. By the end of May, Hicham and Salah MUST be in racing form. If they are not ready, they will soon be found out by the strong competition.
June - September	Racing, racing and more racing. Hard training must be employed carefully during these four months.

This is my very *basic* take on the year of the international distance runner. There are four periods that could be termed as the distance runners' four seasons. Most international distance runners take very little time off. El Guerrouj took a break from running of approximately three weeks at the end of each European track season.

Hicham El Guerrouj took the early stages of 1997 quite seriously. He was keen to repeat as the World Indoor 1,500 metres champion. This season the titles were being held in Paris and the Moroccan's final was scheduled on March 8.

Wanting some warm up races, Hicham raced in Stuttgart in an event that turned out to be a much bigger occasion than most would expect for this time of year. German fans were pleasantly surprised, for you rarely see a confrontation as interesting as this one. You certainly don't anticipate such a

MOROCCAN SUCCESS; THE KADA WAY

great track head to head as was witnessed on February 2, 1997.

Joining El Guerrouj in the 1,500 metres wasn't Noureddine Morceli or Venuste Niyongabo. It was Haile Gebrselassie, the man who many regarded as the greatest runner in the world. Some even spoke of him in terms of all time greatest. Despite being the Olympic champion at 10,000 metres, many felt that he had the tools to give El Guerrouj a run for his money in the Moroccan's specialty. His sprinting ability had been displayed brilliantly in so many longer distances races. One only had to remember Gothenburg to believe that the Ethiopian could be a chance of defeating any of the world's best milers.

The world record was Noureddine Morceli's 3:34.16, set in Seville on February 28, 1991. It was a nice way for the Algerian to celebrate his twenty first birthday and it would be the first of his many world records during the next five seasons.

So how fitting it was that Hicham El Guerrouj should set his first world record by breaking Morceli's original one. He didn't simply break it. Rather he pulverized it, to the tune of almost three seconds. It wasn't really the incentive of running against the clock that made this possible. It was more the presence of an Ethiopian and a raucous, knowledgeable crowd that helped push Kada's miler to a new level.

Haile arguably had a greater, more blazing kick than Hicham, but the way the Moroccan ran his middle distances, didn't allow the opposition to kick down. When competing at his best El Guerrouj was racing hard all the way. Gebrselassie excelled in sitting on sixty two to sixty five second laps and then exploding. Now he was asked to raise that speed to around fifty seven second laps and still find an extra gear at the finish. Everybody discovers their limits, even the greatest. Haile Gebrselassie found that running at this high a speed, even though it was over a much shorter distance than he was used to, was a bumpy ride. In Stuttgart, El Guerrouj took him out of his comfort zone.

Ten athletes are on the starting line and with this indoor circuit having only four lanes, the runners are cramped as they squeeze onto one front line. After one lap (200 metres) the field is well spread out with the first five having a margin on the rest. It is no surprise that the group has been divided when the split at 400 metres is 55.33! The two favourites start in fourth and fifth positions and gradually make their way to the front. Only one rabbit leads them at 800 metres, clocked at 1:52.30. He moves off the track after 900 metres, allowing the superstars to do battle. The good sized crowd are making a racket, no doubt helped by a large Ethiopian contingent, though Haile can not keep on the heels of Hicham as the Moroccan gets to 1,200 metres in 2:49.27. His lead is around ten metres soon after, with his opponent far from spent, but just unable to match this sort of constant heavy pace.

The seven and a half lap event is fast from the start and in the middle stages Hicham really pours on the power. Desperately Haile tries to hang on, but over the final 400 metres the Moroccan proves his superiority at this distance. Stopping the clock at 3:31.18 is a big moment. It is his first race of 1997 and it is sub 3:30 outdoor form. How hard to beat is he going to be come Athens?

Gebrselassie could hold his head up in defeat. His recorded result of 3:32.39 was outstanding for a longer distance runner. It's just that we weren't accustomed to seeing this man lose. El Guerrouj hadn't won with an explosive Morceli type finish with the last lap being only 56.0, but it was the constant lung bursting pace that eventually got the better of Haile.

Being pretty unaccustomed to losing, we might forgive Haile Gebrselassie for not knowing how to react, or not being gracious in defeat. This was never his style. A couple of El Guerrouj's Moroccan contingent had congratulated him and afterwards Hicham started to go off on a lap of honour with the media in close pursuit. However he was quickly stopped by another runner with a big smile on his face who gave him a big hug. It was Gebrselassie! A show of great sportsmanship. Hicham's left hand soon held Haile's right hand in the air. The winner's lap continued once Haile was congratulated by his

MOROCCAN SUCCESS; THE KADA WAY

agent Jos Hermens.

Next on the agenda for El Guerrouj was a mile event in Ghent on February 12. The competition for Hicham was zilch as he won by over five seconds while again demonstrating truly awesome form. When he stopped the clock at 3:48.45, he realized that he had run faster than he ever had outdoors. He had also broken a second world record, this one being previously held by Irishman Eamonn Coghlan who had run 3:49.78 in East Rutherford on February 27, 1983. Two races for two world records. This sort of standard was going to be hard to maintain.

To give a comparison to his Stuttgart run, Hicham went through the 1,500 metres in 3:33.01 in Ghent. It wasn't too much slower and the more solitary effort put this performance on almost the same level. There was no need to over race. His records proved what Abdelkader Kada already thought. That he was at a career best level. Hicham proved there was no need to race again until Paris.

The heats of the World Indoor Championships didn't arrive until March 7. Qualifying was effortless, winning his heat in a time of 3:40.18. The final didn't contain any other massive names in the sport and was really a much smaller event than the Stuttgart race a month before. This made a mockery of these 'World Championships', showing them up to be much less significant than its title suggested. It can be a complicated world at the elite levels of track and field. A European 'Grand Prix' meeting usually holds more meaning than the World Indoors. That's just the way it is. It doesn't help that the championship has the 60 metres as its blue ribbon distance rather than the 100 metres. Nor does it help that no distance exceeds 3,000 metres or that there is no steeplechase event. But what mattered on the 8th of March 1997, was that Hicham El Guerrouj was in the field for the 1,500 metres final. The sport should be privileged to have one of its current day greats to show off, in promotion of this somewhat lacklustre championship.

The Moroccan didn't let anyone down as he won his second

Greg Rowlerson

world indoor gold medal convincingly and with a decent time. His 3:35.31 was well clear of Rudiger Stenzel's 3:37.24. Hicham said, "I'm really happy. The race was very fast. I did not break the record, but after all, I took my revenge after my fall in Atlanta."

In some ways it was unfortunate that the outdoor season was nearly three months away. Hicham El Guerrouj appeared ready for world middle distance domination right now, but some more altitude training wouldn't go astray.

While he was heading home, Salah Hissou was making his final preparations for the World Cross Country Championships. The event was a month away when Hissou had raced in Italy on February 23. This was Hissou's lead up race and it was over the same 10.5 kms terrain that he had reigned on prior to his breakthrough performance in Budapest '94. The Moroccan continued his great form from 1996 and was victorious, finishing in a time of 30:57.80. Behind him was the usual possé of Kenyans, with Douglas Rono second, Ismael Kirui fourth and Shadrak Lagat fifth. Separating them was an Italian in third place named Vincenzo Modica. While not the greatest of fields, it had given Salah an opportunity to demonstrate his quality, which he grabbed with both hands. It showed his real rivals that he was ready for a battle royal in Turin. Ismael Kirui didn't look like being a real rival with his less than impressive run here showing that he hadn't managed to recover from a disappointing 1996.

Hissou went into the World Cross Country Championships on March 23 with Paul Tergat looking set to again be his main opposition. The Kenyan was gunning for three straight victories and it seemed like only this outstanding Moroccan could deny him. But after the Brussels hiding, Tergat was keen to turn the tables on Hissou. Fifteen thousand spectators would have the privilege to see one of the truly great World Cross Country races.

As usual, Kenya has the strongest team, and Tergat uses this to his advantage. Just before the 2 kms mark, Olympic 5,000 metres participant Thomas Nyariki takes off and quickly

MOROCCAN SUCCESS; THE KADA WAY

establishes a lead of about fifty metres. Hissou remains with the main pack as the crazy Kenyan continues on his merry way, going through 5 kms in 13:52. This frenetic pace would usually have been seen in the first half of a major championship 10,000 metres. Nyariki is doing it over cross country terrain.

Morocco has more depth in its team than ever before, but Salah Hissou is its only serious medal threat by the latter stages. Also in contention at this point is Mohammed Mourhit who is putting in a fine performance. The remaining runners in the main pack are Kenyans. They are happy to let their mate stay out in front for as long as he is able.

During the second half of the race Salah increases the pace and gradually reels in Nyariki. In doing so, he drops all the others bar Paul Tergat, who sits and waits, doing quite a good Haile Gebrselassie impression.

The second 5 kms is a little slower, and as Nyariki passes through in 28:04, the 10,000 metres world record holder and the world cross country champion are nearly upon him. Once caught, there is no respite. Hissou immediately gets rid of Nyariki and does his best to do the same to Tergat. This is his first big chance to win a major championship. He has never gotten so close. All he has to do is just drop one more Kenyan.

Hissou speeds through the 11 kms split in 30:46. At one stage it appears that he's prising open a small gap. Yes, Salah has put some metres on the reigning champion! Has Tergat been put into difficulty?

Alas, the great Kenyan recovers and into the final 400 metres is still with Hissou and looking very menacing indeed. It will be a sprint finish and we know that Salah Hissou rarely wins sprint finishes.

Despite his very best efforts, today will be no exception. Distance running unity was restored as Tergat won again, in 35:11. Hissou was right on his heels clocking 35:13, but he would have been slightly disappointed with his second placing, having to be content with a minor placing for the third consecutive year. This only made Salah more determined in his quest for victories at these 'major championships'.

Salah displayed his respect after the race to Tergat and his Kenyan teammates,"I can only congratulate Paul, because today he was the best. I had to try to keep up and once I had taken Nyariki there was only one tactic possible. Try to stick with Tergat, because one Kenyan is easier to beat than four," commented Hissou. Later Salah reflected on his big effort to drop him,"I don't know how he came back to me."

He could take some solace in the athletes he defeated. Nyariki held on for third in 35:20, with Paul Koech next in 35:23. Mourhit and Bernard Barmasai were next to finish with times of 35:35. Barmasai's performance demonstrated the many great runners that the world cross country attracted. Bernard was a future steeplechase world record holder, yet he'd mixed it with the best 10,000 metres runners. Who did he think he was, Henry Rono! Morocco had seven athletes finishing in the first twenty two which displayed its great depth. None of these were named Khalid Skah either. Kenya also had seven in the first twenty two but five of these were in the top seven. Kenya had again comfortably won the team competition but Morocco was the clear winner in the battle for second. Ethiopia's first runner was Habte Jifar in a distant eleventh place. He ran a time of 35:59. The time gaps were not so great this year.

Despite being beaten, this was one of Hissou's truly great performances. Looking back, he may have been defeated by the greatest cross country runner ever, yet he came close to beating him when he was in his prime. Later Paul Tergat would reflect on the battle in Turin. "It was the hardest of my three victories," he declared.

Not wanting to waste his good form, Hissou decided to compete in the 'Shoe Of Gold', a shorter 8.1 kms road race in Italy on the 31st of March. The race held some prestige, with Tergat being one of the former winners. The '94 victor was not

MOROCCAN SUCCESS; THE KADA WAY

present this time around and Salah had a pretty easy time of it competing against the local Italians. The Moroccan was out on his own from the early stages and won in 23:09. Second was Simone Zanon, running 23:34. The rest of the top ten were also Italians. They were honoured rather than upset to have the 10,000 metres world record holder take part in their local race. For a runner as distinguished as Salah, it was a relatively minor event.

Also currently going about his business in relative obscurity was Hicham El Guerrouj. In Ifrane he'd put the finishing touches on his magnificent form. After retaining his indoor title, Kada had added interval sessions at race pace to his star's training schedule throughout March and April, during the second preparation cycle. One of these sessions could be termed as step downs, with Hicham completing one 1,600 metres rep and then 'stepping down' to one 1,200, 800, 600 and finally a 400 metres surge. Recovery or rest periods started at sixty seconds but were reduced to just thirty seconds by the end. Later during the third preparation phase, Kada and El Guerrouj incorporated a 'race pace' session of 10 x 400 metres with 30 seconds recovery. These sprints were run at approximately 53-54 second lap pace. Emphasizing the group aspect of Kada training was the fact that Hicham received assistance in the form of a rabbit for the final 200 metres of each repetition.

It wasn't until May 11 (start of third preparation cycle) when the highest intensity running of official *speed work* was introduced. This is very much anaerobic threshold work. Going virtually all out, Hicham ran sessions incorporating 6 x 500 metres and 10 x 300 metres with rabbits used throughout. The Moroccan middle distance star only ran alone during the last 200 metres of each of his 500 metres reps.

It is interesting to note that the rabbits mixed up the pace during these short sprints, making it feel like a racing environment for their group leader. This was intended to improve reaction speed as well as fitness levels with the races themselves approaching quickly. It must be said though, that with a standard 300 metres rep being run in 36 seconds or faster, changes in pace were probably quite minimal.

Since more intense training was now included, the Moroccan's schedule also added 'warming-up' sessions, which lasted one hour. This was a combined thirty minutes of easy running and thirty minutes of general exercises. This sort of training is very much the exception rather than the rule in the Kada group, with high quality running being the staple ingredient of the coach's training diet.

Hissou's training closely resembled that of El Guerrouj's as he also warmed up for the European track season.

By the 31st of May, Hicham was chaffing at the bit to race. Hengelo was the venue for the start of his and many athletes' European season. None of his main rivals were on the start line for the 1,500 metres and after seeing Hicham explode into action, they were thankful that they weren't. The Moroccan's superiority was self explanatory from the following results:

Hicham El Guerrouj	3:29.51
Laban Rotich	3:32.91
Ali Hakimi	3:33.59
Rudiger Stenzel	3:33.81

To clock sub 3:30 straight away was truly incredible. Even Morceli had never run such a time for his first race in a campaign. It says a lot about Abdelkader Kada, in how well he prepares his athletes for the outdoor Grand Prix season. He had also managed to get Salah into incredible shape for his first sub thirteen performance in Rome last year without having a prior race as a warm up. El Guerrouj and Hissou had their fair share of admirers but now Kada was also starting to gain some serious recognition.

It was business as usual on June 2 as Hicham destroyed Rotich and another good field by over three seconds. It was basically ground hog day. Coming just two days after Hengelo, the Moroccan ran another impressive time of

MOROCCAN SUCCESS; THE KADA WAY

3:31.76. He obliterated an Algerian who recorded a thirteenth place finish, however this wasn't *the* Algerian. It was a nineteen year old named Ali Saidi-Sief.

Hicham continued his domination of his pet event when he raced in Rome's Golden Gala, the first big meeting of 1997 on June 5. Yet the increased relevance of the occasion didn't increase the quality of competition at all. The only concern for Kada may have been that this could all be a little too easy for his superstar. He was fortunate that the twenty two year old he trained remained level headed. The third convincing victory in a week didn't alter Hicham's persona or outlook in the slightest. For El Guerrouj, these races were mere stepping stones to achieving what he so badly wanted, the title of world champion. He didn't need reminding that Morceli, Cacho and Niyongabo had not raced him so far this year. For the record, El Guerrouj's time in the Rome 1,500 metres was 3:30.59, well clear of second placed Hakimi's 3:33.54.

There was another much more interesting distance race being held on this evening. Salah was making his season debut at the Olympic stadium where he held great memories.

Hissou had returned to Morocco following the cross country season for more training as his focus shifted to the track season. Being in the best form of his life, it seemed that winning a major championship was more attainable than ever. But now came his first big test. Could Hissou accomplish back to back wins at Rome in the 5,000 metres? It was the first of many races that would hopefully increase the Moroccan's belief still further, thus aiding his quest to win either the 5,000 metres or 10,000 metres track events at the World Championships later in Athens. This was belief that had been built up over time, in particular through his results in Brussels and Turin. However two events would soon contribute to destroying that belief.

It was exactly twelve months to the day since his breakthrough 12:50.80 performance. On this occasion the third fastest man in history would have to contend with the second fastest man in history. Daniel Komen was also racing and as Salah had discovered in Milan, he was going to be extremely hard to beat.

Komen's track season had already started, with Daniel having clocked a fast 13:03.51, in winning at Osaka, Japan, on May 10. Being the first big Grand Prix meeting of the season meant that there were many other athletes of quality for Hissou to contend with. As it turned out, he needn't have worried about them. Just the twenty one year old superstar.

There was lightning in the sky and plenty of fireworks on the track as the best from Morocco and Kenya careered away from the rest of the world class field, making them look like club runners. The rabbit, Kenya's David Kisang, took them to 3,000 metres in 7:49.2. He was closely followed by Komen, Hissou and a surprise Kenyan named Julius Kiptoo. Sorry, I forgot that the words 'surprise' and 'Kenyan' should never be included in the same sentence.

Once Kisang moved aside, the pace increased and Kiptoo was quickly disposed of. The final 2,000 metres were run at a scorching speed but neither Komen nor Hissou were showing weakness as both shared the pace. They remained together at the bell.

Salah took the lead with 300 metres to go, but was immediately repassed by the Kenyan who proceeded to storm away over the final 200 metres. It was another demonstration of Komen's greatness and Hissou's lack of basic leg speed. Salah could not have run much better, his performance being of a very high quality. But Komen was a freak and won convincingly, with a winning time of 12:48.98. He had run the last five laps in 5:00.58. What was just as remarkable was that this was becoming regulation for Daniel. This year the Kenyan selectors could *not* ignore him. He would be at the start line for the 5,000 metres heats in Athens. Having already experienced a similar defeat in last year's Grand Prix final, Hissou knew that it would be best to avoid Komen at these World Championships.

MOROCCAN SUCCESS; THE KADA WAY

But why should he worry really? He was the world record holder over 10,000 metres. He could win that. He had run faster than everyone else, even Gebrselassie. He could take that knowledge and confidence into his third championship track battle in David vs Goliath.

So for the second big race in 1997, Hissou had lost out to a great Kenyan runner, but he was pretty content with his run saying, "It was raining which made it tough conditions." Just like in Turin, the athletes and the time gaps behind Salah were significant. The top performers from the 5,000 metres were:

Daniel Komen	12:48.98
Salah Hissou	12:52.39
Ismail Sghyr	13:04.52
Assefa Mezgebu	13:05.48
Julius Kiptoo	13:06.12
Fita Bayissa	13:07.20
Mohammed Mourhit	13:07.83
Anacleto Jimenez	13:08.30
El Hassan Lahssini	13:10.47

It was nearly the length of the straight back to third placed Moroccan Ismail Sghyr. Amongst those struggling even further back in the field was Philip Mosima. It was disappointing to see him so far down in fourteenth position, completely out of form. Last year's Kenyan star wasn't anywhere close to being in the same shape now. Another notable was seventh placed athlete Mourhit who was now competing for Belgium. He cited "mutual incompatibility" with Aziz Daouda as a reason for his departure. Morocco had lost an excellent talent.

Hissou continued with the same early racing schedule from 1996, as he next raced over 1500 metres in Nuremberg on June 13. Unfortunately he was also unable to repeat his victory from '96 here. In fact he finished only fifth. The time wasn't great either, just 3:36.58, perhaps showing that for whatever reason, Hissou didn't have quite the form of a year ago. The winner ran 3:35.26 with the name of Driss Maazouzi hardly being a household name in track circles.

Feeling deflated from this result, Salah decided to keep away from the big Grand Prix races in an effort to acquire a win and a confidence boost. On the 18th of June he raced in Helsinki, moving back up to his more familiar distance of 5,000 metres. This wasn't a high quality field and Salah was an established star. Even if not at his best, he should destroy such a field.

Hissou did just that, winning rather easily, but the time of 13:07.16 wasn't anything to be particularly happy about. It certainly wouldn't scare Gebrselassie or Tergat. Second across the line was another top Kenyan, Julius Gitahi who finished well behind him in 13:11.76. It was a nice win but this race was further confirmation that Salah Hissou in June '97, wasn't up to the very high standards of Salah Hissou in June '96.

We were well into the track and field season as the Paris meeting arrived on the schedule on June 25. Back in action was Hicham El Guerrouj, aiming to record another emphatic victory at 1,500 metres. Despite his recent exploits, many expected this race to be a lot different. Noureddine Morceli was in attendance.

The Algerian had endured an interrupted year thus far, having been ill a while ago with anaemia. This had affected his training but he'd decided to compete in Hengelo anyway. He raced in the two miles that was won by Haile Gebrselassie in a world record time. The event was promoted as a match race between the two distance runners with the best pedigrees in the sport. A significant purse of $1 million was offered for any runner breaking the eight minute barrier. Haile just failed to break this, clocking 8:01.08, but he easily broke Noureddine who pulled out early. A lot had changed since Morceli defeated Gebrselassie so easily in Monaco almost three years before.

Paris was Morceli's first competition since Hengelo. It was interesting, some might say gutsy, that he was willing to take

MOROCCAN SUCCESS; THE KADA WAY

on El Guerrouj without proving his form elsewhere first. Perhaps he simply wanted to be in a fast race. If he lost, so be it. The Athens final was still six weeks away.

Anyone who considered themselves a serious fan of middle distance running took full notice of the results from this 1,500 metres in Paris. Hicham had won the pair's last encounter, but it hadn't been a truly run miler's race. The Moroccan made sure that there were no excuses for the Algerian this time.

When it got to crunch time, Morceli tried to go with El Guerrouj but wasn't fit enough to give him a good fight. This was nearly as decisive for Hicham as his previous three wins. He again showed that a slow time from him is a rarity as he stopped the clock at 3:31.87. To Noureddine's credit, his 3:33.98 was comfortably faster than the rest of the field. To be beaten by so much was indeed a setback in his plans to win a fourth consecutive world title but considering his problems, it wasn't a total disaster. He still had more races to run before Athens to rebuild his mindset for the toughest challenge of his illustrious career.

Abdelkader watched the race that some were quickly terming 'the takeover.' His boy was the best miler in the world. Nobody could dispute that. It was now up to them to win what they both felt they deserved.

Another takeover or take back was being declared on this same day. Haile Gebrselassie's major aim for 1997 wasn't the retention of his world title, which was a little surprising. He wanted something belonging to Salah.

The Olympic champion had changed his racing schedule a little this season and so far he had not tangled with Hissou. This was just as well for the Moroccan, as Haile was as dominant as ever. Deciding to avoid the World Cross Country, Gebrselassie instead competed in the indoor track season. The result of this was tremendous, as he won gold at the World Indoor Championships at 3,000 metres, clocking 7:34.71 on March 9. By the start of the outdoor track season he remained indestructible. As well as the 2 miles Hengelo world record, he'd performed well over 5,000 metres. On June 13 he ran 12:54.60 for 5,000 metres in Nuremberg. In that same meet, Hissou had avoided him and run his sluggish 1,500 metres time. Then on June 25, Haile won again at 5,000 metres. His 13:01.51 in Paris was faster than Salah had managed one week earlier in Helsinki. In France Gebrselassie stated, "The World Championships are not that important to me as I have already been to two and won two 10,000 metres titles. My one target for this reason is to get back my 10,000 metres world record."

Haile was non committal in regards to competing in Athens and would not make a decision on it until after he raced in Oslo over 10,000 metres in his world record attempt. His mindset appeared confident, like Hicham El Guerrouj's.

Salah Hissou's current mindset was more like Morceli's than his training partner's unshakeable belief. He decided to keep avoiding the really big players in the distance running scene as he raced in Lausanne on July the 2nd. The 5,000 metres race became a sit and kick affair, not a favourite of Salah's, but good practice nevertheless, for this was his second last race before the World Championships.

At his best, Hissou would have got rid of Paul Bitok before the bell. Here, he hadn't, and despite an improved sprint finish, he lost out to the Kenyan. Finishing second to Kenyans was becoming a habit for the Moroccan whose time of 13:11.84 was nothing to write home about. Bitok wasn't far ahead with his 13:11.31, and at least Salah had defeated Fita Bayissa, 13:12.68, Assefa Mezgebu, 13:13.43, and Philip Mosima, 13:13.74. The double world champion, Ismael Kirui was a shadow of his former self, finishing eleventh. Salah was better off than most others, but there was plenty of work to do if the 10,000 metres world record holder was going to challenge for gold in Athens. Specifically, this meant challenging Haile Gebrselassie.

July 4 was the significant date for the Ethiopian and also a Moroccan. All his previous victories in '97 were just a lead up to the Oslo meeting, and Haile's main ambition. Despite the

MOROCCAN SUCCESS; THE KADA WAY

season's form guide, Hissou still had a slight chance to win gold in Athens. He only had to look at the statistics. Over 10,000 metres, he had run faster than the world champion.

Well Salah *had* run faster than Haile. After the 4th of July the 10,000 metres world record was back with its rightful owner after the 'emperor' from Ethiopia clocked 26:31.32 to win easily in Oslo. Hissou's belief to win a major championship had just flown out the window.

Greg Rowlerson

Athens ~ Confirmation Of What We Already Knew

Haile's record was run at an even pace (13:16.74 and 13:15.58), similar to his Hengelo '95 performance. This differed to Salah's record that was strongly negative split. The Ethiopian's advantage was in being able to go out at a much faster speed for the first half of the race, but his disadvantage was a lack of competition. Brussels '96 was very much a race as well as a record attempt, so when Hissou surged emphatically over the last 3,000 metres, it was done to dismantle Paul Tergat and Paul Koech as much as it was to break the world record. In Oslo '97, the last of Gebrselassie's rabbits, Habte Jafar, was gone after 4,500 metres, leaving Haile to stay ahead of world record schedule on his own. To achieve this with so much running still to go was incredible, especially as he had hoped to be paced through to 6,000 metres.

Hissou hadn't just lost his world record. Gebrselassie had taken nearly seven seconds off Hissou's time, an enormous chunk. What was disheartening was to compare the strength of this performance to Hissou's current form. Gebrselassie's average pace was nearly as fast as Hissou's pace for his most recent 5,000 metres race in Lausanne. The Ethiopian was virtually running at the Moroccan's pace for double the distance! It was going to take an enormous turnaround for things to change in August.

Not needing to change things at all was Hicham El Guerrouj. He competed in the famous 'golden mile' in Bislett and for the first time, he challenged one of Noureddine Morceli's *serious* world records. The current world record stood at 3:44.39, having been recorded in Rieti on September 5, 1993.

Even in this era of amazing record breaking feats, the performance in Italy by Morceli stood out as something special. The previous record was a long standing one, with Britain's Steve Cram owning the mile's fastest ever time when he clocked 3:46.32 in Oslo on July 27, 1985. Eight years is a long time in athletics. Any world record is one to be admired

MOROCCAN SUCCESS; THE KADA WAY

but one that survives for such a lengthy period, especially so. That Morceli broke Cram's mark was not a surprise. Twice in the previous two weeks he had come within one second. Noureddine knew that he could get it. From his 1,500 metres times (faster than Cram) he knew that he should get it. He was very determined to do so and set the record straight, so to speak.

To lower the world record by nearly two seconds was an eyebrow raiser. Many felt that 3:46 would be quite a barrier, yet Noureddine had skipped that and gone straight under the 3:45 barrier. He had set an intimidating mark. For how long would this record last?

Nobody expected that the record would come under threat in 1997. Even come the day in question, the 4th of July, no one was thinking of world records in the mile. Perhaps this had something to do with the distraction of a more realistic record run! Even with the current day's best miler on the start line, few fireworks were anticipated.

Hicham El Guerrouj had other ideas. The weekly victories had become the norm and now he wanted the incredible times to go with them. It was high time he broke Said Aouita's national record of 3:46.76. Having this as a target almost led to something even more significant. The Oslo meeting was a remarkable one and not just for the 10,000 metres record. The results from the mile were:

Hicham El Guerrouj	3:44.90
Laban Rotich	3:47.65
John Kibowen	3:47.88
Venuste Niyongabo	3:48.26
Steve Holman	3:50.40
John Mayock	3:51.46
Robert Kiplagat-Anderson	3:52.39
Reyes Estevez	3:52.61

El Guerrouj had just recorded the second fastest mile ever! Whilst doing so he had eclipsed Aouita's Moroccan mark by an enormous 1.86 seconds. These statistics are impressive enough but consider the following. Kenya's Laban Rotich was nearly three seconds in arrears of Hicham yet prior to this race, only four men (Morceli, Cram, Aouita and Coe) had ever run faster than the time Rotich registered here. Kibowen's and Niyongabo's performances along with his own, were all first class but Hicham El Guerrouj had moved into a different stratosphere.

Finishing fourth in Oslo must have been a tough pill to swallow for the man from Burundi. Three years earlier he had won the same mile race with consummate ease while setting a national record. The next year he also won the 1,500 metres at Bislett in a fast race. Fast forward to 1997 and he was still breaking national records with his run here being superior to that of 1994. But the competition had improved, making it hard for Niyongabo to not feel his age, despite being only twenty three.

This was the first major race for him in the season. His first hit out wasn't until June 24 when he ran a 1:46.93 over 800 metres to register fourth place in Torino. On the 29th of June he followed this up with a 3:53.28 mile, as he defeated a B grade line up in Sheffield. Meeting Hicham in his rich vein of form was a lot to ask of Venuste from this limited preparation. At least he now knew where he stood and how much ground he needed to make up, if he wanted to contend for the 1,500 metres title in Athens. The problem was that he had just sliced more time off his own national record. How could he ever expect to improve much more in the future?

El Guerrouj had indeed ruined Niyongabo's career plan for a miler's domination. The situation was made pretty simple though. Either he raises his standard in order to compete with his Moroccan rival or he becomes a fully fledged 5,000 metres runner. That would mean racing against athletes with far greater pedigrees than those he faced in Atlanta.

Hicham still wasn't totally satisfied and wanted to keep racing. On July 7 he travelled to Stockholm with the aim of another fast 1,500 metres time the target. The same guys who had competed well in Oslo were in this race and the performances

MOROCCAN SUCCESS; THE KADA WAY

registered were of a similarly high level. At least Laban was a lot closer on this occasion. The top eight were:

Hicham El Guerrouj	3:29.30
Laban Rotich	3:30.13
John Kibowen	3:31.24
Robert Kiplagat Anderson	3:32.05
Venuste Niyongabo	3:32.14
Steve Holman	3:33.45
Martin Keino	3:33.94
Fermin Cacho	3:34.26

It was just 0.25 seconds off Hicham's own Moroccan record set in Brussels last year. El Guerrouj wasn't only going for a personal best but also Morceli's world record. That still seemed some way off. Another personal best for Laban Rotich was in fact his second straight race of breaking a Kenyan national record. It looked likely that the twenty eight year old would be El Guerrouj's biggest threat for the World Championships. He was proving that his surprisingly good 1996 season, which included a fourth place in Atlanta, was no fluke. Niyongabo should not be a factor for Abdelkader Kada any longer and Cacho's form was non existent. The pecking order was changing at a rapid rate.

Hicham El Guerrouj was clearly Morocco's current day distance running idol. In the 1980's there was no debate. It was always Said Aouita. Throughout the first half of the 1990's it was always Khalid Skah. As his reign drew to a close, a number of others threatened to take the crown. Now it was firmly on Kada's main man.

Kada's other man remained motivated to also scale even greater heights. Hissou wasn't completely shattered by Gebrselassie's time in Oslo. Salah and Abdelkader were even making plans to regain the 10,000 metres record. However firstly, there was the small matter of the Athens World Championships.

As was often the case, Hissou fine tuned his preparations for the 10,000 metres with a 3,000 metres race. The July 16 meeting in Nice wasn't a Golden League event, but it may as well have been. For many athletes it was their final race before the World Championships because it was the last Grand Prix meeting until then. It would be the best quality race that Salah had competed in since Rome.

The effect that the victories of 1996 had had on his confidence or some might say his ego levels, was fully demonstrated in the lead up to this big race. Not deterred by having his 10,000 metres record obliterated, Salah declared that he was now targeting Daniel Komen's 3,000 metres world record in France. He appeared to be serious in his intentions despite having a personal record that lagged almost ten seconds behind the Kenyan.

Salah Hissou could never run sub fifty nine second laps for seven and a half laps under any circumstances. There was no wind but the high humidity was going to make a really fast time even more of an impossibility. The Moroccan tried hard but simply winning was always going to be a great challenge in itself. The top finishers from the event were:

Khalid Boulami	7:30.99
Thomas Nyariki	7:31.49
Paul Bitok	7:31.78
Salah Hissou	7:32.13
Ismail Sghyr	7:32.27
Enrique Molina	7:33.15
Wilson Boit Kipketer	7:33.96
Mohammed Mourhit	7:34.49
Paul Koech	7:35.23

The fourth placing was a great disappointment, but it was a much improved run, clearly his best since that battle in Rome with Komen. Despite being well outside the world record, times were still fast and a Moroccan did win. No matter who it was, Moroccans were rarely allowing Kenyans to have all the distance running success these days.

Boulami had managed to out sprint Thomas Nyariki, whose 7:31.49 was a tremendous performance, considering his lack

MOROCCAN SUCCESS; THE KADA WAY

of basic speed. This Kenyan often got left behind when it came to a final kick.

About a year earlier, Salah Hissou had run a similar 3,000 metres in Oslo, just losing to Bitok. In Nice, Salah was averaging close to sixty second laps. It was an encouraging sign for Athens. The men ahead of him would be running in the 5,000 metres.

There was plenty going on in this meeting. El Guerrouj again lined up in the 1,500 metres and once again he believed that a world record was possible.

Did Hicham and Abdelkader fully understand just how good 3:27.37 was over 1,500 metres? Or did they both know just how incredibly good *he* was? This time, going for a time almost cost El Guerrouj on the line. Kada's boy had stormed through 1,200 metres in 2:48.53 that was nearly 1.5 seconds off world record pace, but fast enough to potentially break 3:29 for the first time. However in this race, Hicham fell off his tempo and was slightly fortunate to hold on. His winning time of 3:30.32 remained impressive, as was John Kibowen's 3:30.44. The Kenyans seemed in good shape for Athens.

There was another male distance runner competing in Nice who deserves attention. Apparently a 1,500 metres race wasn't enough for this program. But I suppose if the best miler of the last seven years says that he wants to race over the mile distance, it would be fair enough to try to accommodate him. So the mile was also held. Could Noureddine Morceli lay down the foundations for a fourth consecutive world championship title?

There were few reasons to expect a top performance in Nice. Upon losing to El Guerrouj in Paris, Morceli didn't spend any time licking his wounds. Two days later on the 27th of June he raced in a low grade meeting in Zagreb and got back on the winning list while clocking a 3:34.35, finishing nearly two seconds ahead of the rest. Then on June 29, he won at the rarely run distance of 2,000 metres with a 4:54.67. The good news was that Noureddine had won twice. The bad news was that both times recorded showed approximately seven second differentials compared to his world records. But that was seventeen days ago. Those days may have been precious in his attempts to recover his lost fitness. This mile race would provide some sort of an answer.

The Algerian responded with something that closely resembled his old self. As he held onto a strong pace throughout, a young Moroccan was surely keeping a close watch.

When the world champion stopped the clock at a highly respectable 3:48.64, everybody should have noticed. The 'king' had not abdicated just yet. While rediscovering some of his prowess, he'd also brought out the best in a young Kenyan. Noah Ngeny was only eighteen yet able to place second in a fantastic time of 3:50.41. What a talent! The Algerian had aimed for even faster given that the third lap split was 2:50.93 from the rabbit. Morceli said, "I am getting my health back. It is just the beginning of my season."

If Noureddine Morceli could improve so much in those seventeen days then how much more could he improve before Athens? The 1,500 metres heats were still eighteen days away. Forget the Kenyans. The world record holder was again the biggest obstacle in Hicham El Guerrouj's path to becoming world champion.

Abdelkader Kada had an incredibly hectic schedule as everything came about in the early part of the championships. Both the men's 1,500 metres and 10,000 metres heats were scheduled for the second day, which was Sunday the 3rd of August. First up was Hicham at 8:20 pm in the fourth and last qualifier. Salah was in the first of two heats, starting at 10:25 pm. El Guerrouj confidently stated, "I am going to erase the memories of Atlanta. I am going to be the new world champion and I am going to stay there for a long time."

Morceli won his first heat but not in any outstanding fashion. The time of 3:37.26 was reasonable, though he was only 0.49 seconds ahead of the seventh placed runner. The Algerian

MOROCCAN SUCCESS; THE KADA WAY

had recently endured another setback in his preparations when his younger brother Abdelkader tragically died after being hit by a car on July 26. Noureddine managed to spend his final hours with him as Abdelkader lapsed into a coma. Grieving with the family in the aftermath of his death meant that he only arrived in Athens the night before his first qualifier.

The second heat was slower and nearly resulted in a major upset, with Rotich only squeezing into the fifth and final qualifying position by three hundredths of a second. Reyes Estevez took the next heat in a fast 3:36.20. Now it was Hicham's turn. There was no need to do anything dramatic. Get out in front, pour on the power then relax if in a comfortable enough position to do so.

The race could not have gone better. The pace was nice and even for the first three laps. Then El Guerrouj was able to go up a gear and display his form. He was clearly superior to the rest, even though Fermin Cacho's finishing time of 3:37.16 wasn't far behind the Moroccan's 3:36.72. So far nothing had changed. Hicham remained the favourite for the gold medal.

As both he and Noureddine ran similar paced races, we can compare their finishing bursts in the heats. Both had the lead by the 1,200 metres split, a period of the race where an athlete is usually hitting his maximum speed. Morceli clocked 42.38 for the last 300 metres whereas El Guerrouj clocked 40.80. There were no medals up for grabs but this was a significant difference.

Now Kada waited for Salah's turn. He would face greater challenges than Hicham.

When August and the World Championships finally arrived, Salah Hissou incredibly had yet to compete against Haile Gebrselassie or Paul Tergat on the track in 1997. On August the 3rd the Moroccan was lined up in heat 1 of the 10,000 metres alongside the great Kenyan. He would have to wait another three days before coming face to face with the great Ethiopian.

The first heat was a little slow, with Domingos Castro running aggressively and taking it out in 28:07.04. The little power pack turned on the turbo over the final 3,000 metres and won by almost five seconds. Tergat and Hissou took it easy, finishing seventh and eighth respectively. Their times were only 28:13.98 and 28:15.09, well behind the diminutive Portuguese. Only the first eight finishers were automatic qualifiers but Salah was never in danger of missing out. He had almost five seconds up his sleeve on ninth placed Jose Ramos. By running conservatively Hissou had shown none of his cards before the final.

Heat 2 provided no great surprises. Gebrselassie was first over the line in 27:55.36. This was a pretty good time for a heat, yet it was over three seconds per lap slower than he had recently run in Oslo. In comparative terms, the Ethiopian was just jogging.

The semi finals of the 1,500 metres came the following day and Hicham El Guerrouj found himself in the first race at 8:35 pm. It was clearly the less competitive of the two line ups, but Abdelkader may have been slightly concerned when the German Rudiger Stenzel took the pack through 800 metres in a very sluggish 2:03.19. He needn't have worried. Hicham soon put himself at the front and made the long run for home. The third lap was a quick 56.02 and he carried the impressive speed through until he could relax, eventually registering a time of 3:38.92. The last 300 metres were raced in 39.71. It was an excellent kick down.

The second semi was almost as slow, with the first 800 metres covered in 2:02.05 with Estevez doing the leading. Slowly he began to wind it up, but he couldn't shake the field as Morceli passed him on the line, stopping the clock at 3:38.82. The first five athletes were separated by one tenth of a second!

Estevez ran the final 300 metres in 39.63 with Morceli and Cacho both finishing even faster. El Guerrouj was going to be contending with a number of runners who were capable of running a sub fifty-three second last lap if they were given a

MOROCCAN SUCCESS; THE KADA WAY

slow enough race early on. It was up to the Moroccan to make the final more of a test of strength than a test of speed.

Clearly Hicham El Guerrouj was the number one miler in the world and everyone's pick to prevail in his Athens final. But perhaps the Moroccan camp was a little cocky. If nothing else, Aziz Daouda's comments on August the 5th showed no respect for the previous 'king' of the mile.

"He's younger and he's stronger and he's faster," said Aziz in reference to Hicham vs Noureddine. "If he had not fallen in Atlanta, he would have won by 25 metres."

Yes, he was stronger and faster. Now. A year ago it was borderline as to who was the best. Yet in hindsight, it wasn't only Daouda who was trying to rewrite history. Others now wrote articles talking of how the Moroccan 'favourite' Hicham El Guerrouj, had been denied Atlanta gold because of his fall. Opinions had changed about who should have won during the time since then because the Moroccan had indeed knocked the Algerian from his lofty perch. But Hicham was improving all the time while Noureddine was going backwards. It was in Atlanta when the lines were about to cross over. Twenty five metres is almost 3.5 seconds at the end of a 1,500 metres race. According to Daouda, Hicham should defeat his rival by even more than that tomorrow, given that he is at least as strong this season and that Noureddine is discernibly weaker. No, I don't think so!

I will put forward the case for Morceli as the rightful 1,500 metres champion in Atlanta.

There were suggestions that Morceli avoided El Guerrouj during 1996 but these hold little substance. Certainly he would do so plenty of times in the future but prior to Atlanta, it was a different story. Morceli competed in earlier European outdoor meetings in Lille, Saint-Denis, Rome and Moscow. In comparison El Guerrouj competed in Seville and Duisburg. All these races were at 1,500 metres and so far it was Morceli who led with a 3:30.93 in Rome, compared to a 3:32.94 for El Guerrouj in Seville. Nothing really to be scared of there.

Remember that their last contest was won by Morceli with a comprehensive 3.50 second margin in a mile at Zurich.

If Morceli was avoiding anyone at this stage it was Niyongabo. Entering the '96 season the Burundi runner was rated more highly than the Moroccan and most expected him to be the Algerian's major opposition in Atlanta. Both Noureddine and Venuste refused to race each other in Lille and so the organisers conducted two separate 1,500 metres races. How ridiculous!

In the next racing phase again it was the Algerian who competed at the bigger meets. He won in Paris, Lausanne and the massive meeting of Oslo, while El Guerrouj won in Hechtel and Stockholm. His Hechtel win came only two days after Oslo so clearly we can say that Hicham avoided Noureddine here. That is the only reason why he would not have run at the Bislett Games. Morceli edged him out on best times with his 3:29.50 in Paris but for the first time we can say that El Guerrouj possibly intimidated him, as a result of his 3:29.59 performance in Stockholm.

The final European Grand Prix meeting before Atlanta was in Nice and both athletes were in attendance, however they did not race each other. We can accuse Morceli of running scared here, since El Guerrouj won the 1,500 metres while Morceli won the rarely contested 2,000 metres. Form wise there was nothing to separate them though. Hicham ran 3:30.61, defeating Venuste Niyongabo by 1.04 seconds. Noureddine ran 4:49.55, defeating the lesser competition, led by Martin Keino, by 4.29 seconds. The Moroccan was 3.24 seconds off the world record while the Algerian (the 2,000 metres world record is slightly weaker) was 1.67 seconds off his world record. On this day in France, it was the third fastest performance of all time at the distance.

The Algerian's form was hardly waning too much. His earlier win in Paris was in a time that only Said Aouita (and himself) had ever bettered.

Both men went to America with unblemished 1996 seasons.

MOROCCAN SUCCESS; THE KADA WAY

On form it was impossible to separate them, though Morceli's almost four year unbeaten run from distances ranging from 1,000 metres to 5,000 metres gave him the slight nod from most. Everyone was in agreement that we were set for a magnificent confrontation. Nobody was talking of twenty five metres victory margins! I will try to imagine the outcome of that final lap in Atlanta, with all the runners remaining on their feet.

Morceli leads at the bell. El Guerrouj could not quite pass him approaching the turn, so has to relinquish the advantage to the world champion. The Algerian at least leads to the 300 metres mark. Fermin Cacho is close to the duo, not having had to hurdle the fallen Moroccan and he sits close to Hicham. Morceli is running at close to fifty two second lap speed on the back straight (after having run the first bend in 12.84 and the first 200 metres in 25.90 or 51.80 pace). There is no way that anyone is going by him. It would take an enormous burst to get by, so Hicham and Fermin continue to sit. They won't get past on the final curve either so the question is whether they can do so in the home straight. It would be like Lagat trying to get by El Guerrouj eight years later. I think that the Moroccan will challenge. He moves out, but can he get past?

In the *real* race Morceli slowed a lot in the final twenty five metres which resulted in a 53.51 second last lap. That would not be good enough to win in this scenario but he would have pushed all the way under this most intense of pressure and I sense just hold on. He probably could have run a sub fifty three lap if required. It might have been less than a tenth of a second difference but the Moroccan has only just started to dominate and so deep down thinks that he should get another good Olympic winning opportunity. The Algerian on the other hand has dominated for five plus years and should know that he's unlikely to get another good Olympic winning chance. So it is Morceli, by a whisker. Hypothetically of course. Cacho is not too far in arrears and we all talk about what a classic race it was, as opposed to simply pondering over what might have been.

When Abdelkader Kada woke on the morning of Wednesday, August the 6th, 1997, he could be forgiven for being a little nervous. This was the biggest day in his coaching career to date, perhaps the biggest he would ever encounter. Within the space of a single hour his two magnificent students would attempt to become the best in the world. They both had the pedigree required to be amongst the fancied runners. Now it was up to them.

This wasn't only a big occasion for Abdelkader Kada but for Moroccan men's athletics in general. It was a massive night of distance running with the steeplechase final being run before the other events. There were three Moroccans in the twelve men final, which was a tremendous achievement. This emphasized that Morocco was now the second best nation in the world at this event.

Both Brahim Boulami and Elarbi Khattabi struggled to tenth and eleventh place finishes but Hicham Bouaouiche battled on gamely and reaped the rewards of fifth place. His time of 8:14.04 was eight seconds behind the three Kenyans who swept the medals but this was a slightly unfair reflection, as Hicham had stayed in contact until the final 600 metres. If Morocco could continue to progress in this fashion then perhaps it might have someone capable of winning a steeplechase medal in the not too distant future. Abdelkader Kada was possibly thinking similar thoughts as he watched this final take place. Moses Kiptanui just failed in his quest for a fourth consecutive world title, as he won the silver medal behind Wilson Boit Kipketer.

The clock was ticking ever so closer toward 8:15 pm, Hicham El Guerrouj's moment of truth. He had not lost a proper race for almost two years. Logic said that he should win if he made the race suit him. Morceli was the big threat, though Cacho couldn't be totally discounted with his proven record in major championships. Rotich also had good form this season. They were the three men for Kada and El Guerrouj to keep an eye on. Kibowen hadn't qualified, nor had Hicham's teammates Maazouzi and Seddiki. Only Spain had two runners in the final so team tactics weren't expected to play a part. How slow

MOROCCAN SUCCESS; THE KADA WAY

was El Guerrouj willing to allow the race to be run?

Noureddine Morceli had the accolades going into the Athens final. Hicham El Guerrouj had the form. Would the champion hold onto his crown or would there be an emphatic takeover?

The final is a typically slow one early, but El Guerrouj places himself perfectly on the outside of the German Stenzel who leads through 400 metres in 61.08. Robert De Castella comments on Morceli and El Guerrouj, "The big question is can this young Moroccan unseat Morceli from the throne that he's had now for five or six years? Morceli has completely dominated this event winning world championships, Olympic Games and world records, but there is a bit of a question mark. Over the last couple of years he has been vulnerable, and the person he's been vulnerable to, is in second place there."

Estevez soon goes to the front and he takes them to 800 metres in 2:02.04. Suddenly El Guerrouj tears to the front with the clear intention of taking his eleven opponents past their pain threshold. There is no better way to do this than to run the third lap at an unbelievable pace.

With 600 metres to go the pressure is being firmly applied. Nobody in recent times would ever take a major championship 1,500 metres final on so far out. Morceli usually went at the bell. Now he is forced to chase and go close to his red zone earlier than he wants. Initially Noureddine is able to follow the Moroccan into second place. These are good tactics from the Algerian.

Cacho has also passed Estevez to move to third and with 500 metres to go we have a real race on our hands. Then boom! El Guerrouj puts a couple of metres on Morceli in no time. The advantage of youthful legs. Does the world champion really have the necessary speed anymore?

Hicham hits the bell in 2:43.35, though he certainly hasn't broken his rival yet as Morceli clings on, appearing to remain very much in the contest.

Around the bend and there is no let up, yet still no discernible gap shows between the two great milers. The split comes up at 1,200 metres and it's no surprise that Hicham is decimating the rest of the field. The clock says 2:55.63, meaning that he's run the third lap in quicker than 53.59!

At this point he has just a metre on Noureddine, but Hicham continues to pour it on and draws away on the back straight. It is here where the Moroccan wins the race, to the novice viewer anyway. He increases his lead substantially and it's clear that he is too strong for the Algerian.

Yet it wasn't the final 300 metres that won El Guerrouj the race. It was the last 600 metres. Even Morceli at his best would have struggled to run such a strong final one and a half laps. His strength lay more in the final lap where he arguably possessed more explosive speed than El Guerrouj. A 53.59 lap is pretty exceptional for the last 400 metres but Hicham did this from 700-300 metres remaining. There is a huge difference in this style of running. The Moroccan did not take the lead and increase the pace until the 900 metres point, so from the 900 to the 1,300 metres juncture he must have run a 400 metres sectional of well under fifty three seconds, which is phenomenal. This was when the damage was done. He continued to hold that pace to the end.

By the top of the bend it became apparent that he definitely had Morceli's measure as a margin of at least four metres had opened up. Cacho was coming home strongly and passed the Algerian easily on the final straight but kept looking back as he often does. The gold was never an option. The Moroccan had won comprehensively. It was how Hicham deserved to win. The way the victory was constructed was also rather fitting. Achieved on the back of a long run for the line, where once he went for it there was no looking back. Hicham El Guerrouj was now officially the world champion!

He immediately laid his knees and head on the track. Kada was quickly on the scene to hand him a Moroccan flag and congratulate him. El Guerrouj ran into the crowd to share the jubilation with some of his supporters.

MOROCCAN SUCCESS; THE KADA WAY

Abdelkader could rejoice in this magical moment. The feeling for them both was one of relief as much as happiness following the Atlanta result. A great weight of a nation's expectations had been lifted from their shoulders. The results of the 1,500 metres final were:

Hicham El Guerrouj	3:35.83
Fermin Cacho	3:36.63
Reyes Estevez	3:37.26
Noureddine Morceli	3:37.37
Ali Hakimi	3:37.51
Mohamed Suleiman	3:37.53
Graham Hood	3:37.55
Robert Anderson	3:37.66
John Mayock	3:38.67
Rudiger Stenzel	3:38.82
Laban Rotich	3:41.27
Nadir Bosch	3:48.35

Morceli slowed badly over the final fifty metres. Unable to fight on with his title gone, he gave up the bronze medal to the fast finishing Estevez in the last few strides. Rotich was a disappointment. Cacho again proved his great capacity to perform up to his best under pressure.

Hicham eased off as he closed in on the finish. The time gap to Fermin could have been greater. Not once did the Spaniard look like threatening. It was Morceli who challenged the Moroccan but the longer you are on top, the harder it often is to stay there. Unless there was a dramatic change of events Noureddine was a spent force at this distance.

Finally on the subject of the changing of the guard, it was remarkable to look at the margin that Morceli enjoyed over El Guerrouj in Gothenburg and compare it to the reversal of what transpired in Athens. In 1995 it was 1.55 seconds to Noureddine. In 1997 it was 1.54 seconds to Hicham. Both eased up late in their victories. This further emphasised how impossible it was to declare a definite winner if a fair fight had ensued in Atlanta.

El Guerrouj described the final, "It was a classic example of a sit and kick race. My surge was devastating and after that it was just a matter of controlling the race. I am very proud to have won my first major outdoor title. It makes up for what happened at Atlanta. I am very sorry for Morceli. For me today is historic. It's the beginning of a long time on top."

Hicham could now go off and celebrate his ascension to the throne but his coach could do nothing of the sort. The men's 10,000 metres event was about to start at 8:35 pm. What could Salah Hissou accomplish against the likes of Haile Gebrselassie and Paul Tergat?

Despite all that had occurred, very little had actually changed since Atlanta as the usual suspects lined up for the 10,000 metres final in Athens. Skah was gone. In his place were youngsters named Said Berioui and Zitouna Abderrahim who were not in his same class. Just like in Atlanta, Hissou was Morocco's only hope. Joining Tergat was Koech, the men who Hissou had successfully defeated on that marvellous night in Brussels. The third Kenyan was Dominic Kirui, who appeared to be a strange selection.

He had been a very good cross country competitor, where at the world titles he'd placed seventh in 1992, second in 1993 and twelfth in 1994. But the last three years he had not made the Kenyan teams and his pedigree on the track was virtually non existent. Kirui had never broken 27:30 for 10,000 metres, nor even 13:30 for 5,000 metres. Surely there was another Kenyan who could have a greater impact on a world championship final. Joseph Kimani? Josephat Machuka? Luke Kipkosgei?

In this race Dominic Kirui was dropped early and finished twelfth. Someone in high power must have liked him a great deal!

Gebrselassie's teammates were Assefa Mezgebu and Habte Jifar. The 'Belgium' athlete Mohammed Mourhit looked impressive in his heat but was a late withdrawal from the final. The race as always was enthralling and kept everyone

MOROCCAN SUCCESS; THE KADA WAY

guessing until very late. What everyone did know was that this was going to be one hell of a battle.

Twenty one year old Jifar had run personal records of 13:12.88 and 27:30.26 this season, so he expected to be competitive. But more was expected from his even younger teammate, Mezgebu. Despite having just turned nineteen, Assefa had already participated in a World Championships final when he placed fourteenth in Gothenburg. In 1996 he dominated the World Junior Championships by winning the 5,000 and 10,000 metres events. In both races he out kicked Kenyan David Chelule. It was a good sign that he'd repeated the feats of Gebrselassie and Komen. But Athens was his sternest test so far.

'Let's get ready to rumble' is what the stadium announcer could have yelled just prior to 'on your marks'. But in contrast to an angry looking boxer stood the smiling assassin from Ethiopia. Under this picture of youthful exuberance you could put the title, 'The Joy Of Running'. In this moment it was easy to see that Gebrselassie loved what he did and while this was a massive race you could see that he was not nervous. It was as if he already knew what was in store. Perhaps his rivals also knew, for there were no other smiles as bright on the start line.

The race was a slightly slower one than Gothenburg and Atlanta but its quality was pretty much the same. It still had distance runners of the highest pedigree. Just like in the previous two championships it would come down to six survivors in the second half of the race.

Initially Berioui took up the front running. Were these Moroccan team tactics? He led the pack through 2,000 metres in 5:39.99, pretty slow really. Yet he wasn't able to help Hissou anymore and drifted back, eventually running a disappointing time of 29:22.05. Many of the runners ran much slower in the final than they had in their heat. For many, the heat was the final and trying to run at their optimum level again only three days later was a lot to ask. Only the really top Africans could run a twenty eight minute 10,000 metres and have something left in the tank to go faster with such a short recovery time. Men who have run sub twenty seven minutes for example. There were only four of these guys in the field. They were Koech, Tergat, Hissou and Gebrselassie. Even such elite athletes as these can find the championship program energy sapping. Salah describes the difficulties of backing up, "If the IAAF system that was used later (just a 10,000 final with no heat) were in place in the mid '90's, then I would have run my 10,000 metres championship finals more aggressively."

Despite some fatigue, Salah Hissou is showing some authority for the first time in a major championships track race, even though we do not think that he has quite the same form as a year ago. Just before the 4,000 metres split he is checked by Jifar and is clearly unhappy. The Ethiopian is crowding him for room at a time of the race when it's important for the Moroccan to relax. Relax at 2:46 km pace? These athletes are fit! So he spits, rounds the field and then surges for 200 metres. The group is quickly decimated and only Koech, Gebrselassie and Tergat are able to move easily with the Moroccan. Perhaps realising that he's let his emotions get the better of him, Salah steps off the pressure, allowing Koech to carry it on for the remainder of the lap. Many of the athletes find the 62.35 second lap too fast as the field breaks down to an elite group. But the pace slows again and halfway is reached in 13:58.79 with nobody too keen to set a tempo. Little known Australian Darren Wilson (among others) manages to tack back on as the slower laps tick over: 69.28, 70.44, 69.10. The elite athletes are just playing games. On the fifteenth lap Kirui surges, though only on the back straight. Gebrselassie moves alongside with a ridiculously graceful looking ease, then peers at him almost in disdain, in a 'is that all you've got?' manner. The answer to that question proved to be 'yes!'

There are around twelve athletes still in contention as the pack approaches 6,000 metres, which they reach in 16:49.31, that last km having been covered in 2:50.52. Unfortunately for some, a familiar face is back at the front.

MOROCCAN SUCCESS; THE KADA WAY

Hissou jumps out of the pack with real purpose in a 'let's end this jogging' type mode. It's time to get serious. Again it is just another half lap effort but on this occasion Koech carries on with the pace making for good. After just this single 63.81 lap the group is down to eight. A 63.43 lap then disposes of the Spaniard Julio Rey and the Kenyan continues the torture, completing the seventh km in 2:38.61, which is 26:26, or sub world record pace! So how can anybody kick down now?

The Moroccans weren't the only ones perplexed as to how to defeat Gebrselassie on the track. The mental impact that Haile had on his opponents even lessened the confidence of the Kenyans, explained one of their coaches earlier. "We have no idea how to beat him. What you'd have to do is chop both his arms and his legs off."

Haile appears to be having no problems as he clips the heels of Paul Koech while the others look to be straining to remain in contact. The following laps are 64.13 and 64.50, still very fast, as Jifar can hang on no longer, leaving six survivors with six laps to go. Finally there is some brief respite as the twentieth lap is run in 65.60, although the eighth km is still clocked at 2:42.86, or about 27:09 pace.

The pack of six contains Hissou, Koech, Tergat, Gebrselassie, Mezgebu and Castro. Yes Castro, the little man who won his heat is still up there and competing with the best from Africa. Domingos Castro from Portugal is quite a remarkable runner whose top achievements go all the way back to the '88 Seoul Olympics when he placed fourth in the 5,000 metres final. By 1997 he was a marathon man, the fastest in the world at the great endurance event. He had therefore been expected to run the marathon at these World Championships. Yet here he is mixing it with the best in the 10,000 metres, with the truly elite men of long distance running. It is extraordinary to see. While he never stands a serious chance of victory, it is enthralling to see him battle to stay up there (he looks like he is sprinting to keep up, which in truth he probably is). The race is shaping up like the Atlanta final with Paul Koech doing the hard work. We wait for Paul Tergat to make his move.

But it's hard, even for the best to make a major decisive move in a 10,000 metres final when the laps they are now running are consistently around sixty four and sixty five seconds. World record pace is around sixty threes and sixty fours, so you can imagine how hard it must be to try to do a big kick down when already running at this sort of speed. Tergat sits in his customary position at the back of the pack waiting, or perhaps he's barely hanging on.

Bruce McAvaney describes what we are all thinking, "Well, what can Tergat do in third place or Salah because Koech is obviously the worker for the Kenyans. He's done the work, and you'd think that he's sacrificed himself for Tergat."

It's going to be up to Tergat or Hissou to do something, as Koech is doing all the work and Mezgebu and Castro aren't good enough. Do the Kenyan or Moroccan have anything left? Is Koech setting too fast a pace to kick down from?

Tergat has not replicated his move from Atlanta and the fifth last lap is timed at 66.36. Hissou looks good in third and Tergat appears to be struggling momentarily. Ahead of Salah is Haile.

Bruce McAvaney: "Gebrselassie sits. He's like a machine. How do you break him?"

Rob De Castella: "Well I don't know that you can, I mean look at the rhythm. He's just cruising along very comfortably. Compare it to every other runner in the group there. You can see the ease. He's actually talked about moving up to the marathon. God knows what he'll do to the marathon world record, if he maintains the sort of tradition he's set over the 5,000, 10,000 metres."

Koech has gone again, with that lap a 63.77 at 1,200 metres remaining. Surely Salah is unable to kick down from sub 26:40 speed in warm conditions. But he is running smoothly and is nicely tucked in behind the Ethiopian. They slow on the back straight and Salah takes his opportunity to move alongside Haile. This is the moment to go for it if he wants

MOROCCAN SUCCESS; THE KADA WAY

any shot at the gold. However his five opponents would sit on him so he runs the risk of being run over the top, but there is just a km to go. If Salah has anything left, this is the time to show it.

Perhaps this is what Kada is thinking, but Hissou continues to wait. That ninth km is 2:42.71, again too fast to realistically surge off. With 900 metres left Salah looks imposing, again moving onto Haile's shoulder. With two to go he tries to box him in, when really he should have gone to the lead, increased the tempo, thus adding pressure to the opposition.

That lap of 66.57, is much slower. Salah now moves around Haile. 'Go past Koech and go for it!' But go he doesn't and Gebrselassie quickly moves back around him into second spot. The chance is gone. In last year's Brussels form, surely he would have kicked right there and split the pack. It still would not have been enough to defeat Haile but it was always great to try. Here he gave the Ethiopian the opportunity to seize the initiative.

Hissou sits on Gebrselassie who sits on Koech as the six athletes enter the back straight for the second last time. The tension continues to build as Rob De Castella greatly puts it, "Surely something's going to happen fairly soon. You feel as though the tension is building and building, surely mounting on these runners. Gebrselassie is looking, he's waiting. He's looking up at the big screen to see if anything's happening behind him. He knows that Tergat is there. Here he goes. Look at this. Watch this acceleration."

Haile knows what to do. When he looks at his feet with about 570 metres to go, it is all over.

Within 100 metres of kicking, Gebrselassie has gained about ten metres on Hissou who isn't particularly quick to move around Koech. Tergat, starting further back has missed the boat, not passing the Moroccan until the bell, by which time Gebrselassie has the race in his pocket, with a lead of approximately fifteen metres.

Once again at the finish, Salah Hissou does not have the kick. Having gone past him with 450 metres to go, Tergat lengthens away from Hissou in the last lap, even making an impression on Gebrselassie's lead. Yet it is clear that even as he pulls away from the Moroccan, Tergat's chance for gold is well and truly gone. He flies home over the last 200 metres but can never get close enough to have a crack at Gebrselassie who has won yet again. Hissou struggles home yet hangs on for the bronze medal ahead of Koech who has run a great race. The final results were:

Haile Gebrselassie	27:24.58
Paul Tergat	27:25.62
Salah Hissou	27:28.67
Paul Koech	27:30.39
Assefa Mezgebu	27:32.48
Domingos Castro	27:36.52
Habte Jifar	28:00.29
Julio Rey	28:07.06
Stefano Baldini	28:11.97
Darren Wilson	28:20.16
Kamiel Maase	28:23.20
Dominic Kirui	28:28.13
Abderrahim Zitouna	28:29.09
Hendrick Ramaala	28:33.48
Tendai Chimusasa	28:55.29
Carsten Eich	28:59.34
Said Berioui	29:22.05
Jose Ramos	29:49.00

The final km was run in 2:31.09 as the same three athletes repeated the medals from Atlanta. Mezgebu was the big improver in fifth, trailed in by a determined but outclassed Castro. In less than 600 metres Domingos had lost nearly twelve seconds to Haile. For Hissou it was another highly respectable performance in a major championship, but he had hit a brick wall in his running career. His next career moves would be vital. Try as he might, he just could not match the finishing speeds of Haile Gebrselassie and Paul Tergat at the end of a championship 10,000 metres.

MOROCCAN SUCCESS; THE KADA WAY

I say that Hissou struggled home and did not have a kick in the last lap in Athens but this needs to be put into perspective. Gebrselassie ran the final 600 metres in about 1:24. His official split for the final lap was 55.87, although he was only holding his pace from his initial acceleration at best, not increasing it. Therefore the previous 200 metres must have been run in approximately twenty eight seconds. So 'struggling home,' Salah ran a final 600 metres of around 1:28 with a last lap of probably sub fifty eight. This, after averaging just under sixty seven's for the first half and just over sixty five's for the second half, prior to the twenty fifth lap. Therefore to sprint home for well inside a sixty second split after those laps is actually quite a kick down. It's just that in comparison to Gebrselassie and often Tergat, he was lacking when it came to the finishing kick. Even if it was hard to see, Salah had definitely made big improvements on his finishing speed in the two years since Gothenburg.

Paul Tergat's run was another top one. In fact, his last lap was faster than Gebrselassie's, probably sub fifty five, but his strong finish provided more questions than answers. Just why didn't he go earlier? His post race comments provided some insight.

"I have the silver but it is never easy to run in this sort of company. This is the first time for me at these championships and so it is a great moment for me."

It was clear that he was satisfied with finishing second. There was nothing wrong with this way of thinking but it fully explained the impact that Gebrselassie had on him and everyone he raced against. To run for the gold medal by going hard from a long way out could put his silver medal at risk. Atlanta had showed that this all out effort didn't necessarily work in the best possible circumstances anyway.

Rob De Castella attempts to explain the difficulties of making the long run for home and why Tergat didn't go earlier, "Maybe it's just the change in pace, the variation in pace. It takes its toll on all the runners. Often you just don't feel comfortable. You just don't feel able to maintain the rhythm and that lack of confidence. It's a hard run a long run for home. You've really got to be feeling strong and confident to put it to someone of this calibre."

The Australian was impressed with Salah's run, "A bit of a surprise really for Hissou to come up and perform so well. There was really a bit of a question mark this year. He hadn't really performed much on the European circuit but here in Athens, he's demonstrated that he really is a true champion."

Not a bad compliment from a former world champion!

The 5,000 metres contest in Athens was all about incredible threshold running rather than a finishing kick. It was a race much better suited to Hissou's style but the man who made it happen had already proved that he was too good for the Moroccan. Unlike in Gothenburg and Atlanta, Salah's chances of winning the 5,000 metres here would have been very slim. But slim is better than none, as the 10,000 metres had again proven to be. One athlete who was a great front runner was Ismael Kirui. A lot can happen in eighteen months to a Kenyan distance runner. In March '96 he finished third in the World Cross Country, beating a certain Haile Gebrselassie. In August '97 the double world champion was unable to qualify for the Athens 5,000 metres final. Injuries had slightly restricted him but the world's improvement was the bigger reason for Ismael no longer being competitive. Sub 12:50 was now the standard for amazing times as opposed to sub 13 which Kirui had never broken anyway.

It was Daniel Komen who put on a breathtaking display of endurance running in the middle stages. He did so in only 48 percent humidity but 29 degree heat. Dieter Baumann and Thomas Nyariki had kicked it down, running sixty and sixty one second laps. In the process they had destroyed the vast majority of the field. But Komen decided that this wasn't enough. He proceeded to peel off consecutive fifty eight second laps! Nobody had seen something like this in a major championship. Bruce McAvaney described it best when he posed the question, "How can you put such a space, in such a field, so quickly?" With a km to go he was about thirty

MOROCCAN SUCCESS; THE KADA WAY

metres ahead of Nyariki and Khalid Boulami. He tired slightly which was understandable after his mid race heroics but still held on to win, not by much, but comfortably enough. From Hissou's perspective the only way that he would have been a chance is if he had run the race of his life. At his absolute best and running tremendously tactically he might have been able to put it to Komen. After everyone had been destroyed in the middle laps, nobody in that field had the ability to step it up and attempt to bring Komen back. Perhaps if Hissou had sat with Nyariki and Boulami and then made a solo pursuit with three laps to go, things could have been interesting. For all the fast middle laps, the winning time was only average at 13:07.38. Realistically, Komen was on fire and Hissou wasn't quite in the same league. Once again this was a 5,000 metres race that was run for strength runners, not speed ones. Salah might have relished it, you never know. At this stage it remained unclear what Hissou's best distance was. From a major championship's perspective he had yet to give the 5,000 metres a crack.

In hindsight it must be said that Hissou's form was not what it had been in '96 and he would have stood next to no chance of winning the 5,000 metres in Athens. Upon further inspection this becomes even more apparent. The last 3,000 metres were run in 7:34.35. Komen took things pretty easily for the fourth km, running it in 2:28.34. This is actually being rather generous to this split, as Daniel was giving his teammate Thomas a bit of a head start at the 3 kms time check. His splits for the laps when he did the damage were 56.80 and 58.38! Considering the speed was already on in earnest before Komen went for it, he definitely ran a sub four minute mile during the toughest segment of the final (even allowing for the extra nine metres). So yes, Salah Hissou would have needed to run the race of his life to have defeated Komen. It's most likely that he would have been fighting for the minor medals at best.

Komen said post race, "I have based my running on the pace and past feats of the great Kip Keino and Moses Kiptanui. This aspect of my training and racing is very crucial to how I, and the rest of Kenyan runners perform. Obviously, it was the two laps under 60 seconds which were the decisive moments."

Kada could feel doubly proud that he was coaching world championship gold and bronze medallists. Athens may have been over but the 1997 track and field season was anything but. Zurich was arguably the biggest single day of athletics all year and this was the first meeting post Greece. Hissou had never raced here before and this season would be no different. Brussels was again his focus and he had only sixteen days to recuperate before he returned to the Van Damn Memorial on August 22. Zurich held its meeting on the 13th, which didn't suit Salah's preparation. In any case Switzerland witnessed its usual high quality distance running, and then some.

Hicham El Guerrouj went straight back into racing. It felt fantastic to enter a race as the world champion, a feeling that he and Kada hoped they would become accustomed to. The stadium was packed with approximately 25,000 people for this most amazing of athletics nights. Most had purchased their tickets six months in advance. It was always a privilege to be here. Just a little more so in 1997.

The field for the 1,500 metres was a stronger one than the Athens final. Venuste Niyongabo was back, with Laban Rotich the only noticeable absentee. The race was incredibly fast throughout and the competition was fierce. It was the highest standard race in the history of the event.

The first lap is clocked in 53.55, but the leading rabbit is about ten metres up on Hicham who lies fourth. The pacesetter remains well in front, reaching 800 metres in 1:50.03. El Guerrouj probably passes through in 1:52 plus. With 500 metres to go only one rabbit is left ahead of the Moroccan while Morceli is going well in third. He is right with Hicham at the bell.

The 1,200 metres split is 2:48.24 and from here it is up to El Guerrouj to push all the way to the line. With 250 metres to run the Algerian is hanging with him. Just trailing him are

MOROCCAN SUCCESS; THE KADA WAY

Cacho and Niyongabo. This could be interesting.

As the best approach the home straight nothing has been decided. But Morceli quickly loses his power and stumbles through the last 100 metres. This is not the case with Cacho who unleashes a withering sprint to nearly defeat El Guerrouj. Despite the close attention of the Spaniard, Hicham never once becomes distracted by his opponent. He is able to maintain his strong form to the end.

When its conclusion was reached the results were the following:

Hicham El Guerrouj	3:28.91
Fermin Cacho	3:28.95
Venuste Niyongabo	3:29.43
Noureddine Morceli	3:30.23
Robert Kiplagat Anderson	3:31.17
William Tanui	3:31.30
Steve Holman	3:31.71
Mohamed Suleiman	3:32.10
John Kibowen	3:32.15
John Mayock	3:33.21
Reyes Estevez	3:33.40
Ali Hakimi	3:33.87
Graham Hood	3:33.94

El Guerrouj had to run at his absolute best to keep his winning streak alive as he got slightly closer to Morceli's world record. He clocked 40.67 for the final 300 metres. Cacho was truly delighted. Post race he raised both arms with fists clenched into the air in triumph.

Here are some statistics to describe the quality of the performances in Zurich:

El Guerrouj's run was a Moroccan record. Only Morceli had ever run faster and he had only done so on four occasions.

Cacho smashed the Spanish record by 1.97 seconds. In fact he beat his own personal best by a whopping 3.06 seconds!

This was a man who had been at the top of the sport for over five years. It was an extraordinary time from him. In the process of this staggering improvement, he became the third fastest runner in 1,500 metres history.

Niyongabo was the third athlete across the line and the third to set a personal and national record. He defeated his previous best by 0.66 seconds and became the fourth fastest ever, ahead of the likes of Aouita, Cram and Coe.

A total of seven runners in this race broke 3:32. Only elite milers ever reach this standard.

Despite my arguments for this being the greatest race of all time over 1,500 metres, the event was overshadowed by not one, but *three* other races on this most unbelievable of track and field nights.

Wilson Kipketer lowered Sebastian Coe's long standing 800 metres world record from 1:41.73 to 1:41.24. This was a record that he had recently equalled in Stockholm. Moses Kiptanui's 3,000 metres steeplechase world record fell when fellow Kenyan Wilson Boit Kipketer ran 7:59.08. Two world records on the one night by two Kenyan born Kipketers! Bernard Barmasai and Kiptanui pushed him all the way, registering times of 8:00.35 and 8:00.78 themselves. Both these magnificent runs had only ever been bettered by Moses beforehand. The twenty three year old Boit Kipketer (who like Paul Tergat is coached by Dr. Gabriele Rosa) had to run a 58.59 second last lap to achieve the record. His spurt over the concluding fifty metres was amazing. Wilson had made big strides this year, as prior to 1997 his personal record was 8:11.29.

Still the biggest race of the night was yet to come. It was track and field's match up of the season as Daniel Komen and Haile Gebrselassie took on each other in the 5,000 metres with Komen going after Gebrselassie's world record.

The possibility of another record is very real after the Kenyan passes 3,000 metres in 7:38.07. His Ethiopian rival is right

MOROCCAN SUCCESS; THE KADA WAY

with him but by this stage the rest of the field is in tatters. Tergat is just going past Koech and both are ten metres off the leaders. It's another five metres back to Khalid Boulami.

Tergat is really digging in, bringing himself virtually onto the back of Gebrselassie with 1,900 metres remaining. But this is out of his comfort zone and surely he cannot have too much left at this frantic tempo. During this lap Paul's efforts to stay in touch are seemingly encouraging Koech and Boulami to do the same. Komen's lap time is 61.54 seconds.

As always at Zurich there is a large and enthusiastic crowd. The atmosphere is spine tingling. Daniel Komen is applying the pressure on the first half of the fourth last lap, resulting in Tergat slipping ten metres away. Koech and Boulami are out of it but now Komen relaxes a fraction and Tergat surges hard to make it a true three man battle with three laps to go after a 62.08.

Komen never appears to seek any assistance with the pace as Haile Gebrselassie continues to clip his heels. We would find out post race just how frustrating this was for the Kenyan. The 4,000 metres split is 10:12.89, with the last km being covered in 2:34.82.

Tergat begins to drop again and after another good lap time of 62.23, his resistance goes completely. With 700 metres to go, he is fifteen metres back from the two contenders. Still Komen cannot put Gebrselassie under any real difficulty.

The crowd is roaring as Komen clocks a 62.87 penultimate lap. It seems inevitable that Haile will win. The Kenyan has managed to maintain a torturous pace throughout the race's duration, yet the little Ethiopian has kept up without once appearing to be in any sort of trouble.

To be able to explode on the final lap of any 5,000 metres race is impressive. To do so when running at a world record pace is simply mind boggling. What Haile Gebrselassie does on the back straight has to be seen to be believed, as he puts twenty metres on Komen within the space of ten seconds. For a fifty metre burst, think of Gothenburg. Last year Daniel had run away from Haile easily, almost with disdain, but in 1997 the 'emperor' is at his best and untouchable. He clearly gets the better of Komen this time but also receives the benefits of Daniel's hard front running as he clocks a time of 12:41.86, smashing his own mark by 2.53 seconds. Komen trailes home in 12:44.90, a time that is only 0.51 seconds outside of Gebrselassie's old record. Almost forgotten is Paul Tergat who shows his best ever form at the distance, running third in a personal best of 12:49.87. He profited greatly from his efforts of attempting to stay with the leaders, and becomes the third fastest of all time, moving ahead of Hissou on the charts. Both he and Komen were in career best form but against Gebrselassie, it all seemed irrelevant.

The final lap was timed at 55.07 and the concluding 200 metres in 26.80 but what about the last 300 metres? Komen had been running at around sixty two second lap pace so the first 100 metres of this lap would have been run in well over fifteen seconds before Gebrselassie made his decisive move with about 270 metres remaining. Considering that the Ethiopian was behind at the bell, he has got to have run sub forty seconds for this split which is faster than Hicham and Noureddine often finished off their event in. This must be the most impressive finishing kick ever recorded for a track distance race that was a world record run.

Brussels was the next massive Grand Prix meeting of the season but prior to that, there came a significant race in Monaco on August 16. Everybody was aware of the great era we were in the midst of in men's distance running at 5,000 metres and 10,000 metres, but just how great was truly displayed and explained when a 1,500 metres race took place in the city of the rich and famous. It was the 5,000 metres world champion Daniel Komen who was willing to roll the dice and take on the world's greatest milers, save for Hicham El Guerrouj who was resting up for Brussels. At this stage of his career, Komen didn't know the meaning of the word rest. Every race he ran seemed to be monumental and this one was perhaps his masterpiece.

MOROCCAN SUCCESS; THE KADA WAY

Many track experts couldn't believe their eyes when they saw the Kenyan dismantle these speedsters in their own discipline. Komen ran like a long distance runner, but the clock doesn't lie and here it spoke the truth in volumes. A time of 3:29.46 by a strength runner, although a 55.30 final lap clocking showed pretty good speed too! It was hard to comprehend, for Komen had bettered the best of Cram, Coe and Ovett. He'd matched the old world record of Said Aouita. Even greater was his achievement of winning, finishing well clear of Niyongabo's very respectable performance of 3:30.47. Further behind were names such as William Tanui, Fermin Cacho, John Kibowen and Noureddine Morceli. The Algerian ran awfully and placed twelfth in 3:33.98.

If Komen didn't have the necessary speed to take on Gebrselassie at the end of a 5,000 metres, then how could he possibly have the toe to challenge the 1,500 metres specialists? Not just to challenge but to defeat them quite convincingly. It made no sense. A logical explanation was that the long distance runners that were setting the new standards during this period were incredible athletes. This was a golden age for the sport and Daniel Komen shone brighter than most. Besides Henry Rono, there could be no greater talent in the history of Kenyan distance running.

It was Friday the 22nd of August. The long awaited meeting at the Van Damme Memorial had finally arrived. It was the second biggest day of Abdelkader Kada's year, not far short of August the 6th.

Hicham El Guerrouj aimed to continue his dominance of his pet event. Noureddine Morceli was not on the start line, still recovering from what had taken place in Monaco. Venuste Niyongabo had displayed good form since Athens and appeared to once again be the Moroccan's major opposition. This 1,500 metres race was a beauty and was a reminder of the many great battles that these two had engaged in during the previous two years. In some ways little had changed. With Morceli not racing they were the best athletes in the field. The difference being that now it didn't matter whether the Algerian raced them. The top eight finishers from Brussels were as follows:

Hicham El Guerrouj	3:28.92
Venuste Niyongabo	3:29.18
Laban Rotich	3:30.77
John Kibowen	3:31.15
William Tanui	3:31.44
Steve Holman	3:31.52
Ali Hakimi	3:31.70
John Mayock	3:31.86

It was yet another glorious victory but an agonizing one hundredth of a second outside his recent Moroccan record! Hicham and Abdelkader were very satisfied with 3:28's. Even Morceli never made those sorts of times a regularity. For Niyongabo it was another Burundi record. He could scarcely believe his bad luck. He continued to make improvements but this young Moroccan was one step ahead of him. It was frustrating as he was used to often winning with times outside of 3:30. Now inside this awesome barrier he was on the losing side. El Guerrouj was letting him know that he would have to take his game to another level if he wanted to become a regular winner again. The pre Athens trends returned with Rotich and Kibowen performing well. The overall standards came close to matching the Zurich race. There, seven runners broke 3:32. In Brussels there were eight so depth wise, it was arguably even better.

At most meetings a 3:28 1,500 metres would have had Hicham El Guerrouj as the major story. But as in Zurich, he was upstaged by other distance running performances. This meet was anything but ordinary. It had real drama to go with it and most of it centred around Haile Gebrselassie.

The twenty four year old living legend was competing in the 3,000 metres in Belgium and why not? He'd just improved his already intimidating world record at 5,000 metres, shortly after retaining his world title at 10,000 metres. Brussels, being the distance running Mecca that it was, was also holding events over 5,000 and 10,000 metres on this magnificent night, though there was no obvious reason for Haile to run in either

MOROCCAN SUCCESS; THE KADA WAY

of these events so he opted for the shorter distance where he even hoped to challenge Komen's world record. By the night's end there were clear reasons given for why Gebrselassie could have given this decision a bit more thought.

There were no surprises in the 3,000 metres, with the usual suspect setting the track alight. The winning margin was simply staggering.

Haile Gebrselassie	7:26.02
Paul Bitok	7:34.37
Khalid Boulami	7:34.49
Bob Kennedy	7:36.28
Bernard Barmasai	7:36.40
Fita Bayissa	7:36.55

Komen's mark was never seriously under threat with Haile passing 2,000 metres in 4:56.1, so no record, though still a time that only two other men had ever bettered. After easily dispatching of some of the world's best distance runners Gebrselassie watched the remaining events from the stands. The results that unfolded would have left him gobsmacked.

Paul Tergat and Daniel Komen were both keen to exact revenge for their recent defeats and here was the opportunity for them both to get something back on the Ethiopian. Both were planning world record attempts at Haile's 10,000 metres and 5,000 metres standards. Paul Koech and Salah Hissou joined Tergat in the 10,000 metres for their rematch from a year ago. It was always going to be a big night for distance running. But no one could have possibly predicted how big.

When Gebrselassie had set his most recent world record at Zurich, he had done it by going through 3,000 metres in 7:38.30. Komen was just ahead of him at the time and stopped the clock at 7:38.07. Nine days later in Brussels, the Kenyan had no opposition by the 3,000 metres mark. When Martin Keino took him through in 7:37.22, breaking Haile's world record became a distinct possibility. Komen had earned a reputation for being able to sit on a tortuous pace for lap after lap. Running sub sixty one second laps over the final

2,000 metres was well worth the torture for Daniel Komen when he crossed the finish in a new 5,000 metres world record of 12:39.74! Twice at Zurich he had come awfully close to getting this record. Now he had it to go along with his 3,000 metres mind blowing mark. In a period of only fourteen months, this Kenyan had become a legend of athletics and perhaps the greatest runner that his distinguished country had ever produced. Daniel said, "I knew I was going to break the world record, it was in the air. I had the feeling that nothing could go wrong."

There was still the matter of the 10,000 metres to be decided. Mohammed Mourhit was running, attempting to make up for missing out in Athens. The second, third and fourth place getters from that final were all in Brussels. It was a good measuring stick for the Belgium to test just how much improvement he had made this season.

The event's focus had mostly centred on Morocco's former world record man Salah Hissou. He had run 26:38.08 last year. What could he produce in 1997?

The Kenyans weren't all that focused on last year's time. Paul Tergat's concentration was firmly on Haile Gebrselassie's time of 26:31.32 from Oslo. Salah also had the same aggressive mindset saying, "Now I will attempt to break the world record in Brussels on the 22 August. The track is much better than in Atlanta and I am satisfied with my performance".

These were Hissou's comments following his bronze medal in Athens. They portrayed a top runner of contradictions. On the one hand he felt capable of running even faster and had the confidence to break records. Yet that level of expectation of performance far outweighs being satisfied with a third placed finish at a World Championship.

What the perplexing comments came down to was the Haile Gebrselassie factor and the history that Salah Hissou had at the Van Damme Memorial. He knew that he could defeat Paul Tergat.

MOROCCAN SUCCESS; THE KADA WAY

The early pace is scorching, much faster than last year. But when Tergat, Koech and Hissou reach 5,000 metres, they are outside world record tempo. Despite this fact, 13:18.00 at halfway is certainly enough to have all the other athletes holding up the white flag. This is long distance running at its finest, but *without* its finest.

Abdelkader Kada watches on in anticipation. The Moroccan is looking good. Perhaps he can repeat last year's heroics. This is how the situation appears, but deep down Salah Hissou is going through torture, straining with all his strength to hang onto the Kenyans.

The Ethiopian is taking a great interest from the stands, not merely to see if his other prized world record will be stolen. He can watch with fascination, the main men whose major focus during the last three years has been to defeat him. Gebrselassie can admire these men and look at them from a different perspective, as fellow great African distance runners and not just worthy opponents.

The time of 13:18 for 5,000 metres is a tick under 2:40 km pace and the Kenyans keep up the standard, running the sixth km in 2:40.20. The Moroccan remains in contact with his adversaries. For now.

Maybe Salah knows that he is pushing his luck. His previous two 5,000 metres runs had been barely faster than the first half split in Belgium, and now Hissou has sat on sixty four second lap pace for 6,000 metres! The Moroccan is trying to defy his form, defy his body and extend his real capabilities. He's trying to run at a new threshold level. Salah is a great runner and great runners have tremendous pride. His pride is carrying him.

But sometimes pride can only carry you so far.

The 1997 track season has seen setbacks for Salah Hissou. Indeed since 1994 there has been the occasional hiccup in his highly successful career. Mostly it has been good news and great results for the now champion twenty five year old.

Greg Rowlerson

So far there is no race that has crushed him.

Koech and Tergat continue to pile on the pressure, testing out Hissou's reserves of energy. Despite the defeat of last year, this isn't even personal for the two Pauls. They have nothing against Salah, except for the fact that he's Moroccan! The battles going on are not of the kind that you can physically see. These aren't two boxers or two tennis players going head to head. This is a situation where two Kenyans are battling an Ethiopian and one Moroccan is battling himself.

In the end, one battle is won and one battle is lost. The seventh km is run in 2:39.60, by which time Hissou can hold on no longer. The elastic stretches and then breaks. This is nothing like Atlanta, when Tergat had stormed away from him, destroying the Moroccan's dreams of gold or silver well before the bell. Back then, Salah had some fight in him. Sure, his punches couldn't hit their mark, but he could still battle on. By the end of this edition of the Brussels 10,000 metres, Hissou is well and truly on the canvas.

The Kenyans aren't going to rest on their laurels just because the Moroccan has been dropped. They pick up the pace still further and later with 600 metres remaining, Tergat runs away from Koech and into the history books. While doing so, he runs into distance running folklore as his kick down at the end of this super fast 10,000 metres has to be seen to be believed.

When Tergat's example of distance running at its finest was over, he could marvel at this brilliance and his new standing as the 10,000 metres world record holder. A time of 26:27.85 was set, and with that, a new level for Haile Gebrselassie to strive for. Right now, all Haile could do was watch. Not just with envy, but with admiration. Incredibly, this was Tergat's first ever major track victory on the European circuit.

Tergat informed us, "I rested after Zurich because last year, I was lacking a bit of freshness." He had learnt a little here from Kada.

MOROCCAN SUCCESS; THE KADA WAY

Paul Koech confirmed himself as a great runner in modern times, with his 26:36.26 beating Hissou's now ancient mark. He had helped Paul Tergat on many occasions but this probably ranked as his greatest 'supporting' performance.

The statistics were amazing. Tergat ran the last 3,000 metres in 7:50, a phenomenal pace. The second 5,000 metres were timed at 13:09.8! The Kenyan was a lot better now than the Moroccan. This had to hurt Salah since he was virtually at the same level as Paul in Turin. In the last five months things had changed. Salah could feel himself being left behind by the distance running world.

What about the change in only twelve months? From defeating the two Pauls in a world record time to this. This absolute thumping. As Hissou's laps of sixty fours blew out to sixty eights, the Moroccan took the biggest fall of his running career. As an international athlete, this was the most he had hurt, both physically and mentally. He had lost a lot of time. It would take a lot of time to recover.

Some explanation of the various levels of Hissou's performances at Brussels from '96 to '97 can be attributed to the time he had to specifically prepare for the race. His world record run came twenty five days after Atlanta as opposed to his latest effort which came just sixteen days after Athens. His slightly lesser form was exaggerated somewhat by the improvement of the Kenyans. Mentally, it is much easier to continue pushing through the pain barrier during the final 3,000 metres when you are leading, in contrast to when you are being dropped. Salah backs this up, commenting on the Kenyans breaking him, "I gave up."

There is little doubt that Salah Hissou's belief was temporarily destroyed following Brussels, but his dignity and reputation remained well and truly intact. Maybe the best way to analyse an athlete is to not look so much into their best performances, but their worst. The greatest of them all, Haile Gebrselassie, ran a shocker at Zurich in 1996. A 'shocking' 5,000 metres performance, so *bad*, that only two other men had ever run faster! Salah Hissou's run at Brussels in 1997 could be looked at in a similar way. The Moroccan had hit the wall over the last 3,000 metres, but his time still made him the fourth fastest for the year at 10,000 metres. No other Moroccan had *ever* run as fast. Hissou ran the last 3,000 metres in approximately 8:30, but still clocked 27:09.07 at the finish. The time was still fractionally faster than he'd run in the Brussels race of 1995, a race where he had become the Moroccan record holder.

Salah also managed to hold on for third place, finishing well ahead of the rest of the quality field. Fourth was Mourhit in 27:23.58. Fifth was Kenyan Elijah Korir in 27:27.87. Back in seventh place was a familiar name. Khalid Skah was still chugging along and a 27:49.36 was more than respectable at his age. But at twenty five, was Hissou well past his best?

Many Kenyans had been washed up before Salah's age. It was usually the toll of hard training. The speed sessions, the many miles. It would be no great surprise if Hissou achieved little from now on.

But enough of the down side. This night in Brussels was a truly great night for men's distance running and a frustrating one for a particular Ethiopian. Gebrselassie could only wish that he had gone in the 5,000 metres or 10,000 metres. Then he would have had some say in what took place. But this night turned out to be one of the greatest for Haile as well. The bar was raised and 1998's targets had been set for him. Motivation wasn't going to be a problem in the upcoming non championship year.

"This track has been a little better, not as hard as the one in Atlanta. I am proud to have done a triple and I don't care any more about the World Championships. If someone beats my world record I will start to train again. I am not a person from another world. I am a human being."

These were the comments from the great man following his third straight world title. They showed a runner in need of new challenges. To be only twenty four and over the World Championships was unhealthy for not just Gebrselassie, but the sport itself. The breaking of his records gave us the timely

MOROCCAN SUCCESS; THE KADA WAY

reminder that he is human after all. It also gave Haile motivation for next season.

Perhaps the World Championships had lost a little of its meaning having changed from every four to every two years. I think that having one break year out of every four from the major championships is more than enough. And think of the races we would have missed from Stuttgart and Athens!

A final summing up from Brussels. Daniel Komen breaking the 5,000 metres world record wasn't the greatest of surprises. Everyone knew that he was special. Paul Tergat's record was a different story. For the cross country star it was a major step up. Remember that his previous best time was a 26:54 at the same venue a year ago. If not everyone was convinced from Atlanta, then surely now everyone knew that Tergat was an outstanding track runner, as well as a legend in cross country and on the road. His portfolio was nearly complete. All he needed was to become the 10,000 metres world or Olympic champion.

The European track season wasn't over yet. Next up was a small meet in Cologne on the 24th of August. The 3,000 metres steeplechase world record was broken again. This time it was smashed by another Kenyan, Bernard Barmasai who ran 7:55.72, taking over three seconds off the record. It was obviously a highly impressive run by the twenty three year old who had shown his strength earlier this year when finishing sixth in the World Cross Country. Almost regaining his record was Moses Kiptanui who clocked an amazing 7:56.16. He found himself in the unfortunate position of breaking a world record but not holding it. This result again illustrated the enormous leaps and bounds that men's distance running was making. The last three seasons had seen many ground breaking performances.

Keen to make amends from his Brussels disappointment, Salah Hissou went to Berlin to compete in another Golden Four meeting on August 26. It was only four days since he had 'hit the wall'. How quickly could he recover?

Not within four days was the answer.

Competing over 5,000 metres, Hissou was dropped again, only this time it was even worse. The Moroccan was one of the real strugglers in this race, finishing ninth and clocking 13:17.16. He was clearly done for 1997.

One man who was never done was Gebrselassie. Haile took out his Brussels anger in this race to some good effect, winning easily in 12:55.14. The only men who offered any resistance were Paul Koech and Thomas Nyariki. Despite being good strength runners, they could never offer the Ethiopian any real concerns in a 5,000 metres. Koech ran 12:56.59 and Nyariki 12:58.95. Gebrselassie may have only been the *former* world record holder at 5,000 metres and 10,000 metres but he was still the best distance runner in the world. Berlin was yet another fast time and another victory for him over a high quality field.

Berlin was the fourth of the 'Golden Four' meetings and there was some extra cash on the line. Twenty kgs of gold were to be shared amongst athletes who had won their event at each of the venues of Oslo, Zurich, Brussels and finally Berlin. El Guerrouj was still in the running for this attractive prize, which meant added pressure as well as some determined high class opposition.

The mile event in Berlin was a much more interesting affair than the 5,000 metres with the usual Hicham vs. Venuste contest having the added dimension of Daniel Komen in the field. The race was run at close to a world record tempo and incredibly the Kenyan was able to mix it with the Moroccan. He attempted to make a long run for home but with 300 metres left, Hicham was on his heels and then he kicked. The back straight burst from El Guerrouj was becoming as synonymous as Michael Johnson exploding on the bend in the 400 metres.

Immediately he gained a gap on Komen. Venuste Niyongabo was still in contention as he made a valiant effort to go with El Guerrouj, while also passing the Kenyan on the back straight.

MOROCCAN SUCCESS; THE KADA WAY

With 200 metres remaining, Venuste seemed to be a real winning chance but then he ran out of steam. Komen came back at him and overtook him, although was unable to make any great impression on the Moroccan's lead, which was again a winning one. The top three times were:

Hicham El Guerrouj	3:45.64
Daniel Komen	3:46.38
Venuste Niyongabo	3:46.70

Only Morceli had gone faster than El Guerrouj, yet he would have hardly blown out a candle after recording another magnificent win and thus joining Gabriella Szabo and Frankie Fredericks in a share of the gold. Komen and Niyongabo became the fourth and fifth fastest of all time over the classic distance. Komen's elevation on this list added even more to his incredibly high status in track circles. He also ranked equal fifth in the 1,500 metres, first in the 3,000 metres, first in the two miles and first in the 5,000 metres. That's not for the year but all time! The following year he briefly became the fourth fastest ever at 2,000 metres also. The Daniel Komen story is a book in itself!

Even as Morceli was disappearing from the middle distance running map, El Guerrouj was having to defeat some outstanding competition. It was much tougher than what the Algerian had had thrown at him during his halcyon years.

Niyongabo was a tough nut to crack. The Burundi athlete continued to seek improvement when he went to Rieti to race in the 2,000 metres on September 5. With his nemesis absent he finally had a genuine shot at a victory and he was able to take his opportunity in emphatic fashion. He ran a great time of 4:49.00 while totally obliterating the top Kenyans Bitok and Nyariki by over six seconds. Venuste was quite close to the world record of 4:47.88. Noureddine Morceli must have been worried about losing his stranglehold on the middle distance records. If Niyongabo could threaten them, then what could El Guerrouj do?

Morceli wasn't spending all his time worrying about what

others were accomplishing. He too had made the trek to this Grand Prix meeting where he made his return in the 1,500 metres. After the Monaco disaster another poor showing could spell curtains for him at his pet event. But give credit where credit is due. Noureddine managed to turn back the clock and win easily. The 3:31.00 run was super impressive and far too good for second placed Laban Rotich who clocked 3:32.85. Perhaps the 1998 season would have a lot to offer for Morceli. Could he climb atop the mountain again after his twenty eighth birthday?

If this was going to happen, he needed to risk his pride on occasions. The way he ended the 1997 season was disappointing. This year the Grand Prix final took on even less meaning because it was held in Fukuoka, Japan. Most of the best athletes were already burnt out and having to travel to Asia just made for more upsets. Both the men's steeplechase and 5,000 metres events were won by outsiders as was the mile. Now back to Morceli. He travelled to Japan and raced in Tokyo on the 8th of September. In a slow race he out kicked Mohamed Suleiman and Robert Anderson in 3:41.33. The Grand Prix final was only five days later yet the Algerian didn't show up. He probably didn't believe that he could defeat Hicham El Guerrouj any more and Morceli didn't care much for second place. As things turned out, he certainly could have won at Fukuoka and who knows just how important that would have been to Noureddine's future morale?

It was a hot day with the temperature reaching thirty two degrees so it would be understandable to see the race run in a slower pace. However, only the mercury reaching record levels could have excused the athletes for just how slowly they ran. Remarkably the bell was reached with Hicham leading in 3:11.73. When El Guerrouj kicked on the final lap it wasn't with quite the same venom as in past races. Rotich made a massive move on the back straight but was unable to fully pass the Moroccan who kept him out on the curve. On the home straight he pulled clear of the Kenyan with only Niyongabo appearing a threat, although El Guerrouj was holding him off. From even further back came a flashing run from Kenyan born Dane Robert Anderson. The final

MOROCCAN SUCCESS; THE KADA WAY

comments from the race were, "Robert Anderson finishing fast but it's El Guerrouj clear. No he's not clear. El Guerrouj has been pipped on the line."

Everyone watching was stunned when Anderson ended his unbeaten streak. The Danish runner collected $50,000 for his victory, as did all the winners in Japan. The mile times were a disgrace. Anderson, 4:04.53 and El Guerrouj, 4:04.55. Niyongabo couldn't take his chance and placed a close third. Hicham's season had ended on a sour note. Not that it tasted too bitter because the rest of his year had been oh so sweet.

The Fukuoka meeting was a fairly irrelevant one making a mockery of the Grand Prix 'final' title. Not only was it a problem because it had been run outside of Europe but that it took place too late. The 13th of September was over two weeks after the final big European meeting had been run in Berlin. That was too great a gap. It was little surprise that many of the performances were sub standard in Japan.

Before Anderson's upset win, Hicham El Guerrouj had reeled off eleven victories outdoors and three indoors in finals during 1997. All were at the 1,500 metres or mile distance. He had established his clear dominance in this area. In 1998 there were no major championships. As such, Kada felt that it was the perfect situation in which to attack Morceli's records. Hicham was twenty three and entering his prime.

Salah Hissou would soon turn twenty six and was at a career crossroad. The wins had dried up and there were no personal bests forthcoming in 1997. Yet at the end of the year, Salah was still the fourth fastest for the season over 5,000 metres and 10,000 metres. His Rome time had put him behind only Komen, Gebrselassie and Tergat. This was an order that greatly demonstrated the best long distance runners in the world. Since the end of '96 Salah had lost a bit of ground. Time would tell if he could regroup.

There were more important questions to answer for most distance running fans. Could Haile Gebrselassie reclaim his world records and could Hicham El Guerrouj claim some outdoor ones of his own in 1998?

MOROCCAN SUCCESS; THE KADA WAY

Injuries, Development And Domination

1998 saw a year without a major track championship, yet for Salah Hissou it held potentially the biggest race of his career to date. The 1998 World Cross Country Championships were to be held in Salah's home country, in the city of Marrakech. In the previous year, Morocco had come relatively close to Kenya in the team's competition and there was genuine hope that the home ground advantage could tip the balance its way.

Morocco had never achieved anything in the World Cross Country during the 1980's, which made Skah's victory in 1990 all the more surprising. Khalid's win elevated his nation to an all time best fifth placing in the men's team competition. The same result was duplicated in '91 but Morocco slipped to sixth in '92 and remained there in '93. It just didn't have enough depth to support Skah, who always fought a lone hand against the Kenyans and Ethiopians. The Kenyans had won the team's event ever since John Ngugi first triumphed in 1986. Each year since, they had won it easily with results being calculated on the positions of the first six runners.

1994 saw an amazing change in fortunes as Morocco rose to a stunning second place, albeit well behind a still dominant Kenya. In 1995 it was second again with the trend continuing in 1996. Morocco wasn't challenging Kenya for gold, but was nevertheless developing a greater depth of quality. The South African race saw three Moroccans finish in the top ten, with Hissou second, Skah seventh and Sghyr eighth. Their sixth finisher Khalid Boulami, was a respectable fortieth placed runner across the line. Morocco's team tally was 99. Unfortunately Kenya's was a meagre 33! All its six points scorers finished in the first ten! Tergat was first with Kirui third, Koech fourth, Kimani sixth, William Kiptum Mungei ninth and Machuka tenth. Gebrselassie's fifth placing meant that the top ten were filled by runners from Africa's three dominant distance running nations.

But changes were about to take place. Hissou's 10,000

metres world record in Brussels, achieved while defeating two of Kenya's best cross country runners was a small sign. By the 1997 World Cross Country, Morocco had closed the gap on Kenya significantly. In Turin, Hissou had closed the gap on Tergat. Metaphorically, this represented the rise in the rivalry between the two countries. For the first time since 1985, Kenya had not completely dominated the team classification. Morocco had reduced its points total to 70, while Kenya had blown out a little to 51. The victory was still convincing, but Kenya now had a nation that it could call a worthy rival. Names like Hissou, Lahlafi, Sghyr, Skah, and Boulami now meant something. They didn't sound too out of place alongside Tergat, Nyariki, Koech, Kirui and Machuka. So in 1998, was Morocco even closer to Kenya? With the encouragement of home support it was feasible that Kenya's reign could be under threat.

Morocco's great improvements weren't the only reason why experts were considering the possibility of a Kenyan defeat. The IAAF was making changes to the 1998 edition that made the outcome of the team's race harder to predict. Each country was now only allocated six entrants as opposed to nine, with only each team's first four runners being counted in the total points, not six. This would make Kenya's extraordinary depth less of a factor. As well as the twelve kms race there was also the introduction of a four kms event, a short course race. Most fans were happy with the expanded schedule. For traditionalists the move was disappointing. The World Cross Country had always prided itself on attracting the world's best distance runners. The four kms would detract from this. For example in 1998, the 5,000 metres world record holder Daniel Komen ran in the short course. Previously many athletes that had excelled at 5,000 metres had competed in the long course. John Ngugi, Ismael Kirui and Haile Gebreselassie are some fine examples. Some could argue that the IAAF was only adapting to the times. With the 3,000 metres being such a popular track event, why not have a shorter world cross country race? The debate continued about the benefits and negatives of the four kms event for many years. Eventually tradition won out, with the IAAF scrapping the short course in its 2007 edition, which was

MOROCCAN SUCCESS; THE KADA WAY

appropriately held in Kenya.

Despite the changes, Morocco's quest to defeat Kenya remained an enormous challenge. This was distance running's equivalent to climbing Mount Everest. For Hissou and company, perhaps it was even harder. With their incredible lungs giving them amazing oxygen carrying capabilities, the Moroccans probably would have fared better climbing Earth's highest peak! Improvements had been made each year, from 1994 to 1997 to team Morocco, though this didn't necessarily mean that 1998 would bring even better results. Mohammed Mourhit's defection to Belgium was a big setback to Morocco's chances in Marrakech (he would finish eighth). It would need all its remaining top runners to be competing and at their best to stand a realistic chance of winning gold.

All sound logic pointed to Salah Hissou being a big chance to win his first ever major championship. To win the World Cross Country in his native Morocco would be something very special indeed. From eleventh in '94, to third in '95, to second in '96 and a closer second in '97, Hissou had perfectly represented Morocco's overall rise to prominence. All he needed now was to be at his best, perform well on the day and hope that a boisterous crowd could carry him to victory. Aziz Daouda anticipated as many as 100,000 spectators at the championships. Aziz comments on the importance of the event and his and the nation's expectations of the Moroccan runners in Marrakech, "We have not changed the strategy we have adopted for the last three years in terms of schedules and the way our runners have been training, but this year is clearly more important. There is no doubt that the Moroccan squad is more motivated. We obviously want to do well in front of our home fans. The championships are important not only for the Moroccan team but for the Moroccan people. It is an opportunity for the Moroccan people to see many of our stars and also the great names of world athletics. Athletics is very big in Morocco, the second most popular sport after soccer and this is the first major global sporting event that Morocco has staged since the last World Cross Country Championships here."

For an elite distance runner, Salah had experienced no serious injuries. Avoiding this curse had enabled him to compete in the last three major track championships, as well as the last four World Cross Country races and four Brussels 10,000 metres races. Hissou's form at the end of the 1997 track season was disappointing, but with months to prepare for Marrakech, this shouldn't have been a major concern.

However Salah's preparations had not gone according to plan. He had experienced problems with his left ankle and was restricted in his training. He retained hope that he could compete strongly, but in the final week before the race, he was forced to concede that his challenge was over before it had started. With it went a realistic dream. It was a devastating outcome for the proud Moroccan. Taking the advice of his doctor, he would not be on the starting line in Marrakech.

Abdelkader Kada explained to the press that, "He can run, but not well enough to challenge for the podium."

Morocco's slim chance at winning the team gold also vanished. Its chance to do at all well was hampered even further when Khalid Skah was forced to miss the event with his own injury. The team's competition would be a non event and Morocco's peak would remain Turin.

Paul Tergat won the long course World Cross Country, making it an incredible four victories in a row. On the grassy, firm surface he tied Ngugi's record. His compatriot Paul Koech finished second, improving on his fourth placings in the last two editions. Koech ran strongly, taking off during the seventh km and making Tergat really work till the end but the result was never in much doubt. The 10,000 metres world record holder destroyed Koech in the sprint to the line, eventually finishing five seconds clear. He completed the 11.415 kms course in 34:01. After Koech in 34:06, there was a big gap to Mezgebu who won the bronze in 34:28. Kenya then filled the next four places for six of the first seven spots. An amazing domination of the team's competition. Assefa's outstanding performance was the main reason why Ethiopia

MOROCCAN SUCCESS; THE KADA WAY

edged out Morocco for the silver medal. The bronze medal provided little solace, for Morocco knew that its performance in its own homeland was a dismal one. It was the Federation's first real kick in the guts since the 1993 World Athletics Championships.

There was no doubting that Paul Tergat was the best cross country runner in the world but it would have been nice for him to have had some more serious competition in 1998. Although Paul Koech was a great competitor, he was a fellow Kenyan, and one devoid of a good finishing kick. Even his post race comments suggested that he didn't believe he could defeat Tergat. Koech said, "I tried to push, but I knew he was behind me. We've trained together for some weeks. I knew I couldn't leave him, and I knew he had a faster finish."

Salah Hissou may have been able to stick with the first two Kenyans and so might have Haile Gebrselassie, given that the hard terrain would have suited his bouncy stride. Without these two competing it made the race a little dull. Tergat made the following statement years later about the World Cross Country, "Cross country is what I always liked most. It was my world, my passion. Before the IAAF introduced the short course in 1998, all the world class athletes from 1,500 metres to the marathon were in the same race. The World Cross Country Championship was the toughest distance race in the world to win." On April 4, Tergat would break the world record for the half marathon when he clocked 59:17 in Milan.

Salah Hissou's career was at the crossroads. At twenty six, age was becoming a factor and now injury was an added concern. He could drift away into obscurity or he could recover his fitness and form in time for the European track season, less than three months away.

Fortunately for his Moroccan fans, the latter would be the case.

The debut of the short course 4 kms event in Marrakech was most notable for the appearance of Daniel Komen. The outstanding Kenyan may have been a step behind Ethiopia's best as the world's greatest long distance runner at the conclusion of 1997, but already Daniel had produced some extraordinary performances in the early phases of 1998.

The indoor season had seen the Komen vs. Gebrselassie rivalry go to yet another level. On January 25, Haile raced over 3,000 metres in Karlsruhe. He already held the world record at 7:30.72 but this obviously did not satisfy him. What the Ethiopian did now was amazing. He clocked 7:26.15! It was a time that only himself, Morceli and Komen had ever bettered outdoors. In comparison with outdoor records, this was stronger than El Guerrouj's 1,500 metres indoor record. However there was one Kenyan who felt that it was not strong enough.

One week later Daniel Komen competed in Stuttgart on February 1. So high was his confidence that he believed himself capable of dismantling this new and mightily impressive mark straight away. While Gebrselassie's run was effectively a time trial, Komen had former world record holder Moses Kiptanui for company. But Moses couldn't touch Daniel now. As he fell away to a still respectable 7:35.66, his fellow Kalenjin marched on, coming close to achieving his goal. His time of 7:27.93 was another stupendous performance but like Gebrselassie, Komen wasn't easily pleased either.

During the past two seasons it had been quite common for Daniel to make regular world record attempts. Sometimes this seemed to be on a weekly basis. On February 6 he raced again at 3,000 metres, this time in Budapest. He was in career best form. There was a chance that he could take this very difficult record away from his great rival, and take it he did! When this race was over the new standard was 7:24.90. Only he had ever run faster outdoors. The manner in which this record was broken was also abnormal. The rabbit Rotich, reached 2,000 metres in 4:59.82. This was well outside Haile's split of 4:57.51 on the way to his 7:26.15. Yet Komen absolutely blasted through the final km. It was a level of distance running that arguably nobody had ever attained. Most athletes would likely take a break now, return home for some rest before focusing on the outdoor season. Not

MOROCCAN SUCCESS; THE KADA WAY

Komen. There were always more records to be broken.

On February 19 there was an indoor meeting in Stockholm and both Gebrselassie and Komen were ready to race, but not each other. There was some bad blood between the pair following the Zurich battle of last year, with Komen upset that Gebrselassie gave no help during the event. The Kenyan was refusing to race against the Ethiopian. A solution was arrived at in Sweden. Haile would compete at 3,000 metres where he could try to reclaim his record. Daniel would compete at the rarely run 5,000 metres and try to break the world record of 12:59.04, held of course by Gebrselassie. The winners out of these proceedings were the spectators who might be lucky enough to see the most exciting distance running ever indoors.

The 'emperor' remained in outstanding form. On February 15 he'd set another world record, this time at 2,000 metres! His time of 4:52.86 surpassed Ireland's Eamonn Coghlan who'd held the record for almost eleven years. However this record was a much weaker one. For example Morceli and El Guerrouj had never made an attempt on it and they were superior to Gebrselassie over this distance. Nevertheless, it was another world record to add to his incredible resumé.

Haile ran well in Stockholm but couldn't approach the new record. His 7:31.70 paled in comparison. Passing 2,000 metres in 4:59.00, he was clearly attempting a fast time. As well as this minor failure, Gebrselassie also had to watch in dismay as Komen obliterated his 5,000 metres time by clocking 12:51.48. As in Budapest, Komen finished at a furious pace. At 3,000 metres it was fifty-fifty whether he would break the world record. Daniel's split here was 7:47.19, a fraction under 12:59.04 schedule. Yet he eventually sliced more than seven seconds off the mark. This Kenyan was very special indeed. Gebrselassie had continued to dominate and run fantastic times, though in the space of about six months had lost all his major outdoor and indoor world records.

Komen boarded a plane but did not fly back to Kenya. Instead he went to the other side of the world, to Australia, to continue racing. This was crazy! Just six days later, on February 25, he lined up in Melbourne to race outdoors at Olympic Park. The distance of one mile was not his specialty, but being in such terrific form, there wasn't anyone at this meeting with the necessary credentials to defeat him. Daniel ran a 3:53.63 and won easily over second place youngster Noah Ngeny, who clocked 3:56.06. This was pretty much a jog by his standards!

That mile was his warm up for a two mile event in Sydney on February 28 where Komen believed that he could break his world record. He basically had only his personal records to break, but he wanted to lower this one further, which currently sat at 7:58.61.

Assisted by rabbits Julius Kiptoo and Martin Keino, Komen passed the first mile in over 4:01. Keino took over on lap five, but team Kenya still remained outside of record schedule with a split of 5:01.54. Remembering his recent records, we knew that Daniel could kick down even from such a fast tempo. With Martin out, it was all up to the world champion.

At the next split he hit the line in 5:59.54. It was a lap of fifty eight seconds! This man is a freak. Suddenly he was favoured to defeat his Hechtel time. Lap seven was passed through in 6:59.21. Surely he will break it. But alas, no. He couldn't muster a sprint on the final lap yet still clocked 7:58.91. After a month of amazing racing, Komen was fatigued. The splits told us as much. In Hechtel his 3,000 metres split was 7:27.30. In Sydney it was 7:27.00. Though a weaker record than his 7:20.67, this remained another incredible performance with only Morceli and Gebrselassie having run faster for a flat chat 3,000 metres.

At the conclusion of February 1998, Daniel Komen could claim to be the best long distance runner in the world. Not satisfied fully with his Australian venture, he now lined up in Marrakech for the World Cross Country short course event. At a distance of four kms, he was the clear favourite to win. He ran well in the thirty one degree heat and late in the event took up the front running. His familiar bouncing stride looked imposing, but his teammate John Kibowen stayed with him

MOROCCAN SUCCESS; THE KADA WAY

and at the finish, Komen was out sprinted comprehensively. Kibowen clocked 10:43 after a 2:33 final km to Komen 10:46. Regardless, it was another top notch result and a silver medal to put on the mantlepiece.

Despite Salah Hissou's withdrawal from Marrakech, Abdelkader Kada still took an interest in the weekend's events. Also competing in the short course race was another member of his highly talented training group. Ali Ezzine recorded a respectable twelfth place result. To many, this performance (and therefore athlete) might appear to be not worth mentioning, but consider that Ali was only nineteen years old. Also take into consideration that the runners in Marrakech had nothing to jump over. Morocco placed a distant second with 42 points, compared to Kenya's best possible total of 10 points in the team's competition. Brahim Boulami was the best of them placing sixth in 11:06.

Born on September 3, 1978 in a suburb of Meknes, Ali Ezzine was an immensely gifted runner, one who was specializing in the 3,000 metres steeplechase. His talent arguably surpassed that of El Guerrouj and Hissou, so considering what Abdelkader Kada had achieved with them, suggested a very bright future for Ali. But to accomplish much in this event he would have to defy all the recent trends. For you do not expect many victories in the steeplechase if you are not a Kenyan!

In 1995, shortly after taking up the sport, Ali finished sixth in the Moroccan School Championships under seventeen category. His talent was obvious and he soon joined the Sports Club of Meknes to concentrate further on his running. The following year he was recruited to the National School of Athletics in Rabat, though the acceptance of this offer took time, as his parents very much wanted Ali to focus on his studies. Eventually they were persuaded into letting him join the school.

That same year he made his abilities known to many when he won the bronze medal in the 3,000 metres steeplechase at the World Junior Championships in Sydney. This was a surprise to see a Moroccan challenging the Kenyans in *their* event. The results of the medallists were:

Julius Chelule	8:33.09
Kipkurui Misoi	8:33.31
Ali Ezzine	8:35.60

From this race onwards many Moroccans were keen to tutor this young man. He soon found himself in the care of Abdelkader Kada. Being aware of the athletes that Kada coached, Ali had great confidence that Abdelkader was the best advisor who could extract the most out of his God given talent.

1997 was an excellent year of continued improvement for Ezzine. He showed his strength by winning the National Junior Cross Country race and then was far from disgraced when he converted that into an eleventh place finish in the World Junior Cross Country over 8 kms in Turin. With Morocco, he collected a team bronze medal albeit some way behind the dominant Kenyans and Ethiopians on the points table. Later that year, Ali also won a silver medal in the Pan Arab Games in Beirut when he finished behind Saudi Arabia's Saad Cheddad Asmari in the steeplechase. It was the first of hopefully many senior medals in championship events.

On June 20 Ali displayed some versatility when he set a Moroccan junior record over 5,000 metres. In this race in Lisbon he raced against a high quality field and placed sixth in a time of 13:32.56. Some of the guys ahead of him were major runners on the European circuit. Famous names such as Khalid Skah and Domingos Castro. Progress was happening quickly for this Moroccan.

On August the 13th, 1997, Ali Ezzine found himself running at one of the true Meccas of distance running. The venue was Zurich and he performed at his best, recording a Moroccan junior record in his customary event, the steeplechase. This achievement was done under no spotlight because despite a time of 8:23.18, he finished in a lowly fourteenth position. This was the race where Wilson Boit Kipketer set the world record,

MOROCCAN SUCCESS; THE KADA WAY

so very few eyes were on the young Moroccan who was understandably well behind the top Kenyans.

Into 1998 and more improvement appeared on the cards as Ali started his season with an impressive indoor performance in Lievin, France on February 22. The indoor meetings do not include the steeplechase event so Ezzine entered the 3,000 metres flat, using it as a warm up for his cross country race in Marrakech. His time of 7:48.62 and third placing offered further encouragement to himself and Kada that excellent results were not too far away.

Also racing in Lievin was Hicham El Guerrouj and he let the world know that his dominance of middle distance running wasn't going anywhere.

There were many excellent athletes competing in the 1,500 metres here. Maybe they felt this was a good opportunity to score a victory over Hicham, when it was his first race of the year. But as usual El Guerrouj was more than ready for any challenge that came his way. His great rival Venuste Niyongabo again made sure that the mile 'king' brought his A game to France.

Burundi's best produced another top run as he clocked 3:33.17. It was never enough though with Hicham moving away in the latter stages and winning comfortably as his time of 3:32.01 showed. Abdelkader had kept his best runner in the same exceptional form that he had demonstrated throughout 1997. Some order was restored also. Finishing well behind in ninth was last year's Grand Prix final victor, Robert Anderson.

Regardless of his youthfulness, Abdelkader felt that it was time for Ali Ezzine to become a little more competitive in the senior ranks. Training had gone well prior to the European Grand Prix season and now it was time to reap some rewards.

On the 30th of May Ali raced in Seville in a secondary meeting, but this particular event was anything but secondary as the top results show:

Eliud Barngetuny	8:20.76
Wilson Boit Kipketer	8:21.06
Elarbi Khattabi	8:21.42
Ali Ezzine	8:21.60
Hicham Bouaouiche	8:21.96
Yarba Lakhal	8:29.12
Alberto Genoves	8:29.36

The quality of this field undoubtedly contributed to Ezzine running another personal best in the steeplechase. To be very competitive with a sub eight runner (Kipketer) was an incredible confidence boost. Finishing fourth was much better than fourteenth and Ali looked upon the rest of the season a little differently. Kada had a great many races lined up for Ali in 1998, the first major year of his career.

This race also highlighted the gradual mark that Moroccan men were making in the steeplechase as they took the positions third to sixth. At only nineteen, Ali was close to being the first finishing Moroccan with only seasoned campaigner Elarbi Khattabi, a mere eighteen hundredths of a second in front of him.

On June 4 it was onto the Saint-Denis meeting, which often produced some top results. Ali's upward career curve continued on its steady trajectory when he clocked 8:19.26 and placed sixth. As a sub eight twenty runner he could now consider himself worthwhile of a regular spot on the lucrative European circuit. Again the quality of athletes was impressive with the top ten being:

Moses Kiptanui	8:15.62
Eliud Barngetuny	8:17.27
Elarbi Khattabi	8:17.55
Patrick Sang	8:17.81
Hicham Bouaouiche	8:19.06
Ali Ezzine	8:19.26
Mohamed Belabbes	8:23.55
Paul Kosgei	8:27.61

MOROCCAN SUCCESS; THE KADA WAY

Stephane Desaulty   8:27.82
Fabien Lacan   8:29.34

Running alongside Olympic and world champions probably made Ali feel like he belonged in the big time.

Moses Kiptanui was born on October 1, 1970. He had established himself as one of the greatest athletes of the 1990's and perhaps the greatest steeplechase runner of all time. Moses was virtually unbeatable at his pet event throughout the first half of the decade, winning world titles in '91, '93 and '95. Not only that, but his versatility was incredible, having broken world records at 3,000 and 5,000 metres. Olympic bad luck came his way however when in 1992 he missed the Kenyan trials with an injury, during a period when he was considered by far to be the world's best. Kiptanui may have even started the 5,000 metres as Olympic favourite if he'd lined up, such was his stature! World records in the 3,000 metres flat and the 3,000 metres steeplechase came post Barcelona, as well as the third fastest time ever over 5,000 metres in Brussels. In 1996 Moses made the Kenyan Olympic team, but suffered ill health before Atlanta. He still came close to the elusive gold, though had to content himself with the silver.

On times, 1997 had been Kiptanui's best season to date. Unfortunately the Kenyan world had caught up and he lost both his world record and world title. Now a veteran, it remained to be seen if Moses could recapture his number one ranking in the steeplechase. This victory in France was a step in the right direction.

Hicham El Guerrouj was also racing in Saint-Denis. This was his second race of the outdoor season having already competed in Hengelo on the 1st of June.

In Holland El Guerrouj was in superb form. He had previously experienced enormous victories here in 1995 and 1997 but this season he further improved on those winning margins as he recorded a fast time of 3:31.19, well over five seconds ahead of the rest of the field with second man Nadir Bosch of

France clocking 3:36.80.

Following this performance Hicham was fully expected to win easily three days later in France. He did this with aplomb, recording a 3:32.34, while finishing a big distance in front of second placed Russian runner Vyacheslav Shabunin's 3:35.59.

These races were merely preparations for Hicham as he embarked on a successful season at the biggest European athletics meetings. In recent years the season had been based around the Golden Four, which involved the track and field nights in Oslo, Zurich, Brussels and Berlin. The IAAF was taking this concept a step further and making this a proper series where athletes would score points based on their placings and could be ranked in their event by these results. The 'Golden Four' became the 'Golden League' as Rome and Monaco were added to the elite list. The seventh Golden League meeting was the Grand Prix final that this year was to be held in Moscow.

An athlete could also score points towards his end of year ranking in smaller meetings that were now labelled as GP 1 or GP 2. In the Golden League and Grand Prix 1 meetings, the first eight athletes scored points. A Golden League winner tallied twelve points, with second place scoring ten points, and then counting down to eighth who recorded four points. In GP 1 it was simply eight points down to one, while in GP 2, only the top five performers scored, from five to one.

Most athletes did not concern themselves with any points collected from the lesser races. Generally these meetings were used by the top runners to coincide with their training, as lead up races for a bigger race where they would aim for a best performance a week or two later. A less successful athlete would compete in these GP 1 or GP 2 races with the hope of recording a good enough result that may earn them a spot in the next Golden League meeting.

Hicham El Guerrouj was clearly in the first category of these runners. In some ways he was in a category all of his own.

MOROCCAN SUCCESS; THE KADA WAY

Yes, he would race in smaller events to keep him in racing shape for the Golden League, but this does not mean that he took these races less seriously. In 1998 El Guerrouj made two world record attempts in such races.

The Golden League concept also brought more money into the sport of track and field with television rights becoming big business. The athletes deservedly would reap some of the financial rewards as a million dollar jackpot was devised and offered as incentive, not just to keep the athletes interested, but more so the viewing public.

This was a brilliant marketing ploy, for nothing had changed too much out on the track, with the original Golden Four meetings still holding the bulk of the prestige among the athletes. In 1998 304,121,000 viewers tuned in at some stage during the season. In 1999 this figure rose substantially to 827,657,000. The IAAF had indeed created a gold mine. For 2000, the number of countries broadcasting the Golden League had grown to 105. Crucially American network ESPN was one that came on board. America = $'s. El Guerrouj, like Hissou and Ezzine, knew this personally, as they were all sponsored by another giant American company, Nike.

The usual race purses and appearance fees remained, but the jackpot was an extra carrot that dangled in front of the world's best athletes as a possible end of season pay day. To get a slice of the million dollars was not easy. You had to be a truly dominant sportsperson to aim for it and realistically only a dozen or so men or women had a chance of being a part of it in 1998. To stay in the running for this competition meant winning your event at every single one of the Golden League meetings. Abdelkader Kada knew that Hicham had enough superiority in the 1,500 metres to make this a sensible target. The first Golden League event was not until July 9 in Oslo. After Saint-Denis El Guerrouj had five weeks of critical training to complete, by which time he needed to be at his best (or for him at least close to it) for the colossal run of big races that followed. The most difficult task for Hicham would be to remain in awesome form for nearly two months, as the Grand Prix final was not held until September 6. There could be no slip ups. So far there were no youngsters coming through the ranks that appeared capable of challenging the Moroccan for his mile crown. If El Guerrouj could just retain his usual high standards, then the jackpot was his for the taking.

Abdelkader had a lot on his plate with Salah Hissou also competing in the Saint-Denis meeting. The event was only classified as a GP 2 but the results suggested that a higher rating was more appropriate. This was an important period for Salah who was returning from injury setbacks. He needed to prove himself again.

After a long time out of the spotlight, Hissou had returned to Europe on the 30th of May in good condition. He raced in windy conditions over 3,000 metres in Seville but without stiff competition. Athletes often start the track season in poor form and by the latter stages of the race Salah found himself running with just a sole Kenyan. That runner was Paul Kosgei, a youngster who had run a world junior steeplechase best last year. He was no slouch but there was a Moroccan out to prove that he was much better than an 'average' Kenyan. Did Salah Hissou still have what it took to be a major player in the European track distance races?

A resounding yes was the answer as the rebounding Moroccan turned on the power 600 metres from home. Kosgei simply wilted in his wake. Hissou's winning time was 7:36.97, a great first up performance. His outstanding finish was fully explained by his winning margin with Kosgei finishing in 7:43.68. He was well and truly back! The overall time wasn't particularly fast and the field was almost entirely comprised of Spanish runners (though surprisingly finishing a horrible tenth and clocking a very sluggish 8:02.18 was Salah's old teammate, Mohammed Mourhit). The important thing was that he won and won convincingly. Winning was vital for Salah now, more so to rebuild his confidence. To build it to a level where he felt that he could beat the best from Kenya and Ethiopia. There was one man on the other hand who was remaining incredibly hard to beat.

MOROCCAN SUCCESS; THE KADA WAY

In the first two weeks of June, Haile Gebrselassie regained both his 5,000 metres and 10,000 metres world records from his Kenyan rivals Daniel Komen and Paul Tergat. On June 1, two days after Hissou's return in Seville, the Ethiopian created more running history at his favourite circuit. A 10,000 metres race in 26:22.75 at Hengelo was all that Haile could manage! The performance took five seconds off Tergat's mark in Brussels. He was well inside the required pace after 5,000 metres which he reached in 13:11.70. But by the 9,000 metres split (23:51.53) he was struggling to keep ahead. Gebrselassie however, managed to kick down for a 2:31.22 last km, which was amazing. Twelve days later on the 13th of June he was in Helsinki, running a 12:39.36 over 5,000 metres to sneak under Komen's Brussels mark by thirty eight hundredths of a second. Throughout this run he was always a little outside world record pace but Haile managed to record an incredible 56.77 final lap to regain this record. Gebrselassie's sensational times demonstrated that while he remained young, he would go as fast as was necessary to hold the 5,000 metres and 10,000 metres world records.

It wasn't so much a question of could he go faster? It was more a question of whether anyone would push him to do so, particular in the case of the 10,000 metres event. That's how great he was. In some ways it was a shame that neither of Gebrselassie's June '98 records were taken in the next twelve months. Up until 2000, further outdoor world records were a possibility for Haile, but there was no need to largely focus on improving those records that he currently held. The Ethiopian already had enough on his plate to concern himself with for the rest of his '98 season, which was there for him to try to win every Golden League long distance race and with that, a lot of money. 1999 was there for him to do wonders in the World Indoor Championships as well as retain his 10,000 metres world outdoor title. The year 2000 contained the sole purpose of repeating as the 10,000 metres Olympic champion. Nevertheless, the 5,000 metres and 10,000 metres world records had reached such a standard that it was possible they would survive for some time. Perhaps until another East African freak came along.

Haile may have reached his optimum at 5,000 metres, especially when you consider that he had been unable to break 7:25 for 3,000 metres. Or perhaps not. Read about another world record in the next chapter. At 10,000 metres I have a strong suspicion that he had some more time up his sleeve. When you consider his future performances in Paris and Brussels in 2003 at the age of thirty, surely he could have clocked 26:15 if required. Gebrselassie did not attempt a fast 10,000 metres time from 1999-2002. Thinking again of the back end of that Paris 10,000 metres, I believe that 26:10 was possible for the 'emperor' from Ethiopia. On the track and when fully fit, Haile Gebrselassie was more than five seconds better than Paul Tergat over 10,000 metres. Perhaps as much as thirty seconds faster than Salah Hissou.

The Moroccan was currently in the sort of form where he could dispute such a claim. Three days after Gebrselassie broke the 10,000 metres world record, Salah Hissou was racing at 5,000 metres, keen not to let the distance running world forget about him. He would go about this in magnificent fashion as he completely destroyed his opposition. There was no Gebrselassie in attendance, but June the 4th contained one of the distance running performances of the year and was better than anything Hissou had done on the track in 1997. The results from the 5,000 metres were:

Salah Hissou	12:57.73
Assefa Mezgebu	13:06.91
Paul Bitok	13:14.26
Million Wolde	13:14.56
Daniel Gachara	13:16.22
El Hassan Lahssini	13:16.25
Mustapha Essaid	13:16.36
Abdellah Behar	13:21.12
Said Berrioui	13:24.36
Kipkirui Misoi	13:26.83
Halez Taguelmint	13:29.35
Sergey Lebed	13:30.23

In an awesome display, the Moroccan flashed through 3,000 metres in 7:48.80 and eventually finished nine seconds ahead

MOROCCAN SUCCESS; THE KADA WAY

of Assefa Mezgebu and over sixteen seconds clear of third placed Paul Bitok. Mezgebu had run fifth in last year's World Championship 10,000 metres and had improved since then, with a podium place in Marrakech. Bitok had won two Olympic silver medals at 5,000 metres. Salah Hissou has won one Olympic bronze medal. This is why we should not solely rely on Olympic medals when rating athletes. Despite this discrepancy, Hissou was, and is in a different class to the Kenyan kicker and remained a much classier runner than Gebrselassie's lesser countryman. He had proved to himself that once again, he could win big races on the track and do it in his unique style.

There were not many athletes capable of winning quality European 5,000 metres races by such a big margin. You could count them on one hand. Apart from Gebrselassie, Hissou was the form long distance runner on the circuit. I say 'apart from Gebrselassie' a lot when I refer to Tergat and Hissou. Clearly, the Salah Hissou of 1996 was back and he could head to the Golden League, quite certain that he was going to have a good season.

Quite certain? Not certain enough as it turned out. Salah's great form was completely wasted as his ankle pain flared up again, thus ending his season. Just like that. It seemed that the Moroccan's aging legs could no longer handle the strain of the constant training and the hard racing that being a world class track distance runner entailed.

This must have been devastating for Salah. However for Abdelkader, it was more a case of moving forward, there are bigger fish to fry.

The Golden League season had arrived and it was time to see if Hicham El Guerrouj's training had been sufficient enough to build on his already impressive form. On the 9th of July he raced in Oslo at 1,500 metres. There was an excellent field on the start line but the absence of Noureddine Morceli and Venuste Niyongabo was noticeable. Noureddine preferred to avoid racing his conqueror, while Venuste was experiencing some serious injury difficulties.

Greg Rowlerson

This was the first big track race of the year and it remained to be seen if a young unknown Kenyan might appear on the scene with immense talent, or whether another runner might have made big improvements in the off season. Hicham would need to be careful and focused. Even still, when the gun went off, he was the hottest of favourites to win.

It was business as usual for the Moroccan as he went back into sub 3:30 territory. The results from the 1,500 metres were:

Hicham El Guerrouj	3:29.12
Laban Rotich	3:32.12
Daniel Komen	3:33.93
Vyacheslav Shabunin	3:34.13
Reyes Estevez	3:34.19
John Mayock	3:34.71
Kevin Sullivan	3:34.80
William Tanui	3:34.94
Steve Holman	3:35.27
Nadir Bosch	3:35.71
Ali Saidi-Sief	3:35.87
Abdelkader Chekhemani	3:36.77
Noah Ngeny	3:37.69

Three seconds ahead of the best that the world has to offer at this distance is a very long way in front. For example, this equates to eight tenths of a second in a 400 metres or an amazing two tenths (not hundredths) of a second margin in a 100 metres! Hicham was currently as dominant in his discipline as Michael Johnson was in the one lapper. In this race, only Rotich could be reasonably happy with the outcome (as well as Hicham) as he managed to finish easily ahead of the rest of the bunch.

There was a 3,000 metres race in Oslo however the world record holder was not in the field. Instead Daniel Komen had lined up in the 1,500 metres where he placed third. He was really just one of the many who were taught a severe lesson by Hicham about middle distance running. Following this result it was expected that Komen would immediately go back

MOROCCAN SUCCESS; THE KADA WAY

to running the distances that better suited him. Not the case. Before the European track season, Daniel had made it clear that his major ambition in 1998 was to become an even better miler and thus challenge El Guerrouj. Shortly after breaking indoor records at 3,000 and 5,000 metres he said, "I am not satisfied with five world records. I need more, especially in the shorter distances. I think I have the ability to do it." Daniel informed us that it was his outstanding victory in Monaco last season that had inspired him to take up the 1,500 metres full time. "That was my third 1,500 race in a serious field. It encouraged me that, after all, it is possible."

Kenya's best had enormous self belief. One defeat in Oslo wasn't going to make Komen change his plans.

So it was onto Rome, the second of the Golden League meetings. This athletics night took place on Tuesday July 14, which was a shift from its traditional first week of June schedule. Each of the last three meetings there had held large significance for Salah Hissou. It was possibly at the commencement of the 1998 edition that it began to sink in just how much he was missing out on. His mind may have occasionally drifted back to the World Cross Country. He had already missed so much.

Kada's other stars were fully fit and prepared to run at their best for their crucial races. Following Rome there was a brief break from the Golden League meetings and the next one in Monaco wasn't until next month.

Ezzine's steeplechase was another step forward in time, although he had to endure just a ninth place finish as well as the pain of hitting one of the barriers hard with his knee. When he stopped the clock at 8:15.85, he made it three personal bests in a row in his specialist event. Abdelkader was absolutely delighted with Ali's quick progress. This was in the range of times that he'd hoped Ezzine would reach by the end of this season. There were a lot of races to go to build on this even more.

While this Moroccan was reducing his clock another athlete

was turning his back. The greatest steeplechaser of all time, Moses Kiptanui, put on an outstanding display in front of the Italian audience. He completely destroyed his opposition, bolting clear and running a fast 8:04.96. Virtually left stranded were fellow Kenyan Kipkirui Misoi, 8:11.09, and Morocco's own Elarbi Khattabi, 8:11.86. It was another good honest performance from this very consistent athlete, but like many others he simply wasn't in the same class as a Moses Kiptanui.

It was thought that Moses' time at the top of his sport was over. He'd endured a surprise defeat at the Atlanta Olympics (admittedly he wasn't fully fit) and in 1997 lost his world championship crown, which he had kept since 1991. Perhaps the hardest thing to take was his loss of the world record. Twice it was lowered late in the season, in races that he'd almost won. After these setbacks it was expected that the likes of Bernard Barmasai and Wilson Boit Kipketer would stop Moses from ever recovering one of his illustrious titles. Neither was in Rome to test Kiptanui, but the way that he won left nobody in any doubt. This guy was far from finished.

The biggest event in Rome was the men's 1,500 metres and this was not because of the overall field, rather just one man. Hicham El Guerrouj was embarking on the biggest week of his running career. During this week he was to go after not one, but *three* world records, all of which were held by Noureddine Morceli. The Algerian was not competing in Rome, Nice or Gateshead, so he was doing nothing directly to try to hold onto his 1,500 metres, mile and 2,000 metres records. With the form Hicham had showed in Oslo, all were capable of going to the Moroccan.

Abdelkader Kada may not have seen a risk in attempting a world record in Rome. He might reason that Hicham had won so convincingly in Oslo that he could not lose in Rome, even if he went a little too fast early on. He advised Hicham to go with the rabbits, but if he felt in the middle stages that a world record was not on he could slip back into racing mode. El Guerrouj would have to fall apart disastrously to enable any other athlete to defeat him.

MOROCCAN SUCCESS; THE KADA WAY

Never before had Hicham come seriously close to matching Noureddine's excellent mark of 3:27.37 with his 3:28.91 at Zurich last year, his fastest time so far. Still only twenty three, it was thought that more improvement was possible, but often an athlete needs to closely challenge a record a couple of times before he breaks through. As such, a world record in the 1,500 metres was possible in this race, but still more improbable. When the end came on another great night of track and field, it was the result of this race that sparked the most interest and discussion.

It is somewhat disgraceful that a poor crowd has shown up for this meeting. Most of the stadium is sparse as Robert Kibet takes on the pace ahead of Noah Ngeny with Hicham quickly settling into third spot. He stands out in his light black and white uniform with the Kenyans wearing yellow. Remember that these are sporting brands, not country colours!

Tracking the Moroccan is John Kibowen with Daniel Komen well back in seventh place. Behind him, the rest have already settled for the second division by the conclusion of lap one which is split in fifty five seconds. Soon there are even gaps appearing among the leaders and after 800 metres, reached in 1:50.73, none of the Kenyans can keep with the tempo as Kibowen drifts away from El Guerrouj. They are inside the required time as Morceli's corresponding split from his Nice world record is 1:51.80.

Ngeny takes over from Kibet after 900 metres and Komen is making a move up to third with 500 metres remaining, although he is fifteen metres back from the Kenyan and Moroccan. As they approach the bell, the Italians begin to make some noise as those that are there sense the possibility of a very fast time. The bell is hit in 2:32.73. Still inside schedule.

Hicham moves out and passes Noah just after the commencement of the final lap and Ngeny pulls out at the 1,200 metres, which El Guerrouj goes through in 2:46.34. This remains inside the record mark split of 2:47.10. Noureddine did finish very well but if Hicham can sustain sub fifty six second lap pace over the last 300 metres, the record is his!

El Guerrouj continues to surge on the back straight. The spectacle is one that you might expect from a 5,000 metres, perhaps even a 10,000 metres because his lead has suddenly extended to around thirty metres. It seems that he is building his pace, not slowing, with the record about to go. It not only goes but is smashed as Hicham crosses the line and stops the clock at 3:26.00! A final lap of 53.27.

He immediately falls to the track on his back. After being helped into a sitting position he stands up, though only for a second before he kneels to the rubber and kisses it like Salah did two years before. After a couple of more seconds he looks up with his hands outstretched facing the sky. Hicham's face is perfectly illustrated in a 'what have I done?' type of look. Now he stands erect and hugs another supporter.

The fourteen men who completed the three and three quarter laps were:

Hicham El Guerrouj	3:26.00
Laban Rotich	3:30.94
John Kibowen	3:31.08
Daniel Komen	3:31.10
Andres Diaz	3:32.17
Vyacheslav Shabunin	3:33.30
Branko Zorko	3:33.64
Reyes Estevez	3:33.82
Sammy Rono	3:34.73
John Mayock	3:36.74
Adil El Kaouch	3:37.47
Lorenzo Lazzari	3:40.54
Kevin Sullivan	3:45.91
Ali Saidi-Sief	3:47.56

With the help of rabbits, Robert Kibet and Noah Ngeny, El Guerrouj had done it. They say that records are made to be broken but even when this mark is inevitably beaten, Hicham El Guerrouj will forever be a world record breaker. The

MOROCCAN SUCCESS; THE KADA WAY

amount that he had humbled Noureddine's time would have definitely convinced anyone who was still unsure if Morceli's era was really over. The answer that it well and truly was, came right here. El Guerrouj said, "I came here with the idea of breaking the record. I ran 3:33 here in pouring rain last year. This time the weather was perfect."

The time of 3:26 to many was unfathomable. To think just how far ahead of the best of the British milers he would be. This is how incredibly good El Guerrouj was. Beating his previous best by almost three seconds might make this performance seem like a fluke but in many future races, Hicham would prove that it was far from that. This wasn't like Salah arguably performing above himself in his Brussels world record. This was simply the standard at which Hicham El Guerrouj was now at as an athlete. It must have made his rivals cringe.

Rivalry is probably the wrong term to use. For the first time in his career he clearly had nobody who was close to his equal. Anyone competing against him now was simply a part of his whipping brigade. With the challenge of winning gone, chasing records became the only challenge.

The Moroccan's confidence was now sky high. El Guerrouj said, "My dream is to run 3:24. I hope to do it before this season is out; if not, God willing, I will be back to do it here next year. Before it was Aouita's time, then it was Morceli's, now it is Hicham's time. We are all Muslims, all brothers."

Nobody dared argue with his following statement, "Only the clock can beat me. My only enemy is Hicham."

Others were astounded at the performance and of Hicham's capabilities. Steve Cram commented on this world record plus the possibility of one over the mile in Nice, "What I saw in Rome was awesome. This guy can take the world record into another dimension. We used to think that the differential between the 1500 metres and the mile was something like 17 seconds. Now it is closer to 15, which means that El Guerrouj should be capable of running 3:41 for the mile. I'm only glad that I'm not running now."

Thursday July 16 saw the Grand Prix meeting in Nice and in panic mode, Noureddine Morceli decided to enter the mile race, if only as a distraction to Hicham El Guerrouj's world record plans. Perhaps he never planned to race because at the last minute he withdrew. The Algerian had recently come into some form, having won a mile race at Zagreb in a decent time of 3:50.68. This had come after a series of sluggish performances in low grade races. Remarkably he had failed to break 3:34 this season. Instead of racing Hicham head to head in Nice, he journeyed to America where he won the Goodwill Games on July 21, in a championship, which perhaps didn't deserve that title. The time of 3:53.39 was not in the ballpark of what Hicham ran in Nice. To be fair to him, conditions were hot and humid in Uniondale and the race was tactical, with Daniel Komen going to the front after 800 metres before Morceli took over before the bell and won convincingly. However a last lap of 56.09 just didn't compare to his closing speed of seasons past. It was clear to all knowledgeable observers that Noureddine wasn't close to being the best in the world any more, yet he preferred to live the illusion of still winning regularly in easier fields, rather than at least trying to face the best milers and finish his waning career with some dignity. When asked when he would be racing El Guerrouj, Morceli replied, "I don't know. I have a lot of respect for Hicham. Hicham is such a great athlete. He won't be 24 until September. He has great talent and has many years to go. I will see, because I think I did too much in the 1,500 metres, and maybe I'll give it one more try and see what I can do. I believe that I have a lot of chances to run very good in the 5,000 metres later on."

It was sad to see him struggle to handle his recent demise. He was good enough to still race in the best races, so that is where he should have been. In addition, there were (are) the many fans that looked up to Morceli and wanted to see him race, even if that was as a loser. But Noureddine couldn't accept not being the best. It was a sorry sight to later see him firstly, avoid El Guerrouj by racing in the 3,000 metres in Paris and Monaco, and secondly, failing to finish both races after

MOROCCAN SUCCESS; THE KADA WAY

being dropped by his superior opponents. This wasn't the right way for a great champion to bow out.

Now back to the current great champion.

The world record for the mile is 3:44.39. In his current shape a sub 3:43 is a possibility, particularly as the conditions on this night are a perfect twenty degrees Celsius and there is no wind to speak of. The first split is a little too fast at 54.43, but a reasonable 56.40 second circuit gives a 1:50.83 second sectional. There's a record chance. However Hicham finds himself having to cover the final 550 metres all alone, making his task all the more difficult.

It is another marvellous run from the Moroccan but alas, this time he falls just short of eclipsing Morceli's record. Not that a 3:44.60 mile is anything to sneeze at. It's the second fastest time ever recorded and makes him over two seconds faster than the all time bests of such athletes as Venuste Niyongabo, Said Aouita and Sebastian Coe.

Hicham finished about 50 metres ahead of Laban Rotich (3:51.02) and Anthony Whiteman (3:51.90). It was difficult to break world records at the best of times, even harder when there was nobody pushing you. Maybe this would be a tougher record for El Guerrouj to break, not so much because of its standard, but because the mile is raced less often than the 1,500 metres.

Three days later on Sunday July 19, Kada and El Guerrouj took their imposing coach/athlete combination to England and Gateshead with the aim of breaking the rarely run 2,000 metres world record. Morceli's time to beat was 4:47.88. Hicham had never had a serious crack at the distance. To finish off his amazing week of record attempts in England was fitting as many track fans still remembered the exploits of Sebastian Coe, who when at his peak broke three world records within a fairly short space of time. Although even Coe had never attempted such lofty goals within just one week! Again this was an opportunity for the record to go, but Gateshead was an even smaller meeting (GP 2) than Nice, making the chances of someone staying with him for long quite slim. At least Sammy Langat and William Tanui were in the field to offer support as the designated rabbits.

It was somewhat weird that El Guerrouj found himself being assisted by the Kenyans in his attempt to break Morceli's world records. Obviously this was all to do with the money they were being paid by the event organizers who always wanted to see world records broken at their meetings. I wonder whether these Kenyan runners would be quite so willing to help a Moroccan if the records on the line were held by Kenya.

El Guerrouj thrashed his opposition yet again but had to be content with a time of 4:48.36. Again he had come within half a second of a new world record. Maybe this could have been the greatest week of performances by one athlete in the history of track and field. To reach such a lofty target they had failed, although Hicham and Abdelkader could remain satisfied that it was still one of the greatest weeks.

The world champion was unlucky in that conditions were far from ideal, with the weather providing both strong winds and rain. This sapped him of his strength. His last lap wasn't completed with its usual zip but the Moroccan, fully understanding the circumstances commented. "To run 4:48 in these conditions...that means that if the weather was good I would have done something unbelievable. I am not a machine. I cannot run a record every time. I just try to run as fast as I can. World records don't come when you want them to. They come when God wants them to."

Most would not have seen him but the second runner across the line was a surprise to those who noticed. Ali Ezzine clocked for a steeplechaser an impressive 5:00.84. This was a good display following a small setback that he suffered in the steeplechase in Nice three days earlier with the results of that race being:

| Bernard Barmasai | 8:01.53 |
| John Kosgei | 8:09.08 |

MOROCCAN SUCCESS; THE KADA WAY

Hicham Bouaouiche	8:10.10
Eliud Barngetuny	8:10.74
Elarbi Khattabi	8:12.57
Jonathan Kandie	8:15.04
Paul Kosgei	8:15.58
Wilson Boit Kipketer	8:18.50
Ali Ezzine	8:19.49
Bouabdallah Tahri	8:19.75
Joseph Keter	8:22.52

Ali had remained in established company, only just trailing the world champion Wilson Boit Kipketer. Obviously Wilson was not in the same shape this season and the real barometer for all was the world record holder Bernard Barmasai. His performance was brilliant as he destroyed a field that was more like a Golden League meet in quality than an ordinary Grand Prix meeting. Bouaouiche was highly impressive, nearly ducking under the 8:10 barrier. The Kenyans remained the best in the steeplechase by far, but as they had in cross country, the Moroccans were making second best their own. Slowly they were closing the gap to Kenya.

Ezzine's season appeared to have run out of steam when he could manage only seventh place in 8:21.59 at Paris on July 29. There were extenuating circumstances however with Ali's knee flaring up badly. It had been sore after he'd hurt it in Rome but it was thought that no major damage had been done, so on the advice of the team doctors and Kada, he'd continued racing. The jury remained out as to just how serious his injury was.

Running with a full head of steam was Barmasai. For the second straight race he won in a canter. This time the gap was even wider as Bernard ran 8:02.81 in comparison to Paul Kosgei's 8:13.94. Clearly this Kenyan was one of the world's top runners. The first Moroccan home was Brahim Boulami who placed fifth in 8:14.86.

Also competing in Paris was Hicham El Guerrouj. He had initially planned on another world record attempt but some days you just don't have it. There were far less fireworks in this mile than we'd become accustomed to in recent races. Despite there being no threat of a world record, it is not every day that you get to see a sub 3:50 run. The winning time was 3:49.01, with Hicham once again in a class of his own. Second on this occasion was John Kibowen who ran a solid 3:51.96. It is interesting to note that Daniel Komen was competing on this night although chose not to run in this race, as had been his way this season. Daniel instead raced at his familiar 3,000 metres. He duly won, clocking a good time of 7:32.55, accounting for a good field in which the athletes behind him were Luke Kipkosgei, Assefa Mezgebu, Bob Kennedy, Driss El Himer and Brahim Lahlafi. Komen's appearance on this start line and eventual victory may have had a little to do with the fact that Haile Gebrselassie was not at this meeting.

Haile Gebrselassie dominated everything on the track in long distance running during 1998, this being the year when he would win a share of the golden bars (million dollar jackpot). Daniel Komen was racing a new discipline and telling others that this was his new goal, but his racing patterns made it look like he was running scared. So far he had spent nearly the entire season partly wasting his talents by competing over 1,500 metres, where he was never ever going to defeat Hicham El Guerrouj. Maybe he had a fantasy to be a 1,500 metres world champion. Komen was great, at his best truly brilliant, but he lacked the explosive speed to turn such fantasy into reality. Gebrselassie was the only 5,000 metres man who could realistically dream of such things. Seriously. If the 1,500 metres had been his focus, Haile would have been in the mix, but not Komen. Fifteen hundred metres weren't quite long enough for his incredible threshold running to burn everybody off, at least in the majority of circumstances. My advice would have been to stick to the 3,000 metres and 5,000 metres. In other words, don't forget your day job. Even if this meant suffering a couple of defeats at the hands of distance running's finest.

I think that deep down, Komen knew he'd received an advantage when defeating Gebrselassie in Zurich '96. Haile was still battered and bruised from Paul Tergat and the harsh

MOROCCAN SUCCESS; THE KADA WAY

Atlanta track. This was confirmed in the '97 race when Haile took the honours despite Daniel improving his magnificent time a fraction. Now knowing that he was without any such advantages, Komen in the spirit of Jerry Seinfeld, was basically saying that, "I choose not to run!" It wasn't quite that feeble of course, as the Kenyan had taken great offence at the Ethiopian's racing tactics during that Zurich extravaganza. But you shouldn't hold such a grudge forever.

The 1998 season was the easiest that Gebrselassie had ever experienced. Without Komen and to a lesser extent Hissou, most races became a non contest. The athlete who usually finished second this season was Kenyan Luke Kipkosgei. Luke was a quality runner, but he wasn't a Tergat, Komen or Hissou. That, combined with Haile being in career best form made for the no contests.

It is fair to say that Salah would not have been beating Haile during this Golden League season. But if second was the new first, it would be fair to say that Hissou could have enjoyed many 'victories' in 1998.

The Golden League season was a procession for Haile Gebrselassie as he registered times of 7:27 in Oslo, 13:02 in Rome, 7:25 in Monaco, 12:54 in Zurich, 7:25 in Brussels, 12:56 in Berlin and finally a 7:50 over 3,000 metres in the Grand Prix final in Moscow. Nobody could seriously challenge him whether the distance be 10,000 metres, 5,000 metres or 3,000 metres. The 3,000 metres had become such a big event that the Golden League had the distance scheduled at four of their seven meetings.

Was this the best year ever by a track distance runner? Gebrselassie won seven times at the highest level in Europe. His 7:25.09 for 3,000 metres in Brussels was the second fastest ever. In addition, he had taken back his 5,000 metres and 10,000 metres outdoor world records as well as breaking the 3,000 metres and 2,000 metres world records indoors. Perhaps there wasn't any point in posing the earlier question.

The question that was worth posing was whether or not

Komen was deliberately avoiding Gebrselassie. The distance running capital of Brussels later provided a clear enough answer. Like last year the venue held events at 3,000 metres, 5,000 metres and 10,000 metres. For Golden League purposes Haile was running in the 3,000 metres. In this instance Komen decided to stick his hand up to compete in the 5,000 metres. What a coincidence! It could be argued that Komen was wary of being defeated in the event that he was world champion. He thought that Brussels would provide the perfect opportunity for him to ease back onto the winner's list.

On August the 28th Daniel Komen put his huge reputation on the line and raced in the 5,000 metres. It was the same meeting that he had run his 12:39 world record twelve months earlier. A subtle sign that the dominating Komen wasn't quite the same came here when he ran second to Assefa Mezgebu in 12:54.82. The Ethiopian ran 12:53.84. Komen had gone from the Gebrselassie standard to the Mezgebu standard.

Daniel still had very good form during 1998, but the regular racing and flights to all corners of the globe were beginning to take their toll. Throughout this season he would travel to Australia, Morocco, America, Senegal, Malaysia, Russia and South Africa! Plus there were the more common European destinations. In the Brussels 5,000 metres, Komen reached 3,000 metres in an excellent split of 7:40.1 (Noah Ngeny was the rabbit), which was almost as quick as his record split in '97. If not fatigued, he would have surely broken 12:50 as well as broken Mezgebu. Only three days prior, Daniel had also lost by one tenth of a second to Luke Kipkosgei over 3,000 metres in Lausanne. There appeared to be increased hope for Salah Hissou's chances of gold in the 5,000 metres at Seville!

But first Salah needed to return to competition. The Brussels meeting would have been hard to watch for the Moroccan. The last four years he'd done battle in the 10,000 metres, each race being highly significant in the relative success and failure of his career. To miss this year's battle was tough. An opportunity to get some payback on the two Pauls was lost. This was the *big* 10,000 metres race of the year, considering

MOROCCAN SUCCESS; THE KADA WAY

there was no major championship.

Tergat and Koech again scored the quinella in the 10,000 metres with their standards being somewhere between their '96 and '97 efforts. Tergat won in 26:46.44 with Koech just behind in 26:47.89. This was a top run but for Tergat, it was twenty four seconds slower than Gebrselassie had run in Hengelo. It seemed he had lost ground to the 'emperor'. Haile was never more clearly the best long distance track runner in the world than he was right now. The best plan was to avoid Haile Gebrselassie at all costs. Daniel Komen was right!

Back to the 1,500 metres and the Golden League meet in Monaco on August 8. Again Hicham had aspirations of breaking a world record. The only difference was that this one was now his own. In this race he won easily as always, although at least this time there were signs that the Kenyans were bridging the gap. The results of the first fourteen athletes, incredibly all under 3:34 are as follows:

Hicham El Guerrouj	3:28.37
Laban Rotich	3:30.06
Noah Ngeny	3:30.34
John Kibowen	3:30.36
Isaac Viciosa	3:30.94
Reyes Estevez	3:31.34
Driss Maazouzi	3:31.59
Fermin Cacho	3:32.62
Daniel Komen	3:32.81
John Mayock	3:32.82
Branko Zorko	3:33.30
Vyacheslav Shabunin	3:33.32
Nadir Bosch	3:33.52
Steve Holman	3:33.60

El Guerrouj continued to delight his coach and growing worldwide fan base. While this performance didn't threaten his Rome mark, it was still Hicham's second fastest 1,500 metres. The number of runners that he helped drag through to excellent times was astonishing. Five men under 3:31 made this a race of rare quality. Robert Kibet was again on hand to set the pace, but unlike Rome, it was William Tanui who was the second pacesetter. The other rabbit in Rome, Noah Ngeny was allowed to run his own race in Monaco and quickly showed that he was no ordinary rabbit. At only nineteen years old he finished third, defeating established milers like Kibowen and Estevez, and massive names like Cacho and Komen. Laban was again the first Kenyan finisher but Noah was the big story, the first younger athlete showing the potential to one day challenge Hicham.

The future of middle distance running in Morocco looked very bright. Not only did it have El Guerrouj totally dominating the discipline, but on August the 2nd it had also found itself a world junior champion. Born on January 1, 1979, Adil Kaouch won the gold medal with a time of 3:42.43, just getting the better of Kenyan Benjamin Kipkurui who ran 3:42.67. Benjamin had led through 1,200 metres in 3:02.90, meaning that Adil had covered the last 300 metres in 39.53 or quicker. This Moroccan had some serious speed for a nineteen year old.

There was plenty of good news for Moroccan running but Abdelkader Kada was having problems with Ali Ezzine. His knee injury was one hurdle too many as the youngster could only manage an 8:37.02 in Monaco, finishing a second last fourteenth out of those who completed the steeplechase. It was clear that he would need plenty of rest, maybe even surgery. Certainly his season was over. But so long as the injury wasn't too bad, then there were more pros than cons in 1998 for Ali. This frustrating situation could even be a blessing in disguise, giving him an enforced layoff and more time to focus on the 1999 season. At this stage the major aim was to qualify for the Moroccan team to compete at the Seville World Championships.

The wonderful exploits of Bernard Barmasai had continued with the Kenyan almost breaking eight minutes again, in 8:00.67, while finishing well ahead of compatriot Wilson Boit Kipketer who ran 8:04.97. Brahim Boulami was the only Moroccan to impress as he finished fifth and ran a good time of 8:11.30, but being twenty six years old, it was unlikely that

MOROCCAN SUCCESS; THE KADA WAY

he could improve much further. Morocco needed to push through some younger talent.

The always sensational meeting of Zurich arrived on August 12. It was probably the best venue for breaking records. As a result, much hype surrounded the men's 1,500 metres with El Guerrouj looking to improve on his last race in Monaco. Remarkably, Noah Ngeny went back to his position as rabbit. What more did the guy have to do to get a regular gig? With his help the times were extremely fast with the results showing:

Hicham El Guerrouj	3:26.45
Laban Rotich	3:29.91
John Kibowen	3:30.18
Daniel Komen	3:30.49
Reyes Estevez	3:30.87
William Tanui	3:32.02
Anthony Whiteman	3:32.69
William Chirchir	3:33.24

It was excruciatingly close to an improvement on his Rome record. The strength of Hicham El Guerrouj was his most impressive quality. Nobody had ever run this event consistently in the way that he was doing, which was running at his limits for the race's entirety. Well yes of course, others did race at their limits, but Hicham could hold his pace. There were many similarities in the style with which El Guerrouj raced his races and the style with which Komen raced his. That's when Daniel raced at the 3,000 and 5,000 metres.

Laban Rotich joined the exclusive sub 3:30 club, a reward for the constant improvements he had made during the season. In 1998 he was similar to Luke Kipkosgei, performing well and beating the majority, but finding that there was one runner ahead who seemed unassailable.

The invincible Moroccan next took his fast wheels to Brussels for another tune up. This race was a little easier, if you can call running 3:29.67 that! It demonstrated the new standards that he had reached when a sub 3:30 no longer got people excited. The win was as convincing as ever but this time there was a different runner trailing him home. Spaniard Andres Diaz clocked 3:32.48 with Rotich next in 3:33.08. This season was basically a farce as far as a 'contest' was concerned with Hicham easily winning all the time with two of the runners who could get closest to him, Tanui and Ngeny, often setting the pace, which they both did in Brussels and Tanui would again do in Berlin.

Off to Germany for the September 1 track and field action and the pressure was building, though for the sole reason that Hicham now required just two more victories to grab a share of the golden bars. Logically there was little reason for concern. Yes, El Guerrouj had lost in the Grand Prix final last year, which cost him dearly, but the circumstances there were far different. One, there was a greater gap between the previous Golden League meeting and the final making it harder to stay in racing shape. Two, Fukuoka is a lot further from mainland Europe than Moscow, making jet lag a possible factor and three, the temperature was likely to be much cooler in Russia. In distance races, hot conditions often gave the lesser athletes a better chance at defeating the best. These chances are accentuated the greater the distance, which explains why the major championships (usually run in oppressive hot climates) usually throw up a few surprises.

With these factors in mind Hicham should remain quietly confident yet focused on the job at hand. The former trainee mechanic simply needed to keep his machine running smoothly and he would hit the jackpot. From now on he needn't any theatrics so in Berlin and Moscow he made no further challenges to his world record.

Hicham El Guerrouj triumphed with tremendous effortlessness, winning in 3:30.23, a massive distance ahead of the usual rabbit Noah Ngeny's 3:33.54. Almost everyone goes through a similar pain barrier, but in every race on the back straight during the final lap, it appeared that the Moroccan was the only one that was adverse to it. It is here that it really hurts, where the race is often won or lost for anybody still in contention. Some athletes are or were known

MOROCCAN SUCCESS; THE KADA WAY

for a particular style of racing. Take Billy Konchellah's late burst on the home straight as an example. The main image that many track fans will have of Hicham El Guerrouj will be of him going up just one more gear, to a gear that nobody else has, and moving away slowly but surely on the back straight towards yet another victory.

The Grand Prix final arrived just four days later on Saturday September 5. It would be the closest race that Hicham had endured all year, though it wasn't tight enough to worry him. The results from the final race of the Moroccan's year were:

Hicham El Guerrouj	3:32.03
Laban Rotich	3:33.04
William Tanui	3:33.30
John Kibowen	3:33.64
Noah Ngeny	3:33.81
Daniel Komen	3:33.86
Andres Diaz	3:34.02
Driss Maazouzi	3:34.59
John Mayock	3:34.60
Vyacheslav Shabunin	3:39.36

Robert Kibet of Kenya helped again with the pace as Hicham became an even wealthier young man. Now he could look forward to 1999 and hope for much of the same, culminating with the defence of his world championship. The general order of this final race was a pretty fair reflection on the entire season. A Moroccan first with a bunch of Kenyans behind him. This was the only nation of runners which Hicham and Abdelkader needed to keep an eye on. One of these athletes might also wake up and discover that his best abilities lay elsewhere.

Do not flirt with your form, Daniel. Your peak period may be short, so make the most of it.

Greg Rowlerson

The Toughest Barrier Is The Kenyans

Salah Hissou wasn't worried about avoiding a smiling Ethiopian. He was too busy worrying about himself. After many injury free years his body was falling apart. At least he knew that when fit he could still match it with most. Just the two races in 1998 for two wins. It was a good ratio. He had shown that he could still dominate races, at least those that didn't include Gebrselassie. Some belief still existed and with good reason. The door to being the 5,000 metres world champion was becoming ajar. The 1999 World Athletics Championships were on Hissou's horizon and this time he planned to stop Haile's comet from stealing his sunlight. It was Salah's time to shine in Spain. Such a good runner deserved a major championship. Would his body give him one more chance? Would the Moroccan Federation do the same?

Abdelkader Kada had already coached one world champion, but to totally prove to any doubters that his systems worked, he needed to lead another athlete to gold. Salah Hissou had always showed the potential of winning a major championship and one day Ali Ezzine might also reach such heights. Hicham El Guerrouj had reached this level long ago and from now on his career required more of a regular general maintenance, rather than any major service or upgrade. For 1999 it was Salah Hissou who would prove Abdelkader Kada's success or failure as a coach.

Salah had won plenty of races at the top international level but he never seemed to ooze the mentality of someone who expected to win. He needed to change this, to increase his mental competitiveness in order to win a major championship. His performance in Paris last year showed that the 5,000 metres was really his forte but of course Salah had thought this as early as 1996. Despite lacking a finishing kick, Salah had the strength to put in excellent mid race laps and recover, or make a long run for home and carry it through to the end. Plus there was the 'emperor from Ethiopia' factor. The little master hadn't run the 5,000 metres at a major championships

MOROCCAN SUCCESS; THE KADA WAY

since the 1993 world titles in Stuttgart. He figured to only run the 10,000 metres again in Seville. Running the 5,000 metres would also take Paul Tergat out of the equation. Nevertheless, planning to win gold in Seville was going to be much harder than simply avoiding Gebrselassie and Tergat. Getting back to full fitness while avoiding injury had to be top priority.

There were handfuls of runners now running sub thirteen minutes for 5,000 metres. Salah had done so on a number of occasions but even this barrier wasn't a cake walk for him as his personal best was 12:50.80. He wasn't in the Gebrselassie/Komen category of men who had twenty seconds up their sleeve on the thirteen minutes. He also didn't have the luxury of a great kick. Hissou would have to perform at his best while also running a supreme tactical race if he was to have a chance at taking the gold medal. Going into 1999, only Gebrselassie, Komen and Tergat had ever run faster than Hissou at 5,000 metres. To really simplify things the main question would be this. Could Hissou beat Komen in Seville?

Things are never that simple but even as the Moroccan prepared for the cross country season, he would be keeping an eye on Kenya's world champion.

After another long injury layoff Hissou returned to competition on New Year's Eve, 1998. In Bolzano, Italy, Salah raced on the road over an old familiar distance. This was his first 10 kms race since Brussels '97.

It was a decent enough first up performance. Hissou clocked 28:11 and finished third, just losing out to Kenyan Paul Kosgei and Ethiopian Lemma Alemayehu. Both were timed at 28:10. This was a good confidence builder with another top Ethiopian, Habte Jifar, finishing behind Salah in 28:14. The main thing was that Salah got through the battle with his left ankle intact. Despite the setbacks of 1998 he had not undergone surgery, the Moroccan Federation feeling that rest was sufficient to overcome the problem.

Greg Rowlerson

This was the first in a sequence of races that would lead Hissou up to the World Cross Country Championships in Belfast on March 28. The aim was to find the sort of form that would give Paul Tergat something to worry about. The Kenyan was going for an unprecedented fifth straight long course title. This seemed very likely to happen but if a certain Moroccan could return to the form of Turin '97, maybe Tergat wouldn't have things all his own way.

That was Hissou's plan anyway, although plans for Salah hadn't panned out in recent times. In January he turned twenty seven. He wasn't finished, but his window of opportunity wouldn't remain open for too much longer.

By March he was still fit. That's at least three months without an injury! On March the 7th he raced in a 10.2 kms event over cross country terrain, again in Italy. It was the same race that he had won in the lead up to the World Cross Country in '94 and '97. This time Hissou managed a second place result. The man who defeated him was Paul Kosgei, the same Kenyan who had won the 10 kms road race in Bolzano. Nevertheless, it was a good performance from Salah as he attempted to reestablish himself as one of the world's preeminent cross country runners. Some of the runners that he defeated were good cross country runners. Names such as Sergey Lebid, Christopher Koskei and Aloys Nizigama were good scalps to pick up with the World Cross Country Championships just three weeks away.

One week later Hissou was in Milan and it was time to get really serious. March the 14th was the day of his final race before Belfast and Salah was going to be running into a famous Kenyan.

This Milan race had enjoyed some history. The 10.8 kms cross country course was known as the Cinque Mulini 'Five Mills' and some famous names had won the event. It would be a nice feather to add to the Moroccan's cap if he could add his name to the winner's list. The race win became a much easier prospect when Paul Tergat was a late withdrawal, citing a slight muscle injury. Things were looking much

MOROCCAN SUCCESS; THE KADA WAY

brighter for success in both Milan and Belfast for Salah.

Hissou showed signs of a potential world cross country champion when he easily won the Five Mills race. Just before 2 kms he took off and was able to run away unchallenged, recording a winning time of 34:49, well ahead of Kenyan John Korir's 35:03.

With the reigning champion in some doubt, finally becoming the world cross country champion was again becoming a realistic possibility for Salah Hissou.

Unfortunately when the big day came, Salah didn't have it. The Belfast course was in a horrible state, that's if you consider ankle deep mud to be horrible, although for the purists, this was true cross country conditions. Despite the inclement conditions, the Kenyan contingent still took its place at the head of the pack. After one km, Hissou was just remaining in contact and by two kms, he was already off the back and in about tenth place. By three kms the situation had not improved and soon after, he pulled out.

It was another moment at the cross roads for Salah, but not for Paul Tergat who incredibly won, yet again. This achievement was extraordinary. It equalled fellow Kenyan John Ngugi's total wins, although winning five in a row had never been done before.

Tergat as usual did it easily, winning in a time of 38:28, the time being slow because of the conditions. He finished four seconds ahead of the surprise packet Patrick Ivuti. Everyone else was well back although a great performance was put in by Portuguese runner Paulo Guerra, whose third place finish made for a rare sight. It was the first time since 1989 that a non African had finished on the podium.

Hissou wasn't the only significant name to have performed below expectations. Paul Koech finished sixth, but his time of 39:51 was well off the pace and was disappointing considering his excellent lead up form. He had been the pick of many to win the title. Mohammed Mourhit continued his development with seventh place in 40:09. But this cross country produced some weird results. Habte Jifar and Assefa Mezgebu were ninth and eleventh. The latter had placed third only a year ago. Tom Nyariki finished 39th! He was third in '97.

Morocco remained well off its 1997 peak results. In Belfast the highest placed finisher was Lahcen Benyoussef in thirteenth. The team finished a distant fifth with a points total of 108. Kenya scored 12 points. There was plenty of work for the squad to do before the Seville World Championships in August.

Why had Salah struggled so much in Belfast? Was he injured? Was the 1996/1997 version a thing of the past? His two track wins in 1998 suggested that this was not the case. The truth wasn't quite so bad as like many of the athletes, he just didn't cope well with the muddy surface. It was so difficult to get consistently firm footing that Tergat's split at 10 kms was 31:41! That pretty much explains Salah's problems. Hissou has always had the distinctive style of a track runner, possessing good bounce in his stride, his form looking as good as anyone else. Except for Wilson Kipketer! A return to Europe and the track in June might be all he needed to turn his career around.

A lot had gone wrong for him in recent times. Only two years earlier, Salah Hissou was a name on every distance running fans' lips. Now it was more a case of Salah Hiss who?

Hicham El Guerrouj had skipped the indoor season, not racing in the year's early European action for the first time since 1994. 1998 had been a most hectic year and Kada's decision to avoid racing for a while made sense. Hicham would gain nothing by racing indoors this year but burnout was a possibility. Also having El Guerrouj wait until June for a big race was a good way of whetting his appetite. Despite making winning a regular habit, there was never any issue with Hicham lacking motivation when he did race. For this, Abdelkader Kada should be given some credit.

MOROCCAN SUCCESS; THE KADA WAY

The coach took his two star pupils to Milan for their first races of the 1999 outdoor season on June 9. The competition would provide some answers as to how successful the months of training at Ifrane had been. Kada was confident that he'd prepared El Guerrouj and Hissou to the best of his coaching ability and thus had them in outstanding shape. He hoped that Milan would confirm this belief.

For Hicham the 1,500 metres was just a time trial. There was nobody in this field of a Golden League miler calibre and the world champion was able to coast around the circuit untouched in 3:31.34. His victory margin was incredibly over five seconds on Italy's Giuseppe D'Urso and Mohammed Amyn, a Moroccan whose talents were better suited to the longer distances.

It was tough to find a challenge these days for El Guerrouj but not so for Hissou, as this meeting provided him with an intimidating opponent. The first race in Salah Hissou's European track season had often been significant as the Moroccan usually started his track campaign very well. Some athletes struggled to get their body's race ready for June but Salah didn't seem to ever require a warm up.

Here are Hissou's first 5,000 metres races of the season since 1995:

Year	Venue	Placing and Time	Comments
1995	Rome	4th in 13:02.25	Moses Kiptanui and Daniel Komen both went under Haile Gebrselassie's world record. Hissou recorded a personal best time.
1996	Rome	1st in 12:50.80	Hissou defeated practically a who's who of Kenyan distance running at the time. Philip Mosima, Moses Kiptanui, Thomas Nyariki, Daniel Komen, Shem Kororia. Hissou's time was the second fastest in history.
1997	Rome	2nd in 12:52.39	Hissou was beaten by Daniel Komen.
1998	Saint-Denis	1st in 12:57.73	Hissou left the opposition in tatters.

Daniel Komen and Salah Hissou were two of the best track distance runners in the world and had been for four years. Yet they hadn't raced each other since Komen's fantastic victory in Rome 1997. 1999's first significant 5,000 metres race was in Milan and both would be in attendance. It was the first of many memorable contests between the pair in the lead up to Seville.

Had Hissou recovered from his Belfast failure? Was Komen still a world record breaking force?

The Kenyan was coming off a 3,000 metres victory in Stuttgart just three days earlier. There he had clocked an impressive 7:32.72 and out sprinted nineteen year old Ethiopian Hailu Mekonnen who registered 7:33.00.

In Milan the pace was fast from the start and it quickly

MOROCCAN SUCCESS; THE KADA WAY

became a race of two. The rabbit James Kimutai Kosgei, went through 3,000 metres in 7:42.99. Both Salah and Daniel were in good form. With their attractive running styles, the sixty two second laps looked easy. But Salah's outward exterior always gave the impression that he was jogging. It was hard to tell if he was feeling tired or still had something left in his tank. Out went the rabbit and it was one on one for two world champion hopefuls. The situation was similar to the last two occasions where Hissou had raced Komen. Both of them were too good for the rest and on target for a fast time. Then it had been the Kenyan storming away in the dying stages. This time it was a different story.

The Salah Hissou of Rome and Brussels '96 returned in a big way in Milan '99. The Moroccan was in spectacular form as he managed to drop his big rival. His winning time of 12:52.53 further conveyed that he was back to his best. Daniel Komen may have looked sluggish in comparison, but his time of 12:55.18 was still tremendous running. He nevertheless had improvements to make if he was to reestablish himself as the clear favourite for the world championship 5,000 metres.

The rest of the field was fairly irrelevant. Moroccan Mohamed Said El Wardi, 13:10.10. Kenyan's Daniel Gachara and Mark Bett, 13:13.41 and 13:14.27 respectively. It was the first two that mattered. They were the ones that distance running fans would keep an eye on. The 5,000 metres world champion and the guy who used to lose to Gebrselassie and Tergat at 10,000 metres. Those in the know knew that Komen had a worthy adversary as he battled to retain his world title.

To those who understood the sport, this result was of no great surprise. Salah had produced many performances of such a standard in the past. Abdelkader Kada knew better than most as he explained to the press the return to form of Hissou,"I understood that he could recapture his form of two seasons ago when I saw him training in Ifrane with El Guerrouj. Salah had no problem keeping up with El Guerrouj's quick pace."

In 1996 and 1997 Daniel Komen ran some astonishing times. He had broken the world record at 3,000 metres, two miles and 5,000 metres. His 5,000 metres personal best was eleven seconds faster than Hissou's! His superb form had continued into 1998 with those great performances indoors. It was in this rich vein of form that he ran under eight minutes for the second time at two miles outdoors. He was the only man to do this and it seemed all the more incredible, considering how long it took a man to break four minutes for one mile. Less than half a century later, Daniel Komen was running sub sixty's for twice the distance.

Following his sub eight minute run in Sydney, Komen stopped threatening the record books. Gebrselassie dominated the Golden League meetings in 1998 as Komen started to regularly compete in the 1,500 metres. Brussels had best illustrated the drop off in his standards. A year after his 5,000 metres world record Komen could *only* run 12:54.82. What's more, this was his best time outdoors for the year. Daniel finished second here to an Ethiopian but not the usual suspect. Gebrselassie's lesser countryman, Assefa Mezgebu had beaten him by one second in a career best run.

Even still, his outdoor season wasn't half bad. Komen did win the African Championships, World Cup and Commonwealth Games 5,000 metres races, each convincingly. In oppressive conditions at Kuala Lumper, Daniel's time was just 13:22.57 but his run was outstanding. With two laps remaining, he was behind compatriot Thomas Nyariki. In the next lap he left one of the world's best long distance runners for dead and went on to win the Commonwealth gold by more than five seconds.

But 1999 started ominously for the star. Since he owned the 3,000 and 5,000 metres world records (indoors), he decided he might as well go for the 2,000 metres record. On February 5 he not only clocked a decidedly average 4:58.77, but lost to Moroccan Adil Kaouch. On February 14 things got worse at the Birmingham meeting when Komen placed a distant fourth with a 4:59.93. Laban Rotich took the victory in 4:56.09.

Now Salah Hissou had defeated him in their first big confrontation of 1999. Could Daniel Komen turn his form around in the little time left before the Seville World

MOROCCAN SUCCESS; THE KADA WAY

Championships?

This is a book primarily about three Moroccans, but I can never avoid discussing a certain Ethiopian for any great length of time. Hissou may have run well in Milan, but that paled in comparison when a day later, we witnessed another majestic display by Gebrselassie in Helsinki. The Ethiopian won the 3,000 metres in 7:26.03. This form was coming on the back of another incredible indoor season. He'd come pretty close to Komen's 3,000 metres record with a 7:26.80 in Karlsruhe on January 24. Then he went and broke his world record for 5,000 metres with a 12:50.38 in that Birmingham meeting on February 14. There was also the minor matter of him rocking up to the World Indoor Championships and winning the 3,000 metres. There he also decided to give the 1,500 metres a go and he won that too! Even when he wasn't beating him, Gebrselassie would almost always overshadow Hissou.

Not to be outdone, Salah raced in Nuremberg on June 13. Again the distance was 5,000 metres. Only this time there was no Komen. The event was a slower, more subdued affair. That was until Hissou showed the rest what real speed endurance was all about.

He was in intimidating form, recording his second straight win and doing it with consummate ease. The time was 13:09.67, which was not anything special but the winning margin was, as Salah defeated the lesser runners by over five seconds. Richard Limo, 13:15.24, Daniel Gachara, 13:17.83, Luke Kipkosgei, 13:18.12 and Mohamed Said El Wardi, 13:22.31. However this was not the time for over confidence as these athletes would not even make it to the start line of the World Championships in August.

Hissou had done more than enough at this early stage of the season and took a brief break from racing. The rest of June was a period of hard training. By the end of the month nothing had changed on the men's distance running scene. On June 30 in Oslo, Haile Gebrselassie won the 5,000 metres in 12:53.92, just another *average* performance. This was three days after he had won a one mile race in Gateshead.

Also racing in Nuremberg was El Guerrouj and for a change he wasn't quite as dominating, though his time of 3:32.40 was still comfortably faster than regular second place man Laban Rotich. The Kenyan clocked 3:33.64 in another highly respectable performance. But Hicham's next race clearly showed that there was a different Kenyan in a much higher class. Like Salah, Hicham also took some time out from racing. His racing schedule was much lighter this season and he even bypassed some Golden League races, not bothering to chase the golden bars that he most probably would have won again if he had so desired.

After their brief respite, Hicham and Salah returned to one of their favourite venues, Rome. El Guerrouj had something special planned for the meeting, aiming at adding his name to the illustrious list of mile world record holders. The Kenyans Robert Kibet and William Tanui would set the pace which Abdelkader and Hicham hoped could set them up to join the likes of Bannister, Landy, Walker, Coe, Ovett, Cram and Morceli in middle distance running folklore.

Hicham stated pre race, "If the conditions are as good as last year – the weather, the crowd and the pacemakers – then I really think that I can break the record tomorrow. For me it is very important. I owe it to all those who have helped and supported me, especially my family, who need something to boost their morale after my uncle's recent death."

He had just put in a good stint of training at altitude. This world record attempt came just five days after returning to sea level.

As with last year's record attempt, the crowd is poor. The first lap is clocked at 55.07 with El Guerrouj in his customary 'drivers seat' position of third. Ngeny is the next athlete in the long line behind him.

El Guerrouj appears to be straining to hang onto the leaders during the early stages of lap two, which may have caused

MOROCCAN SUCCESS; THE KADA WAY

Kada some concern. Ngeny manages to keep up for now, yet the rest are already giving up fifteen metres. By the end of this lap, Hicham seems to be keeping in contact much easier as Kibet drops out after a 1:51.58 split. Can Tanui run the third lap strongly enough to provide El Guerrouj with a platform to break the record?

This is certainly no problem as William really pours it on down the back straight, appearing to put Hicham briefly into difficulty. Yet looks can be deceiving because Noah now slips three metres behind the Moroccan. It looks to be only a matter of time until he lets go. Into the final 500 metres and El Guerrouj looks as if he's accelerating, passing Tanui just before the bell, which he reaches in 2:47.91. The crucial third lap is fast enough, giving him a great chance at the world record.

Surprisingly, the outstanding young Kenyan Ngeny has remained in touch. Trying to shake him off as well as create history, Hicham produces his usual kick on the back straight and his opponent gives him around four metres advantage. But he is not yet beaten, and as they enter the final bend, Ngeny begins to creep back ever so slowly. El Guerrouj passes through 1,500 metres in 3:28.21 with the Kenyan right on his tail, ready to pounce if Hicham falters at all. He isn't, although the gap isn't growing.

Noah moves out into lane two hoping to take him. For a moment he appears to be a chance half way down the straight, but Hicham still has a mini burst in reserve and keeps him at bay. The results from the Rome mile on Wednesday, July 7, 1999, were:

Hicham El Guerrouj	3:43.13
Noah Ngeny	3:43.40
Rui Silva	3:50.91
Andres Diaz	3:51.15
Laban Rotich	3:51.66
Ali Saidi-Sief	3:51.90
Vyacheslav Shabunin	3:52.23
Mohammed Amyn	3:52.66

Giuseppe D'Urso	3:52.72
John Mayock	3:52.79
Kevin Sullivan	3:52.96
Frederick Cheruiyot	3:52.99
David Lelei	3:53.14
Adil Kaouch	3:53.35
Youssef Baba	3:53.64
Lorenzo Lazzari	3:55.89

The record was his! It was a comprehensive lowering of Noureddine Morceli's 3:44.39 time, a similar amount to which he had taken off the Algerian's 1,500 metres world record at the same track last year. In the way that Haile Gebrselassie had made the Hengelo meeting his own, Hicham El Guerrouj was doing with the Rome circuit. He appropriately declared, "Rome is a magic track for me."

He immediately grabbed the usual bunch of victory flowers before being stopped and embraced by the Kenyans. There wasn't quite the shock of last year's record. This was almost expected.

With the many celebrations taking place it was nearly forgotten that a young Kenyan had almost taken all of the spoils. Benefiting from the Moroccan's strong pace setting, Noah Ngeny was able to follow the champion in a way that was a little too close for comfort for Hicham's entourage. Last year this Kenyan was a more than useful rabbit. This year he was bettering the best of Morceli! Suddenly El Guerrouj had a worthy rival and the Seville 1,500 metres now took on a completely different dimension.

Born on November 2, 1978, Ngeny had age on his side. Noah had made steady, almost expected progress, having gone from a 3:32.91 in '97, to a 3:30.34 in '98 for 1,500 metres. Both these times were set at Monaco with his improvements coming under the guidance of renowned coach, Kim McDonald. His mile run was the equivalent of about a 3:27 time so this was a big jump in standard. Most people were surprised to see him threaten El Guerrouj in Rome. Pleasantly surprised to see this was Steve Cram who said, "What made

MOROCCAN SUCCESS; THE KADA WAY

it better than a lot of races we see on the circuit, was that it was a race. The young Kenyan really did push him all the way to the line."

The 5,000 metres event was greeted with almost as much enthusiasm as the mile. Hicham had also said the following prior to breaking Morceli's mark, "I will not be running the 5,000 metres just yet, though," he laughed with Salah Hissou, seated at his side, "not until Salah retires! Maybe, in fact definitely, it will not be until after Sydney. This year I will run another six or seven races on the Grand Prix circuit, with the ultimate aim of defending my 1,500 metres title in the World Championships in Seville in August."

Nothing that Hissou did could ever match the magnificence of that mile but at least he didn't have to contend with his training partner yet, and we would still be in store for a really top class 5,000 metres without Hicham. For Salah it was his third consecutive hit out at his preferred distance. Basically this field was as good as it got in distance running. Everyone was here except for Gebrselassie. This gave others a chance to win!

Daniel Komen had returned to his imperial best with a thumping win in Lausanne on July 2. Racing over his favourite 3,000 metres distance, Komen simply destroyed Olympic silver medallists Paul Bitok and Paul Tergat. The time differentials were immense. 7:30.62 to 7:36.25 and 7:36.89. Awesome stuff.

As was so often the case, Rome became another chapter in the Salah Hissou versus Kenya saga. For the first time since August '97, Hissou reacquainted himself with Tergat on an athletics track. A confident Komen also showed up, looking to turn the tables from Milan a month ago. In a well paced race the final results were:

Daniel Komen	12:55.16
Paul Tergat	12:55.37
Salah Hissou	12:55.39
Benjamin Limo	12:56.55

David Chelule	12:57.79
Richard Limo	12:58.15
Mohammed Mourhit	12:58.45
Paul Koech	13:01.72
Bob Kennedy	13:08.43
Benjamin Maiyo	13:09.83
Tom Nyariki	13:10.63
Hailu Mekonnen	13:10.98
Alberto Garcia	13:11.10
Philip Mosima	13:12.67
Assefa Mezgebu	13:22.17
Said Berioui	13:22.42

The race was of the highest standard with seven runners breaking thirteen minutes. Among them was Hissou, with another impressive time of 12:55.39. Unfortunately for Salah, two familiar rivals had defeated him. But not by much. This time Komen took the spoils ahead of Tergat, with Paul being only two hundredths of a second ahead of Salah! It was a very close run event and another instalment in the rivalry between Tergat and Hissou. The final km split was 2:31.46.

Many others had remained in the mix until the latter stages of this race, which saw quite a kick down over the final few laps. Benjamin Limo showed that he was an athlete for Salah to watch out for, while the other runners to break thirteen minutes were David Chelule, Richard Limo and Mohammed Mourhit. Anybody running these times was in contention for Seville.

It is worth noting here that neither Limo is related. Benjamin had made a sudden rise to the elite level and was already twenty four years old. Meanwhile Richard was only eighteen and was an athlete with spectacular versatility. In 1998 he'd finished second in the World Junior Cross Country, third in the Commonwealth Games 5,000 metres and second in the 3,000 metres steeplechase at the African Championships.

The many other big names behind the Limo's in Rome highlighted the amazing depth of the event. Nyariki was not the runner of '97 and Mezgebu's fifteenth placing was

MOROCCAN SUCCESS; THE KADA WAY

mystifying, considering that he'd won so well in Brussels last year.

Daniel Komen had posted a crucial victory in the lead up to Seville. This partly erased the memory of the Milan loss and was crucial in the whole scheme of things for the World Championships. His win raised his own confidence while slightly deflating the confidence of his Moroccan rival.

There was still a significant amount of time before Seville, with the 5,000 metres final not being run until the 28th of August. The remaining lead up time would be vital.

Hissou had already shown tremendous form in this 1999 season. His strength over the 5,000 metres was as good as it had ever been and even his relative weakness of closing race speed seemed to be on the improve. Yes, Salah was out kicked by Daniel and Paul in Rome, but he finished within three tenths of a second of the duo. In past years Hissou's losing margin would have been seconds to these guys. His finishing last lap kick had definitely improved.

But this remained his main area of concern when it came to planning to win the 5,000 metres gold in Seville. To try and make it even less of a concern, Salah Hissou went back to the 3,000 metres for some sharper speed work.

Nice always attracted a top class field for its 3,000 metres and the athletics meeting on July 17 was no exception. Salah was up against an assortment of 5,000 metres specialists but most of them didn't seem to concern the Moroccan. Late in the race he was well clear of the likes of Bitok, Nyariki, Richard Limo, Bayissa and Sghyr. Sounds good doesn't it?

However Salah Hissou wasn't ahead of everyone. There was a runner accompanying him who he hadn't seen face to face on a race track for almost two years, yet he more than knew him quite well. If nothing else, this was a good opportunity for the Moroccan to test out his finishing kick. There was a famous little Ethiopian close at hand.

Hissou ran very well. A 7:33.44 is not to be scoffed at, especially when you've finished over three seconds clear of Paul Bitok and over five seconds clear of Thomas Nyariki. But his last lap kick did fail the test. Haile Gebrselassie saluted the French crowd in 7:30.58. This was the ultimate test. Gebrselassie said of his victory, "It's not a fast time, but it is the sort of race I like." A time of 7:30 is pretty fast by most standards!

In his current shape Salah could come awfully close to out sprinting Komen and Tergat but he could barely get within three seconds of Gebrselassie. One may wonder why Hissou would bother racing against an unbeatable athlete.

By the time of this Nice race, he had raced numerous times on the track against Haile. On many occasions he had raced well, but on every occasion he had lost and never had he come seriously close to defeating him. A runner as good as Salah Hissou has to have a lot of confidence in his own ability, but at the same time also remain realistic. He knew that he could not defeat Gebrselassie while the Ethiopian remained at his level of excellence, no matter what he tried to do. It was the way in which Salah lost to Haile here that was arguably more demoralising than any trouncing he'd received from the Ethiopian since Gothenburg. In Nice, Hissou led at the bell and continued to lead into the back straight. It wasn't until 250 metres to go that the decisive move was made, so the final winning margin was quite staggering. But we had seen this before. Take Zurich '97 against Komen as the perfect example.

However there was still a good reason for Salah to keep racing against Gebrselassie. Racing against the best meant often pushing yourself more, therefore getting the best out of yourself. It's unlikely that Tergat and Hissou would have run as many high quality 5,000/10,000 metres races if Gebrselassie had not been around to defeat them.

It was possible that for the first time ever Salah may not compete against Haile in a major track championships. But racing against him remained a good way to get into shape to

MOROCCAN SUCCESS; THE KADA WAY

defeat Daniel Komen who was proving this season to be beatable. The Kenyan preferred to totally avoid racing Gebrselassie. At least Hissou wasn't afraid to lose. Nevertheless he certainly did not want to lose his next race on July 21. It was another 3,000 metres and Daniel Komen's name was in the field for the Paris race.

Now losing on a regular basis was Moses Kiptanui. The former world record holder at multiple distances could no longer keep pace with his younger opponents. In Nice he placed tenth in 7:41.69.

There was an important steeplechase race in Nice and Ali Ezzine was keen to test his form against some of the best that Kenya had to offer. Ezzine had started his season late following surgery, which was required to mend knee ligament damage. His recovery had gone as well as he and Abdelkader could have possibly hoped for. Just four days earlier he had started his season in Dar-el-Beida. On July 13 Ezzine served notice to the rest of the top steeplechasers that he was ready to make an impact on the international scene. Not only did he win the event but he also ran a personal best time of 8:13.43. The result not only raised his confidence, but greatly increased his chances of participating in Seville.

Despite the quality of this performance it was still surprising that Ali was able to contest so strongly in Nice. Only Paul Kosgei got the better of him and his time of 8:09.46 wasn't too far ahead of Ezzine's 8:11.20, yet another personal best for the Moroccan. He easily defeated top Kenyans Christopher Koskei, 8:13.32 and Eliud Barngetuny, 8:13.92. Kada could afford a smile. He knew that he had three potential medal winners in his stable for Spain.

The race was run very evenly with the first 1,000 metres completed in 2:42.88. Ezzine then led at 2,000 metres in 5:26.77. Kosgei took over with two laps remaining and was never headed from there.

The steeplechase race that took place in Paris on Wednesday, July 21, 1999 should perhaps be remembered as Morocco's first big foray into Kenya's stronghold over the event. Ezzine went even faster and was supported by Khattabi as the duo was too good for the majority of Kenyans:

Bernard Barmasai	8:05.71
Ali Ezzine	8:07.31
Elarbi Khattabi	8:09.48
Christopher Koskei	8:11.42
Bouabdallah Tahri	8:12.24
Kipkirui Misoi	8:12.65
Moses Kiptanui	8:12.86
Paul Kosgei	8:14.07
Eliud Barngetuny	8:18.64
Julius Chelule	8:19.62
Wilson Boit Kipketer	8:20.59

Barmasai's victory was convincing but Bernard had been clearly the world's best steeplechaser during the past two seasons. The top Moroccans had defeated the rest of the highly rated Kenyans with Ali writing himself into the Moroccan record books. With Ali still short of his twenty first birthday, Kada now believed that he had three possible world champions for a month's time. Ezzine's development would have been even faster than Kada had planned for, so the goals had to be adjusted. There was certainly no issue with Ali being a part of the national team. Barring injury, he would be on the start line for the steeplechase heats on August 21.

The Paris 3,000 metres was another Kenya vs. Hissou confrontation with Salah putting forward his best efforts but still being denied the win. The results were:

Daniel Komen	7:33.23
Salah Hissou	7:33.47
Paul Bitok	7:34.70
Benjamin Limo	7:34.87
Sammy Kipketer	7:35.08
Bob Kennedy	7:35.41
Brahim Jabbour	7:35.92
Mohammed Mourhit	7:36.89
David Chelule	7:37.36
Philip Mosima	7:38.40

MOROCCAN SUCCESS; THE KADA WAY

Mohamed Said El Wardi   7:38.82
Paul Tergat   7:40.78

It was virtually a repeat of Rome. Daniel edged out Salah. This rivalry was now taking on epic proportions. This was their third great battle of the season. It was another fairly fast race that meant the sprint finish came down to strength as well as basic speed. In an exciting contest, the two adversaries traded the lead three times over the concluding stages. Despite the loss, Hissou's kick was proving to be much stronger than in any previous season. The significant names behind him illustrate this point.

We can safely assume that Tergat was in heavy training, or in any case the 3,000 metres was never as big a focus for him as it was for Hissou. Nine days later he managed to win the 10,000 metres event in Stockholm in a fast time of 27:10.08. But back to the Moroccan. The impressive list of runners trailing him in Paris were now losing to Salah because of finishing speed as well as cross country strength. From the results of this season Daniel Komen seemed to be his only serious challenger for the 5,000 metres gold in Seville, should Hissou decide on that distance.

Paul Bitok and Benjamin Limo were in good form but Hissou was beating them. Salah's Milan time remained the fastest 5,000 metres of the season. Most things were falling into place nicely. It would be even nicer if he could defeat Komen in their next meeting.

The 3,000 metres event was now more popular than ever. But it had never really caught on with the world's best middle distance runners who preferred to live a sheltered existence rather than try something different. This surprises me. I assume that if you are continually seeing Hicham El Guerrouj flying away from you then eventually you might want to try your hand at something else. More of the world's best 10,000 metres runners raced over 3,000 metres than the world's best milers. This doesn't make sense to me. A miler needn't have the 3,000 metres as his main target, but it would have to be good training for their specialty. It works the other way too.

Why not compete in the occasional 800 metres race? Salah Hissou would never solely race 5,000 metres for an entire season. He was pretty versatile, but he never expected to win many 3,000 metres races. He raced the distance often in the hope that it would improve his speed so that he could win more often at 5,000 metres. Paul Tergat's best track distance was clearly the 10,000 metres, but this didn't stop him from competing in the 5,000 metres and 3,000 metres.

Year after year, Hicham El Guerrouj raced at the 1500 metres/mile almost all the time. You could say that you might as well keep racing at the same distance if you never lose, but isn't running about getting the best out of yourself, no matter what your standard? It is hard to argue that El Guerrouj didn't get the best out of himself but I am saying that some variety in your racing can't hurt, while it can help. El Guerrouj did happen to lose a race of some significance the following year and some attribute this to the lack of variety in his racing distances. The man who beat him did do some racing at shorter distances. This may have contributed to Hicham's defeat though for the most part El Guerrouj was just highly unlucky. The runner who defeated him was an outstanding miler in his own right and there was every chance that at some stage he would knock off the mighty Moroccan.

On the 4th of August Hissou raced again in the distance runner's sprint, the 3,000 metres. The month of August in 1997 had proved to be a vital one in the Moroccan's career. August 1999 would be every bit as important.

The long distance race in Monaco was of great interest as far as Seville was concerned and two more men announced themselves as serious contenders for the 5,000 metres World Championship. For the fourth time in two months, Hissou was racing against Komen. Could Salah defeat Daniel in a 3,000 metres? The results of one of the highest standard distance races ever seen were:

Benjamin Limo	7:28.67
Salah Hissou	7:28.93
Brahim Lahlafi	7:28.94

MOROCCAN SUCCESS; THE KADA WAY

Daniel Komen   7:29.43
Mark Carroll   7:30.36
El Hassan Lahssini   7:32.13
Bob Kennedy   7:32.55
Mohammed Mourhit   7:32.65

Although finishing second for the third consecutive 3,000 metres race, Hissou broke Said Aouita's Moroccan record. William Tanui had taken the field through 2,000 metres in 4:58.29 with Salah hot on his heels in 4:58.50. The young Kenyan Benjamin Limo, who split in 4:59.20, was able to cling on with enough of a finishing burst to just out sprint Hissou and fellow Moroccan Brahim Lahlafi. Salah had the honour of taking Aouita's record by one hundredth of a second. Aouita's record of 7:29.45 was once the world record and as the Moroccan record, it had stood for nearly a decade. Hissou's new record wouldn't last quite as long. But for now, he was the Moroccan record holder over 3,000 metres, 5,000 metres and 10,000 metres. This was something of which Salah could be truly proud, especially as he came from a country of now great distance running tradition.

Limo was becoming a real concern with the Seville 5,000 metres final only twenty four days away. He had outstanding basic speed and this gave him the capacity to produce a devastating kick over the last 200 metres of a race. History also showed that it was very dangerous to underestimate young Kenyans. Lahlafi was a seasoned pro who had also run into form at the right time. Komen continued his decent form which was a little off his heyday when Hissou would have found it near impossible to defeat him over this distance. Remarkably eight men went under 7:33 with Irishman Mark Carroll surprisingly taking it up to the Africans. This was a great preview for Seville as all the main contenders for the 5,000 metres came from this race.

Salah Hissou had to feel pretty good about himself. If he could compete so strongly against these runners over 3,000 metres then he stood a good chance of beating them over 5,000 metres. With his excellent pedigree over 10,000 metres of which his rivals had none, the extra two kms would hopefully be enough for Hissou's strength to prevail. At the age of twenty seven, Salah couldn't realistically hope that his speed was ever going to improve much more. He now had to combine it with his natural strength to give him all the ingredients of a 5,000 metres world champion. Yet Hissou still had love for his old event.

Salah said, "It's the national Moroccan record so I'm really happy. I knew I was in good shape because I'm preparing for Seville. I'll be running the 1,500 metres in London and the 5,000 metres in Zurich. I haven't decided yet if I'll run the 5,000 metres or the 10,000 metres in Seville. I'll choose after Zurich."

Not many knew of his true intentions so right now, Salah was acting a little like a Morocco 'mole.'

Ezzine's race in Monaco was somewhat of a setback as the Moroccan could only place sixth in 8:11.77, although all five men ahead were Kenyans, with second placed Christopher Koskei only slightly faster in 8:10.69. The big gap was to the winner with the amazing Barmasai again putting on a hurdling clinic, destroying the field in a way that few greats had ever done before. When the smoke cleared the clock showed 7:58.98, under the magical eight minute barrier. At the moment he was arguably more superior in his event than anybody else was in theirs. However, we all know that anybody can be beatable on a bad day.

The middle distance race in Monaco was more interesting than usual because it did not include Hicham El Guerrouj. This wasn't a criticism of the Moroccan, rather a compliment of how usually superior he was to his opposition. This 1,500 metres did include a who's who of his rivals however, and it was Noah Ngeny who managed to stamp himself further as the world's second best leading up to Seville. He clocked a superb time of 3:29.79 to win comfortably. Behind him there were a number of excellent times run, with seven men going inside 3:33. Bernard Lagat was the next best with 3:30.61 and just a little further back was Noureddine Morceli who registered a 3:30.95. The former world champion was running

MOROCCAN SUCCESS; THE KADA WAY

a lot better than last season. Earlier in Paris, Morceli had finished second to Ngeny in an even faster race. Their corresponding times were 3:30.91 and 3:28.84.

Bernard Lagat was born on December 12, 1974, so his rise to international prominence was a late one, particularly for a Kenyan. But Bernard wasn't your usual Kenyan, having based himself in the state of Washington in the United States since 1996. All his major improvements as a distance runner came as a product of the American system, so credit must be given to them for that, though his natural talent came from his Kenyan genes.

His natural talent did not make him stand out from the rest early on and his progress was slow. In 1996 he recorded a best time of 3:37.7, set at altitude. But in 1997 Bernard's best performance over 1,500 metres was a disappointing 3:41.19. He did not seem destined for any greatness. Lagat graduated from Washington State University (just like Henry Rono before him) in 1999, though he was never an outdoor 1,500 metres champion when at college. He ran a personal best of 3:34.48 in 1998 and he credited this as a breakthrough in his career, "When I ran 3:34, that was a turnaround for me, it showed what I should do in my training to become a world class athlete. So from there I changed my training," said Lagat.

He had come into the Monaco meeting in good shape, having just run a 4:55.49 2,000 metres in Stockholm on July 30. Now his latest performance should have made him an outside medal contender for Seville. Unfortunately Bernard hadn't made the Kenyan team.

All of Abdelkader Kada's three star runners would conclude their Seville preparations in Zurich on August 11. This time Ezzine was much more competitive and finished an excellent third in a race where the competition was just as high a standard as he would see at the World Championships. Barmasai was surprisingly pushed to the line by Christopher Koskei although questions would be asked later as to whether he could have been pushed further. The pair ran times of

8:05.16 and 8:05.43 respectively. A little way back came Ezzine. Critically, he ducked back under 8:10 with an 8:09.19. The fourth athlete under this time was unexpectedly a German by the name of Damian Kallabis who ran 8:09.48. Perhaps the Kenyans wouldn't have the race all to themselves on this occasion. Kada was happy with Ezzine's form and the possibilities that lay ahead.

There was plenty of controversy in the aftermath of this race. Making a slip up during a BBC radio interview, Barmasai said that he'd asked Koskei to "leave it to me" in the finishing straight, effectively meaning to allow him to win the event. Even though both athletes were from the same country, it was debatable if this sort of arrangement should be permitted, since Bernard's unbeaten streak had him in contention for the golden bars jackpot. The circumstances were different as opposed to a championship when athletes specifically compete for their country. The IAAF looked deeply into this issue and it remained to be seen how much the drama would affect Barmasai's future performance in Seville.

Both Salah and Hicham had raced in England before the Zurich meeting. Hissou continued to work on his speed as he took another step down, deciding to run the mile race with El Guerrouj in London on August 7. There was great variety in Hissou's schedule as Kada seemed to be getting everything just right. Hissou could never hope to compete with El Guerrouj in a mile event so once again he wasn't racing to win. He was racing to improve so that he could reach his long term goal which was to win in Seville. Abdelkader was happy with the race results, which were as follows:

Hicham El Guerrouj	3:47.10
Laban Rotich	3:50.79
Adil Kaouch	3:51.62
Sammy Mutai	3:52.19
Salah Hissou	3:52.54
William Tanui	3:53.36
John Mayock	3:54.72
Steve Holman	3:54.86

MOROCCAN SUCCESS; THE KADA WAY

To the expectation of most, El Guerrouj won easily. But the Kada camp breathed a sigh of relief as they knew that Hicham's preparations had been far from perfect. In fact they had been painful with the world champion recently suffering from haemorrhoids. The enforced racing layoff hadn't seemed to do him any harm. His time wasn't close to his best, but it was a time that few others had and could ever beat. The race was another that illustrated how strong Morocco had become in men's distance running.

Well behind Hicham was the Kenyan Rotich with Moroccan youngster Adil Kaouch not far in arrears. Salah's fifth place and good time were impressive. To finish within two seconds of Laban was a good sign. He wasn't putting a foot wrong this season. He even managed to defeat former 800 metres Olympic champion William Tanui and England's middle distance specialist John Mayock, which again displayed his tremendous versatility. But that was enough speed work. Hissou had always avoided Zurich previously, but this year the meeting was on prior to the major championship. In 1999 Zurich fitted perfectly into Salah Hissou's schedule. He would race in the 5,000 metres rather than the 10,000 metres at the World Athletics Championships. It was two weeks before the Seville 5,000 metres heats. There could be no better lead up race for that than a Zurich 5,000 metres, with the greatest distance runner of all time in the field.

Salah took his absolute peak form to the Zurich stadium, a venue that many considered to be the Mecca of athletics for his final race before Seville. He needed a good run here. Physically he was definitely ready but another good performance could give him the mental edge that he required to become the 5,000 metres world champion.

Brahim Lahlafi ran as a rabbit and the early pace was torturous. He went through 3,000 metres in 7:38.88. This was slightly too fast for the main field as Gebrselassie led them through in 7:39.7, just ahead of Hissou, 7:40.0 and Benjamin Limo, 7:40.3. Koech, 7:41.8 and Kipketer, 7:42.8 were losing contact for good and the remaining competitors had been dropped earlier.

With Lahlafi pulling out, it became a race between three. The pace slowed a little, but then Salah picked it up late. He showcased his outstanding form as he dispensed of Limo. Yet when the bell rang, Gebrselassie was still in contact and on the back straight he took off, making Hissou look like a club runner. Haile had done it to Salah again. The final results were:

Haile Gebrselassie	12:49.64
Salah Hissou	12:53.45
Benjamin Limo	12:55.86
Ismail Sghyr	13:04.80
Bob Kennedy	13:05.54
Antonio Pinto	13:05.82
Benjamin Maiyo	13:06.54
Paul Koech	13:07.81
Alberto Garcia	13:08.13
Adam Goucher	13:11.25
Dieter Baumann	13:11.68
El Hassan Lahssini	13:12.23
Sammy Kipketer	13:16.22
Mohamed Said El Wardi	13:16.71
Enrique Molina	13:25.44
Paul Bitok	13:31.01
Mark Carroll	13:31.31

His superiority was almost embarrassing. Haile's burst was so emphatic that he finished almost four seconds ahead of Salah making it the fastest performance of the year. Morocco's multiple national record holder was never going to beat this bloke. Not unless injuries hampered him in the future.

Limo finished well to keep Hissou in sight and in his thoughts for the championships. The remaining athletes were well in arrears as again Salah had proven that he was one of the best long distance runners in the world. Just never *the* best.

At least he accomplished the good performance that he was after and nobody had defeated him in Zurich who he had to worry about in Seville. Haile would not be on the start line for

MOROCCAN SUCCESS; THE KADA WAY

Salah's Seville heats. Hissou had beaten everybody else who mattered in men's long distance running during the season. It was his best chance yet to win a major championship.

The Swiss meeting was just as significant for Hicham El Guerrouj as he faced his toughest opponent, Noah Ngeny in the 1,500 metres. This was their first battle since the Rome mile world record. It was going to be a fascinating dual. Incredibly this was only Hicham's fifth race of the year so he was going to be super fresh for his Seville races. Being just his third race at the championship distance, it was the first time that El Guerrouj had gone under 3:30 in 1999:

Hicham El Guerrouj	3:28.57
Noah Ngeny	3:30.28
Bernard Lagat	3:30.56
Rui Silva	3:30.88
Ali Saidi-Sief	3:30.91
Reyes Estevez	3:31.99
Noureddine Morceli	3:32.19
Steve Holman	3:32.73
Driss Maazouzi	3:34.14
Daniel Komen	3:35.42
Nadir Bosch	3:36.11
Laban Rotich	3:36.89
Fermin Cacho	3:37.96

The emphatic way in which Hicham triumphed was vital as it reconfirmed his strong favouritism ahead of Noah. The Moroccan took over 550 metres out and destroyed the Kenyan. In contrast to El Guerrouj's season, the Zurich meet was Ngeny's nineteenth race in 1999 so perhaps fatigue played its part. The Kenyan still showed good form but it appeared unlikely that he could reduce such a deficit to challenge the Moroccan in the short time left before the Seville 1,500 metres final.

Hicham obviously realized the threat that Ngeny posed, as he declared his joy at reducing the Kenyan's confidence while raising his own. "That was important for me not only as a psychological blow before the World Championships but because some people were suggesting that I was not the same athlete after my illness," Hicham said in reference to his haemorrhoids problem. He added, "But I am confident again now and will return to Morocco for my final preparations."

There were many intriguing sub plots to this Zurich race. If Rotich's form here was anything to go by, he would be unable to offer Noah much support in Spain. That's if he managed to qualify for the final in the first place. Cacho's career seemed to be coming to a sudden end. Morceli was back in good enough form to contend for a minor medal, while Portugal's Silva and Algeria's Saidi-Sief were making nice improvements, but were probably at least twelve months away from giving Hicham and Abdelkader anything to think about. Nothing much had changed from the end of last year. El Guerrouj would go into the final fully expected to retain his world title. Hicham had a lot to lose. How would this impinge on his racing strategy when it came to crunch time?

Kada watched the Zurich 1,500 metres not only with Hicham in mind, but also Salah. He took note of the Kenyan who struggled back in tenth place, running a time that was well outside his previous capabilities. Perhaps they were wrong to simply expect that this guy would be the one to beat in the 5,000 metres. Kada and Hissou needed to look deeper. Maybe his race would be about much more than just Daniel Komen.

MOROCCAN SUCCESS; THE KADA WAY

An Initiation, A Masterpiece And A Final Exam

Abdelkader Kada had set a platform for Moroccan distance running excellence. It was possible that the Seville Championships would be his high point as a coach. A competition where he could stand out from the rest as the best distance running coach in the world. Among male mid/long distance runners he coached one of the top three in the world (Hicham), another of the top ten (Salah), and probably the most recent entry to the top twenty (Ali). To call these championships the World Championships was a little misleading because in a number of races, it was really just a case of Kada vs. Kenya!

Being a head distance running coach at the Moroccan National Training Centre obviously meant that Kada oversaw a great number of quality Moroccan athletes, not just his most famous three. His training squad left no stone unturned when it came to getting the very best out of its talent. Morocco's top runners do not live a normal lifestyle. The athletes live together for the vast majority of the year so that their careers incur no distractions. It is only rarely that they leave the squad to spend time with their spouses and family. Many squad members share rooms with fellow athletes but the best runners are given rooms all to themselves. Seven doctors are on hand to take constant care of the runners.

The focus of Kada's runners remains solely on their targets in competition. For these targets to be reached in peak fitness, there requires a total commitment to training and related activities. Abdelkader Kada is not a trailblazer when it comes to forming ideas for training distance runners, but he is smart. Very smart. He has taken the best ideas from others and used them to help take many Moroccan athletes to dizzy heights.

Many of Kada's training philosophies come from the great British milers of the 1980's. Specifically, we are talking about Sebastian Coe, Steve Ovett and Steve Cram. Some of his other coaching techniques have been adopted from

Morocco's original distance running trail blazer, Said Aouita.

Altitude training has been a major component of Abdelkader's training programs. His squad will go to high altitude training camps around four to six times a year, for a period of three to five weeks per trip. The squad's main altitude training base is Ifrane, situated in the Atlas Mountains in Morocco, at an altitude of around 1,600 metres above sea level.

Font Romeu, France and St. Moritz, Switzerland have been other occasional training places for the Kada group in the past. Here the team live at approximately 2,500 metres altitude, meaning that the athletes also sleep at this height. For training sessions, the runners return to approximately 1,500 metres altitude. Abdelkader's athletes are therefore adopting a form of the live high, train low philosophy. While most coaches believe altitude training to be greatly beneficial, many have the theory that you can train too high. The higher up from sea level that you run, the harder it is to run well because the oxygen in the air is thinner. The argument made is that to train at 2,500 metres or higher will be detrimental to the athlete because the quality or pace of the running will become too slow. Therefore the fast, regular leg turnover that a Hicham, Salah or Ali requires to stay in top shape will be missing from their training. This negative will have a greater impact than the positive of a greater oxygen carrying capacity. Too many slow training runs may even cause an elite track athlete to lose some fitness. The categorization of distance runner can be very misleading as it portrays the vision of jogging for a long time. What Kada's athletes were doing was trying to get into shape to run at close to 2:30 km pace or faster for their races. Compared to the not so naturally gifted runner, they are almost sprinters that run for a longer period. Therefore these athletes must not allow their legs to totally forget was fast running is like.

Abdelkader has found that living and training at about 1,600 metres is the right balance, hence spending so much time in Ifrane. It is high enough to have some impact with the development of more red blood cells in the body which allow a runner to race harder for longer, but low enough to enable

MOROCCAN SUCCESS; THE KADA WAY

the athletes to conduct high quality, fast work outs, whether this be on tempo runs or interval (track) sessions.

There is no written rule that states an exact height above sea level to run at which will be of the most benefit. It comes down to personal opinion. Many athletes train higher than Kada's, at 2,000 metres plus as some believe that you need to be higher than around 1,600 metres in height to receive any positive results. But surely even 500 metres above sea level (for both living and training) is going to be better than being at sea level. A small benefit is still a plus.

The level of impact that the regular altitude trips have had on the success of Moroccan running remains subjective, yet it obviously hasn't done them any harm. Remember that Hicham El Guerrouj set his recent mile world record in Rome just five days after returning from high altitude. By 1999 the Kada group was spending about four months of the year in Ifrane, with the rest of its training taking place in Rabat.

Kada's runners usually train twice a day, occasionally three times. The third run would be very easy. This differs from many of the top Kenyans who often run three times a day. The amount of mileage by Moroccan athletes is not staggering in its volume. It is the quality of the Moroccans' training that really stands out. A normal run which Kada describes as 'jogging', would be running at around three minute km pace! These 30-45 minute runs are termed aerobic endurance sessions and take up about half of the running part of a Kada athletes training. El Guerrouj will start these runs slowly, but by the end is running in the range of 2:50-3:10 km pace. If Hicham El Guerrouj is able to regularly 'jog' ten to fifteen kms at three minute kms pace, it is no wonder that he can run a sub four minute mile with consummate ease. The same can be said for Salah Hissou going out in race conditions and comfortably posting sub twenty eight minutes for a 10,000 metres race. Kada's Moroccans regularly complete three high quality speed sessions a week as well as engaging in plenty of hill training. The hill training is designed to "improve the movement of arms and legs, stride and speed'" Abdelkader states. Often multiple sprints (around ten to fifteen) are undertaken on inclines that vary from 250 metres to 500 metres in length.

To continually back up from this hard training and go again requires plenty of rest. Hicham El Guerrouj sleeps eight hours a night and also has a three hour nap during the day. This extensive extra rest period is a must. The average person does not require a three hour nap to get through the day but these athletes are regularly pushing their bodies to the extreme. Athletes also use swimming at times as another recovery aid.

Running is far from the only form of training that is practised by the Moroccan group.

With the aim being to strengthen all parts of the body, particular the trunk, Kada places huge emphasis on stretching exercises and weight work. During some workouts, El Guerrouj completes an incredible 300 sit ups and 300 back ups to make sure that his back remains strong and aligned. Being distance runners and not weightlifters means that strength exercises are generally completed with a 25 kg or 30 kg bar. The likes of squats and lunges are done in repetition to further improve the condition of the abdominals, back, hamstrings, quadriceps, etc. El Guerrouj speaks about his weight training, "October, November, December I do a series of weight training to adapt the leg muscles to the exercises. I do heavy weight lifting from the early couple of months of the year and after the following months more dynamic exercises, weight lifting that is. I do field track training as well with more kilometres involved."

Kada is against any regular training on the solid bitumen road surfaces. All his athletes undertake the majority of their running on grass and dirt. Abdelkader believes that too much road running puts unnecessary strain on the legs that can cause injuries. He doesn't see any reason why an athlete who competes at 5,000 metres or less should train on a hard road surface. Some training is conducted on synthetic tracks but this is limited so as to reduce the chances of injuries, consequently not all interval speed sessions are done on all

MOROCCAN SUCCESS; THE KADA WAY

weather circuits.

A standard training week for Hicham El Guerrouj is running about 120 kms in total while for Salah Hissou the total is approximately 140 kms. Many of these kms were at a high quality as stated earlier.

Typical interval sessions run at race pace by El Guerrouj, Hissou and Ezzine for example are:

20 x 400 metres, with a 1 minute recovery.
4 x 500 metres, with a 75 second recovery.

Interval distances at race pace can vary, being as extensive as 1,600 metres in length.

Other interval sessions are conducted at less intensity. These are termed lactic threshold runs (same as aerobic endurance sessions) and regularly the intervals are at distances of 800, 1,000 and 1,200 metres. Sometimes lactic threshold sessions are done on the track without intervals. Just a specific distance of running at a solid pace.

Race simulations are often carried out, with lesser squad runners acting as pacemakers for the likes of El Guerrouj and Hissou. A relatively fast pace might be set, so that the group leader can test how well he can kick down from that. This is a great way for Hicham and Salah to practise race tactics while still improving on their high fitness levels.

Moroccan distance running in general was reaching its peak as the 1999 World Athletics Championships arrived. It was time to make the most of all the good work.

When August 21 arrived it was time. It was the running of the heats of the men's 1,500 metres and 3,000 metres steeplechase. These were nervous days for Abdelkader Kada, with virtually nothing to gain but everything to lose. For all intents and purposes his runners should qualify, though 'should' and 'will' have two different meanings. Like Atlanta, all it would take is one fall to destroy his brilliant planning. It was unlikely to be with much enjoyment that the coach viewed today's proceedings.

Hicham was in the first heat at 8:25 pm. The first six were automatic qualifiers so it appeared simple enough as the Moroccan toed the line as one of thirteen starters. The Russian Shabunin led early, taking them to 800 metres in a fast 1:56.61, just the way that El Guerrouj liked it. By the 1,200 metres mark he was in front with a split of 2:54.64. From here, Hicham only got faster and finished with the fastest time ever in a world championship preliminary, a 3:35.63. The gap back to Cacho was an enormous amount for a heat, a full eight tenths of a second. Rotich also safely qualified. Regardless of what happened in the next two heats Hicham would retain his 'favourite' tag for the semi finals.

Reyes Estevez, 3:41.24 and Ali Saidi-Sief, 3:41.34 were the first finishers from a very slowly run heat 2. Attempting a comeback after horrible injury problems was Venuste Niyongabo. Unfortunately he placed seventh, some twenty seven hundredths of a second away from qualification. The Burundi runner deserved better. A stress fracture in his foot had prematurely ended his career. Hicham's teammate Adil Kaouch got through safely in fourth position.

Noah Ngeny was the centre of attention for heat 3 and the Kenyan stayed out of trouble by running the race from the front. Only briefly did Andres Diaz go past him before Noah retook him and crossed in 3:37.41. Also passing the Spaniard in the dying stages was Noureddine Morceli. The third of the Moroccans Salah El Ghazi, failed to progress to the next round.

Ali Ezzine's first experience at a major championship was a complicated one. There were twelve spots available for the final in two days time, and with Ali being the fastest non Kenyan in the event, qualifying shouldn't have been a problem. Forty athletes were scheduled to compete, so there were too many for only two heats. Fair enough then that three steeple heats were held. An easy and reasonably sensible method for a qualifying procedure would be to have the first

MOROCCAN SUCCESS; THE KADA WAY

four finishers from each heat advance to the final. But the organizers didn't want this, preferring to have a fastest loser included as incentive for the runners to make their races faster. I don't have a problem with this but I feel that they went too far with the emphasis on time over placing. Instead of having three automatic qualifiers from each heat with three fastest losers (which would have been a good system), they went with just the two automatic qualifiers. In other words if an athlete finished third and their heat was slow, they might not make the final. This system would probably make the best runners even more agitated and apprehensive than they should have been, as they got ready to race. Ezzine would have to perform at his best just to ensure qualification.

Ali's situation was made even tougher when he was drawn to compete in heat 1 at 9:25 pm. With so few automatic qualifiers it was much better to be in a later heat, when an athlete can see the times already posted and therefore know what time he is required to run. There were four Kenyans in the steeplechase with Wilson Boit Kipketer an automatic entry as the reigning world champion. Fortunately for Ezzine there was just the one Kenyan in his heat, the lesser known Paul Kosgei. But recent sub 8:10 man, Germany's Damian Kallabis was also included. To finish in the first two would be hard, so Ali and the rest of the athletes wanted a fast race to increase the chances of this heat producing more qualifiers.

The pace was fast from the gun with Romanian Florin Ionescu leading the pack through 1,000 metres in 2:43.49. Quickly, an elite group of six established itself and Kada could relax a little with his athlete right in the mix and looking comfortable. By 2,000 metres Kosgei had taken up the running as they remained on pace for a sub 8:15 (5:29.38). The last km was the fastest with the heat finishing in a four man sprint, which Ezzine came out of well to finish second. Ali was safely through to the final.

Kosgei ran 8:10.34, with Ezzine next in 8:10.45, then Kallabis in 8:10.56. These were scintillating times. As a comparison, the fastest preliminary time from the Athens World Championships (where both heats and semis were run) was an 8:17.95! Kosgei had clocked the fastest time in a heat of any World Championships. Yes the racing was exciting, but the excitement should be experienced in the finals, not the heats. This new system was an absolute farce!

There were no major casualties from the following two heats with Elarbi Khattabi running well to win heat 3 in a time of 8:14.22. As it turned out there were six qualifiers from heat 1 so the energy spent on the furious last lap was a total waste. All the Kenyans made it to Monday's final. We were set for a cracking race. Abdelkader was very proud of Ali for having already achieved a great deal. A good result in the final would be a bonus.

The 1,500 metres semis were the following day and Hicham had less to worry about than Ali. Not just because he was the stronger athlete, but because the first *five* runners qualified automatically. His race was first at 9:30 pm.

Estevez led the runners through a very slow first 800 metres. The time of 2:03.25 wasn't exactly El Guerrouj's cup of tea so he went to the front at the 900 metres mark and upped the tempo significantly. Suddenly the entire field was stretched out and with a 1,200 metres split of 2:57.28, showing a last 400 metres of 54.03, it was of little surprise that he was breaking up the field.

Hicham's relentless pace did not slacken and he finished a clear winner in 3:37.34. Cacho clocked 3:37.88. The experienced Spaniard had hit form at the right time after a mostly disappointing year. Saidi-Sief finished a disappointing eleventh but everyone else performed as expected. It was another box that Kada could tick off.

The second semi was fractionally faster with Ngeny winning in 3:36.13. Kaouch managed another good run to finish third to give El Guerrouj a possible ally in the final. Morceli only finished sixth but qualified as a fastest loser. Rui Silva was the real loser from the heats, falling after an incident with John Mayock 600 metres from the finish.

MOROCCAN SUCCESS; THE KADA WAY

The final of the steeplechase kicked off at 9:10 pm on August 23. The temperature was a very hot 32 degrees, which made a slow race more likely. The clear favourite for the gold medal was Bernard Barmasai, although not only was the 32 degree heat on him, but also the heat from the IAAF who had cancelled him out of the running for a share in the $US1 million Golden League jackpot after doubt as to the legitimacy of the win in Zurich. The victory in itself still stood. It was a strange incident for the Kenyan to have asked for a favour as this season he hadn't needed one. He was undefeated in 1999 and most of the world record holder's wins had been by massive margins. For his part, Koskei denied any role in any wrong doing, saying that he could not have heard any message from Barmasai due to the volume of noise from the Swiss crowd.

Koskei, as well as the other Kenyans of Boit Kipketer and Kosgei were considered the best chances for the minor medals in Spain, but a sweep was far from guaranteed, with the German Kallabis and the Moroccans of Khattabi and Ezzine not to be discounted from medal calculations. Kada knew that his boy was in with a real chance.

The race commences at a slow tempo but this soon changes with Floren Ionescu leading through 1,000 metres in 2:48.08. By halfway the Kenyan brigade has taken over, with Barmasai leading the charge. Ali hangs in there and appears comfortable with the good pace but unfortunately Elarbi is struggling and having a very bad day at the worst possible time. Khattabi falls off the back of the pack and eventually finishes in a disappointing eleventh position.

Barmasai goes through 2,000 metres in 5:33.54, running at just around 8:20 pace. This is understandable given the conditions. The race seems to be between Barmasai, Koskei and Boit Kipketer but Bernard starts to drop back a little and Kallabis and Ezzine remain in touch, as the contest becomes a battle of five going into the final lap.

Wilson Boit Kipketer makes the decisive move 300 metres out and only Christopher Koskei is able to respond convincingly.

Sadly Barmasai loses ground. The Kenyan star is having his one bad day for the season, eventually drifting away to an undeserving fifth place finish. His teammates are able to pick up the slack as the two leaders engage in a great battle, with Koskei emerging the stronger over the final 100 metres to become the world champion, making the final step up from the silver medal he won four years ago in Gothenburg when he was still short of his twenty first birthday. Not far back in Seville is another athlete at the tender age of twenty. Finishing powerfully, Ali Ezzine has got the better of Kallabis to win the bronze medal. The full results were:

Christopher Koskei	8:11.76
Wilson Boit Kipketer	8:12.09
Ali Ezzine	8:12.73
Damian Kallabis	8:13.11
Bernard Barmasai	8:13.51
Eliseo Martin	8:16.09
Paul Kosgei	8:17.55
Florin Ionescu	8:18.17
Gunther Weidlinger	8:19.02
Giuseppe Maffei	8:22.65
Elarbi Khattabi	8:24.62
Bouabdallah Tahri	8:25.59

Ali had won Morocco's first ever major medal in the steeplechase event. It was a tremendous honour for both he and Abdelkader to be a part of this small piece of Moroccan running history. Again he proved his finishing strength, going with the leaders despite a sub 2:40 final km. He was never able to seriously threaten for the win but he had finished within a single second of Koskei. To be the future champion of the world was a distinct possibility. The Kenyans were not quite as feared any more so next year's Olympic race promised to be just as open with the likes of Morocco and Spain becoming more of a force. Ali's heat time was faster than the final, which was a rare occurrence.

Ezzine made the following post race comments, displaying his immense confidence, as well as the emotional pride he took in his performance.

MOROCCAN SUCCESS; THE KADA WAY

"At the beginning I took the pace off the Kenyans. For the rest of the race I had a plan already two days ago. If the pace was to be slow I would just follow but with a fast race I wanted to attack in the front. Already 600 metres before the finish line I was certain to be in the podium. I am very proud of my bronze because no other Moroccan has ever got a medal in steeplechase. This medal pleases me personally, too, because last year I was operated after my knee hit the steeple in Rome."

For Kada it was one down and two to go. This was not a time for celebration with Hicham in action tomorrow on August 24, also at 9:10 pm.

Spain and Kenya each had three runners in the final with Morocco having two participants. With this in mind team tactics were a possibility. Excluding anything out of the ordinary only Noah Ngeny would have believed that he had any chance of taking Hicham El Guerrouj's mantle. The atmosphere in the stadium was absolutely electric, in part because of the Spanish athletes competing. Cacho, Estevez and Diaz were all medal chances. Coming off the 1,500 metres world record last year and the mile world record this year, everyone knew that El Guerrouj was an athlete of rare quality, one at the peak of his powers. There was the potential here to witness something special. This was a race that many considered to be the best of the championships.

The height of the expectation and pressure facing Hicham is best summed up by one Sebastian Coe, who comments just seconds before the gun, "Well this is going to be El Guerrouj's night. It would take an extraordinary event here for El Guerrouj not to win this. Nothing short of falling over. He is looking absolutely relaxed but very confident. Look at those eyes and look at the concentration on that man's face."

Hicham quickly settles at the front, edging out Morceli as the runners make an initial fast start for a good position. Ngeny makes a fast start also and now places himself behind the Moroccan. Usually at around 200 metres into a major championship the field bunches as the pace slows and the event becomes tactical with everyone wanting to be near the front but expending as little energy as possible to remain there. It is only during the last 600 metres when a kick down in pace typically occurs. The manner in which this race is run is determined the moment Adil Kaouch storms to the front after 200 metres with a very business like approach. This is serious as the twelve finalists quickly form a single file.

El Guerrouj is in the perfect position right behind his teammate, enjoying the ride of his life. The first split is mind blowing, 54.31 at 400 metres! Athletics fans had seen many great races at championships past involving team Kenya. Previously the Moroccans had mostly run as single entities but here on show we are seeing the first instance of team tactics the Moroccan way.

Ngeny is nestled in behind the Moroccans with Cacho and Morceli also prominent. Kaouch continues at his break neck speed. For his own abilities he is virtually sprinting. When he reaches the 800 metres split his pace has slowed but not too much with a reading of 1:52.15. That lap was 57.84.

While most of the opposition is gasping for air, El Guerrouj steps up the pace once more. Hicham looks like he is doing this easily as he moves out to pass his teammate.

Ngeny continues to keep with him as the Spaniards also move into the reckoning. They are on close to world record pace yet Hicham can still kick down from it! Bruce McAvaney says, "This is one of the classics already, with 500 to go. We haven't seen a final like this in a long time."

Like El Guerrouj, McAvaney is in rare form and says it best with his "Morceli's spent already," quote. The Algerian is losing contact 500 metres out and soon after hitting the bell he despondently steps to the infield. Approaching the bell El Guerrouj is in full flight. McAvaney again, "A mighty roar from a full house here in Spain. A classic distance. A classic runner."

2:33.78 is the 1,100 metres split as Estevez hurriedly makes

MOROCCAN SUCCESS; THE KADA WAY

a huge surge, moving from fifth to second. These tactics are unwise as he catches Hicham but is unable to pass him before the bend. To make such quick inroads off the pace that the Moroccan is setting is crazy. Clearly the Spaniard has terrific form and if he'd run a little smarter he might have been a lot closer in the end to the silver medal. But he is running in a World Championship final in his home country, so we can excuse Reyes for running with a little emotion.

His move onto the world record holder's shoulder hasn't bothered El Guerrouj at all as he launches into his typical surge on the back straight. It is here after going through 1,200 metres in 2:46.79, that Reyes realizes he is out of his depth. The third lap has just been run in 54.64, so this is no surprise! A new world record is only a little out of reach.

Hicham's lead extends to almost ten metres before Noah retakes the fading Spaniard on the bend. As they enter the home straight El Guerrouj has wrapped it up. He continues to steam along in his majestic cadence until the final forty metres when he manufactures a remarkable celebration, blowing kisses into his hands, then touching his shoulders before kissing both together and releasing them out in front of himself. He constructs this while smiling and easing off, without showing any signs of fatigue despite the frantic tempo. Regarding his celebration, El Guerrouj commented:

"I sent two kisses tonight, one for my family and the other for the people watching tonight and in Morocco. I was so happy because I truly think that this was one of the best races of this century."

Hicham's kisses were the only thing that beat him to the line on this night. This was symbolic as the Moroccan was awarded the gold medal. However the real winner from this race was the sport of Athletics. Surely there were many people the world over who were inspired to love running purely from watching this performance.

As Hicham crossed the line, you had to ponder for a moment if he was already the best miler of all time. Sebastian Coe didn't go that far, but the British legend did say that, "It is the greatest 1,500 metres race I have ever seen." The final results were:

Hicham El Guerrouj	3:27.65
Noah Ngeny	3:28.73
Reyes Estevez	3:30.57
Fermin Cacho	3:31.34
Andres Diaz	3:31.83
Laban Rotich	3:33.32
David Lelei	3:33.82
Driss Maazouzi	3:34.02
Steve Holman	3:34.32
Graham Hood	3:35.35
Adil Kaouch	3:47.05

Coe went on further, "That was definitive 1,500 metres running. I've never seen anybody commit themselves in a 1,500 metres championship race like that man. And it's not just about the physical domination. That was a man that was prepared mentally to commit himself at the very highest level and that is the hardest way to run a 1,500 metres."

After being thanked by Kada with kisses to his cheeks, El Guerrouj fell onto his back with the Moroccan flag draped over his head. His chest was heaving which finally showed us that he did have to work hard! Yet his face showed no signs of strain. Upon standing, Kaouch congratulated him and the two commenced a victory lap.

This was by far the quickest time ever at a major championship, easily eclipsing Coe's Los Angeles mark of 3:32.53. Ngeny's performance was not forgotten as he set a new Kenyan record and had kept close enough to the Moroccan to push him, though not quite challenge him. The depth in Spanish middle distance running was extraordinary as its three, four, five placings proved, with Cacho again displaying his ability to perform on the big occasion. The success that they achieved however, was slightly soured by some of Estevez' comments.

MOROCCAN SUCCESS; THE KADA WAY

"The beauty of the final was taken away by the Moroccan because one of them ran as a pace-maker. It was a meeting race pace. If it had been run slower, to a rhythm of 3:37, which I find more comfortable, I would have made thing more difficult to them. El Guerrouj counted on his compatriot help, thing that the rest of runners did not have."

How many times had Kenya implemented such tactics in the past without complaint? Reyes was upset because there was no doubt that he would have been a stronger chance in a slower race but this was a major reason why the Moroccans raced it hard all the way. To say that the other runners had no help is ludicrous. Estevez had two teammates! The reason why he didn't get any specific help was because it was mighty tough to find teammates who can help you while running at 3:27 pace!

I haven't a problem with team tactics in the World Championships or Olympic Games. Since the athletes are competing for their country, it is kind of a romantic notion to have a runner wilfully throw away his own chances for the good of his teammate and nation. In most cases I believe it adds to the spectacle of the event, which is better for the sport. It was the horrendous pace of this final which dragged Estevez through to a personal best time.

Noah Ngeny's race reflection was in much better taste.

"Of course I'm not unhappy. El Guerrouj is a wonderful runner and I have the great pride of beating my national record. I have no problems with how I ran the race. I did everything I could. There was nothing else left in me but I can say that while this was El Guerrouj's year, next year will be mine!"

Bruce McAvaney was also looking into his crystal ball when he predicted, "When he wins the Olympic title next year he will be confirmed amongst the greatest 1,500 metres runners we've ever seen."

The winner also said the following in the post race press conference.

"I didn't have any difficulty. I was sure about winning the race before and throughout my run tonight. It is as simple as that! I thank my parents. I telephoned them yesterday. Their support has been wonderful. My mother prepares me a lot of couscous and I think that is an important part of my diet...I eat a lot of it!!!! I'm proud to be bringing with this medal to my country."

With or without the traditional Moroccan dish I think that Hicham would have been very hard to defeat! But it was nice to hear him give his family much respect. I am sure that his coach was as important as anyone in supplying the high confidence levels that El Guerrouj took with him into the final.

Special mention should be given to thirty year old Fermin Cacho. The experienced Spaniard continued his excellence in major championships with a terrific run to place fourth, adding to his silver medal performances from Stuttgart and Athens. This came on top of his gold and silver medals from the Olympic Games. It was difficult to think of another runner who was less distinguished against the clock that had such an array of medals at the highest level.

The men's 10,000 metres started straight after Hicham's emphatic win. In this final the same thing happened that had occurred for the last few years. Gebrselassie first, with Tergat second. The race itself was nothing much to speak of. The winning time of 27:57.27 was the slowest in a major championship for more than a decade and nobody ever made a significant enough move that could have threatened Gebrselassie. Conditions were warm but spectators had still anticipated more action from the thirty two starters, especially considering there were no heats run. It was the dullest 10,000 metres final of the 1990's though perhaps we (the fans) had been spoiled with the races previously witnessed. Looking at recent history it is hard to say with any great conviction that Hissou could have won this race, but with his new found confidence and aggressive style, the 10,000 metres would have surely been much more interesting with him in it. The penultimate km would have likely been much faster than a slow 2:48.45.

MOROCCAN SUCCESS; THE KADA WAY

The results showed the relatively low quality of the final. Tergat ran 27:58.56, only just beating Mezgebu for the silver, who ran 27:59.15. Mezgebu had finished within two seconds of Gebrselassie. In Athens the gap was nearly eight seconds. The great Ethiopian and Kenyan had come back to the pack somewhat.

The latter stages were still of a very high quality with the last km being run in 2:25.20. Most of the credit for that should go to fifth placed finisher Antonio Pinto. The Portuguese put in a big surge with two and a half laps to go. It wasn't enough for him to break the top Africans, but it did bring a distinct look of pain to the face of Gebrselassie. Pinto was in tremendous form, but marathon men don't often win world championships on the track.

At least he was running for gold. Tergat ran purely for the silver medal. When Haile went with 450 metres left he was languishing in fifth place and even on the final bend Paul was sitting in fourth behind the three Ethiopians. That he finished again so strongly down the home straight made it perplexing as to why he didn't place himself closer to the action (to the front) at crunch time.

The last lap did not appear fast as Gebrselassie did not break away until the final 200 metres. But the clock told us that he ran a 54.37 split. The manner in which he surged away meant that the concluding half lap must have been very close to twenty six dead. Another outstanding, convincing victory.

Pinto was beaten by basic speed on the last lap and he finished in 28:03.42. Either side of him were two Ethiopians. Girma Tolla, 28:02.08 and Habte Jifar, 28:08.82, which gave Ethiopia four of the top six. They clearly had the better of the Kenyans.

Not that the Moroccans had anything to boast about. Their great veteran Khalid Skah was best placed in tenth, running 28:25.10. He remained in the lead group past seventeen laps but was soon dropped. With eight laps left there were almost twenty athletes still in contact. David Chelule threw in a fast nineteenth lap of 62.88 to finally break it up but incredibly the pace reverted back to such a sluggish speed that Skah was nearly able to tack back on with four laps to go. Despite the frustrating racing standard, this was a good effort by the former Olympic champion.

The same couldn't be said for the rest of the team. Ismail Sghyr and Said Berioui finished fifteenth and sixteenth. Outside of Hissou, Morocco did not have a runner capable of running a high quality 10,000 metres.

Not that Abdelkader and Salah were worrying much about the goings on in this race. They were confident that the right choice had been made to compete in the 5,000 metres. Hissou had done everything possible to be in the best shape, physically and mentally for the distance. In the lead up to Seville, Salah had completed the following track session:

3 x 1 km (running each km in 2:30 with only a 45 second recovery)
3 x 400 metres (running each lap in 52-53 seconds with a three minute recovery)

The high class of this sharpening up work proved that Hissou was more than ready for the Seville 5,000 metres. His final was on August the 28th, but first there were the heats, conducted on the 25th. Salah raced in heat 1.

The 5,000 metres heats were a little more cutthroat than the 10,000 metres heats he had raced in at past championships. Only the first five finishers from each of the two heats would be automatic qualifiers for the final so this was at least a lot fairer than the steeplechase. The last five spots in the final went to the fastest 'losers'. If a heat was run really slowly then there would be a greater chance of a favourite missing out in a bunch sprint.

Heat 1 was a slow race. The tempo was more like that of a 10,000 metres heat. Salah didn't want to let it get into a last lap sprint between a big group, yet after 3,000 metres there were still at least a dozen athletes in contention. Kennedy had

MOROCCAN SUCCESS; THE KADA WAY

taken them through the split in 8:26.79. This was nearly 2:49 km pace. Not much faster than Hissou runs when 'jogging' in training!

Not content with jogging, Salah went to the front and upped the ante. He took the pack through 4,000 metres in 11:05.68, meaning that they had gone from 2:49 km pace to 2:39 km pace. Many runners who were not sub thirteen minute men suddenly started to struggle. In the final km, the speed got quicker and quicker. With a lap to go there were eight runners in contact, but Hissou was able to comfortably remain at the pointy end to qualify third in a time of 13:36.60. He clocked 2:30.92 for the last km, much like the sort of pace he ran in his speed sessions.

His teammate Brahim Lahlafi impressively kicked away at the end to run 13:34.26. Veteran Ethiopian Fita Bayissa ran well to place second in 13:35.33. Like many distance runners, these guys possibly had more basic speed than Salah Hissou, but this 'race' was a 3 kms jog, followed by a 2 kms kick down. Hissou was likely to make the final a much different race.

The other automatic qualifiers from heat 1 were Benjamin Limo and Million Wolde. Others would have to wait to see if their time was fast enough to get them through. There had been no big surprises with two Moroccans, two Ethiopians and one Kenyan already into the final. Any distance running fan could have predicted that!

Daniel Komen was in heat 2 and he ran in a remarkably similar fashion to Hissou. The pace of this heat was much more honest, and when Mohammed Mourhit went through 3,000 metres in 8:14.68, it looked like most of the finalists would come from this qualifier. Komen kept the steady tempo going, taking them past 4,000 metres in 10:57.93. There were no concerns about him not qualifying.

Like Salah, Daniel finished his heat in third place. His time was 13:29.39. His final km was 2:31.46. It was a carbon copy of heat 1, the only difference being a more consistently good pace in the early stages of heat 2.

Mourhit crossed the line first in 13:28.96, edging out Ethiopian Hailu Mekonnen who ran 13:29.00. The other automatic qualifiers were Brahim Jabbour and American Adam Goucher. Four fastest losers got through from this heat with only Bob Kennedy surviving from heat 1. Everyone who was expected to, had qualified. The final was set to be a great one.

Africa was dominating distance running even more than ever. In this 5,000 metres final there would be three Moroccans plus their ex, Mourhit. All three Ethiopians had also qualified. Kenya had two representatives. Its third runner Philip Mosima ran a disastrous heat, clocking 13:52.56 to miss out by a long way. This was nearly one minute off his personal best. It added to the Kenyan men's so far disappointing championships by their high standards. Ethiopia had dominated the 10,000 metres while Morocco had dominated the 1,500 metres. There was plenty of pressure on Komen and Limo to restore some pride to the nation. For the first time in fifteen years people could legitimately ask the subsequent question. Was Kenya still the strongest country in men's distance running?

Abdelkader Kada was the man who had gone a long way to ensuring that Salah Hissou was in a good position to become a world champion. Their coach/athlete relationship had developed and strengthened through many years of hard work and planning. Now they had come to this point where Salah's elusive major championship victory seemed a realistic possibility. Could he produce now when it mattered most?

At 9:30 pm on Saturday the 28th of August, Salah Hissou toed the line in Seville. Waiting for the starter's gun he hoped that in about thirteen minutes time he would be a gold medallist. He had experienced six seasons as a top international athlete. He had the pedigree to do it. Abdelkader knew that Salah had it in him, though sometimes it can come down to how you're feeling on the day.

MOROCCAN SUCCESS; THE KADA WAY

The gun sounded and off went the fifteen finalists. Hissou had defeated all of them at one stage or another. He was a much greater runner than everyone else in the field, except for Daniel Komen.

While Komen still had the world title, most of his aura of invincibility was long gone. By making the step down to the 5,000 metres, Salah had instantly stamped himself as the Kenyan's main rival. This reputation had been justified by the Moroccan's two victories over Komen this season. Distance running fans would take a great interest in Hissou vs. Komen in this final. If nothing else they were clearly the most significant names in the field. They were two of the best long distance runners of the last five years.

Komen's teammate Benjamin Limo was the x factor. He was fairly new to top grade international racing, despite having just turned twenty five. He had broken thirteen minutes and contained a potentially devastating kick. He was certainly one for Salah to watch.

Hissou's teammate Lahlafi was arguably in career best form at the ripe old age of thirty one. He had gone close to medalling when he was out kicked into fifth place in Gothenburg '95. Would he run for Hissou or would he run for himself? Twenty eight year old Jabbour was also in career best form, having run a personal best of 13:01.41 in winning at Saint-Denis on the 3rd of July. But this Brahim had never threatened to win a medal at a major championships. Salah had always been far too good for him in the past and this race should be no different. The Ethiopians were handy runners, but were not world beaters. If the race was fast they could be dropped. A particular Moroccan no doubt had this in mind.

The only other runner of note was Mohammed Mourhit. Hissou had never struggled to defeat him in the past, but Mourhit was proving to be a late bloomer. He was making nice improvements and slowly becoming a major player in big distance races. One thing was certain. This 'Moroccan' would not run for Salah in the final.

The early pace is very solid, though not spectacular with American Bob Kennedy doing some of the work. He leads through 1,000 metres in 2:38.16. Feeling that the pace isn't quick enough, Hissou moves to the front. The field immediately stretches out as he pours on the power. The Moroccan glides rhythmically over the track with tremendous authority. The lap is a scorcher for so early in the race, with the 1,200 to 1,600 metres section being clocked at 59.91. Yet it isn't enough to escape the field or even rid anyone of any significance.

This showed the improvement that distance running had made during the 1990's. For example in the 1993 World Championships, Ismael Kirui put thirty metres into the rest of the field with a 60.21 second sixth lap of the 5,000 metres final. Granted, they had gone hard early (two minutes for the first 800 metres), but there was a big difference between running a sixty second lap then and running one in 1999. The field was unlikely to allow Hissou to break away, but Salah could still hurt his opposition by making them run beyond their comfortable tempo too early.

Salah settles back into the pack as the main contenders get into a relatively fast rhythm. The first 2,000 metres are passed in 5:14.26, with Benjamin Limo leading but not surging. Soon Salah is back at the front and puts in a sixty one second lap. The contenders are down to six or seven with five and a half laps to go.

Again Hissou doesn't continue on with his surge, preferring to ease back a little as he takes the contenders to 3,000 metres in 7:52.54. Is he not willing to risk an all out attack which could give him gold, but which could also leave him without a medal? Nevertheless the 3,000 metres split is more than thirty seconds faster than the Moroccan's heat time! Therefore he is doing the right thing in making this a strength race.

What Hissou is also doing is racing with a real stature and belief for the first time in a major championship. Much more so than in Athens '97. In Seville '99 he looks like the athlete with the most dominating presence. By putting in these fast

MOROCCAN SUCCESS; THE KADA WAY

early laps he is showing Komen that he is no longer intimidated by him. Komen for his part has been biding his time, hanging back in about eighth or ninth place for much of the first half of the race, even when the pace is on and everyone strung out. This seems risky, though he had raced in a similar fashion in his own Athens '97 race when he then stormed past and away from the field in the middle stages. However he didn't look as imposing now, although with five laps to go, he is still well and truly in the mix.

As the race edges towards show time Daniel Komen moves to the front with 1,500 metres to go. A younger Komen would put in a fifty eight second lap and destroy the field. However he didn't have such form now. The ridiculous thing is that he is still so young, at just twenty three yet about to be washed up. The first sign of the waves coming in is when Hissou cruises past him with 1,100 metres to go and claps on the pace again. Bruce McAvaney took notice, "Hissou looks really switched on." One by one, other runners are passing the Kenyan and Komen is soon fifth and slowly but surely being dropped. With a lap to go he is well and truly off the back and this time he has no devastating sprint to save him. Fifth place is no disgrace to most, but for Komen, it isn't good enough. He *was* far better than this. Better than these other runners ahead of him on this night in Spain. Unfortunately it would get no better for this superstar who could be added to the list of Kenyan runners who did their best running before they hit their mid twenties. Hissou was twenty seven, yet in his prime. Of course it would get no better for him either. Distance running form and fitness can be fleeting, that's for sure.

Komen certainly hadn't got his timing right as far as preparation goes for these World Championships. In July he'd raced in three high quality meetings and won them all. August was a different story, with poorer performances leading to a horrific situation in Zurich, when he'd chosen to get smashed over 1,500 metres, rather than face Haile Gebrselassie over 5,000 metres. Daniel was holding too much of a grudge, to still continue his stance against racing the Ethiopian two years after their last race. This decision proved to be to the detriment of his own form come Seville. The Kenyan later said that it was just one of those bad days, but it was about more than just biorhythms.

Now back to the battle for gold. Hissou's taking over from Komen is the third time he has taken up the pace. He goes through 4,000 metres in 10:29.68. This is Salah running to the absolute best of his abilities, but not beyond them. His various surges have made the race seem uneven but the km splits have been remarkably similar. The fastest is a 2:36.10 and the slowest a 2:38.28. There's no smarter way for a 12:50 runner without a great kick to race. Tactically, he has laid down a great platform. His hard front running has disposed of the Ethiopians. Now it is the Kenyans' turn to feel the pain.

Hissou continues to push with 800 metres to go. His teammate Lahlafi remains with him, as does Mourhit. These two have done none of the work, which is worrying. There is good news however for Salah. He has indeed put the Kenyans into difficulty as Benjamin Limo is being dropped and so too is Daniel Komen. But can Salah Hissou further increase the pace?

Coming up to the bell Lahlafi takes over from Hissou with Mourhit right behind him. Nothing will hurt Morocco more than an ex compatriot stealing its glory. The Kenyans seemed too far back to challenge. Down the back straight Komen is a forlorn figure as he falls away from Limo, his greatness being unfairly tarnished. Hissou sits on Lahlafi. He didn't particularly enjoy sprint finishes but on this occasion there isn't an Ethiopian singlet in sight. This is his chance!

Sometimes there is justice in sport. Lahlafi, Mourhit and Limo are all top runners, but they aren't in the same class as Hissou. He deserves the title of world champion more than any of them and perhaps he believes it too as he moves out to pass Lahlafi with 100 metres to go. This isn't a sprint finish. It's a strength finish made possible by Salah's great earlier work. He races past Lahlafi easily but without a rocket launcher and holds on for a career defining victory. Salah Hissou is a world champion at last! The results for the 5,000 metres were:

MOROCCAN SUCCESS; THE KADA WAY

Salah Hissou   12:58.13
Benjamin Limo   12:58.72
Mohammed Mourhit   12:58.80
Brahim Lahlafi   12:59.09
Daniel Komen   13:04.71
Fita Bayissa   13:13.86
Hailu Mekonnen   13:18.97
Million Wolde   13:20.81
Bob Kennedy   13:23.52
Pablo Olmedo   13:27.74
Manuel Pancorbo   13:32.12
Adam Goucher   13:39.24
Isaac Viciosa   13:49.59
Mark Carroll   13:52.23

Benjamin Limo came storming home to finish second, just ahead of Mourhit and the unlucky Lahlafi. Hissou's winning time was a championship record, the first time that anyone had gone sub thirteen minutes in any major championship. He had run the perfect tactical race and performed to the best of his ability. You couldn't ask any more from an athlete in the biggest race of his life.

He had beaten a quality field too. Everyone knew Daniel Komen's pedigree but Salah also beat home a future world cross country champion and a future world 5,000 metres champion. It must have been the most satisfying of moments, walking the Seville track with the Moroccan flag draped over his back. It was the rare time that he could step out from some of the large shadows that had engulfed his career. This was his time. It was his time to shine.

The race was another demonstration of Morocco's great rise to power. Runners born in the North African nation held down the first, third and fourth positions. The only let down was Jabbour's failure to finish.

As it turned out, Hissou had just earned enough of a gap on Limo to survive the Kenyan's withering final burst. Benjamin was set to be a regular contender in the years ahead. Just at the moment though, he lacked a little self belief according to his comments.

"I didn't think of having any chance to get a medal until 600 metres before the finish line. I know I have an excellent sprint, I have proven that in cross country races and for example in Monaco (IAAF GL). Tonight I had to struggle a little bit because the others were increasing the pace too early for me, but I was able to recover and draw myself back to them (Hissou, Lahlafi and Mourhit). I am very satisfied with the time and the silver. I know Hissou is too strong for me, oh yes!"

Mourhit earned his first major medal while Lahlafi had the consolation of breaking thirteen minutes for the first time. The rest of the field was a shambles with Komen unable to go with the leaders and Bayissa, Mekonnen and Wolde the next finishers approximately 100 metres further back. Million Wolde ran 13:20.81. Remember that.

There was some confusion in the after race celebrations when Mohammed got involved with his old mate Salah, participating in his victory lap. Hissou knew that this was not appropriate, public relations wise, so he twice pushed the Belgium away when Mohammed attempted to hold the Moroccan flag, although in the end he backed down and wrapped Mourhit in the Moroccan flag regardless! The bronze medallist said about the race.

"The start of the race was normal and I intended just to run in the main pack of runners. In the last 400 metres I knew I would secure a medal but I couldn't run as fast as I would like as I had a problem with one of my calf muscles. I hope to improve next year but as yet I still have concerns about the financial support that allows me to train. This medal is for Belgium but I still have a little bit of Morocco in my heart."

Hissou had run the fifth km in 2:28.45, with the last lap in approximately fifty seven seconds. It was one of the fastest last laps that he had ever run. Normally a fifty seven second last lap would see you miss a medal in a 5,000 metres championship final but Salah had made sure that this final

MOROCCAN SUCCESS; THE KADA WAY

wasn't 'normal'. The champ made this statement post race.

"I had no worries about this race because I was confident of my finishing kick. I was certain of victory and I hoped to prevent the Kenyans from winning again. I was in superb form tonight and I'm glad that I ran the 5,000 metres rather than the 10 kms. My kick was decisive. However, I didn't have to rely on this burst as I had already been increasing the pace before I made my final attack."

I couldn't have summed up the race better myself!

Now he could look ahead to 2000 and the promise of more achievement. Sydney success beckoned for him and this time he wanted more than bronze. So too would Daniel Komen, but this slight dip in his career would become a lot more than that and we would have to remember him for his couple of years of pure brilliance. His fall from grace would be one of athletics' most depressing stories.

There was nothing sad in Seville for Abdelkader Kada and Salah Hissou. The hard work had well and truly paid off. Hissou would forever be a world champion. Nobody could take that away from him. The plans that he had made for 1999 had worked out perfectly.

Now it was time to plan for the year 2000 and the Sydney Olympic Games.

Greg Rowlerson

The Dream: To Emulate Said, Brahim And Khalid

Although Seville didn't conclude the international athletics season, Hissou did not achieve anything of significance during the remainder of 1999. This could have been due to a combination of a lack of motivation after becoming world champion, as well as being a little tired after three months of regular racing. For Ali Ezzine and Hicham El Guerrouj, there were still excellent performances to come.

Abdelkader Kada had quickly become one of the world's most highly regarded and sought after distance running coaches. At season's end he spoke to many of Britain's top track coaches on October 30, 1999, at the BMC (British Milers' Club) Endurance Weekend. Those hearing his lectures came away with an even greater appreciation for what he had achieved in Morocco. He was no longer just the man who coached Hicham El Guerrouj. Kada was able to see the irony in offering advice to the British as he explained to the BMC, "It is ironic that the British invite me here, because I learned by training techniques from the great British runners of the Eighties."

Salah decided to skip his once favourite meeting in Brussels on September 3, withdrawing late from the 3,000 metres. The biggest night in Belgium athletics did not miss him in the slightest. The world's greatest middle distance runner, Hicham El Guerrouj, made the step up to the distance and the result was astonishing. He clocked a 7:23.09 making it the second fastest time in history. In the process he had obliterated Hissou's recent national record.

Hicham had targeted Daniel Komen's world record and for a long time he threatened to take it, only to fall off the pace a little towards the end. It was incredible to fathom that this man was competing in an event which was new to him, but one in which he had ten seconds to spare over the rest of the world class field. Many of the best 5,000 metres athletes were competing. We had the world silver medallist Benjamin Limo, 7:33.86, plus the former fourth best in the world Ismail Sghyr,

MOROCCAN SUCCESS; THE KADA WAY

7:34.14. Other names further back included in seventh, sixth placed runner from Atlanta Bob Kennedy, and eighth, the world record holder for this event Komen. The Kenyan ran 7:36.55, a total of 13.46 seconds behind the Moroccan. Even allowing for some fatigue from his Seville final, this was an embarrassing hammering.

It is interesting to note that El Guerrouj received no help from the usual possé of Kenyans in this race. His pacers were a Frenchman and a Russian. It was the rare example in this era of sport that money couldn't buy everything. No Kenyan was going to help a Moroccan break one of Daniel Komen's world records.

Years later Hicham reflected on this valiant attempt, "I was inside Daniel Komen's fabulous record until the last lap of the race. I completely cracked with 600 metres to go and in the ultimate 200 metres I dropped completely out of world record reach. But, looking back, I'm still proud that I ran 7:23.09, still the second best all-time 3000 metres performance." El Guerrouj had gone through 2,000 metres in 4:53.56, so to say that he'd "completely cracked" was being a bit harsh on himself. Blowing up, Hicham slumped to a 2:29.53 final km!

The disappointment of missing another world record quickly subsided, for Hicham had proved that he would be quite a handful if he decided to try his hand at the 5,000 metres. The potential was well and truly there. This was something else for Salah Hissou to think about as some peoples' thoughts already started to turn towards Sydney 2000. For Abdelkader Kada, it was another feather in his coaching cap.

The 1,500 metres race in Brussels became wide open and it was Noah Ngeny who was able to take full advantage of his rival's absence, winning in magnificent fashion by almost three seconds while obtaining one of the fastest times of the year, a 3:29.19. The top four were Kenyan athletes with Benson Koech, Laban Rotich and William Tanui all breaking 3:33. Only two days later Ngeny continued his incredible form in Rieti by breaking Sebastian Coe's eighteen year old 1,000 metres world record. The Kenyan clocked 2:11.96, erasing the British legends 2:12.18 from the books.

It is a shame that Salah Hissou didn't make a return to the Brussels 10,000 metres. It was a missed opportunity to run another sub twenty seven minute time and rekindle some former glories. When an athlete is in top form he should not waste it. To deny oneself of great racing opportunities by choice can lead to future regret as sometimes that choice will be made for you.

In the race, twenty one year old Kenyan (he was a late starter!), Charles Kamathi ran a superb 26:51.49 to just defeat Mohammed Mourhit who clocked 26:52.30. Both had made startling improvements in quick time. We had seen this on many occasions by young Kenyans so Charles' performance didn't raise too many eyebrows. But to see Belgium's new favourite son break the twenty seven minute barrier was a sporting shock as Mohammed was turning an elite athletic elderly age of twenty nine on October the 10th. Both Kamathi and Mourhit now had good reasons to have high hopes for Sydney.

Charles' sub twenty seven effort was one of the big surprises of the modern era, even for a Kenyan! It highlighted the incredible natural talent that so many from this nation possess for the reason that the Brussels meeting was his debut in a major international competition. He had been entered into the field solely as a rabbit. After setting the pace he kept on going to defeat some well known opposition, while he also improved his personal best by more than two minutes. This of course had been run at altitude.

Parity was restored in the men's steeplechase with Bernard Barmasai bouncing back from his Seville shocker to win convincingly in a time of 8:03.08, easily accounting for Christopher Koskei, 8:07.08 and Wilson Boit Kipketer, 8:07.10. He had enacted some sort of payback. The Kenyans filled the first six places with Ali Ezzine the best of the rest and a little off his recent form, running 8:12.40.

Tuesday, September 7 was the date of the next big European

MOROCCAN SUCCESS; THE KADA WAY

athletics meeting, which was held in Berlin. Kada had his three main charges ready for action and if he thought that things couldn't possibly get any better, he was blissfully wrong. The Grand Prix hosted arguably the most significant steeplechase race in many a year. For a little while now some other nations had been closing the gap on the super power of Kenya. But no matter what challenges were thrown at it, Kenya would come out victorious in any big race. To witness this giant lose at its favourite discipline was akin to witnessing the American 'dream team' lose a basketball match. In Germany the unthinkable happened as Abdelkader Kada added another achievement to his coaching resumé. The first thirteen finishers were:

Ali Ezzine	8:06.70
Bernard Barmasai	8:07.02
Paul Kosgei	8:12.42
Christopher Koskei	8:13.69
Bouabdallah Tahri	8:13.82
Giuseppe Maffei	8:15.11
Damian Kallabis	8:17.43
Elarbi Khattabi	8:17.71
Jim Svenoy	8:17.98
Luis Miguel Martin	8:20.80
Julius Chelule	8:23.69
Casper Vroemen	8:26.59
Wilson Boit Kipketer	8:30.06

Ali Ezzine had just become one of the biggest giant killers in track and field. The greatest thing about his first ever Golden League victory was that he had to defeat the best. There was no more fitting way that he could do it, than to get to go one on one against Barmasai after everyone else had been dispensed with. Abdelkader must have been truly ecstatic. Now anything was possible for Ali. Almost lost in all the excitement was the fast time itself. It was Ezzine's fourth personal best in two months and another Moroccan record.

Also racing in Germany was Hicham, determined to make use of his sensational form by breaking the last of Noureddine

Morceli's world records in the rarely raced 2,000 metres. How strong would his response be to Ngeny's recent record?

Steve Cram comments on the Moroccans chances of setting another new standard; "Well given how fast El Guerrouj has run this year, I think this is well within his capabilities, as long as we have some good pace making."

Robert Kibet and William Tanui are back on hand to offer their support to this cause and the opening lap is a positive one with the split being 56.70, well inside the pace required to run inside the Algerian's mark of 4:47.88.

Kibet continues along at a fast rhythm, with 800 metres reached in 1:54.94, by which time the threesome are some twenty five metres clear of the rest of the field. Robert moves over at half distance, but Tanui keeps the tempo high. The split at 1,200 metres is an impressive 2:52.21.

William is managing to carry through with his duties all the way to 1,400 metres, really striding out towards the end of his stint and not slowing Hicham at all. The rest is up to El Guerrouj. Cram sets the scene as he comes up to the bell; "The crowd are getting behind him which is going to be very important here because he's got nothing behind him to push him. He's only got the clock to run against and let's just see where he gets to at the bell. Morceli, the world record was 3:52 (split). He's going to be certainly inside that (Hicham goes through in 3:49.60). Well within the record schedule that was set, but Morceli ran a brilliant last lap."

Noureddine's final lap was brilliant, but Hicham would need to endure a minor collapse to miss the record now. Instead of that, El Guerrouj gets only faster, powering through the last 400 metres in 55.19 to record an almost unfathomable new world record of 4:44.79. Having taken such a large chunk off Morceli's best, this was a standard that probably even exceeded his previous world record races. His performance had once again well and truly overshadowed his training partner Ali's, despite that win being an historic one. El Guerrouj was certainly assisted by the rabbits who did an

MOROCCAN SUCCESS; THE KADA WAY

awesome job, though in saying that you still need an incredibly gifted runner to carry the early work through to the end.

Some post race praise from Cram; "He's just made a whole bunch of brilliant names over mileing history look very ordinary." Steve added further; "Words almost defy you because he's just setting standards now that I don't think that anyone for quite a while is going to get close to."

Later El Guerrouj would use this world record money to buy a house for his family. Hicham tells us the story of his struggles to please his parents, "I designed the villa and we began to build. But when it was finally finished, my parents told me that they couldn't live there. They said it was too big for them and my kid sister. I have now bought them a nice apartment instead and they are very happy. I think I will move into the villa myself when I get married."

In what has become a minor tradition, after his latest record Hicham knelt to the ground, kissed the track and offered his thanks to Allah. This guy was an extraordinary athlete. Was there no end to his brilliance and capabilities?

Following these celebrations, the 5,000 metres was a slight let down for Kada's group. Salah competed for the first time as the world champion and wanted to do the title justice with a strong performance. The pace was solid and the race evolved into a highly competitive one with eleven runners still in contention late in the race.

Hissou went to the front with purpose 800 metres out but when he wasn't able to prise open a quick gap, it was apparent that he was going to struggle to out kick such a mass number of opponents. With 200 metres to go, there were still nine athletes with a winning chance as Salah tried to break away with Benjamin Limo on his shoulder. This was the big difference in this race. Limo was right with him entering the straight whereas in Seville he had given the Moroccan far too great a start. Hissou was no match for the Kenyan's basic speed and was left standing on the final straight. In the meantime he was swamped by four other Kenyans, led by the other Limo, Richard, and relegated to sixth place. The Limos and Sammy Kipketer all ran sub thirteen with 12:59.54, 12:59.75 and 12:59.90 times. Komen produced a much improved result with his 13:00.69, just ahead of Kipkosgei's 13:00.83. Salah clocked 13:01.07.

Despite it being his worst performance of the season, it was not necessarily a poor result. It merely reflected on just how outstanding his '99 track season had been. Being satisfied with his year's accomplishments, Salah decided to give his spikes a rest until 2000, although little did he know, but finishing 1.53 seconds behind the winner of a Golden League race was something he could soon look back on fondly. It was a long time before the Moroccan would get this close to the winner again.

There were good times registered by all of the top ten. Hissou defeated Lahlafi, Maiyo, Baumann and Sghyr. In eleventh place was Brussels star Charles Kamathi who ran 13:05.29. This was more confirmation that Salah had made a mistake by avoiding the fast 10,000 metres. That is even taking into account the fact that Kamathi's 26:51 was only done four days earlier so he could have been a little tired. But remember that Salah used to race championships at 10,000 metres, where he had to back up from one 10,000 metres, to run another one, only a few days later.

The results of the Berlin 5,000 metres were quite common. To have Kenya completely dominate a high class distance running track race was hardly unique. It was therefore surprising to sometimes see a lack of dominance from this nation in the major championships. One significant difference between a top Grand Prix meet and a major championship is the number of Kenyan entrants. Only three (occasionally four at a World Championships) runners are entered in the championship races. Sometimes their numbers can reach double figures in the Golden League competitions. Since the mid '80's, the Kenyan men have been regarded as the best nation in distance running. However, overall domination has often eluded them.

MOROCCAN SUCCESS; THE KADA WAY

Kenya always has the most depth in men's distance events. Just look at the world lists. The top one hundred times in any recent year from the 800 metres up to the marathon will always include many Kenyan athletes, more than from any other nation. It has the quality of depth too. Narrow it down to top ten lists and you will still get a similar proportion of Kenyan names. Usually this will be about 30-50 percent of the runners on these timesheets.

I think it's fair to say that when people think of long distance running excellence, they think of the 5,000/10,000 metres athletes. How would people who had any interest in track and field, answer the question, which country first comes to mind when it comes to excelling in distance running? A safe assumption would be that approximately ninety five percent would say Kenya.

Yet Kenya's problem over the years is that it hasn't always had the best runner in various eras. Combine that with a lot of bad luck and I can give you the following statistics.

Since the 1976 Montreal Olympic Games, the Kenyan men have won a grand total of *one* gold medal in either the 5,000 or 10,000 metres. I find this to be incredible. So let's look at it further.

They boycotted the '76 Games that were dominated by Lasse Viren. They boycotted the '80 Games that were dominated by Yifter. However in '84 they returned to Olympic competition and since then there have been eight gold medals up for grabs in these events in which Kenya excel. Yet still only a single gold medal.

Over this same period, Kenya has won six world championship gold medals in these men's events. In nearly every year it has won the World Cross Country, but the ultimate Olympic glory has often narrowly eluded this proud long distance running nation. John Ngugi was able to win the 5,000 metres pretty easily in Seoul, but he has been the exception to the Kenyan Olympic rule. Kenya has won six minor medals in these eight races, with four silver and two bronze. There are some factors that have come into play which help to describe the disparity in Kenyan Olympic gold as compared to the gold rush in the World Championships and the World Cross Country. It's not as if Kenyan runners have choked at the Olympics.

Not having the *best* runner has hurt Kenya. In the mid '80's Moroccan Said Aouita was clearly the best track distance runner in the world and he won the 5,000 metres in Los Angeles. By the mid '90's the long distance running crown had been handed down to Ethiopia's Haile Gebrselassie. He won the 10,000 metres in Atlanta.

In the '92 Barcelona 10,000 metres, Kenya felt cheated out of a gold medal when Richard Chelimo was defeated by Khalid Skah in controversial circumstances. In the '96 Atlanta Olympics, Kenya undid itself, bringing back memories of an unfortunate Henry Rono when it didn't select its superstar Daniel Komen for the 5,000 metres.

It could have been even worse. Imagine if Said Aouita had been able to compete in the 5,000 metres at Seoul. Would Ngugi still have won gold?

Of course Kenyan men have won numerous other Olympic events during this time, for example all four steeplechase races. But as it approached Sydney 2000, there must have been a real desire to make its Olympic gold medal record reflect better on its overall dominance as a distance running nation. The poor results in Seville only added to Kenya's motivation.

The Grand Prix Final was held in Munich so the world's best track and field athletes stayed in Germany for the final meeting on September 9. Both Hicham and Salah chose not to race. Ngeny again won the 1,500 metres. His run was so impressive that it made others wonder if Hicham would have beaten him regardless. The Kenyan clocked 3:28.93, well clear of another young star Bernard Lagat who ran 3:32.30. Benjamin Limo produced another great kick to deny Paul Bitok and Mohammed Mourhit in the 3,000 metres. The times

MOROCCAN SUCCESS; THE KADA WAY

of the first three were 7:36.32, 7:36.60 and 7:36.73. Daniel Komen continued to be a shadow of his former glories, falling off the pace to finish eighth in a woeful 7:42.50.

Ali Ezzine was keen to make a repeat of his Berlin breakthrough and he raced fantastically well, but was denied by Kenya's two top names. The top eight athletes in the steeplechase were:

Bernard Barmasai	8:06.92
Wilson Boit Kipketer	8:08.28
Ali Ezzine	8:08.64
Kipkirui Misoi	8:11.36
Paul Kosgei	8:12.89
Moses Kiptanui	8:14.78
Christopher Koskei	8:17.42
Elarbi Khattabi	8:22.94

The results were a fair way to finish the year with Barmasai being the world's best despite not being the world champion. The former master, Moses Kiptanui, was battling on but his days amongst the elite were numbered. Khattabi had enjoyed one of his best seasons, running a personal best of 8:09.03 but the veteran of thirty two was hardly likely to get any better. It was up to Ali to take on the Kenyans himself next year. The fast time made it four runs under 8:10 now for Ezzine. This Moroccan had proved that he was no flash in the pan. He had the Kenyans worried, with the East Africans concerned that they might lose the Olympic title in the event that they cherish the most.

The Moroccan men were riding a great wave of success. Also catching the wave were athletes who had been born in the North Africa country but were now representing rival nations. On the 24th of October, 1999, Morocco established itself even further as a juggernaut of the distance running world. Naturalized American Khalid Khannouchi broke the world marathon record with his time of 2:05.42 in Chicago.

Morocco had enjoyed substantial Olympic success in the past. Aouita had won gold in the 5,000 metres. Boutayeb and

Skah had won gold in the 10,000 metres. Hicham would attempt to become his nation's first 1,500 metres gold medallist and Ali would also try to break new ground in the 3,000 metres steeplechase. But whom would Salah Hissou try to emulate in Sydney?

There was no easy answer. Yes, he was the 5,000 metres world champion but Hissou also had an enormous pedigree when it came to the twenty five lap classic.

Sure, the two men who had so often thwarted him figured to be there again, but Salah had achieved his gold medal so maybe it was time to again try and turn the tables on his old rivals.

Paul Tergat had recently turned thirty, so he was no longer a spring chicken. The track was generally a young man's game. In 1999 the Kenyan recorded a best time for his main event of 27:10.08. While still impressive, this was the first year since '95 that Tergat had not clocked under twenty seven minutes. Haile Gebrselassie did not race a fast 10,000 metres in '99, but still won the World Championships while also dominating the Golden League 5,000 metres and 3,000 metres races. For Salah Hissou, defeating the 'emperor' from Ethiopia on the track remained a dream. A dream that seemed unlikely to come true.

But every great athlete is human and therefore vulnerable. During December, Haile was training in some farmland in his home country. Nothing unusual about that. Unfortunately, during an otherwise innocuous session, he injured his achilles tendon. Gebrselassie was forced to abandon running for six weeks, placing a huge question mark on his entire 2000 season. There was now some genuine hope for Salah's gold medal chances in the Sydney 10,000 metres as well as the 5,000 metres.

Unfortunately, Hissou was to experience problems of his own.

The Moroccan's injury curse returned, again in the form of an ankle injury. It was serious. Serious enough to cost a large

MOROCCAN SUCCESS; THE KADA WAY

amount of time in training and serious enough to force him to abandon any thoughts of contesting the World Cross Country. In normal circumstances it was even likely that Gebrselassie and Hissou would go under the knife in an attempt to recover from their recent afflictions. However this was an Olympic year. The Games were in September. There was not enough time to have surgery and still compete in Sydney. With this in mind, Haile and Salah decided to delay their operations and hope that rest and recuperation would be enough to allow them to race at, or near their best in Australia. The important thing being that Haile could afford to be only *near* his best. Salah could not.

One runner who was ready to compete in the early stages of 2000 was Ezzine. The World Cross County Championships were held in Vilamoura, Portugal and the Moroccan was confident of a high finish in the 4 kms short course on March 18. With the standard of these races being so high, the athletes had to be at the top of their game to be competitive and Ali found it hard going. He was unable to match it with the best and thirteenth place was a little disheartening after his twelfth position two years ago. The event wasn't the major focus for him that it used to be for Salah so it was not a big deal with Ezzine's first Golden League race not until late June.

What was more significant was the men's long course race, which occurred the next day and saw a non Kenyan win for the first time in nine years. Mohammed Mourhit was the surprise winner, becoming Europe's first champion since Carlos Lopes retained his title in 1985. The official results hid the fact that Mourhit was Moroccan and that the North Africans were continuing to thwart Kenya in more and more big distance races. However, there were extenuating circumstances into Paul Tergat's bronze medal, the two second deficit ending his winning streak at five. The Kenyan team had been up all night before the event, debating the final make up of its team and whether it should race at all. Tergat wanted Joshua Chelanga who'd placed eighth in the Kenyan trials while management wanted Charles Kamathi who had finished only thirteenth in the same race. On this occasion it had a valid point in giving Charles special treatment since he had run the fastest 10,000 metres time in the world last year with his fantastic 26:51.49 at Brussels. Clearly he was a special talent. Tergat may also have had personal reasons for wanting him on the sidelines since Kamathi had defeated him in no less than three European cross country races leading up to the Kenyan trials. The reason why this organising of the squad was left until so late was because team management had taken seven runners to Portugal as it hoped to persuade event organizers to give Kamathi or Tergat a wild card entry, even though all teams were to compete with only six members.

Where the selectors made a mistake was in not informing the team members immediately after they'd made their decision to drop Chelanga. Angered at being kept in the dark, as well as the harsh treatment dealt to Joshua, the athletes made a serious threat to pull out of the event. It was Tergat who finally brought some common sense to the situation, persuading his teammates to line up and run the next day. Or perhaps that was now today!

Consequently, Tergat's fight for a sixth world title was always likely to be futile after he arrived at the Vilamoura start line, tired and angry. Yet he still finished third, only losing out in the sprint finish to Mourhit and Mezgebu. For the record, Charles Kamathi improved greatly on his trial's run to place seventh, repaying the faith that the selectors had shown in him. But Tergat didn't care about this and was defiant. Paul felt that individual athletes' agents were having too much of a say these days and that the team concept of Kenyan running was now a thing of the past. In a way he was right. Each runner ran more for his agent and himself than for his country and who could blame them? It was up to the athlete to make as much money as possible during their possible short time at the top of the sport. They needed a future for themselves, their families and their communities.

The result of the long course event wasn't a fair one and we can safely say that another outcome would have been likely under different circumstances. Shortly after this race Paul

MOROCCAN SUCCESS; THE KADA WAY

Tergat remained in Portugal for a half marathon which he won in a fastest time ever of 59:06. Unfortunately the course was judged to be too downhill so the time would not be recognized as an official world record. Despite this, the Kenyan had made his point.

Credit still had to go to Mourhit for his outstanding run in Portugal. Now twenty nine, Mohammed was making up for the many years of lost time with injury problems. He had always possessed tremendous ability. In the early '90's it was none other than Said Aouita who said that Mourhit could handle and produce incredibly hard track work outs better than any other Moroccan runner. Mohammed arguably made the wrong career move when he sided with Aouita after he was kicked out of the Moroccan Federation following disagreements with Aziz Daouda. Throughout the mid '90's he was unable to make the Moroccan teams, during which period he also spent a lot of time in America. His career didn't begin to gather speed until 1997 when he acquired Belgium citizenship and his potential in cross country became apparent. By 1999 Mourhit had transferred that success to the tracks of Europe, which led to his bronze medal run in Seville. Despite the recent upward curve of his career, his victory in Vilamoura was unexpected. To *win* the World Cross Country was a big shock and an amazing accomplishment for this late bloomer of distance running.

For many years Hissou had defeated Mourhit on a consistent basis. He felt that the 2000 race was a weaker field than those he'd pitted his best form against in the mid '90's and felt that it could have been him on the top step of the podium. Despite being a good friend of Mohammed and happy for his success, he could understandably feel a tad unlucky.

Hicham El Guerrouj wasn't having any problems as he went through his usual preparations in Ifrane. Hill training had always been an important part of the Kada schedule. The following is an example of a session that Hicham completed during March 2000:

20 x 350 metres in about 54 seconds up a gradient of close to

15 degrees. Mohammed Amyn paced him through the first 300 metres of each workout on the forest trail.

Quality track work also remained a feature of Hicham's pre racing training. One of these sessions was:

10 x 1,000 metres, each in approximately 2:33 with 2 minutes respite. Houcine Benzriguinet led him through the first 600 metres with Mohammed Amyn and Fethi El Guerrouj trailing the world record holder.

Trailing was the operative word. Mohammed and Fethi were unable to finish the workout while Hicham seemed to grow in strength, even though he soon only had the use of a secondary rabbit after Houcine also became exhausted. The final repetition was completed in a useful time of 2:29. Benzriguinet commented, "That's why he is the champion. You see how he has killed us in the training. Three people, we are all finished, and he is still strong."

For the second consecutive season Hicham El Guerrouj was skipping the indoor season. He didn't make a racing appearance until June 9 when he raced in the Seville 1,500 metres. These weren't the World Championships and Hicham certainly would not need a 3:27 to win this time. He wasn't in quite the same shape on this occasion but nevertheless he won easily and it was a nice way to start his year. The world record holder ran 3:33.48 and had more than two seconds to spare over Kenyan John Kibowen. Abdelkader also likely kept a watchful eye over the 3,000 metres because of the surprise inclusion of Noah Ngeny. The Kenyan showed his versatility by winning in 7:35.46, defeating Moroccan specialists Brahim Lahlafi and Mohamed Said El Wardi.

Two weeks later and track and field became more serious in Paris on June 23. This was the first Golden League meeting and many of the sport's top names came out of hiding for the meeting. The bigger races also brought out the bigger talk and it was the usually quiet Hicham who had a bit to say before his race.

MOROCCAN SUCCESS; THE KADA WAY

"I think I can deliver the world record if the hares do their work. I am here to put up a great performance in a great stadium," he stated confidently.

He also reflected on his most recent world title, "For me that was the greatest race of my life. Everything was in place, the best athletes, good climatic conditions and an important medal at stake. Some people complained that I relaxed at the finish and so missed the world record, but they misunderstood my motivation. I was overjoyed to beat the best in the world that night, men like Ngeny and the Spanish. It was not a night for records."

On his plans for 2000 he said, "At one point, I was interested in trying some races at 3000 metres and 5000 metres as well as the 1500 metres. But of course, I would not have been able to do all this, plus the Golden League and still be in shape for Sydney. So in the end I decided to stick to the 1500 metres. Now I aim to go for the IAAF Golden League Jackpot. The longer distances I will leave to next season."

There had been a significant change made to the rules of eligibility for the jackpot. Instead of needing to win all seven Golden League events, a task which seemed outlandish even for the dominant freaks in the sport, an athlete could afford some losses or a break with a sensible five wins out of seven, now the requirement.

At the Stade de France El Guerrouj was able to raise his level appropriately and win just as convincingly as he had in Spain. Though far from a world record, the winning time was an excellent 3:30.75, showing that Kada already had his champion approaching peak form. Hicham was happy with the result and world leading time as he quoted.

"I was very satisfied with what I achieved here today and thank the crowd for their encouragement. I adore Paris and I adore Parisians. This stadium is everything I hoped it would be."

Hicham had settled straight into third position after 100

metres behind the two rabbits with Mehdi Baala next. But Mehdi instantly allowed El Guerrouj a big break and the Moroccan was quickly out by ten metres. After 250 metres the other athletes began to move around Baala and make an attempt to close down this margin. The first split was 53.85 so little wonder they were giving up five metres to the world champion. Kenyan Bernard Lagat surged strongly with two laps remaining, moving to fourth and quickly cutting into Hicham's advantage. The 800 metres split was 1:51.24 after a slower 57.39 lap with the Kenyan right on the Moroccan's heels in third place as the leader drops out. Then the second rabbit takes off, dragging Hicham away from Bernard who must have gone into his red zone thanks to his recent surge. The Moroccan is left to his own devices with 500 metres left. The gap remained stable at about five metres to Lagat with the rest of the field at least 20 metres in arrears. The time was 2:48.13 at 1,200 metres after a 56.89 lap. On the back straight Bernard closed but on the bend Hicham rose to another level and blew him away. Brilliant. Again. Hicham's last lap was 56.95, though it looked much quicker.

Well behind at the end was Bernard Lagat who clocked a 3:33.14. Impressing in third place was a fast finishing twenty one year old Frenchman who clocked 3:33.67.

Mehdi Baala was born in Strasbourg, but like many of the best French runners he had North African origins, with his lying in Algeria. Earlier this season he'd won the bronze medal in the European Indoor Championships at 1,500 metres. He was young and talented, so obviously a runner for Abdelkader and Hicham to keep an eye on. The Moroccan's number one rival Noah Ngeny, moved down to the 800 metres at this meeting where he placed second.

The steeplechase was jam packed with quality Kenyans but they didn't have the race all to themselves. Ali Ezzine was making his presence felt in a race of very high standards, especially considering it was early in the season.

Ali looks comfortable in the early stages of the race, travelling in sixth position. The rabbit Kipkurui takes them to 1,000

MOROCCAN SUCCESS; THE KADA WAY

metres in 2:41.15 with Barmasai running second. Shortly afterwards and with Kipkurui gone, Ezzine finds himself in a pretty good spot, shifting between third and fourth positions. With four laps to go it appears that Ali might be struggling with Barmasai's pace as he slips behind a little. Reuben Kosgei sits on Bernard. Reuben is just one of five Kenyan Kosgei's ranked in the world's top twenty for this discipline!

For the entire lap Ali is on the edge of dropping off completely, lagging a few metres behind the third Kenyan Raymond Yator. Is he going to be able to hold it together on the third last lap?

The excellent pace remains constant with the second km run in 2:41.31 for a 5:22.46, 2,000 metres split. Still Ezzine flirts with his fans, running some six metres behind Barmasai. It appears that he cannot win, with third or fourth position realistically being the best that he can hope for. Only five runners remain in any sort of contact, though this group is being stretched.

Suddenly Ezzine breaks into his strong stride, moving past Yator and closing the gap to effectively nothing to Barmasai and Kosgei with two laps to go. By the bell nothing has changed. Can this Moroccan defeat the world record holder and the world junior champion?

Kosgei seizes the lead with 300 metres left, something he has been threatening to do for most of the race. Yet Ezzine moves with him, refusing to be dropped. He also passed Bernard before taking the lead as he entered the bend. Ali safely clears the water jump and gains a small break but by the final jump, the Kenyans are still with him. The final top ten results were:

Ali Ezzine	8:03.57
Reuben Kosgei	8:03.92
Bernard Barmasai	8:04.27
Kipkirui Misoi	8:08.00
Raymond Yator	8:09.78
Abraham Cherono	8:16.27

Laid Bessou	8:16.48
Moses Kiptanui	8:16.68
Elarbi Khattabi	8:18.54
Bouabdallah Tahri	8:18.90

Ali Ezzine managed to hold his nerve and form to the line to win and run the fastest ever time for a non Kenyan. The final km was 2:41.12, which included a last lap of 62.33. Magnificent! In the process of finishing second, seventeen year old Kosgei smashed the world junior record.

It was another triumph of enormous magnitude as the Moroccan record went again and Ali became the fifth fastest steeplechaser of all time. Once again Abdelkader Kada had displayed his coaching knack of getting an athlete into sensational form for the start of the season. He had done it time and again with Hicham and Salah. Now it was Ali's turn to deliver his best ever performance first race up. The Kada group often produced its best in a quick period after returning to sea level from Ifrane. It was the recipe for success.

Ezzine was becoming the most regular athlete to defeat Barmasai, having done so in three of their last five contests. He had beaten the best that the world had to offer in his two Golden League victories at Berlin and Paris. Hicham had not even done quite as much at the same age and Ali could see clearly what could be achieved. An 8:03 before he turned twenty two was awesome. Ali Ezzine's potential appeared limitless. His secret for defeating the Kenyans didn't involve rocket science.

"You must be confident and try and upset their rhythm," put Ali simply.

Salah Hissou wasn't ready to resume yet, but his presence would have made little difference anyway to the outcome of the 3,000 metres, won by new sensation Ali Saidi-Sief in an astonishing time of 7:27.67. Komen finished with a very respectable 7:31.47 with Million Wolde next in 7:32.36 as the twenty two year old Algerian improved his personal best by a whopping nine seconds. Ali had shown some potential last

MOROCCAN SUCCESS; THE KADA WAY

season but that was as a miler. Nobody knew that he had this sort of armoury. It would be interesting to see what he could run in his next race.

The first and second km splits were timed at 2:29.14 and 2:31.95. Saidi-Sief picked up the pace 800 metres out and then kicked severely with 500 metres remaining. Only Wolde was still a chance at the bell and with 300 metres left, the race was over. The concluding splits were as amazing as any ever seen for such a fast 3,000 metres. The penultimate lap of 59.88 was very fast considering this is when a hard race really hurts at this distance. From then on Ali just went quicker and quicker, recording a 55.35 last lap! Who else could ever run a 1:55.23 final 800 metres off of such a fast pace?

Komen backed up well from this defeat by winning the 3,000 metres at the Athens Grand Prix on June 28. Daniel ran 7:31.96 to out sprint Benjamin Maiyo who clocked 7:32.36. Also racing were Ezzine's steeplechase rivals Bernard Barmasai and Paul Kosgei who achieved good times of 7:36.79 and 7:39.15 respectively. Struggling to finish with a 7:56.75 was Venuste Niyongabo. He was still unable to get near his former standard and his career seemed to be over. Five days later he competed in a 1,500 metres in Zagreb and the result of fifteenth in 3:39.66 said it all.

Saidi-Sief did race again the following week at the Rome Golden League on June 30. Moving up to compete at the 5,000 metres for the first time, the Algerian was in rare form and arguably even more impressive than in Paris. Winding up an already fast pace with still 700 metres to go, Ali showed El Guerrouj like qualities as he left the Kenyans in his wake. When he stopped the clock at 12:50.86, a new national record, we officially had a new superstar in men's distance running. The guys that he bolted clear from were magnificent athletes. There were junior star Sammy Kipketer, 12:54.07, and all time great Paul Tergat, 12:55.18. Even further behind were the Limos with Richard, 12:58.70 and Benjamin, 13:02.19. Ali Saidi-Sief was going to be a big danger at the Sydney Olympics. Kada had to wonder if he would continue at the 5,000 metres or revert back to his once favourite 1,500 metres.

Hicham was enjoying a break from racing so Noah Ngeny won the 1,500 metres in a fast time of 3:29.99, although he didn't win too easily with his compatriot Bernard Lagat clocking a notable time of 3:30.78. Ngeny was racing with great regularity. Only two days earlier he'd won a 1,000 metres race in the Athens meeting in 2:15.53, defeating 800 metres specialist Patrick Konchellah. Noah was varying his events greatly in an effort to get an edge for Sydney. There were already signs that the Kenyans might be more of a threat to El Guerrouj this year.

Ali Ezzine was unable to continue his great form as he fell apart in the steeplechase. At halfway he led and looked strong, but soon after, he fell off the pace as to everyone's surprise, another Moroccan picked it up. The quality of the field was not as high as Paris but the results here certainly added another name to the list of steeplechase medal hopefuls for the upcoming Olympics.

Brahim Boulami	8:03.82
Kipkirui Misoi	8:07.21
Simon Vroemen	8:13.45
Damian Kallabis	8:14.53
Ali Ezzine	8:14.86
Gael Pencreach	8:14.94
Laid Bessou	8:17.41
Elarbi Khattabi	8:19.42
Vladimir Pronin	8:19.43
Jonathan Kandie	8:20.18

Ezzine hit the lead with four laps to run after a first km split of 2:42.19. The Kenyans in the field were not particularly strong, so Ali was the massive favourite following on from his Paris exploits. Reuben Kosgei and Bernard Barmasai were both absent. The British commentators were making no mention whatsoever of Boulami. Briefly it seemed that Ali was going to break away but soon Brahim took over and piled on the pressure. Misoi also went past and with two laps remaining, Ezzine lost contact for good. Steve Ovett constantly referred

MOROCCAN SUCCESS; THE KADA WAY

to Boulami as Khattabi as he and Misoi put a big margin on the Moroccan record holder. The second km was run in 2:41.77 for a 5:23.96, 2,000 metres split. At the bell Ovett realises that this is Boulami but later as he breaks away from the Kenyan, he comments, "He's got the strength, third in the Olympic 5,000 metres." Now he is confusing him with his brother!

Brahim looked like an absolute powerhouse in the latter stages and certainly didn't look to be huffing and puffing. The last lap was 62.01 and the final km 2:39.86. Now Ovett realises that this is indeed Brahim Boulami. This *was* a surprise result!

Brahim's performance certainly came out of the woodwork. The twenty eight year old's previous best of 8:10.84 had come in 1997. He had shown precious little form since then. In fact his only sub 8:15 performances in the last two years had both come in 1998 when he ran 8:11.30 at Monaco and 8:14.86 at Paris. To say that his victory and near Moroccan record in Rome were a surprise would be the understatement of 2000.

Born on April 20, 1972, Boulami had displayed great strength throughout races in his career, though not the speed necessary to compete with the true elite. His personal record for 3,000 metres was only 7:42.99, yet he'd managed to finish fairly well up in the World Cross Country in 1997, placing twenty second.

Later that season Brahim finished tenth at the World Championships which was a minor setback following his seventh placing in the Olympic final. In 1998 he made some small gains when he finished sixth in the World Cross Country 4 kms event in Marrakech. But the rest of the season was mostly a struggle. He did win a bronze medal at the African Championships but this wasn't a true reflection on his standing in the steeplechase. His time of 8:29.52 was an enormous distance behind world record holder Bernard Barmasai who ran 8:11.74. 1999 had been a year largely interrupted by injury, but in 2000 he had taken his game to another level and was an athlete to look out for come Sydney.

On June the 8th Brahim was presented with a great opportunity to prove that this level of performance was not going to be a once off. He lined up in Nice expecting another good time but in this instance, Ali Ezzine was better prepared for him.

The steeplechase quickly turned into a two man Moroccan battle. The top Kenyans were not here but this wasn't going to stop these men from pushing their own boundaries. A fast pace was on from the outset and the race would be decided in a final kick. To Kada's disappointment, it was Boulami who had the answers and the victory. Not only did he take Ali's confidence but also his national record. The 8:03.30 wiped Ali from the list after a grand total of fifteen days!

It was far from all doom and gloom however. Ezzine had put in a tremendous run with a near personal best of 8:04.06. He was back to his best form with the Olympics less than three months away. In this meeting Ngeny continued to put his stamp on the athletics season by winning the 1,000 metres in a fast time of 2:14.78, three days after winning a 1,500 metres at Lausanne in 3:31.61.

By this stage of the season, things were looking up for Hicham El Guerrouj and Ali Ezzine. However, Salah Hissou was not yet race ready. This was very concerning for the Moroccan with the Olympic Games taking place in late September. Time was running out.

Haile Gebrselassie was already back racing. He had immediately decided to test himself against some strong competition in the Milan 5,000 metres on June 7. His achilles appeared to be fine as he remained a winner, while going close to thirteen minutes with a 13:01.60. Yet he was surprisingly pushed all the way by Kenyan Abraham Chebii who ran 13:01.90.

On June 25, exactly three months before the 10,000 metres Sydney final, Gebrselassie raced again at 5,000 metres, this

MOROCCAN SUCCESS; THE KADA WAY

time in Nuremberg. The result was almost a carbon copy of Milan with another victory and another good time of 13:01.07. Satisfied with his form, Haile reverted back to focusing on some hard training.

Hard training. It was something that Salah Hissou had not been able to do enough of. Into July and the 5,000 metres world champion had not clocked up enough miles, nor had he completed the sheer quantity of quality speed sessions that were required to survive at this level of competition. His ankle had not completely heeled either, but he had to test himself soon or his whole year would simply run out, and what a waste that would be.

Salah didn't like to hide, so on the 28th of July he tried to kick start his Olympic flame with a good performance in Oslo. The meeting had always attracted a top field and this year was no exception, though there was no Haile Gebrselassie on the start line. In previous years this meant that Hissou had a shot at victory, but coming back from injury made this a very different situation.

The race was very fast with the field getting to 3,000 metres in 7:44.91, but Salah was able to hang in there. Soon after he took the lead and went through 4,000 metres in 10:24.86. Unfortunately he was unable to stretch his opposition and it was no surprise that he didn't have the higher gears to switch to on the final lap. The first twelve in the Bislett 5,000 metres were:

Sammy Kipketer	12:55.03
Mark Bett	12:55.63
Benjamin Limo	12:55.82
Brahim Lahlafi	12:56.18
Luke Kipkosgei	12:56.50
Mohammed Mourhit	12:56.60
Ismail Sghyr	12:58.83
Albert Chepkurui	12:59.90
Salah Hissou	13:00.06
Paul Bitok	13:04.15
Patrick Ivuti	13:04.98

Paul Kosgei   13:05.44

In Oslo Salah proved that he had good general fitness. He just didn't have any sort of a kick down in him. To finish ninth might seem like a disaster, but Hissou should have been relatively happy with his time of 13:00.06. He might anticipate that his finishing form would improve greatly with more racing. Sammy Kipketer's 12:55.03 wasn't light years ahead, and everybody else in front of him was also beatable. None of the names of Mark Bett, Benjamin Limo, Brahim Lahlafi, Luke Kipkosgei, Mohammed Mourhit, Ismail Sghyr and Albert Chepkurui had ever put the fear of God into Salah Hissou. It was a question of whether or not he could return to his '99 form.

Sammy was yet another addition to the long list of Kenyan Kipketers. The eighteen year old had already produced good times at Rome and Lausanne this season. In Switzerland Sammy ran 13:01.93 and defeated a crack field that included Paul Tergat and Daniel Komen. Unfortunately Sammy placed fourth in the 5,000 metres at the Kenyan trials, thus missing a spot on the team for Sydney.

Salah was the second Moroccan to finish behind Lahlafi in the Kenyan dominated field but his country should have had far more depth in its distance running. Ahead of Hissou were Mourhit and Sghyr. Both had just broken the Belgium and French records. Both were Moroccan born runners.

Hicham El Guerrouj resumed his racing at Bislett and it was more of the same from the Olympic favourite. Much was expected of the world champion and in the perfect conditions of twenty one degrees and with no wind, Steve Ovett set the scene, "And these other athletes must be now having to swallow hard because at this sort of rhythm very few of them know that they can keep up. In fact they're pushing all their boundaries if they do anywhere near Hicham El Guerrouj. The world record a staggering 3:43.13, set in Rome. A hush falls over the stadium. This could be history in the making."

El Guerrouj did not approach his mile world record which had

MOROCCAN SUCCESS; THE KADA WAY

been discussed as a target pre race, but nevertheless proved too strong for his competitors, leading home Kenyan William Chirchir. The first two ran 3:46.24 and 3:47.94. John Kibowen was the third athlete to go under 3:50 with his 3:49.87. It was incredible that such a great number of Kenyans were now able to run such a time.

That Hicham didn't run closer to his record time wasn't entirely his fault. He concluded the second lap in 1:51.65, just half a second off the first rabbit Robert Kibet. But the second rabbit William Tanui was only able to go to 1,000 metres and the pace slowed to that point before the Moroccan carried it on the rest of the way. 2:49.42 had been the split at 1,200 metres. After that, El Guerrouj slowly pulled away from Chirchir through superior strength.

Only two other men (Ngeny and Morceli) had ever run a faster mile yet the Norwegian crowd was quiet and perhaps unhappy with the performance. Breaking world records should never be expected but I suppose the athletes themselves can be blamed a little for raising expectations on occasions with yet another 'world record attempt.'

Once again avoiding a highly anticipated match up with Hicham was Noah Ngeny. Not that the Kenyan was running scared or in poor form. Noah triumphed in the 800 metres, which certainly stunned the event's usual entrants. Even without Wilson Kipketer competing, it was still an awesome result for Ngeny, whose time of 1:44.49 was excellent for a miler. It compared in some ways to Daniel Komen's win against the milers at Monaco in 1997.

None of Kada's top athletes competed in the Stockholm Grand Prix on August 1 but the meeting still held a first rate steeplechase battle. This was Brahim Boulami's first confrontation with the best Kenyans since becoming a truly world class competitor and the East Africans did not want another Moroccan stealing their thunder. By the latter stages there were down to six survivors with Brahim among them. But when it came time to kick, he wasn't able to quite match it with the top three runners that Kenya had to offer. Youngster

Reuben Kosgei, finishing in 8:06.58, scarcely got the better of Barmasai, 8:06.62, with Boit Kipketer third, 8:07.33. Boulami still managed to post his third best time ever with his fourth place 8:08.67. For the moment Kenya still held the steeplechase title belt.

Surprisingly the first encounter between Ngeny and El Guerrouj in 2000 did not come at a Golden League meeting but rather on a smaller track night in London on the 5th of August. The distance was the mile and the organizers were doing all they could to ensure a fast time by enlisting the services of usual rabbits Kibet and Tanui. Abdelkader didn't want Hicham to lose to Noah under any circumstances, leading up to, and certainly not at the Olympics. The psychological advantage that El Guerrouj had over Ngeny, needed to remain because it was becoming clearer all the time that their abilities were very similar. In England Hicham was able to bring out his best run of the season and vitally, this was enough to win comfortably with the results being:

Hicham El Guerrouj	3:45.96
Noah Ngeny	3:47.67
John Mayock	3:53.44
Hailu Mekonnen	3:53.48
Adil Kaouch	3:54.74
John Kibowen	3:54.74
Kevin McKay	3:55.07
Youssef Baba	3:55.80
Andrew Graffin	3:56.13
Martin Keino	3:57.00
Mohammed Amyn	3:57.32
Neil Caddy	3:58.31
Allen Graffin	3:59.86
Jason Pyrah	4:00.33
Ali Ezzine	4:01.12
Fethi El Guerrouj	4:10.59

It wasn't a particularly close contest but bear in mind that the Olympic 1,500 metres heats were not until September 25. The Moroccan camp had no idea if Ngeny had tapered at all for this race. Regardless, it was a marvellous outcome and

MOROCCAN SUCCESS; THE KADA WAY

strengthened Hicham's resolve that he was soon to become the Olympic champion.

Adil Kaouch was in decent form, which boded well for a similar scenario to Seville, where he could pace El Guerrouj. Adil just needed to make the final, though for his lesser abilities, this was not guaranteed. Hicham's brother Fethi was granted a spot in this field, however he was unable to show that he belonged at this level. Even still, a family whose second best sibling can run a 4:10 mile is very impressive!

Ali Ezzine's run would have probably been a negative for Kada. Despite this being a foreign event to him, he should have been capable of running sub four minutes. His form a month earlier had wavered slightly and with the competition in the steeplechase becoming fiercer, a Sydney medal was going to be mighty hard to come by.

Also running in London was Salah, who decided to again race over the 5,000 metres. Haile was competing here too, back for his first race since Nuremberg and hoping to run under thirteen minutes. This was a crucial race for Hissou. If he wanted to play a big part in Olympic proceedings, he needed to be competitive here. He was competitive, however not highly. As usual, Gebrselassie was victorious. He was far too good for everybody but Kipketer. The top finishers were as follows:

Haile Gebrselassie	13:06.23
Sammy Kipketer	13:06.99
Assefa Mezgebu	13:09.06
Paul Bitok	13:09.54
Salah Hissou	13:09.89
Million Wolde	13:10.99

If the Ethiopian was defeating him this easily at 5,000 metres, how could Hissou realistically hope to challenge him at 10,000 metres, which was Gebrselassie's best distance?

Salah did not have an answer to this right now, but at least fifth place was better than ninth. Finishing within one second of Mezgebu and Bitok was nothing to be ashamed about. Nevertheless, he could not deny that things had previously been so much better. Even during an injury plagued 1998 he had been able to destroy these two.

The new decade (and century) seemed different. The times were not any faster but Salah Hissou could no longer achieve the same results. This wasn't *the* Salah Hissou but a restricted version. Could he shake off that stubborn ankle injury and return to past glories?

Salah did manage to beat Million Wolde in London. Now that *is* really something.

Hissou was getting very little reward for his efforts. He had not been able to return to his best form. He wasn't a long way from it, but being a fraction 'off' meant that contending for victories just wasn't realistic. He wasn't great enough to afford a small lapse in performance.

In 2000, the athletics season was set up differently. All the European Grand Prix meets were on prior to the major championship. In other seasons, big meetings such as Zurich and Brussels had often been held after the Olympic Games or World Championships. The lead up to Sydney was quite a drawn out affair and perhaps it was going to be harder for the athletes to peak at the correct time. Even more pressure would be placed on the coaches to make sure that their runners didn't run into their best form too early.

All these factors should only have helped Salah as he headed to Zurich for the Weltklasse on the 11th of August. His season had started much later than normal but there was plenty of racing time to get into shape, thus making his enforced layoff not so much of an issue. That's if his left ankle did the right thing and healed fully. He, Hicham and Ali all had great belief in their coach. If anyone could get them peaking at the right time, it was Abdelkader. The athletes didn't need to worry a great deal about such matters. They did the hard work as instructed by Kada and had faith that these instructions would lead them all to a best possible Olympic outcome.

MOROCCAN SUCCESS; THE KADA WAY

All the top long distance track runners liked to race in the big 5,000 metres race at Zurich, but sometimes the scheduling didn't allow them all to front up. In 2000, the fact that it was on with still a significant amount of time remaining before Sydney seemed to suit everybody. The field that was on the start line for this race was one of the greatest ever assembled. It described almost a decade of men's distance running. It had been the greatest period of track distance running ever.

There were a couple of handy Kenyans in this race, the final event of the Zurich meeting. The man who was once the third fastest in history in Philip Mosima, and the '93 and '95 world champion Ismael Kirui. Yet these weren't even two of the competitors. They were two of the designated rabbits or pacemakers. What an insult! Kirui looked anything but happy as the television cameras scrolled up and down the race entrants. Next to him was Gebrselassie who as always, looked very happy indeed.

Haile Gebrselassie had every reason to be happy. He had established himself in most people's minds as the greatest distance runner of all time. At twenty seven, he was relatively young to be spoken about in such glowing terms, but this was no exaggeration. His fears about a failure in Sydney had dissipated also. The Ethiopian had survived his achilles tendon scare. Three races in 2000 for three wins at 5,000 metres. It didn't matter how strong the Zurich field looked on paper. Haile wasn't scared by anyone. You can bet that everybody else saw his name on the start list before they read anyone elses. HAILE GEBRSELASSIE always stood out like a beacon even when he wasn't smiling. In approximately thirteen minutes, it would surely be four races, four wins, this season.

Salah Hissou was running out of time and running out of chances. Morocco would select him for the Olympic Games, despite his form slump. He didn't need to worry about that. His country had great confidence in its world champion, but injury and recent performances meant that Salah lacked confidence in himself. He *did* need to worry about that.

Greg Rowlerson

The race is very fast in the early stages with Martin Keino setting the tempo. Mosima and Kirui are next in the long line of single file athletes. The first contenders are Benjamin Limo, Gebrselassie, Richard Limo and Mourhit. Salah settles in midfield behind Paul Tergat. This is quite a handy field.

Steve Ovett comments about the racing style of Tergat and Hissou, "They like to take it easy those two and then come through if they've got the strength later in the race. Try and do battle with Gebrselassie, but Gebrselassie usually has all the cards stacked in his favour when it comes to sprinting against those two."

After five laps a winning time of around 12:50 or faster looks likely. Keino takes them to 2,000 metres in 5:05.29. For most of these quality runners, it is a struggle just to stay in contact. Now what can Mosima do?

Kirui has dropped back behind Gebrselassie, so it's clear that he's not going to be able to provide any support later on. Hissou looks great in seventh place with seven to go. Soon after, Mosima is out. The split at 3,000 metres is 7:44, so the pace has slowed significantly. It is Haile who is forced to take on the pacemaking. Kipketer is second, then Tergat, Mourhit and Richard Limo. Hissou is well placed in sixth.

In the last couple of kms the pace continues to slow, but with two laps to go, there are only six athletes still in contention. Hissou remains in the mix, putting in his best performance of the year. Also running well is Mohammed Mourhit. The Belgium is a little more confident these days and now leads some real legends as the combatants prepare themselves for a final lap sprint. The third and second last laps are only timed at 63.13 and 63.67, so the early hard pace has certainly taken its toll.

For the entire penultimate lap, Salah runs wide. He races alongside Tergat and just behind Mourhit and Gebrselassie. Approaching the bell he makes a serious attempt to take the lead but is eased out by the Belgium and Ethiopian. Mohammed holds the lead until 200 metres left, when

MOROCCAN SUCCESS; THE KADA WAY

Gebrselassie makes his decisive move, and initially only Sammy Kipketer goes with him, just like in London. The final results were:

Haile Gebrselassie	12:57.95
Paul Tergat	12:58.21
Sammy Kipketer	12:58.63
Mohammed Mourhit	13:00.50
Salah Hissou	13:00.75
Richard Limo	13:02.43
Patrick Ivuti	13:02.68
Luke Kipkosgei	13:05.31
Assefa Mezgebu	13:06.13
Benjamin Limo	13:08.53
John Cheruiyot Korir	13:09.58
Mark Carroll	13:12.16
Million Wolde	13:12.26
Ismail Sghyr	13:12.62
Albert Chepkurui	13:17.82
Mark Bett	13:23.37
Fita Bayissa	13:29.56
Paul Bitok	13:29.94

Haile did win again, comfortably pulling away from Sammy over the last fifty metres. But an old adversary nearly got a first track win over Gebrselassie. Paul Tergat finished strongly on the inside to take Kipketer, however he left his run too late to catch the Ethiopian. Nevertheless his good finish was a promising sign for his Sydney chances. Haile was clearly straining and had to pull out all the stops to hold out his rival. The last lap was run in 56.26, completing a 2:32.02 last km.

"When the questions are asked there are always answers from this man," remarked an excited Ovett about another Gebrselassie victory.

Salah Hissou and Mohammed Mourhit were unable to go with the speed but both Moroccan born athletes still should have been quietly happy about the result. They were not too far away and they could look at who they had defeated, many of whom by big margins. A sub par Salah Hissou finished fifth when amongst arguably the greatest distance running field ever assembled. That's not too bad at all.

Track and field had become big business so even a meeting as prestigious as the Weltklasse had to shape up if it wanted to continue to attract the world's best athletes. This meeting had a budget of $6 million Swiss francs. Hosting approximately twenty events, this meant around $300,000 per event. A lot of this would go to the biggest names as appearance fees. For an event as popular as the men's 5,000 metres it's possible that the elite would receive even more than the average quota to compete. As the current world champion, Salah Hissou was on good money. By 2000, Zurich had over twenty different sponsors and a successful television coverage.

The Zurich 5,000 metres highlighted the difficult situations that can often arise in track and field with regards to the television coverage of a meeting. There is often a lot going on, so what exactly should be shown? The British commentators became a little peeved that the director switched to, and then continued to focus on the conclusion of the men's shot put competition, during the latter stages of the men's 5,000 metres. These were some of the comments:

"We're just here Steve for the last three puts of the men's shot competition. I guess that's why the director's come here."

"Adam Nielson here has won the shot. He has got one throw left. It looks like we're going to stay with that while the group of ten still tracks around with three laps to go and we'll obviously be concentrating on that after we take our last look at Adam Nielson, looking for an even better mark in this men's shot put competition."

"Got a new leader in the 5,000, Mohammed Mourhit. Out of the corner of my eye while I look at Adam Nielson (being very sarcastic). Pretty good throw but it's not as good I think. We don't really need to see the replay but we probably will (Steve Ovett laughs in the background). Because there is a fascinating dual going on in this 5,000 metres (hint hint)."

MOROCCAN SUCCESS; THE KADA WAY

The director continues to show Nielson strolling around so the broadcaster becomes quite agitated and still being sarcastic says, "Yep, lots of congratulations. Let's get back to this race."

The field events are usually the ones that take a back seat to the action on the track as far as public exposure goes. These events take time and the argument from the track fans is that these events can be shown later, after being packaged together to show the main jumps and throws. The sprint events get the best deal. The 100 metres will always be shown live and then usually replayed multiple times. Any distance exceeding a mile is where it gets difficult for the television directors. Often the distance races will be interrupted on a number of occasions to show other events. From the distance running fan's perspective, the men's Zurich 5,000 metres contest is always mouth watering and compelling viewing. But try to look at it from a more neutral perspective and you can see reasons why the director may break up the coverage. There wasn't a chance of a world record by the halfway mark of this Zurich race and nobody had made an attempt to break away. The eventual outcome was what most of us would have expected anyway. It would be easy to look at it and think 'the same guy (Gebrselassie) wins all the time, so where is the excitement?'

Most humans by nature are also very impatient and this is to the detriment of the popularity in distance running. Those that aren't obsessed with the sport will generally be more impressed and interested in Maurice Greene breaking ten seconds than in Hicham El Guerrouj running a sub 3:50 mile. The television people know this and understand that they need to cater to the general viewer and not just the knowledgeable one. It is a difficult balancing act.

Haile Gebrselassie was performing another balancing act in the immediate aftermath of another victory. Despite briefly grimacing and shaking his head, he quickly smiled again and walked around the stadium, taking in the crowd's adulation. The important word here is walked. He *couldn't* run, yet Haile forced himself to keep smiling. The game of deception had just started.

After crossing the finish line, the Ethiopian immediately felt great pain in his achilles but was determined not to hobble, not to show his opponents that he was suddenly a weakened version of his super human self. He escaped Zurich that night without his secret being detected and quickly abandoned his remaining planned lead up races in Europe. He would say that he was going back home to train. His operation to defend the Olympic title was in serious jeopardy.

Hissou's own Olympic operation was looking a little more positive. But the improvement in his performance at Zurich needed to continue in his next race.

Hicham's event earlier in this Golden League meeting was every bit as important as Salah's. Only six days after his thrashing of Noah, he had to race him again. It was their final confrontation until the 29th of September, the day of the Olympic Games 1,500 metres final.

This Grand Prix race started differently with Ngeny taking the initiative and sitting in behind the rabbits and in front of El Guerrouj. The 400 metres split was 54.02 and then a still incredibly quick 1:50.16 at the 800 metres, close to world record pace. Hicham was not bothered with proceedings and even now decided to go to the lead with 600 metres remaining. On the final lap the Kenyans of Ngeny and Lagat were stubborn in their efforts, but nevertheless couldn't quite cling onto the Moroccan who edged clear for another resounding victory. The thirteen finishers were:

Hicham El Guerrouj	3:27.21
Noah Ngeny	3:28.12
Bernard Lagat	3:28.51
Andres Manuel Diaz	3:31.79
Driss Maazouzi	3:32.01
Mehdi Baala	3:32.05
Laban Rotich	3:32.93
Benson Koech	3:33.31
Steve Holman	3:33.59

MOROCCAN SUCCESS; THE KADA WAY

Ali Hakimi	3:34.96
Jose Antonio Redolat	3:35.03
Youssef Baba	3:35.21
John Kibowen	3:40.02

It was the fourth fastest time ever, with nobody else having ever run as fast. This was El Guerrouj at his best, which Kada would have surely loved. He knew that his superstar hadn't been in quite the same devastating form as the last two years but this was right back on that extraordinary level. His performance went a long way towards dragging Noah and Bernard through to personal best times, both of which were under the old Kenyan record. The other athletes were not in the same league and Sydney appeared to be a battle between these three plus possibly the other Kenyan William Chirchir. There was also Ali Saidi-Sief if the Algerian decided to run this event. For the moment it was most likely that he would opt for the more winnable 5,000 metres.

Ezzine missed another big steeplechase race, although in this instance the pace was slower soAli didn't miss the chance for a fast time. All his Sydney rivals were in Zurich with the top six finishing as follows:

Wilson Boit Kipketer	8:11.19
Reuben Kosgei	8:11.65
Bernard Barmasai	8:11.77
Raymond Yator	8:12.29
Eliseo Martin	8:13.63
Brahim Boulami	8:14.64

So far, Boulami had been unable to deliver the goods against the top Kenyans as Ezzine had done previously. This was a long way from his national record. Barmasai was proving to be vulnerable in a sprint finish and there was no clear favourite for this event any longer. If anything, this race may have provided Ali with encouragement, as even the Spaniard Martin was highly competitive.

On the 18th of August there was another steeplechase event at the Monaco Golden League but again Ezzine skipped the race, as Brahim Boulami improved further on his Moroccan record. The speed was strong throughout with a 2:40.83 first km, followed by a 2:43.66 second km. With two laps remaining there were six athletes in the mix and it was Elarbi Khattabi pushing the tempo. All kept in it until with 450 metres to go, Brahim Boulami made a decisive move. He quickly burned off all but Kenyans, Barmasai and eighteen year old Raymond Yator. Slowly the two experienced athletes sneaked away from him, and then between them, they enjoyed a tremendous fight to the line. Brahim held the lead at the final hurdle, though in the final stretch, it was Bernard who had the greater strength, but only just.

For the first time Brahim had seriously threatened the best Kenyans. Bernard Barmasai's winning time of 8:02.76 barely edged him out with Boulami running 8:02.90. A very fast last lap of 59.64 was required to save Kenyan pride. Raymond Yator stayed relatively close to clock 8:03.74 in third place.

None of the big guns competed in the 1,500 metres but William Chirchir continued to impress as he won in a decent time of 3:31.02. The first lap was run in a blistering 53.60, with Chirchir pushing hard in third position behind the rabbits in 54.10. At that point he enjoyed almost ten metres advantage on his opponents, however his and the pacesetters tempo fell away, and upon reaching 1,200 metres in 2:49.54, he had Andres Manuel Diaz and Driss Maazouzi still within striking range. The two challengers closed right up on William entering the home straight but again he was able to pull clear for the victory. Diaz clocked 3:31.48 with Maazouzi running 3:32.06. There were highly disappointing performances for Silva, eleventh in 3:35.18, and much worse still for Estevez. Reyes' time of 3:40.64 made him a distant fourteenth and last place finisher.

Noah Ngeny continued on his search for extra speed when he placed sixth in the 800 metres with a 1:44.80. Ali Saidi-Sief, still unsure whether to compete in the 1,500 or 5,000 metres in Sydney, carried on his winning ways in the 3,000 metres, though not only did he win, but his time of 7:25.02 was a personal best, an Algerian record and the third fastest ever

MOROCCAN SUCCESS; THE KADA WAY

run! For such a great overall time, the finale was amazing with the penultimate lap clocked at 59.47 and the final one in 55.52 after Ali kicked hard just prior to the bell. Mohammed Mourhit produced a great trial run for Sydney with second place and a super fast 7:26.62. Next was Daniel Komen who showed some form by clocking 7:28.92. Unfortunately this was too little too late for the Kenyan as he had already missed Olympic selection again after falling ill during the selection trials.

These were held in late July in Nairobi and the 5,000 metres event was an intriguing affair. Going into the latter stages were Komen, Sammy Kipketer, Julius Gitahi, Richard Limo and Paul Tergat, all in contention for the three prized Olympic positions. It was surprising to see Tergat, predominantly a 10,000 metres runner, competing instead at the shorter distance. The crowd of 25,000 was even more surprised when Komen pulled out with a mile to run. Daniel later explained, "I could not breathe properly, so I decided the best thing to do was to retire. I know I have disappointed my fans but there's nothing I can do."

Tergat would be out kicked by both Gitahi, 13:24.40 and Limo, 13:25.00, but managed to hold off Kipketer to claim the final spot.

Back to Europe. From El Guerrouj's point of view, it would have been interesting to see Bernard Lagat place a strong fifth behind Saidi-Sief with a 7:33.51. In the process he'd defeated many of the distances top specialists. One of these was Benjamin Limo whose form had disappeared since last season. In Monaco the Seville silver medallist could only finish eleventh in a sluggish 7:40.16.

After being so scintillating at Zurich, the Brussels mile was a let down for Hicham El Guerrouj and Kada on August 25. With no Noah Ngeny in the field, the Moroccan was expected to win easily but this certainly did not eventuate with El Guerrouj unable to clear away from Chirchir, but still capable enough to hold on to win in 3:47.91 to the Kenyan's 3:48.23. It was another excellent result for William who was becoming a major player for next month's Games. Other Kenyans Benjamin Kipkurui and Bernard Lagat also ran fast times of 3:49.34 and 3:49.84. Back in the pack there were some surprises with Rotich finishing twelfth, Estevez fifteenth and Silva sixteenth. With the Olympic events still over four weeks away, it was highly likely that many athletes were in heavy training, so it was possible for some minor improvements in performance. But to improve from where these runners were currently placing, to become a medal contender was going to take more than just a minor improvement.

Hicham commenced this race with the intention of breaking his own world record, so it was no surprise that he had three Kenyans on hand to pace him for as long as possible. The rabbits did their bit, but being not in quite the shape that he thought, El Guerrouj was left lagging behind. The first lap was a scintillating 53.79 and the leader passed through the second lap in a perfect 1:49.47, but with the Moroccan falling ten metres behind, it became clear that he didn't have the strength for a record tonight. However he did have a seven metre advantage over Lagat and Chirchir at this juncture.

On the third lap the pacesetters opened up to around a twenty metres lead. They were doing their job well but an athlete needed to be in unbelievable world record shape to go with them. The other Kenyans remained a little adrift of the Moroccan until Chirchir suddenly closed at the bell and with 300 metres to go, it was evident that El Guerrouj had a big fight on his hands. Lagat was well beaten but Chirchir managed to stick like glue all the way to the line, though he never seriously threatened to pass. Despite the close finish, Hicham didn't look too tired afterwards.

After many of his opponents congratulated him, Salah Hissou who was about to get ready for his 5,000 metres race, came over to him. They carried out the traditional Moroccan half kisses and Salah patted him on the back in a nice embrace.

It was crunch time for Salah as he lined up for the start. Finally, three years after his most soul destroying race, Hissou had returned to the Van Damn Memorial in Brussels.

MOROCCAN SUCCESS; THE KADA WAY

This was an opportunity to extinguish some demons as well as break thirteen minutes.

Brussels by tradition usually held a highly competitive 10,000 metres but because the meeting this year was being held before the Games, most of the best long distance runners chose not to run it in this instance. It was not the perfect preparation for 10,000 metres athletes to race the distance so close to the major championship. The runners preferred to prepare with shorter 5,000 and 3,000 metres races.

Mourhit and Lahlafi were in this 5,000 metres field of twenty five athletes, as was Daniel Komen who was admirably attempting to shrug off the disappointment of missing selection for the Sydney Games. In some ways Hissou was fortunate to run for Morocco rather than Kenya as it was much easier to qualify for the major championship teams.

Both these champions had enjoyed much better days than what they had endured this season. They were rivals, yet very friendly ones. Before the gun Daniel walked over to Salah, shook his hand and offered a few words of encouragement. The Moroccan patted the Kenyan on the back in return. For Hissou, this was common courtesy from the best distance runners, particularly the Kenyans. For a nation that was so competitive, its athletes were remarkably pleasant. The Barcelona 10,000 metres final had long been forgotten.

The speed is on from the start in this most critical of lead up races with James Kosgei, Martin Keino and Elarbi Khattabi, the designated rabbits. The first km is 2:30.79 with the competing athletes not too far behind. This is a little too fast, but the next lap slows to 63.50, giving the runners some respite. Komen, Mourhit and Kipkosgei are the men keeping closest watch on the rabbits. Salah is about tenth in the early stages.

There is a moment of humour as the British broadcaster comments on Kosgei sprinting away from the pack on the back straight at the end of his 2 kms stint, "They tend to do that, don't they? They're told to go to 2,000 metres in 5:05

and he's determined to get his bonus by hitting that spot on. And he's done it!" 5:05.67, how's that?! He and Ovett have a chuckle.

Khattabi has dropped back so obviously will be of no help with the pacemaking later. It is Keino leading Komen, Lahlafi, Mourhit and Kipkosgei. That lap is 62.93. The big pack is beginning to split and now Salah makes a concerted effort on the bend to round a couple of strugglers and tack onto the back of Kipkosgei in sixth position. Another solid 62.48 lap is recorded and Hissou looks in good shape.

Soon Kipkosgei is losing touch so another determined effort from Salah is required as Ovett comments, "43 we're just seeing for the first time, Salah Hissou. The wiley tactician. Twenty eight years of age. He's the reigning world 5,000 metres champion, picking himself up in fifth."

Keino disappears at 3,000 metres, clocked at 7:43.38. The third km is 2:37.71. The first four of Komen, Lahlafi, Mourhit and Hissou are separating themselves from the rest. On the back straight Salah is clipping the heels of Mohammed, seemingly feeling great although things can change quickly when you are on your limits.

The grace with which Hissou runs, makes it most difficult to tell how he is feeling during a race. The free, bouncy stride looks to be achieved with ease, whether he is running a sixty five or a sixty second lap. His facial expression never gives anything away either but you can be sure he is trying and hurting just as much as anyone else.

Suddenly Lahlafi kicks hard past Komen and the Kenyan quickly finds himself in trouble. Mourhit follows well in his friend's footsteps but Salah now requires another big effort to go with this. Hissou passes Komen and is almost back onto his fellow Maghrebs as they reach four laps to go after a 62.86 lap. But with 1,500 metres left, Salah goes into his oxygen debt. He quickly loses many metres as Komen retakes him. It is all over. Salah Hissou's season has gone up in smoke.

MOROCCAN SUCCESS; THE KADA WAY

This was just as bad as the '97 race, only this time it was more expected, considering his ankle woes. In some ways it may have hurt more, for this were Lahlafi and Mourhit running away from Salah, rather than Tergat and Koech. The Moroccan record holder could have regarded himself as a superior runner to Brahim and Mohammed, because he almost always had been. Now other factors had come into play.

That punishing lap is a 61.32 and now Lahlafi hands the lead to Mourhit. In that lap Salah loses a good twenty metres and is now falling behind Komen also. The fourth km is an excellent 2:34.90 giving a 10:18.28 split at 4,000 metres. Mourhit looks to be slowing with 900 metres left so Lahlafi kicks past again, yet that lap was still a 61.57. Not exactly slow! Both of their personal bests are 12:56. The pace is held with a very fast 61.62 penultimate lap as Lahlafi again moves out to allow Mourhit to lead at the bell. The Belgium spectators are roaring as they realise that their man is going to break the European record. Brahim surges ahead again, entering the final bend and hangs on to win.

In the end it was Lahlafi's strength that prevailed. His finishing time was 12:49.28. At the age of thirty two, he had become the new Moroccan record holder!

Mourhit too went inside 12:50 with a 12:49.71, also bettering Hissou's old mark. This performance confirmed him as one of the best distance runners in the world. In the last twelve months he had done it all. A 26:52 at 10,000 metres, victory in the World Cross Country and now a supersonic 5,000 metres time. The only sore point I found was that some people made a big deal about him holding the 3,000, 5,000 and 10,000 metres European records simultaneously and matching Paavo Nurmi's achievement. To compare Mourhit to Nurmi was committing a little track blasphemy in itself but come on, the guy is not *really* European!

Komen came in third, running 13:01.78, a little ahead of Kipkosgei's 13:03.60. Next was a Spaniard named Jose Rios who ran 13:08.28. Sixth was a dejected Moroccan, limping home in 13:09.37. It would take a miracle for Salah to do any more than make up the numbers in Australia.

The long season was throwing up some strange results with June and July's hot man, Sammy Kipketer, struggling into ninth position with a 13:15.11. Near the tail of the group there were other runners with good credentials performing way outside their optimum capabilities. It was a great surprise to see the twentieth, twenty first and twenty second placed names be Philip Mosima, Mohammed Amyn and Charles Kamathi, with the fastest time of Mosima's being 13:39.76. Perhaps Hissou's run wasn't so bad after all.

Earlier in the day the 10,000 metres had a familiar winner with Paul Tergat victorious in 27:03.87. The race was a bit of a struggle for the Kenyan as he fell off a very fast early pace of 13:18.98 at 5,000 metres. But as Paul said, "It was too hot for really fast times but this was a good run for me in preparation for the Olympics."

His other quote was more interesting, "I still have high hopes of going to Sydney for this event. I love the 10,000. But if I can't go then for sure this was my last 10,000," he said.

It was common knowledge that Tergat was abandoning the track for the road from next year onwards. But it would be a great shame if Brussels was to be his swan song at his favourite distance. Anybody with common sense would have Tergat competing in the 10,000 metres in Sydney. After all, he'd been Kenya's number one for the previous five seasons and nobody in the world had run as fast as 27:03 in 2000. The problem was that at the Kenyan selection trials, Paul only raced and qualified in the 5,000 metres. He quite rightly pointed out that to race the twenty five laps in the oppressive conditions might have an adverse effect and ruin his season. For now the Kenyan committee was holding firm and Tergat was seemingly compelled to race the 5,000 metres at the Olympic Games and not face his great rival Haile Gebrselassie one more time. Hopefully some old fashioned common sense would eventually prevail.

MOROCCAN SUCCESS; THE KADA WAY

The final Golden League meeting was in Berlin the following week on September 1. Again El Guerrouj was drawn into a closer battle with Chirchir than he would have liked. William wasn't threatening to become the conqueror, but Hicham almost looked tired as he slipped away from the initial fast pace to finish with 3:30.90. His new rival was the only athlete within three seconds of the world champion. Chirchir clocked 3:31.72.

Hicham's split at 800 metres of 1:52.84 was not too dissimilar to the pace of his famous Seville race. Alas, his finishing power wasn't the same right now. Not to worry. He remained unbeaten this season and had four weeks to freshen up for Sydney and what was being built up as the most important race of his life.

Salah Hissou could have walked away from his 2000 season after his Brussels race but he didn't give up that easily. Such desired dreams are not easy to walk away from. He also competed in Berlin to give his ankle and patchy form another test.

For the first time this year, Salah raced over 3,000 metres event and in attendance was the best performed distance runner of 2000, Ali Saidi-Sief. Just four days earlier the Algerian had produced another first class performance, this time in a 1,500 metres at Gateshead. In wet conditions he won by over five seconds in a good time of 3:30.82. This probably only further confused Ali as to which event he was best suited for at the Games. Regardless, it was hard to see him being defeated in Berlin. The pace was a good solid one the whole way, with laps generally around the sixty one's. Salah actually looked good. He was staying up near the front and doing his best to mix it with some high class opposition. With one lap to go he was right in contention.

The first km had been very fast with Keino again setting the tempo. Saidi-Sief sat behind him, with Mourhit, Lahlafi, Komen and Hissou next in line. The first split was 2:28.64 for the rabbit as Salah passed in 2:30.54. Mourhit suddenly lost his rhythm approaching four laps to go and soon found himself at the back of the field, so he stepped to the infield. It was obvious that he had reaggravated an injury or created a new one. Not a good sign with Sydney soon upon us.

The pace dipped and Hissou slowly made progress, moving to third behind Saidi-Sief and Lahlafi after 2,000 metres, which was reached in 5:04.89. Despite being a strength runner it can be good for Salah to have a lull in the tempo, as then he has an opportunity to kick down from that. Provided he has the necessary strength.

The pace had now dropped enough for Daniel Komen to make a move 900 metres out and lead with two to go after a 62.94 lap. But his burst was short and on the back straight Ali and Salah moved past him. This was the best that Hissou had appeared all season, as he seemed very relaxed. Yet can he kick?

No! The penultimate lap was timed at 60:73 and already Salah was losing big ground once the Algerian increased the pace 500 metres out. The final lap was amazing. Only Lahlafi could get near Saidi-Sief. With 300 metres left Ovett observes, "Well look at this. Saidi-Sief has stepped it up again and in doing so he's dropped Hissou like a stone." This was very true. Salah sunk faster than the Titanic! He lost twenty metres in no time at all.

The last lap was a little quick at 53.87! Even at his very best this was something that Salah could never contend with. In his reduced form it looked very embarrassing. But the others were in the same boat except for Lahlafi, who continued his career best form. The rest were blown away by Ali's explosive sprint. It was phenomenal. The top eight finishers from Berlin were as follows:

Ali Saidi-Sief	7:30.76
Brahim Lahlafi	7:31.98
Daniel Komen	7:35.80
Luke Kipkosgei	7:36.76
Salah Hissou	7:37.16
Ismail Sghyr	7:37.99

MOROCCAN SUCCESS; THE KADA WAY

Benjamin Limo   7:38.90
Mark Carroll   7:41.03

Even though he had completed five races this season, Salah continued to experience pain in his ankle when he returned back to Morocco. Despite his condition, the Moroccan Federation still wanted him to compete at the Olympic Games. He would contest the 10,000 metres where doubt surrounded the participation of Haile Gebrselassie, although his opposition didn't know about this and were expecting him to be there. Hissou travelled to Australia with the Moroccan squad. However soon after arrival, he experienced further ankle pain. There was no way that he could race competitively. Hence the toughest of decisions was made. Salah Hissou decided to withdraw from the 2000 Sydney Olympic Games.

Greg Rowlerson

Testing Times For So Many Reasons

Atlanta now seemed so long ago. Back then it seemed like just the beginning for Salah Hissou. But the career of an international sportsperson can be fleeting, particularly for one competing in such a physically demanding sport as long distance running.

The Moroccan world champion was unable to challenge in Sydney. If he was better than an Olympic bronze medallist, he could not prove it. Haile Gebrselassie's major opposition in the 10,000 metres wasn't substantial at the best of times. Now it was reduced further. Yet the more pressing issue was whether or not the Ethiopian himself, would be on the start line to compete.

Gebrselassie's achilles problem had worsened severely following his victory in Zurich. He was hardly able to train, with speed sessions on all weather tracks certainly out of the question. He scarcely looked like a world beater but his predicament remained a secret to most. Paul Tergat was kept in the dark.

While the Kenyan trained as intensely as ever before, Haile rested, hoping for a miracle. He drew strength from his Atlanta heroics, when he overcame significant foot pain to win gold. Yet some setbacks are too much for even the most mentally strong sports champion to triumph over. The world record holder missed a full month of training. Gebrselassie decided to be realistic about his situation, much in the same way that Salah Hissou had been. He approached the Commissioner of Sport in Ethiopia and revealed that he would not be competing in Sydney. Not defending his Olympic title. The door was now wide open for Paul Tergat.

But not so fast. Haile Gebrselassie wasn't only a doer. He was also a listener. The Commissioner convinced him to keep an open mind about his Olympic participation by telling him that he truly believed that if he came to Sydney and decided to run, that he would win the gold medal. Haile would think

MOROCCAN SUCCESS; THE KADA WAY

about it some more. The 'emperor' from Ethiopia wasn't giving up yet.

Haile's coach, Dr. Wolde-Meskel Kostre, had expressed disappointment upon hearing of Salah's absence from the Games. "We are very sorry Salah will not be here. He is a good competitor and it is right to have the best competitors at the Olympic Games," Kostre stated.

This disappointment was probably genuine. The Salah Hissou of 2000 would have been a welcome addition to the 10,000 metres starting list for Gebrselassie. A big name and a certain scalp. He and Kostre might not have felt the same if the Moroccan's recent form had not been restricted by his ankle soreness. A fully fit Hissou might well have been a scary prospect in Sydney.

Abdelkader Kada now needed to focus all his attention on the athletes that he could help in Australia. He still had a strong medal prospect in the steeplechase plus everyone's overwhelming choice for the 1,500 metres gold medal. The schedule showed that both Ezzine and El Guerrouj were set to race for gold on the same day of September 29.

The final European Grand Prix meeting was in Rieti, Italy, on September 3, and it was here that Noah Ngeny fine tuned his Olympic preparations. He ran a fast time of 3:30.42, although it wasn't a particularly impressive performance as he was unable to defeat Benjamin Kipkurui, 3:30.73, too convincingly. In the 5,000 metres Daniel Komen turned back the clock as he put on a vintage display to destroy a second rate field. The former world champion recorded 13:04.43, finishing over fourteen seconds ahead of Spaniard Enrique Molina. After him came Ethiopians Kenenisa Bekele and Alene Emere, then another former world champion Ismael Kirui whose 13:26.23 wasn't in the ball park of the sort of time that the twenty five year old should have been capable of running at his peak.

There was quite a large break between this meeting and the commencement of track and field at the Games. The athletes would have a longer wait between racing than usual. Let's take a look at Hicham El Guerrouj as an example.

In the World Championships at Gothenburg, Hicham's heat took place twenty days after his final lead up race in Oslo. In the Olympics at Atlanta, his heat occurred nineteen days after competing in Nice, which was again his final race before the Athens World Championships. This time the gap between competition was eighteen days.

Seville contained different circumstances with El Guerrouj racing at Zurich just ten days before his first qualifier. This year was poles apart with a two week differential. With the heats of the men's 1,500 metres not until September 25, it meant a racing gap of twenty four days for the Moroccan miler. Okay, so the other athletes were in the same boat, but there was no questioning the fact that it was going to be harder to stay in top racing shape this time around. It also gave a runner more time to potentially over train.

Hicham was extremely worried about his Olympic dream not eventuating. He was meticulous about getting himself into the best possible form to make sure that nothing could go wrong. He travelled to Brisbane straight after the Berlin 1,500 metres. In the weeks prior to the Games his training was more intense than Abdelkader had ever seen. In particular, his track sessions such as multiple 1,000 metres repetitions. Also 400 metres repeats were being run in 49-50 seconds. With speed being more and more the sole focus, sessions of 300 metres intervals were also run. His coach was concerned and he advised his athlete to back off a little. But it can be hard to back off when you want something as badly as El Guerrouj wanted this Olympic gold. Sometimes it is possible to try too hard. Abdelkader had mentioned previously that, "He needs a coach to tell him he is doing too much, not too little." Just prior to Sydney, El Guerrouj commented on his training in 2000, "This is a special year for me. It's an Olympic year. I concentrated a hundred percent or a million percent on this objective of the Olympic Games. I worked the first six months for the rhythm mainly. Body building. The last few months I worked on speed, focusing on the 300 metres later on."

MOROCCAN SUCCESS; THE KADA WAY

After falling in Atlanta he was devastated but refused to try and forget the race. Hicham had kept a photo of that pivotal moment on a wall in his home. He had taken this picture with him to Sydney for extra motivation.

Qualifying for the semis of the 1,500 metres was going to be easy with the first six from each of the three heats progressing. There was also the 'get out of jail' clause of being one of six fastest losers. El Guerrouj raced in heat 1 on the Monday morning at 10:40 am. His main opponent was expected to be William Chirchir, but the Kenyan ran a poor tactical race and was knocked around by the big bunch. He was impeded so much late in the race that he was only able to place eighth in a slow time of 3:40.22, thus being at risk of elimination. Hicham had no such problems, sensibly running wide for the first two laps as Chirchir led in 2:01.16. The Moroccan then took up the pace and ended up winning in 3:38.57, just ahead of Spaniard Jose Antonio Redolat who ran 3:38.66.

Chirchir did fail to qualify, missing out by 0.47 seconds, but was quickly reinstated by the organizers. Unfortunately for William, a protest was lodged by the Spaniards and it was a successful one. Good news for Abdelkader as now he only had to concern himself with two Kenyans. The other athlete who could have been a major threat, Ali Saidi-Sief, had chosen the safer option of competing in the 5,000 metres.

The second heat was of most relevance to El Guerrouj because his favourite rabbit, Adil Kaouch, only finished seventh and when the third heat turned out to be faster, he was eliminated. A reenactment of Seville was out of the question. Adil missed out on a safe sixth place by one tenth of a second.

Bernard Lagat made it through without any trouble placing second in 3:40.42 behind Mehdi Baala's 3:40.35. Noah Ngeny won heat 3 in 3:38.03 with Noureddine Morceli a surprise second in 3:38.41. The Algerian had not been expected to race having not done so since he retired from the Seville final, but he was here defending his Olympic title. El Guerrouj's other teammate Youssef Baba qualified in fourth position, so Hicham may still have a rabbit for the final. Finishing a horrible thirteenth was the talented Portuguese Rui Silva.

On this night we saw a spectacular finale to the men's 10,000 metres final. Paul Tergat had been granted his wish by the Kenyan Olympic officials who swapped his spot in the 5,000 metres with Patrick Ivuti. Haile Gebrselassie also lined up for his heat despite the constant pain in his right achilles tendon, showing some form to win his qualifier.

Morocco only had the one entrant, but Said Berioui qualified easily for the final and then put up a good fight, keeping up with the leading pack until the final few laps and eventually placing sixth in 27:37.83. His performance was better than that of another Maghreb, as Mohammed Mourhit became the major disappointment of the race. Starting as the third favourite, the Belgium runner looked composed and dangerous throughout but suddenly fell off the back late in the race and withdrew. As a result it became a battle of Kenya vs. Ethiopia and primarily Tergat vs. Gebrselassie. There was no move of great significance until very late, when with less than 300 metres to go and five athletes still in contention, Tergat took off with a tremendous turn of speed. With Gebrselassie and Mezgebu in his slipstream, the Kenyan led them around the final bend and for a while it appeared that he was going to win. But Haile moved out to lane 2 and as the pair ran clear of Assefa, the world record holder gradually inched his way closer to the former world cross country champion. They both dipped and by a slender nine hundredths of a second, the 'emperor' had retained his Olympic title.

The winning time was 27:18.20 with the last lap and final 200 metres being timed in 55.56 and approximately twenty six seconds respectively. Even with the ravages of injury (Haile) and age (Paul) they had kept their finishing kicks. A fit Salah Hissou would have had no answer to this burst of speed, but it was the rest of the race that informed us that the two legends were no longer in career peak condition.

The final km was a solid, although hardly spectacular 2:34.11

MOROCCAN SUCCESS; THE KADA WAY

with the penultimate lap timed at 65.37. The overall time was slower than Atlanta and despite the cooler conditions the final 5,000 metres was run in 13:32 as opposed to the awesome 13:12 of 1996. Off the decent though not devastating 13:45.88 pace of the first half, I believe that Salah in 1999 form could have kicked down to around a 13:25 back half. Whether that would have been enough to dislodge the medallists we will never know, but I suspect that Hissou and Kada saw this race as a missed opportunity.

Yet this race was about the gold and silver medallists, and what great runners they were! It was the end of a tremendous era with the two certain to never compete against each other again on the track. Many called it a great rivalry, though whether rivalry is the correct word is debatable, since on the track Tergat never once conquered Mt. Gebrselassie. However he had pushed him to great championship performances and the current 10,000 metres world record. Of that there was no doubt.

"The race was really tough. My friend Paul Tergat really surprised me when he kicked earlier than I expected. I have never run a ten thousand like this. You normally only get a sprint like that in the 1,500 metres!" said Haile after the memorable finish.

Tergat, satisfied that he had given it is all said, "I'm happy with this silver medal because I won it after a beautiful race, that was extremely difficult tactically."

The steeplechase heats were run under much more sensible conditions than in Seville, with the first four athletes from each of the three heats to qualify for the final with another three gaining entry as fastest losers. Ali Ezzine was drawn in heat 1, at 11:55 am on September 27. His main opposition was likely to be Kenyan Reuben Kosgei. Ali's form to the public was somewhat of a mystery, having not raced since early July, but Abdelkader was confident that he had his youngster in good shape for qualification and a high placing in the final. We were about to get some answers.

The early pace was very slow, but after Ali led them through 2,000 metres in 5:44.63 the tempo increased dramatically. By the final lap there were just five runners in the leading pack and Ezzine was able to finish strongly to place second behind Kosgei. The times of the first two were 8:23.17 and 8:23.79.

There were no major surprises from the other heats with all the Kenyans plus Brahim Boulami making it through. Thirty three year old Elarbi Khattabi did not have things so easily and ran an awful time of 8:43.46, a distant 17.76 seconds away from making the final. But even without him the Kenyans knew that they had to watch out for the remaining green and red singlets. The final looked like an open and exciting one.

The 1,500 semi finals were held that evening and El Guerrouj was entered in heat 2, commencing at 6:40 pm. In the first heat there was little to discuss, with Ngeny winning comfortably in a slow 3:39.29. Hicham's fellow Moroccan Youssef Baba, ran well to qualify for the final in fourth position. The sad story was of Noureddine Morceli, who in the final lap was bumped out of position by the desperate bunch that trailed the Kenyan. As he entered the home straight and realized that he could not qualify, he simply gave up, finishing his Olympic days as a jogger, trudging home in 4:00.78. The Algerian reflected, "Obviously I was spiked. I am depressed, as I did not come here just to run. I came expecting a medal. This was my last 1,500 metres ever. Next year I am going to go for the 5,000 metres and if that does not work out, then I will retire."

Hicham El Guerrouj had no problems in his race, despite competing in a tougher heat. By the 1,200 metres split, reached in 2:57.51, he was well in control of proceedings and from there he finished strongly to record a time of 3:37.60 with Bernard Lagat close behind with 3:37.84.

All the favourites had made it through and Abdelkader Kada could begin to draw up his strategy for the final.

The men's 3,000 metres steeplechase and 1,500 metres

MOROCCAN SUCCESS; THE KADA WAY

Olympic finals both took place on the night of Friday, September 29. The first Moroccan to attempt to join the illustrious list of Aouita, Boutayeb and Skah as a distance running gold medallist was Ali Ezzine. His race started at 7:25 pm.

The steeplechase favourites were easy to group. The race was expected to be mostly Kenyan dominated, but if they didn't perform up to expectations then it was the Moroccans who were expected to take the spoils. Next in line were the Spaniards with the two Martin's. The other potential medallist was German Damian Kallabis.

His chances were quickly cancelled out when he fell at the first barrier. Kallabis managed to get straight back up and catch up with the pack, but understandably this took too much out of him and he soon fell back to an eventual last place finish.

The speed was never really on, even with the Kenyans being prominent early, although it was Luis Miguel Martin of Spain who led a congested pack through 1,000 metres in 2:55.85, which is over 8:45 pace. It is no wonder then that the others were able to mix it with the East Africans so far. In the early going Ezzine was happy to sit in the middle of the field.

Soon the Kenyans take over, but without their usual level of domination previously displayed in the middle stages of these races. Bernard Barmasai is doing much of the pacemaking with Ezzine settling into sixth position as they start to spread out into single file. On lap four Ali makes his first move and on the back straight is up to third on the outside of the Kenyans. He draws alongside them. It appears to be a good time to put on a spurt and take the lead if he has it in him. Ali has managed to stay out of trouble but is covering extra ground by running wide.

Ezzine does not take the lead and is happy to lie second behind Reuben Kosgei at the 2,000 metres split, which is passed in only 5:43.91. Most of the runners remain in medal contention. With the pace so slow it's almost a certainty that the final km will be run in sub 2:40 and this turns out to be the case. Without possessing a strong kick an athlete has no chance for a top six finish. However going from past performances, Kada should have plenty of confidence in Ezzine's finishing abilities.

Brahim Boulami isn't appearing as comfortable as his teammate. He has kept to the back of the lead pack throughout, perhaps close to being dispensed. He is only placed seventh yet soon Ezzine is also up against it. By the second last water jump he is back to about fifth and badly boxed in. Ali is forced to again move out wide. He makes a concerted effort to recover to third at the bell, with still eight athletes surviving.

On the back straight the Moroccan loses his position and finds himself sixth behind three Kenyans and the two Spanish Martin's. Kosgei leads but remarkably is being challenged by one of the Spaniards approaching the final water jump.

As the leaders fly over the water jump, Ali loses some ground and eighty metres from home Barmasai and Boit Kipketer pass the fading Martin. At this moment, Ezzine is a few metres off the medals. Yet he clears the final steeple well and quickly storms past Martin himself. Kosgei and Kipketer are having a great battle for the win, having cleared out from Barmasai who is on the inside lane and starting to struggle. With only thirty metres to go, he has a couple of metres on the Moroccan. Can Ali become Abdelkader's second Olympic medallist? The final results were:

Reuben Kosgei	8:21.43
Wilson Boit Kipketer	8:21.77
Ali Ezzine	8:22.15
Bernard Barmasai	8:22.23
Luis Miguel Martin	8:22.75
Eliseo Martin	8:23.00
Brahim Boulami	8:24.32
Gunther Weidlinger	8:26.70
Jim Svenoy	8:27.20
Khamis Abdullah Saifeldin	8:30.89

MOROCCAN SUCCESS; THE KADA WAY

Laid Bessou	8:33.07
Simon Vroemen	8:37.87
Manuel Silva	8:38.63
Gael Pencreach	8:41.19
Damian Kallabis	9:09.78

Yes, yes, yes! Ali powered home on the finishing straight to pinch the bronze medal from Bernard and stop a Kenyan sweep! To have repeated his result from Seville in such a strong field was fantastic and Abdelkader Kada surely was happy with his performance. It was obviously the country's first Olympic medal in this event. Ali looked delighted with his result as he crossed the line. The Spaniards ran well and could not be discounted in the future. The poorest outcome was for Boulami. After so many great performances in Europe, he could not produce the goods in Australia. Perhaps he was better suited to a faster overall pace, with this big change of tempo late, advantageous for the younger legs in the field.

Kosgei's kick was every bit as impressive as Ezzine's and enabled him to take the gold. The final sprint was close to a disaster for Reuben, with him running into Wilson. Fortunately nobody fell and it was the youngster who came out of the exchange better, finishing the race full of running. The victory was quite convincing in the end. Kipketer said of the incident, "We were both so excited we did not realise how close we were."

The last lap was run in 61.38 and the last 1,000 metres were clocked at 2:37.52 which is very good. The sit and kick style that we saw in Seville had not suited Bernard Barmasai and with this style even more prevalent here, he was again out of form and luck. When the sprint was on he could not match his rivals and therefore missed a medal.

The most important race to Abdelkader was yet to come and he wished so badly for Hicham to win. He had been the best for nearly four years, since the 1996 Grand Prix final, perhaps for even longer and now it was time to reap the reward of years of dominance. The Olympics only come around every four years. Athens '04 seemed like another lifetime away. If the Games were held every year then El Guerrouj would not have felt the same extreme nervousness as he toed the line at 8:00 pm. Neither would have Kada.

As well as being nervous, the world champion had concerns with his left quadriceps during his time in Sydney. Now just before the final he felt cramp in his leg, but as Hicham would say later, "It is not an excuse." Only days before the final, El Guerrouj had broken down in tears. He knew that physically he was not in as good a shape as he should have been.

His coaching mastermind had planned for a similar race to Seville, with Youssef Baba replacing Adil Kaouch as the sacrificial lamb. Right on cue the support act sprints into the spotlight and as if all of this was being staged, El Guerrouj follows with Ngeny the man on his heels. The first split at 400 metres is almost suicidal at 54.14. The field is already being well strung out with Lagat the only other athlete looking comfortable, but on the next lap Baba is unable to keep up a good pace. This turns out to be crucial. By the 700 metres mark Hicham is running awkwardly close to him because the rabbit is no longer doing a sufficient job. The rest of the field has also closed up. El Guerrouj stays behind Baba for a little while longer as Youssef hits the 800 metres mark in 1:54.77. The second lap of 60.63 has given the field and vitally the Kenyans, a brief respite. Hicham now ventures into the lead and pours on the power.

With 600 metres to go he begins to sink the boots in and is able to gain a small gap over Ngeny. Lagat looks good in third with Baala the only other athlete threatening to keep with them. Everybody else has been beaten. El Guerrouj looks fantastic with 500 metres left, though at the bell he enjoys only a couple of metres advantage. He had kicked, but not with the same venom as in previous years and is still unable to break Ngeny, Lagat and Baala. Now at the commencement of the final lap, this is his moment to kick it down further. Alas he is unable to do so and at 1,200 metres, reached in 2:51.67, the Kenyans are looking relaxed and dangerous. This must have been extremely concerning for Kada. The

MOROCCAN SUCCESS; THE KADA WAY

third lap is only timed at 56.90. Compare this to Seville, which was 54.64 off a faster pace, or Athens, at 53.59 off a much slower pace. There is a great difference and now what he requires is a Morceli type of acceleration in the back straight.

With the slower third lap, the Moroccan needs to finish off with a sub 39.75 (or sub fifty three second lap pace) final 300 metres to be safe of holding off the Kenyans. Unfortunately as Hicham enters the final bend he doesn't seem to be moving at such a speed. There is no kick down left. It's a matter of holding his form as best as he can. His strength has always been his strength and this is when he most needs it. Into the final straight and still the pesky Kenyans don't yield. It is here that Noah Ngeny moves out wide, in a similar vein to Haile Gebrselassie, appearing very menacing indeed. We can see that he believes he can win. El Guerrouj still leads and can see the finish line and the gold medal possibility. But the red vest quickly creeps into his field of vision and with less than seventy metres remaining, has pulled alongside of him. 'Come on Hicham, dig deep!' The Moroccan searches deep inside for another effort but finds nothing. Soon the Kenyan moves past and the crowd gasps. With twenty metres left they know that the hot favourite is beaten. The results are:

Noah Ngeny	3:32.07
Hicham El Guerrouj	3:32.32
Bernard Lagat	3:32.44
Mehdi Baala	3:34.14
Kevin Sullivan	3:35.50
Daniel Zegeye	3:36.78
Andres Manuel Diaz	3:37.27
Juan Carlos Higuero	3:38.91
John Mayock	3:39.41
Jason Pyrah	3:39.84
Driss Maazouzi	3:45.46
Youssef Baba	3:56.08

Hicham immediately slumps to the track and sits down. He attempts to remove his shoes and is showing little emotion, probably in a state of shock. Slowly, the vast majority of athletes walk across to him and shake his hand. Ngeny and

Lagat also do this after first going to their supporters. This is fantastic sportsmanship. In the Olympic spirit!

It wasn't the greatest performance in the history of the event by the Kenyan and it wasn't one of the Moroccan's worst either. El Guerrouj was slightly off his game and Ngeny was in good enough shape to take advantage. The last lap was run in 54.57. Fast, yes, but super human? Far from it. If Hicham had run a sub fifty four which he often did from a fast tempo, he would have won. There was very little in it and at least on this occasion he was allowed a fair fight for the Olympic gold.

However nothing could console the mighty Moroccan in the race's aftermath. The media pointed more to the fact that he had lost, rather than that Ngeny had won. Also lost in the shock was that a silver medal should still be something to cherish. Throughout most of the last four years Hicham El Guerrouj was the world's best miler but on this day he was second best. There were far worse things that can happen in this world.

"Next year I'm changing my specialty," El Guerrouj stated. "I give my throne to Noah."

This comment was made straight after his defeat. Abdelkader was likely to give his runner plenty of time to get over this before deciding on his future plans.

The winner, who clocked a 26.7 second final 200 metres had the following to say about his supposed upset victory.

"I was following Hicham all the way, I stuck close to him until the end. I wasn't thinking about the Olympic record. I was too busy watching Hicham. I didn't beat him before even if I could maybe have won. But I had a plan in my mind. I am not surprised by my win at all. I am fit and I was really thinking about the gold."

Noah also added, "For a Kenyan to make the mile gold medal is very big. When I go back home it will be amazing."

MOROCCAN SUCCESS; THE KADA WAY

His teammate Lagat had come close to making it a Kenyan one-two. Although this had a bit to do with El Guerrouj switching off in the final metres when the gold was lost, it was still a big improvement from Bernard.

There were the obvious claims that Hicham had choked in the concluding stages when he had a gold medal within reach. These claims were harsh and not entirely fair. El Guerrouj hadn't exactly faded in the home straight or even tied up. He simply did not have his usual zip, which he later explained was due to over training. He put a large distance into Baala by the end. Does this mean that the Frenchman choked?

Years later Hicham reflected, "I had over-trained. I put too much pressure on myself because I wanted that gold medal too much. If I had trained 15 per cent less, I would have won. I was training like a crazy person. There was a lack of self confidence and a lack of maturity. An athlete does not only train with his body. He trains with his mind."

Hicham El Guerrouj performed to the best of his ability on the night of September 29, 2000. The choking was done during the "crazy" training sessions that preceded it.

The truth is that in the wrong race Hicham was fractionally off his best and Noah was there ready to pounce. If because of Sydney you decided to completely disregard this man as potentially the best miler ever, I ask you to broaden your narrow horizons. Go back and watch the Seville final. Really watch it. You don't have to rate Hicham El Guerrouj as the greatest miler ever but don't say that he isn't, simply because he lost a race in Australia.

You may have noticed a common theme throughout this book. I believe many people over emphasise the importance of the Olympic Games when rating an athlete. This is not to say that I don't rate the Olympics. It is the pinnacle of our sport. Just remember that a world champion represents exactly what an Olympic champion does. That on a particular day, you are the best in the world. Please do not rate athletes' careers solely on a race every four years.

Greg Rowlerson

The men's distance races in Sydney did not bode well for most of the fancied athletes. It was bad enough for Bernard Barmasai missing a medal in the steeplechase after having been the best in the world for most of the last three years. Then there was Hicham El Guerrouj having to settle for silver in the 1,500 metres after a few years of supremacy. But the unluckiest or most unfortunate runner was Kenyan born Wilson Kipketer. The Danish citizen was unrivalled as the world's best at 800 metres since 1995, but contracting malaria during 1998 had diminished his ability slightly. By 1999 he was being challenged strongly, yet he still managed to retain his world title after out dipping Hezekiel Sepeng of South Africa on the line. In 2000 he endured a leg injury setback but still came to the Games in reasonable form and as event favourite. In the final, he ran what could be described as a slightly misjudged race. Tactically he left his run too late, evoking memories of Sebastian Coe in Moscow twenty years earlier. Running wide and out of position, he attempted a Billy Konchellah like finish which left him with the silver medal, behind Germany's European champion Nils Schumann who enjoyed the benefits of a much more efficient journey to the line in clocking 1:45.08.

The 'unlucky' part of Wilson's race was that he only lost by six hundredths of a second and his sit back tactic wasn't helped by the very slow pace of the first lap. It was only 53.43, with a sub fifty one usually being the norm for a top class 800 metres. If it had been fast, Kipketer could have run over the top of his opponents much easier. As it was, the speed was faster on the second lap so not only did Kipketer have to cover extra distance to pass runners, but do so while they were increasing their pace.

Incidentally, a remarkable coincidence is that the two greatest male 800 metres runners in history (Coe and Kipketer) both failed to win Olympic gold at that distance. The Games outcomes for the two lap event have often amounted to surprise results. In fact in more recent times, the dominance of African runners in terms of world rankings (times) has not always been converted into victory at the Olympic Games with unfancied European athletes taking the spoils in Atlanta

MOROCCAN SUCCESS; THE KADA WAY

(Kipketer was not allowed to participate following his switch of nationalities) and Sydney. If there ever was a sure thing for an Olympic gold medal, then Wilson Kipketer was it in '96. Too often politics has reared its ugly head in the face of sports *greatest* international show (my apologies if I've offended soccer World Cup aficionados and Victorians thinking of that last Saturday in September!).

A similar story concerning upsets has occurred in the marathon, where non African athletes have still been able to emerge victorious in many of the Major Championships. The oppressive conditions have obviously played their part.

The curse for the favourites in Sydney continued in the 5,000 metres, with Ali Saidi-Sief losing out in a sit and kick race to the much lesser credentialed former world junior champion, Million Wolde. The Ethiopian's performances in 2000 were not within a bull's roar of the standards of the Algerian but Saidi-Sief had won all his big Grand Prix races in fast paced races. This Olympic final was nothing of the sort, with the majority of it being run at close to fourteen minute pace! This was truly abysmal considering the capability of the runners in the field. The athletes who have themselves to blame are Saidi-Sief and the Moroccan Brahim Lahlafi who both had the best form coming into the event. A strong contender must go into a championship race with a back up plan, which these two obviously did not. Their finishing kicks which had looked deadly in sub thirteen minute races had been effective to a certain degree because the vast majority of their opponents were already well beaten by those final laps. Once the pack had gone through 3,000 metres in 8:21.79, about half a minute slower than expected, the Algerian or Moroccan should have kicked it down then, rather than wait for the last 600 or 400 metres. At that early pace it should have been quite easy to throw in a sixty second lap and perhaps run the fourth km in around 2:35, just to take something out of the finish of the kickers. The fourth km however was run in 2:48.05, so the race came down to a contest of who had the most basic speed. In the end that man was Wolde, an athlete who had not shown the Saidi-Sief type capacity to run 2:35 km pace on a consistent basis. His winning time was 13:35.49

and he finished with nearly a full second to spare over Saidi-Sief and Lahlafi after a fast final km of 2:25.65.

In fairness to the minor medallists, the circumstances that they faced here were not the greatest. The Kenyans (who often push the pace) in this field were the weakest that the country had provided for a major championship 5,000 metres in decades. The Ethiopians all wanted a slow race. Ali only had one teammate (Reda Benzine) who was not good enough to help him and surprisingly, Brahim was the only Moroccan in the final. If the current world champion had been competing, the final would have been totally different. Even in his reduced capacity of this season, Salah Hissou would not have allowed the race to drag out like this and the middle laps would have been considerably faster. On what we have seen in 2000 it was impossible for him to win the gold but his involvement would have surely seen the victory go to one of his fellow Maghrebs.

The Sydney Olympics were abnormal as far as the winners went in many of the races. The performances also paled in comparison to Atlanta. Many proclaimed the Games as 'the best', but what does the best mean? This is a sporting competition. Should it therefore be rated on the quality of performances of its sports men and women? Track and field is the jewel in the Olympic crown. On this basis alone, Sydney lost out to Atlanta.

Of course this is not solely how 'experts' rate an Olympics. The best also refers to how well it is organized. How well the competitors and spectators are treated. Effectively, did things run smoothly? Along these lines it is unanimously agreed that Atlanta lost out to Sydney.

But this book is not about politics. It is predominately about what goes on in the middle. On the track.

Something that was of major significance *off* the track concerning distance running was the introduction of testing for the illegal performance enhancing substance Erythropoietin, otherwise known as EPO. This is produced naturally in the

MOROCCAN SUCCESS; THE KADA WAY

body by the kidney and is a hormone that regulates the production of red blood cells in the bone marrow. Increasing the number of red blood cells in the human body has the impact of increasing endurance levels, as the body has a greater oxygen carrying capacity. Red blood cells carry oxygen from the lungs to the muscles, thus improving an athlete's aerobic capacity and endurance. When an artificial form of the hormone called Epogen was created with the help of doctors John Adamson and Joseph W. Eschbach, distance runners suddenly had a potentially very helpful aid.

Despite it being approved in 1989, the general sporting public had little knowledge of its existence for many years. The drug of course had not been created with the intention of improving performances in endurance sports. Rather it was designed to treat anaemia.

Epogen's use in sport first came to widespread attention during the 1998 Tour De France. Cyclists had long been suspected of practising with illegal substances and it was during the three week classic that one of the high profile teams Festina, was caught in a drugs storm. The team car revealed large quantities of Epogen, which threw the whole event into total chaos.

The IAAF had been a little slow in catching up with the situation. Only now at the Sydney Games was an EPO test in place. Many of the excellent performances of the 1990's were viewed with some scepticism. Making a decision as to whether an athlete had tested positive to Epogen wasn't as clear cut as with other banned substances such as steroids. This was due to EPO being produced naturally in the body, so determining if artificial Epogen had been introduced was rather difficult. Therefore the IAAF decided the format would be based on a human's hematocrit levels.

Hematocrit is the percentage of blood cells that are red. For a male, the normal figure is between 41-50%. Any test that shows a percentage of greater than 50% is viewed with suspicion. Pharmaceutical EPO can have a positive affect on increasing an athlete's hematocrit levels for up to six weeks, but it is only thought to remain detectable for around one week. This posed a major problem for those fighting illegal drug use in the sport. EPO is easily injected through the skin. The athlete's blood is tested and if this appears abnormal then a urine sample is taken also. It is here that the decision is made as to a positive or negative test.

Altitude training has become increasingly popular during the last decade and time spent at high altitude naturally increases the red blood cell count. Some say that a positive test can therefore never be totally conclusive. However the IAAF determined that there was a point (or a red blood cell count percentage) at which no amount of training or living at a high elevation could naturally get you to. Despite this, some are still not convinced as to the reliability of EPO testing, even with testers continually improving procedures, making false positives highly unlikely.

The 2000 Olympic Games did not produce any EPO positive tests to significant track and field athletes. The subject of performance enhancing drugs in long distance running will be raised in greater detail in a later chapter.

The results from the men's distance races in Australia were a massive let down for North Africa, most specifically Morocco. El Guerrouj, Mourhit and Lahlafi had all under performed. With Hissou out of the picture, Morocco had gone from potentially being the major player in the men's distance races to a clear third in the pecking order. All the good work had not exactly been wasted, but the full rewards had not been reaped. The big winner was Ethiopia. Its success was phenomenal. From the 5,000 metres up, it was the 'major player' as it also won the marathon with Gezaghne Abera.

The fallout or lasting effect of a disappointing performance in Sydney was to some extent longer than in previous Games. This was due to the sudden ending of the athletics season, which didn't allow an athlete to right a wrong or at least prove a point. After Barcelona, Noureddine Morceli showed that his seventh placing was far from an accurate reflection on his abilities by breaking the world record for 1,500 metres at Rieti.

MOROCCAN SUCCESS; THE KADA WAY

Moses Kiptanui, who missed those Games altogether because of injury, followed up by breaking the steeplechase world record at Zurich.

In the Atlanta aftermath there was the absentee Daniel Komen putting together a set of consecutive performances at 3,000 and 5,000 metres, the likes of which nobody had ever seen, or witnessed since. Hicham El Guerrouj was able to partly make up for his fall when he defeated Noureddine Morceli for the first time in the Grand Prix final at Milan. To a lesser extent, Salah Hissou made up for *only* claiming a bronze medal when he broke the world record on the way to defeating Paul Tergat in the Brussels 10,000 metres.

Following Sydney there was only the Grand Prix final, held in far away Qatar. The meeting assumed little relevance with Ngeny winning the 1,500 metres in 3:36.62 and Luke Kipkosgei being a surprise winner in the 3,000 metres with a time of 7:46.21. To venture all this way to run one slow race was not worth it for El Guerrouj.

After Sydney, Salah could not race anyway but Hicham could and it was going to be tough having to wait eight months for the 2001 European outdoor season. So he didn't wait that long. With too much to prove, El Guerrouj went back to racing during the 2001 indoor season.

But it was most difficult for the champion to come back to running. Aziz Daouda had predicted as such. This is what he said about the importance of Hicham winning gold in Sydney, prior to his second place finish, "He needs this medal. He is the world record-holder. He can't miss this. If he does, it will be a big problem. Psychologically, it will be the end of his career."

In the initial aftermath of his Olympic defeat El Guerrouj was so distraught that he wanted to quit the sport. His spirits weren't helped either by the harsh Moroccan press. Hicham remembers, "I will never forget what they said after Sydney."

El Guerrouj had even had his character dragged through the

mud. Despite losing in Sydney, Hicham was offered 750 acres of orchards by the King in his local area of Berkane. After accepting the gift he was ostracised by his community. This hurt him deeply, for El Guerrouj didn't live too extravagant an existence. While he owned two homes in Rabat, he lived mainly at the national training centre where he had just a single bedroom to himself. Hicham drives a small Honda sports car, not a Ferrari, BMW or Mercedes. El Guerrouj comments on his lifestyle, "In my mind, if I don't do the same things as before, if I don't stay in my environment, I won't be as good. I want to be close to the people, to live a simple life. In my country, there are many poor people. You can't be bigger than the others."

Also, in some part to being a devout Muslim, El Guerrouj had always given generously to those less fortunate. Each year he would pour $10,000 into his father's restaurant during the month of October, which coincided with Ramadan, the major fasting period of the year for Muslims. This money helped to feed many of Berkane's local poor residents. Now that he had endured this slanderous attack on his character, he'd gone very public with his giving. It wasn't going to be easy to return to the sport he loved.

Yet time heals many wounds and his sister persuaded him not to throw in the towel, saying that, "it would be wrong to walk away." El Guerrouj later added, "After Sydney it was very difficult for me. Psychologically, it was very hard to handle. I even considered seeing a psychologist because I wanted to stop running. But with the help of my family, my friends and particularly my coach, I have got through this dark period. I now understand that defeats are important for an athlete. They help him to come back even stronger."

By the start of 2001 he had a totally different mindset and soon he was ready to step out onto a track to compete again. On February 23, 2001, Hicham sent out two messages. One, that he had partly recovered from his Olympic heartache and two, that he might indeed be looking at longer distances in the future.

MOROCCAN SUCCESS; THE KADA WAY

The Moroccan competed in the 2 mile event in Ghent and ran an excellent time of 8:09.89, which was almost enough to beat Hailu Mekonnen's weak, as far as world records go, mark of 8:09.66. El Guerrouj won easily with Paul Bitok second in 8:20.55.

Two days later came a greater test, as Hicham moved down to his pet event and waiting for him in Lievin was a top class field. El Guerrouj was up to the challenge as he came away victorious in 3:37.20, with the handy names of Rotich, Lagat and Baala over one second adrift.

These races led onto the World Indoor Championships, which this year, were held in Lisboa, Portugal. Rather than contest the 1,500 metres, El Guerrouj decided on trying for the 3,000 metres title. This would be something different and he was more than capable of winning this event, especially without Saidi-Sief or Gebrselassie competing. His heat was on March 9 and it was by far the slowest of the two, with Hicham easily qualifying first with 8:05.50, ahead of the Olympic 5,000 metres champion Million Wolde. The final on March 11 was shaping up to be an interesting test in just how the Moroccans kick would compare to the Ethiopians.

If you have other abilities to utilize, which make tough questions irrelevant, then why not use them? This indoor final gave a minor lesson as to how others could have run in Million's Sydney final. Hicham has a teammate, Said Berioui in the race and he acts as a rabbit, not taking the pace out too fast, but making sure that the others have to work at a reasonable rhythm. The first km split is only 2:39.62, yet from here the pace slowly increases. By the time El Guerrouj takes over just before 2,000 metres, which is reached in 5:12.98, the tempo is fast enough to have the majority of the runners on the ropes. But Wolde is the athlete currently sitting on him.

It is useful to have in your arsenal an ability to throw in a lung collapsing surge a long way from home. With a lap that would have impressed Daniel Komen, Hicham surges the next 200 metres in 28.0 seconds or at a fifty six second outdoor lap pace. This proves far too great for the Ethiopian to handle but moving into his position is the world cross country champion Mohammed Mourhit, with Spain's Alberto Garcia also in contention. Into the last lap and it is down to the leading pair. It's here where El Guerrouj breaks Mourhit's final resistance with a 28.51 second lap as he eases away for a magnificent victory. The results were:

Hicham El Guerrouj	7:37.74
Mohammed Mourhit	7:38.94
Alberto Garcia	7:39.96
John Mayock	7:44.08
Million Wolde	7:44.54
Bernard Lagat	7:45.52
Mark Carroll	7:46.79
Craig Mottram	7:48.34
Mohamed Khaldi	7:52.76
Paul Bitok	7:54.16
Bouabdallah Tahri	7:57.84
Antonio Jimenez	8:04.01
Said Berioui	8:04.38

Hicham ran the final km in a staggering 2:24.76 in what was one of his best ever performances, this coming from an observer who usually doesn't rate indoor races too highly. It is interesting to note that the minor medallists, who had stuck close to El Guerrouj, would prove to have more in common than just standing on the same podium. The winner had plenty to say about his future ambitions.

"After the (outdoor) World Championships, I will run the 5000 metres in Zurich. And from next year, the 5,000 metres will be my main event. I will run the 5,000 metres in the Athens Olympic Games," said Hicham.

He also added that, "I am planning to attempt the world 5000 metres record in Zurich."

Certainly couscous for thought!

The rest of the championships also provided a positive for Abdelkader and Hicham as they prepared to retake their

MOROCCAN SUCCESS; THE KADA WAY

1,500 metres crown in Edmonton. The event in Portugal provided one of the worst races seen in a recent final, with the first lap being run in 1:10.36. The pace did not improve greatly until a final 300 metres burn up. Rui Silva was the surprised but delighted winner in front of his home crowd in the abysmal time of 3:51.06. Just behind him were Reyes Estevez and a lacklustre Noah Ngeny. The average speed of the Kenyan's 3:51.63 would make for a 7:43.26 3,000 metres time, much slower than El Guerrouj's final. It is a fair assumption that the Moroccan was a little less satisfied with his Sydney medal than the Kenyan and was therefore a much hungrier athlete at this stage of the year.

Hicham returned to Morocco and was soon back at Ifrane, putting together the many hard miles, which Kada hoped would lead to another successful season. Abdelkader was extremely confident about his superstar's future prospects, enough to say, "Maybe Hicham can run 3:40 in the mile, and maybe 3:24 in the 1,500 and in the five kilometres, 12:30. He works hard, he focuses on his objectives, and he does what he wants."

Despite declaring his intentions to compete at 3,000 and 5,000 metres, El Guerrouj remained solely a middle distance runner for the 2001 outdoor season. This commenced for him on May 27 in Eugene, Oregon, USA.

Before the race El Guerrouj discussed the 2001 season further, "The first objective this season is the world championship ...to prove I am still number one at the distance."

But before Edmonton he had another major goal, "I will try to beat the record in the 1,500 in Rome."

Yet even these accomplishments wouldn't totally atone for Atlanta and Sydney. El Guerrouj gives his opinion on the value of the Games, "An Olympic gold medal is 50 per cent of a champion's career, even if you have world records and world championships."

The mile event saw another easy win for the world record holder in a satisfactory time of 3:49.92. The only surprise was that the second placed athlete was not Kenyan! Kevin Sullivan from Canada produced a nice run of 3:51.82 to comfortably defeat Bernard Lagat who clocked 3:53.14.

A sub 3:50 was difficult for most, apart from this Moroccan. Hicham had said pre race, "At this time of the season, if you want to run the mile in 3:48 to 3:50, you have to run the 1,500 in 3:32. And for someone who is able to run the 1,500 in 3:26, that's not hard...It's not a tremendous effort." This wasn't arrogance. Just plain honesty.

The Kenyans confirmed their team for the Edmonton World Championships on June 23 in Nairobi, or so we thought at the time. Bernard Barmasai ran brilliantly to win the steeplechase in 8:16.0 but Wilson Boit Kipketer struggled into a lowly seventh place and was out of the squad. Charles Kamathi was first in the 10,000 metres with a 27:47.33 while Richard Limo won the 5,000 metres in 13:17.20. These were good times for races at high altitude, particularly in the case of Kamathi. Benjamin Limo failed to qualify in the 5,000 metres finishing fourth. The most interesting action took place in the 1,500 metres where the field was jam packed with talent. The top eight were:

William Chirchir	3:40.15
Laban Rotich	3:40.22
Noah Ngeny	3:40.27
Leonard Mucheru	3:40.42
Bernard Lagat	3:41.00
Robert Rono	3:41.34
Sammy Mutai	3:41.42
Musa Kimeli	3:41.72

The Olympic champion was a relieved man after grabbing the third and final spot. Ngeny had yet to return to his top form of 2000 but now he had six weeks to prepare for another crack at El Guerrouj. Lagat was the big name to miss out and he would not get the chance to add to his medal tally in Canada.

MOROCCAN SUCCESS; THE KADA WAY

Hicham did not race again until June 29, when the Golden League season kicked off in Rome. After the Prefontaine Classic in Eugene, El Guerrouj returned to Ifrane for a block of training specifically designed around improving his world record in the Olympic stadium.

El Guerrouj came reasonably close, before finishing with the outstanding time of 3:44.95 for the mile. It was just as well he performed at close to his best as by now Lagat was in much better shape as the stopwatch showed. The Kenyan ran 3:47.28. This field was first class with the first six all going under 3:50. The Spaniards, Andres Diaz and Jose Redolat finished third and fourth, clocking 3:48.38 and 3:49.60 respectively. With Noah Ngeny slow out of the blocks, El Guerrouj had once again defined himself as the world's premier miler.

In other races Hailu Mekonnen surprised the Kenyans when he won the 5,000 metres in 12:58.57. Daniel Komen wasn't in the same form as four years ago but his twelfth placing was a little harsh, considering that he still ran 13:07.50. In the steeplechase Bernard Barmasai once again lost out in a sprint finish. Olympic champion Reuben Kosgei won in 8:09.12, just ahead of Raymond Yator, 8:09.20. Barmasai finished with 8:09.78. Ali Ezzine was again absent but he made his return at the next Golden League meeting in Paris on July 6.

Ali performed admirably, out kicking Kenyan Misoi and Spaniard Jimenez as he recorded a good time of 8:11.40. Unfortunately this was only enough for fourth place as the Moroccan was some distance behind the Kenyans of Boit Kipketer, Kosgei and Yator. The 1997 world champion ran a time of 8:08.13. Abdelkader may still have been happy with Ezzine's result, believing that improvements were possible during the rest of the season.

El Guerrouj was in ominous form as he romped away with the 1,500 metres, proving to be as unbeatable as ever. The Kenyans tried their best to stay with him but this was a lost cause with Hicham running very powerfully and stopping the clock in the rarified air of 3:28.38. Only Morceli and Ngeny had ever run faster. Bernard Lagat and William Chirchir ran well, but they may as well have been in a different race. Their times were 3:30.83 and 3:31.20. Adil Kaouch was the first of the rabbits in this race and his early splits were 54.49 and 1:51.19. At the bell Lagat was close to El Guerrouj but on the bend he was quickly dispatched and a massive gap of fifteen metres soon appeared. Hicham's split at 1,200 metres was 2:47.01 and Adil was waiting to congratulate him on the victory after crossing the line. The world champion decided to take a short two week break before his next assignment in England.

Ezzine was keen to better his Paris performance so remaining in France, he went to Nice on July 9 for the Grand Prix meeting. The steeplechase drew a top class line up and Ali did make some advance on his previous time, although was unable to improve his position. The results from the race were:

Wilson Boit Kipketer	8:05.78
Bernard Barmasai	8:06.12
Kipkirui Misoi	8:08.90
Ali Ezzine	8:10.23
Elarbi Khattabi	8:13.27
Frederic Denis	8:22.03
John Langat	8:22.07
Stephen Cherono	8:24.58
Abraham Cherono	8:32.56
Tom Chorny	8:47.04
Ramiro Moran	8:56.48

Kenya was reasserting its total dominance of this event as this season the Moroccans were struggling to match it. The fifth placing of thirty four year old Khattabi was a great performance but his country now expected more from Ezzine. Perhaps in the next race he could break back into the sub 8:10 range. The Kenyan Cherono's were brothers with the youngest Stephen, only eighteen years old. The fast genes ran even further, for their older sibling was Seville world champion Christopher Kosgei!

MOROCCAN SUCCESS; THE KADA WAY

Amazingly, Khattabi had run faster than Ezzine this season. Starting his track campaign early in Portland on June 3, Elarbi won the meet in 8:12.95, defeating Stephen Cherono by ten seconds. He had followed up with an even better victory in Seville on June 8, when he clocked 8:09.49. This time was only one hundredth of a second off his personal best. This result also made him the second oldest runner ever, behind Patrick Sang, to break 8:10.

Nice again highlighted the waning form of Noah Ngeny. Competing in the 1,000 metres as the world record holder, Noah was unable to win, finishing second in 2:16.93, behind countryman William Yiampoy, 2:16.53. His time was a great deal slower than the 1999 world record of 2:11.96.

The same meeting witnessed the return to form of Ali Saidi-Sief who won the 1,500 metres easily with a 3:31.16. He backed this up when he won arguably the biggest distance race of the season so far, the Bislett Games mile in Oslo on July 13. Racing against everyone bar El Guerrouj, the Algerian produced a terrific run with his winning time of 3:48.23. Lagat was the only guy that could keep with him and he ran 3:48.57. Trailing badly in third was Ngeny. The Kenyan just could not flick the form switch as he ran 3:50.29.

With Saidi-Sief recommitting to middle distance and Gebrselassie and Hissou on the injured list, the 5,000 metres was Kenyan dominated. The nation boasted the first six finishers with the ageless Paul Bitok winning, but just missing out on a career goal to break thirteen minutes. As he hit the line the official time said 13:00.10. Benjamin Limo had returned to form in 2001 and was the second placed man with 13:01.88. Struggling to finish nineteenth was nineteen year old Ethiopian Kenenisa Bekele who ran 13:25.86. Twentieth and last placed finisher was the talented Kenyan Charles Kamathi who could only manage a time of 13:31.56. This was very confusing as previously, the young star had easily broken twenty seven minutes for 10,000 metres.

Ali Ezzine found that he was simply incapable of reproducing the sort of times he had run during the past two seasons when he again finished fourth in the 3,000 metres steeplechase. Running a disappointing 8:15.93, the Moroccan was no match for the finishing kicks of three Kenyans in what was turning out to be a groundhog day type of season for him. The winner was Nice victor Wilson Boit Kipketer whose time was 8:12.63. The result would have left Abdelkader Kada scratching his head, trying to work out why the twenty two year old appeared to have already peaked.

Kada's top men did not compete in the next Golden League meeting in Monaco on July 20. The 1,500 metres was a return of sorts for Morceli but the Algerian again confirmed his liking for giving up when he failed to finish the race. Up ahead was Bernard Lagat who ran a good time of 3:31.08. Surprisingly he was defeated by Benjamin Kipkurui and Rui Silva, who both impressed with great times of 3:30.67 and 3:30.36. The form of the Portuguese was astonishing as he'd shown nothing recently to hint at such a performance. Back on the 11th of June he was just one of the many mere mortals being thrashed by Saidi-Sief as he finished a distant ninth while recording 3:35.76 in Athens.

Brahim Boulami returned to good form with a fast 8:07.28 and a third placing in the steeplechase. Wilson Boit Kipketer continued to make a mockery of the Kenyan team selection procedure as he carried on with his winning ways with a magnificent 8:01.73 run. Compatriot Kipkirui Misoi clocked 8:06.81. I will keep harping on the following issue. Why doesn't Kenya keep *one* spot open for an athlete in outstanding form? Since the trials Wilson had recorded three consecutive Golden League victories in Paris, Oslo and Monaco. He had also won at Nice and Stockholm. These five races were all in the last two weeks! After a slow start to the season, it was obvious that he was now the form steeplechase runner in the world.

Boulami's result was a major upgrade on his 2001 performances as so far he had only managed an 8:17.32 in Athens and an 8:15.70 three days earlier in Stockholm. Now he appeared to be in much better shape than Ezzine and a more likely world championship medallist.

MOROCCAN SUCCESS; THE KADA WAY

On July 22, Hicham El Guerrouj returned to the circuit. The moment had finally arrived. He would race against Noah Ngeny for the first time since that fateful day in Sydney. The event was a mile and the venue was London. Despite the Kenyan carrying the tag of Olympic champion, there was no surprise when the results of the first eight were:

Hicham El Guerrouj	3:49.41
Noah Ngeny	3:51.19
Craig Mottram	3:53.90
John Mayock	3:54.05
Vyacheslav Shabunin	3:54.18
Frederick Cheruiyot	3:54.79
Paul McMullen	3:54.94
Anthony Whiteman	3:55.16

Nobody could get near El Guerrouj in 2001. So far no one had finished within a full second of him. Ngeny seemed to be a completely different athlete this year and looked as if he might become just another highly talented Kenyan that burned out at a young age. It was worrying for him as to just how far away he was consistently from his personal bests. Yet there were the Edmonton World Championships to look forward to but as it turned out, Noah would not be a part of them.

Greg Rowlerson

Edmonton & Abrupt Endings

Noah Ngeny was made a scapegoat in an attempt by the Kenyan Athletics Federation to retain its power over its athletes. Noah had refused to go back to his homeland for a squad training camp, preferring (and rightly so) to remain in Europe, not solely for the money, but because this was where the best competition was and racing in the Golden League might bring him back into form. Travelling all the way back to Africa to train in arduous conditions before flying back to Europe was unlikely to do him any favours. The selectors threatened him with exclusion from their World Championships team if he didn't follow their orders. Initially Noah probably thought that the selection committee would back down on its threat but he would have been well advised to have heeded that Daniel Komen had been omitted from the last two Olympic squads. There were some hard heads amongst the Kenyan power brokers and Ngeny was forced to sit Edmonton out. Despite his form being patchy in '01, it remained unfortunate that the Sydney champion and Seville silver medallist was not on the starting lists for the heats of the men's 1,500 metres, especially since he had also qualified at the Kenyan trials. Noah had ticked plenty of boxes. I would have picked him even if he hadn't placed in the first three, as I believe there should always been one national spot left open in each event for selection by logical interpretation or plain common sense. Ngeny was still one of Kenya's best milers. He wasn't injured and he'd proven that he could defeat Hicham El Guerrouj in a major championship. I would have picked him, but maybe that's just me.

There was added confusion when the selectors didn't take the most obvious replacement, which was the fourth placed Leonard Mucheru from the trials. The man that took Ngeny's spot was instead fifth placed Bernard Lagat. Granted, I would have picked the Olympic bronze medallist over Mucheru, but it was the inconsistency of their selection process that was frustrating. The Kenyan selectors were a walking contradiction as they seemed to have one rule for one and one rule for another.

MOROCCAN SUCCESS; THE KADA WAY

Another athlete going through a difficult phase was Salah Hissou. The year 2000 had been frustrating and in many ways, wasteful. Not only did he miss the Olympics, but not pulling out until the last minute would potentially destroy his 2001 season as well. If Salah had undergone surgery at the start of 2000, when his latest ankle problem first surfaced, it was likely that he would have been back to full fitness for the 2001 World Cross Country Championships. Now that he was expected to go under the knife post Sydney, he was certain to miss the event. Again. That really hurts.

But the Moroccan Federation was unwise enough to take yet another gamble. It insisted that Salah not undergo surgery, and that after some rest, he would be ready to race during the entire 2001 season. This seemed most ambitious considering the pain he had endured throughout much of the past three seasons.

While training in Morocco, Hissou re-injured his delicate left ankle and missed the World Cross Country Championships anyway. He was now in a race against time to be fit for the entire European track season that most importantly, included the defence of his 5,000 metres world title. Remarkably, Salah did not undergo surgery until the end of May! His entire track campaign was a write off and the man management skills of the decision makers in the Federation had to be seriously questioned.

In the end they refused to help Salah with the costs and arrangements of his surgery. This was why there was such a big delay before he went under the knife in Antwerp, Belgium. You would think that a nation would be keen to greatly support one of their reigning world champions. Unfortunately in Salah's instance, this wasn't the case.

The 2001 season was the best time in many a year for a track long distance runner to be arriving at his peak. Gebrselassie and Hissou were laid low with injury. Komen hadn't gone close to his personal records since early '98 and his career was at a crossroad. Tergat had given up the track for good in preference for the longer distances of the roads where he'd finished second in his debut marathon in London, recording a great time of 2:08.14. Also of significance was his abandoning of the World Cross Country as well. The opportunity was certainly there for a quality distance runner to enjoy plenty of success in 2001. Salah fitted that description and he could surely see the possibilities of some career defining victories.

Haile Gebrselassie was severely restricted by injury between 2000 and 2002. His recovery from surgery would take longer than Hissou's yet during this period, the Ethiopian missed none of the events that really mattered to him. The Moroccan missed almost everything.

Bad luck and poor circumstances had condemned Salah to being merely a spectator at the Olympic Games, World Cross Country (twice), the Golden League season and the World Athletics Championships. It was one of the toughest periods of Hissou's career.

Yet there was still more drama and career confusion ahead for Salah. It is all well and good for a coach and athlete to get along during times of success. The real question is how well does the relationship work through the difficult times?

The answer in relation to Abdelkader and Salah was that it didn't.

Kada had his hands full, simply dealing with his star miler, El Guerrouj. Not wanting the added complication of an injured runner, the pair went their separate ways following a decade of association, which included some outstanding accomplishments. After such a long and successful partnership this was far from an easy decision, but it was probably for the best. For starters, it is extremely rare for any elite sportsman to have the same coach for such a long time. Approaching thirty, Hissou needed a fresh start as he contemplated the idea of a move to the roads, which meant his career would require a major overhaul. At this time of Kada's coaching career, he didn't have the time to devote that Salah obviously required.

MOROCCAN SUCCESS; THE KADA WAY

The issue of El Guerrouj certainly played its part in this break up. Hicham's career had clearly overshadowed Salah's and this was a factor in determining where Kada's attention lay. It was doubtful whether Salah could return to the top level with his career seemingly in disarray.

Retaining some level of stability was Haile Gebrselassie, who underwent surgery on his achilles tendon immediately after the Games, hoping that he could recover in time to defend his 10,000 metres world title. His operation was considered a success but Haile's injury was so serious that just getting back to an international level was a question in itself. Despite his extremely slow recovery, everything seemed to work out satisfactorily for the Ethiopian. He declared himself fit to race at Edmonton despite not having raced at all prior to the championships.

It was clearly a new era in men's long distance running. By now there was a dearth of real quality from the 3,000 metres up to the 12 kms of cross country. There was one particular runner of extraordinary quality who could have been dominating the 3,000 and 5,000 metres in 2001. Who knows what Hicham El Guerrouj would have done post Sydney if he had won gold as expected in the 1,500 metres?

If he had been victorious, he probably would have considered his middle distance career complete. As such, he could have made a full commitment to the longer distances. After time had healed some of his pain from Sydney, he knew that he had to continue his journey in the 1,500 metres because of unfinished business. He had to give himself a chance for redemption in Athens. As a result Hicham's 5,000 metres plans were put on the backburner.

Another athlete capable of outstanding performances at 3,000 and 5,000 metres was Ali Saidi-Sief, but the Algerian also had to overcome his *failure* in Sydney. Like El Guerrouj, silver wasn't good enough. If he could recapture his form of pre Sydney, then domination of these events was possible in 2001. Whether the defeat changed his racing attitude we can not be sure, but so far this year, Ali had restricted his distances almost solely to the 1,500 metres and mile, with sensational results. He had not only won in Nice and Oslo. On June 11 he defeated Ngeny and Rotich easily in the Athens 1,500 metres with a 3:30.78. This was a performance that he replicated to an even greater devastating effect when he clocked 3:29.51 in Lausanne. The Algerian had nearly four seconds up his sleeve on Rotich and more on Ngeny. He also produced a more than handy run on June 19 in Strasbourg when he ran a 4:46.88 over 2,000 metres. It was the second fastest performance of all time, taking him exactly one second ahead of Morceli's old world record. Clearly his form was good enough to provide El Guerrouj with a serious challenge in Edmonton.

Unfortunately track fans were again the losers as Saidi-Sief opted out of this battle to contest what he thought was a more winnable 5,000 metres race. Without having raced at more than a mile this season, it was a strange decision. Why display such brilliant middle distance form without putting it all on the line? Ali had defeated everyone who mattered with the exception of the Moroccan who he had avoided thus far.

Hicham El Guerrouj didn't care whom he raced against in 2001. He was a man on a mission, determined to do everything in his power to remain dominant in his pet event. He couldn't totally make up for last year's missed opportunity, but continually winning would slowly help.

The 5,000 metres became one of the tough races to predict in Edmonton. As the form runner, Saidi-Sief became the first choice of most pundits. Yet with a large group of East Africans waiting for him and conditioned for the distance, nobody could back Ali with too much confidence. His main challengers could be any number of athletes, as nobody was running consistently well in the event this season. Perhaps Million Wolde would prove that his Olympic victory was no fluke.

The 10,000 metres event was even more open. Mourhit had performed dismally at the Games and since retaining his world cross country title, his track performances had left a lot

MOROCCAN SUCCESS; THE KADA WAY

to be desired. In fact his form was almost non existent. He was under an enormous injury cloud having failed to finish his last 3,000 metres race in Monaco with a calf problem. Previously he'd retired from the Rome 5,000 metres. With Haile's form unknown and Paul Tergat out, the distance was almost left with an identity crisis. The bronze medallist from Sydney, Assefa Mezgebu was prepared for Edmonton and Gebrselassie's support act suddenly found himself as a potential favourite. There weren't many obvious challengers to Ethiopia's new 'number one'. Maybe Charles Kamathi could get it together. His 26:51 in Brussels had displayed his fantastic potential. He was only twenty three and so much younger than all his rivals. His European form was mostly horrendous having placed tenth in Rome and twentieth in Oslo but earlier this season, he did win the Kenyan trials with a time of 27:47, the fastest run ever recorded at high altitude. He'd also performed well on June 4 at Hengelo. That 10,000 metres race appeared to be Edmonton's best guide with Mezgebu winning in 27:22.30, less than a second ahead of Kamathi and Girma Tolla. There were no heats at this distance so we had precious little to go from, making for even greater guess work as to the event's outcome.

The Kenyans were the clear favourites in the men's steeplechase, even without the in form Wilson Boit Kipketer. The top two left were world record holder Bernard Barmasai and Olympic champion Reuben Kosgei. Bernard appeared to be slightly past his prime while Reuben was expected to be entering his peak period.

Ali Ezzine was in heat 1 at 3:05 pm on August 6. The task of qualifying was made easier than ever when the organizers chose to run only two heats, with the first six getting through automatically and another three as fastest losers. In past World Championships, there had been only twelve finalists but in Edmonton there were fifteen. Even in average form, Ali shouldn't have any problems here.

Abdelkader would have been happy that Ezzine drew only one Kenyan, although he would have to contend with Boulami and the two Spanish Martins, who are not related by the way.

Even if defeated by that group, there were still two positions left to make certain of a final's spot. Not surprisingly, there was little pace on early as Reuben Kosgei led the pack to 2,000 metres in 5:39.96, almost 8:30 tempo. Late in the race, only eight of the twelve starters remained in contention and it was now that Kosgei and Boulami put the foot down. They moved well ahead of the rest in a show of strength and it was the Kenyan who crossed the line first in 8:21.96, just two hundredths of a second ahead of the Moroccan. The next six fell over three seconds behind, with Ezzine not convincing at all, but safely through in fifth place. His time was only 8:26.86, giving him an automatic qualification by merely four tenths of a second.

Antonio Jimenez of Spain won an even slower second heat with 8:25.37. The upset was Elarbi Khattabi's inability to qualify. He only clocked 8:32.70 for eighth position, leaving him 1.13 seconds off the third of the fastest losers.

The final was held only two days later on Wednesday, August 8 at 8:00 pm. Ali was given just an outside chance at winning a medal and with good reason. He had failed to impress in any race since coming within a second of Kosgei and Boit Kipketer in Sydney. Regarding form, he would be hard pressed to finish top eight but he did have a reputation for performing on the big occasion. All he could do was give his best and see what transpired.

The Kenyan trio of Reuben Kosgei, Bernard Barmasai and Raymond Yator were the obvious favourites. Not without a chance were the Spaniards and the Moroccans. There were six sub 8:10 athletes in the final.

There are no fireworks at the beginning but Ali is relieved that the pace isn't too slow. In fact it is Ezzine himself who leads the field through 1,000 metres in 2:48.72. Earlier, Brahim Boulami had made a quick move on the first lap to lead with Ovett commenting, "Well Boulami is a good runner. He's really the only thorn in the Kenyan side as it were. I mean world records, he's up there amongst them. He's one of the fastest non Kenyans ever so if anybody's going to start taking

MOROCCAN SUCCESS; THE KADA WAY

it to the Kenyans it will be this guy." With five laps to go Ezzine takes over with Ovett saying, "Yeah he's a good runner. And this is an unusual thing to see the Moroccans dominating or leading in the steeplechase."

But this is not for long. As is the trend, the Kenyans start to bunch together at the front and slowly the speed picks up. By 2,000 metres, reached by Barmasai in 5:33.81, the majority of athletes are still in touch, including Ali who appears much more relaxed than in his heat.

The steeple style of today's elite athlete is very much to clear the hurdles, rather than step on them. Ezzine and Boulami jump over them, as do the Kenyans. What is most admirable is the hardly noticeable difference the barriers make to the runners' fast rhythm. Despite having five of these hindrances a lap (less on lap one) the best times are sub eight minutes, which is not too far behind the best performances without the steeples, which break 7:30. Allowing for fatigue, which sets in from jumping throughout the race, the actual time lost when passing over the obstructions is very minimal.

Barmasai is doing a fantastic job at the front and with two laps to go, Ezzine is giving up a couple of metres to the last of the first five runners, seemingly struggling to hang on. Boulami on the other hand, appears strong and threatens to move forward.

Brahim is fourth on the back straight and Ali, while still in sixth position, is perhaps not so much struggling, but instead running smartly and giving himself plenty of room to clear the barriers without interference. He's also enabling himself to coast along on the inside without covering extra ground. Barmasai slows as he approaches the water jump and Kosgei takes the lead. However going with him easily are Boulami and Martin. The group of six are tightly packed. This is anyone's race.

Steve Ovett remarked, "Well, this is a bit of a scramble now. The Kenyans are letting the others sort around them which is a big mistake. Because some of these guys if it's slow, will

probably have a fairly good kick."
Nic Bideau predicted, "I think we're going to see an upset."

After the bell it's Kosgei leading Barmasai, Luis Miguel Martin, Yator, Ezzine and Boulami. The split is 7:11.18. There is never any dramatic speed on in this race and the concluding stages are more of a gradual kick down. Still, as the athletes enter the back straight, it's clear that only one Moroccan can medal with Boulami dropping off. Brahim is having one of his off days.

Ali on the other hand looks composed and attempts to go with the Kenyans as they begin their sprint. On the third last jump Ezzine moves way out, almost into lane three as he tries to move closer to the medals while passing the fading Spaniard Martin. Kosgei establishes a break following the water jump but here Yator falls while alongside Ezzine, leaving medals up for grabs. The Moroccan is on the heels of Barmasai.

Reuben has the race won at the last hurdle, clearing out to about a seven metres lead. Just as he's moving comfortably away from Bernard, Ali starts to move through his gears. Clearing the final jump smoothly and kicking again, Ezzine strides past the fading Kenyan to record a spectacular second place finish! The results from the steeplechase final were:

Reuben Kosgei	8:15.16
Ali Ezzine	8:16.21
Bernard Barmasai	8:16.59
Luis Miguel Martin	8:18.87
Bouabdallah Tahri	8:19.56
Antonio Jimenez	8:19.82
Khamis Abdullah Saifeldin	8:20.01
Raymond Yator	8:20.87
Ralf Assmus	8:21.73
Brahim Boulami	8:21.95
Tim Broe	8:23.07
Eliseo Martin	8:27.78
Christian Belz	8:31.43
Joel Bourgeois	8:36.38
Gael Pencreach	8:41.51

MOROCCAN SUCCESS; THE KADA WAY

As Ali crossed the line he threw his right arm forward with his finger pointing in a gesture of celebration. He and Brahim shook hands. The last km was 2:41.36 with the final lap only 63.99. Ovett concluded, "A strange race really that one and the Kenyans won't be happy with that. That was a disappointing performance. Not from Reuben Kosgei but the others really." Only gold and bronze, pretty poor really. The Kenyans face pretty high expectations!

Ovett offered his praises in his usual deadpan manner, "Ezzine did a good job really. He just bided his time. He came wide around the final water jump when all the fracas was going on around him and then poured it on down the home straight to get the silver medal. Good performance."

Ali had become the first non Kenyan in fourteen years at a major championships to finish as high as second in the 3,000 metres steeplechase. To medal in three consecutive championships was amazing in itself as the Kenyan dominance of this event went back to the 1968 Olympics when they first won the gold medal. Since then, no other country had ever won a Kenyan participated steeplechase at the Olympics (remembering that Kenya boycotted the '76 and '80 Games).

Ali obviously understood the history of his event as he said, "This is the peak of my athletic career. The steeplechase has always been a Kenyan event, and for someone just north of Kenya to take the silver is a near miracle."

His total elation at securing the silver also highlighted the stranglehold that Kenya had on the event. For any other country a silver medal was as good as a gold was for Kenya. Ezzine also revealed a reason for his below par heat run.

"I was feeling a little sick during the semi-finals, but luckily I became healthy again for today."

Reuben Kosgei was establishing a super resumé as the reigning world and Olympic champion at twenty years of age. The world was his oyster and now his big challenge was to try to break the world record at some stage. Yator's bad luck and subsequent eighth placing at least had given Barmasai a medal after the Kenyan had shockingly failed to medal in the last two championships. Though for a runner of his talent, bronze didn't seem enough and he had probably missed his chances to ever become a gold medallist at the highest level. Boulami flopped again at the highest level. His form was up and down like a yo-yo. At least Ezzine had raced with some consistency. Morocco's reliable championship's performer was looking ahead and aiming for one step higher.

"My next goal is to improve on this performance and win gold at the Olympics in Athens."

Abdelkader Kada would have been delighted with Ali's exploits, and he still had his main man yet to compete. The men's 1,500 metres heats were scheduled to commence the following day.

At the conclusion of the steeplechase final we saw the running of the 10,000 metres. Any logical reasons for picking the event's winner would go out the window once we saw the competitors on the start line for the final. As soon as we saw the distinctive smiling face perched above a green singlet we remembered the past and that was enough to sway our selection towards the four time world champion.

However logic prevailed over sentiment with Haile Gebrselassie losing out in a slow, tactical race to Charles Kamathi and Assefa Mezgebu. The unpredictable Kenyan revealed his great talent at an opportune time to dethrone the 'emperor', triumphing in 27:53.25. His kick over the final 120 metres was explosive and decisive but the previous 9,880 metres were hardly spectacular. The first half was 'jogged' in 14:15.11, the second half was a barely respectable 13:38.24 with the final km timed at just 2:36.01. There was a small excuse of Edmonton being at 2,000 feet altitude, but this certainly wasn't considered significantly high. For the 10,000 metres and marathon events it would have a small effect on performance.

MOROCCAN SUCCESS; THE KADA WAY

The race basically further emphasized Gebrselassie's greatness despite his loss. As he did during last year's Olympics, the Ethiopian ran in an ungainly style, far removed from the graceful, characteristic technique that we saw dominate the classic event in the 1990's. That he had earned a medal after surgery without any lead up races, was a pointer to knowledgeable fans as to both the weakness of the race's standard and to how easily a younger, healthier Haile would have destroyed this field. Amazingly it was revealed post race that Gebrselassie was suffering from the flu until two days before the final. I believe it is fair to say that he won the bronze rather than *lost* the gold!

Mohammed Mourhit didn't finish and was the event's major disappointment. He appeared to be finished as an international athlete only shortly after retaining his world cross country crown. Strange. The Spaniards of Fabian Roncero and Jose Rios were ridiculously allowed to mix it with the Africans until the final lap. Morocco's Jauad Gharib, with little track pedigree was also able to contend for a long period. He even led during the latter stages only to be blown away by basic speed in the last few laps, before finishing eleventh in 28:05.45. Salah Hissou would have cringed as he watched a final golden opportunity slip by.

Not having any regrets was Hicham El Guerrouj, whose focus was firmly on winning his third consecutive world championship. His heat was the first of three at 7:25 pm on August 9. The Moroccan wanted to make a point that he was taking no prisoners as he thrashed his opposition with an excellent kick down. After James Nolan led at 800 metres in 2:00.34, Hicham released most of his awesome power with a 56.44 third lap (2:56.78 at 1,200 metres) and sped up even more over the race's remainder to win in 3:36.97, well clear of Mehdi Baala who ran 3:38.18. There were no surprises in these early rounds. Jose Antonio Redolat clocked the fastest time when he won heat 2 in 3:36.24.

The Spaniard was drawn in El Guerrouj's semi final, which was the second run at 10 pm the next day, August 10. The race was very slow. Even with Hicham leading by 800 metres, the split was a miserable 2:06.17. Now came the proof that the Moroccan was as strong as ever. On this third lap he took off, bringing the sixty three lap pace down to a 53.24. By the finish he looked to have plenty left in the tank as he clocked 3:39.54, though also appearing comfortable was Redolat who followed him in with 3:39.75. The third of the Moroccans, Abdelkader Hachlaf, did indeed finish third here with a 3:40.16, making it a great heat for the North Africans. Missing out on the final after placing seventh was Kenyan Laban Rotich.

The first semi was run at a solid pace throughout with Bernard Lagat dictating the terms and eventually winning in 3:35.82. Hicham's favourite pet rabbit, Adil Kaouch, was right with him, running an impressive 3:36.01. All the big names made it through this time resulting in Morocco having three representatives in the final. It had four semi finalists with Youssef Baba finishing last in heat 1.

This had come about due to the recent introduction of the World Championships wildcard, which automatically granted the reigning champion a spot in the heats. On top of this advantage, that nation could also select three further participants. This rule applied in Seville but two of Morocco's four 1,500 metres runners did not get past the first round. Many reigning world champions still did not show up to defend their titles. Salah Hissou obviously missed out in the 5,000 metres and suddenly finding itself struggling for depth, Morocco selected only two athletes for those heats. Even as world champion, an athlete still had to often satisfy demanding team coaches. In the steeplechase Kenya did not include Seville champion Christopher Koskei. But in this case I must side with the selectors! Koskei's best result after 1999 was a poor 8:20.49 at Stockholm in 2000. Often the Kenyans were still too stubborn for their own good.

Daniel Komen was the 5,000 metres world champion from Athens and thus an automatic qualifier for Seville. Kenya had more depth than any other country in this event yet it chose to only pick three athletes. This move backfired when Philip Mosima failed to make the final, the race that Hissou won,

MOROCCAN SUCCESS; THE KADA WAY

when he defeated Benjamin Limo and Komen. This wasn't a golden year for Kenyan men distance running but consider the other runners that could have been there, some of whom may have been serious contenders or at the very least provided some support to Limo and Komen. Below are the best performances that the following athletes produced in the 5,000 metres before the World Championships during 1999.

Name	Venue	Date	Placing	Time
Julius Gitahi	Osaka	May 8	1st	13:05.45
Sammy Kipketer	Oslo	June 30	2nd	12:58.10
Thomas Nyariki	Saint-Denis	July 3	2nd	13:04.07
Richard Limo	Rome	July 7	6th	12:58.15
Paul Koech	Rome	July 7	8th	13:01.72

There are four runners here who comfortably broke 13:10 within two months of the Seville final. Taking the season's bests of all the thirty five Seville competitors (prior to the championships), Sammy Kipketer and Richard Limo would have been the fourth and fifth fastest athletes, behind only Hissou, Komen and Limo. Selecting either man as an extra would have been pretty handy. Richard Limo even finished third in the selection trials and still couldn't get a gig, being forced to run in the All-African Games instead.

The Ethiopians had not surprisingly made better use of the wildcard. The last two World Championship 10,000 metres did not include heats, so the East Africans automatically entered four men in both finals. In 1999 they placed first, third, fourth and sixth. In 2001 they followed up with second, third, fourth and ninth. Sometimes it's amazing what can be achieved with the use of common sense.

The 1,500 metres final in Edmonton started on Sunday, August 12. Disappointingly it was held at 4:00 pm, near the hottest part of the day, with the temperature at thirty degrees. Running for only a few minutes wasn't going to kill anyone, but the finals for any event exceeding 400 metres should be held at night as conditions are cooler and more conducive to the best performances.

Hicham El Guerrouj probably wasn't perturbed by this situation as his form had been immaculate and he was highly confident of victory. Before the race Kada had decided that he was calling for a Seville replica. Adil Kaouch would run at a fast pace for 800 metres, stringing the field out in the manner of a Golden League race. With his opponents at his mercy, the world champion would take over and continue the torment.

This is exactly what happened. After 200 metres Kaouch sweeps around the field to lead El Guerrouj with the 400 metres split timed at a fast 55.41. The tempo remains only slightly slower than the Seville burn up, as Adil runs a strong second lap, registering a 1:53.69 time at 800 metres. Hicham makes his move with 650 metres remaining and Lagat, Chirchir and Estevez all react well to the acceleration. Nic Bideau on Lagat, "Lagat's gone with him and he'll be there until the very end but I just don't think he has the belief in his ability to win it. I think he knows he can run with El Guerrouj. I just don't think he thinks he can get past him."

The third lap with Hicham has always been the key to his victories. To the viewer it looks like he does most of his damage in the final 300 metres but he is able to hurt his competitors the most after (and because of) a fast third lap. In Sydney El Guerrouj ran this in 56.90 seconds. In Edmonton he ran it in 55.66 and this made all the difference. Rather than have a couple of athletes sitting on him, Hicham is already moving majestically away from Lagat, gaining a break of five metres as he reaches 1,200 metres in 2:49.35.

The 55.66 sectional is run at a gradual kick down. Approaching the bell, El Guerrouj still has the three opponents in his slip stream but from the 1,100 to the 1,200 segment he runs 13.42, or 53.68 lap pace, too quick for the rest. It is a deceptive speed increase, with the early section being run in fifty six second plus tempo. It isn't the rapid surge of Morceli, who used to throw in a sub thirteen second

MOROCCAN SUCCESS; THE KADA WAY

hundred metres to open the final lap in devastating fashion. El Guerrouj is different, using a longer run for home, using strength to defeat speed. Usually we would only see this style of running succeed at 5,000 metres or further but Hicham El Guerrouj is a different miler to anyone who has come before him.

By the 1,200 metres mark, the race is virtually all over and now the Moroccan goes in for the rest of the kill on the back straight, clearing out to a big lead of around twelve metres. Nothing has changed once he enters the home straight. In the final forty metres El Guerrouj completes the script, celebrating in the same method as Seville, switching off and blowing kisses into his hands before releasing them. It is his unique way of displaying his love for running. The results from the 1,500 metres final were:

Hicham El Guerrouj	3:30.68
Bernard Lagat	3:31.10
Driss Maazouzi	3:31.54
William Chirchir	3:31.91
Reyes Estevez	3:32.34
Jose Antonio Redolat	3:34.29
Rui Silva	3:35.74
Abdelkader Hachlaf	3:36.54
Gert-Jan Liefers	3:36.99
Paul McMullen	3:39.35
Adil Kaouch	3:48.45
Mehdi Baala	3:55.36

The victory was far more emphatic then the times suggest as Hicham took things very easily over the final stretch as he seemed to take in the enormity of his third world championship gold medal. In the aftermath he knelt and bowed to the track, then sat up and symbolically wrote 'I love you all.' Not all of us could understand Arabic but anybody could understand that when they watched El Guerrouj run like this, it was something to be truly appreciated.

Hicham explained further.

"It was a very easy race for me today. I came in confident and I knew if I can run my own race I can win it. It has been a hard year for me, but my family kept on supporting me through the bad times. When I crossed the finish line, I wrote 'Thank you' with my hand to show my appreciate to all of them for believing in me." El Guerrouj's loyal pacemaker Houcine Benzriguinet had also been important, encouraging Hicham to get back into training during his lowest time post Sydney. "He is even better than a psychologist because he understands me. After the Olympics, Houcine played a very important role in getting me back on the rails, waking me up in the morning and taking me to training, but it took four months to recover my enthusiasm."

The last lap in Edmonton was run in only 54.75, nothing too stupendous for 1,500 metres running. This further emphasized the distinctive way that Hicham dominated his event. Steve Ovett hit the nail on the head when he said, "He's got this very deceptive speed over the last lap you know. I mean he's not accelerating like a sprinter. He just lengthens his stride and the others just almost seem to wither down that back straight."

The world champion's Moroccan teammates, Hachlaf and Kaouch walked with Hicham to join Kada in the stands. Abdelkader hugged Hicham and handed him the Moroccan flag. The three then jogged together in celebration.

Now everybody's attention was turning to next Friday's meeting in Zurich where a major focus was going to centre around El Guerrouj entering the 5,000 metres for the first time as a senior. Just what time could the Moroccan manage if he maintained the standards he has set as a miler and in his once off 3,000 metres race in Brussels?

"My goal is to be the best runner of all time at both 1,500 and 5,000. I'd like to run the 5,000 both in Paris in two years and then at the Olympics in Athens. I still feel young. If I could have run both events here, I would have done it. But the time schedule did not allow this possibility."

MOROCCAN SUCCESS; THE KADA WAY

Hicham also commented on his waning interest in his pet event while admitting a difference of opinion with Abdelkader.

"I think this was my last 1,500 metres race at the World Championships," he began, cautiously. "But my coach doesn't agree. He'll have to convince me either one way or the other, and we'll see what comes of it."

Kada still wanted El Guerrouj to keep the door ajar for another Olympic 1,500 metres campaign at Athens in 2004. That was another three years away, by which time the Moroccan would be almost thirty. It was likely that his legs may have slowed by then, making a successful foray into increased distances more realistic.

Age hadn't wearied the legs of Moroccan born French runner Driss Maazouzi, the surprise bronze medallist who would turn thirty two on October 20. Driss made the Olympic final back in 1996 when competing for Morocco, placing tenth in 3:39.65. He had shown signs that he could finish higher in the future after he'd clocked a fast 3:34.35 in those semi finals, almost his personal best time. But being close to twenty seven, he likely needed to improve now, especially as the 1,500 metres was generally an event for young legs.

He failed to make any further impression during the remainder of that season and after 1997 his career appeared to be over, after he failed to make the Athens World Championship final. He also did not run a sub 3:35 that season. Now turning twenty eight, it didn't seem possible that he could make the necessary improvements required to become a truly world class miler.

In 1998 Driss made major changes in his career as he started to compete for France. Suddenly he raised his game to another level when he registered a big personal record, clocking 3:31.59 in Monaco on August 8. Now he was able to compete more strongly in the big races. Maazouzi became a regular championship finalist, finishing eighth in Seville with a good time of 3:34.02 and eleventh in Sydney. It still came as a shock when he ran his second fastest time ever to collect the bronze at Edmonton, but Driss was an example for persistence. If things aren't working out for you, change your circumstances and perhaps try out new strategies. The new French hero commented.

"I'm 31 years old, and just won my first world championship medal. Age plays no part if you really want something."

Age was the furthest thing from twenty year old Richard Limo's mind when the Kenyan won an exciting 5,000 metres final. Reverting back to its tactics of 4-10 years ago, Kenya ran aggressively early, making this a strength race as opposed to the boring, slow final in Sydney a year ago. Limo initially went to the front and ran a first lap of 59.07, which was extreme. He quickly settled back into the pack but the speed did not ease up much because his teammate Sammy Kipketer took on the pace and led at 1,000 metres in 2:32.51. Slowly he began to creep ahead of the opposition, gaining a lead of about fifteen metres by the 2,000 metres mark, which he reached in a fast 5:09.48.

It was no surprise when Sammy was unable to maintain the fast laps and by 3,000 metres he was engulfed by a still significantly large group. The pace had slowed and it remained that way even with Saidi-Sief going to the front. The Algerian played a game of patience, until with two laps left he started to wind it up. With 500 metres to go he was firing on all cylinders and only Richard Limo and Million Wolde could stay in contact. On the back straight for the final time, Ali gave it everything and disposed of the Ethiopian but could not shake off the Kenyan who had another gear in the home straight and won convincingly. The time was an outstanding 13:00.77, with the final km run in 2:26.12. The first Moroccan was really Ismail Sghyr in sixth, but as he was competing for France, officially it was Mohammed Amyn who ran below his capabilities to finish twelfth in 13:28.90.

Many criticised Saidi-Sief, saying that as in Sydney, he had failed in a major championship. This is most harsh considering he ran just over thirteen minutes and was the man responsible for a very fast final km. What more could

MOROCCAN SUCCESS; THE KADA WAY

have been expected from him? On this day Richard Limo was very strong and deserved the victory.

Where the Algerian did fail in Edmonton, was in his test *off* the track. It soon became known that Ali had tested positive for Nandrolone and was stripped of his silver medal.

Nandrolone is an anabolic steroid, occurring naturally in the body, but in small quantities. The testing procedure for this steroid contains even more pitfalls than with EPO. Taken via a urine sample, an athlete is suspected of doping if he exceeds 2 ng per ml of urine of Nandrolone. Studies have shown that this normal urine limit can be breached, simply with high protein diets and hard cardiovascular exercise. This is long distance running! A lot of other supplements also contain Nandrolone. There had recently been many strange cases of positive tests to the drug. Former stars such as Linford Christie, Merlene Ottey (who was later cleared) and Dieter Baumann had all failed tests while protesting their innocence. Nothing unusual about that.

Steroids are thought to enhance brute power and strength, not endurance, therefore they are linked to sprinters more than distance runners. However they do also assist in recovery and Nandrolone is a different beast, not only improving muscle growth, but also increasing red blood cell production. Consequently there are definite benefits to the long distance runner who abuses this banned product. On the other side of the coin, to take it would be considered most careless, since Nandrolone is stored in the body fat for months, making it far more likely to be detected than EPO or other steroids.

To the disappointment of many, Hicham El Guerrouj did not compete in the Zurich 5,000 metres on August 17 as expected. However he did race in the 1,500 metres and he certainly did not disappoint anyone with his performance. The world champion ran a superb 3:29.06 to easily defeat Bernard Lagat who ran 3:30.61. But we know that he can do this. That's why it would have been nice to see the Moroccan line up in the longer race. Noah Ngeny was the surprise from the race as he placed twelfth in a sluggish 3:42.80.

We can only guess as to whether or not Hicham would have won the 5,000 metres, but he would have needed to produce something special to defeat the recent world champion Richard Limo who kicked away effortlessly to win a fast race in 12:56.72. Actually it was the fastest time of 2001. The other man to run under thirteen minutes was Mark Bett who achieved a 12:58.72. This was proving to be a strange meeting with the last runners proving to be as famous as the winners. In fifteenth place was Daniel Komen. The former world record holder ran a horrible 13:28.11. There was no doubting now that his career was finished.

The men's steeplechase produced a performance that even outshone the runs of El Guerrouj and Limo. Ali Ezzine struggled to reproduce his form from Canada but he would still be a part of some Moroccan athletics history. He got to view it first hand, although during the latter stages, he could only see from a distance. The results from the 3,000 metres Steeplechase at Zurich were:

Brahim Boulami	7:58.50
Reuben Kosgei	8:03.22
Kipkirui Misoi	8:04.47
Bernard Barmasai	8:05.00
Raymond Yator	8:09.94
John Kosgei	8:12.11
Bouabdallah Tahri	8:12.37
Ali Ezzine	8:12.96
Khamis Abdullah Saifeldin	8:18.86
Ralf Assmus	8:19.32
Tim Broe	8:24.24
Wilson Boit Kipketer	8:27.04

Brahim became the first non Kenyan runner to ever break the eight minute barrier. It was possibly 2001's most surprising result, given that he had just finished tenth nine days earlier in Edmonton. Boulami became the third fastest of all time and only the fourth athlete to break eight minutes. Bernard Barmasai's world record of 7:55.72 suddenly didn't seem too

MOROCCAN SUCCESS; THE KADA WAY

far away.

The Kenyans, led by world champion Kosgei, were as puzzled as anyone that they were made to play second fiddle in *their* event. Kenya had lost big steeplechase races before, but never (in the modern era) by such an emphatic margin. The best Kenyan athletes in the world were unable to compete against the Moroccan.

Ezzine's performance was also unexpected, though on the opposite end of the performance scale. He had been incredibly proud of his run in Canada and maybe that took away some of his hunger for Zurich. Ali had a week to ponder over this result before he raced in Brussels on August 24.

Boulami was also in Brussels and waiting to take him on were many of the top Kenyans, however on this occasion there was no Boit Kipketer and Barmasai. Bernard should have been given a special invitation, meaning that he could have been there in person to congratulate the man who broke his world record. The results from the 3,000 metres steeplechase in Brussels were:

Brahim Boulami	7:55.28
Reuben Kosgei	7:57.29
Stephen Cherono	7:58.66
Kipkirui Misoi	8:01.69
Julius Nyamu	8:07.59
Luis Miguel Martin	8:08.74
Bouabdallah Tahri	8:09.23
Ali Ezzine	8:10.53
Eliseo Martin	8:19.20
Jose Luis Blanco	8:22.73
John Kosgei	8:27.62
Simon Vroemen	8:30.13
Elarbi Khattabi	8:36.44

In just two races Boulami had gone from being a solid, good steeplechase performer to the world record holder! It was one of the more perplexing turnarounds in sport but there it was, right before our eyes. The overall standard of this race was astonishing with Brahim helping to drag two Kenyans under eight minutes, as much as they helped to push him to the new mark. Poor Kipkirui Misoi ran 8:01.69 and finished a distant fourth. Luis Martin broke the Spanish record in sixth place. The select group of athletes to have broken eight minutes for the 3,000 metres steeplechase was now as follows:

Moses Kiptanui
Wilson Boit Kipketer
Bernard Barmasai
Brahim Boulami
Reuben Kosgei
Stephen Cherono

For Kosgei to break through was no great surprise, even though he bettered his personal record by almost six seconds. Given his youth and major titles, many felt that he had this sort of ability. Cherono's result came as almost as big a shock as Boulami's. The Kenyan was only eighteen (turning nineteen on October 15) but his previous best time was recorded in Zurich two years earlier at 8:19.12. He had knocked over twenty seconds off that. Distance wise, this is the equivalent of a ten second improvement at 1,500 metres or close to seventy seconds at 10,000 metres.

Big improvements from youngsters, particularly Kenyans are not uncommon. Some are almost expected, but Cherono's case was a surprise because the twenty seconds he gained did not come during the full two year period from when he recorded his previous best run in Zurich on August 11, 1999. He failed to break 8:25 in 2000 but then had some reasonable results early in 2001, running times of 8:19.23 and 8:20.28 in May. Stephen followed up with an 8:22.98 in Portland on June 3. So far he hadn't competed against the truly world class athletes, but this changed when he competed in Nice on July 9. However Cherono was only able to register an 8:24.58. No wonder I am surprised when he ran 7:58.66 in Brussels forty six days later!

Ali Ezzine went close to his season's best but could only register another eighth place finish. Disappointingly, he

MOROCCAN SUCCESS; THE KADA WAY

concluded his year of competition before the Grand Prix season was over.

Hicham El Guerrouj was far from done. In Brussels he produced a run that was incredible even by his own high standards. Despite a year of true excellence, Hicham had not seriously challenged one of his own world records thus far. In Belgium he set this record straight, making an all out assault on his 3:26.00 from Rome over three years earlier. The outcome hung in the balance, all the way to the line, and not just whether or not the record would go.

Graham Hood from Canada is the man who is going to make the pace for the first 800 metres. He's aiming for a split around 1:50. Steve Ovett sets the scene for the Golden League event; "Now this sort of temperature and these conditions should be perfect for the mile and the 1,500 metres and if they're out for a fast time they're not going to get any better conditions than this tonight."

Off they go with David Lelei the second rabbit behind Hood. El Guerrouj sits third and Lagat fourth. It's the usual procedure. No surprises.

The opening lap is a terrific 53.65. Ovett remarks; "El Guerrouj really hasn't been in the sort of scintillating form that he was maybe three or four years ago, but he's still in a significant shape to take most of these races fairly comfortably, but I've yet to see anybody challenge him down the home straight as Ngeny did in the Olympics and that's when the real pressure is on this man."

The second split from the rabbit Hood is 1:50.08. It's the sort of pace that a world record could be set off.

With 600 metres to go Lagat and William Chirchir are remaining right with Hicham, which is a bit surprising and might even be a little disconcerting for the three times World Champion.

Chirchir begins to drop off just prior to the bell. Lelei takes El

Guerrouj all the way to this point.

Into the last lap Ovett says; "Hicham El Guerrouj, this is his trademark. A long, long, drawn out surge for the line."

The Moroccan is indeed surging, this being highlighted by a 2:46.10 clocking at 1,200 metres, meaning a third lap of 56.02 whilst on world record tempo! However Lagat is still right on his hammer. Hicham continues to accelerate but still cannot shake his rival.

As they're about to enter the home straight Ovett takes up the commentary on this great contest; "Hicham El Guerrouj must sense that he's there. It's not often you see this. It's not often you see El Guerrouj under pressure (now with seventy metres left). Has Lagat got anything in his legs? The crowd realise that he may have because they're standing up. But El Guerrouj is still striding out, he's still working hard and he's going to take it. Lagat just cannot get past the man." The results from the 1,500 metres were:

Hicham El Guerrouj	3:26.12
Bernard Lagat	3:26.34
William Chirchir	3:29.29
Laban Rotich	3:31.64
Driss Maazouzi	3:32.15
Juan Carlos Higuero	3:32.30
Gert-Jan Liefers	3:32.89
Vyacheslav Shabunin	3:33.01
Benjamin Kipkurui	3:33.12
Enock Koech	3:33.43
Abdelkader Hachlaf	3:33.59
Andres Diaz	3:33.64
John Mayock	3:34.43
Jurgen Vandewiele	3:34.93
Reyes Estevez	3:35.61
Paul McMullen	3:36.37

MOROCCAN SUCCESS; THE KADA WAY

Lagat really did run out of his skin on this night, knocking more than two seconds off his personal best. Thus he became the second fastest ever at the distance and kept up with the Moroccan all the way, in much the same manner that Noah Ngeny had done during El Guerrouj's mile world record. Hicham even moved slightly into lane 2 on the home straight, making it fractionally tougher for the Kenyan to get by. The final lap was completed in 53.4 seconds. Bernard was never more than a stride behind, but could never quite get to El Guerrouj. The gap of twenty two hundredths of a second was a little more convincing than it sounds.

How much help had Hicham been to Bernard? That's up for debate. Nevertheless, no matter how much help somebody gets, not many athletes are capable of running a 3:26 over 1,500 metres, period. Chirchir also took a large chunk off his best time that had previously stood at 3:31.02. Maazouzi continued his impressive form in fifth place.

Noah Ngeny was absent and this was a little surprising as the Kenyan had displayed some form at Gateshead five days earlier when he won the 800 metres in 1:45.97. Maybe he'd conceded that he could no longer match the Moroccan and like a previous Algerian, decided that it was best to stay away.

The 3,000 metres was a quality race that saw the winner, Ethiopian Hailu Mekonnen, almost go under 7:30. He clocked 7:30.53 to marginally get the better of his younger countryman Kenenisa Bekele who ran 7:30.67. This was a nice step up for the cross country star as previously he hadn't displayed quite the same potential on the synthetic surface. The nineteen year old figured to be a major player on the Golden League circuit in 2002. Finishing sixth in this highly competitive field was Morocco's Abderrahim Goumri. At twenty five his development was slow but he was now a future prospect for the North Africans at future championships as a 5,000 or 10,000 metres runner. Like Khalid Skah he'd spent a lot of his time in Norway, even competing for the same athletics club IL i BUL. In 1999 Goumri had only been a 7:48.97 athlete but after a year troubled by injuries in 2000 he had come back a different runner.

The 10,000 metres event in Brussels was a shadow of its former self though it remained Kenyan dominated. The surprise was that the Edmonton winner, Charles Kamathi, did not win an average paced race. The world champion clocked 27:26.55, behind Mark Bett and Robert Kipchumba who finished in 27:24.68 and 27:25.55 respectively as Kenya filled the top five spots.

The next week the circuit shifted to Germany and the meeting in Berlin on August 31. El Guerrouj was scheduled to race in the 2,000 metres and many felt that after his Brussels form, another world record attempt might be on the cards. This proved not to be the case as Hicham instead settled into 'racing' mode. Despite clocking a rather modest 4:51.17 he was far too quick for the rest of the small ten man field which was led home by Driss Maazouzi. The Frenchman recorded 4:55.55.

If this was a little sub standard for the above average Moroccan then his next race was anything but. Competing in Rieti on September 2, El Guerrouj was in his element. Going back to the 1,500 metres, Hicham went straight back to sub 3:30. In registering 3:29.08 he totally devastated his opponents as second placed Spaniard Andres Diaz was a long way in arrears with his 3:33.79. It was a shame that we had become so accustomed to this standard of performance that we viewed it as just another El Guerrouj victory. The reality is that such convincing victories in fast times are rarely produced by anybody else, bar the king of the mile.

As is often the case, the Grand Prix final was held in a distant location, Melbourne Australia. The world's best athletes were encouraged to embark on another all Aussie adventure. But this time the IAAF had got things right with a scheduled date of September 9, basically straight after the European season. This was also a sensible decision because the Goodwill Games were held in Brisbane just four days prior. Subsequently some athletes were able to use the Games as a warm up event to shake off the jet lag.

MOROCCAN SUCCESS; THE KADA WAY

El Guerrouj did not race in Brisbane, which saw some bad and reasonable standard distance races. The men's 5,000 metres event was embarrassing with the winner Paul Bitok running 15:26.10. This is not a misprint! Noah Ngeny won a slow mile with a 3:56.64, while the steeplechase was more interesting with Brahim Boulami continuing his magnificent form by winning with an 8:17.73. He was able to hold off his Kenyan Brussels rivals as Reuben Kosgei and Stephen Cherono finished with 8:18.63 and 8:19.98 times.

The same three athletes repeated the positions in Melbourne with Boulami being far too strong on the final lap. His winning time was 8:16.14, comfortably ahead of Kosgei's 8:17.64. This made it four defeats of the Olympic champion within a month so the Kenyans were not at all happy! Next year was going to be an all out war. Could Kenya stop this Moroccan from dominating its pet event?

El Guerrouj's victory was far from his finest, but he nevertheless defeated his Kenyan opponents with minimal fuss. Hicham ran 3:31.25 with Bernard Lagat again second in 3:32.10. Noah Ngeny concluded his poor season with fourth position in 3:34.76. He required a major overhaul during the off season if he was to become a factor in the Moroccan's career again in 2002.

Abdelkader Kada might have been a delighted man. His favourite athlete had produced masterful performances the world over in 2001. This wasn't quite the same scenario, but at least Hicham finished this year off in Australia as a winner.

Does El Guerrouj remain a middle distance specialist next season or does he move up in distances to where the East Africans are arguably better suited? Will moving up to 5,000 metres take away his middle distance kick, therefore making a move back down to 1,500 metres impossible? These were just some of the many questions clouding the mind of Kada at the close of 2001. What was clear was that there was no longer any room for much else. His decision was made. The talents of Abdelkader Kada's coaching would be applied solely to Hicham El Guerrouj from 2002. Ali Ezzine would have to do without him.

Having been under his care for his entire senior career, it was going to be tough for Ali to deal with the split. The twenty three year old should have the majority of his career still ahead of him so choosing his next mentor was going to be all important if he was to keep his dream alive of winning gold in Athens '04.

October 7, 2001. The comeback.

This wasn't the cross country or the track. It was the World Half Marathon Championships in Bristol. There had been no lead up races for Salah Hissou. He was throwing himself straight back into the highest level of competition. He had last competed in these championships way back in 1994. On that occasion the race had helped prepare him for a great 1995 cross country and track season. Salah hoped that 2002 would see a similar outcome.

There were a good many issues for the Moroccan to overcome. Could his suspect left ankle and the rest of his aging body hold up against the rigors of international competition? If so, did he still have the speed in his legs to keep up with the younger generation?

His operation had apparently been a success but since nobody in the Moroccan Federation knew much about such an injury, rehabilitation was an issue. Salah was told to return to training shortly after surgery and it was soon obvious that not enough time for rest was allowed. Hissou experienced discomfort for two to three months after resumption.

However he was feeling better by the Bristol race and was excited at the prospect of racing again. This was a cracking field and a large one, much like a World Cross Country. Salah was able to keep pace with the leading runners in the early stages. He could do this solely on his extraordinary natural ability. Even with little training, a former 10,000 metres world record holder is going to be capable of keeping up with 2:55 km pace for a while. But eventually the questions will be

MOROCCAN SUCCESS; THE KADA WAY

asked. Is your body strong enough to hold the pace? Has it endured enough miles in the preceding months? Did Salah Hissou have enough gas in the tank?

The answers were an emphatic no. Hissou wasn't a factor as he slipped away from the high class opposition, though he didn't exactly hit the wall. By finishing in eleventh place in a time of 61:56, he had at least re-established himself as a world class distance runner. Critically he had no issues with his problematic ankle so the surgery was paying dividends so far. The Moroccan could still be one of the fastest machines. He just required a more thorough service.

One machine that was again finely tuned was a vehicle named Haile Gebrselassie. The Ethiopian added yet another dimension to his repertoire, winning in the fast time of 60:03. It proved that he was more than a track specialist and would be a pointer to his future marathon success. He had only needed one warm up race (the Edmonton 10,000 metres) to get back to his world beating best. To do this after surgery on his achilles tendon would have been considered quite remarkable if anyone else had managed it. Yet nobody in distance running circles was completely surprised by anything that 'the greatest' accomplished any more.

This latest miracle put further doubts on Salah Hissou's hopes of returning to the top on the track. Everything Salah did seemed to be a little behind or a little slower than Haile. Hissou came into the world after Gebrselassie yet arrived into the big time of distance running a year later. The Moroccan was a little slower on the track when they raced each other and usually when they raced apart. Now Salah was proving to be slower in recovery when it came to serious injury. In distance running, timing is all important. This Moroccan was very fast but at times in his career, his timing was very poor.

Gebrselassie had out sprinted his teammate Tesfaye Jifar who clocked 60:04. It was another example of Ethiopia reigning supreme over Kenya and a severely weaker Morocco.

The next two runners were both Africans, but they weren't

fellow Ethiopians, Kenyans nor Moroccans. John Yuda and Hendrick Ramaala ran 60:12 and 60:15 to finish third and fourth correspondingly. They both largely carried the long distance running hopes for their respective countries of Tanzania and South Africa.

The man who finished ahead of Salah Hissou in tenth place is worth noting. Khalid Skah's little legs were still churning over at a good tempo. The time of 61:41 was more than good for a thirty four year old.

Losing to Skah now should be an insult to Hissou, with or without an ankle injury. There was no quick fix for his hurt pride either. His next race was a long way away. The season was over, just when Salah was getting started.

The most important thing now was to buckle down and do the really hard yards. Negative thinking wasn't going to get him back to where he wanted to be. Salah decided to do his own thing and had not requested the services of another coach. This was surprising but with his vast experience it wasn't necessarily a bad idea. After seven seasons at the top he should be able to organise and operate his own training program.

Hissou got through the rest of October without any setbacks, with November and December resulting in highly productive months of training. With each passing day, Salah could feel himself getting stronger. The 2002 World Cross Country Championships were on the horizon.

But the 1999 edition seemed to have left some mental scars. Rather than use the confidence gained from his peak years, Salah decided that the event wasn't a viable goal for him. At least in 2002.

He reached the conclusion that the many injuries and subsequent time off had likely sapped him of his cross country strength. There was also the issue of avoiding injury. One more serious problem would probably end his career. On January 16, 2002, Salah Hissou turned thirty. For an

MOROCCAN SUCCESS; THE KADA WAY

international athlete, this is not a milestone to be celebrated. The sand was rapidly falling through the hour glass. Any time back at the top was likely to be short. If he stayed fit he needed to make the most of it. After a good block of training, Salah was desperate to feel the excitement of regular competition again. So, what would he compete in instead of cross country?

On February 3, 2002, Hissou found himself back on a start line. It was the first time since a Berlin race during the September of '99, that he could have certain confidence in his body, in his fitness levels. But nothing could substitute for the racing that sharpens an athlete. Haile Gebrselassie and Daniel Komen had given the longer races indoors some much needed credibility. Now Salah was giving it a try. Was it worth trying to teach this old dog a new trick?

The race was over 3,000 metres in Stuttgart. Now into the dreaded thirties, there was a slight concern that Hissou might not even be able to keep up with his younger opposition at this relatively short distance. Going from his last race, the half marathon, to this shorter distance, was going to be a shock to the system.

The field wasn't of the highest quality but still had runners of definite class. Most of the world's top long distance runners don't bother with the indoor season, particularly when it is not a year of a World Indoor Championships. These were held every two years, the same seasons as the World Outdoor Championships (this later changed as in 2004 the championships moved to even years to alternate with the outdoor championships.). For any success indoors, an athlete needs to be in good form at a fairly inappropriate time of the year. To peak in March and then do so again in June/July/August for the European outdoor season is not easy. Athletes like Tergat and Hissou have certainly peaked previously around March/April for the World Cross Country and then gone on to have very successful summer track seasons, but this was a strength peak, then a speed peak. These peaks require different forms of training. The training for the strength peak in December/January/February doesn't only help the athlete for the cross country season. This heavy load of training also builds a tremendous base for the runner to call upon in the months ahead, when the focus shifts to speed. To train for the indoor season, Salah Hissou may not have run quite the same level of mileage as in previous years. We would soon see if the heavy training in April/May gave him enough of a base for a successful lengthy Golden League season.

Hicham El Guerrouj and Haile Gebrselassie are good examples of distance runners who have been able to follow up highly successful indoor seasons with an equally successful outdoor one. However these guys are freaks and arguably two of the greatest five distance runners ever. They are also primarily speed based runners as opposed to Hissou and Tergat whose forte is their strength. To perform well on the track, these two needed their strength first of all, to stand a chance of combating the speedsters. In possibly leaving his really heavy bulk training until March, Salah risked not being at his strongest for June. He wasn't going to get three months of pure strength training to build his season platform. Remember that he would likely require at least a few weeks to sharpen up before the outdoor season commenced. This season's training schedule might be a little more like Jan Ullrich's for the Tour De France. Jan was notorious for getting into shape late for his anticipated July peak. The German's natural ability and strong support from his team always enabled him to get away with it!

But training was still training. Whether there was more emphasis on speed work or long miles, running is running. You may have noticed that I don't always describe things very technically! If Salah could avoid injury through to June, he would have enjoyed approximately nine months of regular running. He had not enjoyed such a period for nearly five years. But there was a lot to do before June.

The Stuttgart race was a good one for Hissou. He remembered what it was like to run around sixty one, sixty two second laps with a big crowd cheering him on. Yet this was a totally new experience. Fifteen short 200 metres laps

MOROCCAN SUCCESS; THE KADA WAY

around a tight circuit.

The Moroccan proved he could handle this new format as he remained in contention until the sprint finish, where he didn't fade at all. It was a case of being beaten by younger legs and basic speed. 3,000 metres was too short to expect a victory. Sixth place didn't sound great but Salah should have been happy enough. For the Moroccan it probably felt great just to run fast again. The top six were as follows:

Luke Kipkosgei	7:38.77
Abderrahim Goumri	7:39.58
Million Wolde	7:40.16
Abiyote Abate	7:40.54
Dieter Baumann	7:40.68
Salah Hissou	7:40.80

If it felt bad to lose to thirty four year old Skah, then how bad did it feel now? Fifth placed Baumann was six days shy of his thirty seventh birthday!

Getting beaten by the elderly aside, things were looking up for the experienced Moroccan. One race indoors was not enough, and Salah wanted better than sixth. Hence he went to England and Birmingham for another indoor meeting on February 17. The field for the two mile event was weaker than he had faced in Stuttgart and Salah was more race ready. As such, a better placing was more feasible.

The British crowd saw one of the very best at close to his best. The race wasn't particularly fast, but Salah destroyed his opposition in the latter stages, earning himself a most satisfactory comeback victory. He was far from a spent force.

It was his old quality front running style in full display. The crowd was appreciative, even though he defeated one of its own. The athletes were widely strung out, emphasizing Salah's strength on the day. He had established his winning break by the start of the final 200 metres circuit. Hissou wasn't remotely close to emulating the feats of Gebrselassie and Komen. His time of 8:15.60 just didn't compare, but in this day and age it was good enough. Haile was focusing on his marathon debut in London in April. Daniel was trying to figure out where his form had gone. It wasn't the greatest of victories but it was still a win against an international field. If Salah retired today, he should be content knowing that he had made a triumphant return from a serious ankle injury.

England's John Mayock wasn't far behind in 8:17.06, which was a new British record. The rest were a rabble. Hissou's teammate Mohammed Amyn ran 8:19.57 while Paul Bitok was fourth in a sluggish 8:22.49. Then came another Moroccan Jaquad Gharib, who clocked 8:29.23. Jaquad soon realized that his speed wasn't sufficient for the track and tried his hand on the longer distances of the roads.

It was a nice overall result for Morocco as well as for Hissou. It was a small indicator that the country was getting back to its esteemed position in the long distance track running world of pre Sydney.

That was enough indoor racing for Salah. His focus now shifted to the outdoor Golden League season where he would be truly tested both on the track and off. He had also targeted the African Championships in August as a major goal.

In the meantime, Ali Ezzine's form had lapsed. Regardless, he travelled to Dublin for the short course World Cross Country on March 23. In hindsight, this may not have been a wise decision for the outcome was devastating. Ali placed fifty fourth in the big field, an indictment on a world championship silver medallist. His time of 13:01 was very poor for the albeit difficult 4 kms event.

The runner stealing all the limelight in Ireland was the new sensation Kenenisa Bekele. He won this event with a time of 12:11, finishing seven seconds clear of Luke Kipkosgei. Not only was this a spectacular performance, but it came on the back of his victory in the 12 kms long course event the day before. The Ethiopian was the first man to achieve this double since it had become a possibility in 1998. He was running in the footsteps of Haile Gebrselassie and already he had

MOROCCAN SUCCESS; THE KADA WAY

climbed a mountain that was even too high for his predecessor.

Born on June 13, 1982, it was scary to think just how dominant Bekele may well become. How can a nineteen year old win back to back races of the highest quality which suit a strength runner, therefore usually an older one? Kenenisa had shown track speed too, with a World Junior 3,000 metres record of 7:30.67 at Brussels last season. He was an amazing talent. Like Gebrselassie he was being managed by Jos Hermens.

By the commencement of the European summer season, Ali Ezzine's condition was no better than it was for the cross country season. Returning to the steeplechase for a race at Hengelo on June 2, the Moroccan finished fourth but in a poor time of 8:27.98. He was an absurd distance behind the first two athletes, Kenyan's Reuben Kosgei and the new man on the scene Paul Kipsiele Koech. Both ran excellent times of 8:05.87 and 8:05.91. Ali decided that he was too far off the pace to recover during only a few months so he abandoned the rest of the season. This was highly disappointing but perhaps it was better to train hard while rebuilding his shattered confidence in Morocco than to continue to take a hammering in Europe. There wasn't a major championships this year which probably encouraged him further to make this big decision. Age wasn't against him so this could simply be a lull in his career. He hoped for much better in 2003.

The Hengelo meeting was more notable for a different reason as another tradition looked set to continue. Haile Gebrselassie had broken world records here in the '90's. He arrived in Holland in superb shape, looking surprisingly fresh so soon after his marathon debut. It was decided that to shift straight down to his favourite distance would be too much of a change in pace for his first race after London, so Jos Hermens had set Gebrselassie the goal of breaking a record that he had once held, that of the one hour. It was not a distance record, in that there wasn't a set distance to be completed. The challenge was to see how much distance a runner could cover during the sixty minutes. The event once held some lustre, but in recent years it had become meaningless. As its prestige reduced, more emphasis was placed on the half marathon, which was held on the road. When Arturo Barrios set the record in 1989 it was at a decent standard in comparison to the world records of the 10,000 metres and half marathon. But then the half marathon begun its own annual world championship and the hour barrier was soon broken. Then Paul Tergat made the distance even more famous. Nobody was even remotely interested in the one hour on the track any more. As Haile Gebrselassie lined up in Hengelo, Barrios still held the record. This was a joke, as Haile alone had taken over forty five seconds off Arturo's old 10,000 metres world record. The half marathon record had also improved by over a minute since 1989. This world record would be far inferior to Haile's ones at 5,000 metres and 10,000 metres. Unless he totally obliterated it. In any case another world record would add more legend to his story. Plus he would join the likes of Zatopak, Nurmi, and Hermens. Famous runners who had extended the one hour track world record.

Alas, things didn't go according to script. In the middle of an apparent record run, his achilles injury flared again, causing Gebrselassie to break down and subsequently retire. As it eventuated, his Golden League season was over before it had started with a strong chance that his glittering career might be over with it.

This was grim news of the highest order for distance running fans around the globe. However there was one Moroccan who may have had a smirk on his face.

After Birmingham, Hissou had returned to his native land to engage in some serious altitude training. In Ifrane, Salah went through his paces, making the final preparations that he hoped would bring him success in the high stakes competition of the Golden League. His biological clock said that he was up against it. Not many thirty year olds had enjoyed success at the highest level of track distance running, at least not in recent years. The majority of Kenyans that Hissou would be competing against would be approximately ten years his

MOROCCAN SUCCESS; THE KADA WAY

junior. A couple of disappointing races was all it would take for the Moroccan to feel his age and to feel finished. He had made it through the indoor races quite well, but the competition was set to improve significantly in standard. To offset that, was an anticipated improvement from Hissou, following the few months of solid training. Plus he knew that he could win big races. Mentally, Salah would be strong. Would his body be able to deliver what it once could?

Salah did exactly what he'd done during many seasons of the past. When with Kada they'd targeted a race in the first week of June to kick off the European campaign. As he had in '99, Hissou was racing in Milan over 5,000 metres. The meeting was to be held on June 5.

With the news of Gebrselassie's injury still reverberating, the Golden League season was now potentially an open one for long distance running aspirants. The race in Milan would show that it could be unpredictable as well as lesser in quality to its usual high standards.

Salah Hissou finished second in Milan. That's a good start. He ran 13:17.70, in comparison to the winner's 13:07.12. Not so good.

The field wasn't exactly loaded with class. Even still, the slow times and the time gaps were a big surprise. Either the distance running world had lost its mind or this was a once off. The victor was Kenyan Benjamin Maiyo who won with an ease that he couldn't have previously even dreamt of. What was just as surprising was Hissou's advantage over the third placed runner. The new superstar Kenenisa Bekele struggled to a 13:26.58.

Something was definitely amiss on this night. The double world cross country champion running 13:26 for 5,000 metres is hard to comprehend. The most logical explanation was that the Ethiopian was tired. He had peaked for the cross country season and expecting a runner to carry his peak through for a few months was asking a bit too much. Particularly one that was still eight days shy of his twentieth birthday.

Kenenisa went home and skipped the Golden League season. Salah's major two anticipated rivals were now disposed of, without the Moroccan even attempting to deliver a killer kick down. But Maiyo would need to be watched, and there were always other Kenyans ready to step up and give Hissou a hard time. Besides, 13:17 wasn't truly world class. Running that sort of time was unlikely to win him any Golden League races. Most importantly Salah needed to improve before he started focusing on other athletes.

Salah was well aware of the progress that was required. It was over three weeks before he raced again, and this was a much more serious affair. The venue was the famous Bisslet Stadium in Oslo and the date was June 28. The distance was again 5,000 metres. Maiyo was in the field and certain to be a threat although it was unknown whether he would be the main competition to Salah.

Hissou managed to pass this initial test. He defeated Maiyo, reversing the spanking he copped in Milan. Hissou was also the first Moroccan across the line but there remained far tougher questions for Salah to answer.

This is his first race in the really big time since 2000 and he is immediately determined to make an impact. Hissou is the runner who follows the pacemaker at the start. The pace is a frantic one, 2:34 for the first km. While the rabbits remain at the front, the pace tends to remain fast, certainly too fast to kick down from. This is the case here as another 2:34 km brings the lead pack to 2,000 metres in 5:08, or 12:50 schedule.

The rabbit drops out and understandably the fast tempo drops also. Salah takes over as the third km is covered in 2:40. Hissou looks composed, but there is a pack of Kenyans snapping at his heels.

Sammy Kipketer takes up the pace soon after and the fourth km is clocked at 2:37. Nobody endeavours to make a long run for home as the contenders ready themselves for a final lap

MOROCCAN SUCCESS; THE KADA WAY

sprint. This is not going to be Salah's preferred way of finishing, but this is his first 5,000 metres race of this quality for a long time. He is on his upper limits, trying to stay on thirteen minute pace.

At the bell Hissou is near the lead, but is soon overtaken by the Kenyans who race away from him. It is not a destroyed runner who eventually finishes sixth in a time of 13:01.10, rather an athlete without a kick. Whether the thirty year old could rekindle such a weapon was doubtful. But at least Salah still had his track threshold strength. The best performers from the 5,000 metres in Oslo were:

Benjamin Limo	12:57.50
Sammy Kipketer	12:57.90
John Kibowen	12:58.61
Paul Bitok	12:58.94
Mark Bett	13:00.38
Salah Hissou	13:01.10
Benjamin Maiyo	13:02.95
Assefa Mezgebu	13:04.15
Abderrahim Goumri	13:06.38
William Kiptoo Kirui	13:18.06
Ismail Sghyr	13:19.52
Roberto Garcia	13:20.00
Alberto Garcia	13:22.77

Hissou couldn't manage much under sixty seconds for the last lap, while his opposition exposed this deficiency. The winner was the silver medallist from Seville, Benjamin Limo. He had arguably improved since then with Kipketer being his only challenger on the home straight. The fourth athlete to run sub thirteen is worth noting. At thirty two years old, Paul Bitok recorded a personal best. After a decade at the top he had finally gone under thirteen minutes. It was a great personal achievement for the double Olympic silver medallist.

Assefa Mezgebu was the Ethiopian who hoped to challenge in the absence of Gebrselassie and Bekele, but here the Edmonton silver medallist was well off the pace. The early signs were that Salah's 2002 opposition would be solely

Kenyan, though the season was only just starting.

Not needing to show as much concern for his opposition was Hicham El Guerrouj. Rejuvenated from the sensational results of 2001, he skipped the indoor season and started outdoors on May 26 in Eugene. There was a 5,000 metres event at this meeting but this season would again be one of no surprises. The Moroccan would focus solely on the 1,500 metres and mile. Some might suggest that specifically he and Abdelkader Kada were chasing the dollars on offer during the Golden League season.

Hicham settles into his customary third position behind two rabbits. Lagat and Chirchir are next as the first lap of the mile is timed at 57.10. The rabbits are really taking off now and there is a significant break of about ten metres back to the Moroccan after 500 metres. Already we can see that El Guerrouj is not in peak shape. Soon the gap is closer to twenty metres to the pacesetters.

Clearly Hicham has given up on any sort of fast time and will now race tactically for the win as Lagat surprisingly goes past him. Very un El Guerrouj like. Chirchir is clipping his heels as the lead is twenty five metres over the proper pack by 700 metres. Yet the rabbit's time is only 1:54.70 at the half. It's around 1:58.50 for Hicham. The now sole rabbit is slowing up on lap three in an attempt to let them catch up. Suddenly with 550 metres remaining, Hicham moves out and passes Bernard. Together with Chirchir, they have cleared out by about ten metres from the rest. The rabbit is jogging in the second lane and is caught at the bell, which is hit in 2:56.10. The kick down is very much on and Chirchir is dropping off ever so slightly. Now Lagat also loses two metres by the back straight but entering the final curve the race is still alive. Suddenly Hicham looks to be slowing and Lagat looks to take him. El Guerrouj moves out into lane two pushing Lagat out further but forgetting that he is opening up the inside for Chirchir who is back with them. Lagat hits his wall with fifty metres to go, yet Chirchir almost draws level before El Guerrouj edges away over the final twenty metres. The results of the first three were:

MOROCCAN SUCCESS; THE KADA WAY

Hicham El Guerrouj   3:50.89
William Chirchir   3:51.03
Bernard Lagat   3:52.63

Hicham came out of the blocks a little sluggish in 2002 though still prevailed. It was a good example of his current day dominance that in most cases he had to be well off his best to lose. The last lap was a strong 54.79 and the large American crowd was highly appreciative of the great contest that it had witnessed. William embraced Hicham, who then went to Bernard where the two exchanged pleasantries.

His next race was another mile event and it didn't come until that Oslo meeting. Bernard Lagat and William Chirchir didn't attend so it was considered to be a non contest if Hicham had been able to round himself into top shape in the month following Eugene. One Kenyan who was contesting at Bislett was Noah Ngeny so it would be intriguing to see how he performed.

For the second straight race El Guerrouj was unsuccessful in running sub 3:50 though he did win more convincingly in this instance. The Moroccan recorded a 3:50.12 to finish over ten metres clear of Rotich whose time was 3:51.99. Putting in a good performance in third place was Moroccan Abdelkader Hachlaf who ran 3:52.42.

Unfortunately Ngeny was struggling even more so now as his 3:57.39 was only fast enough for eleventh place. Noah was having problems getting his body right after a car accident in Kenya last November that left him with damage to his back and pelvis. It remained to be seen whether or not he could return to the upper echelon of his event.

Hicham was still the best around but not yet at his own upper echelon of performance as his victory in Sheffield, England showed on June 30. Racing a B grade field, El Guerrouj allowed himself to take it easily and not push too hard. It was a site rarely seen since 1996. When he eventually stopped the clock at 3:40.20 it was hard to believe. It would be almost more realistic to hear of Hicham running a 3:40 mile than a

3:40 1,500 metres. Finishing second was Kenyan Michael Too who registered 3:41.03.

There were more names of note in the 3,000 metres but the standard was much the same. Salah went into the race as a potential favourite because none of the Kenyans who had defeated him in Oslo were here. The pace was very slow throughout, as most of the seventeen man field remained in contention for the win, well into the final km.

The last lap was a great test of Hissou's finishing speed and he showed some nice improvements from Bislett to finish second in a bunch sprint. The first four athletes were separated by less than a second with Salah's countryman Mohammed Amyn taking the victory in 7:57.83. The self coached Moroccan recorded a 7:58.30. Craig Mottram, Tim Broe and Ismail Sghyr all came in within a full second of Hissou. Daniel Komen was still in the doldrums, running 8:03.46 in twelfth place.

The following week the cream of the athletics world ventured to Paris for the Saint-Denis meeting on the 5th of July. The European season was in full swing. Hissou was hungry to keep racing and improve further on the progress he'd seen thus far.

Benjamin Limo was aiming for a second consecutive Golden League win, while his world champion teammate Richard Limo remained absent. His twenty two year old countryman, Abraham Chebii, was making his first appearance of the season at this level after finishing sixth in the Sheffield 3,000 metres. The Moroccans hoped they could give the best Kenyans more of a contest this time around.

The race is run in a similar fashion to Oslo only it's a little slower. The pace is constant and solid though not startling. The first 2,000 metres are reached in 5:12 and 3,000 metres in 7:52 with Limo leading.

Hissou now takes up the front running, with support from his teammates, Goumri and Amyn. However the pressure isn't on to any great extent as the 4,000 metres split arrives in 10:29

MOROCCAN SUCCESS; THE KADA WAY

with Limo still racing comfortably.
However many of the others are struggling. Morocco is proving to be a force again with Hissou, Amyn and Goumri all in contention going into the last lap. Limo sits and waits. The real fireworks don't even start until the final 200 metres. Salah is unable to go with the speed. Despite the other Moroccans putting up a good fight, in the end, they are never able to gap Limo, and the Kenyan is able to coast through for the victory on the final straight. His winning time is 13:02.34. Pretty good, but the last lap of around fifty eight seconds isn't amazing. Behind him are Goumri, 13:03.17, Amyn 13:03.80, and Chebii 13:05.08.

Hissou trundled in for fifth place and a time of 13:05.58. It wasn't bad, but was some way off his halcyon days of the '90's. Still, it wasn't yet time to pack up and go home. He was being very competitive and would endeavour to produce a better performance in the months ahead. Tactically, it was clear that just being with the leaders in the latter stages wasn't going to give him a chance of a victory. He needed to be more ambitious. Of course, there was no point in having a tremendous plan if you didn't have the talent required to follow it through.

Salah was still an elite athlete, even if winning a big race was now beyond his capabilities. He was struggling on the final lap, but others were having bigger problems well before the bell. Well behind him in Paris were athletes such as Mark Bett, Luke Kipkosgei, El Hassan Lahssini, Assefa Mezgebu and Benjamin Maiyo.

Lahssini was one of the many Moroccans now running for France. As the depth in Moroccan men's distance running became greater, it became much harder for athletes to force themselves onto their national teams, hence numerous Moroccans had recently abandoned their country in an attempt to further their international careers.

Mezgebu was finding the European season tough going, but to be fair, he tended to excel more at the 10,000 metres. Even still, I don't believe that 13:14.43 and ninth position would have impressed him. Maiyo's current form highlighted the potential fragility of an international long distance runner. His Milan victory was exactly one month ago and now he was clocking 13:22.79. His form had completely deserted him.

Returning to magnificent form was El Guerrouj who won the 1,500 metres with a brilliant 3:29.96. He helped to drag Lagat into a faster rhythm and the Kenyan finished in 3:31.59. The rest, led by Mehdi Baala's 3:33.55 were at least twenty five metres adrift of the Moroccan. They weren't in the same class.

Abdelkader Kada would have been extremely happy with this result as Hicham had been able to clearly establish his dominance once again in an illustrious field. If there was even better to come then it was almost impossible to see him losing, with his rivals appearing to be at their least threatening since the 1998 season.

On the 12th of July, 2002, the Golden League took its show to Rome. The Olympic stadium was one of Hissou's favourites and Salah soaked up the atmosphere as he stood near the 200 metres mark on the track that had also hosted a World Athletics Championships. The actual track surface was different to the one that the Moroccan had made his reputation on with his breakthrough performance in 1996. A new synthetic track had recently been laid down. In previous editions the Moroccan had single handedly taken on the best that Kenya had to offer. He never failed to put in a good performance. It was perhaps appropriate then, that Salah should be the only Moroccan in this field. There was no Amyn and no Goumri (both raced four days later in Stockholm with Abderrahim winning in an excellent time of 13:00.76). It was Hissou's moment. He wanted something special from this meet. For any extra sign of this you only had to look at his uniform on this night. The Golden League wasn't a championship and to most fans the athletes were really competing for Adidas, Nike or Asics. These were the brands that were paraded on the sportswear of the world's best athletes at these European affairs. But here, Hissou proudly sported the colours of Morocco. The green Nike singlet

MOROCCAN SUCCESS; THE KADA WAY

displayed 'MOROCCO' across the top, above his bib number '73 Roma.' Having been denied the opportunity to compete in Sydney and Edmonton, Rome had became 'his championship.'

The field is unusually large. Twenty five athletes take to the line, with at least two of these being rabbits. The Kenyans stride to the front and Hissou settles into sixth position, right behind Benjamin Limo. As in Oslo and Paris, the pace is consistently good in the early stages. There is no point trying to surge when the laps are regularly in the sixty one second range. Sensibly, Salah tries to relax and feel at one with the rhythm of the race. Running sub thirteen minutes. It is what he's born to do.

The recent race in Paris suggested a changing in Moroccan fortunes. Kenya had not had things all its own way. The one constant had been Benjamin Limo, the comfortable winner of Oslo and Paris. He was in great form, proving unstoppable in the latter stages of the 5,000 metres. His kick wasn't an explosion like Gebrselassie's in the '90's but instead he seemed to glide past his competitors with his short, choppy stride. It may have been ungainly, but it was getting the job done. Somebody was going to need to do something out of the ordinary to defeat him.

Richard Limo was competing for the first time this season, which meant double trouble for the opposition. One Limo had been more than enough in the previous races but Richard was arguably a better runner than Benjamin. His presence meant an even greater likelihood of a Kenyan victory.

The race continues along at a fast cadence, each km being covered in around 2:37. Runners are slowly being dropped. As they enter the last three laps, less than ten competitors remain in contact.

We are set for a Paris repeat with another Limo win in a tick over thirteen minutes. Only the man in the red singlet poses any sort of a threat to this result and that threat is based more on a past reputation. But the Moroccan looks bouncy as he starts to round the field with 1,000 metres to go. The 4,000 metres split is 10:27 with Benjamin Limo coasting along in the lead.

Woooooosh! That's what Benjamin Limo now hears as Salah Hissou flies past on the eleventh lap of the 5,000 metres. The Kenyan is not following the Moroccan, for this is beyond his capabilities, as it is the rest of that field in Rome. The pace had slowed slightly, to approximately sixty two's and sixty three's, so a gap immediately opens up as Salah goes into overdrive, with the next 200 metres being covered in twenty nine seconds!

No wonder he's escaped the Kenyan's clutches. In the space of one lap he's put twenty metres on the Limo's and much more to the many others. "They've got to make their move now because he's looking very good indeed Steve," declared the British broadcaster.

"They're not going to catch him," replied Ovett. "I think he's learned his lesson from the last two Golden Leagues when he left it too late. This time he's thrown the gauntlet down when it really hurts with two laps to go, and Limo looks a spent man. I don't think he's going to take him tonight."

It is one thing to break away. It is another to hold the gap. There is a reason why athletes rarely take off with over a lap to go in long distance races. The build up of lactic acid. It's a rare runner indeed that has the capacity to carry out a long run for home at such a highly sustained speed. Hissou had been able to do this in the past. Could he successfully turn back the clock?

A definitive yes is the answer as Salah careers away. The full power in his stride is back. This is a beautiful thing to watch for distance running purists.

The Moroccan clocks 59.21 seconds for the penultimate lap. Not many can do this, with the knowledge they still have another 400 metres to survive. Yet Hissou is strong and his lead is significant. He's now about twenty five metres clear of

MOROCCAN SUCCESS; THE KADA WAY

the Limo's, both of whom have raced away from the rest of the pack.

There isn't a stunning sprint to conclude proceedings, but the power remains on, all the way to the line. A 60.09 second last lap completes a comfortable victory and the fastest time in the world this year. The smile of satisfaction is one of the more sincere emotions that Salah has ever displayed. He felt unbelievably great to be back on top.

It turned out that winning a big race was not beyond a thirty year old Salah Hissou's capabilities. He had proved that just once, he could do it, with or without Abdelkader Kada.

Greg Rowlerson

The Three Letters That Taint Distance Running

Hissou had regained a spot amongst the world's best distance runners. His Rome romp was clearly the best performance over 5,000 metres during the last couple of seasons. The time of 12:55.85, though quite fast, was not what made it so impressive. As Ovett said, "under thirteen minutes, now almost common place, which was a far cry from my day when it was almost unbelievable." It was the way in which it and the victory were produced that made it special. "That was a magnificent run really," acknowledged Britain's former 800 metres Olympic champion.

There are plenty of runners who can run similar standard times to Salah Hissou over 5,000 metres and even over 10,000 metres. But it is the way in which he won in Rome (and has won other races) that separates him from many of his rivals on the all time lists. There simply aren't many athletes in top class international distance running who can make the long run for home and sustain it. For every ten or so runners who can run a fast last lap off a thirteen minute pace, there is only one type of runner who can do what Hissou did on this night in Rome. Running on the upper limits of his enormous threshold capacity, Salah clocked 2:28.22 for the final 1,000 metres. It was a nice reminder to the distance running world of his great quality.

It is worth emphasizing that despite firing on all cylinders, Salah's last lap was *only* 60 seconds. It highlights his lack of basic top line speed. He ran a faster last lap in the '97 Athens final after running twice the distance, yet he seemed to be dawdling in comparison to Rome '02. This highlights the quality of the opposition of then as compared to now. It also highlights how very good Hissou was in the 1990's. Yes, almost anyone who was any good in 2002 was competing in the Rome 5,000 metres, but 2001 and 2002 had seen a drop off in standards in men's track distance running. In the late '90's there were Gebrselassie, Komen and Tergat, all of whom had set new standards. In 2000, Saidi-Sief performed brilliantly, ensuring that the 3,000 and 5,000 metres events

MOROCCAN SUCCESS; THE KADA WAY

remained at a remarkably high level. Consider the list of men's distance runners who weren't competing or would have zero impact on the 2002 Golden League season for various reasons. There were Haile Gebrselassie, Kenenisa Bekele, Paul Tergat, Ali Saidi-Sief, Mohammed Mourhit, Daniel Komen, Ali Ezzine, Noah Ngeny and Million Wolde. These weren't runners that were all old and past it. This list in many ways had dominated recent track racing. Some were also expected to be the sport's flag bearers of the next few years. To take such an illustrious list of runners out of European competition was obviously going to have some effect on the Golden League distance running standard. There were still quality runners for an athlete such as Salah Hissou to defeat, but the absolute pinnacle of track distance running performance had dipped slightly. The results of the top ten from the Rome 5,000 metres were:

Salah Hissou	12:55.85
Benjamin Limo	12:57.24
Richard Limo	12:57.52
Sammy Kipketer	13:01.56
Abraham Chebii	13:03.01
John Yuda	13:03.62
John Kibowen	13:04.13
Alberto Garcia	13:10.90
Assefa Mezgebu	13:13.18
Driss El Himer	13:16.31

Not surprisingly, Benjamin was able to out kick his brother. The gap of 1.39 seconds to Hissou wasn't a fair reflection on the dominance of the Moroccan. The Limo's only made a big impression on his lead in the last fifty metres. The surging final km was even tough enough to drop Sammy Kipketer, never an easy thing to do. The Tanzanian John Yuda managed to split the Kenyans in sixth place. This was a great effort considering that his domain of excellence was really the half marathon on the roads. Mezgebu continued his very uninspiring season. He was made to carry the burden of the responsibility of Ethiopian leadership and hadn't adapted well to the added pressure, without Haile Gebrselassie for company. As a whole, the Ethiopian men's contingent was proving to be the big disappointment of the athletics season.

There was little debate that Salah Hissou's display in Rome was the best long distance track running performance seen so far in 2002. But other matters would soon take the public's interest, over anything produced on an athletics track. The Golden League headed to Monaco for its next meeting on July the 19th, but as its athletes readied themselves for battle, there broke news of a doping scandal. Mohammed Mourhit had tested positive to the banned substance erythropoietin, otherwise known as EPO or Epogen. Now we knew why he was a late withdrawal from the Rome meeting.

The Belgium champion had failed a surprise test which took place before the World Half Marathon Championships in May. The event was held in Brussels in front of his *home* fans.

Sometimes sporting stories that seem too good to be true are just that. Whilst Mourhit was a talented junior, he just wasn't able to go on and quite bridge the gap that existed to the world's best distance runners at senior level.

Early on, Said Aouita guided him. Mohammed said of his idol, "Said Aouita really inspired me. I trained with him for four years. We followed the same program. I learned a lot from him. He is a great champion. He always told me that if I continue to train hard, to be as willing and determined as well as nice as I am now, I would break his records and approach the world marks." However by the end of his Moroccan career, Mourhit still had a personal best 5,000 metres time of only 13:29.20, produced in Oslo during 1991.

He blamed reoccurring injuries for his delayed improvement whilst being a Moroccan athlete, suggesting that his late career improvements came as a result of realising and amending this problem. Mohammed had discovered that one of his legs was longer than the other.

However, it's unlikely that Mourhit spent most of his time injured during the first half of the decade, since he managed to fit in national championship victories at 5,000 metres in

MOROCCAN SUCCESS; THE KADA WAY

1993 and 1,500 metres in 1992 and 1995.

When he started competing for Belgium in 1997 he immediately began showing signs of great promise, particularly in cross country where he placed fifth at the World Championships in Turin. He also placed fifth in the World Half Marathon where he clocked an impressive time of 1:00.18. But it was in 1999 when things seriously changed. Nearing his twenty ninth birthday, Mohammed became a force to be reckoned with. His form improved throughout the European season and in Seville he qualified impressively for the 5,000 metres final, winning his heat. Mourhit had never before threatened for a major championship title, but here in a high quality race that produced a championship record he finished third, collecting his first major medal. He was in contention for the gold all the way to the home straight.

Greater success still lay ahead for this ex Moroccan. Shortly after the World Championships Mourhit became the seventh fastest 10,000 metres runner in history when he ran 26:52.30 in Brussels. The Belgiums were more than happy to claim him as their own as this not surprisingly smashed the European record. Twice during 1997 Mohammed had raced at the fastest venues for this event and his best time was a 27:17.09 from Oslo.

Mourhit had previously been a strong cross country runner but nobody ever considered him a potential winner of the World Cross Country. In the 1998 race he'd finished eighth followed by a seventh place result in 1999. Yet in 2000, Mohammed shocked the running world when he became the world champion, ousting Paul Tergat from his pedestal in the process. It was the first time since 1994 that Tergat had been defeated in the championships.

Mourhit had reached the rarified air of a distance running superstar. Many of us believed that much of this had been achieved due to the many miles run in rarified air. In other words, enduring plenty of high altitude training.

The glory continued to rain down on Mohammed. His next

major accomplishment was a 12:49.71 over 5,000 metres in Brussels on August 25, 2000. He became the fourth fastest ever at the distance, whilst beating the career best times of Paul Tergat and Salah Hissou. This result further improved his recent personal best of 12:56.60 from Oslo.

In 2001, Mourhit won a silver medal in the World Indoors over 3,000 metres and defended his world cross country title, much to the disgust of the Kenyans. Even after his thirtieth birthday Mourhit seemed to be improving.

But some good things must come to an end.

With the public being made aware of the positive drug test, the 'clean' distance runners would be a secondary story in the sports pages, no matter what happened in Monaco. Nevertheless the show must go on. Nobody is bigger than the sport.

Salah Hissou moved down to 3,000 metres, where he encountered many of the athletes he had faced in Rome. The race witnessed something strange, though Salah had seen it before. There were two rabbits in the field and they set off at sixty seconds per lap tempo. Only one runner went with them, a Kenyan named Benjamin Maiyo. The three 'leaders' went through the first km in 2:29.63, with the rest of the field lagging about twenty five metres in arrears. Hissou had seen Maiyo race successfully as a front runner to his detriment in Milan.

Sammy Kipketer makes a brief attempt to make some inroads but the lead remains about the same for Maiyo. It is surprising to not see Salah go with the rabbits. The fourth last lap is a fast 59.64. Consequently Maiyo drops five metres behind Martin Keino. With his lead now thirty metres the question remaining is can he sustain this lead on his own?

Perhaps attempting to replicate his last race, Hissou moves to the front of the group with 900 metres to go and starts pushing the pace. But 3,000 metres is too short an event for the Moroccan. He will need more speed as opposed to more

MOROCCAN SUCCESS; THE KADA WAY

strength to burn off a field at the end of a 3,000 metres instead of a 5,000 metres. Salah is unable to escape from the field. Nevertheless the British broadcaster becomes a little excited and declares, "Well if anybody can catch him, it is Hissou. He ran a great last 600 metres last week in Rome but they've got to work together if they're going to catch him now."

With Maiyo's assisting pacesetters out of the race, he is starting to tire. He clocks 63.77 and 62.61 second laps yet as he hears the bell, his lead is still massive. However a horde of runners are grouped behind Hissou, waiting to launch an attack.

Down the back straight they go for it with Salah taking them to the curve before being well beaten. With 300 metres left, Maiyo's lead had been reduced to a still significant space of twenty five metres. Alas, this is swallowed up in no time. On the bend Ukrainian Sergey Lebed makes the break from the pack and appears set for the victory. He soon takes the fading Kenyan, but the pack is still coming. In the last fifty metres, Benjamin Limo comes out of hiding and with his short quick strides, he powers away to another win. It is his third Golden League win of the season. His finishing kick is absolutely frightening. The top twelve are as follows:

Benjamin Limo	7:34.72
Sergey Lebid	7:35.06
Salah El Ghazi	7:35.71
Sammy Kipketer	7:35.91
Paul Bitok	7:35.94
Abraham Chebii	7:36.11
Abderrahim Goumri	7:36.25
Mohammed Amyn	7:36.52
Salah Hissou	7:36.98
James Kwalia	7:37.18
Craig Mottram	7:37.30
Benjamin Maiyo	7:37.94

The victor's time was the fastest of the season, surprising given the spate of sub 7:30 performances we'd seen in recent years. El Ghazi showed that there was another Salah with tremendous ability. He was the first of four Moroccans in the top ten.

This was another good performance by Hissou, despite only a ninth placing. This distance wasn't long enough for the thirty year old to hope to win against a quality field but his time still showed decent speed in his legs. The signs were good as he came to the end of his initial European campaign. Salah was on his way back to Africa to compete at the African Championships in Tunisia.

Hicham El Guerrouj was also in Monte Carlo to compete in the 1,500 metres and Bernard Lagat was ready to take him on. The Kenyan had skipped the Rome race when the Italians had held a mile event. El Guerrouj seemed to be getting better and better with each race as the results of the top ten confirmed:

Hicham El Guerrouj	3:48.28
William Chirchir	3:49.49
Rui Silva	3:49.50
Laban Rotich	3:50.16
Cornelius Chirchir	3:50.69
Reyes Estevez	3:51.82
Abdelkader Hachlaf	3:52.20
Juan Carlos Higuero	3:52.49
Bouabdallah Tahri	3:52.95
Hudson de Souza	3:52.97

Hicham had immediately settled into third position behind the Kenyan rabbits David Lelei and Sammy Mutai. The time of 54.98 was the first lap split. Many of the others stayed in contact with Hudson de Souza of Brazil who was doing particularly well to stay with the Moroccan as the second split registered 1:51.96. With 500 metres remaining, there were three athletes still with Hicham, but then Mutai pulled out wide and El Guerrouj began to clear away.

The third lap split was timed at 2:49.99 when suddenly, Hicham surged to a fifteen metre advantage upon entering the back straight. Rui Silva and William Chirchir started to

MOROCCAN SUCCESS; THE KADA WAY

give chase, but even with the leader stagnating a little, they made very little impression. 3:32.80 was the 1,500 metres time for El Guerrouj. His Rome victory was very convincing with Chirchir stealing second place from Silva on the line. Thirty three year old Rotich remained a very good consistent athlete as he battled against all the sub thirties! The Kenyan names appeared to be becoming familiar now with another Chirchir (Cornelius) making a middle distance impact.

Back to Monaco where the French crowd saw the best race in this discipline so far in '02 as another Kenya vs. Morocco chapter was written into athletics history. Lagat had not displayed any great form recently and so it was a somewhat bolt from the blue to have him challenge El Guerrouj so strongly when the Moroccan was also putting in his season's best result. This wasn't far from world record territory for the top two. The depth of the field was also magnificent as the first six times showed:

Hicham El Guerrouj	3:27.34
Bernard Lagat	3:27.91
Rui Silva	3:30.07
Cornelius Chirchir	3:30.24
William Chirchir	3:30.88
Driss Maazouzi	3:31.45

Most of the athletes were quickly dropped after the pacesetters concocted a 53.04 first lap. It was Lagat who sat in position A, behind the two leading Kenyans with his Moroccan rival following next and he being tracked by Chirchir. These five were quite close to one another and were not surprisingly going away from the others. Steve Ovett observed that, "the pacemaking is really laying it on a plate for El Guerrouj and does detract from the racing but nevertheless, great performances from anyone who's tried to keep up with him."

The next split was timed at 1:49.82 with the three contenders still close together. Ovett commented about the importance of the third lap, "Well it's on world record pace if they keep this rhythm going but this is crucial this third lap is kept to a reasonable speed. They can tend to let it drop and that's when records are lost. You can see now that El Guerrouj is moving wide as if he sensed that the pace is dropping. There are not many athletes who can run a really hard third lap and El Guerrouj should really take this race by the scruff of the neck if he's going for a world record and get out there and really start pushing it on."

With 500 metres remaining Hicham did take off, shooting past Lagat and the final rabbit, quickly destroying the field. The time of 2:45.78 was his 1,200 metres split after an excellent 55.96 third lap. By now he had over five metres on Lagat. Bernard closed in the final 150 metres but the Moroccan still won again. The last lap of 54.80 was just awesome off that tempo. Ovett further commented post race, "This is his trademark. He goes with about 400 or 500 to go and they just don't go with him when that initial acceleration goes. Lagat lost about six or seven metres there in that 100 metres. They all know it's coming, which is even more bewildering."

For Bernard, it was his second fastest time ever while for Hicham, it was merely his fifth quickest! Knowing that the major part of his season extended to almost a period of three months, Kada had done a tremendous job in getting El Guerrouj into peak shape a little slower this time around. The victory made it four Golden League wins with the next meeting in Zurich nearly one month away. It was a handy little phase where the pair now had to recharge the batteries and work towards another peak that would need to last thirty days in order to finish the year well at the Grand Prix Final in Paris.

Moroccan success in men's middle distance running continued on July 21 in Kingston, Jamaica where Yassine Bensghir won the World Junior Championships gold medal in the 1,500 metres by a full second. His victorious time was a 3:40.72, which was concluded with a final 300 metres split of 40.15.

There were plenty of good times being run in the absence of Ali Ezzine in the men's 3,000 metres steeplechase during 2002. On May 15 in Doha, Qatar, an outstanding Kenyan

MOROCCAN SUCCESS; THE KADA WAY

battle took place with the top eight finishers being:

Wilson Boit Kipketer	8:05.98
Reuben Kosgei	8:06.58
John Kosgei	8:08.13
Stephen Cherono	8:08.73
Paul Kipsiele Koech	8:09.05
Julius Nyamu	8:11.13
Thomas Kiplitany	8:12.91
Khamis Abdullah Saifeldin	8:29.67

After starting this season strongly, the Olympic champion Reuben Kosgei hurt his left achilles that adversely affected his year. His problem persisted into 2003 and he would not race at the Kenyan trials, yet under the wild card system he was able to line up in Paris.

Brahim Boulami started 2002 in red hot form when he clocked 8:04.51 for victory in Portland on May 18. Cherono put in another terrific performance here, running 8:05.75.

These races led to a confrontation between Boit Kipketer and Boulami in Ostrava on June 12. Kenya finally got the better of Boulami when Wilson clocked 8:06.14 to Brahim's 8:07.91. Yet the battle was only just beginning.

The biggest steeple race of the season had come on July 16 in Stockholm, when the following nine runners broke 8:20:

Wilson Boit Kipketer	8:00.56
Brahim Boulami	8:00.77
Stephen Cherono	8:01.65
Saad Shaddad Al-Asmari	8:08.14
Julius Nyamu	8:11.82
Paul Kipsiele Koech	8:15.00
Kipkirui Misoi	8:16.71
Thomas Kiplitany	8:17.62
Antonio David Jimenez	8:17.77

It was a good comeback victory from Wilson after he'd placed third in 8:11.27 at Lausanne on July 2, behind Ezekiel

Kemboi, 8:10.32, and Reuben Kosgei, 8:10.36. The clash between the first three in Sweden was of the highest quality and in the end, Boit Kipketer again defeated the world record holder. Yet arguably the most incredible run was from Saudi Arabian Al-Asmari, who achieved a personal best at the age of thirty three. He ran just inside his 8:08.26 that he'd run at the same venue five years earlier.

This Stockholm race had set up the Monaco encounter just three days later and it produced perhaps the most exciting finish to any steeple event ever run. So far during his young career, Stephen Cherono just couldn't quite defeat Boulami, though on this occasion he was doubly determined to do so. The two men pushed themselves into the rare sub eight minute zone which would usually guarantee that others would remember the entire race. It was only the final metres that would stick in the memories of most who saw it, for Cherono hit the line to record an outstanding personal best of 7:58.10. The only thing to detract from this performance was Boulami edging him out in 7:58.09! These were the fifth and sixth fastest times ever recorded. Also for the second consecutive race a thirty three year old registered a personal best. Holland's Simon Vroeman ran 8:06.91. It was a result that virtually came out of nowhere, considering his previous best was 8:13.45. He became the fastest non Kenyan and Moroccan ever!

Many of the best African runners went back to their continent for the August African Championships in Tunisia. Salah Hissou had never competed in these championships but in 2002 he had a desire to compete in the World Cup. To qualify, he had to win the 5,000 metres at the African Championships.

The World Cup in athletics sounds more significant than it is in reality, with only one athlete from each continent or area of the world to race in each event. It decides many of the races before they have been run and is often like the Grand Prix final in that it doesn't rate alongside the biggest European meetings of the year. Since 1994, the championship has been held every four years in an attempt to fill in for the World

MOROCCAN SUCCESS; THE KADA WAY

Championships and Olympic Games. This it will never be able to do. With all the other championships taking place in this 'off' year (African Champs, Commonwealth Games, European Champs, etc) I do not see the relevance of a World Cup.

It did hold some meaning when it was first introduced in 1977, as the World Championships did not exist. Steve Ovett won the 1,500 metres in 1977 and 1981 and had to defeat John Walker and Olaf Beyer to win the second time, so there was some significant competition. Miruts Yifter won the 5,000 and 10,000 metres in 1977 and 1979. But in the modern era the cup has become a throw away event. Noureddine Morceli won the 1,500 metres in 1994 by over five seconds. Brahim Lahlafi had to defeat the big names in the 5,000 metres such as John Nuttall and Martin Bremer to win the same year. Daniel Komen only ran 13:46 in 1998, yet this still put him over seven seconds clear of Shaun Creighton. Khalid Skah also had a difficult time winning the now defunct 10,000 metres in 1994 when he edged out Antonio Silio by more than thirty seven seconds!

So why did Salah Hissou wish to compete in it anyway?

The factors were age and injury. The realisation that he probably only had a short time left at the top gave him the desire and determination to strive for any rewards possible. The African Championships themselves were going to be much more significant regardless, as there was usually some top opposition to contend with. The dominance of Africa was another reason for the meaninglessness of the World Cup because in most distance races, it was logical that the African would win.

It was not a surprise that Hissou had never raced in the African Championships. Since Salah had reached the lofty heights of an international standard, they had been held in 1996, 1998 and 2000. On two occasions he was in Europe, busily preparing for the Olympic Games and in 1998 he was injured. With the World Cup no longer containing a 10,000 metres event, it wasn't a shock to see Hissou on the start line for just the 5,000 metres, though it was another indicator that he was totally done with racing the longer track distance.

While there was an abundance of tough competition to overcome, there was also the matter of handling the oppressive Tunisian heat. The race was sure to be slow. It could come down to which athlete was feeling the best on the day.

Hissou's event was raced on August 10, twenty days after his previous race in Monaco. For whatever reason, he was unable to adapt to the change in conditions and the style of racing. It was slow, but that shouldn't have completely cancelled him out of the reckoning. A slow race can allow for a bigger kick down over the last few laps that could have worked to the Moroccan's advantage. But when it was time to kick, Salah had nothing in reserve. The great Kenyan Paul Bitok pulled off a surprise victory, triumphing at the age of thirty two. What further added to this coup was that he out kicked the best runner of the season in Benjamin Limo. It wasn't a convincing margin, but Bitok couldn't care less about that or the time. He ran 13:31.95. Limo clocked 13:32.10 with Amyn third in 13:33.98. Ten years after winning Olympic silver in Barcelona, Paul Bitok was the African champion at 5,000 metres. What tremendous longevity. The kind that most Kenyans are unable to replicate.

Salah was mightily disappointed with his fifth placing in 13:36.79. Perhaps it was just a case of peaking for Italy, rather than Tunisia. However deciding that his form remained good enough, he travelled back to Europe with the intention of winning in Zurich for the first time on August 16.

There were other intriguing results from Tunisia with Boulami turning the tables on Boit Kipketer in the steeplechase. The duo registered times of 8:19.51 and 8:20.92, with Cherono next in 8:23.85. Bernard Lagat won a slow 1,500 metres in 3:38.11, out sprinting Laban Rotich, 3:38.60 and Abdelkader Hachlaf 3:38.78.

Hicham El Guerrouj and Abdelkader Kada had stayed in Europe, deciding that to compete in Africa would be too great

MOROCCAN SUCCESS; THE KADA WAY

a risk to the rest of their Golden League campaign. This proved to be a sensible decision, as many of the athletes who performed well in Tunisia could not convert a similar good result in Zurich. This was as clear as day when looking at the outcome of the 1,500 metres race in Switzerland:

Hicham El Guerrouj	3:26.89
Cornelius Chirchir	3:30.88
Rui Silva	3:31.22
Bernard Lagat	3:31.52
William Chirchir	3:32.76
Reyes Estevez	3:33.08
Robert Rono	3:33.10
Abdelkader Hachlaf	3:33.78
Fouad Chouki	3:35.41
Laban Rotich	3:36.84
Craig Mottram	3:37.34
Peter Philipp	3:38.01

Laban in particular suffered from the Tunisian trip as a fresh Hicham produced one of the best performances ever seen in middle distance running to come within a second of his world record, despite not having anyone push him at all for the race win. The first lap was a fast but sensible 54.34 and Hicham wasn't far off this in third with Lagat fourth. The second split was 1:50.25 at 800 metres. The world record seemed a real chance of going and soon it was only Lagat who was maintaining contact with El Guerrouj. At the bell he was only a metre down. This did not last for long, with the Moroccan steaming away from the Kenyan, then reaching 1,200 metres in 2:45.27 following a 55.02 lap. We were seeing an awesome piece of middle distance running. By the conclusion of the back straight, his lead was at least fifteen metres. He continued to increase it to an astonishing margin as Bernard fell away badly. What Hicham showed us was a turn of speed for which Noureddine Morceli would be proud and this was while going at well under 3:30 speed! Despite running a final lap of 54.33 he just missed the record. After finishing, the world record holder immediately stopped and bowed to the ecstatic Zurich crowd. Magnificent!

Brussels was next on the Golden League schedule and in this sort of form why not try again for the record? Especially if there wasn't an athlete who could provide serious competition.

The 5,000 metres race also clearly favoured those who had remained in Europe over the runners who had put too many eggs in one basket and decided to race in Tunisia. It wasn't only that the African Championships had sapped these athletes of their energy. It was also the matter of handling the change from thirteen thirty racing to thirteen minute racing. Hissou hoped he was up to the challenge and early on was able to settle in to the fast Grand Prix rhythm. The race turned into a battle of strength rather than a bunch sprint and the results were:

Sammy Kipketer	12:56.99
Richard Limo	12:57.86
Abraham Chebii	12:58.98
Benjamin Limo	13:01.31
Salah Hissou	13:01.50
Charles Kamathi	13:02.51
Ismail Sghyr	13:05.80
Paul Bitok	13:06.39
Hillary Chenonge	13:06.47
Dieter Baumann	13:07.40
Jose Rios	13:08.60
Jose Manuel Martinez	13:13.57
Abderrahim Goumri	13:18.39
Alberto Garcia	13:20.54
Mohammed Amyn	13:28.47
Benjamin Maiyo	13:35.76

Sammy Kipketer proved the strongest while going close to achieving the fastest time of the season. A Limo was again prominent. This time it was Richard who ran the best, clearly defeating the rest of the field apart from Sammy. Chebii was the third Kenyan under thirteen minutes. It was the twenty-two year old's first time under the barrier.

The first African Championships competitor was Benjamin

MOROCCAN SUCCESS; THE KADA WAY

Limo who didn't have the reserves to hang onto his teammates. His run was nevertheless a solid one. Fourth place with a 13:01.31 was nothing to be scoffed at. Hissou battled on valiantly to finish just behind his new nemesis. This fifth place finish was much better than the last one but Zurich pretty much confirmed that he had spent all his energies for 2002. It was time to rest the body and the mind and focus on 2003 with the hope of having one more shot at a World Championships.

Zurich was another race in which Hissou had the dubious distinction of being the first non Kenyan finisher. He defeated many top names. Special mention can be attributed to Dieter Baumann with the German's tenth placing being outstanding for a thirty seven year old.

Best highlighting the effects of Tunisia was the performance of Benjamin Maiyo. The front runner had raced in the physically draining 10,000 metres in Africa, placing third, just losing to Paul Kosgei and John Korir by under half a second. On his return to Europe the bounce that he had in his stride in Monaco was completely gone and he hit the wall completely. This is not uncommon as a runner can often over race, resulting in this outcome.

Salah's Moroccan teammates were of little help to him as he single handedly took on Kenya. Goumri was thirteenth and Amyn fifteenth with both being dropped well before the final lap. With Mourhit testing positive to EPO there was always going to be speculation about a big variance in performance. However, not all of Hissou's countrymen were struggling.

As well as Hicham El Guerrouj they had Brahim Boulami. In the 3,000 metres steeplechase, Kenyan's Cherono and Koech ran fantastically well, running times of 8:05.14 and 8:05.44. These performances would guarantee victory in approximately eighty percent of high class European races, but on this occasion, these guys were not even remotely competitive. Distancing them by almost eighty metres was the world record holder. Yes, Brahim had done it again. The Moroccan took a large slice off his own world record when he crossed the line in a staggering 7:53.17!

Moroccan athletics was on a high and Hicham continued the good vibes when he won the mile event at London on August 23. The victory made it an incredible twenty consecutive wins since his Sydney silver. This man was an absolute machine. In this contest he wasn't able to match the levels of his recent runs, yet he was proficient enough to again defeat a strong field. His time of 3:50.86 was too fast for the new best Kenyan Chirchir, Cornelius, who ran 3:51.68.

The date for the Brussels meeting was August 30 and El Guerrouj looked forward to competing at the Van Damme Memorial where Moroccan runners had built a tremendous reputation, always receiving a good reception. This year would be a little less comfortable for Hicham and his compatriots because on August 29, another bombshell was dropped. A drug test that Brahim Boulami had submitted just a day before setting his new world record in Zurich showed traces of the performance enhancer EPO. It was a massive day for the sport, revealing that Mourhit wasn't a one off. A second Moroccan born runner had also profited from the benefits of Epogen.

Surprisingly, the Kenyans were still pushed in the steeplechase event in Belgium. No, Boulami was not competing, though technically he could have until his B sample tested positive. It was the Spaniard Luis Miguel Martin who clocked a Spanish record of 8:07.44 to defeat all but Ezekiel Kemboi who emerged victorious in 8:06.65. Again, track and field had shown that no athlete was bigger than the sport itself. There would be great steeplechase races in the future, with or without Brahim Boulami.

Even under a big cloud of suspicion, Morocco managed to win races in Brussels. El Guerrouj came through with the goods in the 1,500 metres by running a regulation time (for him) of 3:29.95. He had not run it in a regulation manner, although the first lap was clocked at an outrageous 53.30 (the first rabbit was under fifty two seconds). Hicham slowed significantly in the middle stages before flying home with a

MOROCCAN SUCCESS; THE KADA WAY

52.40 last lap, which he certainly required in order to defeat the Kenyans again. This time, he was closely followed by Lagat in 3:30.39, with his teammates Robert Rono, 3:30.99 and Cornelius Chirchir, 3:31.02, not far behind. Entering the home straight, El Guerrouj was under severe pressure from Lagat but was able to put in another burst to extend out to the winning margin. Kada probably knew that this was a difficult race for his athlete and must have been very proud of how Hicham had been able to deal with the added pressure. Remember, there was still the normal pressure of trying to win every Golden League event!

Abderrahim Goumri produced the performance of his career to defeat the Kenyans in a major upset over 3,000 metres. The Moroccan showed there were yet more fish in this talent pool as he ran a time of 7:35.77, which wasn't far from the season's best. Seven athletes from Kenya trailed him in. From Abraham Chebii in 7:36.58, to the disappointment of the race, Benjamin Limo in 7:40.72. The manner in which this event was raced was surprising. Goumri had been given the latitude of following the rabbits, while the rest of the field chose not to keep with the pace. When he passed through 2,000 metres in 5:04.43, his lead was a winning one. As the chasers did not close until late, the victory was achieved much more convincingly than the time gaps suggest.

Kenya was victorious in a fantastic 10,000 metres that reached the levels of the Brussels era from '96-'99. For the first time in a single race there were five men breaking twenty seven minutes and ten men breaking twenty seven thirty. The results of those runners were:

Sammy Kipketer	26:49.38
Assefa Mezgebu	26:49.90
Richard Limo	26:50.20
Ahmad Hassan Abdullah	26:50.67
John Cheruiyot Korir	26:52.87
Patrick Ivuti	27:05.88
John Yuda	27:06.17
Gebre-egziabher Gebremariam	27:25.61
Sileshi Sihine	27:26.12

Kamiel Maase 27:26.29

The depth of high standard was a dismissal to those who suggested that the EPO test was slowing down the times in distance running. Sure, there were no sub 26:40's recorded but the four men who had achieved that level were not competing.

Mezgebu finally flew the flag proudly for Ethiopia, almost pulling off a sensational victory. Kipketer and Limo had shown this level of feat before at 5,000 metres on many occasions. Abdullah and Korir had taken their game to a new level.

Berlin was next on the track and field calendar on September 6. It was the final race that Hicham El Guerrouj needed to win if he was to gain a share of the Golden League jackpot. This he was fully expected to do, especially with both Chirchirs not competing. During the final 300 metres there were never any worries as the world champion streaked away for one of his usual commanding victories. As if to further emphasize his perfection, the clock stopped at 3:30.00 exactly. Lagat came in at 3:32.91 and Rotich 3:33.81. It was just another day at the office for Hicham, except in this instance he and Abdelkader were rewarded with some extra cash. Just to ensure they could afford the plane trip back home to Rabat!

Before taking that flight there were still other meetings to take care of. Next on Hicham's 'to do' list was the small matter of breaking his 1,500 metres world record in Rieti, Italy. Despite the challenge coming on September 8, only two days after Berlin, El Guerrouj was confident that he could head into 3:25 territory.

Bernard Kisilu and David Lelei are the rabbits and they do a superb job, taking the Moroccan through to 800 metres in 1:49.14, which is under record schedule. If there could be any complaint, it would be that the Kenyans have gone fractionally too fast because after 1,000 metres, Hicham is on his own. Yet at 1,200 metres a new record is there for the taking as El Guerrouj reaches the split in 2:44.75! He's running at just under fifty five second lap pace. Alas, he fades a little over the

MOROCCAN SUCCESS; THE KADA WAY

concluding stages and hits the line in 3:26.97. What a disgrace!

It was yet another sensational piece of running from the master. The gap back to the second placed athlete Vyacheslav Shabunin was massive even by his standards, with the Russian clocking 3:34.63. The last 300 metres were El Guerrouj's slowest in this honourable record attempt. To have set a new mark, the Moroccan didn't have to increase the tempo with a dramatic sprint finish. If he had done so, a sub 3:25 was possible. Running the final segment (300 metres) at exactly fifty five second lap pace would have resulted in a finishing time of exactly 3:26.00, the current record time. This really was a big opportunity to break it, not that I say this in disappointment at Hicham's performance. I pose the question as to how much stronger he could have been over the final lap if the gap between the Berlin and Rieti races was a few days longer.

The 800 metres at this meeting is worth mentioning because Danish superstar Wilson Kipketer set a season's best mark of 1:42.32. Of more interest to El Guerrouj's future was the result of the fifth placed runner who clocked 1:43.15. Mehdi Baala set a French record and showed the very high speed that he possessed for a mile athlete.

It was next on to the Grand Prix final in Paris on September 14 for the season's finale. The 1,500 metres was as we'd become accustomed to, Hicham vs. Kenya with the usual conqueror prevailing. The results were:

Hicham El Guerrouj	3:29.27
Bernard Lagat	3:30.54
Cornelius Chirchir	3:31.51
Robert Rono	3:32.70
Laban Rotich	3:34.09
Abdelkader Hachlaf	3:34.46
Vyacheslav Shabunin	3:34.63
Rui Silva	3:37.31
William Chirchir	3:39.11
Seneca Lassiter	3:54.38

There were some odd performances at the tail of the field but the common thread remained with four Kenyans following El Guerrouj in. It was another flawless year for Hicham, the only shame being that Abdelkader didn't encourage him to spread his wings a trifle further distance wise. As a miler it was all positives. The only negatives about Hicham El Guerrouj were the results of his regular drug tests. For the second straight season Hicham was named the best athlete of the year by the IAAF. The way in which the Moroccan had responded to his silver medal in Sydney was inspirational.

Salah Hissou was listed as a starter for the 3,000 metres despite not being in attendance. As it turned out he didn't miss much.

This final was a farce. Quite often the Grand Prix final includes a slowly run distance race. This is understandable being the end of the season with the athletes already having raced many times in the months prior. The Grand Prix final doesn't mean a lot to some athletes. The fact that it is called a *final* is very misleading since most runners focus far more on the meetings in Zurich and Brussels. In this race the high class field went out and 'jogged' seventy plus second laps. The first km was run in 3:06.79, the equivalent of seventy four second laps. A slowly termed race would be throwing in the odd lap of sixty nine, seventy. This pace was utterly ridiculous.

It may have been quicker if Hissou had competed. He might not have tolerated too much of this nonsense. As it was, the second km was only fractionally faster as the Kenyans kicked it down to just under three minutes for that split. Considering this tempo, the last km of just under 2:28 was disappointing also, being only slightly faster than Salah's last km in Rome, which of course was done after a longer distance and slicker earlier lap pace.

The small field of nine was separated by just over two seconds. The race was won by Abraham Chebii in 8:33.42. He was timed at 50.68 seconds for the final lap! Paul Bitok and Mark Bett trailed him home. The season's best performer,

MOROCCAN SUCCESS; THE KADA WAY

Benjamin Limo could only manage sixth, one place ahead of his brother Richard. Kenya filled the first seven places with Mohammed Amyn running 8:35.03 for eighth. After a season of turmoil, it was a dismal way to end the season for distance running in general.

There was one significant race that took place during the '02-'03 off season. It was in a usually uneventful road race, but this time it had the greatest of all time in attendance.

Haile Gebrselassie returned to racing on December 11 in Doha, testing himself over his preferred distance of 10 kms. This time it was on the road, not the track. His winning time was nearly as fast as we were all used to anyway. After the splendid 27:02 run, the Ethiopian was most experts' favourite for next year's World Championship 10,000 metres. The titles were to be held in Paris.

January 16, 2003 came and went for Salah Hissou. Another year older. Another year wiser. Was it a case of another year slower?

The indoor season would provide an early indicator. Salah enjoyed his short stint indoors in 2002 and it led to a pretty good season outdoors. He decided to give it another go in 2003. First up was a 3,000 metres event in Stockholm, Sweden, on February 18.

The class of the field was typical for an indoor meet. Nothing particularly special but Hissou wasn't the favourite, just one of a few possible winners.

The race had the same outcome for the Moroccan as many had in the past. He was able to hang with the elite for the race's majority, but when the question of a kick was raised, he had no answer. Salah clocked a 7:46.08 as he finished fourth, well behind the first three who were Rui Silva, Luke Kipkosgei and Gunther Weidlinger. The trio registered times of 7:42.55, 7:43.46 and 7:44.19.

Silva showed off all of his miler speed with a devastating

sprint. Even the aging Kipkosgei (now twenty seven) could still kick a little. The Austrian Weidlinger was the surprise packet. The results above were a rarity indeed. Two non Africans in the first three of a 3,000 metres race. Perhaps Hissou lowering his colours to Europeans was the first sign that his days were numbered.

There were eight athletes behind him in Stockholm with fifth placed Mark Bett, 7:49.35, the only runner with a significant pedigree. At least the result had proved that Hissou's off season training had given him a decent base to work from. He had the strength but speed was always going to be harder to find. At least there was plenty of time in which to find it.

Racing over 2 miles was a rarity for most of the world's best distance runners. As a result, the world record for the event has often been very soft. In the outdoors, Gebrselassie was the first to bring this to everyone's attention. On the 28th of May, 1995, he ran 8:07.46 in Kerkrade to comfortably beat Kiptanui's world record of 8:09.01. In light of the fact that Haile set mind blowing records at 5,000 metres and 10,000 metres that year, it was understandable that this performance received little attention.

It probably didn't deserve it anyway. At least that's what Daniel Komen thought. On the 14th of July, 1996, he clocked an 8:03.54 in Lappeenranta. Now that was more like it.

Gebrselassie doesn't take his records being broken lightly. It always seemed to invigorate and inspire the Ethiopian to greater deeds. If ever there was a sign that the two mile event was becoming a serious one, it was on the 31st of May, 1997. Haile was competing at his favourite location Hengelo, but instead of running a 10,000 metres or a 5,000 metres he decided to have a go at Komen's world record. Not the 3,000 metres event mind you. Gebrselassie is an athlete with high intelligence. It is much easier to run 8:03.54 for two miles than it is to run 7:20.67 for 3,000 metres! The rich carrot of $1,000,000 that Adidas dangled in front of him (required to break eight minutes) was also rather enticing.

MOROCCAN SUCCESS; THE KADA WAY

Haile rarely failed when he targeted a record. This night was no exception as he lowered the mark to 8:01.08. Yet still it wasn't safe.

On the 19th of July during that same year, Komen was in Hechtel with the aim of putting this record closer to the level of his '7:20'. Daniel managed to achieve this in brilliant fashion, becoming the first man to run back to back miles in under eight minutes. Distance running times had been lowered substantially in the '90's, but to many people a world record was just a world record. Older fans could remember the struggles in the 1950's as man tried to run one mile in under four minutes. The improvements in men's distance running were therefore explained to great effect with Komen's 7:58.61 for two miles.

Contradictory to the spate of outdoor records, indoors, the event was lagging. Little known Ethiopian Hailu Mekonnen held the world record with an 8:09.66, set in Birmingham in 2000. For the 2003 meeting Gebrselassie wanted another world record and so he targeted this 'soft' mark.

Even after his many injuries, Haile was able to demolish his teammate's time when he ran 8:04.69 on the 21st of February. Mekonnen tried in vain to hold on to his record, running 8:09.39, a good effort as this was also inside the old standard. However, this was another record that Gebrselassie might not hold for too long.

Hissou had not tried to defend his victory in Birmingham from a year ago. Instead he was in Lievin, aiming to help Hicham El Guerrouj to the world record. His attempt came on February 23, only two days after the Birmingham race. The Moroccan was more than capable of taking it off the Ethiopian.

Unfortunately Salah and the rest of the field were not up to helping Hicham sufficiently enough to break the record. In Birmingham, Haile had to some extent been pushed. In Lievin, El Guerrouj was left to fly solo for far too long and as a result, fell just short of the record. His winning time of 8:06.61

remained impressive, especially considering that second placed Kenyan Laban Rotich ran 8:28.25! It must be added that the rabbits did get Hicham to halfway in 4:02.8, so his finish wasn't quite as strong as expected.

Abdelkader Kada was happy with Hicham's run, in view that he was to move up in distance (yes!) in 2003. Kada even used an excuse for the non record run saying, "If we had anticipated he would need 8:04 instead of 8:09, we would have stopped the weight training three weeks ago instead of only one week ago." That comment was arguably a little sour. In regards to moving up, El Guerrouj would still base himself at 1,500 metres in 2003 but his plan at this stage was to contest both that, and the 5,000 metres at the World Championships. Kada had scheduled 3,000 and 5,000 metres races to open his European outdoor season.

It was a little hard to gauge Salah Hissou's form at this early stage of 2003. It didn't seem that he was in the condition of twelve months ago but we had yet to get conclusive proof. There were some important events coming soon that would give us and Salah more information. The World Indoor Championships and the World Cross Country Championships were fast approaching.

The Indoor Championships, which were also held at Birmingham only scheduled a 3,000 metres event for the long distance runners that Haile Gebrselassie won again in 7:40.97 on March 16. For Salah, a 5,000 metres distance would have been more attractive. With that in mind he decided to return to cross country. It was four years since he had competed in the discipline and six years since he had finished the actual world race. Was this the genuine comeback of a podium athlete or one who was about to be put out to pasture?

Hissou was well renowned as a superstar 12 kms cross country runner, but it seemed that he no longer saw himself in the same light. Salah decided that he was better suited to the 4 kms short course. For an athlete whose performances relied more heavily on strength than speed, it was an unintelligent

MOROCCAN SUCCESS; THE KADA WAY

decision.

Perhaps the race at Brussels in 1997 still had an impact at this point of Salah Hissou's career. In some ways it had persuaded him to become a full time 5,000 metres runner. The success that followed had convinced him to completely ignore who he used to be as an athlete. He had built his reputation from the ages of twenty two to twenty five as a 10,000 metres and cross country star. Since then he had achieved nothing in these events and he had hardly even tried to rectify that.

The comparatively weak years when Mourhit won the long course event were over. Now it was the era of Kenenisa Bekele.

Salah's race came on March 29. It was an absolute shocker. Not so for the new 'emperor' from Ethiopia who completed another 'double double'. But the once competitive Moroccan was humbled in the class field and clearly didn't belong. Finishing thirty fifth was disappointing enough, yet the time gaps put it into perspective in an even blunter fashion. Hissou clocked 11:48. The podium placers went to:

Kenenisa Bekele	11:01
John Kibowen	11:04
Benjamin Limo	11:06

Last year Salah was competitive against Benjamin. In 2003 he was the equivalent of 250 to 300 metres behind. It is difficult to imagine Hissou nearly being lapped at 3,000 metres or 5,000 metres. That's how much he had slipped. This sort of form was unlikely to grant him an entry into the Golden League races let alone allow him any sort of respectable performance if he did race in them. A huge turnaround was required and some good signs needed to be shown by June or the thirty one year old would be well and truly finished with the track.

Greg Rowlerson

Should It Always Be Guilty Until Proven Innocent?

The success that the Abdelkader Kada group had achieved during the past decade was under question. Well, not that success had been achieved, for that was beyond debate. Rather, exactly *how* it had been achieved.

As discussed earlier, Morocco did not have all the same natural advantages as its East African rivals. It had advantages over other countries yes, but not over Kenya and Ethiopia. The principle disadvantage that most Moroccan distance runners had was to be born at a lower altitude. Admittedly, much of Morocco is mountainous, just not on the same scale as the aforementioned nations.

The great rise of Morocco's athletics and cross country teams throughout the 1990's was greatly attributed to their superb commitment and specific approaches to training. Much of this training was conducted at the high altitude of Ifrane and it was said that the many hours spent here had helped to close the gap, if in fact there was any in natural talent as far as the East Africans were concerned.

Living at high altitude increases a human's red blood cell count. This helps to improve endurance. As such, altitude training has become an increasingly popular pastime for runners, both at the elite and 'fun run' levels. It was the 1968 Mexico City Olympics, which first made us aware of the impact that an environment with thinner air (less oxygen) can have on various track and field events. Most famously, on the positive side of the ledger came the stand out leap in the men's long jump, when Bob Beamon flew a distance of 8.90 metres, recording a world record that lasted until the 1991 World Championships. For the majority of events, conditions were conducive to good performances. However, these controversial Games also brought to everybody's attention the major difficulties that many athletes faced when running long distances at high altitude. The man who was generally regarded as the best long distance runner in the world, Ron Clarke, *failed* to perform up to expectations. Unfortunately for

MOROCCAN SUCCESS; THE KADA WAY

the Australian, he was unable to cope with the severe challenges that he was *forced* to encounter in Mexico and found himself being defeated by opponents with far less impressive resumés, but had been born at altitude. A similar situation was faced by the American Jim Ryun, the favourite to win the 1,500 metres, who was upset by Kip Keino. As a result of these surprises, it could be safely assumed that by living well above sea level, athletes gained an advantage over those living at sea level when racing at a 'Mexico City', a place of high elevation. Back then it was unknown if those same advantages could be converted into performances at sea level. Of course decades later, we learned that growing up in such an environment could also give an advantage to a long distance runner when competing at sea level.

Not everyone believes in the benefits of altitude training. Yet during the last decade you would be hard pressed to find a 5,000 metres or 10,000 metres medal contender who was not undergoing some of their major championship lead up training at a high altitude venue. It is in the exact practices of this training where some runners vary in their application, such as how high to live and train and how hard to train at various levels of elevation as discussed previously.

Now getting back to the Moroccan training. By the mid '90's Moroccans all swore by altitude training. As more of their runners enjoyed success, more people wanted to know about their training secrets. According to most Moroccans there was nothing secretive in how they were able to compete with the East Africans. Good organization and strict commitment seemed to be enough. Encouraging its talented athletes to eat well, sleep well and train well at various height levels (Rabat and Ifrane), had established Morocco as a tremendous distance running nation.

Or were we all missing something?

The catching out of Mohammed Mourhit and Brahim Boulami with EPO positive tests immediately led to some fans labelling Morocco as a cheating country. The likes of Aziz Daouda and Abdelkader Kada had always sprouted that much of the success was due to its regimented training camps. Systematic doping was the thought that came to many an athletics fans' mind.

'Ha! Ha!' some outsiders said. 'EPO is how Moroccans compete with their more talented rivals. It was never just the altitude training'.

Of course Mourhit and Boulami have never admitted guilt and have always said that high altitude training is all that they can be accused of. But their guilt is close enough to 100% to be safely assumed as certain.

Following the 2003 World Cross Country Championships, there was an announcement made that four more athletes had tested positive to EPO. A Moroccan newspaper claimed that all four runners were Moroccan. The IAAF would neither confirm nor deny this, which added even more fuel to the 'Morocco EPO' fire. Was Salah Hissou about to be caught out?

In May the names were released and only one of the four was a Moroccan. Her name was Asmae Leghzaoui. Still, one was more than enough for many to now proclaim that all her teammates were cheats.

Hicham, Salah and Ali were up against it. It was nearly as bad to be a Moroccan athlete in 2003 as it was to be an East German athlete twenty to thirty years earlier!

However they, along with many of their counterparts shouldn't be instantly labelled as drug cheats. We should delve more deeply into what has transpired. Nobody should judge Abdelkader's boys too quickly, either as innocent or guilty.

Let us look at the possibility of systematic doping in Morocco. We know who has been caught so let's look at the backgrounds of those athletes. The great Said Aouita also has a case to answer for. Not necessarily because of his remarkable achievements in the 1980's but because of what has emerged since.

MOROCCAN SUCCESS; THE KADA WAY

By 1994 Said Aouita had long finished his career as an athlete and had moved into coaching. His experience would surely only be beneficial to the many young Moroccan runners who looked up to him as an idol. His country instantly appointed him as its top coach.

However, Said did not last long in his role. After six months and therefore very little time spent with the likes of El Guerrouj and Hissou, he was booted out, citing differences with Aziz Daouda. At the time many were sympathetic to Aouita and saw him as the great athlete being bullied by the team manager.

Mohammed Mourhit was also having problems with Aziz, so he left the official Moroccan national training program and sided with Aouita. Together they worked diligently to try to bring Mohammed up to the international level. It was a level that eluded him for many years. Later Mourhit blamed injuries and his difficult relationship with Daouda for his lack of development during this period. It was a period in which Hissou and El Guerrouj stepped to the fore and into the international spotlight.

In 1997 Mourhit parted ways with Aouita and changed his nationality. He earned Belgium citizenship and hired his brother Hassan as his full time coach. Quickly he started to see improvement in his times and results. He still conducted a lot of his training in Morocco at Ifrane, but he was certainly not part of the Moroccan system.

Aouita later had problems of his own. He was hired to be the AIS (Australian Institute of Sport) National Distance Coach by Athletics Australia in 2002, to commence after the Manchester Commonwealth Games. Immediately his appointment was considered dubious because Said claimed to have coached many Moroccan stars, including Hicham El Guerrouj and Salah Hissou. This was partly true, but it was the great responsibility that he alleged he'd had for their success which was dubious. Aouita even went as far to say that he'd changed El Guerrouj from a 3:53 1,500 metres runner into a world class performer. Yet of course he had very little to do with them, and the work and their success was very much a product of Abdelkader Kada. Kada and Daouda both downplayed the role that Aouita claimed to have had with the huge recent Moroccan successes. Initially Australia ignored the Moroccan legend's suspect situation. Kada and Daouda both stated that Aouita had only played a large role in the success of Brahim Boutayeb, and not all the other Moroccan champions whom Said alleged to have been responsible for.

It didn't take long for Aouita to get Australians offside with him also. Young miler Mark Fountain claimed that Said had advised him that he must take performance enhancing drugs to have any chance of competing at an international level. Fountain sent an official letter of complaint to Athletics Australia. The walls had fully caved in on Said Aouita's coaching career.

Unlike Mourhit, Brahim Boulami was competing for Morocco when he tested positive to EPO in 2002. But like the Belgium competitor, Brahim was not deeply involved with the Moroccan training camps. Boulami was self coached, distancing himself from his teammates. You could say that he was doing his own thing.

The IAAF was prepared to keep Boulami's positive A sample under wraps until the result of the B sample was known. That this news came to the public's attention immediately, was due to none other than the Moroccan Athletics Federation who received the news as soon as Brahim. It seems a little strange that a country with a systematic doping program would go completely against its athlete in portraying them as guilty!

The latest Moroccan to make EPO famous was Asmae Leghzaoui. Asmae spent most of her time in America. Here she had enjoyed enormous success on the roads. In 2002 she shocked the world by breaking Paula Radcliffe's 10 kms record. Like Mourhit and Boulami, her big improvements had come at a fairly late age and as such were suspicious, even before a positive test came to light.

Most road races do not test for EPO. It was only when she

MOROCCAN SUCCESS; THE KADA WAY

competed in the IAAF sanctioned World Cross Country Championships that she was caught out. This unfortunately cast a cloud over the road runners that were producing great results legally.

Aouita, Mourhit, Boulami and Leghzaoui. All athletes with strong links to performance enhancing drugs. None of them had strong links to the Moroccan Athletics Federation when it enjoyed such great results in the mid to late 1990's.

Abdelkader Kada has always coached under the umbrella of the Moroccan system. None of Kada's athletes have *ever* tested positive to EPO or any other illegal performance enhancing substance. Let's take a look at each of his star runners individually.

Unlike Mourhit and Boulami, Hissou's major improvements came as a twenty two year old. His best times generally came at twenty four. He has been tested on numerous occasions, including during the period of time since the EPO test has become available. All his tests have returned a negative reading.

Ali Ezzine was already a good international performer as a junior. He continued to improve in his early days as a senior yet has made no real improvements since turning twenty one. Regular tests have discovered nothing and as you will soon read, he returns to compete regularly on the European circuit, after the IAAF has proved that it can catch out the EPO users.

Hicham El Guerrouj was like Ali Ezzine, a world junior bronze medallist. He made a significant improvement as a nineteen year old and since then his performances have been very consistent, leading to his fastest times as a twenty three and twenty four year old. While not setting any new world records, his standards have basically remained at the same level since track and field started testing for EPO. His performances from race to race and season to season are highly consistent. If you were to compare Hicham's races on a graph you would get a fairly flat line, like an early stage of the Tour De France. Draw the same graph for Mohammed Mourhit and you will see a layout that strangely parallels many of the stages in the Alps and Pyrenees!

Salah, Ali and Hicham have competed in a multitude of championships and Golden League meetings that are all very stringent in their testing procedures. On this evidence, we must conclude that these athletes are unquestionably clean and have achieved their results through natural talent and hard work.

Performance enhancing drugs are often used for their recovery benefits as opposed to strictly enhancing an athlete's performance in a speed or endurance aspect. Many people ask the question, "How can you complete your regular training runs at close to a three minute kms pace average and also produce three quality speed sessions a week?" Well, Kada's runners were forced to have plenty of rest. Spending nearly half their twenty four hour day sleeping may make recovery drugs irrelevant.

The three Moroccan runners mentioned who tested positive to EPO give conclusive proof that the substance and other performance enhancing drugs are used in distance running today. But there have not been enough athletes test positive to suggest that EPO use is rife in the distance running scene. Those to have been caught are not the best going around. It's a popular theory that those who are most likely to cheat are those who are just below the top echelon. Not those at the top echelon. It is a theory with real substance.

Brahim Boulami and Mohammed Mourhit were outstanding runners for many years. They just weren't quite good enough to match it with the best from Kenya in their domain of the steeplechase and cross country. There is no shame in that.

In these disciplines they were in the top ten in the world for a period, but never in the top three. They were close enough to know that great success was possible, but in order to attain such success, they would have to resort to extreme means. These extreme means brought magnificent results. Two world records in the steeplechase and two world cross country

MOROCCAN SUCCESS; THE KADA WAY

titles. Plus the ire of the Kenyans!

But not everyone gets away with it. The EPO test had only become available in 2000, so the recent spate of positive tests raised an obvious question. Just how clean had the 1990's been?

That decade saw the men's distance running times tumble to an extent not seen since the 1960's. As the '80's had been stagnant, many felt that the limits of human endurance had been reached. Logically world records would be broken, but improvements should only be in small increments.

This was obviously not the case during the '90's. On the 10th of July, 1993, the first big chunk was taken off a record in a men's track distance event. In the 10,000 metres Yobes Ondieki ran 26:58.38, smashing Richard Chelimo's five day old mark of 27:07.91. Chelimo had edged out Arturo Barrios' time of 27:08.23. This record was set back on the 18th of August, 1989.

The following year William Sigei and Noureddine Morceli took significant amounts off the 10,000 and 3,000 metres records. From then on, there was rarely a dull moment with Haile Gebrselassie singlehandedly changing peoples' perceptions on what was possible with his stunning world record double in 1995.

Daniel Komen helped push Gebrselassie to even faster times in the 5,000 metres, while Salah Hissou and Paul Tergat had a similar influence on the Ethiopian, motivating Haile to bring down his 10,000 metres personal record also. These times just happened to be the world records. By 1998, these numbers bared no resemblance to those of the records at the start of the decade. In fact the major improvements had taken place within a five year period.

During the 1990's there were at least ten world records in men's distance running that could be described as extraordinary, especially when we also remember some performances in the steeplechase, Komen's 3,000 metres mark and El Guerrouj destroying Morceli's already imposing middle distance records. EPO became available around 1990 so many people point the finger at the substance as the sole reason for what happened during this time. But there is a lot more to consider.

Point 1 - The Africans had been held back in their development. They also had not been involved in the sport for as long as the rest of the world. Thus, they had a lot more scope for improvement.

As discussed earlier, the Kenyans, Ethiopians and to a lesser extent the Moroccans, have natural advantages in distance running. For starters, there are many explanations as to why the best 5,000 metres runner from each of these nations can usually run better than the best from America, Australia, Spain, Germany, etc.

The 'white man' has been racing long distances since the 1896 Olympic Games when Athens famously held the men's marathon. By the 1920's Paavo Nurmi and his Finnish teammates were starting to push closer to the limits of human endurance. The second world war held back development, but by the 1950's it was all systems go. Emil Zatopak took distance running to even greater levels. His triple gold (winning the 5,000 metres, 10,000 metres and marathon) effort at Helsinki in 1952 remains one of the most amazing achievements in Olympic history.

By 1960 the Olympics Games were becoming truly international. As soon as Africa gave competing a shot, it instantly showed to the rest of the world its immense natural gifts. Ethiopian Abebe Bikila won the marathon easily and in the process set a world record, all the while running barefoot. It demonstrated perfectly that Africans were born to run. It is like their natural pastime. For the western world it seemed like it was much harder work. But Bikila was only one African and who was to know if there would be any others? But doesn't it say something when the western world has been trying to run marathons for so long and one African gives it a go and runs faster than all of them?

MOROCCAN SUCCESS; THE KADA WAY

Some Africans had of course run marathons prior to 1960, but not with the same levels of commitment to the event that were showed by the world's elite.

In 1964 Bikila won the Olympic marathon again but the 10,000 metres event was the domain of American Billy Mills and Australian Ron Clarke. Over the next couple of years, Clarke rewrote the record books and went into the 1968 Olympics as the clear favourite at both the 10,000 metres and 5,000 metres.

Kenya made a small impact in Tokyo but it was at Mexico City where its legend started. Kip Keino in particular shocked everyone when he defeated America's favourite Jim Ryun in the 1,500 metres. Ron Clarke was given little chance in the longer distances and Africa dominated most of the events, which was due mostly to the altitude. By the end of the decade, Clarke's times of 13:16 and 27:39 remained faster than anybody else could manage or previously imagine as possible.

It soon became apparent that Clarke's times were close to the optimum in endurance performance, in non African performances anyway. Lasse Viren was the star of the 1972 Olympics, but during this period the world records only improved marginally. The depth in Kenya's running was improving slowly. Ethiopia had shown its talent and Tanzania even had a great runner in Filbert Bayi. However in 1976 the continent suffered a big blow when it boycotted the Montreal Games. It was very unfair on the likes of Mike Boit and Murits Yifter.

Without the Africans, Viren didn't get the full test that he should have had. Being excluded from the Olympics was going to take time for Africa to recover, as it would reduce the development in its young talent. Countries need international competition to inspire them.

In 1978 Kenya possessed the greatest runner in the world and perhaps the greatest all round talent of all time. Henry

Rono broke the world records at the 3,000 metres, the steeplechase, the 5,000 metres and the 10,000 metres in the same year. It was quite an accomplishment!

Rono had improved the times to be significantly faster than Clarke's records. The 5,000 metres was now 13:08 and the 10,000 metres was 27:22. However Rono wasn't remotely close to representing the pinnacle of potential from Kenya.

Henry had significant problems with alcohol which no doubt hampered his career. Also discouraging him was his enforced absence from the 1980 Moscow Olympics. We would never know how fast his records could have been if he'd been inspired by Olympic competition and stayed abstinent and more committed to his training.

Kenya boycotted the Moscow Games. Since they had also boycotted Montreal, they were denying a whole generation of runners from competing at the highest level from 1972 to 1984. It was a big gap in Olympic involvement.

Ethiopia's Murits Yifter dominated in Moscow, his two gold medals earning him redemption from Moscow. But like Viren four years earlier, his double was slightly soft because of who wasn't in attendance. In 1983 the World Athletics Championships took place for the first time. This was a competition on a par with the Olympics. It would give the African nations even more encouragement to make the most of their God given talent.

By 1984 there was some normality restored to the Games. Being held in Los Angeles meant that Russia boycotted, though Africa were there in force. Yet it wasn't a Kenyan or Ethiopian who was the biggest star in a distance race. This time it was a Moroccan called Said Aouita who triumphed in the 5,000 metres running close to a world record time of 13:05.59. Aouita proved to be another level up from Rono.

The 1986 World Cross Country Championships were a big sign that things were changing. Ethiopia had often been competitive in the past but Kenya had been disappointing. Not

MOROCCAN SUCCESS; THE KADA WAY

so on this occasion, as John Ngugi took out the title and Kenya won the team gold. The following year Ngugi won it again and Kenya repeated as the dominating victors of the team title. Kenya continued their reign in cross country while Aouita set the track alight, setting world records at distances as diverse as 1,500 and 5,000 metres. He won the latter event (where he was virtually unbeatable) at the 1987 World Championships, a competition which fully displayed the dominance of the African's. Somalia's Abdi Bille won the 1,500 metres, while Kenya's Billy Konchellah won the 800 metres. His teammate Paul Kipkoech convincingly won the 10,000 metres by ten seconds!

Kenyan success carried over to 1988 when Ngugi won Olympic 5,000 metres gold in Seoul. Peter Rono took out the 1,500 metres title and Kenya also went one-two in the steeplechase. This was the start of Kenya's complete supremacy in the event.

Morocco showed it had more talent than just Said Aouita with Brahim Boutayeb winning the 10,000 metres in a very fast time of 27:21. Conditions were very warm in Seoul so it was very conceivable that if Brahim could produce this performance here then someone should be able to break twenty seven minutes soon. Considering that Boutayeb was no Aouita, it was logical that the barrier could be obliterated. If a Moroccan could do that then potentially so could an Ethiopian or Kenyan. Africa was unstoppable in the men's distance races in Seoul, even with another boycott from Ethiopia.

All these performances were achieved before the availability of EPO. By the end of the '80's it was clear that Africa was the dominant continent in men's distance running. This was after approximately only thirty years of any serious application to the sport amongst numerous Olympic boycotts. Countries such as Ethiopia and Tanzania had also been unstable. Most of these circumstances were not perfect situations for athletics teams to prosper, yet the incredible talent, particularly of the Kenyans, had been able to push through these barriers. Defeating the westerners, many of whom had less national issues to deal with, was an issue that was quickly becoming irrelevant.

Henry Rono ran 13:06.20 and 27:22.47. It's not difficult to imagine that those times could have become approximately 12:55 and 26:55 without the problems he endured, plus having greater competition from today's runners. Said Aouita ran 12:58 and 27:26.11 with the latter being off just one attempt. With greater competition I believe that he could have run, or at least come closer to 12:50, and 27:05. Something like that. Remember that Said edged inside Dave Moorcroft's record by just one hundredth of a second in 1985. Nobody took his world record until after his career with Aouita himself making one further minor (when compared to Gebrselassie!) improvement to the time in 1987. What if like Gebrselassie, he'd had another athlete to break his record, a la Daniel Komen? 12:50 for 5,000 metres might have been possible for an athlete who ran a 3:29.46 for 1,500 metres.

Yes, the records did come down astronomically from 1993, but Africa had been building to this point throughout the 1980's and again I state that EPO was not available then. Most of the amazing performances were largely due to two men in Haile Gebrselassie and Daniel Komen. It is natural for great athletes to inspire others to better performances. Of course you also need to have the necessary talent and not just the belief. Kenya, Ethiopia and Morocco had earlier displayed that they possessed that required talent on many occasions.

We shouldn't always lower the ceiling too much on just what the possibilities are as far as times go by clean athletes. I am sure that when some fans saw Paavo Nurmi compete, they thought that nobody could ever improve much on his times. The same goes for Emil Zatopek, Ron Clarke and Henry Rono. It is ridiculous to draw a line and say that 'those are the cheats and the rest are the clean runners'. It doesn't work like that and people do have different natural levels of ability.

Point 2 - No non Africans are breaking twenty seven minutes and only a few have barely broken thirteen minutes. If EPO

MOROCCAN SUCCESS; THE KADA WAY

was rife in distance running then isn't it reasonable to think that distance runners across the globe would be improving their times substantially and not mainly just the East Africans?

Why would only the Africans be taking EPO and not the rest of the world's athletes? This makes no sense. Americans and Europeans take performance enhancing drugs in many other sports so why not in distance running if the sport is so rife with illegal substances? Some say that the western world is more of a target for out of competition tests but since when has that ever stopped elite sportsmen from crossing the murky line to gain an unfair advantage? In recent years, the sport of cycling has become arguably the leader in endeavouring to stamp out drug cheats but we still get many of the sport's top names getting tangled up in scandals.

As I have said, the 'white man' had gone close to his limits after Ron Clarke's exploits in the 1960's. Therefore in recent times the improvements have been fairly normal. Today in 2008, Australia's best 5,000 metres runner Craig Mottram has a PB of 12:55.76, just more than twenty seconds faster. And Craig is hardly the perfect prototype for distance running. Why can't Daniel Komen, with a build that is obviously far better suited, run sixteen seconds faster?

If EPO was the main reason for the big drop in times, then wouldn't there have been at least one non African running a sub 12:50, or a sub 26:40? There are reasons why the Africans have improved the world records that have nothing to do with EPO. The main reason as to why the rest of the world didn't follow suit is because the rest of the world had run out of improvement. By 2007, the Africans seemed to have hit that wall also, after about fifty years at the top level. From now on expect that most of the world record improvements will be minimal. However great performances are still possible from great athletes.

Point 3 - The endurance levels of the best distance runners have not improved as greatly as the times would suggest. It's just that the men who are now leading the packs at the longer track distances, have got fantastic middle distance speed that

Ron Clarke could have only dreamt of. Clarke's best mile time was 4:00.20 and back in his day, the event was raced regularly. Salah Hissou in one attempt clocked 3:52.54.

Also, do you think that Ron had 49 to 50 second quarter speed? No. He is reported to have run a 53.1 second 440 yards which equates to 400 metres. The sub fifty second speed is what the vast majority of current day top distance athletes have in their arsenal. If you convert the advantage that many Africans have over Clarke at this short distance, then guess what? You get a differential or an improvement of about thirty to fifty seconds on Ron's 13:16.60 for 5,000 metres!

The improvements in the marathon world record are also not only due to improved endurance levels. It's because the best 10,000 metres runners are converting that track speed to the marathon distance. Robert de Castella's personal best stands at 2:07.51, which is a long way off the sub 2:06 marathons that we were starting to see and would continue to in the future. But this does not mean that the Australian can't match the strength or endurance levels of the Africans that are now setting the standard. Later Paul Tergat would record a 2:04.55 time in Berlin, almost three minutes faster than de Castella's time at Boston in 1986. Firstly, Boston is a slower course than Berlin. Secondly, Rob never broke twenty eight minutes for 10,000 minutes! Now the Aussie was fully focused on the marathon, not the track, but even with more concentration on speed, he could not have come within eighty seconds of the Kenyan's then world record time of 26:27 on the track. So if these runners had approximately the same endurance levels, then Tergat would be able to run at least five minutes faster than de Castella, given that the marathon is more than four times the distance of the 10,000 metres.

Point 4 - Most of the EPO positive tests in men's long distance running have come from Moroccans (as explained previously) and Europeans. There would be little reason to cover up any systematic doping by the IAAF as far as the East Africans are concerned. Distance running is not particularly popular in America because there is too much

MOROCCAN SUCCESS; THE KADA WAY

dominance from the Kenyans and Ethiopians. It makes no sense to protect these athletes and therefore put a limit on the popularity of the sport in Europe and the USA. America, just like any other country, would prefer its athletes to be winning, or at least being competitive. Look at how the popularity of the Tour has increased since Lance Armstrong started winning.

There would later be controversy surrounding Kenyan Bernard Lagat, but we know that he is a product of the American system.

Point 5 - There have still been many fast times clocked since the EPO test came in.

In 2000, at the Sydney Olympics, track and field started to test for EPO. Considering the drug became available around 1990, it was a long time coming. In these first three years distance running times slowed. But there are good reasons for that as I have explained earlier. The times have soon become fast again. Kenenisa Bekele has broken Gebrselassie's world records, records that I thought would stand for many more years. Nobody has broken El Guerrouj's world records because he has been such a better miler than everyone else except for Morceli. If his records were all due to EPO, then wouldn't his times be significantly slower after 1999? This is not the case. The world record is 3:26.00 for 1,500 metres. Hicham broke 3:27 in 2001 and 2002.

The amazing talent of the Africans still shines through with new examples. Runners from Eritrea and Uganda would later run superb 10,000 metres times. Zersenay Tadesse and Boniface Kiprop have personal records of 26:37.25 and 26:39.77.

I cannot say for certain that all the world record holders and other best performers of the last fifteen years who didn't test positive, are clean. That would be ignorant and fanciful. It is human nature to lie and in some cases cheat to benefit each of our own situation. Just not necessarily everyone, and all of the time. What I am saying is that with the evidence we have, we should believe that EPO is not rife within the sport of distance running.

I will get back to the actual running/racing side of things. Salah Hissou coming back to run the fastest 5,000 metres of 2002 was a great achievement. Yet how was this allowed to happen?

1999 had been an outstanding year for Salah with very fast times at 3,000 metres and 5,000 metres, all being capped off by that win in Seville. He was able to strongly contend for race wins in all meetings that didn't include Haile Gebrselassie.

After a serious injury and being on the wrong side of thirty, it was unreasonable to think that Salah should return to the top. Nonetheless, unforeseen circumstances had given him a chance to do this. 2000 and 2001 saw big lulls in the standards of distance running, but unfortunately for Hissou, he was injured and couldn't cash in. Fortunately the lull continued for one more year and he was able to reap his reward with his magnificent win in Rome.

But things didn't look quite so promising for 2003. Abdelkader Kada was letting Hicham El Guerrouj loose to move up to the 5,000 metres. Haile Gebrselassie had recovered from his injuries and was back to running very fast times indoors. Kenenisa Bekele had done the 'double double' again in the cross country and looked set to make his mark on the track. There were also some young Kenyans on the rise that might prove to be stronger competitors than the Limo's. Even in his 2002 form Salah was likely to struggle, and getting anywhere near that form seemed unlikely given his horrible short course race.

The Moroccan still had hopes of being in the Paris World Championships at the 5,000 metres. More than just being there, he wanted to be competitive as a former champion.

Ali Ezzine hoped to firstly regain some sort of his old confidence before he remotely thought about the Paris Championships. He needed to perform to a reasonable

MOROCCAN SUCCESS; THE KADA WAY

standard at a lower grade meet before embarking on a Golden League race. He had targeted a race at Rabat in June as the start of his comeback.

Hicham El Guerrouj was excited about the new challenges that were coming his way. He in particular, was looking forward to his June races in Turin, Italy, and Ostrava, Czechoslovakia. So were fans of distance running the world over with the events being over 3,000 and 5,000 metres. On June the 6th Hicham lined up in Turin, where an average field had been assembled.

The best credentialled athlete that the Moroccan was racing against was Charles Kamathi, the current world champion at 10,000 metres. However the Kenyan had no pedigree at this distance, having never recorded a sub 7:40 time. This was surprising even though this athlete tended to be inconsistent. El Guerrouj was likely to run faster so this would be a good test of Charles' true capabilities. The other runners on paper, appeared to be out of their depth.

True to form, Hicham slaughtered this bunch. He transferred his massive victory margins in his pet event, to enjoy an even superior margin here, due to the greater distance and time that he had to build up such a cushion. Wearing an all red Nike uniform, Kada's superstar ran 7:30.23. Not too bad first up! Kenyan Mushir Salim Jawher ran 7:41.55, yet came in second! El Guerrouj's superiority was almost embarrassing. Also inside 7:42 were Said Berioui and Kamathi. The Edmonton race proved that he had a good finishing kick, however that doesn't always convert to good overall speed at the shorter distances.

The pace was pretty quick all the way with Hicham passing through 2,000 metres in 5:02.52. He finished strongly, completing the last lap in 58.19. About this race and his upcoming one, the winner commented, "I hoped to run faster than 7:30 tonight, perhaps I could have clocked 7:26 but the pace set by the pacemakers in the first 2 kms was a bit slow, so I decided to increase it. If pacemakers help me keep a fast pace, I can attack the 12:45 barrier in the Ostrava 5000 metres."

We now looked forward with even greater anticipation to the Ostrava meeting on June 12.

Hicham's manager, Frenchman Laurent Boquillet gave greater clarity into the track star's future plans.

"Hicham still wants to be Olympic 1,500 metres champion. Firstly the 5,000 metres is of course one for the future but secondly, it is about breaking the monotony. So instead of doing yet another season at 1,500, he now has a new challenge."

El Guerrouj also added, "The first objective is to just run the 5,000 metres, then to find pleasure from running the 5,000 metres, and then and only then can we start thinking about records...the 12:39 of Haile Gebrselassie was quite remarkable."

There are some notable Kenyans in the race but as Hicham sets out at close to world record pace, it quickly becomes clear that only one athlete might test him. Initially running behind rabbits, El Guerrouj goes through 1,000 metres in 2:31.16, which is slow compared to his middle distance speed, but lightning fast for this distance. Maybe this will take its toll later on. His rhythm remains immaculate as 2,000 metres is reached in 5:05.42. With the pacesetters still playing their supportive role, El Guerrouj continues to threaten the world record a smidgen as he passes through the 3,000 metres split in 7:37.65. The two front runners leave the race and Hicham discovers that only steeplechase specialist Stephen Cherono remains on his hammer. The pace begins to slow slightly as the feeling of a real contest grows to be evident.

Now into the latter stages, Cherono is still in contact with El Guerrouj who reaches 4,000 metres in 10:15.17. Stephen decides to prove that he's having no trouble with the fast pace as he moves ahead of Hicham with two laps to go. Perhaps angered at the Kenyan's boldness, the Moroccan retakes the

MOROCCAN SUCCESS; THE KADA WAY

lead immediately but finds that he can't shake this athlete from his back. Into the back straight for the final time and there is still no breaking of Cherono. To the surprise of most, on the home straight it is Stephen who finishes over the top of Hicham and in the process, becomes the third fastest athlete in the history of the distance. The results from the top ten in the 5,000 metres were:

Stephen Cherono	12:48.81
Hicham El Guerrouj	12:50.24
James Kwalia C'Kurui	13:04.72
Abiyote Abate	13:05.13
Benjamin Limo	13:11.97
Charles Kamathi	13:15.33
Solomon Busendich	13:16.02
Boniface Kiprop	13:16.21
Benjamin Maiyo	13:20.88
Mohamed Said El Wardi	13:30.31

Only Gebrselassie and Komen headed Cherono on the all time list.

El Guerrouj made the following statement after his first defeat since the Olympics, "I saw today I am not yet a 5,000 metres runner...I have a good feeling from my first 5,000 metres. I have to work on my rhythm. I will continue running the distance."

Perhaps Hicham was disgusted with *only* becoming the seventh fastest of all time! In one attempt he had bettered his old training partner Salah. This was a great run and instantly made him one of the favoured athletes in the event for Paris later in the year and Athens next year if he chose to also try for a double at the Games.

The 1,500 metres was a battle of the Chirchir's with Cornelius defeating William 3:31.17 to 3:31.70. Lagat, who often started his seasons slowly, finished fifth with a time of 3:34.24.

It was desperate times for Salah Hissou who had returned to Morocco subsequent to his disaster of a run in the World

Cross Country. He couldn't afford any setbacks in his training as he prepared for the track season. Running in Ifrane usually had a positive impact on his mental state. It was peaceful and he could be reminded of many of the great sessions during past years. Spending time in this environment would enable Salah to regain some confidence, most of which may have been taken away from him in Lausanne.

For some reason the big Golden League meetings of the season were starting later in the year of this era. In the '90's Salah had liked to start racing in late May or early June yet in 2003 he didn't race until June 27 in Oslo. In this instance it was a good thing, as it gave him more time for preparation and mental recovery after the cross country debacle.

The Moroccan's racing schedule was log jammed with 5,000 metres races. There were no plans to compete over 3,000 metres or in any middle distance events for speed work. Salah aimed at continuous 5,000 metres racing in order to give him some good strength for the World Championships. He was a little fortunate to get an invite from the Bislett organizers given his last race. Was he able to justify their faith in him?

Salah felt at home back on the track. But doubts abounded about the thirty one year old. Was he even capable of running at 13:20 pace these days?

In the past the thoughts in the Moroccan's mind may have been, 'When is the right time to attack and drop these runners?'

Now the mindset was different. It was likely more a case of, 'How long can I hold onto the pace that is being set?'

Salah performed most admirably in Oslo. He hung in tenaciously, metaphorically showing that he was not a spent force. After five laps he looked comfortable, despite the pace being anything but. It was a fast 5:08.67. After ten laps he was still in contact, with the tempo slowing slightly to 10:22 at 4,000 metres. This was a total form reversal to his condition

MOROCCAN SUCCESS; THE KADA WAY

earlier in the year. Was asking for an attack now expecting too much?

It certainly was. Despite Haile Gebrselassie being absent from this race, the field was a significant step up from the ones Hissou had competed against in 2002. Kenenisa Bekele, the man who many considered the heir to the throne, was looking in ominous form as he mixed it with the pacesetters.

Salah soon lost touch as the speed was applied in a kick down. Up ahead, Bekele was having a fierce battle with a bunch of Kenyans. On the penultimate lap he found himself boxed in, but managed to extract himself from the trap as they got the bell. It was a race of six that was soon to become a race of four. Abraham Chebii stormed to the lead with 250 metres to go and looked the winner as he opened up a small gap. Unfortunately he had played all his cards and was unable to maintain his form. In the final straight he had nothing left as Bekele, Kipketer and Eliud Kipchoge all went past him. A final burst over the last few metres was enough to give Kenenisa a narrow victory over Sammy. It was his first big win on the track.

Bekele made the following significant comments after the race.

"It was a very good competition tonight with a lot of Kenyans. I am very happy because I have improved my personal best. Going into the race I was aiming at a time around 12:45. I am not the new Haile Gebrselassie. I am a different athlete. Haile is a fantastic athlete but I am not him. In Paris at the World Championships I will only compete in the 10,000 metres because doubling up with the 5,000 metres would be too difficult."

He was very quick to declare that he was, and always would be his own man. His career was a very separate one to Gebrselassie's, even though they were managed by the same man and conducted much of their training together.

The top ten in this Bislett race were as follows:

Kenenisa Bekele	12:52.26
Sammy Kipketer	12:52.33
Eliud Kipchoge	12:52.61
Abraham Chebii	12:52.99
James Kwalia	12:54.58
Albert Chepkurui	12:56.27
Salah Hissou	13:05.89
Sileshi Sihine	13:09.90
Gebre-egziabher Gebremariam	13:14.54
Abiyote Abate	13:16.80

The last km was run in 2:30 with the final lap clocked at 54.64. It was little surprise that Hissou was unable to keep up. Still, this was a very encouraging performance from the veteran. He wasn't far off thirteen minutes and as such wasn't a long way off his best from last year. Afterwards he could breathe a huge sigh of relief, for this confirmed that he was still an elite athlete. Following Lausanne he may not have been so sure.

One runner who was far from elite here was the 2000 Olympic champion Million Wolde. In Oslo he finished a destitute nineteenth in 13:36.96.

Eighteen year old Kipchoge's 12:52.61 was a world junior record, highlighting the quality of the race. A twenty year old Ethiopian also ran well. Coming home eighth, only about twenty five metres behind Hissou was Sileshi Sihine.

The Norway race confirmed to Salah that he still belonged with the best and that he was in decent shape. It was only once the kick down started that his older legs were laid bare. Finishing seventh was still an excellent return, with the time of 13:05.89 more than promising. As such he should have felt invigorated and thus excited about his next race in Paris.

The Saint-Denis meeting was held on July 4 and again Salah was in great company. His run at Bislett had already put him into the ball park for selection to the World Athletics

MOROCCAN SUCCESS; THE KADA WAY

Championships. His excellent reputation also gave his chances an additional boost. Another good 5,000 metres performance in front of this 50,500 strong crowd in the Stade de France might seal the deal.

The race was conducted in a similar fashion to its Golden League predecessor. The top names were Kenyan dominated, but this time the race did not include Kenenisa Bekele. In his place was a more than handy replacement in the form of Haile Gebrselassie.

As usual the pace is fast from the gun and many of the fifteen man field is struggling early with the high standard. Haile is wearing his Adidas blue while Salah wears the Moroccan national colours. As the best runners distance themselves from the rest, these two stand out, though not just for their distinctive running styles, as most of their opposition wear red, distinguishing them as Kenyan.

The tempo is a virtually identical one to Oslo, as the pack reaches 3,000 metres in 7:44.62. Salah appears to be in solid shape. His stride is full as he matches it with the big guns.

The rabbits have exited and with Gebrselassie at the head of the field, the tempo takes a small dive. The 4,000 metres split ticks by in 10:23.38 with Hissou holding onto the elite group. Last year's top man Benjamin Limo now goes to the front and from there, everyone sits and waits for somebody else to make the decisive move.

Yet even as the runners hear the bell, there are no significant cards played. The pace gradually picks up regardless and Salah finally loses ground. He is already done before the real fireworks begin. Gebrselassie starts it all with a characteristic burst on the back straight. Like Chebii a week ago, he looks the winner. But last week's late fader has learnt his lesson and watches attentively. Abraham closes the gap on Haile and then delivers his own devastating sprint to win with relative ease. The full fifteen finishers in Paris were:

Abraham Chebii					12:53.37

Haile Gebrselassie	12:54.36
Benjamin Limo	12:54.99
Eliud Kipchoge	12:55.52
Salah Hissou	12:59.15
Gebre-Egziabher Gebremariam	13:03.19
Luke Kipkosgei	13:06.92
Ismail Sghyr	13:10.79
Abderrahim Goumri	13:11.39
Richard Limo	13:14.75
Charles Kamathi	13:20.43
Assefa Mezgebu	13:22.42
El Hassan Lahssini	13:22.89
Jose Manuel Martinez	13:24.88
Mohammed Amyn	13:25.34

The winning time was excellent and Abraham had the following to say after his big breakthrough.

"It's a good feeling to win a race and especially to beat Haile. You know Haile has been a great athlete, the greatest ever. He has done fantastic things on the track but I think it's now time for him to let the youngsters win. Before the race I thought that today would be my chance to beat him. I had planned to try and finish ahead of Haile and now that it's done, I am a happy man. I will run the 5,000 metres hopefully at the world's while Haile will run the 10,000 metres. But I am sure another one of my Kenyan fellows will give him a hard time at the world's."

In a nice way Chebii was suggesting that Gebrselassie's rule on the track was over.

Five men broke thirteen minutes in this 5,000 metres, but not many thirty one year olds ever achieve such a result. Well Salah had just done it, being the fifth placed athlete, tailing off from the stars while still holding a significant margin on the rest of the field. Winning at this level was likely to be beyond him now but good runs should always be cherished. Despite being past his peak, Hissou had been the first Moroccan home in both Golden League 5,000 metres events.

MOROCCAN SUCCESS; THE KADA WAY

He was probably happy to know that Aziz Daouda would hear about his second race of the season and realising the continued improvement, would see that the inner drive to succeed was still a part of his athlete. It's just that no amount of effort could adequately provide an answer to the pure speed that the first four finishers possessed. Nevertheless, this was a tremendous morale boosting run.

Some fans might not see it that way. They may say that this guy was a world champion and a regular winner at the distance. That he was the fastest in the world a year ago. We must keep in mind that it is incredibly difficult to remain competitive at the highest levels of this distance. You only had to scroll down the list of names behind Salah to reach that understanding.

Tenth, eleventh and twelfth were Richard Limo, Charles Kamathi and Assefa Mezgebu. They had been gold and silver medallists from Edmonton. None were over twenty five, yet here they were, just fifty five days out from the 5,000 metres heats of the next World Championships getting spanked by an elderly Moroccan! Post thirty, it was almost expected that Salah Hissou would fall from grace. That he remained competitive was almost more of a surprise.

Hissou was approaching his best form from 2002 as if right on cue. The Rome Golden League meeting was only one week away.

With Hicham El Guerrouj taking a short racing break, it gave Bernard Lagat an opportunity to win the 1,500 metres in Paris. Despite clocking 3:31.40, he was unable to prevail as he was upstaged by French star Mehdi Baala. His 3:30.97 was a personal best by one second for the twenty four year old. Given that the world's were in his home country, it was possible that Mehdi might lift his running to another level, thus providing Hicham with a potential threat. This season had already been most productive for Baala. On June 26 in Strasbourg he'd become the seventh fastest ever at 1,000 metres, clocking an impressive 2:13.96. On February 18 in Stockholm he'd also run a fast 800 metres indoors. His

1:44.82 third place performance wasn't far off event specialists Yuriy Borzakovskiy, 1:44.34 and Wilson Kipketer, 1:44.68.

Ali Ezzine was returning to the big time in the steeplechase event at Paris, without too much in the way of form going into it. His sole victory had come at the North African Championships that were held in Rades, Tunisia for the first time since 1990 where they were then known as the Maghreb Championships. The quality of competition was fairly weak for a runner of Ezzine's capabilities. The best athletes from Morocco and Algeria did not appear and Tunisia and Libya weren't exactly renowned for their talents in men's distance running. Ali was expected to win the steeplechase which he did, though not with any great authority. His time was just 8:32.71 with Tunisian Lotfi Turki, 8:33.90, pushing him most of the way.

Ali commenced his season proper in Rabat on June 14 and came through with a pretty good result of 8:19.58 to place third behind Abel Cheruiyot, 8:18.43 and Abdelkader Hachlaf, 8:16.51.

Hachlaf's first name reminded Ezzine of what he was missing. It was a surprise to see this athlete in this event as he was mostly known for being a pretty good middle distance runner, having won the bronze medal earlier in the year at the World Indoor Championships over 1,500 metres. This was just his third race over the barriers and he was adapting well.

Ezzine's first race in Europe at Lausanne on July 1 was a different story to Rabat in that it did not go well at all. Ezzine was not remotely competitive against the first three Kenyans who were led by Ezekiel Kemboi's very fast time of 8:06.37. Ali was basically only making up the numbers as he finished seventh in 8:25.01. Some improvement needed to be shown in Saint-Denis or it might be a case of concluding another track campaign early.

Fortunately the Moroccan had something in reserve and on July 4 an improved performance was seen in Paris. Despite

MOROCCAN SUCCESS; THE KADA WAY

slipping to an eighth place finish he was able to finish closer to his opponents this time around. The results of the twelve finishers in the steeplechase were:

Stephen Cherono	8:06.41
Paul Kipsiele Koech	8:06.63
Bouabdallah Tahri	8:06.91
Kipkirui Misoi	8:07.74
Ezekiel Kemboi	8:14.87
Abdelkader Hachlaf	8:15.33
Pavel Potapovich	8:15.54
Ali Ezzine	8:17.12
Vincent Le Dauphin	8:17.48
Michael Kipyego	8:18.81
Abel Yagout Jawher	8:24.23
Khamis Abdullah Saifeldin	8:31.68

Ali could take something from this. He wasn't far from being the first Moroccan who in this race was again Abdelkader Hachlaf. A realistic goal was to get back to being his nation's best before even concerning himself with the best Kenyans.

Kemboi was the disappointment in this race. It was strange to see him trailing so far behind because the Commonwealth Games silver medallist was expected to be a leading contender for the world title. Tahri performed brilliantly to equal Simon Vroeman as the fastest non Kenyan and Moroccan ever. The Commonwealth champion Stephen Cherono, continued with his outstanding form of 2003. Only three days earlier he had also been in Lausanne. Already a proven steeplechaser and the third fastest ever at 5,000 metres, Stephen wanted to show another string to his bow and competed in the 1,500 metres. Whilst not retaining his lofty standards of the longer distances, Cherono was nevertheless competitive and placed fifth in a time of 3:35.15, not too far behind winner Cornelius Chirchir's 3:34.06.

Also racing in Switzerland was Kenenisa Bekele who produced a devastating kick to win the 5,000 metres in 13:06.05. The Ethiopian recorded a last lap of 52.63, giving Sammy Kipketer, 13:07.78, no chance. Bekele now returned to the Golden League for the Rome 5,000 metres, where with the help of Gebrselassie, he hoped to defeat the posse of Kenyans, led by Paris winner Chebii. The stage was set for a memorable contest.

On the 11th of July, 2003, the time was right for Salah Hissou to make his mark at this old Olympic stadium which was like his Coliseum. The question was did he still have the same armoury that had served him well here in years past?

The 3,000 metres mark is passed in 7:45.60. Salah seems to be struggling to remain with the leaders but is suddenly thrown a surprising lifeline by Bekele who ventures into the lead yet opts to slow the pace. The fourth km is covered in 2:43.78, which brings the seven survivors to a ten lap split of 10:29.38.

Shortly afterwards Haile shoots into the lead, proceeding to run the second last lap in sixty seconds. Salah is well and truly beaten and so are many others due to this change of gears. The battle is now between Gebrselassie, Bekele and Chebii.

Despite his best efforts, Haile is unable to break away from the youngsters. But his actions now suggest that he'd expected this because he begins to shift out from lane 1. Moving aside with 100 metres to go, Gebrselassie releases Bekele and Chebii who close the race with devastating speed. The top ten place getters were:

Abraham Chebii	12:57.14
Kenenisa Bekele	12:57.34
Haile Gebrselassie	13:00.32
Gebre-egziabher Gebremariam	13:05.47
Albert Chepkurui	13:05.96
Sileshi Sihine	13:06.53
Salah Hissou	13:08.38
Hailu Mekkonen	13:10.16
Abderrahim Goumri	13:11.42
Assefa Mezgebu	13:14.60

MOROCCAN SUCCESS; THE KADA WAY

Again it was the Kenyan who triumphed, once again in under thirteen minutes, having closed the final 200 metres in under twenty five seconds! Injuries and age eventually catch up to all athletes. Haile Gebrsellasie was proving to be human after all.

That Haile ran for Kenenisa wasn't the greatest shock, since many considered that he'd passed his crown over to his protégé back on the 1st of June, when Bekele out kicked Gebrselassie in the 10,000 metres at Hengelo. His winning time of 26:53.70 (Haile, 26:54.58) was his first performance under the twenty seven minute barrier. Now he clearly seemed to have his elder statesman's measure, but Abraham was a different story.

Hissou tried his utmost to truly match the best of '03 but it was to no avail. This turned out to be a step back from his great output in Paris. It wasn't devastating. Simply another reminder that what he was attempting to accomplish was very much against the odds. Salah finished seventh in this one, the same placing as in Oslo. The big guns were putting him back in his rightful position.

Salah was generally unaccustomed to seventh place finishes. He usually only finished that lowly if he was lacking fitness, but fitness in this instant wasn't the problem. It was an age old problem. Age itself.

He was performing as well as he could. How could he improve on what he had produced so far? Salah didn't know if he could pull something out of the bag but he did know that he needed a brief respite from racing. Three 5,000's in two weeks was a big commitment. He would put his spikes away until August 5.

What really stood out from Rome was the revival of the Ethiopians. So poor in 2002, here they filled six of the top ten spots. Chebii's win was big for Kenya, but behind him Chepkurui was his only countryman in the top ten. Richard Limo was another talented Kenyan whose varying form was mystifying. It was tough to work out what was wrong with the reigning world champion, thirteenth here in 13:20.71.

El Guerrouj returned to the European circuit after nearly a month out, with the Rome meeting being his first attempt at his preferred distance this year. Subsequently Kada and he might have been slightly unsure just what to expect, so it surely was a relief when the world record holder was able to instantly revert back into his usual rhythm to win the 1,500 metres easily in 3:29.76. It was confirmation that the twenty eight year old was not losing any of his feared leg speed, even after contesting longer races. The Golden League field was left in tatters, which was a familiar scene, as the event became more of a time trial for Hicham. In second place was Kenyan Benjamin Kipkurui, 3:32.59. Trying to decipher what his best event was, Abdelkader Hachlaf didn't exactly succeed on his move back down to 1,500 metres. He finished seventh in 3:35.12.

The ease with which El Guerrouj won in Rome was staggering, considering the concerns that he and his support team had regarding his back. On July 7, Hicham was diagnosed with arthritis in his fifth vertebrae. It obviously sounded a lot worse than it actually was, for most runners would take a sub 3:30 under any conditions!

Just two days after Rome he took his crippled body to Gateshead and on the rarest of occasions he struggled. Perhaps his back injury was more serious as Hicham wasn't able to run freely when competing after the quick turnaround. The quality of his opposition wasn't particularly significant but the Moroccan was never allowed to break clear of Kenyan Paul Korir who almost produced one of the year's biggest upsets. Kicking down to a 40.68 final 300 metres, the world champion barely survived this scare to defeat Korir 3:33.41 to 3:33.63. Given that it was not a Golden League meeting, and the fact that ten athletes finished within five seconds of the champion, highlighted his laboured run.

Kada often showed great common sense and now was a good example. He gave El Guerrouj another respite from racing. His next event was again in England with a mile at

MOROCCAN SUCCESS; THE KADA WAY

London on August 8, which would lead into the big meeting at Zurich on August 15 where Hicham would contest the 1,500 metres. This was the final track and field action before the World Championships.

Stockholm hosted track racing on August 5 and Ali Ezzine returned to action in the 3,000 metres steeplechase for what was a vitally important test with the Paris steeplechase heats now not far away on August 23. This and Zurich were his lead up races to the championships and he needed good performances now to give him a realistic expectation of making the final. Only then could he start to dream again of what he had accomplished in Seville and Edmonton under Abdelkader Kada.

The Swedish meeting attracted a great field and Ali performed admirably, yet this was still nothing like his running from a few years ago. He registered a fifth placing and an 8:17.71. He even defeated some big names with Dutchman Simon Vroeman finishing seventh with 8:19.68 and Kenyan Ezekiel Kemboi taking ninth, whose time was a horrible 8:21.20. Could Kemboi get himself right to be amongst the medals in Paris?

Four Kenyans closed in front of Ezzine with the first two well ahead of the Moroccan. Stephen Cherono ran a world leading 8:04.75 to edge out Paul Kipsiele Koech, 8:05.28.

Hissou was also racing in Stockholm and had hopes of a high placing in his track campaign's first non Golden League event. For his confidence he needed a top three finish somewhere before going back to Paris for the World Championships.

Sadly Salah wasn't remotely close to challenging the top runners in his latest 5,000 metres competition. Perhaps he was rusty after a racing break of a few weeks. He could only pray that this was all it was. Running a time of 13:11.94 to register another seventh place finish was a major disappointment. Salah was really trailing off badly towards the end. It wasn't just the lack of a kick. Adding to the disappointment was the fact that this field was clearly the weakest he had raced against this season. The World Championships would be much tougher. Kenyan youngster Eliud Kipchoge won in a time of 13:00.63. Things looked very bad for Hissou's Paris prospects.

Not that any major successes had ever seemed realistic for him in 2003. It was pretty clear that he had missed his chance, although through no fault of his own. At 5,000 metres he was the second best in the world in 1999, which he fully confirmed when he became world champion. With the best (Gebrselassie) not interested in competing in the event at the major championships, there were going to be opportunities for Hissou to achieve even more success. There would be no guaranteed victories, but likely medals, whether they be bronze, silver or gold. 2000 and 2001 could have been anything for him but alas, injuries stood in his path. The competition remained relatively weak in 2002 but that was a year without a World Athletic Championships or Olympic Games for Salah to potentially capitalize on.

Now it was 2003 and the competition had risen a notch. At thirty one Salah was past improvement. He appeared unable to keep up any longer.

Medalling in Paris was highly unlikely. A respectable top eight finish was the best that he could realistically aim for in his current form. Not being one of the truly elite runners for the first time in many a year also raised another possibility With his great teammate Hicham El Guerrouj trying to do the 1,500/5,000 metres double, would Hissou be willing to work as a domestic and help him? Salah had always run for himself. Would a runner with such a great pedigree lower himself to the level of 'rabbit' in a major championship?

It was obvious that Salah Hissou was having major problems with his lack of basic speed. Wouldn't it have been common sense to compete in a 3,000 metres race in the Paris lead up? Not to win of course, but running a 7:35 or at least a sub 7:40 wasn't going to do his form any harm. It had always been a regular practice of Salah's to compete at the distance as a

MOROCCAN SUCCESS; THE KADA WAY

fine tuning for his major championship event. In any case, Hissou decided to race yet another 5,000 metres. Like most athletes his final lead up competition would be at Zurich on August 15.

Abderrahim Goumri produced a good run to finish as the first Moroccan in Sweden with fourth position and a time of 13:05.81. He was the third runner selected for Morocco's 5,000 metres squad in Paris. Still in the wars was Assefa Mezgebu who recorded a 13:18.70 for eleventh place. His enormous fall from grace was confirmed when he failed to make Ethiopia's team for Paris. He had medalled at the last three major championships and now seemed over the hill despite having just turned twenty five.

Showing a return to winning ways was Bernard Lagat who registered a 3:32.99 to be the first of five Kenyan runners home in the 1,500 metres. Abdelkader Hachlaf was best of the rest in sixth with a 3:35.10. He was to compete in the steeplechase at Paris. Lagat on the other hand would not be competing at all.

Another runner not racing was Hicham El Guerrouj, who was a late withdrawal from the London Grand Prix meeting on August 8. He continued to have problems with his back and the question was being asked as to whether he would even compete in Paris. Nobody was talking much now about his chances of winning two gold medals. It was all about defending and winning one.

The mile event was won by Paul Korir in 3:48.17. This was a terrific time and he defeated Cornelius Chirchir, 3:50.40, comprehensively. Korir was another Kenyan who seemed to have come out of nowhere. He hadn't produced anything of great substance until this year. He'd just turned twenty six, qualified and then been selected for the World Championship 1,500 metres. Coming into form at the perfect time, Abdelkader and Hicham could rightly consider him a dangerous man.

The 5,000 metres in London was won by Haile Gebrselassie

who rediscovered some of his finishing speed to dispose comfortably of Sammy Kipketer and John Kibowen and return to the winner's circle. His time was a fast 12:57.23, whereas the Kenyans clocked 12:59.13 and 12:59.74. Despite suffering losses earlier in the season, Haile figured to be a major factor in the World Championship 10,000 metres.

Usually it is the racing at Zurich that raises all the hot topics of discussion, but this year the meeting was held under different circumstances. Two of the world's leading distance runners of 2003 were the subjects of conjecture, though not for anything done on an athletics track. Nor had these men tested positive for a performance enhancing substance. The controversy surrounded their changing of allegiances that had many people questioning their morality.

Kenyan athletes, Stephen Cherono and Albert Chepkurui were both outstanding runners and just twenty one and twenty two years old respectively. This season Cherono led all athletes with his times of 12:48.81 at 5,000 metres and 8:04.75 for the steeplechase. His personal best was an even more impressive 7:58.10! Chepkurui had run a 12:56.27 for 5,000 metres and last year clocked a 26:50.67 for 10,000 metres. Quite clearly they had the talent that most other nation's best runners could not match. Yet in Kenya they were just two of the many great talents going around. There is no doubt that other countries would have wished to have athletes of this quality running for them.

Consequently, Qatar took things a little further and made their wish a reality. The middle east nation was donating some money to its athletics program, although this didn't only mean funding Qataris that showed potential. Instead it decided to recruit or poach other athletes that were already at an international level. This was common practice in the big money games of club teams for sports such as soccer and basketball but even in those instances, international competition was different. Competing for your country was sacrilege.

Track and field was a little different to the aforementioned

MOROCCAN SUCCESS; THE KADA WAY

sports. In Europe there wasn't a significant club competition where say a Hicham El Guerrouj could bargain and then command upwards of five million dollars per season guaranteed. There wasn't so much guaranteed money in the sport so the best athletes had less power and less financial security. Good money could be made while at the top, but particularly in Kenya's case, where the depth is huge, it is quite easy and common for an athlete to slip from his country's number one ranking in his discipline to outside the top ten with a relatively small drop off in performance. This means that suddenly an elite athlete can be struggling to make a living as they disappear from the national teams.

When Qatar approached Cherono and Chepkurui, the offer that it posed was a mighty attractive one. 'Come and compete for us and we will take good care of you financially.' The offer to Stephen of financial incentive even went beyond his athletics days with a guaranteed $1,000 (US) per month payment to last throughout his entire life. It was only $12,000 a year, but to ninety nine percent of Kenyans, this was the equivalent of becoming an instant millionaire. As both runners also knew that they would never have trouble making the national Qatar teams, they accepted the offer and by the 15th of August 2003, were ready to race for their adopted country.

Although this created widespread criticism in Kenya, some could see the good sense in the athletes' moves. World steeplechase champion Reuben Kosgei later remarked, "To me, I think it's something normal. That is not a surprise, because everyone in Kenya is very strong."

Not only would the Qataris run under new colours in championship races, but under new names in all races. The names were given to them, of Said Saeed Shaheen (Cherono) and Abdullah Ahmed Hassan (Chepkurui). It was no revelation that all of this had caused quite a stir.

However Kenya was not going to be a total loser throughout this unstable period. After being helpful to Qatar in making the switch of nationalities a fast process, the middle eastern country had agreed to build a tartan track at Eldoret, Kenya's high altitude training Mecca.

The move of Shaheen all of a sudden, created a rivalry in men's steeplechasing. Previously we had Ezzine and Boulami taking Kenya on, but with them falling by the wayside, the event had again become predictable this season. Now Kenya was threatened with losing its world title in Paris. The only thing worse than losing to a cheat (Boulami) could be losing to a traitor (Shaheen). The purists may not have liked what we were about to see but for sports fans wanting good contests, Shaheen's move was a Godsend!

Ali Ezzine's most important race of his season thus far, intertwined with all this political action. Even if it was impossible to do so, the race itself did its utmost to match the interest of national matters. The finish was incredible. If this was the start of a Qatar vs. Kenya war, then I can't imagine it starting in a much better way. The results of the Zurich steeplechase were:

Saif Saaeed Shaheen	8:02.48
Ezekiel Kemboi	8:02.49
Paul Kipsiele Koech	8:09.54
Abraham Cherono	8:13.14
Bouabdallah Tahri	8:13.65
Ali Ezzine	8:16.52
Wilson Boit Kipketer	8:17.84
Abel Yagout Jawher	8:19.24
Kipkirui Misoi	8:19.62
Pavel Potapovich	8:37.17

Now Shaheen was the fastest non Kenyan ever! The head to head battle helped to push Kemboi through to a personal best. Ezekiel was a different athlete to the one who raced at Stockholm only ten days earlier. Here he did everything in his power to try to retain his country's iron grip on the event. What a contest! This was only battle number one. The 3,000 metres steeplechase had all of a sudden become one of the most intriguing events in the World Championships.

Kemboi had now competed in eleven steeplechase races

MOROCCAN SUCCESS; THE KADA WAY

during 2003 for seven victories. He had won the Kenyan trials and clearly stamped himself as their number one man for Paris. Unfortunately, all his four season defeats had been at the hands of Shaheen whom he had yet to beat. The Zurich result indicated that the tide may be turning in this rivalry. The twenty one year old was a fast improver, having only been running for three years.

Shaheen's brother Abraham Cherono wasn't capable of duelling with his bro here but he had been selected for the Paris heats so perhaps he might be able to raise his standard there. So then we may have countries and families combating! Abraham had this to say about his brother during the World Championships, "It is strange. We have to compete against one another, and I have to do my best to beat him. I won't call him by his new name. He is still Stephen to me, because it's in the blood."

The man now known to the rest of the world as Saif said, "I really wanted to run under 8 minutes today and I certainly could have done it if I had run a different race but I could feel Ezekiel Kemboi on my heels and I know he's a very fast finisher so I decided to control the race and save my energy for the final sprint. If you really want me to be honest with you I don't think I am a very good steeplechase runner. I am definitely a better 5,000 metres runner. I will still compete in the 3,000 metres steeplechase in Paris, though. In 2004, I might do both but by 2005 I will definitely concentrate on the 5,000 metres."

It sounded like Shaheen was contemplating his own double in Athens. He concluded by saying. "My name? I didn't choose it; they just gave it to me. Do I like it? (laughs) Well the thing is that Cherono is more famous, everyone remembers Cherono. My heart feels Qatari now but all my fans are still back in Kenya."

Ali Ezzine managed his fastest time of the year, though the improvement was minimal and baring any miracle, it was not enough to hoist him into medal contention in Paris. A sixth position at Zurich was still okay and meant that the Moroccan was certainly capable of qualifying for the fifteen man final. Ali could look back on his fantastic record in major championships and draw belief from that.

Hicham El Guerrouj was on the start line for the 1,500 metres and the feeling was that he was vulnerable to losing his first race at this distance since Sydney 2000. After the 3:33 at Gateshead and withdrawal from London his opponents could smell blood. Hicham had dare not show any weakness at Zurich. Abdelkader knew that this event was vital, perhaps more so than the Paris final because what happened in Switzerland would likely lead on to a similar result at the World Championships. Had the injury curse taken down the king of the mile? The results from the Zurich 1,500 metres provided an emphatic answer:

Hicham El Guerrouj	3:29.13
Bernard Lagat	3:30.55
Fouad Chouki	3:30.83
Alex Kipchirchir	3:32.35
Paul Korir	3:33.25
Robert Rono	3:33.38
Vyacheslav Shabunin	3:33.69
Laban Rotich	3:34.37
Rui Silva	3:34.77
William Chirchir	3:35.19

No! His back was A Okay. It was the fastest time of the season and a comfortable winning margin to Bernard Lagat. Chouki was the race's surprise as he broke Baala's French record while improving his personal best from 3:33.05! Mehdi had competed in the 800 metres where he again showed that he was fleet of foot by finishing fourth in 1:44.46. France had replaced Spain as El Guerrouj's European threat.

Hicham had plenty to talk about after this significant victory.

"More than the time and the win, I am happy and proud of the way I ran and won this race today. 3:29 is not that great a time for me but this is not a track for a 3:25 or 3:26 run. But believe me the way I was controlling I know I can run 3:25.

MOROCCAN SUCCESS; THE KADA WAY

That is for sure. The doctors diagnosed arthritis in my fifth vertebrae but now I am back in perfect shape. I am still young and still motivated to run races and win races. Inch Allah, the World Championships in Paris will offer an excellent show for the fans and I will be able to win my fourth consecutive world title. My plans have not changed; I will still double 1,500 and 5,000 in Paris. I am now heading to Brussels for a four-day training session and will arrive in Paris on 20 August."

So to the disappointment of his rivals, nothing had changed.

Salah Hissou hoped otherwise. He had regarded the Stockholm race as a warm up for this big meeting in Zurich. The 5,000 metres event was to sharpen him up before Paris. But it couldn't have gone much worse.

Everything is going to plan. The 3,000 metres split is 7:47.32 with all the main contenders together. The Ethiopians are surprisingly absent, giving the Kenyans a chance to reassert their dominance.

With one mile to go we are down to nine runners, a large group at this latter stage of the event. Salah is keeping with the Kenyans and without an Ethopian in the field, here is his realistic opportunity at a top three finish.

Abraham Chebii is keeping towards the back of the long pack, seemingly not concerned about the front runners. On form he is the favourite to win here and at the World Championships. Recently he won the Kenyan trials in a great time of 13:24.8, considering the event was held at 1,500 metres altitude. This made it seven wins from his past eight races. Unfortunately he had since aggravated his left calf so was under an injury cloud as the Zurich race headed towards a sprint finish. Again the fourth km is slower, with the 4,000 metres split being almost identical to Rome at 10:29.09. Hissou remains in touch.

Not for long however. Approaching two laps to go he slides off the back with little resistance. There is no increase in speed up at the front. The legs just don't have it any more. They are no longer moving with the same cadence, no longer recovering as quickly from all the training and racing. In Switzerland Salah Hissou looked like an old athlete. He wasn't even dropped in the true sense. He'd just hit his own wall. This time the finishing speed is irrelevant. The Moroccan is done before the race is really on. It is his worst race (that he's finished) since 1997.

Not everyone else was having a great time of it either. Hissou's teammate Abderrahim Goumri had been long left behind, on his way to a last finishing sixteenth place in 13:36.08. Abraham Chebii wasn't faring as badly as the Moroccans but his form wasn't what it had been. With 400 metres to go he was threatening to lose contact with the dwindling elite pack. He wasn't going to win but there was never any threat that a Kenyan wouldn't.

It came down to a fantastic fight between four of them, with John Kibowen out sprinting Nicholas Kemboi, Sammy Kipketer and Leonard Mucheru. The overall standard of the race didn't match Oslo, Paris and Rome. This made Salah Hissou's run all the more second-rate. The top eleven finishers were:

John Kibowen	13:01.01
Nicholas Kemboi	13:01.14
Sammy Kipketer	13:01.44
Leonard Mucheru	13:01.76
James Kwalia	13:03.79
Abraham Chebii	13:04.39
Ahmad Hassan Abdullah	13:04.65
Zersenay Tadesse	13:09.27
Dieter Baumann	13:15.07
Ismail Sghyr	13:15.61
Salah Hissou	13:16.87

Despite this result Salah remained determined to race in Paris. He felt he deserved that much. After all, he was unable to even be on the start line to defend his title in Edmonton. So he would *be there* this time, but only in name really.

MOROCCAN SUCCESS; THE KADA WAY

If Salah was thinking along these lines then you could imagine how Goumri must have been feeling. In comparison Salah had destroyed Abderrahim in Zurich who was also set to race in Paris. So perhaps all was not lost for Hissou.

Behind the Kenyans but well ahead of the Moroccans in Zurich came one of Qatari's finest. Abdullah's debut didn't quite match it with Shaheen's but his good time in the 5,000 metres showed that he was in decent shape to be a factor in the Paris 10,000 metres. Immediately after Ahmad in eighth place was Eritrea's Tadesse. Zersenay, like the Qatar athlete, broke his national record.

Greg Rowlerson

Hicham Attempts To Outdo The Great Said

The heats of the men's 1,500 metres at the 2003 World Athletics Championships commenced at 6:00 pm on August 23. There was drama even before a gun was fired. Kenya's Bernard Lagat was drawn to compete in heat 1 but withdrew, the Kenyan Federation citing illness as the reason for his sudden departure.

This should have had Abdelkader Kada doing cartwheels! Hicham El Guerrouj would now be a stronger favourite to win a record fourth world title at the distance.

Nothing of significance occurred in the heats and for this the IAAF should be blamed. There were twenty four qualifiers for the semi finals but only twenty eight athletes started after Lagat's late scratching. The heats should have been scrapped altogether.

To ask a runner to race three of these events in a short period is quite demanding. Here, the IAAF was handed a fantastic opportunity to show some initiative and have the best milers in the world fresher for the final by having them complete only one preliminary round. Unfortunately sanity doesn't always prevail and the heats were a total waste of time and energy for El Guerrouj and the athletes in the class below him.

The first heat was won in a pedestrian time of 3:47.26 by New Zealander Adrian Blincoe. El Guerrouj won heat 2 with a 3:42.24. The farcical nature of this 'training run' was apparent when learning that if his race was faster than the previous one (which it was almost certain to be) he need only finish in the first eight of nine competitors to guarantee a birth in the semi finals, even if everyone in heat 3 broke 3:30!

Rui Silva won that heat in the fastest time of 3:41.35. When all this excitement was over, the final qualifier of the twenty four was Kirghizistan's Valery Pisarev who ran a personal best time of 3:50.89. The fastest runner to miss out was Pakistan's Miran Atta Atta who clocked 3:51.34. It was good

MOROCCAN SUCCESS; THE KADA WAY

to know that so many important questions had been answered before the semi finals. Kada could sleep well tonight knowing that Atta Atta was out of the reckoning!

The steeplechase heats were of course much more serious and Ali Ezzine faced up to his potential landmine at 7:00 pm later that night in heat 1. The first four were automatically through to the final and with two Kenyans and some worthy Europeans, this wasn't going to be easy. The race started at a good tempo with France's Vincent Le Dauphin taking the bunch to 1,000 metres in 2:46.50. The pace slowed significantly in the middle km with 2,000 metres being reached in 5:39.67 and Jose Luis Blanco of Spain now at the front. The latter stages were awkward times for Ezzine as seven athletes remained in contention for those automatic places. Unusually for Ali, he was unable to finish strongly and only managed sixth. At least the final km was quick and his time of 8:20.10 was pretty good. There was a chance that he could make it as one of three fastest losers, but all that was required now was to have two runners finish outside the first four in faster times than Ali in the next two heats. It was extremely disappointing that the Moroccan had left himself in this predicament. Hopefully he could run much better if given a second chance.

The second heat was very slow in the first 2,000 metres and even a big kick down couldn't bring the winner down to Ezzine's time, so it came down to heat 3.

The situation looked very grim for the Moroccan when a big pack went through 2,000 metres in 5:37.69, faster than heat 1. However the pace failed to increase in quite the same manner as its predecessors and Ezzine was safely into the final. Despite the winner (Luis Martin) clocking 8:19.09, the fifth and sixth athletes were outside of Ali's performance. He would get an opportunity at a third World Championship medal in three days time.

Abdelkader Hachlaf was the second Moroccan qualifier for the final with Zouhair Ouerdi missing out. Saif Saaeed Shaheen won heat 2 with his teammate Khamis Abdullah

Saifeldin also qualifying. Three Kenyans made it with a fourth, Michael Kipyego, surprisingly finishing just ninth in Ezzine's heat. Despite that, we had the makings for Paris' most interesting final with Qatar taking on Kenya!

On August 24 the men's 10,000 metres final took centre stage and again there was a lack of a presence from Morocco. Should Salah have been competing in the 10,000 metres, rather than the 5,000 metres? It seemed logical that Hissou could achieve a better placing in the longer race but he had long since done away with his former favourite event. Maybe he would finish a couple of spots higher but that wouldn't mean a lot anyway. Morocco had a chance to win the 5,000 metres and Hissou may have wanted to give some help to that cause.

The non participation of Morocco in the longest track event didn't adversely affect the race as a spectacle for it was quite extraordinary. This was the race that guaranteed Haile Gebrselassie's status in many peoples' minds as the greatest long distance runner of all time. This, in a race that he didn't even *win*. It still rated as one of his best ever performances. Haile made this final the greatest 10,000 metres race ever, even better than Atlanta '96.

After a comparable pedestrian pace for the first 5,000 metres in 13:52.23, Kenenisa Bekele and Haile Gebrselassie ran the second half in under thirteen minutes! This was almost impossible to imagine, let alone accomplish! Bekele ran the final 5,000 metres at a speed which surpassed Hissou's championship record for a *sole* 5,000 metres as well as Aouita's old world record time!

The action was red hot, right from the moment that Bekele ran the fourteenth lap in sixty one seconds, leaving just his teammates Gebrselassie and Sihine, and the Kenyan world champion Kamathi with him. Haile took the lead for the next lap and the pace barely slowed as the quartet stormed through 6,000 metres in 16:26.85 following a 2:34.52 km! That in itself is ridiculous. Yet there was much more to come.

MOROCCAN SUCCESS; THE KADA WAY

Kenenisa went back to the front and the result was a sixty three second sixteenth lap. Haile still wasn't satisfied so he took up the front running again and produced another sixty two. This was torturous. But Kamathi was still there. Haile wanted to make sure that this was an Ethiopian trifecta. He pushed on, running a sixty four for lap eighteen, with the seventh km clocked at 2:38.29. He had forgotten about tactics to win the race. He was truly running for his country.

This was vastly different to when Haile first competed in the World Championships, where he had no support in the 10,000 metres. Now it were three Ethiopians vs. one Kenyan. Haile was going to make sure that he ran Kamathi into the ground for defeating him two years earlier.

On the nineteenth lap Haile moved out to let Kenenisa take the lead but he refused to accept the offer. Gebrselassie surged harder still and for this lap they ran a sixty one, which resulted in Charles Kamathi raising the while flag (he would eventually finished seventh). Haile continued with his front running, something that the athletics world hadn't been used to witnessing. He ran the next lap in sixty three which made for a 2:37.44 eighth km.

As the three surviving Ethiopians came up to one mile to run, Haile moved out to lane 2, encouraging one of his teammates to pass, but again they refused to assist him. The rest of the field was now over fifty metres behind. Gebrselassie could run tactically. Why didn't he?

Still pushing on with the hard work, Haile ran the ninth km in 2:37.98 for a 24:20.56 split. He continued to push harder, registering another punishing sixty one second lap as they heard the bell. The youngster Sileshi was now twenty metres off the back, but Bekele was sticking to his idol like super glue.

Kenenisa went past Haile with 200 metres to go with Gebrselassie no longer having his famous kick to call upon. Bekele's winning time was 26:49.57, with Gebrselassie recording 26:50.77. It was amazing stuff. Kenya had never before been embarrassed like this. Haile may have finished second, but to most athletics fans he remained a winner in every sense.

Sihine finished with an outstanding time of 27:01.44 and to add further insult to Kenya the fourth placed finisher was from Qatar! Yes, Ahmad Hassan Abdullah finished strongly to register a 27:18.28. The next three were Kenyans with John Korir, 27:19.94, Wilberforce Talel, 27:33.60 and finally the forlorn figure of Charles Kamathi, 27:45.05.

Hicham El Guerrouj raced in the first semi final of the 1,500 metres at 8:50 pm on August 25. The interesting situation (or for Abdelkader, a potentially worrying situation) that Hicham found himself in at these championships, was that he was the sole Moroccan in the event. In the past he had usually relied on the help of a teammate to make the race fast, as he was used to in a European Grand Prix meeting. It was the one criticism that some had of Hicham. In spite of his wonderful record there were many who believed that he couldn't win 'an honest race', when the pace was slower and more tactics came into play. It was for this reason that some thought him to be vulnerable in Paris. Realistically, this was the only reason to doubt him, for his form at Zurich confirmed that he remained the finest athlete in this discipline.

Many were talking up the chances of Mehdi Baala, citing his excellent 800 metres speed and how that may come more into play in a slowly run final. This sounded logical, but like we had seen before, it doesn't always equal the end result. For example we may have thought that in previous 5,000 metres races a slowly run race would likely suit Ali Saidi-Sief, who had superior 1,500 metres speed compared to his rivals. But converting that at the end of a longer race is sometimes more difficult than it sounds and Saidi-Sief's advantage in 1,500 metres speed might not be the same over 800 metres. It was the same with the El Guerrouj vs. Baala confrontation. The Frenchman's supposed superior speed over 800 metres does not necessarily mean that he has superior speed over 400 metres, or that he can produce close to his 800 metres best after running 700 metres prior, no matter how slow the tempo.

MOROCCAN SUCCESS; THE KADA WAY

These scenario's related to many other athletes. For example Salah Hissou had great 1,500 metres speed for a 10,000 metres runner but was often out kicked by Paul Tergat and others who had slower personal records at the middle distance. Ali Ezzine had slow 3,000 metres flat speed compared to others in the steeplechase yet he often produced fast finishes in the last 200 metres of races. Khalid Skah never possessed daunting times at shorter distances but everyone feared his finishing sprint.

Hicham produced a nice turn of foot to win his semi final, completing the final 300 metres in 39.54 seconds for an overall result of 3:38.25. It was close however, with sixth placed man Gert-Jan Liefers clocking 3:38.61. The Dutch runner would have to wait and see if he qualified as a fastest loser.

Mehdi Baala was arguably more impressive in the second semi that was fractionally slower. He ran the last 300 metres in 39.28 for a total time of 3:39.73. There were no surprises from both races so we had learned nothing at all before the final that we didn't know when we started in Paris.

The only minor point of discussion was some bleeding seen coming from arguably the most valuable feet in the world. Hicham had blood showing on his right foot that resulted from an incident during his semi. One of his staff informed the media that it was nothing serious even though the Moroccan was seen to be limping a little. El Guerrouj had two days to get fully right for the final.

Tuesday, August the 26th was a day that saw one of the greatest finals in the history of the World Championships. The men's 3,000 metres steeplechase kicked off at 9:30 pm. Usually in any event that exceeds 800 metres there is a lull in proceedings during some part of the race. This final was a rare example of a race that contained no lapses. The entire final was an explosion of activity, with the pace and positioning of athletes varying throughout. That it contained country and family in fighting was an added bonus. Could Ali Ezzine perform well enough to be amongst the action?

Ezzine quickly settles into a reasonable position, in about sixth place but already finds himself way behind the two leaders before the first lap is completed. Both are the athletes running for Qatar! Saifeldin is acting as a rabbit, pacing Shaheen and after 300 metres they are over fifteen metres in front with the Kenyan's in third, fourth and fifth, not knowing what to do about these crazy front running tactics.

Adding further humour to the situation is the point that Saifeldin isn't Qatar born either. Khamis is from Sudan but is making good money in his adopted country having said that, "I made $180,000 in bonuses last year!"

Into the second lap and one Kenyan begins chasing but he's almost twenty metres down with the pack another ten metres behind him! Abraham Cherono is the Kenyan chasing after his brother Stephen and before the end of the second lap he has latched onto the leaders despite them keeping up the same insane pace. Saifeldin is done for after only 800 metres. Well he is only an 8:18 athlete after all. Shaheen takes off and immediately puts ten metres on his brother! This is truly incredible stuff. He reaches the first km in 2:36.24. This is way under world record pace. Try sub 7:50! Shaheen has about forty metres on the main bunch that is led by Ezekiel Kemboi who is expected to be his major challenger. Ezzine is next, going well in fourth position. Soon Shaheen is twenty five metres ahead of Cherono and appears to be sprinting down the back straight.

With four laps remaining, Shaheen still looks like Superman. Kemboi is realizing the urgency of his situation and has put five metres on Ezzine. Most of the field is a further fifteen metres back. The athletes are spread out in the manner that you might expect during the second half of a 10,000 metres, not halfway through a steeplechase!

Shaheen heads down the back straight again and his lead measures about thirty five metres, but that is over his brother who appears spent. Kemboi has just taken off and passed Abraham and is in pursuit of the Kenyan traitor.

MOROCCAN SUCCESS; THE KADA WAY

Ezekiel's comments after the heats had added even more fuel to the Qatar vs. Kenya fire. The national champion said that, "It will not be good for Kenya if this man wins. It will be very hard for us. It will demoralise Kenyans. Yes, I am angry. To do this, at this time, when the World Championships are on, is not right. He could have waited until he was running slower, around 8:20. Yes, what is being spoken about is a lot of money in Kenya, but I would never do this. I am happy to run for Kenya for $200 a month. What he has done is sell his country."

Certainly didn't mince his words!

Approaching three laps to go Shaheen finally looks to be tiring. He still has a margin of twenty metres on Kemboi and 50 metres on most of the field, but now Ezekiel is literally sprinting down the back straight to make contact with Saif. The surging in this race is unbelievable. Admittedly Shaheen is now struggling but the speed at which Kemboi is running is astonishing. Can he go on with it and defeat his rival on this occasion?

The 2,000 metres split is 5:19.58 after a 2:43.34 second km which is still very fast, but they are now a little off world record pace. Bare in mind that this is Shaheen's split. Kemboi probably ran the second km in around 2:36! He is motoring and straight after the split takes the lead and immediately sets about destroying Shaheen. There is no cat and mouse game here. It is just all out effort! But now approaching two laps remaining, Kemboi is tiring as well. He slows and Shaheen is able to sit on him. Suddenly they are jogging, but despite being in recovery mode, still have at least twenty five metres on the third place athlete who remains Abraham Cherono. He is nearly being caught by two of the Spaniards, the Martin's. Ali Ezzine is still thereabouts in seventh place but now he begins to drop away from the medals. He is not at his best, which is unfortunate, as he is still giving it his all. Up ahead the show goes on and with 700 metres left, Shaheen retakes the lead but is no longer able to surge now. In a show of defiance, Kemboi instantly regains the lead.

At 600 metres to go, the leaders are back into a genuine jog (for this level!) and the two Spaniards suddenly surge up behind them. By the bell they are only five metres in arrears. Another ten metres back is Bouabdallah Tahri of French and the Paris crowd is really cheering him on. However he can never get into the frame to contend for the victory. Cherono has dropped a little behind him and is cooked. Ezzine was put on a plate a lap ago!

Just as the Spaniards consider themselves a chance, Kemboi kicks with 300 metres left and puts a small gap on Shaheen. Yet then he himself (this guy is a nutcase!) sprints back on to, and passes his Kenyan rival. This is all happening within 60 metres mind you! They now have fifteen metres on the closest of the Martin's. Nothing changes until the last jump as Kemboi attacks it and sneaks past Shaheen. However the Qatari battles back again on the inside in the final 30 metres to win. What a race! The results of the thirteen finishers were:

Saif Saaeed Shaheen	8:04.39
Ezekiel Kemboi	8:05.11
Eliseo Martin	8:09.09
Bouabdallah Tahri	8:10.65
Abraham Cherono	8:13.37
Luis Miguel Martin	8:13.52
Simon Vroemen	8:13.71
Jose Luis Blanco	8:17.16
Jukka Keskisalo	8:17.72
Ali Ezzine	8:19.15
Yoshitaka Iwamizu	8:19.29
Khamis Abdullah Saifeldin	8:28.37
Abdelkader Hachlaf	8:35.17

Kenya lost two of the medals in its pet event so it was far from happy with the outcome. The result was arguably harder to take since the new Kenyan team coach for the championships was none other than steeple legend Moses Kiptanui. The reigning world champion Reuben Kosgei failed to finish (still suffering from his achilles injury) and Cherono's early burst effectively ruined his medal chances. Generally, Kenyan born athletes remained supreme. The change from Edmonton was

MOROCCAN SUCCESS; THE KADA WAY

the improvement of the Europeans and the fall of the Moroccans.

Compared to where he was at a year ago, tenth best in the world was a good conclusion for Ali Ezzine. With Hachlaf having a shocker he was back to being his nation's best also. But the big story was the gold medallist.

Soon after he crossed the finish line, Shaheen celebrated by grabbing his 'national' flag. A broadcaster made the comment, "Now Shaheen with a flag that a couple of weeks ago he wouldn't even have recognized!" He looked very proud of 'his country', which was a bit of a joke really. Kemboi looked on despondently though he did accept the result as another Kenyan win. "To me, it was a Kenyan gold medal. He is Kenyan born, and until earlier this month he ran for Kenya, so I see this as another Kenyan victory."

Shaheen disagreed with his sentiments, saying, "You can call it a Kenyan medal, but it is the Qatar flag that will be raised tomorrow. I admit I have never heard the national anthem of Qatar, but I look forward to doing so tomorrow at the medal ceremony."

Saif also admitted that Abraham was not too pleased with the result observing, "He is Kenyan. I am running for Qatar. We are two different people now so there were no congratulations. Fifty per cent of my family are so happy for me, the others are not, but I have been given a great welcome by Qatar."

It was going to be tough to top that drama but having an athlete attempting his fourth consecutive world title was a good way to go about it. Hicham's final started at 9:00 pm on Wednesday, August 27.

The pace is fairly slow as initially Baala takes up the front running. Hicham is right behind him. Then after 250 metres, Estevez storms to the lead and claps on the pace leading to a solid 57.70 first lap split. El Guerrouj sits in third spot with Baala fourth on his inside. Hicham is covering extra distance in this race, something that he rarely does. This is developing into a more tactical affair.

With 800 metres to go El Guerrouj moves past Estevez with Baala following in hot pursuit. The pace is not on yet as the 800 metres split is only 1:56.29. I say *only* in comparison to other major championship races involving Hicham. Compared to previous eras this is a more than respectable split time. With 500 metres left he is starting to wind it up. This is a gradual thing. As they hear the bell it is Baala and Estevez trailing the Moroccan but they are very much in contention. The next split is 2:51.28 at 1,200 metres and now is where he really does go.

To the naked eye it appears that Hicham has only moved into top gear now, yet the previous lap was covered in 54.99, a very fast speed indeed! This is the subtle, deceptive nature of El Guerrouj's running style. The legs don't all of a sudden turn over at a much faster rate but he lengthens his stride a fraction. This is how he gives the impression that he can cruise at fifty five second lap pace, unlike any before him.

As Hicham continues to build up pace on the back straight, only Baala can match it to the top of the turn. The Paris crowd is wildly cheering on its hero as it anticipates him challenging the marvellous Moroccan. The Frenchman stays with him, yet never seriously threatens to pass until the final fifty metres when the gap inevitably grows. This is history as El Guerrouj surpasses Morceli's three world titles. Who said that he requires a rabbit? He took the race by the scruff of the neck and prevailed. Again. The results of the 1,500 metres final were:

Hicham El Guerrouj	3:31.77
Mehdi Baala	3:32.31
Ivan Heshko	3:33.17
Paul Korir	3:33.47
Rui Silva	3:33.68
Reyes Estevez	3:33.84
Gert-Jan Liefers	3:33.99
Vyacheslav Shabunin	3:34.37

MOROCCAN SUCCESS; THE KADA WAY

Isaac Kiprono Songok   3:34.39
Roberto Parra   3:35.02
Juan Carlos Higuero   3:38.49

With another fast run Hicham now had the three fastest winning times in major championship history! After being congratulated by Mehdi, Hicham sank to the track, knelt and bowed his head in prayer. This is a very Islamic custom for Moroccan runners. After proudly carrying the Moroccan flag, El Guerrouj does a little celebratory jig. He won't ever become the lord of the dance but it is humorous and entertaining all the same. Abdelkader Kada would have been ecstatic that his man is still the king!

Hicham made reference to the 'me against them' battle when he acknowledged in his post race comments, "It wasn't easy. I was against 60,000 people out there. Since I arrived in Paris I have not been able to sleep. I have found it impossible to sleep for five days, and as well as that, I was up against the whole of France. I rang home last night and said, 'All of France hates me,' but my sister said, 'God loves you and he will help you win'. 'Bring me back the gold,' she said, and that's what I did. This is fantastic. I have protected my kingdom. I am still king of the 1,500 metres."

He gave credit to Baala while also taking a shot at his critics, some who said he was finished due to his back injury and some who even suggested that he was exaggerating the problem. "Mehdi made it a wonderful race and was given fantastic support by the crowd, but I never doubted I would win. The race was crazy, but it is the most beautiful day of my life. There have been criticisms of me this year, but when you are facing a challenge you have to deal with a few things like that. Some people said I was finished, but look at me, I am young, beautiful, and classy. The whole of France was supporting Mehdi and I understand that, but it is disappointing there have been so many negative comments about me this year. I am an ambassador for the sport and we should be sending out positive messages."

El Guerrouj was generally regarded as a great ambassador of

his sport and two days later this was highlighted when he was voted in by his peers as one of twelve athletes to represent them on the IAAF Athletes Commission. Only Haile Gebrselassie received a greater number of votes from the twenty six candidates.

Hicham had further enhanced his reputation as a person of tremendous character when during his lap of honour he picked up and hugged Baala's daughter. This was an amazing gesture that had the Frenchman in tears. Baala said of El Guerrouj, "His generosity of spirit and humanity is an example to us all of how we can better ourselves."

Some other comments from the silver medallist were, "Having everyone cheering for you gives you an advantage, but also brings a lot of pressure. It was like being in a concert hall. My ears were almost hurting from the noise and I was nearly brought to tears. Hicham is a fantastic runner. Thinking you are going to beat him is dreaming, but I ran the right race. I don't think the Olympics next year will be as stressful as this."

Maybe not for you Mehdi but I'm not sure that Athens will be quite as relaxing for Hicham!

The race's latter stages again showed that while the Moroccan's pure speed wasn't the greatest ever seen at the distance, his strength was without peer. The final lap was timed at 53.90 seconds. This wouldn't have been extraordinary for Sebastian Coe and Morceli often ran sub fifty two second laps during his prime. It was the fact that Hicham could run at close to this speed for 600 metres or a little longer in some instances that separated him from past greats.

Following this, El Guerrouj now had to back up for the 5,000 metres heats. It was an exhausting program, but having got the 1,500 metres out of the way, he could race the longer event for enjoyment. There would not be the same pressure to face, despite there being potentially a fantastic opportunity to create even more history. Kada had no concerns on him backing up. "He will definitely be there because he is not tired

MOROCCAN SUCCESS; THE KADA WAY

at all after the 1,500 metres final."

The heats took place the following evening on Thursday the 28th of August. Hissou was in heat 1, commencing at 6:45 pm local Paris time. El Guerrouj took centre stage again at 7:05 pm.

Going by a well proven assumption, automatic qualification for Sunday's final shouldn't have been an issue. The first five finishers from the two heats went through, with an additional five fastest losers. Salah was one of five runners in heat 1 that were competing for one of distance running's three power house nations. There was one Ethiopian (Kenenisa Bekele), two Kenyans (John Kibowen and Eliud Kipchoge) and two Moroccans (Abderrahim Goumri joined Hissou). In the past decade it was rare for any athletes from these nations to miss making a final of the 5,000 metres or 10,000 metres. As the gun sounded, some wondered how Salah, Abderrahim and Hicham would work together once we got to the final. Qualification was made to sound even easier when three of the scheduled fourteen competitors in Salah's heat withdrew.

The situation wasn't that simple for Hissou, for on this season's form he was unlikely to defeat the Kenyans or Bekele, so already three of the five guaranteed finals places were gone. Goumri was unpredictable and then there was the quality of the other Africans to consider. Zersenay Tadesse of Eritrea and Boniface Kiprop of Uganda were both emerging athletes of real distance running calibre. We have thus established that six competitors have a great chance at beating Salah. Perhaps if Abdelkader were still his coach he would have suggested to the experienced Moroccan that setting a reasonable pace in his preliminary race would be in his best interests, rather than risk a bunch sprint in a slow contest.

However the heat started at a woeful pace and Hissou found himself leading at 1,000 metres in 2:58.83. It already seemed like a good chance that no fastest losers would come out of this heat. In this situation it's up to an athlete who doesn't believe in his kick to pick up the tempo, therefore increasing his chances of qualification. Salah didn't look concerned. Racing in the later heat was always advantageous because the pack could set a pace that was a little quicker and potentially get more qualifying runners through from that heat. Finishing outside of the first five in heat 1 was going to be more than risky.

The pace did pick up substantially as the distance wore on with 2,000 metres reached in 5:48.91, then 3,000 metres passed in 8:32.33. The fourth km is very fast, a 2:35.79 for an 11:08.12 split at 4,000 metres with Kenenisa leading the charge. By this stage there were still eight of the eleven starters in contention. Hissou was in the bunch but could he finish ahead of three of his rivals?

There were no surprises with the heat winner. Kenenisa Bekele stormed home, clocking 13:38.03, comfortably ahead of Eliud Kipchoge's 13:38.73. Two distance stars of the future finished sixth and seventh in Tadesse and Kiprop. A distance star of the past faded behind them in eighth position, stopping the clock at 13:44.27. It was improbable that Salah's run would be good enough for a final's berth.

Heat 2 also had three runners pull out, leaving only twelve athletes to compete. Sub thirteen minute man Abdullah of Qatar didn't start, which was understandable if he was too tired from the pulsating 10,000 metres final.

The depth in this heat was slightly less impressive, though El Guerrouj still had to face two Ethiopians (Gebre-egziabher Gebremariam and Abiyote Abate) and two Kenyans (Richard Limo and Abraham Chebii). Hicham was comforted to know that at least Goumri had safely qualified after he'd placed fourth in heat 1. However a faster tempo here would likely send Hissou packing early.

Significantly the first km is much faster as the pack records a 2:48.47 split with Suarez of Mexico leading. The pace remains fairly consistent and by the latter stages there have been only two runners dropped. As the bunch goes through 4,000 metres in 11:04.49 with Limo in front, it is a near

MOROCCAN SUCCESS; THE KADA WAY

certainty that most of the qualifiers will come from this race.

Hicham looked superb, as if converting to an event more than three times his usual distance was totally natural. Being largely a strength/endurance runner, it made sense that he could have more success at this discipline than others that had tried before him. The great British milers couldn't reproduce the same levels of performance at longer distances and Morceli, while breaking the 3,000 metres world record, had never run sub thirteen minutes in this event. Aouita had of course dominated it, but it is up for debate as to whether Said was better suited to middle distance or longer.

El Guerrouj was now in the middle of a quest that he hoped would result in an historic double. No man had won both the 1,500 and 5,000 metres at a major championship since the legendary Finn Paavo Nurmi did it at the 1924 Olympic Games. Symbolically these championships were also in Paris. Kenyan Kip Keino had come the closest in the seventy nine years since, with his exploits at the 1968 Mexico City Games. Like Hicham he'd already triumphed in the 1,500 metres when he embarked on the 5,000 metres. After another great performance, he won the silver medal in his second final after losing to Tunisian Mohamed Gammoudi by a mere fifteen hundredths of a second! Said Aouita certainly had the potential to achieve such a double. From 1984-1989 he was one of the best in the world at both events. In 1987 he was virtually unbeatable and won the 5,000 metres at the Rome World Championships with consummate ease. He would have started the shorter event as nearly as big a favourite, however during this era the finals of the 1,500 and 5,000 metres were held on the same day, making his task impossible in the modern professional age. Times had changed since Nurmi won his 5,000 metres gold approximately one hour after the 1,500 metres final!

El Guerrouj frequently ran his middle distance races at sub 2:20 km pace so it wasn't hard to explain why he would appear comfortable now running at 2:46 km pace. A sub 2:30 final km should be like a walk in the park, even taking into account that this heat was within twenty four hours of his latest gold medal winning run. Though of course a famous Finn would have laughed at the suggestion that the Moroccan might be tired!

The Moroccan did go sub 2:30, finishing in fourth place with a time of 13:32.88. The five favourites finished as expected and were all within one second of each other with Gebremariam taking it in 13:32.46.

Behind the first seven athletes there were runners being dropped. During the final lap there suddenly appeared a chance that Salah might get away with a great escape. But his poor performance and lack of initiative cost him dearly. Effectively, the sluggish first 1,000 metres was the difference between the two heats and Hissou was out. Out of the World Championships. Out of Paris. His time on the track had run out.

The former world champion could hardly consider himself unlucky as there were two runners faster than him who also did not make the final. Boniface Kiprop had to console himself after missing out by less than half a second. The Ugandan was still short of his eighteenth birthday. What a talent. His future looked bright and this small failure need only be a minor career setback.

A common perception was often that Moroccan men's running was all about Hicham El Guerrouj but the true strength of its teams was that there were always others to step up and perform at the major championships.

On August 30, Morocco had its first championship marathon success in the modern era when thirty one year old Jaouad Gharib won the gold medal in an outstanding time of 2:08.31. This was a championship record, however the victory was far from easy with Spain's Julio Rey finishing only seven seconds adrift. Gharib had never quite made it as a track runner, but a 7:39.22 personal best for 3,000 metres is good leg speed if you can combine it with strength for the marathon. Last year he had begun his road quest with an excellent second place at the World Half Marathon Championships. He was being

MOROCCAN SUCCESS; THE KADA WAY

coached by Brahim Boutayeb, someone who certainly knew about performing at a major championships. Jaouad's move up from the track was obviously a highly successful one. Would it entice another Moroccan track runner to consider making a similar move?

It was surprising that Morocco had not enjoyed recent success in championship marathons, not the fact that they did break through in Paris. Abdelkader El Mouaziz was the one guy to have made an impact, placing seventh in Sydney and sixth in Edmonton. Mouaziz had clocked fast times also. In 2002 he ran a 2:06.46 at Chicago. Khalid Khannouchi had of course broken the world record there three years earlier with his 2:05.42 making him the first ever sub 2:06 athlete. In 2002 in London he knocked his own mark down to 2:05.38 while competing for America. Mouaziz ran 2:06.52 in the same race. Abdelsalam Serrokh had registered a 2:08.59 at the 1999 Rotterdam Marathon. The Mahgreb nation had plenty of pedigree and after the result of Paris there would be future expectations, starting with the Athens Olympics next year.

The 5,000 metres final that Salah Hissou failed to qualify for was an extraordinary race. It was almost of a similar ilk to the men's 10,000 metres final. Even at his best, Salah would not have medalled. It was further confirmation that his track career was over.

It started at 6:40 pm on Sunday, August 31. All the talk was of Bekele and El Guerrouj. And why not? Both were trying for rare doubles and both had realistic chances of pulling it off. Bekele's double was more common since his two events are more similar than Hicham's though nobody had won both the 5,000 and 10,000 metres at a major championships since Miruts Yifter at the Moscow Games in 1980. Kenenisa had two teammates while Hicham had one. These were considered to be only supporting runners as none had the capabilities of actually winning.

This wasn't like a heavyweight boxing duel. Kenenisa and Hicham embraced each other during their pre race warm up, appearing to be more like teammates than rivals. Nic Bideau on Hicham. "The thing about El Guerrouj is he doesn't actually have an extremely fast finish. I mean in 1,500 metres running it's not really required because you're going so quickly already and there's such volumes of lactic acid in your legs. You finish in fifty four, that's pretty quick in a 1,500 and his last 800 was a 1:49, but he might find that these guys at the end of a 5,000 can run fifty one or even faster and that will trouble him. So I've heard that his plan is to try to make a very hard last 800. There's talk that he's going to try to run the last thousand in 2:20. Well it's going to have to be pretty slow if he's going to run 2:20 for the last thousand. I think he might have to readjust that plan because I don't think the Ethiopians will allow it to get that slow, nor will the Kenyans."

To say that a fast finish is not required for a 1,500 metres is very misleading but I know what Bideau meant. You are not necessarily going that quickly already in that event but the athletes have to because that is how El Guerrouj dictates for those races to be run. For that reason sometimes the last lap of the 5,000 metres will end up faster than the last lap of a 1,500 metres. Many of Hicham's races are run at close to world record speed. We don't get to see him run a lot of *really* fast last laps in sit and kick situations.

Bideau also added, "He's much more relaxed about this. The pressure's off him. He's got a gold medal. He's won the main event. That was a lot more pressure than the 5,000. This is just enjoyable for him and it's going to be a hard race but he's not so concerned if he doesn't win this. It's just something that he wanted to do and a challenge for him."

El Guerrouj said pre race, "Beating Bekele in this event is a real challenge for me, but anything can happen. Stay tuned and you may see a surprise in the final."

As well as Bekele and El Guerrouj, there were the Kenyans, four of them, all of whom possessed the firepower to take gold. Richard Limo was the reigning world champion. John Kibowen was another 1,500 metres runner who had moved up and he had proven his extra endurance by winning the World Cross Country short course event in the past during the

MOROCCAN SUCCESS; THE KADA WAY

'98 and 2000 editions. He'd also won bronze over this distance in Edmonton. Abraham Chebii was the best performed 5,000 metres runner of the season having defeated Bekele and Gebrselassie in the Golden League. Eliud Kipchoge was the Ismael Kirui of this group. Only eighteen years old but prodigiously talented, although aren't all Kenyan's? He had already run a 12:55.52 on this track in July, which followed his stunning world junior record of 12:52.61 in Oslo.

With this array of talent, team Kenya may have planned for all sorts of tactics in this final. But any tactics that it had became meaningless because of the almost reckless way that Kenenisa Bekele raced. I say 'almost', because if anybody else had run this way, it would have been reckless. But we are talking about a guy who has doubled at the last couple of World Cross Country Championships and just won the most remarkable 10,000 metres race in championship history. He is far from an ordinary athlete.

Hence when Bekele purposely went to the front, immediately we took it seriously. Anybody who didn't would quickly change their minds after the first km split, which is run at nearly world record pace, in 2:31.94. Many felt that after the exhaustion of recently running a sub twenty seven, that Kenenisa might prefer a slower, sit and kick type race. Maybe it was the inclusion of a 3:26 1,500 metres runner who scared him, but Bekele should have referred back to the history of Saidi-Sief. That faster shorter distance speed doesn't always reflect at the end of longer races!

This was possibly the greatest 5,000 metres field ever assembled. Certainly it was for a major championship. The only men missing from this year's top performers were Haile Gebrselassie and Saif Saaeed Shaheen. The steeplechase gold medallist tried to enter this event late but was disallowed. Despite having so many other sub thirteen minute runners behind him, Bekele has so much confidence in his ability that he firmly believes he can just burn them all off. Sometimes a gap can be gained by a sudden change in pace but what the Ethiopian is doing is taking the tempo and effectively saying to the others that 'I am going to set a searing pace that none of you are going to be able to handle.' After going through 2,000 metres in 5:07.27 and finding that all his main opposition were still in toe, the thought might have crossed his mind that he could have put a little more consideration into his gung ho tactics. The Ethiopian made the following comments just prior to the championships and now they seemed very relevant.

"A competition is a competition. There really is no major difference between cross country and track. This is of course my first experience, but I don't see any difference."

Bideau had doubts with these tactics suggesting, "This is a brave tactic by Bekele but it's a little bit dangerous, unless he starts to get a little bit of a gap. At the moment they're all still there. He's got a lot of laps to go."

It is more difficult to break rivals on the track than in cross country and here is the definitive proof. Even though he is producing standard laps of sixty one to sixty two seconds, Bekele is never able to establish any margin over the pack and there's no discernable sign of struggle from El Guerrouj or the Kenyans. Still he does not let up much, taking an elite group to 3,000 metres in 7:45.44. He has slowed but they remain on schedule to break the championship record. Now Kenenisa allows himself to settle into the bunch and give himself some respite in preparation for a sprint finish. If any other runner had raced in this manner and not succeeded in his ambition, we'd cancel him out of the reckoning for the victory. In most cases such a front runner would soon be dropped or if not, then they certainly wouldn't have anything left to produce a significant kick. Again I emphasize that Kenenisa Bekele is not just any other runner!

In spite of his awesome talent I suspect that Hicham would have been relieved that Kenenisa took his foot slightly off the accelerator and later relinquished the lead. He like the Kenyans must have been close to bursting point even if the smoothness of his stride never looks like wavering. Everyone seems content that the fourth km is slow, as Kipchoge takes

MOROCCAN SUCCESS; THE KADA WAY

eight contenders to the split in 10:28.46. Bideau approaching three to go remarks, "He's done a good job El Guerrouj. He hasn't made a mistake yet. He's run very efficiently and evenly. He's concentrated well. He looks relaxed. He looks comfortable. I give him a strong chance."

Goumri has been long since dropped but team tactics have been made irrelevant due to the horrific early speed. El Guerrouj has been running relaxed throughout, staying in about third or fourth position without covering extra ground. Owing to the fast pace, it is likely that a final sprint will be left until later, probably after the bell because the runners will feel too tired to try for a long run for home. But Abdelkader and Hicham always race with a plan and they like to carry it out, no matter what. They had reasoned that the Moroccan's best chance for victory lay with him running the concluding laps as he would a 1,500 metres event. So approaching two laps remaining, the four time world champion eases into the lead as he naturally always did. His opponents react as if they totally expect this and get in line to catch the Moroccan express. How much can he kick down, considering the fast early pace?

It doesn't seem a lot to the naked eye, but the clock doesn't lie. The sixty second lap between 1,000 to 600 metres left appeared so easy.

Hicham is utilizing his normal, gradual pick up in tempo style and looks magnificent as he piles on the pressure. Bideau isn't so confident though as Hicham approaches 500 metres remaining. "I think that's a bit of a mistake by El Guerrouj. I think they'll get past him. It's just a tactical advantage to be coming from behind and once they go, if they get a gap he'll never recover from it."

He still has five men on his back. However soon this becomes three, as Kibowen and the dangerous Chebii are dispatched as the Moroccan produces his patented, killer, back straight surge. Many fans may have reflected on a missing ingredient from all these years, of not having had El Guerrouj adding his grace to this event.

Kipchoge had moved into second place at the bell and even with the King of the mile doing his very best, he can't shake him, or Bekele. Regardless of this super speed they aren't budging. The spilt from the 4,400 to 4,800 metres is 57.39 and the latest 200 metres has been run in a scorching 26.77, but this is the Moroccan's optimum speed that Bideau had referred to and he is unable to gap his rivals by more than three metres. Now they reach him on the bend. Can El Guerrouj hold this speed to the line?

El Guerrouj continues to lead into the home straight and in sight is the incredible track double, something to separate him from Aouita, Gebrselassie and Bekele. Kenenisa moves out wide to intimidate, but the real threat is coming from the youngster Kipchoge who progresses onto Hicham's shoulder. It's Kenya vs. Morocco yet again, as the two race side by side over the final fifty metres. Eliud edges in front as Hicham makes a desperate dive. They hit the line and the difference is less than most winning margins over 100 metres. The results of the 5,000 metres in Paris were:

Eliud Kipchoge	12:52.79
Hicham El Guerrouj	12:52.83
Kenenisa Bekele	12:53.12
John Kibowen	12:54.07
Abraham Chebii	12:57.74
Gebre-egziabher Gebremariam	12:58.08
Richard Limo	13:01.13
Zersenay Tadesse	13:05.57
Juan Carlos de la Ossa	13:21.04
Abderrahim Goumri	13:23.67
Abiyote Abate	13:23.81
Alejandro Suarez	13:24.51
Christian Belz	13:26.02
Moukheld Al-Outaibi	13:38.92
Jorge Torres	13:43.37

Kipchoge, just! What a race!

MOROCCAN SUCCESS; THE KADA WAY

For a change the medal may not have been gold but this race definitely had a silver lining for Hicham. It was one of his great runs and he appeared every bit as delighted with this as his 1,500 metres gold, as he went to the stands where he was congratulated by a number of supporters, including his highly appreciative coach. The quality of his performance was underlined further with his long run for home leading to an incredible 2:24.33 last km split. Holding his form to the conclusion, Hicham's final 200 metres were run in 26.79, making his final lap a 53.56. Everyone performed up to expectations or better, save perhaps for Chebii who when he won here in July, was many people's pick for gold. Kipchoge reminded us again to never underestimate *any* Kenyan in a major championship, while Bekele should be commended for coming so close to his own double despite doing most of the work in this final. Eliud's victory gave the Kenyan men their only gold medal at the championships. The eighteen year old who very few selected as the winner had this to say, "I knew that everybody is watching Chebii, Bekele and Hicham, so I took the prize. I have never raced Hicham. I have raced with Bekele, and he beat me in Oslo. If Bekele and Hicham are watching Chebii, let me go, they won't get me."

Kipchoge did appear to be a little surprised as he bowed to the grateful Paris crowd. Like Bekele, Kipchoge is managed by Jos Hermens. The Dutchman expected both to medal, though not in the order that eventuated. Jos said, "But we know he is very good and that he has a good kick. He ran a smart race tactically."

Hicham made the following evaluation of the race, "I guess that the only mistake that I made was to focus too much on Bekele and possibly to have broken away too soon. I think that if I had waited to 400 metres out to break then I could have won the race. As it is, I started to pull away at 600 metres and then the Kenyan caught me and I had to kick again. Then I was concentrating on Bekele and Kipchoge just sprinted past me – he was going like crazy – I came back but just could not catch him on the line."

Bideau commented further, "I think El Guerrouj has got to be proud of that performance. That was a terrific run. Did everything he could, almost got up. He handled Bekele who I think made a bit of a mistake leading those early laps. That didn't help him in the end and they were both stunned by Eluid Kipchoge who just a few months ago was winning the World Junior Cross Country."

When shown a replay of Kipchoge and El Guerrouj hugging, Craig Mottram gave his reasons for the greater camaraderie between distance runners as opposed to sprinters, "I don't reckon there's as high a testosterone levels out there. I reckon when you're spending weeks and weeks together, training at altitude, running 200 or 180 kms a week, living together. You just learn to respect each other and when you go out and race each other you know that everyone out there is working just as hard, giving it 100 percent."

Aussies know what they are talking about!

El Guerrouj received very little time to soak in the enormity of his achievements as by September 5 he was back in Brussels to compete in the 1,500 metres. It was expected that the Moroccan would race over 3,000 metres, just as he had here in 1999. Hicham gave his reasons for the change of plans. "I really wanted to run the 3,000 metres this time around, but I have just not recovered sufficiently from Paris. Doubling really took it out of me and I do not feel that I could live up to the expectations of the crowd here in Brussels over seven and half laps. I was really pleased with my performances in Paris, but there was a huge amount of pressure and stress for me at the Championships."

The world record holder enjoyed getting back to the traditionally fast, rabbit races of the Golden League, though he would not have things all his own way, with Mehdi Baala fresher and still carrying the good form that took him to the silver medal in Paris.

The early splits are 54.80, then 1:51.54 as Hicham runs behind two rabbits. With 450 metres remaining, he takes control and by the time he passes 1,200 metres in 2:47.73,

MOROCCAN SUCCESS; THE KADA WAY

only Baala is with him. El Guerrouj surges on the back straight though is still unable to shake the Frenchman, but in the home straight his strength prevails. The end product is an outstanding final lap of 54.35 seconds. The results from the top twelve in the 1,500 metres in Brussels were:

Hicham El Guerrouj	3:28.40
Mehdi Baala	3:28.98
Paul Korir	3:30.72
Robert Rono	3:31.33
Alex Kipchirchir	3:31.42
Juan Carlos Higuero	3:31.61
Benjamin Kipkurui	3:32.58
Vyacheslav Shabunin	3:32.63
Rui Silva	3:33.04
William Chirchir	3:33.61
Cornelius Chirchir	3:34.16
Isaac Kiprono Songok	3:34.85

It was the fastest time of 2003 and El Guerrouj needed it to hold off the strong French runner. Mehdi was becoming consistently better and better. He appeared likely to become a very serious threat to Hicham's main goal of finally turning into the Olympic champion at the classic distance next year. This hard fought victory was a true testament to the incredible consistency of El Guerrouj. Many athletes suffering from fatigue and a lack of motivation may have allowed themselves to produce a slightly sub standard performance. It was something that this man almost never did. It was another testament to Kada's coaching. In spite of the many competitions that his athlete entered, Abdelkader never seemed to push him too hard and over the edge. Thus Hicham El Guerrouj was a runner whom meeting organizers always wanted above most other big names. Not just because of his pedigree but because he could be trusted to perform at his best. The winner had this to say about recent events and future ones:

"I am extremely pleased with my run tonight. I was so tired after the World Championships that at first I didn't even want to come here. But then I decided to come and run the 1500 metres and offer a great show to the crowd. I have had 12 days of constant stress and pressure in Paris and it really has been very difficult. I went back to Morocco and slept for twelve hours each night. Tonight I ran with an exceptional ease, I was only running at 50% of my ability but was still pushing the pace setters. It felt like jogging to me. I am also very pleased for Medhi Baala who came 3 hundredths of a second short of the European record. He ran the perfect race and really deserved to improve on the record. I believe he is capable of breaking the European record soon. He is not quite ready yet to beat me though."

"Next year will be very important for me. I want to go to Athens and win both the 1,500 metres and 5,000 metres. My only aim at the Olympics next year is to win two gold medals. I know I am not an Olympic champion but maybe the double win next year will pay back for the two Olympic titles I lost in my career."

The Moroccan's *only* aim at the Olympics is to win two gold medals? He is not asking for much!

During Hicham's interview Maria Mutola was victorious in the women's 800 metres, completing her year of dominance and confirming her as the sole winner of the million dollar Golden League jackpot. Showing that he doesn't simply focus on himself, El Guerrouj suddenly stated, "And there you go! Mutola has won one million dollars. I am very pleased for her. She has had an excellent year, and deserves the Jackpot. Isn't track and field beautiful?"

A great ambassador for the sport indeed.

Even without Hicham, the 3,000 metres was a fascinating race. Much of this was due to the inclusion of Ali Saidi-Sief, the Algerian, who was returning after a two year doping suspension. He faced stiff competition from the usual posse of Kenyans but surprisingly defeated them all, including world champion Eliud Kipchoge, in a good time of 7:30.79. The gap to the junior athlete was marginal as the Paris champ registered 7:30.91. John Kibowen finished third with a

MOROCCAN SUCCESS; THE KADA WAY

7:32.01. In most cases the jewel in the Brussels crown was the men's 10,000 metres and the participation of a well loved individual made sure that 2003 was no different.

Haile Gebrselassie was not the slightest bit perturbed by his incredible teammate Kenenisa Bekele defeating him in Paris. If anything, the silver medal had only added to his confidence and he believed that he was in good enough shape to break his own 10,000 metres world record. The annual 10,000 metres championship was regarded by most to be held by Brussels and the Van Damn Memorial stadium. Despite its prestige Gebrselassie hadn't raced here at the distance since 1994. But in 2003 the race fitted into his schedule perfectly and the meet organizers were excited to have the Ethiopian in their always high class field. There were other quality runners competing but it was expected that Haile would be racing on his own for most of the second half of the race.

This did not eventuate, though it wasn't as if Haile wasn't on for a fast time. He went past 5,000 metres in 13:15.58 and continued on with that fast cadence, but come the final few laps he had to focus on other things, as Kenya's Nicholas Kemboi and Qatar's Ahmad Hassan Abdullah were still in tow. Most knew of Abdullah's talents and particularly in light of his recent fourth place in Paris, his strong performance wasn't a great surprise. Kemboi was a different story. Like Kamathi did in '99, his run had come straight out of left field. He had never recorded a sub twenty eight minute time, let alone a sub twenty seven. Even the most astute fans of the sport would have likely been whispering and asking, 'Who is this guy?'

Haile was probably asking himself the same thing as he slowed the pace and wondered if he could rid himself of this opposition that included a 28:19.77 athlete.

After a consistently fast pace there were some games played on lap twenty which resulted in a 67.32 second lap time, which cancelled out any slight chance of a world record. Kemboi and Hassan were unwilling to help Haile who was forced to soldier on at the front. As he paraded around, the broadcaster comments, "So there he is, the greatest distance athlete of all time. Now thirty. What a lot he's crammed into those thirty years."

Nothing happened until with 600 metres remaining, Gebrselassie kicked viciously and left the Qatar athlete for dead. What acceleration! This was almost as impressive a burst as the one in Athens '97, yet in this race he was running at an overall pace of nearly one minute faster!

Yet Kemboi didn't waver and it was highly possible that the Ethiopian would be out sprinted by younger legs again. On the final turn Kemboi tried to overtake him, which wasn't wise. Gebrselassie kicked again and then with fifty metres left he kicked once more, finally extracting a gap to earn him his best win of the season. The time was a sensational 26:29.22. Even after all his injury problems he had just produced a run that only Paul Tergat and himself had ever bettered. That it came shortly after his breathtaking, punishing Paris race gave Haile and the rest of us a strong feeling that a third straight Olympic title next year was not beyond the 'emperor'.

He had run a 2:28.92 last km and a 56.6 second last lap, in the third quickest time ever! There could be no doubt. This was indeed the GREATEST DISTANCE RUNNER OF ALL TIME.

Kemboi and Abdullah's times were 26:30.03 and 26:38.76, so the previous unknown became the third fastest of all time. Richard Limo put in a tremendous run to be the fourth man under twenty seven minutes with 26:56.63. The quality of the depth in this event was underlined by Charles Kamathi. The former world champion placed a horrible thirteenth, though his time remained a decent enough 27:29.47.

Backing up from a reasonable result in Paris was Ali Ezzine, who lined up in the steeplechase in Belgium. Again it was a case of Shaheen vs. a Kenyan and another close finish kept the rivalry simmering along nicely. The results of the first twelve were:

MOROCCAN SUCCESS; THE KADA WAY

Saif Saaeed Shaheen	8:00.06
Paul Kipsiele Koech	8:00.42
Simon Vroemen	8:09.18
Julius Nyamu	8:10.33
Ezekiel Kemboi	8:12.87
Ali Ezzine	8:13.31
Bouabdallah Tahri	8:14.44
Zouhair Ouerdi	8:14.81
Kipkirui Misoi	8:17.27
Wilson Boit Kipketer	8:17.86
Luis Miguel Martin	8:20.89
Steve Slattery	8:24.99

It was an additional world leading time for the world champion and he agitated his old country further by just winning another close finish. The only difference was that this time it was Koech rather than Kemboi. Despite the outcome, Saif's comments were mostly negative, "I am still not pleased with the result. I was aiming at a sub eight minutes performance around 7:55 or 7:57. I do not like the steeplechase because you get a lot of problems, a lot of injuries and it inevitably leads you to missing important races. Tonight was my last steeplechase run of the year. Six races a year is enough for me."

For Ezzine, the result was an excellent one, a clear season's best. He was ending 2003 in an encouraging way and should approach 2004 believing that he can break 8:10 once more. For Ali there was still the Grand Prix final to come in Monaco.

On September 7 Hicham El Guerrouj raced in Rieti. He initially considered a 1,500, before opting for the mile distance. It was now that the effects of his hectic Paris schedule showed, as he endured a mighty struggle to defeat Kenyan junior Alex Kipchirchir. The Moroccan posted a 3:50.20, barely holding on to oust his opponent, whose 3:50.25 set a new world junior record. Robert Rono, 3:50.98, also came close to defeating the best.

Realising that fatigue had set in, Kada and El Guerrouj did not engage in the Grand Prix final a week later, now known as the

World Athletics Final. Taking the opportunity in his absence was Paul Korir, whose winning time of 3:40.09 was dreadfully slow. However, the Kenyan did cover the last 300 metres in a scorching 38.25 seconds, or exactly fifty one second lap pace. It proved once again that there were milers out there with at least as much basic speed as Hicham, though if he'd been in this race, it's likely that the earlier pace would have been around ten seconds faster, thus the final fifth of the race wouldn't have been nearly as quick.

For the second consecutive steeplechase race, a tremendous contest ensued between Saif Saaeed Shaheen and Paul Kipsiele Koech. The competitiveness of the Kenyan again helped the event's pacesetter achieve another new season's best. In fact Shaheen's winning time of 7:57.38 was quite close to Boulami's first world record. Despite the positive test his performance from Brussels during 2001 still stood as the official record. Koech could consider himself unlucky not to have won the year's final race, after he clocked 7:57.42. Saif was not regularly dominating his event like Kiptanui and to a lesser extent Barmasai once did, but he often seemed to have a knack for emerging as the victor in close finishes. On September 14 in Monaco, the other nine competitors were beaten well before the start of this exciting sprint finish. Third place man Ezekiel Kemboi only recorded 8:11.79. The first km was run in 2:38.31 and 2,000 metres were reached by Shaheen in 5:19.81. This was a rarely seen event of the highest quality for the final meeting of a season but here there were extenuating circumstances that helped produce it.

Hicham El Guerrouj was leading the IAAF rankings and on course to be named as the top male athlete of track and field in 2003, but by skipping the World Athletics Final he gave Shaheen an outside chance of stealing the award. The problem was that the Qatar superstar not only needed to win the steeplechase, but record a time of 7:54.49 or better. Obviously he fell just short of this very difficult target. That Hicham could still top the list despite missing this meeting illustrated his greatness further. It was an unprecedented third consecutive time that he'd been named as the world Athlete of the Year. Not only that, but no male had ever won the

MOROCCAN SUCCESS; THE KADA WAY

award on three occasions, with Carl Lewis and Michael Johnson having each achieved two wins.

Ali Ezzine did not conclude his year in any great fashion as he clocked an 8:18.05 to place seventh in the steeplechase burn up, though at least he was regularly pitting himself against the best again. To improve sufficiently, so as to challenge the Shaheen's of the event was a lot to ask, yet if he could return to his best times as a youngster, then he wouldn't be too far away in 2004.

The male Athlete of the Year was not satisfied with his season and so went to Russia well rested to race in the small Moscow Challenge Grand Prix on September 20. He ran into most of the Monaco athletes including the winner Paul Korir, with whom he had a terrific contest. Like Shaheen, El Guerrouj seemed to be able to will himself to victory when things got tight and this race was no different with Hicham edging out Paul by a mere four hundredths of a second! The times were fairly slow, 3:36.44 to 3:36.48. He was still the King and this fighting win was going to be important for his mental strength. He wasn't getting any younger and so might not expect to cruise to victory quite as often. Who knows? He may need these fighting qualities to fend off someone during an all important race next year.

Fighting off a surprise opponent on September 28 was Kenyan great Paul Tergat. Competing in the Berlin Marathon, he combated with supposed rabbit Sammy Korir all the way to the line, only winning by one second. That Korir could keep with Tergat would have been a shock under any circumstances but it was especially so in this case. Tergat stopped the clock at the conclusion of his 42.195 kms journey on 2:04.55! With the help of his countryman he had smashed Khannouchi's world record by thirty seven seconds. It added further to the glittering credentials of the man who had already broken records on the road, the track, and dominated cross country. Maybe now he could mount a case as the greatest distance runner ever? He sure looked to be in an ideal position to claim an Olympic gold medal in the Athens marathon. However the marathon is a far more unpredictable event than the 10,000 metres. Historically, the favourite rarely wins.

An old adversary of Tergat's took notice and admired yet also found inspiration from the breaking of the 2:05 wall in Berlin. Apparently it was not the end of Salah Hissou's running career. It was time for the Moroccan to hit the road.

Since his career had often been engulfed by Tergat and Gebrselassie, why not follow in their footsteps? Tergat was a full time road runner, having given up the track after the Sydney Olympics. This wasn't a case of throwing in the towel because he'd lost to Haile again. Paul was thirty one and it was time to move on and see how much he could achieve in the latter part of his career in a new event. Being a proven superstar in the half marathon made the decision to move up a no brainer. Gebrselassie on the other hand hadn't put all his eggs in one basket. Injuries reduced his time at the helm of track distance running and it was this that first made Haile consider the road. He was an instant success, winning the World Half Marathon in 2001 and running the fastest debut marathon ever in London 2002. He had since returned to the track in an attempt to win back his 10,000 metres title. What versatility!

There is no easy answer as to what makes a great marathon runner. It certainly helps if you can run a twenty six something for 10 kms, but this doesn't guarantee success over the Olympic event's most demanding distance.

The fastest times are run at approximately thirty minute 10 kms pace for the 42.195 km event. This converts to about a 2:06.36. But history shows us that many good marathon runners haven't broken twenty eight minutes. In contrast, many that have gone sub twenty eight have struggled with the transition.

Salah Hissou only had a 'so so' pedigree at the longer distances, those further than the long course cross country. However, he had never focused fully on the road and never raced over this while at his peak. He had still compiled some

MOROCCAN SUCCESS; THE KADA WAY

decent results, being reasonably competitive in the 1994 and 2001 World Half Marathon Championships. In 1994 he also set the world record for the rarely run 20 kms. With his full attention on the roads, perhaps Hissou could be a giant killer in the marathon.

Obviously planning for a long season on the track was Ali Ezzine. The Moroccan came out of hiding early in '04 to race in a couple of indoor meets. First up was a 3,000 metres race in Stuttgart on January 31 and the opposition was incredibly strong for this period of the season. Ali finished well down the pecking order but check out the names. Zurich would have been proud of this line up. The results were:

Kenenisa Bekele	7:30.77
Sileshi Sihine	7:41.18
Paul Bitok	7:43.23
Abderrahim Goumri	7:44.00
Abiyote Abate	7:44.30
Mark Bett	7:45.44
Hailu Mekonnen	7:46.58
Ali Saidi-Sief	7:48.20
Ali Ezzine	7:48.36

This was a pretty good start for Ezzine and was proof that his training was going well during the winter. He was only comprehensively beaten by one of these flat specialists. Whilst not coming close to the previous times of Komen and Gebrselassie indoors, winning with in excess of ten seconds up his sleeve was extraordinary, even for Kenenisa's standards. In this sort of form it was unlikely that he would be losing either of his cross country titles during the spring.

Ezzine next raced in Stockholm on February 12, also at 3,000 metres. He improved his time marginally by clocking a 7:47.17, which placed him seventh. The winner was Mark Bett who also improved on his run in Germany by registering a 7:43.38. As you can see, Ali was a lot closer to the pointy end on this occasion.

Hicham El Guerrouj had only one indoor race scheduled for

this Olympic year and like last season it was in Lievin. He raced over 3,000 metres on February 28 and immediately sent out a warning to anyone who planned on winning either the 1,500 or 5,000 metres in Athens. He won in a good time of 7:34.71 but it was the margin of victory that like Bekele in Stuttgart, was most impressive. Best of the rest was Robert Sigei Kipngetich who recorded 7:43.09. It seemed that the twenty nine year old Hicham still contained as much fire power as when in his early and mid twenties.

Now thirty two, Salah Hissou was embarking on a brand new challenge. After seeing what Jaouad Gharib achieved in Paris, he took note of what he had done prior to becoming world champion. The Moroccan had recorded a fast time of 2:09.15 in the 2003 Rotterdam Marathon. While this was only good enough for sixth place on that day, it was good enough to qualify him for the World Titles where anybody who is a sub 2:10 runner can win if everything goes well for them on the day after a meticulous preparation.

Rotterdam was known as a fast course so where better for Hissou to commence his marathon career in April, 2004? After five months of specific training for the daunting distance he felt ready to go through an initial test. Salah decided to race over 20 kms on the road in Holland on March 7. It was the sensible choice to undertake this small challenge, to prepare him a little for Rotterdam. Of course, Salah could never be fully prepared before he actually gave it a go.

His lead up race informed us that the marathon training had Hissou in good stead. He lined up against two of his future marathon opponents, Felix Limo and Salim Kipsang from Kenya. In the important confrontation, Salah came out the winner. An incident that was crucial to the end result reminded us that distance running doesn't contain the etiquette of cycling. By the second half of the race, Hissou and Limo had broken away, but at about twelve kms, Felix was forced to stop briefly to tie up his shoelace. Immediately, Salah reacted and made a gap, from which he was able to extend to the winning margin. His time was a new course record 57:54, only seventeen seconds outside of

MOROCCAN SUCCESS; THE KADA WAY

Khannouchi's world record. Felix ran 58:20, the same time that Hissou had run in 1994 when setting the record. Salim Kipsang finished well to close in 58:28. It was an impressive victory, a tremendous confidence builder, though it didn't exactly mean that the Moroccan was back to career best form. Twenty kms is far different to forty two.

Hissou commented post race,"I'm feeling fine. It was a good test for Rotterdam. Now I'm going to train again in Ifrane in my country. And I will be well prepared for Rotterdam. I hope there to follow the same scenario as my countryman Jaoud Gharib did last year. He ran Rotterdam and became later the world champion in Paris. What Paris was for him, I hope Athens will be for me."

April the 4th was the big date on Salah Hissou's calendar. It was an opportunity to discover if he was in fact suited to the marathon. As discussed earlier, Moroccan men performing prominently at the distance was no longer uncommon and nine athletes had already run the qualifying time of 2:12 for the Athens Olympics. He and his manager Aziz Daouda were targeting a time in the low 2:09 range for the debut effort. Salah said at the press conference:

"After the surgical operation that I underwent in 2001 (on ankle), I decided to go up to the marathon to complete my career. If I carry out the minimal requirement to go to Athens, I will prepare intensely to dispute one of the medals. In the contrary case, I will be satisfied with some participations in races on road and leave the Olympics to other Moroccan athletes in Athens."

Hissou wasn't the only track star attracting attention from the Rotterdam organizers. Surprisingly Bernard Barmasai was also competing. He was certainly a classy enough athlete to be worthy of discussion, but the Kenyan had never converted his steeplechase results into anything of note at the longer track distances. It seemed a big jump, even for a steeplechaser, to go straight to the marathon.

Conditions were not perfect on race day. The strong winds of the night before continued into the day and blew straight into the runners' faces as they took off at 11:00 am.

A pack of approximately twenty runners establish themselves, going through 5 kms in 15:17. The athletes soon receive the benefit of the wind at their backs and the second split is faster, with the group reaching 10 kms in 29:56, about 2:06 schedule. By 15 kms, timed at 44:52, there are just seven leaders and two of these are rabbits. The five contenders are Romulo Wagner da Silva of Brazil, Kenyan's Stephen Cheptot, Michael Rotich and Felix Limo, plus Morocco's Hissou.

The fast tempo persists, with 59:48 being the split at 20 kms. Shortly after, the competitors get the half way split of 1:03.13.

Salah seems composed and relaxed at this stage of the race. It looks like he belongs at this discipline. The full length of his stride is noticeable and his natural bounce makes this caper appear far easier for him than those around him. Is 2:06.26 pace too fast first up? Only nine athletes had ever completed the marathon in as fast a time.

"Salah Hissou never runs more than one hour of continuous running."

This was a quote derived directly from Aziz Daouda. It seems pertinent here because Salah Hissou is in the middle of a marathon, a race more than two hours in duration. This comment was offered nearly eight years ago. Would it still be relevant today as the Moroccan dug deep into his resources, trying to maintain the tortuous tempo?

Back in his heyday as a track star, Salah focused on short but high quality sessions. Long runs weren't a part of his program as they were for say a Paul Tergat. The overall weekly mileage remained high as a result of training twice a day.

By now the wind is at its fiercest and blowing directly into the leaders as the pace understandably slows a fraction. Cheptot drops off and the 25 kms split arrives in 1:15.12.

MOROCCAN SUCCESS; THE KADA WAY

Soon Salah begins to drift off the back of Rotich and Limo. Something is definitely wrong. This far out from the end, trouble is brewing as it's nigh on impossible to simply tough it out in a marathon if you are spent with over ten kms to go. He hangs in for a while but eventually lets go along with da Silva. The two pass through 30 kms in 1:30.09, still sub 2:07 pace. The Kenyans had clocked 1:29.59 at the same point.

The possibility of the race win is gone for the Moroccan but there is still a little something called an Olympic spot up for grabs. Salah uses this as incentive as he battles to keep what remains of the smoothness in his stride. Mental strength eventually counts for nought however, as he slips away from the Brazilian and into his own purgatory.

The way that he felt at 30 kms would soon feel like the ease of a morning jog in comparison to what his body is going through by 35 kms. In a marathon, once you hit the wall you don't get better. There is no second wind. The only respite is gained from withdrawing, and doing so means that you've failed the event completely. Hissou was never in the regular habit of quitting a la Morceli so he pushes on. For a long time he thinks that maybe things aren't so bad in spite of his waning form. He is still running in fourth position as he approaches 40 kms.

However the event does not end here. In fact the final two kms are an event in itself for Salah who later mentioned that, "The last two kilometres each felt like an entire twenty five laps of the track." This distance could do that to the best of runners. Hissou finishes the race moving at close to the speed of your average fun runner, only this is not fun. The top twenty finishers from the Rotterdam Marathon were:

Felix Limo	2:06:14
Michael Rotich	2:09:07
Romulo Wagner da Silva	2:11:28
Peter Kiprotich	2:11:52
Stephen Cheptot	2:11:52
Tom van Hooste	2:11:55

Luc Krotwaar	2:11:56
Zebedayo Bayo	2:12:23
Willy Cheruiyot	2:12:28
Philip Singoei	2:12:36
Salah Hissou	2:12:45
Kamel Kohil	2:13:40
Wilson Chelal	2:14:23
Shane Nankervis	2:14:45
Bernard Barmassai	2:14:49
Gabriel Jose Amedo Garcia	2:14:52
Salim Kipsang	2:14:55
Hugo van den Broek	2:14:59
Claudir Rodrigues	2:15:27
Alejandro Gomez	2:16:22

At 32 kms Limo had broken away from Rotich and from there he seemed to only get stronger. His seventh five kms split was run in 14:22, which was amazing. He was able to carry that through to register a course record and become the sixth fastest man ever. Felix reflected on his great performance, "I think I ran a fantastic race. I'm sure that if there had not been such a strong wind I could have been close to the world record. After 35 kms there was a lot of wind and I lost a lot of time there. I will be back here."

The wind most certainly played a role in Salah's demise but this wasn't the major reason why he fell away to an eleventh place finish in 2:12.45. Some athletes are just not cut out for this discipline, despite their ability. Not everyone can run marathons.

Nevertheless, this result still gave Hissou an outside chance to compete at the Games. He had finished inside the official 'A' qualifying standard of 2:15, though with so many other Moroccans running faster, it would take a dubious decision from the Federation to allow him to run. Salah did not want to back stab anyone so as he had said prior to Rotterdam, 'leave the Olympics to other Moroccan athletes.'

One of these athletes was Ali Ezzine who was set to commence his outdoor season. His racing program was

MOROCCAN SUCCESS; THE KADA WAY

complicated and intense, starting in Morocco, going to Europe, then back to Morocco before returning to Europe in the final lead up to Athens.

On May 23 Ali recorded his best ever time for the flat 3,000 metres when he clocked a 7:45.9 in Rabat. This result confirmed that he hadn't lost any speed since the indoor season. However, when he raced in Holland he wasn't able to convert this potential into a good steeple. Competing at Hengelo on May 31, Ezzine could manage just an 8:19.93 for fifth place, way behind the top Kenyans Brimin Kiprop Kipruto, 8:05.52 and Paul Kipsiele Koech, 8:05.92.

While the meeting wasn't memorable for Ali, it certainly was for Kenenisa Bekele, who knocked off Haile Gebrselassie's world record in the 5,000 metres. His time was 12:37.35 and verified his standing as the 'king' of Ethiopian men's distance running. It was very difficult to see him losing the 10,000 metres race in Athens. The rabbits took him through 2,000 metres in 5:05.47, but soon after, Kenenisa was on his own, yet he improved the pace to 7:37.34 at 3,000 metres. This was fractionally off the average speed of Haile's time but he didn't wilt, reaching 4,000 metres in 10:07.93 and kicking down to a 2:29.42 final km. Bekele commented, "I was very self-confident today. I felt very strong. At 3,000 metres, I was convinced I would break the record. I have been training very hard in the last three weeks with the idea of breaking this record. This result is from hard work. I am very happy."

The vanquished record holder raced in his favoured 10,000 metres and 'Mr. Hengelo' did not disappoint, running a time of 26:41.58. Unfortunately for Gebrselassie, another of his 'protégées' had made the step up in class and Paris bronze medallist, Sileshi Sihine was able to not only match him, but out sprint him quite easily. The so called 'third' of the Ethiopians powered home to record a 26:39.69. The pair ran close to an evenly paced race with the first 5,000 metres coming in 13:19. Haile was not disappointed but realistic as he spoke of his future in the sport, "I still have a chance at 10,000 metres which I will run in Athens, but the future for me is the half marathon and marathon, and 26:41 is pretty good speed for a marathoner!"

Kenenisa Bekele continued with his staggering form, as he took Gebrselassie's other major world record, the 10,000 metres, in Ostrava on June 8. His time of 26:20.31 was all the more incredible considering that he reached 5,000 metres in 13:14.42. His second half was a considerably faster 13:05.89. The last lap of 57.20 wasn't bad either.

Hicham El Guerrouj was postponing his start to the season and here, the 1,500 metres event was being contested by Eliud Kipchoge, the 5,000 metres man. The world champion was the man of the moment. Already this season, on May the 14th, Eliud had achieved something that would have to be regarded as one of the toughest things to do in track and field in 2004. Not only had he defeated Saif Saaeed Shaheen, but had done so at the star's home Grand Prix in Doha, Qatar. The race was 3,000 metres without the steeples and in a tremendous contest, for a change it was Shaheen who lost out. The Kenyan recorded a 7:33.37 to restore some East African pride. The Qatari ran 7:34.67.

It was still a huge shock when Kipchoge got the better of Isaac Songok and Bernard Lagat as five athletes contested the bunch sprint in Hengelo. His winning time was 3:33.20. This was outstanding, considering it was so far outside his comfort zone.

Lagat was still trying to come to terms with a tumultuous ten months in his career and life. The Kenyan had really missed last season's World Championships because of a positive test for EPO, not a stomach illness, which was stated by the Kenyan Federation so as to not distract the rest of the Kenyan team. The 'A' sample result was discovered just before the championships and Bernard's career appeared to be over. But five weeks later the 'B' sample was revealed and surprisingly, it showed no trace of the banned drug.

This case had Lagat and others saying that the EPO test needed to be re-evaluated as it may be unreliable. Even though he was exonerated, Bernard Lagat could never be

MOROCCAN SUCCESS; THE KADA WAY

completely cleared in the minds of those who took a large interest in distance running. His name would always be muddied and we would never know the true answer to the question, 'Which sample was the correct one?'

As it was, Lagat had already made a successful comeback to his sport, winning the 3,000 metres at the World Indoor Championships in Budapest on March 6 in a time of 7:56.34. He was probably again the major threat to Hicham El Guerrouj in the 1,500 metres.

An additional athlete that recently tested positive to EPO was another Moroccan, Abdelkader Hachlaf. His result was known in April though it wasn't until October that everything was given the all clear and he was suspended for two years. It made Ezzine's task of Olympic qualification all the more easier.

Ali made some gains with his form in his next race in Seville on June 5. He registered a time of 8:16.65 and finished third, with only Koech, 8:05.31, severely beating him in the largely Spanish field.

Ezzine headed back home where he raced again in Rabat on June 19. Wins had been few and far between with only one since his Paris victory almost four years ago. To cross the line first here was nice, with the time not highly convincing but a reasonable 8:18.31. Fellow Moroccan Zouhair El Ouardi stayed with his better known opposition and clocked 8:18.68.

Only five days later he was in action again, competing in Algiers on June 24. His performance here was a minor failure. If he still had desires to be a sub 8:10 runner again, then registering an 8:24.72 wasn't a good sign. Ali placed second, losing to Justus Kiprono Kipchirchir who ran 8:23.96. Losing to a Kenyan, particularly one with two 'kips', two 'chirs' and a 'rono' in his name wasn't a great surprise!

Ali shouldn't have had high expectations when he lined up in Rome on July the 2nd for his first Golden League competition of the season. It was tough to know what to make of the result when it was all said and done. The Moroccan had finished fourth, which at this level had to be respected, though his time was only an 8:19.01 and he wasn't within sight of the winner, Koech. The Kenyan produced a rare sub eight performance of 7:59.65 to destroy the field by more than fifteen seconds. On the other hand Ezzine did defeat Kipchirchir this time around. Perhaps Ali's next race in Lausanne would give us a better indication of where he was at.

Hicham El Guerrouj was also commencing his season in Rome. He enjoyed a marvellous record there, winning ever since 1997, every year except for 2000 when he didn't attend the meeting. As Hicham had set two world records there the Romans always expected a good performance and El Guerrouj always delivered. This year's 1,500 metres event was shaping up as a different race, a greater challenge for him. 2004 was not running as smoothly as the Kada camp had hoped, just Hicham's luck being an Olympic year.

Early in the season El Guerrouj discovered problems with his breathing and after a health check from a French doctor, he was diagnosed with about ten allergies and put on a three month treatment program. This affected the quality of his training somewhat, but continue to train he did, and Hicham went to Spain to compete in Zaragoza on June 8, confident that he was still in good enough shape to win.

Maybe the enforced reduction in training was a blessing in disguise. Hicham would endure less training in 2004 than in 2000. Kada commented on the pre Sydney madness, "I had to walk away from some training sessions. Hicham would run 10 times 1 km and want to do more. I tried to explain that more was not better. Now he understands."

El Guerrouj elaborates further on what is necessary for Athens success, "This year, I need to train five per cent less than I did in 2000. To train at 40 per cent would be enough to put me among the world's best - 95 per cent is enough to make me the best."

Last year his training had included specific work for the 5,000

MOROCCAN SUCCESS; THE KADA WAY

metres but this year he would revert back to only working on the 1,500 metres as Kada explains, "This year, Hicham will double but training is concentrated on the 1,500 metres. We will not do much specific work for the 5,000 metres and he will not race over 5,000 metres before the Olympics. The 1,500 metres is his job, the 5,000 metres his toy."

Hicham had been spending three weeks out of every month at Ifrane where even in March and April the temperature would usually be a chilly 0-5 degrees. The major bulk of his training came during his late morning runs, which would sometimes go for as far as eighteen kms. Here, he enjoyed the peaceful surroundings of the Curcuil Royale Forest where monkeys and wild boars wander. Cedar trees line the forest route. Some afternoons would involve speed sessions on the track at 1,600 metres altitude. These were also conducted on the plateau at 2,100 metres. On other occasions a weight session would be thrown into the mix.

The constants at his training sessions were Abdelkader Kada and Houcine Benzriguinet. El Guerrouj really appreciated Houcine who he'd bought an apartment for in Rabat. Hicham says, "He is very professional and better than a psychologist. This guy is everything for me. The relationship is so intense that he is part of my success. He is like a brother."

To give you an idea on the sort of speed sessions being conducted, this is one from late March, 2004.

20 x 300's - sub 45 seconds each, or sub 60 second lap pace.

This was done on the track at the standard 1,600 metres height, with the dedicated Houcine Benzriguinet leading the way. Hicham Bellani and Anis Selmouni also kept Hicham company. Resting periods were forty five seconds in length.

The session was viewed by a British journalist David Powell. As the rain turned to sleet he questioned Hicham on the trying conditions. The Moroccan answered, "I have trained in worse than this. Once, during Ramadan, I trained at 11 o'clock at night when it was minus 6."

As well as breathing difficulties there was another more personal issue that had distracted El Guerrouj's lead up to the European outdoor season. But this distraction was of the best kind. On June 5, Hicham's wife Najoua Lahbil gave birth to a daughter, named Hiba. As a result he was sleep deprived but joyously happy. What would have a greater impact on his Spanish race?

The former so it seemed. The Moroccan did not go with the rabbits from the gun and ended up barely defeating Kenyan Alex Kipchirchir, 3:36.46 to 3:36.49. It could best be described as a lacklustre showing from the Olympic favourite.

Later Hicham offered some explanation, "You know, Zaragoza was just three days after the birth of my daughter. I had been sleeping on the hospital floor by my wife's bed for two days because I didn't want to miss anything of my baby. I wanted to feel her, to hear her breath, to see her move, I felt like I was on a cloud. And when I was in Spain, I wasn't concentrating at all. I spent all my time on the phone arranging my daughter's naming, inviting people, making sure everything was perfect for this celebration. When the pacemaker went, I didn't react. I wasn't in the race, my head was elsewhere. So when I saw all the other runners sprinting at the end I just gave everything I had not to lose the race."

"Had I been my usual self I would have easily clocked 3:31 because I am in great shape both physically and mentally. The birth of Hiba was like winning the most prestigious medal in the most important meeting but now I want to think about tomorrow. I want to think about the future and what it holds for me."

Hicham's marital situation was also a story in itself. He'd married in 2003, just six months after first setting eyes on Najoua. El Guerrouj was obviously more steadfast with running than with women for he immediately decided to ask her to marry him, before the two had uttered a single word to each other! "I saw her in the street and liked her. I didn't even meet her before asking her parents for her hand. At first, she

MOROCCAN SUCCESS; THE KADA WAY

was shocked and didn't like the idea but she accepted a week later."

The nineteen year old Najoua studies business at the University of Akhaouayene in Ifrane and lives on the campus.

Hicham was discussing Hiba and Zaragoza just a day before his big race in Rome, a contest which would contain Bernard Lagat. The Kenyan was the winner of the first Golden League race in Norway on June 11, though his time was only 3:34.08 and his margin of victory was like Hicham's, just three hundredths of a second over Ukrainian Ivan Heshko. The Bislett Games were now held in Bergen rather than Oslo. El Guerrouj commented further about Rome and the future.

"My season starts tomorrow. I am a much more relaxed person than I used to be and I know that from tomorrow and until Athens you will see a great El Guerrouj. I usually tend to improve my form as the season advances so by the time the Olympics come around I should be at the peak. I feel physically and psychologically stronger than last year. Last year I had huge rhythm problems. I couldn't kick and yet I won the world title. This year my training program has slightly changed and I feel like my rhythm is a lot better. This year I have been preparing specifically for the 1,500 metres, the 1,500 metres and the 1,500 metres!"

El Guerrouj was his same old confident self before Rome. Going from his apparent frame of mind we should expect another run that we could describe as great from Hicham. Yet in hindsight something was amiss. The strength of past years was gone, for now. The results of the 1,500 metres in Rome were:

Rashid Ramzi	3:30.25
Bernard Lagat	3:30.81
Mehdi Baala	3:31.25
Isaac Kiprono Songok	3:31.94
Rui Silva	3:32.13
Alex Kipchirchir	3:32.35
Michael East	3:32.37

Greg Rowlerson

Hicham El Guerrouj	3:32.64
Nicholas Willis	3:32.68
Mounir Yemmouni	3:32.97
Gert-Jan Liefers	3:33.87
Kevin Sullivan	3:34.43
Juan Carlos Higuero	3:34.48
Vyacheslav Shabunin	3:35.50
Anis Selmouni	3:37.36
Paul Korir	3:37.69

MOROCCAN SUCCESS; THE KADA WAY

From The Greatest Never To The Greatest Ever?

Some of Hicham's other comments on the day prior to his disastrous eighth place finish were:

"The idea of doubling 1,500 metres and 5,000 metres in Athens remains. But attempting the double doesn't necessarily mean I will succeed in the double. I am not a robot. I am a human being. My training has been excellent and everything has been great for me but don't forget that I am not a machine."

Was the king's reign over? It seemed a reasonable question to ask after being beaten by not one, but seven athletes. Then again it may just have been a bad run under difficult circumstances given his medical treatment and birth of baby daughter Hida.

El Guerrouj had raced in his usual fashion, from the front. Approaching the bell there was a surprise when Baala went ahead and into the lead. This had never happened in the past. Hicham threatened to return to the lead on the back straight but was held off by the Frenchman. The Moroccan was unable to have an impact on the bend and slipped well behind Baala on the home straight as many athletes ran over the top of him. Baala was also comfortably defeated by Rashid Ramzi and Bernard Lagat. The Moroccan born Rashid in particular flew home to win well against the top notch line up.

However Ramzi was another talented runner that Africa had lost, as he was competing for Bahrain, for the same reasons that Shaheen was competing for Qatar. His victory in Rome came as a surprise, not on recent form, but on anything he'd achieved before this season. Just recently in Algiers he had smashed his personal best when he won with a 3:31.87 on June 24. Prior to 2004, Ramzis' personal best was only 3:37.26. He would turn twenty four in fifteen days time.

It was a remarkable improvement from a man who years ago,

was used as a regular rabbit by Hicham El Guerrouj. Yet this wasn't even in races, but during the Moroccan's heavy speed work sessions. As a result, he earned a living but did not get to compete internationally. Rashid had been injury prone and it were these reasons that were given for his fairly late burst onto the scene. No matter what his past, we all knew that in 2004 Ramzi was going to be a potential gold medallist in Athens. Even when El Guerrouj was defeated, a Moroccan born athlete still won!

The 5,000 metres race in Rome didn't contain such drama but it did produce a standard that was more than worthy of a Golden League event. Kenya's Eliud Kipchoge and Ethiopia's Sileshi Sihine fought out a wonderful battle that saw them become the fourth and fifth fastest men ever and ended with another massive victory for the Kenyan superstar. His time of 12:46.53 only slightly eclipsed Sihine's 12:47.04. It was a huge personal best for Sileshi whose previous standard was the 13:06.53 that he ran at last year's Rome meeting. Clearly he was a major threat for the 10,000 metres gold in Athens. Qatar's purchase failed, with Ahmad Hassan Abdullah finishing only thirteenth in 13:10.62. Maybe Bahrain was the new giant of distance running. Up ahead, placing an impressive sixth was Mushir Salim Jawher who clocked 13:00.59. Goumri ran well for Morocco but in this field 13:01.73 was only good enough for eighth position. Yet the results were even harsher for Norwegian Marius Bakken who ran a national record of 13:06.39 though only finished eleventh! Having a shocker in the big line up was Benjamin Limo who placed nineteenth and was timed at 13:31.25.

Only two of the seven men who enjoyed the rare taste of victory over El Guerrouj in Rome were in the Moroccan's next race on July 6. Hicham was keen to show the world that he was not a spent force at the Lausanne Grand Prix meet. Isaac Songok and Alex Kipchirchir were the men who he needed to turn the tables on if he aimed to return to the winner's list. To win though might be expecting a bit much after coming eighth. What Hicham required from this race was a little more competitiveness. Second or third placing would not be so bad.

MOROCCAN SUCCESS; THE KADA WAY

He made the following comments before racing in Switzerland, "I'm very worried about going or not going to the Olympics. I hope tonight will be ok and I'll be able to run under 3:30. If I don't, I'll make my final decision on the 6th of August in Zurich."

One defeat had certainly made a difference to the Moroccan's psyche. Once Noureddine Morceli lost ('96 Grand Prix final), he was never able to defeat the best again. Was El Guerrouj made of sterner stuff?

The Lausanne result was inconclusive, as it didn't tell us if Hicham was going to remain the best miler in the world. However it did remind us of his fight and determination. Still not in terrific shape, El Guerrouj was able to struggle to the finish line, where he barely held off a late challenge from Songok. It was only a well timed dip that saved him, as the times of 3:32.20 and 3:32.22 showed. The rabbit had set a very fast pace of 1:52.32 for the first 800 metres, so it was more a case of which athletes could hold on the best, rather than who might kick it down. Despite toiling to run out the distance, Abdelkader Kada would have been very happy with his athlete's effort. He knew that 3:32 form wasn't too far away from winning against the absolute best and that there was plenty of time to get Hicham strong enough to run under 3:30 again. The Olympic 1,500 metres title remained very much a realistic goal, not just a dream.

Ali Ezzine also had renewed hope after this meeting as a result of his fourth placing in the steeplechase. His time was only 8:20.05, but he defeated some Kenyans and finished closer to the winner than he had for a long time in Europe. The winner incidentally was world silver medallist Ezekiel Kemboi who recorded an 8:17.46. This was much better from Ali, to be in contention until very late.

The Golden League had a three week break and its next edition was in Paris on July 23. Things were getting continually better now for Ali Ezzine after he produced his fastest time of the season and second fastest since 2001 to finish in sixth place in the steeplechase. The Lausanne form held up nicely with the results of the first eleven finishers being:

Ezekiel Kemboi	8:11.03
Julius Nyamu	8:11.29
David Chemweno	8:11.44
Kipkirui Misoi	8:13.38
Wesley Kiprotich	8:14.49
Ali Ezzine	8:14.74
Antonio David Jimenez	8:14.81
Bouabdallah Tahri	8:16.73
Vincent Le Dauphin	8:17.57
Wilson Boit Kipketer	8:19.21
Eliseo Martin	8:19.60

There were some handy scalps taken by the Moroccan who was the first of the non Kenyans. Ali just had the one race in Stockholm to go before he commenced his Olympic campaign. Kemboi appeared to be rounding into form just at the right time.

El Guerrouj chose to sit out the Paris 1,500 metres race, though interestingly, so did Ramzi and Baala. That left Lagat as the clear favourite and the Kenyan did not let anyone down. Not only did he win, but did so with the season's best time of 3:29.21. Bernard had laid down the gauntlet. This was a big statement pre Athens.

His countrymen filled the first five positions with Timothy Kiptanui and Cornelius Chirchir the most impressive, registering times of 3:30.04 and 3:30.60 respectively. Well behind in seventh and eighth places were two of the biggest names of the last Olympics, Ali Saidi-Sief and Noah Ngeny. Both were timed at 3:34.06. Both had endured massive problems since their glory days and it seemed impossible that either could play a major role in the 2004 Games.

The Stockholm Grand Prix meeting came about on July 27 and it was here that Ali Ezzine ran his best time since 2001. The Moroccan finished third in 8:12.93, only a small margin behind Julius Nyamu, 8:12.14. He even defeated Kipkirui

MOROCCAN SUCCESS; THE KADA WAY

Misoi, 8:13.33 and Luis Miguel Martin, 8:13.55, amongst the sixteen finishers. The only downside was the enormous gap to Paul Kipsiele Koech who ran solo for an 8:03.10. It was another of this Kenyan's dominant victories and he looked set to play a major role at the Olympics. For Ali, this form was good enough to aim for a top six finish and dream of a medal.

The 1,500 metres held two races at Stockholm and surprisingly it was the 'B' race that was the faster. Ethiopian Mulugeta Wendimu clocked 3:32.38 to upstage the bigger names of the opening 'A' race. Often, Grand Prix meetings will conduct two races at the same distance when there are too many athletes to include in the one field. This regularly happens in the 100 metres.

The biggest name in this 'A' race was Rashid Ramzi, but when he was asked to really kick off this slower pace he was unable to produce the sort of finish that had blown away his opposition in Rome. The first eight runners finished within two seconds of one another and it was Ukrainian Ivan Heshko who won out in 3:35.31. Alex Kipchirchir came closest with a 3:35.50 while Ramzi was next in 3:35.57. This result showed that the new kid on the block was clearly beatable and this would have given Kada and El Guerrouj more encouragement as they prepared for their next test in four days time.

The 5,000 metres event in Sweden contained interesting competitors left, right and centre. The Moroccans produced a decent showing with Goumri finishing fifth in 13:05.78 and Amyn finishing eighth in 13:10.18. The race was won by Kenya's Boniface Kiprotich Songok, who ran a good time of 13:01.47. However, the real interest surrounded the athletes competing for Qatar and Bahrain, and those who were planning on doing so in the future.

Qatar's Abdullah and Bahrain's Jawher took second and third places with times of 13:02.03 and 13:03.46. Both were in good enough form to contend for medals at Athens. Just like Abdullah, Jawher was actually Kenyan born. As recently as last season he was still competing for the East African giant, when he recorded a personal best of 13:01.76 in Zurich under his original name, Leonard Muchero Maina. Now twenty six, Leonard or should I say Mushir, had improved slightly on that time in Rome and had already won in Lausanne earlier in the month. He seemed to be in his prime as an athlete. Runners with this talent were a dime a dozen in East Africa but for other nations, it was almost a blessing to have someone so good to call their own. He did not have to worry about earning a living, and making the Bahrain national team was as certain as other countries wanting their oil supplies. Any links to the old amateur days had clearly been squashed. Track and field had become more of a money game.

Usually runners who place fourteenth and fifteenth can be glossed over but in Stockholm those athletes were Kenyan's Nicholas Kemboi and James Kwalia C'Kurui. That they had clocked only 13:19.65 and 13:26.61 was strange enough. Kemboi had pushed Gebrselassie at Brussels to run 26:30, a faster average pace than he could manage here. Kwalia had run 12:54.58 at Oslo last season. Mainly because of those performances they became some of distance running's most wanted. They both attracted interest from the Bahrain Athletics Federation and were both apparently going to compete soon for their new nation. Yet in March this year, they had a change of heart after Qatar offered them better conditions. With their recent form being so poor, would Qatar now try to back out of the deal? Later Kemboi would reverse his plans and continued to compete for Kenya.

The tenth placed athlete from this 5,000 metres event was actually the biggest name in the field. Saif Saaeed Shaheen was unlike his usual self, uncompetitive in recording a 13:14.65. Perhaps the Qatari runner was still trying to get over his disappointment of being unable to race in Athens. The IOC was not budging on its ruling which stated that athletes are required to be nationalized for a specific period of time before they are allowed to compete for that country at the Olympic Games. The IAAF had a different ruling, which was why Saif had been able to race last year in Paris. Unfortunately the IOC had the authority over the Athletics Federation when it came to the Games. Despite Shaheen's and Qatar's protests he was going to have to sit this out. This

MOROCCAN SUCCESS; THE KADA WAY

was a shame. We want to see the best athletes competing at the Olympic Games, which is the so called pinnacle of our sport. It is useful to reflect back on some comments made by Shaheen after his first race under his new name at Zurich last year, "Today was my first race for Qatar, my new country and yes, it did feel a bit different. I am not surprised that the decision came so quickly because both Federations were in agreement and both countries are happy about the situation. My family is also very happy about my decision. My fans back in Kenya are happy as well."

The majority of track fans wanted to see Shaheen on the track and not up in the grandstands. Perhaps there were too many people on the IOC committee who were sticklers and hated change, even stubborn enough to stand up and put a stop to what most wanted. An athlete's life can be short and Beijing 2008 was a long way off. Shaheen was unlikely to be in such terrific form by then. The one thing that we can say is that it was *his* decision to switch nationalities, so he knew the possibilities of what he could miss. His case reminded us of Wilson Kipketer's plight eight years earlier.

Despite the poor performance in Stockholm, Saif's form over the barriers was great. On July 4 in Athens, he'd won by over ten seconds in a fast 8:01.97. He had also won in Ostrava on June 8. On that day his time of 8:11.54 was over three seconds faster than his rival Kemboi. The Olympic situation wasn't only unfair on Shaheen but also his competitors. For whomever the gold medallist in Athens turned out to be, that steeplechase champion would always have an invisible asterisk next to his name.

July 31 was the date of the Heusden-Zolder 'night of athletics' meeting and Hicham El Guerrouj expected a fast time from himself in the 1,500 metres. The world champion was quoted on recent developments before the important race. "My allergy problems are solved and things are going unexpectedly well in training. I want a pace that can bring me inside 3:28, because I want to arrive in Athens as the world leading performer. If any 1,500 metres runner deserves to be the Olympic champion, it must be El Guerrouj. But I will take on the tournament like any other race, with as little pressure as possible. My next races in Heusden-Zolder and Zurich must help me to enjoy racing again. If you see me smile after Saturday's 1,500 metres, then I will feel relieved and confident."

His confidence had returned but only recently. Hicham made a late change in his racing schedule and decided to compete in Belgium just one week ago. The meeting organiser Wilfried Meert was of course happy to oblige. Former top Kenyan performer Laban Rotich was bought in to act as a rabbit, with El Guerrouj asking for an incredible 1:49 first 800 metres.

The early speed was nothing quite like that, but it was still fast enough, faster than the Olympic final was sure to be run at if Hicham did not have a teammate in support. The field sat on approximately 3:32 tempo until the Moroccan showed that he still had the fast wheels as he burned off everyone with a fifty four second final lap!

It was a magnificent performance with bonuses too. As he hit the line in 3:29.18 he became the season's fastest. This could be important psychologically going into Athens. The only athlete who remained at all close to him was a new Ethiopian star named Mulugeta Wendimu. Ethiopians tended not to excel at the middle distances yet this nineteen year old ran a national record of 3:31.13. Could he continue to improve enough to pose a threat in a month's time? The world leader had little concern about Mulugeta as his ecstatic post race quote shows:

"I am extremely happy today. I was running very smoothly. At a certain moment the pace dropped dramatically which left me 1.5 seconds behind schedule at the bell. It felt as if I could run below 3:27 today. My finishing speed proved to be very reliable; I'm prepared for all sorts of tactics now. Will I double 1,500 metres and 5,000 metres in Athens? Inch Allah, if God wants it. There has never been any doubt in my mind about my ability to do it."

Bring on Zurich!

MOROCCAN SUCCESS; THE KADA WAY

Morocco's Zouhair Ouerdi produced an excellent run in the 3,000 metres steeplechase, clocking 8:13.67 and finishing in second position behind Kenyan Richard Kipkemboi Mateelong, who wasn't too far ahead in 8:11.33. Third place went to Musa Amer Obaid in 8:13.91. Perhaps Qatar had unearthed another star!

Bahrain's Jawher continued his top form to win the 5,000 metres in 13:03.09. Again Morocco placed second. In this race it was Hicham Bellani whose time of 13:05.72 was a good sign so close to the Games. Things weren't going quite as smoothly for a former teammate. Discovering his attempted comeback to be one almighty struggle was Mohammed Mourhit. The Belgium boy registered 13:44.18, finishing a distant nineteenth. In front of his home crowd, this was quite a fall from his halcyon days.

The Zurich meeting contained greater opposition for Hicham El Guerrouj with Bernard Lagat and Mehdi Baala on the start line. This race on August 6 would likely show us the gold medal protagonists for the Games to follow at month's end. Rather than a tactical race, this battle was conducted in the manner of a time trial, with the pacesetters going at a torturous tempo. There was no opportunity to relax and think about when you might decide to sink the boot in, for the speed was simply too great.

The split at 800 metres is 1:49.0 and soon it's clear that only the season's sub 3:30 men can keep close to sustaining the pressure. As we've seen on many occasions, this is quickly becoming the Hicham vs. Bernard show. Sometimes in the past, the Kenyan has managed to go with the Moroccan at this type of speed, but he's never been able to get by him at the end. Surely the world record holder is a little more vulnerable this year. Lagat needs to show us, and more importantly himself, that he believes he can be an Olympic champion.

Considering the early pace, a fifty seven second third lap is very good as Hicham reaches 1,200 metres in 2:46.0. He has his opponents beaten, bar Lagat, and now it's just a question of who is the stronger on the day. El Guerrouj continues to lead into the final straight and whilst maintaining a good rhythm, he gets that familiar Sydney feeling of having an East African move up on his right shoulder. The two run side by side before the constant pressure from Lagat wins out, causing El Guerrouj to fall behind in the last fifteen metres. When he requires another major effort, there is nothing left in reserve. The results from the fourteen finishers at Zurich were:

Bernard Lagat	3:27.40
Hicham El Guerrouj	3:27.64
Isaac Kiprono Songok	3:30.99
Paul Korir	3:31.32
Mehdi Baala	3:32.54
Alex Kipchirchir	3:32.74
Laban Rotich	3:34.11
Nicholas Willis	3:34.53
Kevin Sullivan	3:34.69
Vyacheslav Shabunin	3:36.25
Michael East	3:36.92
Rui Silva	3:37.99
Noah Ngeny	3:40.46
Craig Mottram	3:46.80

Just before Athens, Lagat spoke about the value of this victory, "That win really boosted my confidence. El Guerrouj is one of the greatest athletes in the world ever. I really wanted to win that race and it's given me massive motivation for the Games. If I can continue to run as I did in Zurich, then I know I will get a good result." Just before the heats he declared: "I have improved a lot since I won the bronze medal in Sydney and I think the time has come for me to win the gold."

Finishing second with Hicham was an uncommon feeling for Abdelkader Kada. He shouldn't feel absolutely delighted about the loss, though he should be far from dejected by the outcome. His boy had run incredibly well. It was his fastest time of the season, continuing the improvement shown in Belgium. That they had lost to Lagat in spite of this

MOROCCAN SUCCESS; THE KADA WAY

performance told Kada that the two rivals were now for all intents and purposes, equal in ability and form. What the Athens final might come down to is mental strength, or to better put it, sheer will. Abdelkader may well have prayed to Allah, to give Hicham the strength on that day. It was certain to be the most important race of his life.

Zurich may have been just a lead up event to Hicham El Guerrouj, but to Saif Saaeed Shaheen it meant much more. "Zurich is my Olympics," he was quoted as saying prior to the 3,000 metres steeplechase. It was a race where he endeavoured to break the world record of Brahim Boulami.

In this quest he failed, though in every other facet of running, he succeeded. Shaheen demolished the class field with a consummate ease rarely seen at this level. But when he finished in the fast time of 8:00.60, nearly the length of the straight ahead of Ezekiel Kemboi, 8:12.75, he looked highly disappointed. There were no medals handed out in Switzerland.

Athens was finally upon us. There were many points of discussion among the men's distance races. Could Kipketer, El Guerrouj and Tergat finally win gold? Could Gebrselassie defy all the odds to win a third straight title? Would Bekele and El Guerrouj both again attempt to double (both were expected to)? Would Kenya sweep the steeplechase in the absence of Shaheen?

One of these questions was answered on August 20, the night of the 10,000 metres final. The Ethiopians were favoured to win the medals, however to the majority of viewers, there was really only one favourite. Haile Gebrselassie was not the favourite to win, but most hoped that the 'emperor' could add to his already congested resumé with another memorable Olympic performance.

The race certainly was a memorable one and Haile was very much caught up in the drama, though not in the mode of Atlanta and Sydney. As Kenenisa Bekele forced the pace during the race's second half, he reduced the contenders to only five men. These included his teammates Sihine and Gebrselassie. Remarkably the resistance of the Kenyans had already ended with over 3,000 metres remaining and Uganda's Boniface Kiprop and Eritrea's Zersenay Tadesse were the only potential spoilers of an Ethiopian sweep.

Soon Kenenisa put in another spurt, seriously damaging Tadesse and Gebrselassie. The Athens crowd was stunned and an uneasy, almost sad atmosphere overtook the race. The two Ethiopians quickly realised that something was amiss and after looking up on the big screen, they actually slowed down and waited for Haile to catch up! In this day and age of professional sport such respect for a fellow competitor was rarely seen. By giving Gebrselassie a second chance, they in turn allowed Tadesse to recover, thus putting their own Olympic medals at risk.

Despite the assistance Haile continued to struggle, and with a km to go the youngsters kicked again. Soon they had fifteen metres on Tadesse and Kiprop, with Gebrselassie well beaten, some thirty five metres adrift. The gaps continued to increase, which came as no surprise after Bekele showed off his own rocket launcher with a 53.02 second final lap! This gave him an Olympic record 27:05.10 and left him comfortably ahead of Sihine who recorded 27:09.39. Tadesse finished well to take the bronze medal, becoming his nation's first ever Olympic medallist, though he was around 100 metres behind his conquerors. Gebrselassie ended up fifth, in 27:27.70. It wasn't the great performance that we so often associated with him, but there was nothing to be ashamed of. After appearing initially distraught once crossing the line, Haile's beaming smile again broke out, soon after being embraced by his teammates. It officially ended the era that had unofficially finished last year. Time catches up with all the greats eventually.

Nearing thirty, El Guerrouj hoped that his legs would retain their sharpness for just one more week. The 1,500 heats had been run before the 10,000 metres final. Obviously Hicham was expected to progress easily, though he knew that disasters were possible as he spoke with caution but also

MOROCCAN SUCCESS; THE KADA WAY

excitement about what was to come, "The thing with our distance over three rounds, anything can happen. Even athletes who have run 3:30 can not make it to the final, so we all have to be ready. But I don't really want to speak about anyone else. I am ready and I think the 1,500 metres will be the race of the Games."

Abdelkader Kada fought off negative talk of El Guerrouj's earlier health problems as he explained, "There is no problem now. Nothing at all. This is going to be the end of his bad luck." He also noted that, "His racing has been improving a lot recently."

I am sure that many Moroccans echoed these same sentiments.

The heats were action packed for a change, though fortunately Hicham kept out of trouble to win heat 1 in 3:37.86. Yet even he was reminded of how close trouble could lurk. Just after the start, Mounir Yemmouni of France hit El Guerrouj's heel and tumbled to the track, taking with him American Grant Robison. Both were out of contention.

The pace was very slow with an 800 metres split of 2:02.96, almost fourteen seconds slower than the same split in Zurich. The Moroccan soon bounded into the lead and from there he did what he liked. It was a most impressive run and there were never any issues in regards to him not taking one of the four automatic qualifying spots. The same could not be said for a big name in heat 2.

For some reason this heat had been packed with quality performers. There were Lagat, Baala, Wendimu, Estevez and a young American talent named Alan Webb. Lagat and Wendimu put themselves in the front positions on the last lap but trouble ensued when Webb tried to sneak through a small gap on the back straight. Here he hit Lagat's heel and lost his impetus, unable to kick on thereafter. Baala was also boxed in but didn't seem in any trouble until the home straight, when his strength completely deserted him and he faded to thirteenth place. The qualifiers finished up being Estevez, who won in 3:39.71, Lagat, Nicholas Willis, Kaouch and Wendimu. Adil's run was potentially more good news for Hicham. British athlete Michael East was the winner of heat 3, in a decent time of 3:37.37. Rashid Ramzi left his run late, but managed to come home safely in fourth spot.

The steeplechase heats on August 21 contained no great surprises, which was good news for Moroccan hopeful Ali Ezzine. The enforced absence of Shaheen would have added to his belief that a repeat of his bronze medal from Sydney was not totally out of the question. Yet there were still four Kenyan born athletes in the event, with Qatar including another former Kenyan, Moses Kimutai. The nineteen year old now went by the name of Musa Amer Obaid. With a personal best of only 8:13.91, he was not expected to pose as tough a competition as the three that were running in the Kenyan uniform. He was however a world junior silver medallist.

Ezzine raced in heat 1 and the pressure was on with only the first three positions given as automatic qualifiers. This made the heats like a final for everyone except the Kenyans and Ali had to give it his all just to survive. The pace was pretty good and this enabled him to qualify despite placing only fifth in a time of 8:20.18. Qatar's other import, Khamis Abdullah Saifeldin showed good finishing speed to win in 8:17.89. Kemboi was next with 8:18.11 and in the end, the first seven athletes progressed to the final.

Kenyan Brimin Kipruto produced a faster time of 8:15.11 to win heat 2, but the overall depth in this preliminary was not great enough to worry Ali. The third heat was by far the slowest, so Ezzine could breathe easily, even before the final km was over. It was won by Qatar's Obaid in 8:23.94. Morocco's Zouhair Ouerdi placed fourth but his time of 8:27.55 was too slow to make the final. Ali was the only Moroccan to qualify after Abdelatif Chemlal could only achieve ninth position in heat 2. In contrast, all the Kenyans had made it to the final in three days time. There wasn't anywhere near the excitement surrounding this race as there was last year in Paris.

MOROCCAN SUCCESS; THE KADA WAY

Far greater anticipation surrounded Hicham El Guerrouj's bid to erase the ghosts of 1996 and 2000. August 22 was the day of the 1,500 metres semi finals and it proved to be a fantastic day for he and Abdelkader.

The first semi commenced without the world champion, though even without him, the pace was surprisingly fast. Eight hundred metres were reached in 1:56.74 but drama was soon on the horizon. With 600 metres remaining Algerian Tarek Boukensa hit the heels of Rashid Ramzi and fell. Bahrain's hope was able to continue but only struggled from then on and finished eleventh. One of Hicham's main threats was extinguished.

In a minor upset, the heat was won by Kaouch who registered a fantastic time of 3:35.69, with Lagat just behind in 3:35.84. East and Songok were the runners that got through as fastest losers.

The second semi was a comparative cruise as El Guerrouj led the tight bunch to 800 metres in 2:07.19. This pedestrian run pace may well have been of some concern for Kada, but sure enough Hicham soon started his long familiar surge for home and eventually won in 3:40.87. Rui Silva finished well to record a 3:40.99, with Timothy Kiptanui running 3:41.04. It was all set up for a magnificent final in two days time. Hicham said after his semi, "I am confident it will be third time lucky for me. Just wait and see, I'll make you believe me."

Tuesday the 24th of August, 2004, was a monumental date for Hicham El Guerrouj. It was the day where he would find out if he'd join Sebastian Coe and Noureddine Morceli, the recent truly great milers, to win Olympic gold at the 1,500 metres. Morocco also had yet to win this event so there was a lot hanging on a race that would last only a few minutes.

Despite his coaching credentials, Abdelkader Kada had never experienced involvement in an Olympic gold, although of course he had coached three different athletes to minor medals. Not that any Olympic medal should be considered minor. His viewing entertainment for today did not only include Hicham's race to whet his interest. A nice prelude was the men's 3,000 metres steeplechase where Kada could watch his former student Ali Ezzine.

The first 300 metres are taken cautiously but then the three runners competing for Kenya all push to the front with Kipruto making the initial move. This fast pace remains, leading to a brisk time of 2:42.55 for the first 1,000 metres. Not many athletes would be capable of sustaining this speed, least of all Ali who will be hoping that the second km is slower. The Moroccan soon moves up to seventh place and looks good in the middle of the pack. Paul Kipsiele Koech is setting the pace and as the season leader, this makes some sense. A fast tempo throughout might increase his chances of victory. There is the issue though of his countryman Kipruto and Kemboi sitting on him.

Clearly the Kenyans are trying to destroy the entire field early, to make sure of the medals. In this they are succeeding with all the athletes spread out by the fourth last lap. It is here that Ezzine makes his bid, moving into fifth position and hanging on to the leaders, as is the Qatari Musa Amer Obaid in fourth. But Ali's progress stagnates at the water jump and he falls back to sixth, now fifteen metres behind Obaid. This is the desperate time of the race for him. If he has any chance of a medal he must put everything into the next 300 metres or so.

The second km is faster than the first and the 2,000 metres split is an excellent 5:24.27. This speed from the leaders is close to the fastest race tempo that Ezzine has ever run at and he is no longer in that same shape, hence he's losing ground. With two laps to go, Ali is back in fifth place but now twenty five metres behind the fourth placed runner. It's clear that medalling is now beyond him. On the back straight he starts to 'hit the wall', falling to sixth behind Luis Miguel Martin of Spain who quickly drops the Moroccan. Ezzine still has 20 metres over the rest but if he had anything left he would have gone with the Spaniard's valiant move as he makes an attempt to catch up with the leading four.

MOROCCAN SUCCESS; THE KADA WAY

Koech leads Kemboi at the bell with Obaid posing a serious threat in third and Kipruto fourth, but even he has a chance as together they are all separated by no more than ten metres with Martin now only five metres behind Kipruto. Ezzine still has twenty metres advantage over seventh but is running in 'no man's land'. This is when you are out on your own and it's tough. For a reference, think of Salah Hissou in Atlanta. In the battle for gold Kemboi takes off at the top of the bend and looks a winner. Martin drops twenty metres back and out of the medals. But there is still the matter of the Qatari runner. Ezekiel eases away and strolls it in, yet regularly looks back, seemingly more interested in the clean sweep of the medals than his own individual glory. His teammates finish strongly enabling the clean sweep and all are delighted as they embrace. I can't ever remember a distance runner winning a sprint finish so easily at this level without even looking as if he was sprinting! The results from the steeplechase final were:

Ezekiel Kemboi	8:05.81
Kipruto Brimin	8:06.11
Paul Kipsiele Koech	8:06.64
Musa Amer Obaid	8:07.18
Luis Miguel Martin	8:11.64
Simon Vroemen	8:13.25
Bouabdallah Tahri	8:14.26
Ali Ezzine	8:15.58
Eliseo Martin	8:15.77
Vincent Le Dauphin	8:16.15
Daniel Lincoln	8:16.86
Radoslaw Poplawski	8:17.32
Mustafa Mohamed	8:18.05
Antonio David Jimenez	8:22.63
Khamis Abdullah Saifeldin	8:36.66

Kemboi took a step up from his silver medal in Paris. Koech was another example of a Kenyan with the best form not necessarily being the first Kenyan in the major championship. Obaid was another example of a world junior medallist finding the transition to senior competition a comfortable one. Ali Ezzine's eighth place was neither a pass nor a fail. In doing his best to go with the leaders he'd arguably run beyond his limits. Running at a more even pace may have resulted in a higher finish but why settle for sixth when you've been a medallist previously? The Moroccan ran gamely and could be satisfied that he had remained in contention for as long as possible.

Now there was the small matter of another final.

He'd exceeded Morceli by winning four world titles and surpassing all of Noureddine's outdoor world records. His longevity outweighed Herb Elliott's by so much that it had to out rank Herb's brilliant yet short domination of the discipline. His times were far enough superior to Sebastian Coe's, more than making up for the approximate fifteen year gap of their eras. When strictly discussing the greatest 1,500 metres/miler of all time, Hicham El Guerrouj was now the choice of most knowledgeable athletics fans. Most couldn't ignore the sheer quantity of sub 3:30 performances that clogged up the all time 1,500 metres list. But there were still some that said, "He's never won the Olympics." It was the one blight on an amazing career. Unfortunately this one blight was a major one. Athens was providing Hicham with a final chance and it was coming under different circumstances.

Hicham went to Atlanta aiming to become the world champion (number one in the world). He didn't know if he was the best, but he knew he was awfully close. Hicham went to Sydney as the world champion but with what must have felt like the weight of the world on his shoulders. He knew that he should win and that he was expected to win. In 2004 Hicham went to Athens with worse winning form than he took to Atlanta and Sydney. Both of those previous campaigns were unblemished ones, as the entire 1996 and 2000 seasons were filled with victories except for the Olympics themselves. This year things were different and Hicham must have felt a little like Noureddine did in Atlanta. It was the concerning feeling that your days at the top may be numbered. But Morceli would have only had these thoughts due to general talk and hype as the Algerian went into those Games undefeated. He had doubtless heard about the young Moroccan who had been ripping up the Grand Prix circuit with impressive results. In

MOROCCAN SUCCESS; THE KADA WAY

2004 Hicham had been given the physical evidence that he wasn't as superior as seasons past. He'd received the shock of his career when he placed ninth in Rome, the sort of result that he hadn't experienced in a decade. Even once in top form he had lost to Lagat in his final tune up race in Zurich.

The pressure here was still immense, though it was a dissimilar pressure to Sydney. It was the pressure of a last opportunity rather than of an expectation to win.

Steve Ovett predicted, "It will probably be the classic El Guerrouj scenario, where he takes it out with a lap and a half to go, kicks in hard to the bell, and then kicks in even harder from there. I could write the script now. It just depends whether anybody else wants to change it."

The gun sounds at approximately 11:40 pm and the race quickly resembles one from a bygone era. There are no early fireworks as it quickly becomes clear that Adil Kaouch is running for himself this year, and why shouldn't he? His form in the semi final was perhaps as impressive as we'd ever seen from the long time second string Moroccan. It is a cagey El Guerrouj that we see running wide in midfield on the opening lap as the three Kenyans head the pack in 1:00.42. Now comes a moment that Hicham is hoping for. Estevez makes a surprise move to the front and instead of having to take an early initiative, all the world champion has to do is follow the Spaniard's path.

Reyes stops short of taking the full brunt of the pace, preferring to stay on the outside of the leading Kenyan Lagat. As a result, El Guerrouj is forced to sit out wide, covering more ground as he has all race. He moves onto Estevez' shoulder as they approach two laps to go.

Abdelkader Kada nervously watches his charge with pride. Hicham's patience here is impressing him. There is no sign of panic. The average viewer knows that this is his most important race ever and we are told that a slow tempo is unlikely to suit him. Yet with 800 metres remaining El Guerrouj's face is a picture of concentration, but not concern.

The fan wants him to push the pace now but crucially he waits just that little longer.

At exactly half distance Hicham takes up the front running but he doesn't surge yet. As he gets to 800 metres the split is only 2:01.93 after a slow 61.51 lap. Had this race become too much like an 800 metres, giving the speed merchants the advantage over the pure milers?

Into the back straight and the Moroccan begins to stride out with intent. Lagat has positioned himself on the inside, perfectly placed behind his great rival. Looking at the field, it is difficult to see that El Guerrouj is really pouring it on, for with 500 metres to go the majority of his opposition are sticking to him like they never have in years past. However most would remember that his distinctive surge is usually a continuous one. Once Hicham kicks, he keeps kicking, so there is rarely a let up in pressure. That's why his previous victories mostly showed a gradual lengthening of his lead, as opposed to a sudden explosion of speed, which shot the likes of a Coe or Morceli on their way to glory. It's a question of sustaining a lung bursting surge for 700 metres. Who can handle that?

Nearing the bell, the Moroccan's pressure starts to show its effect, as the first five athletes establish a small gap. Barring a big turnaround, this is where the medals will be. Into the turn and further damage begins to show, with only Lagat and the Ukrainian Heshko toughing it out with El Guerrouj. The split at 1,200 metres is 2:55.21. Hicham has just covered the third lap in 53.28! This is similar to his previous massive win on this track in 1997, his first world championship.

Unfortunately seven years on the competition is stronger and Lagat still shows no signs of being put into difficulty. At the top of the final turn Heshko can no longer hang on, but replacing him in third position is Portugal's Silva, making a late run. As the combatants enter the home straight Bernard moves out to attack Hicham. He looks like he will take him, just as he did in Zurich. Rui can't quite get to them as the Kenyan edges alongside the Moroccan. Didn't we see this four years ago?

MOROCCAN SUCCESS; THE KADA WAY

For a moment, with about fifty metres remaining, it appears that Lagat hits the lead. You could almost hear the groans from Hicham's supporters, 'Oh no, not again.' But importantly, the thinking in the mind of one man was in the mode of 'no, not this time.'

From somewhere very deep inside, El Guerrouj finds something extra over that final stretch and etches his name forever in Olympic history. It isn't an extra kick. This isn't something he'd trained for. This is sheer determination, perhaps even desperation. In these final strides he has belief, and this is enough to prevail, just barely over his worthy opponent. The results from the 1,500 metres final were:

Hicham El Guerrouj	3:34.18
Bernard Lagat	3:34.30
Rui Silva	3:34.68
Timothy Kiptanui	3:35.61
Ivan Heshko	3:35.82
Michael East	3:36.33
Reyes Estevez	3:36.63
Gert-Jan Liefers	3:37.17
Adil Kaouch	3:38.26
Mulugeta Wendimu	3:38.33
Kamal Boulahfane	3:39.02
Isaac Kiprono Songok	3:41.72

Hicham had claimed what he and many others felt was rightfully his. The last lap was clocked at a magnificent 51.91 seconds. This was astonishing, considering the entire final 700 metres was run at break neck speed. After crossing the line El Guerrouj sank to the track and was instantly overcome by emotion and no doubt, relief. For many people, not only track fans, this was their greatest moment of these Games. After bowing his head to the track he looks up and is hugged by Bernard Lagat.

Later he was able to venture to the stands where he was met with joy by his nineteen year old wife Majuva and their daughter Hiba. El Guerrouj spoke of the love for his newborn,

"Today I ran for her and for my family. In shallah (God willing), she will be happy for her Papa."

The world record holder, world champion and now *Olympic* champion commented, "This is the greatest day of my life. I can't express my feelings. It is finally complete."

Lagat offered his congratulations and respect to the greatest, "I am very happy for him. He has now achieved it all. He deserves it." On the finish the silver medallist stated: "In the last 100 metres I knew it was going to come down to the kick. I was right behind him all the way. With 50 metres left I thought this could be another Zurich, but he had the strongest kick today."

El Guerrouj: "In the last 50 metres I had the image of Sydney in my mind. In Sydney I didn't have the energy to accelerate at the end. This time I had the energy. I felt I could push it. I knew I would win. The last few metres I just refused to let him go. I was so desperate for the title that I had to hold on, such was the desire in me to win."

He also added, "I lost in Sydney because I had trained too hard and run out of gas. This time I had extra. Four years ago in Sydney I cried tears of sadness. Today I cry tears of joy. I'm living a moment of glory. I'm overjoyed for myself and for my country."

Abdelkader Kada gave his stamp of approval, "It had become a psychological complex. The Olympic medal was all that was left. Now for me today, he becomes the best miler in history."

Many were thankful that Hicham now had his Olympic gold medal. Four hundred metres Los Angeles champion Nawal El Moutawakel said, "This means so much for the youth of the country. Hicham is a hero, a great role model for generations yet to come. He has worked for this for a long time. It was all about dedication and will power and guts." El Guerrouj also received the obligatory phone call from his King, Mohammed VI. "He was super happy. He will go on supporting me."

MOROCCAN SUCCESS; THE KADA WAY

As was the situation in Paris, there was little opportunity to bask in the glory of such an achievement. The next night, on August 25, Hicham El Guerrouj was back on the track in the heats of the 5,000 metres. He ran in heat 1. Joining him was Kenenisa Bekele.

The Africans allowed Austrian Gunther Weidlinger to set the pace and he lead all the way past 3,000 metres in 8:07.42. This was a good steady pace and made it likely that more than just the five automatic qualifiers would progress to the final. This was a good thing for the non stars in the field, as there were still twelve athletes in contention during the race's latter stages. By 4,000 metres, reached in 10:53.34, Abraham Chebii was in front with nobody having yet played any significant cards.

Soon the speed kicked in severely as Bekele took the lead 600 metres out. The quality of this event was now displayed with the fact that even producing a 2:30 final km in your heat may not be adequate as to guarantee qualification. For Bekele, such running was easy enough, and it was the Ethiopian who crossed the finish first in 13:21.16. The other automatic finalists were Gebremariam, El Guerrouj, Mottram and Chebii. Hicham was happy with his time of 13:21.87 and now he had three days to recover before he gave it everything for that historic double.

Craig Mottram proved that he had indeed gone to the next level. The Australian was the first runner in a long time from that nation who had showed the necessary ability to take it up to the best from Africa on the track. While Robert de Castella and Steve Moneghetti had recently flown the flag proudly in the marathon, no Aussie had made much impact over the shorter distances since Ron Clarke re wrote the record books in the 1960's.

Initially, Craig spent his teenage years as a triathlete, but some persuasion from Nic Bideau encouraged him to take up distance running full time. Nic took on the role of coach and agent, believing that Mottram had what it took to compete at an international level. His first major international race was in the 1999 World Junior Cross Country in Belfast. Out of the one hundred and fifty one finishers, Craig placed eighteenth over 8 kms in a time of 27:49. This was over two minutes behind the leading Africans, with Hailu Mekonnen and Richard Limo taking the first two spots. For someone just starting to take the sport seriously, he'd shown enough for Bideau to think that his initial instincts were correct. This was a kid worth working on.

Mottram first showed track potential in the 1,500 metres, and this was the event that he unsuccessfully tried to qualify for before the Sydney Olympic Games. 2002 was the year when Craig showed that he was better suited to the longer distances. Firstly he ran brilliantly to place fifth in the 2002 World Cross Country short course event, won by Kenenisa Bekele. Later that season he ran a national record of 13:12.04 for 5,000 metres. It wasn't quick enough to have the East Africans take notice, but it was good progress all the same.

Injuries curtailed his 2003 season and he missed the Paris World Championships. Now in 2004 he was fully fit and a different athlete. On July 30 he became the second fastest white man ever when he clocked 12:55.76 to finish second in a 5,000 metres event in London, only being out sprinted by Haile Gebrselassie. Now he had the attention of the dominant Africans. The tall Australian did not look too out of place as he mixed it with Kenenisa and Hicham in heat 1. Could he contend for a medal in the final?

Moroccan Hicham Bellani performed very well in the first preliminary though his time of 13:22.64 only earned him sixth position. It would be unfortunate if that time did not survive the second heat.

That race was slightly faster and it was Algerian Ali Saidi-Sief who showed some semblance of his old form by taking it in 13:18.94, just ahead of Eliud Kipchoge. The last km was timed at 2:26.25! Abderrahim Goumri finished fifth in 13:20.03 and with just the seven athletes bettering Bellani's time, he was through also. It was a good day for Moroccan distance running.

MOROCCAN SUCCESS; THE KADA WAY

All the favoured athletes survived the day's proceedings so all was in readiness for the final which some were predicting would be the race of the Games.

Having broken both of Haile Gebrselassie's outdoor world records earlier in the season and produced the most stunning of final lap kicks to win gold in the 10,000 metres, most were picking Kenenisa Bekele as the clear favourite to win the 5,000 metres also. One man who had a better insight than most into the difficulties that milers encountered when moving up was Steve Ovett, the British champion who was an Olympic medallist at both the 800 and 1,500 metres at the Moscow Games. Always a straight talker, Ovett had this to say about Hicham's chances in the race, "I can't see him beating Bekele, no. Moving up to five is not an easy route. In my era the 5,000 was on the cusp of changing to the super heroes we've got now. I think he's got to accept the simple fact of life that he is a miler. But if he does win, it really will be going off the deep end."

Any fears some may have had about the Moroccan being too satisfied from his previous victory had been quickly dispelled with Hicham having this to say in the aftermath of his 1,500 metres triumph. "I'm really hungry. I have a huge desire to win the gold. It will be a great battle with the Kenyans."

The world champion, Eliud Kipchoge was the third of the main contenders. After his giant killing effort in Paris, nobody would be too surprised if he stood atop the rostrum in Athens. Earlier this season Eliud had qualified for the Games in spectacular fashion, winning the 5,000 metres at the Kenyan trials in 13:14.00, while totally destroying John Kibowen, 13:22.60, and Abraham Chebii, 13:27.80.

So just like last year, Hicham El Guerrouj attempted to join Paavo Nurmi in achieving the ultimate perfection in middle and long distance running by winning both the 1,500 and 5,000 metres gold medals in the same major championship. At 9:05 pm, on Saturday the 28th of August, 2004, his quest for true immortality began.

The final is conducted in nothing like the same manner as the Paris burn up. Again Bekele moves to the front, yet on this occasion he doesn't do anything remotely spectacular. El Guerrouj is happy to sit wide in about sixth place, alongside Mottram. Gebremariam shoots to the front and looks as if he wants to get things moving but the clock doesn't lie. This is dreadfully slow, the first km being run in 2:58.46. This will suit Hicham just fine. Post race, the Moroccan gave us his thoughts during this period, "When I saw that Bekele got through the first 400 in 1:06 and the second 400 in 2:26, I said to myself, 'Hicham, you are going to win this.'"

Soon the pace becomes solid, with Chebii making the difference in front. El Guerrouj is not under any pressure, and is happy to remain in seventh position for now. He is gliding along the inside, covering as little distance and conserving as much energy as possible. Historically, we all expect him to make a concerted effort from about two laps out. The slower the better for his winning chances until the concluding laps.

Kipchoge takes the large pack to 2,000 metres in 5:35.99. But shortly thereafter comes the final's first significant move. Kenenisa Bekele strides into the lead, completing the seventh last lap in 60.97. This appears to be serious. Eliud is not letting him have his way in front and retakes the lead, shortly relinquishing it again to the Ethiopian who reaches 3,000 metres in 8:10.89. The latest km is a pretty fast 2:34.90, a pace which has many of the athletes working hard to stay in contact. This will certainly need to continue if they wish to disturb Morocco's finest.

Bekele remains at the front while a fifth last lap of 62.23 is recorded. It's a good pace but nothing more than that. Remember back to 1997 when Daniel Komen was running fifty eights during a similar period of the race.

There are still eight men in the lead group with only Tadesse in noticeable difficulty. This is no surprise given that he is backing up from third place in the 10,000 metres. Goumri and Bellani have dropped off. Kipchoge again goes to the lead, but very little is happening as they arrive at three laps to go.

MOROCCAN SUCCESS; THE KADA WAY

El Guerrouj appears to be in his element and looks like he wouldn't burn out a candle. As one American broadcaster observes, "Sixty threes aren't going to bother El Guerrouj. El Guerrouj could eat a candy bar running sixty threes!" That lap was indeed another sixty three (63.25). Tadesse has recovered and now tries to move up, passing Mottram who is starting to show the strain. The 4,000 metres split is 10:48.62. How long will Hicham wait?

With two laps remaining Kipchoge is moving quickly whilst leading, but this is troubling only Tadesse and Mottram. The six Africans look comfortable enough. Hicham is sitting fourth behind Bekele with Gebremariam constantly on his outside in an annoying position, blocking his space. He is boxed in badly with 600 metres to go, at about the time when he usually does go! Can he break free and then break clear?

The third of the Ethiopians, Dejene Birhanu, is very much a prominent player in fifth place, as is the dangerous Kenyan John Kibowen behind him. There still remain six contenders with 500 metres left. The penultimate lap is run in 61.43 and at the bell the waiting game continues. Nobody is yet willing to make a decisive move on the leading world champion Kenyan, while Hicham remains trapped on the inside. It has come down to a final sprint over 300 metres, something that the Moroccan doesn't always feel comfortable with in his pet event. But as Kenenisa finally lets fly, a space appears and Gebremariam is soon out of Hicham's way. He himself is free to fly. But can he fly as fast as the Ethiopian?

At the top of the curve it is the cross country legend who seizes the initiative, rounding Kipchoge during the early phase of his final decisive kick. Sihine was blown away in the 10,000 metres but Bekele can not inflict the same damage here as Kipchoge stays in touch. Here comes El Guerrouj! With 150 metres to go he attempts to take the Kenyan on the outside. Not such a wise move on the bend, but exiting the curve, he goes by him and soon he is in the Bernard Lagat position, of trying to chase down a gold medal in the home straight.

Suddenly he is right on Bekele and is absolutely flying. The greatest *ever* to win the 1,500 metres now has no burden on his shoulders and his running shows it. Hicham gets to Kenenisa at sixty metres. This is a moment suspended in time. Two champions, each so close to writing their own major piece of Olympic history. Here they stay as equals for around five tense strides before the Moroccan master delivers his final piece of athletic brilliance. The results from the 5,000 metres final were:

Hicham El Guerrouj	13:14.39
Kenenisa Bekele	13:14.59
Eliud Kipchoge	13:15.10
Gebre-egziabher Gebremariam	13:15.35
Dejene Birhanu	13:16.92
John Kibowen	13:18.24
Zersenay Tadesse	13:24.31
Craig Mottram	13:25.70
Hicham Bellani	13:31.81
Ali Saidi-Sief	13:32.57
Tim Broe	13:33.06
Alistair Ian Cragg	13:43.06
Abderrahim Goumri	13:47.27
Samir Moussaoui	14:02.01

Hicham El Guerrouj's first reaction upon his extraordinary double is to show us a two finger salute. "Two," he declares to the camera, stating that he is now a double Olympic champion.

Kada explained how Hicham was able to win his second gold of the Games, "There was so much pressure before, but after the victory in the 1,500, he could run free. He knew he was strong compared to the others."

Yet who better to sum up the Moroccan's Athens Games than his great predecessor, Noureddine Morceli. The Algerian was watching in the stands and with great respect for his former rival he said:

"To make that double at these Games is amazing. Hicham is such a great athlete and such a great man too. He deserves

MOROCCAN SUCCESS; THE KADA WAY

it. He has a great talent and great desire to win. He has carried that sadness for eight years but he never gave up. Now he is a true successor to Nurmi."

Afterword

There was another significant men's distance final that took place on August 28, 2004. Like Hicham El Guerrouj in the 1,500 metres, Wilson Kipketer was trying to finally claim Olympic gold in the 800 metres. Alas, the Kenyan born Dane failed in his quest, though a bronze medal was a pretty satisfying result, considering that he was no longer the dominant athlete in this discipline. Still, to retire without an Olympic gold was unfortunate for a runner who had been the world's best for much of the last decade. The victory went to Russian Yuriy Borzakovskiy. On this occasion, Kipketer was two tenths of a second behind the winner. Those who remembered him at his peak knew that he was highly unlucky. For Wilson Kipketer was much more than just an Olympic minor medalist.

I have commented only sparingly on the 800 metres event throughout this book, in part because my three Moroccan athletes did not specialise in it. Also, my greater interest on the track lies in the longer events, hence my discussion of major 5,000 and 10,000 metres races, even when they did not include any of Kada's runners.

The following date of August 29 was the day of the men's marathon. Again this is a distance event that has been given little mention, but I will talk of the Athens result, due to the inclusion of former track star Paul Tergat and Morocco's Jaoub Gharib.

Tergat's career had everything except for a gold medal from an Olympic Games or a World Athletics Championships. This was his chance to complete his career, and do so in the grandest fashion. Paul was happy with his preparation and as the world record holder, he started the race as favourite. Gharib was one of many other athletes also considered a strong chance to win, thanks to his World Championships victory in Paris.

Both were looking good for a high finish for the majority of the

MOROCCAN SUCCESS; THE KADA WAY

journey, but both struggled in the closing stages and finished well out of the medals. At 35 kms the Kenyan appeared the most likely to win, given that he was in the chase group with Stefano Baldini and Mebrahtom Keflezighi, gaining ground on the lone leader Vanderlei de Lima. However, Tergat had to battle hard from then on and he soon fell away from contention. He later said this was the result of something he'd drunk.

There was plenty of action up ahead, with the most disgraceful incident of the Games taking place some four or five kms from the finish when De Lima was pushed off the course by a mad Irishman (perhaps also as a result of something he drank!). The leader was stunned and obviously affected by this heartless intruder. Nevertheless the Brazilian valiantly continued, but inevitably was soon caught by Baldini and Keflezighi. The Italian went on to win gold, yet the biggest cheer was reserved for Vanderlei, who held off a late challenge by Britain's Jon Brown (his second straight fourth place finish in the Olympic marathon!) to claim the bronze. I doubt that he could have held on to win even if he hadn't been impeded (Stefano was really motoring), but it's a shame that he will never truly know the answer to this himself. What he endured certainly wasn't in the Olympic spirit.

On a side note, the motives of the 'pest' weren't terribly clear, given that some four years earlier he'd caused a similar commotion by disrupting the Formula One Grand Prix race in Germany. On that occasion he'd given great assistance to *Brazilian* driver Rubens Barrichello by putting a stop to the charge of runaway leaders Mika Hakkinen and David Coulthard. Despite being a Coulthard fan I must admit to having found some humour in this incident. However, in the case of De Lima I was simply infuriated.

Post Athens, there was a big Golden League meeting at Brussels on September 3, which produced some fantastic performances. The Ethiopians and the Moroccans were largely absent, deciding to take the rest of 2004 off. Kenya was therefore expected to dominate and it did triumph in the 1,500 and 3,000 metres, with Timothy Kiptanui clocking

3:30.24 and Eliud Kipchoge 7:27.72. Bernard Lagat only managed fourth place behind Kiptanui, despite El Guerrouj missing in action.

However, Kenya had to be content with second place finishes in the steeplechase and 10,000 metres. Saif Saaeed Shaheen produced an incredible effort to remove Brahim Boulami from the record books. The Qatari's time of 7:53.63 was not surprisingly a long way ahead of the next athlete, Paul Kiepsiele Koech who ran 8:02.07. Surprising in third position was the return of Boulami himself. The Moroccan gave a good account of himself to finish in 8:02.66. Perhaps even more astonishing than a new world record, was the result from the longer event, which saw another Qatar runner, Ahmad Hassan Abdullah, defeat Kenya's best Charles Kamathi, 26:59.54 to 26:59.93. Plenty of others also produced great times in the 10,000 metres, with eight athletes going sub 27:10.

In Brussels Ali Ezzine placed a distant eleventh, though produced a reasonable time of 8:16.63. However it would prove to be the beginning of the end for Ali. He had no results of any note in 2005, failing to perform well at the Mediterranean Games, then not even competing at the World Championships. In 2006 he could only manage third in Rabat, running 8:19.37. His career petered out.

El Guerrouj did not compete at the highest level again. He continued training after his Athens double gold, but found that he was now unable to maintain his usual high standards due to a lack of motivation and perhaps age. He announced that 2005 was to be a break year, though to the surprise of very few, Hicham declared his retirement in 2006.

Hissou did not return to any former glories either, placing third in the 20 kms road race (won by Felix Limo) in Holland 2005, which he had won the previous year. Salah did not back up for another marathon, preferring to compete in the Stramilano half marathon instead. He did not fare any better, as his time and placing of 1:02.39 and seventh showed.

MOROCCAN SUCCESS; THE KADA WAY

In 2006 Abdelkader Kada was recognised for his coaching excellence, selected as one of the four best athletics trainers in all of Africa. This meant a lot to Kada, as the survey was carried out by the Association of the African trainers of athletics (AEAA). The president of the African Confederation of Athletics, Hamad Kalkaba Malboum, awarded Kada a gold medal, appropriately in Rabat. It was the first time that this survey had been conducted. For future editions, one trainer would receive a gold medal each year.

Putting their inability to win plenty of Olympic gold medals aside, Kenya's men remained the best distance runners in the world. To give you an example of their depth of high talent, here are some statistics from the world lists of 2004:

5,000 metres – Kenya had thirty seven of the top one hundred times.
10,000 metres – Kenya had forty of the top one hundred times.
Half Marathon – Kenya had seventy two of the top one hundred times!
Marathon – Kenya had forty eight of the top one hundred times.

Haile Gebrselassie underwent further surgery on his achilles tendon in September 2004, yet was able to resume his career with some spectacular performances on the roads. In 2005 and 2006 Haile ran the world's fastest marathon times with wins in Amsterdam and Berlin. His results of 2:06.20 and 2:05.56 showed that if anything, he was getting better with age. Clearly, he was focused on taking Paul Tergat's world record. The build up to his return to Berlin in 2007 was huge. At the age of thirty four, Haile still possessed good leg speed. He'd been producing fast half marathon times also. In 2006 he set a world record with a magnificent 58:55 performance and warmed up for his marathon assault by winning in New York with a 59:24 on August 5, 2007. He'd even broken twenty seven minutes again earlier in the season in the 10,000 metres at Hengelo with a 26:52.81. So could Gebrselassie break the marathon world record on the same course on which it had been set and overshadow his great rival one more time?

The record stood at an imposing 2:04.55, but the Ethiopian took to his task with confidence on September 30. He had good reason to, for his form was as magnificent as ever. He broke the tape in 2:04.26. We had run out of superlatives for this man.

In a touching moment Haile spoke and apologised to Paul, shortly after his latest record run. The Kenyan had initiated the conversation with a phone call to congratulate him. Later Gebrselassie said to the press, "I am sorry - this record belonged to Paul Tergat. Paul is my friend."

Into 2008 and 'the emperor' continued on with his fast times, breaking 2:05 for the marathon in Qatar, and *again* breaking twenty seven minutes for 10,000 metres in Holland. 'Mr. Hengelo' was only beaten by his outstanding countryman Sileshi Sihine in a sprint finish. The younger athlete had produced many great runs since Athens, highlighted by his silver medals in the 2005 and 2007 World Championship 10,000 metres.

Kenenisa Bekele continued with his dominance of the World Cross Country Championships, winning the short and long course events again in 2005 and 2006. This made it five straight doubles, perhaps making it the greatest of all the men's distance running deeds of the modern era. 2006 was the final year of the short course, so Bekele was arguably an even stronger favourite to win the 12 kms race in 2007. The only factor against him appeared to be the event's location, which was Mombassa, Kenya. Conditions on the day were oppressive, and Kenenisa felt the pressure, though not from any of the Kenyan runners. It was Zersenay Tadesse of Eritrea who was putting up a strong fight against the Ethiopian. However, by the latter stages, Bekele had broken clear and seemed certain to record victory number six at this discipline, and number eleven overall. But Kenenisa showed us his mortality. Having an off day, he suddenly began to slow and fell back into the clutches of Tadesse, shortly after pulling out of the race. There was no shame in his abandonment as

MOROCCAN SUCCESS; THE KADA WAY

he was one of many starters who failed to finish. In 2008 Bekele reclaimed his world title, winning a record sixth long course crown, one more than Ngugi and Tergat. In between times Kenenisa ran some brilliant races on the track, improving his world record in the 10,000 metres to 26:17.53 and retaining his world title at the same distance in the 2005 and 2007 World Championships. The Osaka victory was perhaps his best ever because Kenenisa was struggling a little, but still managed to emerge triumphant over his great rival Sihine (who must have been sick of finishing second to Bekele), despite appearing to be dropped during the penultimate lap. His overall career record was quickly closing in on his famous predecessor Gebrselassie.

One of the other major achievements in recent times was Bernard Lagat's performance at the 2007 World Championships. The Kenyan finally went from bridesmaid to bride when he won the 1,500 metres. This wasn't a surprise, but perhaps feeling relaxed from this result, Lagat was able to perform well in the 5,000 metres and emulate El Guerrouj's double from Athens. Bernard was certainly helped however, by the lacklustre display from the 5,000 metres specialists. Nobody was willing to set any sort of decent pace throughout the first 4,000 metres, which Lagat showed his liking for with a very fast finish. The overall time was just 13:45.87, yet the final km was clocked at a scintillating 2:23.41.

The state of Moroccan men's distance running didn't appear great. The Athens Olympics was all about Hicham El Guerrouj, so with the track legend no longer competing, who was going to replace him?

In the 1,500 metres a surprising athlete did a reasonable job at filling his shoes. Adil Kaouch continued on with his improvements from 2004, suddenly becoming one of the world's best during 2005. At the World Championships Adil won the silver medal, a major step up from anything he'd achieved previously. However this achievement became seriously tainted when Kaouch tested positive before the 2007 World Championships.

Greg Rowlerson

Morocco was struggling to have any impact in track events, but on the road it was coming to the fore. Jaoud Gharib defended his World Championship in the marathon, a stunning accomplishment. Abderrahim Goumri moved up to the tortuous event and also found that he was greatly suited to it. After clocking 2:07.44 in London 2007, he raised his game to another level by breaking the Moroccan record when he ran 2:05.30 the following year at the same race. It was a remarkable performance.

Brahim Boulami produced a good run in the twilight of his career to finish fourth in the steeplechase at the 2005 World Championships, missing a medal by an agonising two hundredths of a second. He also won the event at the Mediterranean Games. Mohammed Mourhit did not fare anywhere near as well in his comeback. Some slow times on the track were followed by a failure in a move up to the marathon, as he clocked 2:19.43 in the 2005 Rotterdam Marathon. Hamid Ezzine, a brother of Ali, made the rise to international ranks, also as a steeplechaser. While he attained this high standard, the medalling accomplishments of Ali have thus far remained out of reach. Time wise though, Hamid hasn't been far away, as his excellent run of 8:09.72 on July 2, 2007 in Athens showed.

A Moroccan born athlete who has achieved great feats since 2004 is Rashid Ramzi. The Bahrain competitor not only won the 1,500 metres at the 2005 World Championships, but also the 800 metres. It was a major surprise, especially considering his lack of experience at the shorter distance. On the 1,500 metres, we can look back to his outstanding victory at the Rome Golden League during 2004, and realise that his taking of this World Championship crown from Hicham El Guerrouj wasn't a shock.

It is interesting to note the dominance that the maghrebs, (people of Morocco, Algeria and Tunisia) have enjoyed over the rest of the world, and in particular the East Africans, in the 1,500 metres in men's competition during the modern era.

In 1983 Said Aouita was becoming one of the world's best at

MOROCCAN SUCCESS; THE KADA WAY

the distance. For the next three years he was arguably *the* best, though this was not conclusive. However by 1987 he was definitely the world's number one, and he carried this through until 1990, when Noureddine Morceli took over his mantle. It wasn't until 1997 that Hicham El Guerrouj categorically took the crown, which he held right through to Athens 2004. So, also considering Ramzi's win in 2005, it can be said that a North African was the world's best for a period of nineteen seasons, and that might be a slight understatement.

From this discovery we realise that the maghrebs tend to excel more at the middle distances than the longer track events. Morocco's track talent has at times extended through to the 5,000 metres, with Aouita, Hissou and El Guerrouj all winning at the highest level. Yet despite providing Olympic champions at 10,000 metres (Boutayeb and Skah), the depth of elite athletes from Morocco just doesn't compare to the East Africans at these longer distances. Even Algeria's best performer in recent times relates to this. Ali Saidi-Sief, while very successful at 5,000 metres, was arguably more adept at 1,500 metres. No North African has come close to matching the times of Bekele, Gebrselassie and Komen in the 5,000 metres, while Hissou remains the only non East African to have broken twenty-seven minutes for 10,000 metres.

The extraordinary domination that East Africa enjoys here seems to extend through to the half marathon, yet the marathon itself remains a little different. This region of the world still provides the bulk of fastest times in the event (led by Gebrselassie and Tergat), but in major championships, particularly those held in adverse conditions, the gaps in talent are reduced and we still see a great mix of nations on the podium.

Now onto some hypotheticals.

Who is the greatest Moroccan male distance runner of all time? This is certainly a case of Said vs. Hicham.

It seems a pretty clear cut victory to El Guerrouj given that in major championships (Olympic Games and World Championships), he won six gold and three silver medals to Aouita's two gold and two bronze ones. That is a spanking!

Yet there are other factors to speak of, such as the World Championships only being held every four years during Said's time. So let's look at hypothetical World's in '85 and '89. How would have Aouita likely performed?

In '85 he would have run just the 5,000 metres, being a little wary of Steve Cram to run in the 1,500 metres. We will give him the gold medal here.

In '89 Aouita may have tried to be more versatile, given his attempt at the 800 and 1,500 metres in Seoul. To race in the 5,000 metres as well as the 800 metres wouldn't have been feasible either there or here, given the great differences in these events making it difficult to train for both. His best option would be to compete in the 1,500 and 5,000 metres.

Said's problem was that these finals were held on the same day so this option was not available. So I predict that he competes in the 800 and 1,500 metres again. I will give him another bronze in the 800 metres and a gold in the 1,500 metres.

Even with these additional 'free' medals, Aouita's total of four golds and three bronzes still pales to El Guerrouj who has two more golds and silver medals instead of bronze medals. It can be argued that Said missed out on a 1,500 metres medal in '88 through bad luck (injury), though the same can be said about Hicham falling in '96.

Aouita has a slight advantage in the number of world records run, though Hicham almost makes up for this deficiency when you consider that the 1,500 metres, mile and 2,000 metres records he set in the late '90's continue to stand around a decade later. Overall versatility is where Aouita's argument as Morocco's best comes in. Here are some examples:

1   He won big European 800 metres races throughout

MOROCCAN SUCCESS; THE KADA WAY

    1988.
2   He won the 10,000 metres in Oslo in 1986 at his first (and only ever) attempt at the event.
3   He finished a close second in a steeplechase race during his best season of 1987, running a national record.

El Guerrouj cannot match these feats and he never broke the 3,000 metres and 5,000 metres world records either, but he did run the second fastest 3,000 metres of all time (which remains the second fastest) and his 5,000 metres best rates pretty highly on the all time list, especially considering that this was his sole attempt at a fast time for this distance. Despite only two 5,000 metres competitions as a senior before Athens (Ostrava and Paris) he was able to take the gold, the sort of thing that Said never accomplished (for example he tried a similar, if not greater challenge in '88 at the 800 metres). Remember that Aouita's major championship wins all came at his preferred distance.

Hicham wins out when comparing career longevity, being truly world class from 1995-2004. Said was at this level from '83-'89 and perhaps was at a good enough level in '91 for that season to classify (his '90 season was destroyed by injury).

So there you have it. It is not an overwhelming victory, but convincing enough. Hicham El Guerrouj is the greatest Moroccan male distance runner of all time.

This leads me to another point of discussion. Who is the third best Moroccan male distance runner of all time? I believe this is a case of Khalid vs. Salah.

I suspect that most would choose Skah without giving it much thought, though I (perhaps not surprisingly!) disagree. I will attempt to explain my reasons.

Yes, Skah won a lot more races than Hissou. No argument there. But how many championships and big Grand Prix races would have Skah won if his peak years directly coincided with the peak years of Haile Gebrselassie, Paul Tergat and Daniel

Komen? My guess is not too many. Probably less than what Hissou won. Yes I hear you. Skah was a double world cross country champion. How highly do I rate that? I rate this very highly. To win in consecutive years despite the best efforts of the Kenyans was a mighty accomplishment. However let's look at the circumstances surrounding these victories.

The champion from 1986-'89 was John Ngugi who was a truly dominant cross country runner. Yet he wasn't in shape and wasn't a factor during Skah's winning years. When he returned to his best in '92 he thrashed Khalid. Skah's main opposition in '90 and '91 was Moses Tanui who he out kicked in both races. Tanui was a great runner but not one of the best ever. I rate Salah Hissou's performances in the '96 and '97 world cross country races higher than Skah's aforementioned results. Particularly in the case of the '97 event when he nearly defeated Paul Tergat who was a level up from Ngugi's standard at a time when Tergat was at his peak. Also look at the quality of runners that Hissou was finishing ahead of. Kirui, Koech, Gebrselassie, Nyariki, etc. Salah was a better cross country runner than Khalid in my opinion.

On the track, both men won major championships at different distances. Skah the 10,000 metres, Hissou the 5,000 metres. Hissou ran faster times than Skah, but because his career started later, he had an advantage in this regard. As the years go on, times generally are on the improve. So simply talking about Hissou running thirty-four seconds faster than Skah over 10,000 metres is fairly irrelevant. However, let's look at records. They *are* relevant.

During the early '90's, men's distance running records were not all that strong (taking into account the improvements that soon came). Yet Skah only ever held one world record, which was the rarely run two miles. His record was quickly obliterated. Hissou held the 10,000 metres world record, taking it from Gebrselassie while defeating Tergat and Koech in the same race. Skah never quite reached that sort of level. Salah also ran the second fastest 5,000 metres ever and would eventually run a faster 3,000 metres time than Said

MOROCCAN SUCCESS; THE KADA WAY

Aouita. He briefly held the Moroccan records at all three distances. Hissou's two best races over 10,000 metres and 5,000 metres were achieved by his own doing. He wasn't dragged through to a fast time by a superior athlete, nor did he require too much help from pace makers. At his best, Hissou could run at a near Komen type level and that is something that Skah could never have stayed with.

As we are talking of a period of about five years (between the Skah/Hissou eras) I believe a fair comparison can be made between these two. There were no great improvements in track surfaces or running shoes throughout the '90's. These improvements mostly came decades earlier. Yes, Salah raced in a more competitive era than Khalid, so it's natural that he would run faster times. But I wasn't just talking about times.

A just way of rating athletes from any era is to see the highest position reached on the all time lists. Obviously a world record holder has reached number one, as Hissou did in the 10,000 metres. Despite being an Olympic champion, Skah's highest ranking here was only ninth. In the 5,000 metres Hissou once ranked second to Skah's fourth. In the 3,000 metres Salah was as high as sixth, Khalid only eleventh.

With the injuries Hissou suffered, Skah arguably had greater career longevity. His fans can also point out his very good results in the half marathon (far superior to Salah's) as evidence of greater versatility, but on the opposite end of the spectrum, Skah couldn't get close to Hissou's personal record at 1,500 metres, 3:38.10 to 3:33.95. Granted, it could be argued that Khalid didn't focus at all on this event, yet the same could be said for Salah in the half marathon. But with an 8:19.30 in the steeplechase, I will give Skah the nod in regards to versatility! Overall though, I think I've given enough evidence to support Salah Hissou as Morocco's all time number three distance runner.

There is no argument as to who Morocco's greatest ever steeplechase athlete is. Given Brahim Boulami's positive test, Ali Ezzine is clearly his nation's best. In fact, even when disregarding the positive, there is no contest between the two, with Boulami's superior times being made irrelevent due to the massive discrepancy between them in major championship performances.

Ali Ezzine and Hicham El Guerrouj could have very few career regrets, whereas Salah Hissou, with his injuries and versatility may feel a little differently. As a further argument as to his supremacy over Khalid Skah, I will explore just how Salah might have gone in the 10,000 metres major championships of the early '90's.

Consider Hissou's performance in Athens '97. It was first class. He was competing against two of the greatest long distance runners ever. Nobody argues with that. You couldn't possibly compile an all time list and not have these two (Gebrselassie and Tergat) in your top ten. Salah didn't look too flash in their company over the last 600 metres in this World Championship, but looks can be highly deceiving. So let's put Hissou in another era.

The 1991 Tokyo World Championships 10,000 metres was won in a lot slower time than 27:28.67 (Hissou's time from Athens '97), of 27:38.74. The 1992 Barcelona Olympics and 1993 World Championships 10,000 metres races were run in even slower times. Granted, Barcelona was stinking hot, but it wasn't winter either when Athens held the World Championships in 1997. Hissou, the '97 version, potentially was good enough to win any one of these three major championships. This version of Salah, that wasn't quite as good as in '96 or '99 either. Perhaps you are saying. 'Good enough to beat Tanui, Skah and Gebrselassie ('93 version)? I can't see the logic.'

Well let me explain how the Salah Hissou of '97 (who some people said couldn't kick) could have won these 10,000 metres championships. The best runner to look at here is again Skah, not just because he is Moroccan, but because during this era, he was generally regarded as the man to beat in the big races. His finishing kick was feared, so the tactics of the Kenyans generally revolved around getting rid of Khalid. Skah finished off a 'slow' Barcelona 10,000 metres with a

MOROCCAN SUCCESS; THE KADA WAY

scorching twenty-six second final 200 metres. There is no way that Hissou could have ever gone with that. But the Athens race was different. Make no mistake. For a start it was faster so therefore it can be assumed that Skah wouldn't have finished quite as quickly as he did in Barcelona. Khalid did finish an even faster 10,000 metres in Gothenburg '95 in approximately 26.68 for the last 200 metres. So I will work off that.

Hissou never clocked a final half lap in the vicinity of that split as he didn't have the necessary basic speed. But Athens '97 was a different type of sprint finish. It came down to the final 600 metres, not the final 200 metres. Skah was a great runner, but he was never of the ilk of a Gebrselassie (few are) who could go 200 metres, or 400 metres, or 600 metres out. Haile at his peak probably could have taken it out hard with three laps to go or more (see Zurich '95) and still won without much concern. Salah ran the last lap of Athens in about fifty-eight seconds. In a good quality 10,000 metres, this is much closer to the Skah standard who would maybe run a fifty-seven or so in such a situation. Salah ran the last 600 metres of Athens in about 1:28 and this puts him borderline with the Khalid of Barcelona. This of course is only hypothetical.

Take Gebrselassie and Tergat out of that race and Hissou would have looked very impressive, very much like Skah in his prime. It would have been very much like the early '90's, with a Kenyan (Paul Koech) leading a Moroccan (Hissou), an Ethiopian (Assefa Mezgebu) and a Portuguese (Castro). The Kenyan (as was/is often tradition) had set a tough pace in the lead up to the finish and had his rivals at their limits. Then with 600 metres remaining (or about 570 metres if you want to be more exact), Hissou rounds Koech and puts in a significant surge (as much as anything this is describing just how good Gebrselassie and Tergat were) which earns him a small gap over the others. With 400 metres to go he is on his limits, but he manages to hold his form (though in contrast to Haile and Paul it didn't appear like he was) and win with a small but clear margin to Koech, a big gap to Mezgebu, while completely blowing Castro away. This hypothetical win would have been just as impressive as any 10,000 metres major championship that preceded it, save for perhaps Kipkoech's solo front running effort in Rome '87. Would he have beaten the Khalid Skah of the early '90's, specifically of Barcelona '92? It's a close call, but certainly the possibility was there to do so. Remember too that Hissou's form at other times was better than it was during 1997.

Putting Ali Ezzine into the early '90's likely would have limited impact on his major championship results. There is no way that he could have defeated Moses Kiptanui looking at any of the form the Kenyan displayed in his three World Championship victories. So at best, Ali would have again been going for the minor medals.

Throwing Hicham El Guerrouj at his peak into the path of Noureddine Morceli during the Algerian's three world titles would be the fantasy of many a distance running fan. The result of this would be totally subjective, hence the fascination of exploring it. The argument could go on forever as to who would win a major championship 1,500 metres out of Morceli and El Guerrouj at their peak levels of performance. El Guerrouj overall is the greater athlete, though to me, Morceli is the definitive miler, with the perfect balance of endurance, explosive speed and some strength. El Guerrouj was always geared a little more towards strength, which is why he was able to become so successful at 5,000 metres. For example, I believe that Noureddine at his absolute best might have won the Athens 2004 final, with the first 800 metres being conducted slowly enough to give him the eventual edge. However, when the race was run in the manner of Seville '99, Hicham wins hands down.

Some more general opinions. Bringing a short course event into the World Cross Country Championships was a wrong move. The only major purpose was to get the best 1,500 metres runners involved, who naturally were not inclined to race in the 12 kms race. But for the most part, the middle distance elite still stayed away, even with the temptation of a 4 kms event. Hicham El Guerrouj never entered it. As a result, the great tradition of the 12 kms event lost some of its gloss, while there was no worthwhile benefit that I can see, to having

MOROCCAN SUCCESS; THE KADA WAY

introduced a second race to the schedule.

The IAAF took too long to get a women's steeplechase into its track schedule for the Golden League and World Championships. It puzzled me, that once women were allowed to race over 5,000 metres, 10,000 metres and the marathon, why not the steeplechase? Women naturally have less power than men, though not less endurance. There is no reason why they shouldn't compete at the same distances as their male counterparts. A worthwhile reason to scrap tradition would be to have women compete over 12 kms in the World Cross Country, rather than 8 kms. This book has hardly given mention to distance running on the female side, though this is no slight on the elite women runners themselves. To have also discussed the women's side of things would have made the book far too long, if it wasn't already!

On other event changes/additions. How about a 10,000 metres steeplechase? For the sprint hurdling there are two events (110 metres, 400 metres) so why not have two for the distance runners also? It could provide some fascinating racing, with the men probably running it in about twenty-nine minutes. It would be a terrific test of endurance as well as concentration, considering all those barriers that are to be cleared, even in the face of extreme fatigue.

How about a 4 x 1,500 metres relay? A total amount of fifteen laps, covered in just over fourteen minutes. The concern for organisers would be of big victory margins, but a closely fought race would be an enthralling spectacle. Again, the sprinters get to carry a baton at an Olympics and World Championships, so how about giving the distance athletes a go? Or another possibility is to not have any relays at all, since athletics is an individual sport. Why try to be something you're not? We didn't see Jordan vs. Pippen in the one on one basketball championship in Barcelona, and not only because the result may have been a little one sided.

References:

I used relevant quotes and information from many internet sources. A big thank you goes to the following sites where most of my research was conducted:

www.iaaf.org - great links to various competition sites
www.alltime-athletics.com - track and field all time performances lists
www.letsrun.com - message board led to contact with Driss and Andreas
www.apulanta.fi/matti/yu/ (other all time lists site) - national lists
www.mariusbakken.com (Marius Bakken Online) - great information from the Norwegian distance runner on Moroccan training, in particular Hicham El Guerrouj's
www.kingofthemile.com - website dedicated to Hicham El Guerrouj
www.athletics(sporting)-heroes.net - good bio's on athletes
www.wikipedia.org - various athlete bio's

www.ingramcontent.com/pod-product-compliance
Lightning Source LLC
Chambersburg PA
CBHW021713300426
44114CB00009B/118